PENGUIN BOOKS

AMERICAN COLONIES

Alan Taylor's previous books include *William Cooper's Town: Power and Persuasion on the Frontier of the Early American Republic*, which won the 1996 Bancroft and Pulitzer prizes for history. He is a professor of history at the University of California at Davis. *American Colonies* is the first volume in the Penguin History of the United States, edited by Eric Foner, award-winning author of *Reconstruction: America's Unfinished Revolution* and the DeWitt Clinton Professor of History at Columbia University.

Booklist Selection, Best Books of 2001

Praise for *American Colonies*

"Drawing on the latest scholarship, Taylor expands our understanding of our own history in this comprehensive and exciting book. Full of surprising revelations, this superb book is history at its best."
—*BookPage*

"A balanced synthesis of recent schol[illegible] Taylor expertly weaves together the arguments and [illegible]s of historians and anthropologists . . . plac[ing] th[illegible] early American history within a broad context cr[illegible]ction of the histories of Africa, Europe, and the [illegible] strategy allows him to highlight the histories of [illegible] neglected in accounts of colonial North America. [illegible]ormidable work of historical synthesis, *America*[illegible] us to contemplate the ways in which residents o[illegible]ave dealt with diversity."
—*The New York Times Bo*[illegible]

"At long last, we have an overview of colonial North America that addresses its full geographic, international, and multicultural sweep. In *American Colonies*, Alan Taylor transcends the heroic saga of freedom-loving Englishmen clustered along the Atlantic coast with a full-blown narrative that extends from the continent's earliest inhabitants through Christian-Muslim interactions in fifteenth-century Africa and Europe to the onset of the American Revolution and Captain Cook's Pacific voyages. Taylor challenges us to rethink the complexity and significance of America's colonial past."
—Neal Salisbury, Professor of History, Smith College

"Alan Taylor puts everything we thought we knew about early America in a refreshing international context. All over the country, teachers will be throwing out stale lecture notes. Students will be sitting up attentively. Here is a history that responds to the skeptical questions we ask in the twenty-first century."

—Linda K. Kerber, author of *No Constitutional Right to Be Ladies: Women and the Obligations of Citizenship*

"[A] superb overview of colonial America. Alan Taylor . . . draws upon an extraordinary array of recent scholarship to present a much more comprehensive and complex story. In the process, he punctures many myths and misperceptions. Taylor skillfully integrates social history into his narrative. His accounts of gender roles, family life, and religious beliefs help illuminate the political and economic processes that shape America's role within the international community. Perhaps Taylor's greatest contribution to our understanding of early American history is contextual. He is one of the few colonial historians to devote a whole chapter to the settlement of the West Indian islands and their role in the development of South Carolina, and perhaps the only one to include developments on the Great Plains and in California, Alaska, and Hawaii before the Revolution. He also broadens our understanding of the multinational aspects of early American history. American Colonies provides the most comprehensive and textured account of the diverse strands that formed the fabric of early American history. It is destined to become the standard work in its field."

—*The Christian Science Monitor*

"Crammed full of fascinating material uncovered by historians, archaeologists, and anthropologists in the past half-century."

—*Newsday*

"Alan Taylor has ranged widely over the best new scholarship in ethnohistory, environmental, imperial, Atlantic, Pacific and Borderlands history, using it not simply to inform, but to transform the narrative of early North America. Compelling, readable, and fresh, *American Colonies* is perhaps the most brilliant piece of synthesis in recent American historical writing."

—Philip J. Deloria, Associate Professor History and American Culture, University of Michigan and author of *Playing Indian*

"Even the serious student of history will find a great deal of previously obscure information. The book offers a balanced understanding of the diverse peoples and forces that converged on this continent and influenced the course of American history."

—*Publishers Weekly* (starred review)

AMERICAN COLONIES

ALAN TAYLOR

The Penguin History of the United States

Eric Foner, Editor

PENGUIN BOOKS

Overleaf: *Taino Indians panning for gold, using Spanish tools.*

PENGUIN BOOKS
Published by the Penguin Group
Penguin Group (USA) Inc., 375 Hudson Street, New York, New York 10014, U.S.A.
Penguin Group (Canada), 90 Eglinton Avenue East, Suite 700, Toronto, Ontario, Canada M4P 2Y3 (a division of Pearson Penguin Canada Inc.)
Penguin Books Ltd, 80 Strand, London WC2R 0RL, England
Penguin Ireland, 25 St Stephen's Green, Dublin 2, Ireland (a division of Penguin Books Ltd)
Penguin Group (Australia), 250 Camberwell Road, Camberwell, Victoria 3124, Australia (a division of Pearson Australia Group Pty Ltd)
Penguin Books India Pvt Ltd, 11 Community Centre, Panchsheel Park, New Delhi – 110 017, India
Penguin Group (NZ), 67 Apollo Drive, Rosedale, North Shore 0632, New Zealand (a division of Pearson New Zealand Ltd)
Penguin Books (South Africa) (Pty) Ltd, 24 Sturdee Avenue, Rosebank, Johannesburg 2196, South Africa

Penguin Books Ltd, Registered Offices: 80 Strand, London WC2R 0RL, England

First published in the United States of America by Viking Penguin, a member of Penguin Putnam Inc. 2001
Published in Penguin Books 2002

34 35 36 37 38 39 40 41 42

ILLUSTRATION CREDITS: James Ford Bell Library, University of Minnesota: title page; Peabody Museum of Archeology and Ethnology, Harvard University, Cambridge, Mass.: p. 3; from Rhys Isaac's *The Transformation of Virginia, 1740-1790* (Chapel Hill, 1982), courtesy of the University of North Carolina Press (Chapel Hill): p. 138, right and left; American Antiquarian Society, Worcester, Mass., courtesy of the Abby Aldrich Rockefeller Folk Art Center and the Colonial Williamsburg Foundation (Williamsburg, Va.): p. 222; Rauner Special Collections, Dartmouth College Library: p. 388. All others courtesy of the American Antiquarian Society, Worcester, Mass.

Map illustrations by Jeffrey Ward

THE LIBRARY OF CONGRESS HAS CATALOGED THE HARDCOVER EDITION AS FOLLOWS:
Taylor, Alan, 1955–
American colonies / Alan Taylor ; Eric Foner, editor.
p. cm.—(The Penguin history of the United States ; 1)
Includes bibliographical references (p.) and index.
ISBN 0-670-87282-2 (hc.)
ISBN 978-0-14-200210-0 (pbk.)
1. United States—History—Colonial period, ca. 1600–1775.
I. Foner, Eric. II. Title. III. Series.
E188 .T35 2001
973.2—dc21 2001017552

Printed in the United States of America
Set in Janson
Designed by Helene Berinsky

For Emily

CONTENTS

Part III

EMPIRES

INTRODUCTION

Christopher Columbus and the worlds he bridged, as imagined by a European artist of the early seventeenth century. From Caspar Plautius, Nova Typis Transacta Navigatio *(n.p., 1621).*

TO WRITE A HISTORY of colonial America used to be easier, because the human cast and the geographic stage were both considered so much smaller. Until the 1960s, most American historians assumed that "the colonists" meant English-speaking men confined to the Atlantic seaboard. Women were there as passive and inconsequential helpmates. Indians were wild and primitive peoples beyond the pale: unchanging objects of colonists' fears and aggressions. African slaves appeared as unfortunate aberrations in a fundamentally upbeat story of Englishmen becoming freer and more prosperous by colonizing an open land. The other colonies of rival empires—Dutch, French, and Spanish—were a hazy backdrop of hostility: backward threats to the English America that alone spawned the American Revolution and the United States. And no colonial historian bothered with the eighteenth-century Russian colonization of Alaska or the English probes into Hawaii, although both places later became absorbed into the United States.

By long convention, "American history" began in the east in the English colonies and spread slowly westward, reaching only the Appalachian Mountains by the end of the colonial period. According to this view, the "seeds" of the United States first appeared with the English colonists in 1607 at Jamestown in Virginia, followed in 1620 by "the Pilgrims" at Plymouth in New England. Earlier Spanish and contemporary French settlements were fundamentally irrelevant except as enemies, as "foreign" challenges that brought out the best in the English as they made themselves into Americans. What we now call "the West" did not become part of American history until the United States invaded it during the early nineteenth century. Alaska and Hawaii made no appearance in national history until the end of that century.

That narrow colonial cast and stage made for the fundamentally happy story of "American exceptionalism": the making of a new people, in a new land. By emigrating to the colonies, white men escaped from the rigid customs, social hierarchies, and constrained resources of Europe into an abundant land of challenge and opportunity. That story persists in our national culture and popular history because it offers an appealing simplification that contains important (but partial) truths. Many English colonists did find more land, greater prosperity, and higher status than they could have achieved in the mother country. After about 1640, the great majority of free colonists were better fed, clothed, and housed than their common contemporaries in England, where half the people lived in destitution. And English colonial societies were truncated, lacking the gentry and aristocracy of the mother country, creating a political vacuum at the top to be filled by prosperous merchants and planters.

But the traditional story of American uplift excludes too many people. Many English colonists failed to prosper, finding only intense labor and early graves in a strange and stressful land of greater disease, new crops and predators, and intermittent Indian hostility. And those who succeeded bought their good fortune by taking lands from Indians and by exploiting the labor of others—at first indentured servants, later African slaves. The abundant land for free colonists kept wage labor scarce and expensive, which promoted the importation of unfree laborers by the thousands. Between 1492 and 1776, North America lost population, as diseases and wars killed Indians faster than colonists could replace them. And during the eighteenth century, most colonial arrivals were Africans forcibly carried to a land of slavery, rather than European volunteers seeking a domain of freedom. More than minor aberrations, Indian deaths and African slaves were fundamental to colonization. The historian John Murrin concludes that "losers far outnumbered winners" in "a tragedy of such huge proportions that no one's imagination can easily encompass it all."

Moreover, not all of colonial America was English. Many native peoples encountered colonizers not as westward-bound Englishmen, but as Spanish heading north from Mexico, as Russians coming eastward from Siberia, or as French probing the Great Lakes and Mississippi River. And each of their empires interacted in distinctive ways with particular settings and natives to construct varied Americas.

Historians have recently broadened their research to recover the enormous diversity and tragic dimensions of the colonial experience. Instead of lurking beyond the colonies in a "wilderness," Indians have come back into the story as central and persistent protagonists. Instead of dismissing slavery as peripheral, recent historians have restored its centrality to the economy, culture, and political thought of the colonists. And new scholarship illuminates the essential role of women in building colonial societies. With the expanded cast has come a broader stage that includes attention to New France, New Spain, and New Netherland.

Colonial societies *did* diverge from their mother countries—but in a more complex and radical manner than imagined within the narrow field of vision once traditional to colonial history. The biggest difference was the unprecedented mixing of radically diverse peoples—African, European, and Indian—under circumstances stressful for all. The colonial intermingling of peoples—and of microbes, plants, and animals from different continents—was unparalleled in speed and volume in global history. Everyone had to adapt to a dramatic new world wrought by those combinations. In their adaptions to, and borrowings from, one another, they created truly exceptional societies (which is not to say that they were either better or worse than European societies, just new and different).

To divide the peoples in three, into the racial and cultural categories of European, African, and Indian, only begins to reveal the human diversity of the colonial encounter. For each embraced an enormous variety of cultures and languages. For example, the eighteenth-century "British" colonists included substantial numbers of Welsh, Scots, Irish, Scots-Irish, Germans,

Swedes, Finns, Dutch, and French Huguenots—as well as the usual English suspects. Moreover, during the eighteenth century those nationalities were still inchoate, still complicated by powerful local cultures within each kingdom. Both the Londoner and the rural peasant of Cornwall, in far western England, were English subjects of the same king, but they could barely understand one another. Thrown together as neighbors in a distant colony, they had to find a new commonality of identity, dialect, and customs. Until lumped together in colonial slavery, the African conscripts varied even more widely in their ethnic identities, languages, and cultures. A very partial list of West African peoples includes Ashanti, Fulani, Ibo, Malagasy, Mandingo, and Yoruba. In general, their languages differed from one another more than English did from French or Spanish. Most diverse of all were the so-called Indians. Divided into hundreds of linguistically distinct peoples, the natives did not know that they were a common category until named and treated so by the colonial invaders. All three clusters—European, African, and Indian—were in flux when they encountered one another in the colonies; in the process of those encounters they defined an array of new identities as Americans.

European ships served as the medium, and European profit-seeking and soul-seeking as the motives, for bringing Europeans, Africans, and Indians together on the natives' lands, breaking down the hundreds of localized identities and cultures that had formerly framed their lives. Thrown together in unexpected and kaleidoscopic combinations, the peoples struggled to make sense of one another as they tried to survive in a strange land of strange peoples. As James Merrell has shown, even Indians—no, *especially* Indians—lived in a new world transformed by the intrusion of diverse and powerful newcomers bearing alien diseases, livestock, trade goods, weapons, and proselytizing beliefs. By necessity, those in the encounter developed a composite culture borrowed in part from their new neighbors. African words and music infiltrated the popular culture of their enslavers, while the African-Americans adapted Christianity to their own needs. In such exchanges and composites, we find the true measure of American distinctiveness, the true foundation for the diverse America of our time.

In these cultural and environmental encounters, the various peoples were not equal in power. In most (but not all) circumstances, the European colonizers possessed tremendous ecological, technological, and organizational advantages, which demanded disproportionate adjustments by the Indians in their way and the Africans in their grasp. But the colonial elites never had complete power. Instead, they constantly had to adjust to the cultural resistance, however subtle, of those they meant to dominate.

Over time, race loomed larger—primarily in British America—as the fundamental prism for rearranging the identities and the relative power of the many peoples in the colonial encounters. A racialized sorting of peoples by skin color into white, red, and black was primarily a product, rather than a precondition, of colonization. At first, during the sixteenth and early seventeenth centuries, colonizing elites thought of their superiority primarily as cultural—as the fruit of their European mastery of civility and Christianity. On those scores, the elites thought of their own peasants, laborers, sailors, and soldiers as only a little better than Indians and Africans. Therefore, the leaders left open the possibility that Indians and Africans could, through cultural indoctrination, become the equals of the European lower orders. Such elites did not yet ascribe status and limit potential primarily on the basis of pigmentation.

From the start, the English subtly differed from the French and the Spanish in a greater readiness to detect fundamental difference in color and to share some political rights with common "white" people. In the colonies, that difference grew stronger over the generations as British America developed an especially polarized conception of race in tandem with greater political power for common whites. Unlike the French and the Spanish, the British colonies relied in war primarily on local militias of common people, rather than on professional troops. That increased the political leverage of common men as it involved them in frequent conflicts with Indians and in patrolling the slave population. In those roles, the ethnically diverse militiamen found a shared identity as white men by asserting their superiority defined against Indians and Africans conveniently cast as brutish inferiors. To avoid alienating the militiamen, British colonial elites gradually accepted a white racial solidarity based upon subordinating "blacks" and "reds." Once race, instead of class, became the primary marker of privilege, colonial elites had to concede greater social respect and political rights to common white men.

In sum, white racial solidarity developed in close tandem with the expansion of liberty among male colonists. The greater opportunity and freedoms enjoyed by white men in the British colonies were a product of their encounter with a broader array of peoples—some of whom could be exploited in ways impossible back in Britain. Confronting that linkage has been the painful challenge faced by the American republic since 1776. Recognizing both linkage and challenge certainly does not diminish the subsequent achievements of the American people. On the contrary, remembering the painful and powerful legacies of the colonial past can only highlight the progress made in the past two centuries—as well as underline how difficult further progress will be. And in addition to recovering the tragedies and exploitations of colonial America, we can find hope there in the development of popular liberties and representative institutions that made possible the American republic. Although originally limited to propertied white men, revolutionary republicanism claimed to promote human rights universally. Over the generations, those claims have enabled more Americans—including the descendants of slaves and dispossessed natives—to seek justice.

BOUNDARIES

American Colonies draws upon three especially productive lines of recent scholarship: an Atlantic perspective, environmental history, and the ethnohistory of colonial and native peoples. The Atlantic approach examines the complex and continuous interplay of Europe, Africa, and colonial America through the transatlantic flows of goods, people, plants, animals, capital, and ideas. Environmental history considers the transformative impact of those flows on the landscape and life of North America. And ethnohistory focuses on the cultural encounters between Africans, Europeans, and natives in colonial North America. Because all three inquiries are rich and complex, they ordinarily belong to distinct specialists, but their combination is indispensable in any effort to understand the bigger picture of North America in the colonial era.

By design the title speaks of plurality, *American Colonies*, rather than the singular, traditional *Colonial America*. The chapters present a series of regional explorations that gradually move forward in time. I favored a regional, rather than a topical, organization lest I confuse myself and my readers by leaping back and forth over broad regions and distinct centuries, comparing British apples to Spanish oranges without first creating a context for understanding both. By exploring regions in sequence and in some detail, I have tried to show how culture, economy, politics, and society *fit together* in each region, have tried to re-create human places coherent and cohesive to the reader. As that picture becomes clearer and more comprehensive, I increasingly compare the various colonial Americas: Spanish, French, Dutch, British, and Russian.

In recent years, the escalating integration of North America—by treaty, investment, trade, migration, travel, mass media, and environmental pollution—renders our national boundaries more porous. As a result, we may now be prepared to broaden our historical imagination beyond the national limits of the United States, to see more clearly a colonial past in which those boundaries did not yet exist. In attempting a more North American perspective on our history, this book is also a half step toward a more global (and less national) sensibility for our place in time.

That goal is somewhat at odds with the mandate for this volume, as the first in a series meant to cover the history of the United States down to the present. That nation-state defines the subject, setting boundaries for the authors of the subsequent volumes—a luxury not available to the colonial scholar, who writes about a period before the United States existed or was even conceivable. Reading the United States back in time and geography to frame the colonial story has the distorting effect known as "teleology": making all events lead neatly to a determined outcome, in the colonial case to the American Revolution and its republic. Teleology costs us a sense of the true drama of the past: the "contingency" of multiple and contested possibilities in a place where, and time when, no one knew what the future would bring. As late as 1775, few British colonists expected to frame an independent country. And very few Hispanics and fewer Indians wished for incorporation within such a nation.

Rejecting teleology, however, to wallow in pure contingency is an equal folly. Hindsight affords a pattern to change over time that readers reasonably seek from the historian. As their author, I cannot and should not treat the coming of the United States as utterly irrelevant to the colonial era—just as I cannot and should not allow that knowledge to overwhelm the other possibilities in that past. Instead, my job is to balance the creative tension between teleology and contingency.

Although British America does not warrant *exclusive* attention, it does deserve relatively *greater* coverage than that afforded the French, Spanish, Russian, and Dutch colonies. For British America became the most populous, prosperous, and powerful colonial presence on the continent—a development that made the American Revolution possible and successful. That revolution transformed the British colonists into the continent's premier imperialists. British America left powerful legacies for the United States, which empowered its nineteenth-century conquest of most of the other peoples, both colonial and native, on the North American continent.

Striking a balance between the emerging power of British America and the enduring diversity of the colonial peoples requires bending (but not breaking) the geographic boundaries suggested by the United States today. Hispanic Mexico, the British West Indies, and French Canada receive more detailed coverage than is customary in a "colonial American history" (which has meant the history of a proto–United States). All three were powerful nodes of colonization that affected the colonists and Indians living between the Gulf of Mexico and the Great Lakes. The internal cultures, societies, and economies of the Spanish, French, and Dutch colonies also warrant attention lest they again appear only in wars, reduced to bellicose foils to British protagonists. Such internal description also affords the comparative perspective needed to see the distinctive nature of British colonial society that made a colonial revolution for independence and republicanism possible first on the Atlantic seaboard.

As I wrote this book, several colleagues asked, "When does your book end?" Although it seemed to me that the end to my writing was nowhere in sight, I knew that they meant "At what year does your version of colonial America conclude?" The question implied the Anglocentric perspective that I hope, in some measure, to shift. So long as the subject was simply the English-speaking colonies on the Atlantic seaboard, the answer was relatively simple and finite: either 1763, when the British imperial crisis heated up, or 1776, when thirteen colonies declared their independence as the United States. But neither date marks an end point for the colonial experience west of the Appalachians. In 1776, the colonial encounter with native peoples was just beginning on the Pacific rim. Consequently, my ending has a sliding scale: about 1775 in the east, where and when the imperial crisis broke into revolution, and approximately 1820 in the west, when colonialism had taken root in California, Alaska, and even Hawaii. By 1820 the United States had emerged from an anticolonial revolution to exercise its own imperial power on the Pacific coast. The former British colonists became the American colonizers of others in their path. In that transition, I end the book.

Ultimately, my geographic and temporal bounds for colonial America are open-ended because *process*, as much as *place*, defines the subject as I understand it. A cascade of interacting changes make up "colonization" as the Europeans introduced new diseases, plants, animals, ideas, and peoples—which compelled dramatic, and often traumatic, adjustments by native peoples seeking to restore order to their disrupted worlds. Those processes ranged throughout the continent, affecting peoples and their environments far from the centers of colonial settlement. In turn, resourceful responses by native peoples to those changes compelled the colonizers to adapt their ideas and methods.

Indian peoples were indispensable to colonizers as guides to local plants, landscapes, and animals; as converts for missionary institutions; as trading partners; and as allies in wars with other empires. By the late seventeenth century, when multiple empires competed for advantage in North America, each needed to build networks of influence over native peoples. Rather than imposing a pure colonial mastery, those alliances involved the mutual dependence of both colonists and natives. Although natives increasingly relied on European trade goods, they also compelled colonizers to accommodate to native protocols and alliances—often imposing costs and compromises on imperial visions.

Recovering native importance, however, has sometimes come at the cost of underestimating the importance of European empires to the colonial story. Historians once exaggerated the power of empires to enforce their will upon distant natives and their own colonists. But in recent years, historians have tended toward the other extreme to debunk empires as impotent and irrelevant on the colonial frontiers. The historian John Robert McNeill offers a more balanced perspective. Referring to Europe as the "metropolis" and colonies as its "periphery," he trenchantly defines a colonial empire as "the product of metropolitan logic and decisions imperfectly inflicted on people and places poorly understood by the metropolitans."

As McNeill so nicely put it, imperial visions were "imperfectly inflicted." Imperialists never achieved the full mastery they dreamed of; but the flawed pursuit of their illusions bore powerfully upon peoples in their way—just as those people inevitably deflected the blows of empire. Colonial empires unleashed powerful forces of disease, trade, missionaries, livestock, and war that, although often beyond imperial control, fundamentally disordered the natives' world. Indians responded to the stresses with remarkable agility, but they did not have the option of ignoring the powerful changes imposed upon their continent by the newcomers. Over time, the natives lost land and freedom to the growing numbers of colonists, especially the proliferating British Americans of the Atlantic seaboard. As catalysts for unpredictable change, empires mattered, even if they were never quite what they claimed to be.

Part I

ENCOUNTERS

1

Natives

★

13,000 B.C.–A.D. 1492

Temple and cabin of the chief of the Acolapissa, 1732, by Alexandre de Batz. In the lower Mississippi Valley, in the early eighteenth century, French colonizers found vestiges of the Mississippian culture featuring powerful priest-chiefs and elaborately decorated temples.

SCHOLARS USED TO THINK of Native American cultures as relatively static, unchanging for centuries until encountered and overwhelmed by the European invaders after 1492. Those scholars assumed that the descriptions of Indian cultures by early explorers could be read backward to imagine their predecessors from centuries past. With the help of recent archaeology and anthropology, we can now see that the explorers encountered a complex array of diverse peoples in the midst of profound change. Far from being an immutable people, the Indians had a complicated and dynamic history in America long before 1492.

Because so much remains controversial about native origins and so many new discoveries are daily made, all of the statements in this chapter are highly speculative and the dates are approximations. The archaeological evidence is fragmentary and limited, suggesting multiple possibilities. In general, I have favored the more cautious interpretations advanced by the debating archaeologists. And we should bear in mind that many contemporary native peoples entirely reject the scholarly explanations for their origins, preferring instead their own traditions that they emerged in the Americas and so literally belong to this land.

Writing about pre-Columbian America is also fraught with controversy because we often enlist ancient natives in contemporary debates over our own social and environmental problems. To highlight the social inequities and environmental degradation of our own society, some romantics depict the pre-1492 Americans as ecological and social saints living in perfect harmony with one another and with their nature. To refute that critique, more conservative intellectuals eagerly point out every example of native violence, human sacrifice, and environmental waste. By generalizing from such examples, the conservatives revive the mythology of the European colonizers: that Indians were warlike savages with a primitive culture that deserved conquest and transformation. Often the debate deteriorates into a competition over who was innately worse: the Indian or the European. In fact, it would be difficult (and pointless) to make the case that either the Indians or the Europeans of the early modern era were by nature or culture more violent and "cruel" than the other. Warfare and the ritual torture and execution of enemies were commonplace in both native America and early modern Europe.

Without pegging Europeans as innately more cruel and violent, we should recognize their superior power to inflict misery. By 1492 they had developed a greater technological and organizational capacity to conduct prolonged wars far from home. They also possessed imperial rivalries and religious ideologies that drove them outward across the world's oceans in search of new lands and peoples to conquer. Superior means enabled, and ideological imperatives obliged, Europeans to cross the Atlantic and invade North America after 1492. In the process, the newcomers escalated the bloodshed in the Americas to a level unprecedented in the native past.

And although Indians lacked the perfection of environmental saints, they did possess a culture that demanded less of their nature than did the Europeans of the early modern era. Almost all early explorers and colonizers marveled at the natural abundance they found in the Americas, a biodiversity at odds with the deforestation and extinctions that the Europeans had already wrought in most of their own continent. Colonization transformed the North American environment, which had already experienced more modest changes initiated by the native occupation.

MIGRATION

With the exception of frozen and isolated Antarctica, North and South America were the last continents occupied by people. All of the human fossils found in the Americas are almost certainly less than fifteen thousand years old and belong to the biologically modern form. Dental, genetic, and linguistic analysis reveals that most contemporary Native Americans are remarkably homogeneous and probably descend from a few hundred ancestors who came to North America within fifteen thousand years of the present (with the exception of the later-arriving Athabascan, Inuit, and Aleut peoples).

Most scholars believe that the first Americans migrated from Siberia in northeast Asia. Genetic and skeletal (especially dental) evidence suggests special affinities between Native Americans and the peoples of Siberia. And the proximity of Siberia to Alaska offers the readiest passage between the Old and the New World, indeed the only practicable route for peoples without the marine technology to traverse the Atlantic or Pacific Ocean.

About fifteen thousand years ago the inhabitants of Siberia lived in many small bands that ranged far and wide in pursuit of the roaming and grazing herds of large and meaty (but dangerous) mammals, especially mammoths, musk oxen, and woolly rhinoceroses. It was a hard, cold, and generally short life in which hunger alternated with the episodic binges of a big kill. Because the people had to remain on the move (on foot) in pursuit of the herds, they could not develop permanent villages and did not accumulate heavy possessions.

In their pursuit of the herds, some hunting bands passed into what is now North America. Today the oceanic Bering Strait separates Siberia from Alaska. But between about twenty-five thousand and twelve thousand years ago, a colder global climate—an Ice Age—locked up more of the world's water in polar icecaps, which spread southward as immense glaciers, covering the northern third of North America. The enlarged icecaps lowered the ocean levels by as much as 360 feet, creating a land bridge between Siberia and Alaska.

Of course, the first people who trekked into Alaska had no notion that they were discovering and colonizing a new continent, nor that they were crossing a land bridge that would subsequently vanish beneath the rising

Pacific Ocean when the global climate warmed. The newcomers naturally regarded the flat, gently undulating, cold, and arid grassland as simply an extension of their home.

The period between fifteen thousand and twelve thousand years ago was an ideal time for a crossing into North America, because the global climate was slowly warming and the glaciers were in gradual retreat, sufficiently so to permit an easier passage into the continent but not yet so far as entirely to refill the Bering Strait with water. By about ten thousand years ago the glacial ice had retreated to approximately its present limits in the arctic, and the climate and sea levels stabilized close to their modern configurations. As the icecap receded over the centuries, the migrants found it easier to spread southward and eastward into North America and beyond. Remarkably similar archaeological sites of human encampments suddenly became common about twelve thousand to ten thousand years ago in distant places, from California to Pennsylvania and Florida.

As the land bridge submerged, migration from Siberia became more difficult—but not impossible for people possessing small boats made from animal skins stretched over a wooden framework. At its narrowest, the Bering Strait is only three miles wide. Contemporary Native Americans who speak an Athabascan language descend from a second pulse of emigrants, who arrived about ten thousand to eight thousand years ago. Settling first in the subarctic of Alaska and northwestern Canada, some Athabascan bands gradually worked their way down the Rocky Mountains, reaching the American southwest about six hundred years ago. These people later became known as the Navajo and Apache.

A third surge of colonization began about five thousand years ago and featured the ancestors of the Inuit (or "Eskimos") and Aleut. Skilled boat builders, they specialized in the hunting of sea mammals—walruses, seals, and whales. The Aleut settled the Aleutian islands southwest of Alaska, while their Inuit cousins gradually expanded eastward along the Arctic coasts of northern Alaska and Canada, reaching Labrador and Greenland by about twenty-five hundred years ago.

PALEO AND ARCHAIC AMERICA

We do not know what the people in the first pulse of migration named themselves, but scholars call them the Paleo-Indians. As in their Siberian past, the Paleo-Indians lived by hunting and gathering in small bands of about fifteen to fifty individuals: the optimum size for far-ranging travel in pursuit of animals as well as for cooperation in the hunt and butchering. Their basic weapon and tool was a spear with a sharp, flaked-stone point (usually flint) bound tightly to a wooden shaft. Most of their archaeological sites were temporary encampments near perennial springs, waterholes, and river

— North America, c. 1492 —

crossings—places where big game came to drink or to pass. After consuming a kill, they moved on in pursuit of another herd.

At first, the Paleo-Indians primarily found in North America a vast, cool grassland that sustained large herds of slow-moving herbivores initially inexperienced in defending themselves against a predator as cunning, numerous, and cooperative as humans. The beasts included immense mammoths, mastodons, bison, horses, and camels, as well as caribou, moose, and deer. The Paleo-Indians found beavers as big as bears: seven feet long. The giant bison had horns spanning six feet, and the mammoths stood twelve feet high and could weigh ten tons, nearly as big as their modern relatives, the elephants. The Paleo-Indians truly experienced the discovery and occupation of a vast new domain of "free land": free from other humans and abounding with plant and animal life. After centuries of subarctic hardship and recurrent hunger, the first Americans had found the hunters' Eden.

But no Eden lasts for long. An abundant diet permitted an explosive population growth, which, in turn, pressed against local supplies of plants and animals. As bands grew too large for a locale to sustain, they subdivided, with new bands hiving off in pursuit of more distant animal herds. By about nine thousand years ago, people could be found from Alaska to the southernmost tip of South America, a distance of some eight thousand miles.

Through some combination of climatic change and the spread of highly skilled hunters, almost all of the largest mammals rapidly died out in the Americas. The extinctions comprised two-thirds of all New World species that weighed more than one hundred pounds at maturity—including the giant beaver, giant ground sloth, mammoth, mastodon, and horses and camels. It is ironic that horses and camels first evolved in North America and migrated westward into Asia, where they were eventually domesticated, while those that remained in the Americas became extinct. The giant bison died out, leaving its smaller cousin, the buffalo, as the largest herbivore on the Great Plains. Of the old, shaggy great beasts, only the musk oxen survived and only in the more inaccessible reaches of the arctic.

At the same time that the largest mammals became extinct, the environment became more diverse. Over the generations, the global warming gradually shrank the grasslands and expanded the forests. The revival of complex forest environments expanded the range of plant and small animal species that could be gathered for food.

The changing climate and the demise of the mega-animals induced the nomadic bands to pursue more diversified strategies to tap a broader range of food sources. The natives had to learn their local environments more intimately to harvest shellfish, fish, birds, nuts, seeds, berries, and tubers. The Indians obtained more of their diet from fishing as they developed nets, traps, and bone hooks. Their hunting evolved into the patient and prolonged tracking of more elusive mammals, especially deer, pronghorn antelope, moose, elk, and caribou. Beginning about nine thousand years ago the Indians adjusted to their smaller, fleeter prey by developing the *atlatl*—a spear thrower that provided increased thrust, velocity, and distance.

American archaeologists distinguish the peoples leading this more complex and more locally framed way of life between about nine thousand and three thousand years ago as "Archaic" to distinguish them from their "Paleo-Indian" ancestors. As the Archaic Indians exploited a broader array of food sources, they more than compensated for the loss of the great mammals. Obtaining more to eat, more reliably, they resumed their population growth. The more local and eclectic Archaic way of life could sustain about ten times as many people on a given territory as could the Paleolithic predation on herds of great beasts. From a late Paleolithic level of about 100,000 people, North America's population probably grew to one million by the end of the Archaic period. Obliged to change by the potentially disastrous demise of the megafauna, native peoples innovated to develop a more efficient and productive relationship with their diverse environments.

In the temperate climes, people began to live for longer periods in semi-permanent villages located beside rivers and lakes or along seacoasts, at places where fish and birds and shellfish and wild food plants were most abundant. They also settled in larger groups within smaller territories. Each band developed a seasonal round of activity and movement within a more defined territory, harvesting those plants and animals as they became abundant at different seasons. For example, in the southwest during the summer and fall the people dispersed to hunt rabbits, deer, elk, bighorn sheep, and antelope. The onset of winter with its cold rains led them to gather in larger groups in caves and rock shelters in the sides of canyons, where they harvested prickly pear and piñon nuts. In the spring, they scattered again in pursuit of roots and berries and game.

Archaic Indians also began to modify the environment to increase the yields of plants and animals that sustained them. In particular, they set annual fires to reduce small trees and encourage edge environments that, by providing more browse and better grazing, promoted a larger deer herd for the people to hunt. In some places the Indians weeded out inedible plants to encourage clusters of edible plants such as wild onions, sunflowers, and marsh elder. These practices brought a people to the verge of horticulture.

Gender structured work roles: men were responsible for fishing and hunting while women harvested and prepared wild plants. In general, men's activities entailed wide-ranging travel and the endurance of greater exposure and danger, while women's activities kept them close to the village, where they bore and raised children. We can intuit this from burials, for the dead were interred with the tools they needed in the afterlife: men with hunting, fishing, woodworking, and leatherworking tools; women with tools to dig and grind nuts and roots. Women probably gained in status as their gathering activities became more critical to their band's survival.

The Archaic way of life was a decentralizing phenomenon as many far-flung peoples figured out how best to exploit the mix of resources peculiar to their locale. The immense continent of North America offered extraordinary climatic and environmental diversity. Peoples living along the Atlantic or Pacific coasts, on the Great Plains, in the Rocky Mountains, in the interior deserts, on the edges of the Canadian arctic, or in temperate forests had to pursue different strategies for survival, had to adapt to different seasonal cycles affecting distinctive sets of plants and animals.

As the Archaic Indian bands proliferated and specialized in harvesting the particular local resources, they became distinguished culturally, developing different languages, rituals, mythic stories, kinship systems, and survival strategies. The native peoples of North America spoke at least 375 distinct languages by 1492. The process of cultural differentiation proceeded most elaborately and rapidly in the Pacific northwest and northern California, where the general abundance and the subdivision into many localized microenvironments led to the development of some five hundred culturally diverse communities speaking nearly fifty distinct languages.

Cultural differentiation did not mean cultural isolation. Trade networks developed over very long distances. Archaeologists have found that some relatively small and highly valued objects could pass hundreds and even thousands of miles through multiple bands. At Archaic sites in the midwest or Great Basin, archaeologists find marine shells from the Atlantic and Pacific coasts; on the coasts they uncover copper from the Great Lakes and obsidian from the Rocky Mountains. Ideas and innovations traveled along with these objects so that the trading peoples influenced one another over long distances.

HORTICULTURE

Through trial and error, over many generations, horticulture evolved from the practices of gathering wild plants, rather than by sudden and conscious invention. As some Indian bands protected, watered, and harvested productive patches of wild plants with edible seeds, they also gradually developed hybrids of increasing reliability and productivity. For example, wild maize has a single inch-long ear with fifty tiny kernels. By 1500 B.C., Indians in central Mexico had learned how to cross maize—"Indian corn"—with other wild grasses to create hybrids with multiple ears, protective husks, and cobs with multiple rows of kernels.

The Indians of central Mexico pioneered the three great crops of North American horticulture: maize, squashes, and beans. As these domesticated plants became more important in their diet, the peoples of central Mexico devoted less time to hunting, gathering, and fishing. Indeed, the expansion of cleared fields and the growth of the human population reduced the habitat for wildlife. By expanding the food supply, horticulture permitted a renewed surge in the human population and a more sedentary life in larger and more permanent villages. Indeed, maize requires permanence, for unless carefully tended, guarded, and watered through its growing season, the crop will succumb to pests, weeds, and drought. As people became dependent on corn, they had to live most of the year in villages near their cultivated fields. The new horticulture also promoted economic differentiation and social stratification as the food surplus enabled some people to specialize as craftsmen, merchants, priests, and rulers.

But the new dependence on horticulture also had negative consequences. The crops were vulnerable to catastrophic collapse from a prolonged drought or infestations of insects and blights. Horticulture also demanded more sustained and repetitive work than did the hunting-and-gathering life, in which temporary bursts of exertion alternated with longer stretches of rest. And a horticultural diet that relies too heavily on one plant, particularly maize, is not as healthy as the diverse diet of hunter-gatherers. The skeletons of early farmers reveal a want of sufficient salt or protein, episodes of early childhood malnutrition, and an overall loss of stature. Moreover, the denser populations of horticultural villages facilitated the spread of communicable diseases, principally tuberculosis, which was less common among dispersed hunter-gatherers.

Consequently, native peoples were often slow to adopt Mesoamerican horticulture. By about 1500 B.C., peoples in the American southwest and midwest had begun to cultivate some maize and squash, but only as a minor supplement to their hunting and gathering. Not until about 500 B.C. did native peoples north of the Rio Grande develop strains of maize better suited to their cooler climate and shorter growing season. Thereafter, cultivation spread more rapidly. Between about A.D. 700 and 1200, maize, beans, and squash became fundamental to the native diet in the American southwest, midwest, and southeast and the more temperate portions of the northeast.

In Mexico and the American southwest, where maize cultivation was most advanced, Indian men reduced their hunting and became the primary cultivators. In those relatively arid regions, maize fields required the laborious construction and maintenance of extensive irrigation ponds, dams, and ditches. In the more humid stretches of central and eastern North America, maize cultivation arrived relatively late and required less labor. Consequently, there the native peoples regarded horticulture as an extension of gathering, which was a female responsibility, while the men remained preoccupied with hunting and fishing.

Horticulture never spread universally among the Indians. Some lived where the growing season was too short: in the vast arctic and subarctic regions of Alaska and Canada or in the high elevations of the Rockies and Sierra Nevada. Or they dwelled where there was too little water: in the western Great Plains and in most of the Great Basin between the Rockies and Sierra Nevada. Where either the growing season was too short or water too scant, the inhabitants continued to live in small, mobile, highly dispersed, and relatively egalitarian groups. Rather than horticulture, the most significant development for these people was their adoption of the bow and arrow after about A.D. 500.

Natives also did not develop horticulture in the temperate and humid coastal zone of California and the Pacific northwest, despite its sufficient growing seasons and abundant water. Along the Pacific coast, the hunting-gathering-fishing complex was so productive that the native peoples did not feel the pressures that elsewhere led to horticulture. In California an abundance of acorns and other edible wild plants supported an especially large population. Similarly, in the mild and rainy Pacific northwest, the people lived plentifully on fish (especially salmon) and sea mammals. Endowed with a bountiful diet and leisure time, the Indians of the northwestern raincoast could develop and sustain elaborate rituals, art, and status hierarchies without developing horticulture.

HOHOKAM AND ANASAZI

Between about A.D. 300 and 1100 two especially complex and populous cultures emerged in the American southwest: the Hohokam and the Anasazi. The names are scholarly conventions, for we do not know what those peoples called themselves. "Hohokam" and "Anasazi" signify broad cultural similarities rather than linguistic and political unity. Neither constituted a nation-state, to say nothing of an empire. Instead, both cultures consisted of several linguistic groups and many politically independent villages or towns (later called *pueblos* by the Spanish). Neither the Anasazi nor the Hohokam had beasts of burden (other than dogs), developed a system of writing, or employed the wheel. Nonetheless, both built substantial stone and adobe towns directed by a social hierarchy headed by men who combined the roles of chief and priest.

The Anasazi and Hohokam annually conducted public rituals meant to sustain the harmony and productivity of their world. Far from taking harmony and abundance for granted, they regarded constant ritual exertion as essential to prevent nature's collapse into chaos. Their arid land of limited resources and competing villages afforded good cause for their existential anxiety.

Both the Anasazi and the Hohokam manifested, to varying degrees, the influence of central Mexico, the preeminent cultural hearth of the continent. In trade with central Mexico, they exchanged turquoise stones for parrots, copper bells, and maize seed. In addition to transmitting their food crops, Mesoamericans taught the Hohokam and Anasazi how to cultivate cotton and to weave cloth. The largest Hohokam villages constructed ball courts and platform temple mounds resembling those of central Mexican cities.

In the arid southwest, horticulture required elaborate systems of dams, reservoirs, and ditches to catch, retain, and channel water to irrigate the plants. In the Gila River and Salt River valleys of southern Arizona, the Hohokam built and maintained over five hundred miles of irrigation canals to water thousands of acres devoted to maize, beans, and squash. To the north, the Anasazi occupied upland canyons that captured more moisture in winter than did the low desert. The Anasazi irrigation system caught and retained winter's rainwater on the mesa tops for spring and summer release via diversion channels to low-lying fields beside the intermittent streambeds, where the people cultivated their crops.

The irrigation works demanded extensive, coordinated labor to build and maintain, while the abundant crops enabled many people to live clustered together. The preeminent Hohokam pueblo, known as Snaketown, had about a thousand residents living in adobe row houses, some of them two and three stories tall. The Anasazi constructed even larger, rectangular pueblos of mortared sandstone blocks roofed with rafters and adobe tile. The largest pueblo, at Chaco Canyon, required thirty thousand tons of sandstone blocks, stood four stories tall, and contained at least 650 rooms.

During the twelfth and early thirteenth centuries, both the Hohokam and the Anasazi experienced severe crises that began in environmental degradation associated with local overpopulation and an excessive reliance on maize. Although highly productive, corn rapidly depletes the soil of nutrients, especially nitrogen. Repeated crops in the same fields led to diminishing yields. In the southwest, between 1130 and 1190, an especially prolonged period of drought years exacerbated the subsistence crisis, setting off a chain reaction of crop failure, malnutrition, and violent feuds.

The Hohokam apparently concluded that their leaders could no longer win favor from the spirits of the plants and the rain. The hard work of supporting their chiefs and priests and maintaining the irrigation systems or the earthworks came to seem futile. During the thirteenth century, most of the Hohokam abandoned their towns and dispersed into the arid hinterland, where they reverted to a mobile strategy of hunting and gathering that shifted with the seasons. They harvested cholla, yucca, saguaro fruit, prickly pear, and mesquite pods, and they hunted for rabbit, deer, and pronghorn antelope. Sixteenth-century Spanish explorers found the probable descendants of the Hohokam divided into many small villages. They called themselves some variant of "O'odham," which simply means "the people," but the Spanish named them the Pima and the Papago. Some lived beside the rivers and maintained smaller-scale versions of the ancient irrigation system, but most lived in the hills.

Between 1150 and 1250, the Anasazi responded to their growing violence by shifting their pueblos to more defensible locations atop mesas, which they fortified. Skeletons from this period reveal a surge in violent death, mutilation, and perhaps ritual cannibalism. At the end of the thirteenth century, most of the Anasazi abandoned their homeland and fled south and east, seeking locales with a more certain source of water and with soils not yet exhausted by corn. Some regrouped in western New Mexico and eastern Arizona to build the Acoma, Hopi, and Zuni pueblos. Founded in 1300, Acoma is probably the longest continuously inhabited community within the United States. Other Anasazi traveled still farther east to settle along the upper Rio Grande, which offered sufficient year-round water to sustain irrigation even in drought years. Later collectively called the Pueblo Indians by the Spanish, the Rio Grande peoples in fact belonged to dozens of autonomous villages, and they spoke at least seven different languages. Instead of "collapsing," the Anasazi culture *moved*, shifting into impressive new pueblos to the south and east of its former homeland. The oral traditions of the Pueblo, Zuni, Hopi, and Acoma agree that their ancestors were uprooted from old homes by a combination of drought, famine, disease, and violence.

MOUND BUILDERS

In contrast to the arid American southwest, the Mississippi watershed enjoys a humid and temperate climate. The great river collects the waters of wide-ranging tributaries, including the Tennesee, Cumberland, Ohio, Missouri, Arkansas, and Red rivers, to drain an area of nearly 1.25 million square miles. Unlike the Hohokam and Anasazi, the Mississippi people did not need irrigation systems to sustain horticulture. Indeed, the mild and moist conditions probably delayed the advent of horticulture by sustaining the inhabitants with an abundance of wild plants and animals. Beginning about 2000 B.C., Mississippi Valley farmers experimented with the cultivation of marsh elder, goosefoot, sunflowers, and gourds. But they continued to depend upon hunting, fishing, and gathering for most of their diet until about A.D. 800, when they adopted the trinity of maize, beans, and squash. The broad floodplains of the Mississippi Valley proved ideal for the new horticulture: well-watered, well-drained soils easily tilled with stone hoes and replenished with fertile silt by annual spring floods. The highly productive new horticulture permitted the population to quadruple, as the Mississippi Valley became the most densely settled region north of central Mexico.

Drawing upon Mesoamerican precedents, the Mississippian peoples built substantial towns around central plazas that featured earthen pyramids topped by wooden temples that doubled as the residences of chiefs. Like the people of central Mexico, the Mississippians regarded the sun as their principal deity, responsible for the crops that sustained their survival; they considered their chiefs as quasi-sacred beings related to the sun; and they practiced human sacrifice. When a chief died, his wives and servants were killed for burial beside him, as companions for the afterlife.

Paying tribute in labor and produce, common people erected the earthworks, built the towns, and sustained a local chief. In turn, the local chiefs usually paid tribute to a paramount chief, who dwelled on top of the largest pyramid in the region's largest town.

The great valley was a vibrant and diverse landscape of paramount and local chiefdoms, of rising and falling power, never stable and never united. There was a "cycling" process by which certain towns emerged for a century or two to dominate their region only to decline in favor of a rival chiefdom. The chiefdoms conducted chronic warfare. Burials reveal skeletons scarred with battle wounds; many towns were fortified with wooden palisades, and their art often celebrated victorious warriors displaying the skulls, scalps, and corpses of their victims. Of course, none of this rendered them more warlike than their contemporaries elsewhere in the world; European graves, cities, and art of the same period ("the Middle Ages") also displayed the prominence of war and the honors bestowed upon victors.

The largest, wealthiest, and most complex of the political and ceremonial centers was at a place now called Cahokia, located near the Mississippi River in Illinois just east of St. Louis. Cahokia arose in the midst of a broad and fertile floodplain, extending over about 350 square miles. In addition to hosting cornfields, the floodplain featured dozens of oxbow lakes and marshes, rich in fish and waterfowl. Located near the junctures of the Missouri, Tennesee, and Ohio rivers with the Mississippi, Cahokia could also dominate both north-south and east-west trade in precious shells and stones.

Developed between A.D. 900 and 1100, Cahokia and its immediate suburbs covered about six square miles and had a population of at least ten thousand (some estimates run as high as forty thousand). Even at the smallest calculation, Cahokia ranked as the greatest Indian community north of Mexico. At its peak, Cahokia contained about one hundred earthen temple and burial mounds as well as hundreds of thatched houses for commoners. The city was surrounded by a stockade, a wall of large posts two miles in circumference with a watchtower every seventy feet. Outside the palisade stood a precise circle 410 feet in diameter, featuring forty-eight large posts. Called "Woodhenge" by archaeologists, this was a calendrical device to determine the solstices and equinoxes—apparently to guide the ritual cycle of the city.

Cahokia's greatest monument was an immense earthen pyramid containing over 800,000 cubic yards of earth, covering sixteen acres, and rising 110 feet high. The Cahokia pyramid was the third-largest in North America, ranking behind two in central Mexico. The flat top bore a wooden temple with a thatched roof. The temple contained a sacred fire representing the sun, and it housed the chief, along with his family and servants. The chief served as the town's preeminent priest, responsible for conducting rituals to maintain a spiritual harmony between the people and their cosmos. The inhabitants sought a supernatural security from catastrophic variations in their climate, especially droughts and crop blights. Endowed with great structures,

Cahokia appeared as a center of great spiritual and temporal power that must be honored and sustained.

During the twelfth century, however, Cahokia began to decline in population and power, and it was abandoned in the middle of the thirteenth century—at the same time that the Anasazi and Hohokam experienced their crises. As in the southwest, the archaeological evidence suggests that environmental strains initiated the demise of Cahokia. The growing population gradually depleted the local resources, initiating a destructive cycle of malnutrition, disease, demoralization, and infighting. Too many hunters killed the nearby wild animals faster than they could reproduce, reducing animal protein in the people's diet, which led to an unhealthy overreliance on maize. The people also chopped down most of the nearby forest, exhausting the wood needed for fires and to repair their homes and the defensive stockade. Urban concentration also accumulated the wastes that bred the pathogens of some endemic diseases. The environmental strains became exacerbated into a severe crisis in those years when unusually hot and dry summers withered the crops. As the people's material circumstances decayed, they doubted the efficacy of the paramount chief in securing favor from the sun. Doubts encouraged dissension and rebellion, especially by the subordinated villages on Cahokia's periphery. In the elaborate and strengthened stockade there is evidence of growing external resistance. Burials throughout the upper midwest also indicate a greater frequency of violent death.

Although in decline around Cahokia, Missisippian culture remained vibrant in substantial southern towns, including Moundville in Alabama, Etowah in Georgia, and Spiro in eastern Oklahoma, which surged in size and apparent power after Cahokia collapsed. The southern Mississippian culture survived for description by the chroniclers attached to a Spanish expedition commanded by Hernando de Soto in the years 1540–42. They were impressed by the numbers of the Indians, the extent of their maize fields, the quantities in their storehouses, the dignity and power of their chiefs, and their disciplined warriors. From the top of one town's temple mound the Spanish could usually see the palisades and mounds of several neighboring towns. "That country is populous and abundant," concluded a Spaniard.

Soto foolishly claimed that he could command the sun and summoned a paramount chief to his camp. The chief contemptuously replied:

> As to what you say of your being the son of the Sun, if you will cause him to dry up the great river, I will believe you: as to the rest, it is not my custom to visit any one, but rather all, of whom I have ever heard, have come to visit me, to serve and obey me, and pay me tribute, either voluntarily or by force. If you desire to see me, come where I am; if for peace, I will receive you with special goodwill; if for war, I will await you in my town; but neither for you, nor for any man, will I set back one foot.

A Mississippian chief could be as imperious as any European warlord. But the arrival of the Europeans, bent on conquest and bearing disease pathogens, introduced a radical and catastrophic acceleration of change. Within a century, European diseases, supplemented by European violence, killed most of the Mississippian peoples and transformed the world of the survivors.

BELIEFS

The Anasazi, Hohokam, and northern Mississippians all put excessive pressure on their local environments, leading to increased violence and the collapse or relocation of their largest communities. Although their experiences contradict the romantic myth of the Indian as environmental saint, it would be equally misleading to depict *all* natives as just as environmentally destructive as their European contemporaries. In their urban concentrations and dependence on maize, the Anasazi, the Hohokam, and the Mississippians were conspicuous exceptions to the general pattern in native America. North of central Mexico, most native peoples lived in smaller, more dispersed, and more mobile bands that placed less of a burden on their local nature. And even the urbanized peoples produced less long-term, accumulative damage than did their European contemporaries. The urban centers tended to collapse within two centuries of their peak, which obliged their inhabitants either to relocate or to revert to a more decentralized and less hierarchical mode of life, which allowed the recovery of wild plants, animals, and soils. Because native peoples more promptly felt the negative consequences of their local abuse of nature (relative to Europeans), they more quickly shifted to alternative environmental strategies.

Natives could and did damage their local environments, but they certainly did less enduring harm than the colonizers who displaced them. By all accounts, the nature found by European explorers was far more diverse and abundant in plants and animals than the nature they had left behind in their Old World. Having depleted the forests and wildlife of Europe, the colonizers came to do the same in their New World.

When the Europeans invaded, the native North Americans painfully discovered their profound technological and epidemiological disadvantages. They lacked the steel weapons and armor and the gunpowder that endowed the invaders with military advantage. Native peoples also could not match the wind or water mills that facilitated the processing of wood and grain. Lacking horses and oxen, native North Americans knew the wheel only in Mesoamerica as a toy. For maritime navigation, the natives possessed only large canoes and rafts incapable of crossing an open ocean in safety. Their lone domesticated mammal was the dog, which provided far less protein and less motive power than the cattle and horses of the Europeans. Only the elites in parts of Mesoamerica possessed the systems of writing that facilitated long-distance communication and record-keeping. Consequently, in the North America of 1492, only the Aztecs of Mexico constituted an imperial power capable of governing multiple cities and their peoples by command. In addition, no Native Americans possessed an ideology that impelled them far beyond their known world in search of new lands and peoples to conquer and to transform. Finally, compared with Europeans, the natives of America carried a more limited and less deadly array of pathogenic microbes.

By contrast, the Europeans of 1492 were the heirs to an older and more complex array of domesticated plants and animals developed about nine thousand years ago at the eastern end of the Mediterranean. The European mode of agriculture featured domesticated mammals—sheep, pigs, cattle, and horses—endowing their owners with more fertilizer, mobility, motive power, animal protein, and shared disease microbes. Building on a long head start and the power of domesticated mammals, the Europeans had, over the centuries, developed expansionist ambitions, systems of written records and communication, the maritime and military technology that permitted global exploration and conquest, and (unwittingly) a deadly array of diseases to which they enjoyed partial immunities. Lacking those peculiar ambitions, technologies, diseases, and domesticants, the Indians did not expand across the Atlantic to discover and conquer Europe.

The technological differences reflected contrasting spiritual commitments. Compared with Europeans, Indians possessed a more complex understanding of the interdependent relationship between the natural and supernatural. Where Europeans believed that humanity had a divine duty and an unchecked power to dominate nature, North American Indians believed that they lived within a contentious world of spiritual power that sometimes demanded human restraint and at other moments offered opportunities for exploitation.

North American natives subscribed to "animism": a conviction that the supernatural was a complex and diverse web of power woven into every part of the natural world. Indeed, Indians made no distinction between the natural and the supernatural. In their minds, spiritual power was neither singular nor transcendent, but diverse and ubiquitous. Their world was filled with an almost infinite variety of beings, each possessing some varying measure of power. All living things belonged to a complex matrix that was simultaneously spiritual and material. Indeed, spirit power could be found in every plant, animal, rock, wind, cloud, and body of water—but in greater concentration in some than others. This power pulsated, ebbing and flowing from interaction with every other being—including the ritual magic practiced by humans bent on exploiting their nature. If properly approached and flattered (or tricked), the spirit "keepers" of animals or plants could help people find, catch, and kill what they needed.

Because of their animistic convictions, Indians lived very differently within their nature than Europeans did within theirs. Natives believed that humans lived inside, rather than apart from, that web of the natural and supernatural. They conceived of their actions with all other-than-human beings as essentially social, as involving creatures more like than unlike themselves. Indeed, in their myths and dreams, people and the other-than-human could metamorphose into one another. As in all aspects of native life, the fundamental principle in harvesting nature was the pursuit of reciprocity. People felt justified in claiming a share in the other life around them, but felt obligated to reciprocate by paying ritual honor and by minimizing waste.

Indians understood that humans could live only by killing fish and animals and by clearing trees for fields, but they had to proceed cautiously. Natives usually showed restraint, not because they were ecologically minded in the twentieth-century sense, but because spirits, who could harm people, lurked in the animals and plants. A healthy fear of the spirits limited how the Indians dealt with other forms of life, lest they reap some supernatural counterattack. Offended spirits might hide away the animals or the fish, afflict the corn crop, or churn up a devastating windstorm. Any success in hunting, fishing, or cultivating had to be accepted with humility, in recognition that the fruits of nature were provisional gifts from temperamental spirits.

Indian animism should not be romantically distorted into a New Age creed of stable harmony. In fact, the natives regarded the spiritual world as volatile and full of tension, danger, and uncertainty. To survive and prosper, people had to live warily and opportunistically. Engaged in an always difficult balancing act, humans had to discern when they could trick and manipulate the spirits and when they should soothe and mollify them. Sometimes people could take fish or kill game with exuberance; more often they had to limit their take. The logic of restraint was animist rather than ecological—but that restraint tended to preserve a nature that sustained most native communities over many generations.

Dreams and visions enabled native people to communicate with the spirits to enlist their aid in hunting, gathering, cultivating, and war. Natives regarded the nocturnal dreamworld as fundamentally more real and powerful than their waking hours. They also provoked visions by prolonged fasting and isolation (sometimes aided by ingesting psychotropic plants). The most adept dreamers and visionaries became shamans, who acted as intermediaries between people and the other-than-human beings. Shamans conducted rituals to promote the hunt, secure the crops, and protect their warriors. Shamans could heal or inflict illness, and could predict, and sometimes magically influence, the future. But even the most skilled shaman often failed in the complex contests to influence, lull, and propitiate spirit beings. Only constant effort and varying tactics could preserve the reciprocities between people and other life.

An animist perspective discouraged the sort of mechanistic development practiced by Europeans. Lacking domesticated animals and metal tools and weapons, the Indians seemed a primitive people to the Europeans. The natives, however, regarded themselves as more intelligent and resourceful than the Europeans. Animism both derived from and encouraged the distinctive forms of perception and ingenuity demanded by hunting and gathering—practices essential to almost all native peoples, even those who also cultivated domesticated plants. Native peoples keenly observed the diverse forms of edible or healing life in the forest and waters, and they mastered the best times and techniques for finding and harvesting wild plants and animals. Because Europeans lacked these skills and that knowledge, they struck the Indians as clumsy babes in the woods. From the native perspective, it seemed that the colonizers had exhausted their intelligence in making their metal and cloth goods. Preoccupied with dead matter, they appeared insensitive to living nature.

A few colonizers recognized that native intelligence and creativity ran in different channels. William Wood concluded that the natives were "by nature admirably ingenious." Another seventeenth-century New Englander, Thomas Morton, decided, "The Salvages have the sence of seeing so farre beyond any of our Nation, that one would almost believe they had intelligence of the Devill."

Even a relatively sympathetic observer like Morton could not accept native beliefs on their own terms. Instead, Europeans forced animism into their polarity between the divine and the diabolical. They generally regarded the Indians' beliefs as dictated by the devil and considered their shamans to be witches, possessed of an evil power to inflict harm on other Indians but not on European Christians.

In contrast to the animism of the natives, the Europeans had begun conceptually to segregate the natural and the spiritual. Christianity fundamentally invests supernatural power in a single God located away in heaven, above and beyond the earth. Even the evil power of the devil and his minions was subordinate to God: allowed in the short term but ultimately doomed to destruction. Most sixteenth- and seventeenth-century Europeans continued to believe in supernatural intervention, both divine and diabolical, in human events. But they regarded the supernatural intervention as coming from without, rather than from within particular plants, animals, and places. Belief in a transcendent God enabled educated Europeans to disenchant the world, to treat it as purely material and its animals as without souls. Of course, many European peasants continued to merge old pagan beliefs in fairies and other nature spirits with their Christian notions. But such rustics exercised no intellectual, political, or economic power in the hierarchical societies of Europe and their colonial ventures.

The Christian alienation of spirit from nature rendered it supernaturally safe for Europeans to harvest all the resources that they wanted from nature, for they offended no spirits in doing so. In wild plants and animals, the colonizers simply saw potential commodities: items that could be harvested, processed, and sold to make a profit. Indeed, European Christians insisted that humanity had a divine charge to dominate and exploit the natural world. In the first book of their Bible, God ordered people to "subdue the earth and have dominion over every living thing that moves on the earth." As a result, colonizers regarded as backward and impious any people, like the Indians, who left nature too little altered. By defaulting in their divine duty, such peoples forfeited their title to the earth. They could justly be conquered and dispossessed by Europeans who would exploit lands and animals to their fullest potential.

The "anthropocentric" implications of Christianity enabled western Europeans to develop the economic culture of capitalism (to varying degrees) during the sixteenth and seventeenth centuries. Spain, Portugal, and France were hybrid economic cultures in which capitalist enterprise remained inhibited by feudal traditions and especially powerful monarchs. By comparison, England and the Netherlands more quickly and more fully developed capitalist societies, in which the means of production—land, labor, and capital—were privately owned, available for sale, and devoted to harvesting or making commodities for sale in pursuit of profit. Although neither the Dutch nor the English had yet developed the mature form of capitalism characterized by industrial production and a propertyless proletariat, both nations had passed into that early stage known as mercantile capitalism. During the sixteenth and seventeenth centuries, the Dutch and English merchant classes were constructing innovative combinations of land, labor, and capital meant to accumulate profit for yet further investment and production. Their ambitious new ventures included trading voyages to, and plantations within, the North American colonies.

Capitalist societies compel much more work from common people and extract far more energy and matter from nature than do the less ambitious economies of aboriginal peoples subscribing to animism. Capitalism demands ever greater production and innovation in a relentless drive for increased profits. Competitors who cannot keep up go bankrupt. Unless regulated, capitalism encourages individuals to harvest wealth from nature as quickly as possible.

Seventeenth-century capitalism already had its discontents. Although Christianity was compatible with the emergence of capitalism, that does not mean that they lacked tensions. Indeed, the materialism and individualism encouraged by capitalism profoundly troubled early modern clergymen. Catholic friars, as well as Protestant ministers, worried that the pursuit of wealth distracted people from attending to their proper goal: the salvation of their souls for an enduring afterlife in heaven. People were supposed to labor diligently at their worldly calling, yet never mistake its rewards as their ultimate purpose in life.

In the less hurried, more egalitarian, and less propertied ways of Indians, some critics saw an opportunity to score points against their own uneasy culture. A French priest in Acadia noted of the Indians, "They are never in a hurry. Quite different from us, who can never do anything without hurry and worry; worry, I say, because our desire tyrannizes over us and banishes peace from our actions." Similarly, Thomas Morton, a fur trader in New England, observed: "These people lead the more happy & freer life, being voyde of care, which torments the minds of so many Christians. They are not delighted in baubles, but in useful things." He added, "If our beggars of England should with so much ease (as they) furnish themselves with foode, at all seasons, there would not be so many starved in the streets. Neither would so many gaoles be stuffed, or gallows furnished with poor wretches."

But neither the priest nor the trader deserted European society to embrace life among the natives. Both men remained fundamentally committed to the superiority of the Christian faith and the European economy. For all their criticism of European materialism, these critics insisted that natives must eventually forsake their own culture and accept that of their invaders. However astute, their critiques were the fleeting indulgence of men bent upon converting Indians or upon trading with them for profit.

By offering such moral criticism, however, Christians helped to preserve a capitalist society from consuming itself. Indeed, without some moral counterweight and some sense of a higher purpose, capitalist competition degenerates into a rapacious, violent kleptocracy. Without a God, the capitalist is simply a pirate, and markets collapse for want of a minimal trust between buyers and sellers. The seventeenth-century English minister Thomas Shepard aptly commented that self-interest was a "raging Sea which would overwhelm all if [it] have not bankes." Shepard did not wish to abolish self-interest, merely to strengthen its restraining banks. Christianity provided the banks that permitted capitalist enterprise to persist, prosper, and expand into the Americas.

2

Colonizers

1400–1800

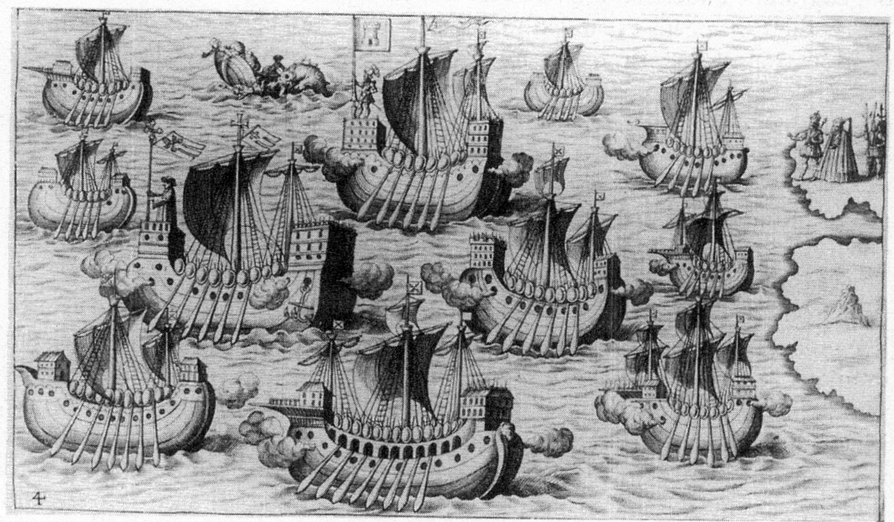

The departure for Columbus's second voyage, with representations of Queen Isabella and King Ferdinand on the shore of Iberia. Although a fanciful depiction of the ships, the image conveys the European mastery of the Atlantic and determination to colonize the Americas. An engraving from Caspar Plautius, Nova Typis Transacta Navigatio *(n.p., 1621).*

DURING THE LATE FIFTEENTH and early sixteenth centuries, Europeans developed the maritime technology and imperial ambitions to explore and dominate the world's oceans. Long a barrier to Europeans, the Atlantic became their highway to distant lands and unknown peoples. Between 1450 and 1500, European mariners, in dozens of voyages, found the Americas and rounded Africa to cross the Indian Ocean to India and the East Indies. In the years 1519–22 the Spanish sailors of Ferdinand Magellan's voyage first circumnavigated the globe, confirming that the oceans formed an integrated system that European ships could probe. On distant coasts, the mariners established fortified outposts to dominate local trade, creating the first transoceanic global empires. It was an extraordinary and unprecedented burst of geographic understanding, daring, and enterprise.

As the Europeans expanded their geographic range, they also developed a combination of science, technology, and commerce that gave them growing mastery over what they found. The various advances fed upon one another as the mariners tested innovations in mathematics, astronomy, geology, medicine, and weaponry. And the distant discoveries brought new commercial riches to Europe: precious metals, sugar, tobacco, vital new foods such as maize and potatoes, and new sources of slave labor. By enriching Europe, the new resources financed further exploration and conquest.

The discovery and exploitation of the Americas and the route to Asia transformed Europe from a parochial backwater into the world's most dynamic and powerful continent. Europeans delighted in the sudden and dramatic change in their circumstances, perspective, and prospects. A sixteenth-century Italian physician marveled "that I was born in this century in which the whole world became known; whereas the ancients were familiar with but a little more than a third part of it." Perceptive Spaniards celebrated their new centrality in the world. During the 1560s, Tomás de Mercado commented that "previously, [the Spanish provinces of] Andalusia and Lusitania used to be at the very end of the world, but now, with the discovery of the Indies, they have become its center."

The first European explorers were stunned by the distinctive flora, fauna, and human cultures found in the Americas. In the West Indies, Christopher Columbus marveled, "All the trees were as different from ours as day from night, and so the fruits, the herbage, the rocks, and all things." Subsequent explorers recognized the obvious: that the Americas constituted a distinctive, hitherto unknown hemisphere. During the 1550s the explorer Jean de Léry reported that America was so "different from Europe, Asia and Africa in the living habits of its people, the forms of its animals, and, in general, in that which the earth produces, that it can well be called the new world."

But the differences began to diminish as soon as they were recognized. The invasion by European colonists, microbes, plants, and livestock eroded the biological and cultural distinctions formerly enforced by the Atlantic

Ocean. Newly connected, the two "worlds," old and new, became more alike in their natures, in their combinations of plants and animals. In 1528 the Spanish writer Hernán Pérez de Oliva explained that Columbus's voyages served "to unite the world and give to those strange lands the form of our own." American colonization wrought an environmental revolution unprecedented in pace, scale, and impact in the history of humanity.

The environmental revolution worked disproportionately in favor of the Europeans and to the detriment of the native peoples, who saw their numbers dwindle. Although never under the full control of the colonizers, the transformation enhanced their power by undermining the nature that indigenous communities depended upon. Colonization literally alienated the land from its native inhabitants. In particular, the colonizers accidentally introduced despised weeds, detested vermin, and deadly microbes. All three did far more damage to native peoples and their nature than to the colonists. While exporting their own blights, the European colonizers imported the most productive food plants developed by the Indians. The new crops fueled a population explosion in seventeenth- and eighteenth-century Europe. Part of that growth then flowed back across the Atlantic to resettle the Americas as European colonies.

EUROPE

The stunning expansion of European power, wealth, and knowledge would have seemed improbable in 1400, when the Europeans were a parochial set of peoples preoccupied with internal and interminable wars. Europe was also slowly recovering from a devastating epidemic of bubonic plague, known as the Black Death, which during the 1340s had killed about a third of the population. Moreover, relative to Asian peoples, the Europeans had shown less interest in new science and technology. Their spiritual and intellectual leaders usually insisted that everything worth knowing had already been discovered by the ancient Greeks and Romans, or had been revealed by their God and recorded in the Bible. Men who indulged in innovative scientific speculation risked prosecution for heresy by church courts.

European Christians also felt hemmed in by the superior wealth, power, and technology possessed by their rivals and neighbors the Muslims, who subscribed to Islam, the world's other great expansionist faith. Dominated by the Ottoman Turks, the Muslim realms extended across North Africa and around the southern and eastern Mediterranean Sea to embrace the Balkans, the Near East, Central Asia, and Southeast Asia. The long and usually secure trade routes of the Muslim world reached from Morocco to the East Indies and from Mongolia to Senegal. Within that range, Muslim traders benefited from the far-flung prevalence of Arabic as the language of law, commerce, government, and science.

Fifteenth-century Christians felt beleaguered, on the losing end of a struggle for the future of humanity. During the preceding three centuries, European crusaders suffered bloody and humiliating defeats in their botched attempts to capture and hold Jerusalem. Worse yet, during the fifteenth century, the Ottoman Turks invaded southeastern Europe, capturing the strategic Greek city of Constantinople in 1453. The Turkish advance created in Europe a powerful sense of geographic and religious claustrophobia, which generated a profound longing to break out and circumvent the Muslim world.

European leaders concluded that the Muslims' power fed upon the wealth generated by their control of the most lucrative trade routes. By paying premium prices to Muslim merchants for the gold and ivory of sub-Saharan Africa and for the silks, gems, and spices of Asia, European consumers enriched the Islamic world while draining wealth from Christendom. Moreover, the Turkish sultan collected taxes on the luxury trade passing through his vast empire to Europe. Visionary Europeans hoped to weaken their enemy and enrich themselves by seeking an alternative trade route by sea to bypass Muslim merchants and Turkish tax collectors to reach sub-Saharan Africa and East Asia.

Popular literature reinforced the European longing for a new trade route to the fabled riches of the Far East. During the second half of the fifteenth century, the development of the printing press immensely lowered the cost and increased the volume of book publishing. More people learned to read, as books became available to more than the wealthy and leisured elite. By the end of the century, Europeans possessed twenty million copies of printed books. Readers especially delighted in vivid accounts of the wealth and power of India and China. These included the real travels of Marco Polo, an Italian merchant, as well as the pure fictions attributed to John de Mandeville. Inspired by their literary fantasies, European visionaries longed to reach the Far East to enlist their peoples and wealth for a climactic crusade against Islam. As a fabulous land that could fulfill Europeans' dreams, eastern Asia (and especially China) rendered the intruding barrier of the Muslim world all the more frustrating.

European expansionists could find hope to the southwest, on the Iberian Peninsula, where the kingdoms of Aragon, Castile, and Portugal gradually rolled back the Muslim Moors. In 1469 the marriage of Queen Isabella and Prince Ferdinand united Aragon and Castile to create "Spain." Zealous, able, and expansionist, Isabella and Ferdinand in 1492 completed the *reconquista* ("reconquest") by seizing Granada, the last Muslim principality in Iberia. They also looked westward, into the Atlantic, for new opportunities to extend their crusade. Close to Africa and facing the Atlantic, Spain and Portugal were well situated to lead the maritime expansion of Europe. In addition, the long and violent *reconquista* had institutionalized a crusading spirit in Iberia, developing an especially militant clergy and an ambitious warrior

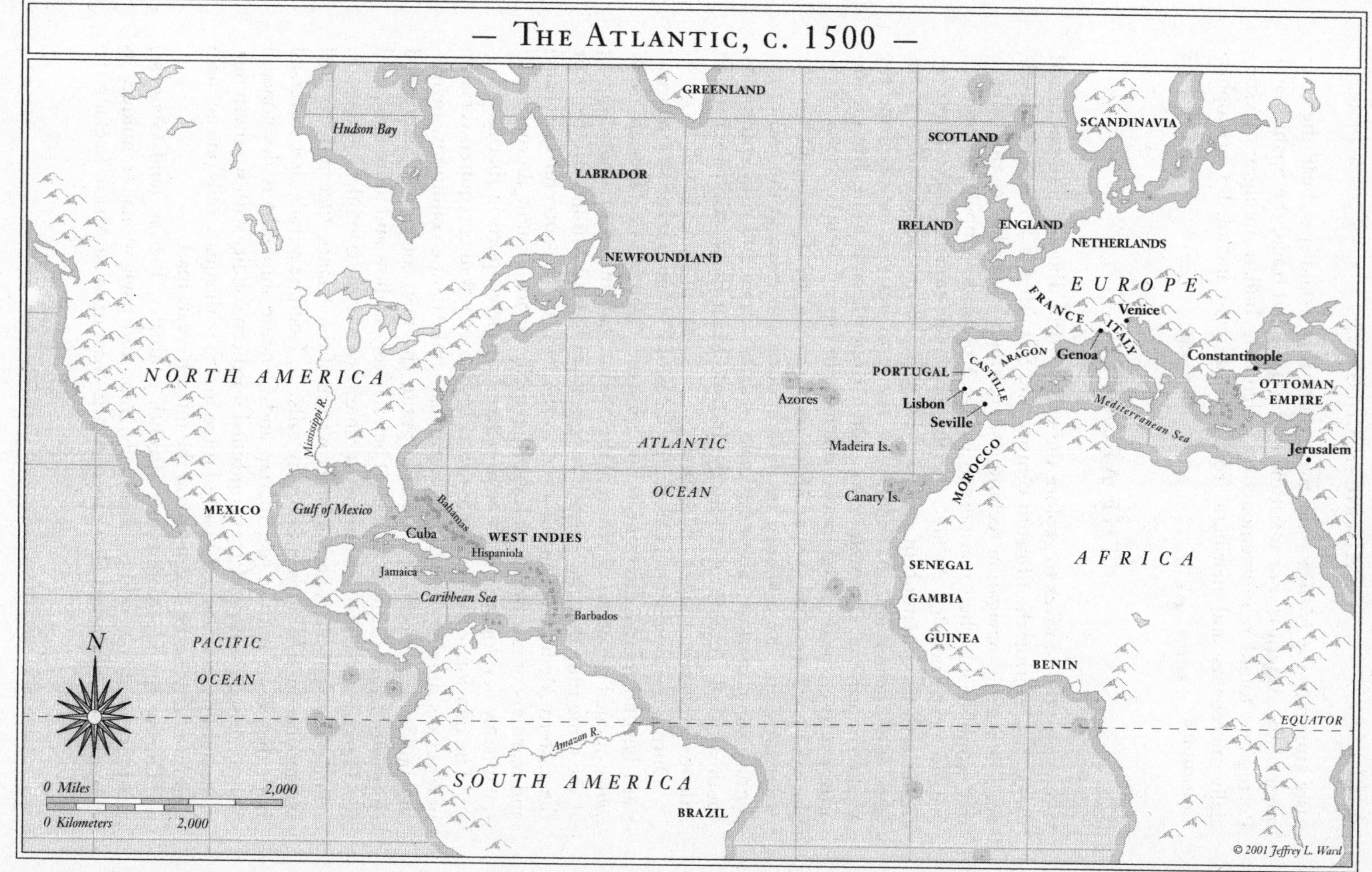
— The Atlantic, c. 1500 —
GREENLAND
Hudson Bay
LABRADOR
NEWFOUNDLAND
SCOTLAND
SCANDINAVIA
IRELAND
ENGLAND
NETHERLANDS
EUROPE
FRANCE
Venice
ITALY
Genoa
ARAGON
CASTILLE
PORTUGAL
Lisbon
Seville
Constantinople
OTTOMAN EMPIRE
Mediterranean Sea
Jerusalem
NORTH AMERICA
Mississippi R.
Azores
Madeira Is.
Canary Is.
ATLANTIC
OCEAN
MOROCCO
MEXICO
Gulf of Mexico
Bahamas
Cuba
WEST INDIES
Hispaniola
Jamaica
Caribbean Sea
Barbados
SENEGAL
GAMBIA
GUINEA
BENIN
AFRICA
PACIFIC
OCEAN
N
EQUATOR
Amazon R.
SOUTH AMERICA
BRAZIL
0 Miles 2,000
0 Kilometers 2,000
© 2001 Jeffrey L. Ward

caste known as the *hidalgos*—the two groups that would spearhead the conquest of the Americas. For maritime exploration and trade, the Spanish and Portuguese found reinforcements by welcoming Italian immigrants, especially merchants and mariners from Genoa, who included Christopher Columbus.

THE ATLANTIC

Along with the motives to explore the wider world, Iberians also cultivated the means. During the fifteenth century, the Spanish and Portuguese developed new ships, navigation techniques, geographic knowledge, and cannon that would enable their mariners to voyage around the globe and dominate distant coastal peoples. At first, the Iberians made none of these improvements with the intention of crossing the Atlantic. Instead, the innovations were incremental and stimulated by the growing commerce from the Mediterranean into the Atlantic to trade with northern Europe. But the improvements enabled daring Iberian mariners to expand their horizons, to explore the northwestern coast of Africa and to exploit newfound islands in the eastern Atlantic. Emboldened by those modest successes, at the end of the century some mariners attempted two especially bold and risky extensions: southeastward around Africa into the Indian Ocean and westward across the Atlantic in search of Japan and China.

During the fourteenth century, the focus of European trade shifted westward beyond the Mediterranean and into the Atlantic. The Iberian *reconquista* opened the western mouth of the Mediterranean to Christian shipping at the same time that the Turkish conquests tightened Muslim control over the eastern Mediterranean. Blocked to the east, the resourceful merchants and mariners of northwestern Italy, principally Genoa, sought alternatives to the west by developing a trade to northern Europe via ports in Iberia.

The new long-distance trade routes into stormy waters required versatile new vessels suitable to both Mediterranean and Atlantic conditions. Involving bulkier commodities, especially grain, the new routes also demanded ships with larger cargo capacities. The relatively shallow and more protected Mediterranean Sea favored maneuverable vessels with triangular lateen sails, while the longer hauls and stormier waters of the Atlantic Ocean demanded strong and durable ships with square sails. To facilitate a trade that traversed both the ocean and the sea, Iberian and Genoese shipbuilders developed a hybrid vessel, the *caravel*, that combined northern solidity with southern maneuverability. The caravel boasted three masts, with square sails on the main and fore masts and a lateen sail on the mizzen (rear) mast.

During the fourteenth and fifteenth centuries, Iberian (and Genoese) mariners gradually refined their new ships and navigational techniques as they pressed southward along the Atlantic coast of West Africa. Lacking the means to organize and finance maritime exploration, the monarchs of Portugal and Castile relied on the private enterprise of profit-seeking merchants and adventurers willing to pay fees in return for royal licenses. Practical men, the adventurers did not pursue exploration for a pure love of geographic knowledge. Rather than launch especially risky voyages directly into the Atlantic unknown, they invested in more modest voyages that seemed likely to generate profits quickly. They proceeded incrementally along the northwest coast of Africa, seeking the sources of known commodities: fishing grounds and the gold, ivory, pepper, and slaves that Muslim North Africans had long tapped by their overland caravan trade with sub-Saharan Africa.

While probing along the northwest coast of Africa, Iberian and Italian mariners discovered three sets of islands in the eastern Atlantic: the Canaries, Azores, and Madeiras. Surrounded by rich fisheries and heavily forested with trees that yielded valuable dyes, the Atlantic islands provided immediate commodities. In turn, the Atlantic islands provided safe harbors and bases that facilitated voyages farther along the coast of Africa.

From bases on the Atlantic islands, Portuguese sailors took the lead in the contest to explore and exploit the western coast of Africa. By 1475 they had passed the equator to reach the powerful and prosperous West African kingdom of Benin. At first, the Portuguese practiced hit-and-run raids for plunder, but staunch African resistance obliged them to reconsider. Superior ships and guns enabled the Portuguese to dominate the coastal trade but did not suffice to overcome the immensely superior numbers of Africans on land. To procure gold, ivory, pepper, and slaves more securely, the Portuguese needed the cooperation of local rulers, who could bring the commodities from the interior. After 1450 the Portuguese wisely negotiated commercial treaties with African rulers, who permitted the construction of a few small fortified trading posts on the coast. The fortifications served primarily to keep away rival European vessels. Indeed, the Portuguese treated interlopers brutally, confiscating vessels and cargoes and casting crews into the sea.

The small but fertile Atlantic islands tempted exploitation by another, more intensive mode of colonization: settlement. In this mode, Europeans emigrated by the thousands to establish permanent new homes for themselves and their slaves. By hard labor, the settlers and slaves transformed the colonial environment to cultivate commodities for the European market. The absence of native peoples facilitated settlement on the Azores and Madeiras, which the Portuguese began to colonize in the early fifteenth century, but a people known as the Guanche inhabited the Canaries.

Numbering perhaps thirty thousand in 1400, the Guanche were an olive-complexioned people related to the Berbers of nearby North Africa. After emigrating to the islands about 2000 B.C., the Guanche neglected their means of navigation, losing contact with the continent. They cultivated wheat, beans, and peas and raised goats, pigs, and sheep. But the Guanche lacked cattle and horses and, for want of metallurgy, depended upon stone tools and weapons. They were not politically united, but divided into rival chieftainships not only between but also within the seven major islands.

The Canaries had been known to the ancient Romans as the Fortunate Islands, but the fate of the Guanche at the hands of the Iberians was anything but fortunate. The Iberians turned Guanche resistance to colonial advantage by capturing them for sale as slaves to work on sugar plantations. In effect, enslavement converted the Guanche from an obstacle into a valuable asset that could finance the further process of conquest and colonization. Iberian slave-raiding expeditions began in the late fourteenth century and escalated early in the fifteenth.

Conditioned by the *reconquista*, the Iberians believed that the Guanche deserved to be conquered and enslaved for two reasons: they were neither civilized nor Christian. Making his own culture the standard of humanity, the Portuguese king assured the pope that the Guanche were "like animals" because they had "no contact with each other by sea, no writing, no kind of metal or money." The techniques and technologies that facilitated the Iberian conquest were also, by their absence among the natives, invoked to justify that conquest. In addition, the Iberians argued that they were obligated to spread the Christian faith to unbelievers. Any people who resisted that faith could justly be enslaved for the greater good of their souls and the profit of their Christian conquerors. By exposing the Guanche to Christian indoctrination, slavery might save their souls from hell, rendering their brief bondage on earth a small price to pay for their eternal salvation. But, with more greed than consistency, the Iberians also enslaved Guanche who had converted to Christianity in the vain hope of living peaceably beside their invaders.

In the mid-fifteenth century the Spanish pushed out the Portuguese and took over the further conquest of the Canary Islands. In 1483, after five hard years of fighting, the Spanish overcame the guerrilla resistance on the largest island, Grand Canary. The Guanche on La Palma and Tenerife did not succumb until the 1490s—at the same time that Columbus sailed west via the Canaries to America.

Mounted on horses and armed in steel, the Iberians possessed military advantages over the unarmored Guanche fighting on foot with stone weapons. But the deadliest advantage enjoyed by the invaders was unintentional and beyond their control. Within their bodies the Iberians carried especially deadly and secret allies: an array of microscopic pathogens previously unknown to the Canaries. Lacking the partial immunities enjoyed by the Iberians from long experience with the diseases, the Guanche died by the thousands from epidemics of bubonic plague, dysentery, pneumonia, and typhus. Death and demoralization undercut their ability to resist invasion. A Spanish friar reported, "If it had not been for the pestilence, [the conquest] would have taken much longer, the people being warlike, stubborn, and wary." In their invasion of the small and long-isolated Canaries, the Iberians reaped the perverse advantage of their relatively large population located at a nexus of commercial exchange, which made for an especially diverse and regularly reinforced pool of diseases.

Although welcoming the reduction of Guanche armed resistance, the Spanish regretted the loss of so many valuable slaves. By the middle of the sixteenth century, the Guanche were virtually extinct as assimilation and intermarriage enveloped the few survivors into the settler population and colonial culture. So complete was the cultural destruction that only nine sentences of the Guanche language have survived. The Guanche's fate did not bode well for subsequent native peoples who would experience European colonization.

During the fifteenth century, Iberians settled on the Azores, Canaries, and Madeiras in growing numbers. Colonists cleared the forest to cultivate fields of domesticated plants—especially wheat and grapes—and to pasture grazing animals introduced from Europe. The products of these activities were not just for their local subsistence but for profitable export in ships to markets in Europe. Although lucrative to landowners and merchants, the transformation proved ecologically costly. By 1500, trees were so scarce that the colonists lacked sufficient firewood and timber for building. Deforestation also induced erosion, depleting the soil on the hillsides. Droughts increased, for want of the trees that formerly captured the moisture in the oceanic fogs.

On the semitropical Madeiras and the Canaries (but not the cooler Azores), the Iberians succeeded in raising sugar, which was in great and growing demand in Europe. Enjoying high value per volume, sugar could be transported over long distances and still reap a profit at sale. Offering a warmer climate superior to the Mediterranean for the cultivation of sugar, the Madeiras and the Canaries became Europe's leading suppliers by 1500.

To produce sugar, the colonists developed the plantation mode of production. A plantation was a large tract of privately owned land worked by many slaves to produce a high-value commodity for export to an external market. As plantation colonies, the Canaries and Madeiras depended upon long-distance merchants and their shipping to carry away the sugar and to bring in tools, cloth, food, and new slaves.

At first, most of the slaves were Guanche, but they inconveniently and rapidly died from the new diseases. To replace the dead, the colonists imported Africans to work the sugar plantations. West African societies had long enslaved war captives and convicted criminals for sale to Arab traders, who drove them in caravans across the Sahara to the Mediterranean. This caravan trade was relatively small in scale, with a volume of only about one thousand slaves per year in the early fifteenth century. After 1450, however, the advent of European mariners along the West African coast expanded the slave trade. By 1500, the Portuguese annually bought about eighteen hundred African slaves, primarily to labor on the Canaries and Madeiras.

The conquest and transformation of the Atlantic islands prepared for the discovery, invasion, and remaking of the Americas. To colonize the islands (especially the Canaries) the Portuguese and Spanish learned how to organize and sustain prolonged oceanic voyages that were predatory as well as exploratory. The expeditions successfully tested steel weapons, mounted men, and war dogs upon natives on foot armed with stone implements. The invaders also learned how to exploit rivalries between indigenous peoples as well as their devastation by disease. By turning native peoples into commodities, for sale as plantation slaves, the invaders developed a method for financing the further destruction of their resistance. In the Atlantic islands, the newcomers also pioneered the profitable combination of the plantation system and the slave trade. In the fifteenth-century Atlantic islands (and principally the Canaries), we find the training grounds for the invasion of the Americas.

The discovery and profitable exploitation of the Atlantic islands also set precedents that encouraged Europeans to seek more islands just over the horizon to the west. Optimistic mapmakers began to enter imaginary western islands called Brazil and Antilla—names that would become attached to real places in the Americas by the end of the century. Indeed, such acts of European imagination inspired the discovery and conquest of those real places, which proved far larger, richer, and stranger than anticipated. For in 1492 no one in Europe had any idea that the next islands farther west lay close to two immense continents inhabited by millions of people.

COLUMBUS

As the colonizers of the Azores and Madeiras, the Portuguese might have maintained their westward momentum across the Atlantic. Instead, they turned south and east, probing along the African coast in search of a trade route to Asia. Their decision made perfect sense. Along the way they could reap the immediate and profitable commodities of Africa to finance further voyages to the ultimate prize: the trade of India, the East Indies, and China. By comparison, voyages due west into the Atlantic were shots into the unbounded unknown.

In 1487 the Portuguese mariner Bartolomeu Dias discerned how to use the counterclockwise winds of the South Atlantic to get around southern Africa. In 1498 Vasco da Gama exploited that discovery to enter and cross the coveted Indian Ocean, the gateway to the trade riches of the East. The profits kept the Portuguese focused on the southern and eastward route to Asia, leaving the westward route largely unguarded for their Spanish rivals to explore by default.

Spain pioneered transatlantic voyages, thanks to the aggressive ambition, religious mysticism, and navigational prowess of the Genoese mariner Christopher Columbus. In popular histories and films, Columbus appears anachronistically as a modernist, a secular man dedicated to humanism and scientific rationalism, a pioneer who overcame medieval superstition. In fact, he was a devout and militant Catholic who drew upon the Bible for his geographic theories. He also owned, cherished, and heavily annotated a copy of *The Travels of Marco Polo*, which inspired his dreams of reaching the trade riches and the unconverted souls of East Asia. Columbus hoped to convert the Asians to Christianity and to recruit their bodies and their wealth to assist Europeans in a final crusade to crush Islam and reclaim Jerusalem. Such a victory would then invite Christ's return to earth to reign over a millennium of perfect justice and harmony.

A man of substance as well as vision, Columbus was a talented navigator and experienced mariner. He had sailed the Atlantic northward to England and Ireland (and perhaps even to Iceland), west to the Azores, and as far south as the Guinea coast of West Africa. Everywhere he investigated stories and clues about mysterious islands presumed to lie farther west. If Columbus did indeed make it to Iceland, he probably heard something about the transatlantic voyages and discoveries of the Norse people of western Scandinavia.

During the ninth and tenth centuries, the Norse had explored and colonized a succession of austere islands, progressively larger, colder, and farther west and north: the Faroes, Iceland, and Greenland. About the year 1000, Norse mariners from Greenland discovered the northeastern margin of North America: Baffin Island, Labrador, and Newfoundland. The Norse called the southern reaches of the new land Vinland, asserting that they had found wild grapes there. At Vinland the Norse established a small and short-lived colony—the first European settlement in North America. The Vinland colonists could not endure their isolation, their long and vulnerable supply line to Greenland, and the hostilities they provoked with the numerous natives, whom they named Skraelings (which meant "ugly wretches"). During the 1950s, archaeologists found the remains of a Norse settlement at the northern tip of Newfoundland—the probable site of Vinland.

The settlement collapsed within a generation, and Greenland entered a long, steady decline that reversed the Norse advance. An epidemic of bubonic plague reduced the Greenland Norse, and an increasingly cold global climate curtailed their agriculture and reduced their livestock. They also suffered from debilitating conflict with the more numerous Inuit (Eskimo) peoples of the north. At the end of the fifteenth century, the last Greenland Norse died out, just as Columbus was pioneering a new, more southern and enduring route across the Atlantic to America.

As early as 1484, Columbus hatched his scheme to head west across the Atlantic to find East Asia and open a profitable trade. Because no private merchants possessed the capital or the inclination to finance such an expensive and risky voyage, Columbus sought royal patronage. He first approached the Portuguese crown, the leading promoter of long-distance exploration. After a careful hearing, the Portuguese authorities declined, regarding the western route as too speculative and dangerous. Columbus then tried the royal courts of France and England, without success, before turning to Spain as a last resort. Queen Isabella and King Ferdinand approved, providing three small ships and most of the funding. They reasoned that even if Columbus failed to reach Asia, he might instead find valuable new islands like the Canaries.

Contrary to popular myth, fifteenth-century European intellectuals and rulers did not think that the world was flat. On the contrary, since the ancient Greeks, learned men had agreed that the world was round. They also accepted the theoretical possibility of sailing west to come up on the East Asian side of the known world. Although they expected to find some more Atlantic islands to the west, no Europeans anticipated that any large continents would obstruct a westward voyage to Asia. And given the high value of Asian commodities, there was a powerful commercial incentive for testing Columbus's theory.

What deterred Europeans from sailing due west for Asia was not a fear of sailing off the edge of the world but, instead, their surprisingly accurate understanding that the globe was too large. Ancient Greek mathematicians and geographers had determined that the world had a circumference of about 24,000 miles, which suggested that Asia lay about 10,000 to 12,000 miles west from Europe. Fifteenth-century European ships were too small to carry enough water and food to sustain their crews on a 10,000-mile voyage beyond contact with land.

Breaking with geographic orthodoxy, Columbus dared the westward trip to Asia because he underestimated the world's circumference as only 18,000 miles, which placed Japan a mere 3,500 miles west of Europe. In other words, a critical, and potentially fatal, mistake in calculations inspired his eccentric confidence that he could sail westward to Asia: the exact opposite of the popular myth that Columbus understood world geography better than his allegedly benighted contemporaries. Columbus was fortunate indeed that the unexpected Americas loomed at about the 3,000-mile mark to provide fresh water and provisions before his men mutinied. It is one of the ironies of world history that profound misunderstanding set in motion Columbus's discoveries.

In 1492, with three ships and about ninety men, Columbus followed the well-tested route southwest from Spain to the Canaries. Exploiting the trade winds, he turned west into the open ocean and had clear, easy sailing, reaching a new land after just thirty-three days. He first landed at the Bahama Islands, just east of Florida. Turning south, Columbus encountered the West Indies, islands framing the Caribbean Sea. But Columbus supposed that all of the islands belonged to the East Indies and lay near the mainland of Asia. Although the native inhabitants (the Taino) were unlike any people he had ever seen or read about, Columbus insisted that they were "Indians," a misnomer that has endured.

The colonial enterprise arrived in the Americas in Columbus's mind. From the start, he treated the Caribbean Islands and their Taino inhabitants exactly as the Spanish had treated the Canaries and the Guanche—as places and people to be rendered into commercial plantations worked by forced labor. He rationalized that such treatment would benefit the Indians by exposing them to Christian salvation and Hispanic civilization. To justify their enslavement, Columbus emphasized their weakness:

> They do not have arms and they are all naked, and of no skill in arms, and so very cowardly that a thousand would not stand against three [armed Spaniards]. And so they are fit to be ordered about and made to work, plant, and do everything else that may be needed, and build towns and be taught our customs, and to go about clothed.

To impress and intimidate the Taino, Columbus publicly demonstrated the sound and fury of his gunpowder weapons.

Columbus unilaterally declared the natives subject to the Spanish crown. He reported, "I found very many islands filled with people innumerable, and of them all I have taken possession for their highnesses, by proclamation made and with the royal standard unfurled, and no opposition was offered to me." Of course, not understanding a word of Spanish, the Indians failed to recognize any cue to oppose Columbus's ceremony. As a further act of possession, he systematically renamed all of the islands to honor the Spanish royal family or the Christian holy days. Columbus even renamed himself, adopting the first name "Christoferens"—meaning "Christ-bearer," testimony to his sense of divine mission.

After his largest ship ran aground, Columbus decided immediately to start a colony by obliging thirty-nine crew members to remain on the island he called Hispaniola. They built a crude fort from the timbers of their wrecked ship. In the two remaining vessels Columbus sailed home, taking a roundabout route north and then east, to catch winds bound for Europe. He reached Spain in March 1493 to receive a hero's welcome from King Ferdinand and Queen Isabella.

What happened next rendered Columbus's voyage of enduring and global significance, far beyond the achievements of his Norse predecessors. The Norse discoveries proved a dead end because they remained largely unknown outside of the northwestern fringe of Scandinavia. Thanks to the newly invented printing press, word of Columbus's voyage and discovery spread rapidly and widely through Europe. Eagerly read, his published report ran through nine editions in 1493 and twenty by 1500. Publication in multiplying print helped to ensure that Columbus's voyages would lead to an accelerating spiral of further voyages meant to discern the bounds and exploit the peoples of the new lands.

Intrigued by Columbus's glowing reports of the Indians' gold jewelry and their supposed proximity to Asia, King Ferdinand and Queen Isabella promptly decided to send Columbus back with another, larger expedition of exploration and colonization. The king and queen declared Columbus admiral and governor of the new islands and promised him a tenth of all profits made by exploiting them. Devout Catholics, Ferdinand and Isabella also vowed to convert the Indians to Christianity, dreading that otherwise so many thousands would continue to die in ignorance to spend their eternity in hell. The monarchs acted so quickly from a well-founded fear that the newly alarmed Portuguese would soon send their own expeditions to the west.

With the assistance of the pope, the Spanish and the Portuguese negotiated the 1494 Treaty of Tordesillas, which split the world of new discoveries by drawing a north-south boundary line through the mid-Atlantic west of the Azores. The Portuguese secured the primary right to exploit the coast of Africa and the Indian Ocean, while the Spanish obtained Columbus's western discoveries. Further exploration determined that South America bulged eastward beyond the treaty line, placing a land called Brazil in the Portuguese sphere. In dividing the world, no one bothered to consult the Indians, for the Iberians and the pope considered them pagan savages without rights under international law. The other western European kingdoms refused to recognize the treaty, for they denied that the pope could exclude them from exploring and exploiting the new lands. But no European leaders thought that the Indians could, or should, be left alone in their former isolation and native beliefs.

In September 1493, Columbus returned to the West Indies with seventeen ships, twelve hundred men (including farmers and artisans, but no women), sugarcane plants, and much livestock. The new colony was supposed to feed itself; recoup the costs by remitting hides, gold, sugar, and slaves to Spain; and serve as a base for further exploration in search of Japan and China. The Spanish were coming to stay, to dominate the land and its natives, and to weave the new lands into an empire based in Europe.

At Hispaniola, Columbus discovered that the Taino Indians had killed the thirty-nine men he had left behind the year before. In the Spanish deaths, Columbus found the pretext for waging a war of conquest. Employing the military advantages of horses, trained dogs, gunpowder, and steel, Columbus killed and captured hundreds of Indians on Hispaniola and adjoining islands. In 1495 he shipped 550 captives to Spain for sale to help pay for his expedition. Because most died during the voyage or within a year of arrival from exposure to European diseases, Columbus had to abandon the project of selling Indians in Spain. Instead, he distributed Indian captives among the colonists to work on their plantations and to serve as sex slaves.

By 1496, Hispaniola's surviving "free" natives had been rendered tributary—obliged to bring in a quota of gold for every person over the age of fourteen.

Columbus's slaughter and enslavement of Indians troubled the pious Spanish monarchs, who declared in 1500 that the Indians were "free and not subject to servitude." But Ferdinand and Isabella failed to close the legal loophole exploited by Spanish colonizers. It remained legal to enslave Indians taken in any "just war," which the colonists characterized as any violence they conducted against resisting natives.

In addition to killing and enslaving the Taino, Columbus antagonized most of the colonists, who bristled at his domineering manner and hot temper. As a Genoese upstart, Columbus commanded little respect among the Spanish colonists, especially when he sought to enrich himself by restricting their undisciplined pursuit of easy wealth. Violent mutinies and more violent reprisals by Columbus induced the monarchs to revoke his executive authority in 1500. Hispaniola became a crown colony governed by a royal appointee, rather than the feudal fiefdom of Columbus. Although displaced as governor, Columbus continued to serve the Spanish as a maritime explorer. In 1498 and 1502 his third and fourth transatlantic voyages revealed long stretches of the South and Central American coast. Nonetheless, to his death in 1506, Columbus stubbornly insisted that all of his discoveries lay close to the coast of Asia.

Other explorers, often working for rival powers, expanded upon Columbus's discoveries to demonstrate that he had, instead, found a "New World." In 1497 the English king employed John Cabot, a Genoese mariner, to seek a northern route across the Atlantic to Asia. Instead, Cabot also ran into a continent, rediscovering the northern shores previously explored and briefly colonized by the Norse. In ignorance of the former Vinland, Cabot called his landfall Newfoundland. Far to the south, in tropical waters, a Portuguese fleet commanded by Pedro Alvares Cabral discovered the coast of Brazil in 1500. A year later, Amerigo Vespucci, a Genoese mariner who alternated between Spanish and Portuguese employ, explored enough of the coast of South America to deem it a new continent. Consequently, European mapmakers began to call the new land by a variant of his first name—America. But the Spanish avoided the new term, clinging instead to Las Indias (the Indies), as Columbus had insisted.

Although Columbus had not reached Asia, he did find the substance of what he sought: a source of riches that would, in the long term, enable European Christendom to grow more powerful and wealthy than the Muslim world. During the next three centuries, the mineral and plantation wealth of the Americas financed the continuing expansion of European commerce, the further development of its technology and military power. Moreover, the very encounter with strange lands and people contributed to the broadening horizons of Europe's intellectual leaders, spurring the sustained pursuit of scientific advances.

HISPANIOLA

The Spanish invaded America with remarkable rapidity as their growing shipping, cargoes, and colonists connected the European and the American shores of the Atlantic. In 1508 alone, forty-five vessels crossed from Spain to the Caribbean islands. With the Canaries as their colonial model, the Spanish aggressively modified Hispaniola, introducing new crops, especially sugarcane, and new animals, including cattle, mules, sheep, horses, and pigs. Assisted by their plants and animals, the invaders remade the environment to sustain themselves, to obtain commodities valuable enough to ship to market in Spain, and to dominate and convert the local natives, the Taino. A Spaniard explained, "Without settlement there is no good conquest, and if the land is not conquered, the people will not be converted. Therefore the maxim of the conqueror must be to settle." The conquest of nature and the domination of natives worked reciprocally.

Transatlantic colonization was difficult and often deadly. The first colonists on Hispaniola suffered severely from malnutrition and sickness. Crowded into small, filthy ships for long voyages, they arrived weak, hungry, and diseased. Barely able to work, they failed to grow enough food during the early years, prolonging their vulnerability to sickness. Probably two-thirds of the Hispaniola colonists died during the first decade of settlement, 1493–1504. But the natives suffered even more severely, as the colonists shared their diseases and forced the Taino to provide food and labor.

As with the Guanche on the Canaries, colonization rapidly destroyed the Taino people of Hispaniola. In 1494 a Spaniard reported that more than 50,000 Taino had died, "and they are falling each day, with every step, like cattle in an infected herd." From a population of at least 300,000 in 1492, the Taino declined to about 33,000 by 1510 and to a mere 500 by 1548. The great missionary friar Bartolomé de Las Casas mourned the virtual extermination "of the immensity of the peoples that this island held, and that we have seen with our own eyes."

Like the Guanche, the Taino died primarily from virulent new diseases unintentionally brought to the Americas by the Spanish, but the colonizers compounded the destructive impact of the diseases by callous exploitation. With armed force, the Spanish drove the Taino to labor on colonial mines, ranches, and plantations, where they suffered a brutal work regimen. Natives who resisted Spanish demands faced destructive and deadly raids on their villages by colonial soldiers. Abandoning their crops and villages, thousands of Taino refugees starved in the densely forested hills. Dislocated, traumatized, overworked, and underfed, they proved especially vulnerable to disease. Las Casas interpreted the 1518 smallpox epidemic as sent by a merciful and angry God "to free the few Indians who remained from so much torment and the anguished life they suffered from, in all types of labor, especially in the mines, and at the same time in order to castigate those who oppressed them." In sum, the natives suffered from a deadly combination of microparasitism by disease and macroparasitism by Spanish colonizers, preying upon native labor. Although not genocidal in intent—for the Spanish preferred to keep the Taino alive and working as tributaries and slaves—the colonization of Hispaniola was genocidal in effect.

EPIDEMICS

Although extreme in its rapidity and thoroughness, the depopulation of Hispaniola was far from unique in the Americas. Everywhere the first European explorers and colonists reported horrifying and unprecedented epidemics among the native peoples. For example, in New England during the 1620s, a colonist reported that the Indians

> died on heapes, as they lay in their houses; and the living, that were able to shift for themselves, would runne away and let them dy, and let their Carkases ly above the ground without burial. . . . And the bones and skulls upon the severall places of their habitations made such a spectacle after my coming into those partes, that as I travailed in the Forrest, nere the Massachusetts [Bay], it seemed to mee a new found Golgotha.

The observers also marveled that so few of their own people succumbed to the same diseases.

The epidemics spread in association with the newcomers. First colonized, the Caribbean islands suffered the first great epidemics. Spanish soldiers unwittingly exported the diseases to the mainland between 1510 and 1535, when they conquered Central America, Mexico, and Peru. During the mid-sixteenth century, Spanish invaders introduced epidemics into the American southwest and southeast. Epidemics afflicted the natives of New England and eastern Canada during the early decades of the seventeenth century, as they encountered European fishermen and fur traders. Along the Pacific coast and in the Great Plains, deaths peaked when explorers, traders, or missionaries arrived in the late eighteenth century. In 1793 an English explorer in the Pacific northwest found the beaches littered with skulls and bones and saw the faces of Indian survivors pocked by the scars of smallpox. The Mandan Indians of the northern Missouri Valley (in present-day North Dakota) escaped the worst ravages until 1837, when, in the course of a few weeks, smallpox destroyed all but forty of their two thousand people.

In any given locale, the first wave of epidemics afflicted almost every Indian. Within a decade of contact, about half the natives died from the new diseases. Repeated and diverse epidemics provided little opportunity for native populations to recover by reproduction. After about fifty years of contact, successive epidemics reduced a native group to about a tenth of its precontact numbers. Some especially ravaged peoples lost their autonomous identity, as the few survivors joined a neighboring group. Consequently, the Indian nations ("tribes") of colonial history represent a subset of the many groups that had existed before the great epidemics. Historian Alfred W. Crosby, Jr., vividly characterizes the population collapse as "surely the greatest tragedy in the history of the human species."

Recognizing this demographic catastrophe, recent scholars have dramatically revised upward their estimates of the pre-Columbian population in the Americas. Because the natives lacked statistical records (and their first conquerors rarely kept any), all calculations of the contact populations are highly speculative. Early in the twentieth century, most scholars were "low counters," who estimated native numbers in 1492 at only about ten million in all of the Americas, including about one million north of the mouth of the Rio Grande (i.e., the present United States and Canada). More recent scholars, the "high counters," claim that their predecessors neglected the abundant evidence for the dramatic depopulation of the Americas during the sixteenth century. The high counters also draw upon archaeological evidence that much of the Americas was densely settled in 1492, and upon generous calculations for the capacity of given environments to support large human populations.

At a minimum, the high counters double the estimated population of the pre-Columbian Americas to twenty million. Some insist upon 100 million or more. Narrowing their view to just the lands north of the Rio Grande, the revisionists claim that the future United States and Canada together contained at least two and perhaps ten million people in 1492. Most scholars now gravitate to the middle of that range: about fifty million Indians in the two American continents, with about five million of them living north of Mexico. Even this middle range represents a fivefold increase over the former "low count."

Our revised understanding of a well-populated North America in 1492 belies the former characterization of the continent as a "virgin land" virtually untouched by humans and longing for European settlement. According to the nineteenth-century historian George Bancroft, in 1492 the future United States was "an unproductive waste . . . its only inhabitants a few scattered tribes of feeble barbarians." Ideologically charged, such a description celebrated colonization as entirely positive. More recently, the historian Francis Jennings aptly describes colonial America as a "widowed land," rendered so by the deadly microbes that accompanied the European invasion.

The exchange of infectious diseases between the invaders and the natives was remarkably one-sided. American pathogens did not kill the colonizers in anything approaching the proportions that European diseases claimed among the natives. Apparently only one major disease, venereal syphilis, passed from the Americas into Europe with the returning explorers and sailors. If so, syphilis exacted a measure of revenge on behalf of the native women raped by the invaders. Although painful and sometimes fatal, syphilis did not kill enough people to stem Europe's population growth during the sixteenth century. After about 1600, the disease lost much of its virulence as European bodies adjusted to it and as the pathogen adapted to a longer life within its hosts. The Europeans died in far greater numbers when they tried to colonize sub-Saharan Africa, where they did encounter relatively novel and especially virulent tropical diseases, principally *falciparum* malaria and yellow fever. Unwittingly, the Europeans imported those African diseases into the American tropics and subtropics with the slaves brought to work on their plantations. Those African maladies then added to the epidemics that devastated the Native Americans.

In part the exchange of pathogens was so one-sided because the Indians lived in a hemisphere with fewer and less virulent diseases. Passing from Siberia into North America about twelve thousand years ago, the Paleo-Indians spent many generations in the subarctic, where the long and bitter winters discouraged many pathogenic microbes that thrive in warmer climes. Moreover, the arctic rigors tended quickly to kill humans suffering from debilitating diseases, leaving a healthier population of survivors. And as nomadic hunter-gathering peoples scattered over an immense territory, the Paleo-Indians did not sustain the "crowd diseases" that need a steady succession of hosts. In the Americas, the natives gradually developed new diseases. Studies of pre-Columbian skeletons reveal the marks of rheumatoid arthritis, osteoarthritis, pinta, yaws, hepatitis, encephalitis, polio, tuberculosis, intestinal parasites, and venereal syphilis. All were formidable but endemic enemies that killed their share of natives every year, but not enough to prevent the overall growth of the Indian population. Meanwhile, in Europe and Asia the world's champion killers evolved after the Paleo-Indians had emigrated from Asia to the Americas. The newer Eurasian diseases included smallpox, typhus, diphtheria, bubonic plague, malaria, yellow fever, cholera, and influenza.

Three factors helped develop especially powerful pathogens in the Old World. First, long-distance trade and invasions were more routine in Europe and Asia, providing vectors for the exchange and mutation of multiple diseases. In effect, the Old World diseases benefited from a much larger pool of potential hosts. Passing to and fro, these pathogens gradually strengthened the immunities of the disease-embattled peoples of the Old World, rendering them deadly carriers when they passed into places where those diseases were not endemic.

Second, urbanization was older and more widespread in the Old World than in the New—and especially virulent diseases develop where people live in permanent concentrations. Crowded populations keep diseases cycling among numerous inhabitants, which is especially important to deadly diseases with only human carriers, such as smallpox. Concentrated human populations also accumulate more garbage and excrement, which breed many microbes that inflict gastrointestinal diseases. And the filth also sustains enlarged populations of vermin—mice, rats, roaches, houseflies, and worms—which serve as carriers for some diseases. The most notorious example is bubonic plague, which is borne by fleas carried by rats (as well as people).

Cities were fewer in North America, largely restricted to central Mexico, and usually much cleaner than their European counterparts. By living in filth, urban Europeans paid a high price in steady losses to endemic disease and occasional exposure to new epidemics. But they also rendered themselves formidable carriers of diseases to distant and cleaner peoples with far less experience with so many pathogens.

Third, the people of Europe, Africa, and Asia (but not the Americas) lived among large numbers of domesticated mammals, including cattle, sheep, goats, pigs, and horses, which share microscopic parasites with humans, encouraging the development of new and especially powerful diseases as viruses shift back and forth between the species. We call one strain of influenza "swine flu" because pigs exchange it with humans. By domesticating several mammals, the early herders and farmers of the Old World helped breed new pathogens unknown to their hunting-and-gathering ancestors. In contrast, North American natives domesticated only one mammal, the dog, which rarely shares diseases with its best friends.

Beginning in 1492, Europeans suddenly carried their legacy of more extensive and virulent diseases to the Americas. The breath, blood, sweat, and lice of the colonizers (and of their livestock and rats) conveyed especially deadly pathogens that consumed Indians who lacked the immunological resistance of past experience. The greatest killers were eruptive fevers, especially smallpox, measles, and typhus. But Indians also suffered from new respiratory infections, such as whooping cough and pneumonia. Even the mild childhood ailments of Europeans, such as chickenpox, killed Indians of all ages. One disease often weakened a victim for a second to kill. For example, many Indians barely survived smallpox only to succumb to measles, pneumonia, or pleurisy.

Because nearly everyone in a village became ill at the same time, few could care for the sick. During the 1630s in New England, a colonist described a smallpox epidemic among the Massachusetts Indians:

> They fell down so generally of this disease as they were in the end not able to help one another, not to make a fire nor to fetch a little water to drink, nor any to bury the dead. . . . They would burn the wooden trays & dishes they ate their meat in, and their very bows & arrows. And some would crawl out on all fours to get a little water, and sometimes die by the way and not to be able to get in again.

For want of healthy people to tend the sick, to fetch food and water and keep fires going, many victims died of starvation, dehydration, or exposure.

Smallpox was the most conspicuous and devastating of the new diseases. A highly communicable virus, smallpox passes through the air on moisture droplets or dust particles to enter the lungs of a new host. Consequently, the breath of victims conveyed death to those in their vicinity. After an incubation period of twelve days, the victims came down with a high fever and vomiting, followed three to four days later with gruesome sores over their entire bodies. Painful, incapacitating, and disfiguring, smallpox transformed people into a hideous mass of rotten flesh. In sixteenth-century Mexico an Indian described smallpox victims:

> They could not move; they could not stir; they could not change position, nor lie on one side; nor face down, nor on their backs. And if they stirred, much did they cry out. Great was its destruction. Covered, mantled with pustules, very many people died of them.

Survivors bore scars for the rest of their lives, and some suffered blindness as well. In addition to depleting the Indians' numbers, the new diseases sapped their morale. After one epidemic, a New England colonist said of the Indians, "Their countenance is dejected, and they seem as a people affrighted."

Neither sixteenth-century natives nor colonizers knew about the existence of microbes, much less that some caused disease. Instead, both assumed that the epidemics manifested some violent disruption of supernatural power. Colonists interpreted the diseases as sent by their God to punish Indians who resisted conversion to Christianity. Indians blamed the epidemics on sorcery practiced by the newcomers. When the native shamans failed to stop or cure a disease, they became discredited as ineffectual against the superior sorcery of the newcomers, who survived epidemics that slaughtered the natives. Because kinship ties defined native society and culture, the rapid destruction of so many relatives was profoundly disorienting and disruptive. Natives lamented that their guiding elders were all dead "and their wisdom is buried with them." In search of new wisdom, a new supply of supernatural power, the most devastated native peoples gave Christian missionaries their desperate attention.

During the sixteenth and seventeenth centuries, the colonizers did not intentionally disseminate disease. Indeed, they did not yet know how to do so. Especially during the sixteenth century, the colonizers valued Indian bodies and souls even more than they coveted Indian land. They needed Indians as coerced labor to work on mines, plantations, ranches, and farms. And Christian missionaries despaired when diseases killed Indians before they could be baptized. Only later, and almost exclusively in the English colonies, did some colonists cheer epidemics for depopulating the lands that they wanted for settlement.

During the sixteenth century, the European colonizers had expected to live as economic parasites on the labor of many Indians, but the epidemics upset their best-laid plans. Left with large tracts of fertile but depopulated lands, the colonists cast about for a new source of cheap and exploitable labor that was less susceptible to disease. Beginning in 1518 to Hispaniola, the colonizers imported growing numbers of slaves from West Africa. Prior to 1820, at least two-thirds of the twelve million emigrants from the Old to the New World were enslaved Africans rather than free Europeans. Most of the slaves were put to work on tropical or subtropical plantations raising cash crops—primarily sugar, rice, indigo, tobacco, cotton, and coffee—for the European market. By 1700, people of African descent prevailed in the American tropics, especially around the Caribbean.

In the temperate zones, the epidemics opened up lands for colonial settlement by free European farmers. In one famous example, the Plymouth colonists of New England in 1620 had their pick of recently abandoned Indian villages with conveniently cleared land. One colonist remarked, "Thousands of men have lived there, which died in a great plague not long since: and pity it was and is to see so many goodly fields, and so well seated, without men to dress and manure the same." Imagine how much more difficult the colonists' lot would have been if instead they had come to a crowded land of well-defended villages, or to a truly virgin continent without any already cleared lands.

American colonization tapped Europe's growing population, which swelled from about 80 million in 1492 to 105 million in 1650 and nearly 180 million by 1800. The increase was especially dramatic and significant in the British Isles (including Ireland), the greatest source of North American emigrants prior to 1800. From a population of 5 million in 1492, the inhabitants of Great Britain surged to 16 million by 1800, when another 5 million Britons already lived across the Atlantic. The post-1492 growth nearly doubled Europe's share in the world's population from about 11 percent in 1492 to approximately 20 percent in 1800. At the same time, the Native American proportion of the global population collapsed from about 7 percent in 1492 to less than 1 percent in 1800. The forced marriage of the two hemispheres meant a demographic boom for Europe but a demographic disaster for the Americas, with enduring consequences for world history.

The demographic and colonial history of Africa offers an instructive contrast to North America. Despite inferior firepower, until the nineteenth century the Africans more than held their own against European invaders because African numbers remained formidable. Unlike the Native Americans, the Africans did not dwindle from exposure to European diseases, with which they were largely familiar. On the contrary, African tropical diseases killed European newcomers in extraordinary numbers until the development of quinine in the nineteenth century. Thereafter, European soldiers conquered most of Africa, but European colonists remained small minorities amid immense African majorities. Without a demographic advantage, colonial rule proved short-lived as the Africans reclaimed power during the twentieth century. In stark contrast, by 1800 in present-day Canada and the United States, only about 600,000 Indians remained, already a small minority in a region dominated by five million Euro-Americans and one million African-American slaves.

FOOD

What can account for the dramatic new growth of Europe's population after 1492? We cannot credit advances in medical science or public hygiene, which were few and barely affected the mass of the population prior to 1800. Indeed, the Europeans were proverbial for their backward medicine and filthy cities. In 1519, Spanish soldiers marveled that the great Aztec city of Tenochtitlán was much larger and yet far cleaner than anything they had known at home.

An expansion of the food supply offers a better explanation for the European growth. As Thomas Malthus noted in the late eighteenth century, human populations tend to grow up to the limit of their food supply and then stagnate as malnutrition, famine, and disease keep pace with reproduction. But populations surge whenever people can increase their supply of nutrition, for an abundant diet encourages good health and rapid reproduction.

After 1492 the European diet improved, in part from enhanced long-distance transportation for produce and better techniques for rotating and fertilizing traditional grain crops. But above all, the improvement derived from the adoption of new food crops first cultivated in the Americas.

Native Americans had developed certain wild plants into domesticated hybrids that were more productive than their Old World counterparts. Measured as an average yield in calories per hectare (a hectare is ten thousand square meters, the equivalent of 2.5 acres), cassava (9.9 million), maize (7.3 million), and potatoes (7.5 million) all trump the traditional European crops: wheat (4.2 million), barley (5.1 million), and oats (5.5 million). By introducing the New World crops to the Old World, the colonizers dramatically expanded the food supply and their population.

A tropical plant, cassava (also known as manioc) could not be cultivated in Europe, but it thrived in Africa after its introduction (along with maize) by Portuguese mariners during the sixteenth century. The resulting surge in African numbers supplied the outflow of slaves to the American tropics and subtropics, where enslaved Africans replaced the natives decimated by the pathogens recently introduced from the Old World.

In Europe, maize and potatoes endowed farmers with larger yields on smaller plots, which benefited the poorest peasants. It took at least five acres planted in grain to support a family, but potatoes could subsist three families on the same amount of land. In addition, the new crops were more flexible, enabling European farmers to cultivate soils hostile to their traditional grains. Unlike wheat, maize can grow in sandy soils and thrive in hot climes, and potatoes prosper in cold, thin, damp soils unsuitable for any grain. In effect, maize and potatoes extended the amount of land that Europeans could cultivate either to feed themselves or to produce fodder for their cattle.

From a slow start, maize and potatoes proliferated in European fields. In 1498, Columbus wrote of maize: "There is now a lot of it in Castile." During the sixteenth and seventeenth centuries, maize cultivation spread eastward around the Mediterranean to become fundamental to the peasant diet in Italy and southern France by 1700. Potato cultivation expanded more slowly, primarily after 1680 in northern, central, and eastern Europe—often with encouragement from governments eager to alleviate famines and promote population growth. During the eighteenth century, the potato first gained its close association with Ireland, and Irish numbers grew from 3 million in 1750 to 5.25 million in 1800. The Irish then became vulnerable to any blight that devastated their potato crop. When such a blight struck during the 1840s, thousands starved to death and millions fled overseas, primarily to North America.

In microcosm and in exaggerated form, Ireland tells a common European story. The new crops developed by Native Americans and introduced to Europe by their conquerors contributed to a great surge in the Old World's population. That growth eventually caught up to the food supply, producing renewed hunger. But, in contrast to the past, the European hungry could seek relief by emigrating thousands of miles over the ocean to help settle the Americas. There they found underpopulated lands, recently rendered so by the diseases that Europeans had exported to the New World.

In sum, although disastrous for American natives, the post-1492 exchange of New and Old World microbes and plants provided a double boon to Europeans. First, they obtained an expanded food supply that permitted their reproduction at an unprecedented rate. Second, they acquired access to fertile and extensive new lands largely emptied of native peoples by the exported diseases. In effect, the post-Columbian exchange depleted people on the American side of the Atlantic while swelling those on the European and African shores. Eventually, the surplus population flowed westward to refill the demographic vacuum created on the American side of the Atlantic world.

ECOLOGICAL IMPERIALISM

The colonizers brought along plants and animals new to the Americas, some by design and others by accident. Determined to farm in a European manner, the colonists introduced their domesticated livestock—honeybees, pigs, horses, mules, sheep, and cattle—and their domesticated plants, including wheat, barley, rye, oats, grasses, and grapevines. But the colonists also inadvertently carried pathogens, weeds, and rats. The unwanted imports spread rapidly and voraciously through the American landscape to the detriment of native plants, animals, and peoples. In sum, the remaking of the Americas was a team effort by a set of interdependent species led and partially managed (but never fully controlled) by European people.

Because land was more abundant than labor in the colonies, the colonists reduced their work by building their fences around their relatively small crop fields. The settlers then allowed their livestock to roam freely in the hinterland, foraging for wild plants. In 1518 a Spaniard reported that thirty stray cattle ordinarily multiplied to three hundred within four years on a lush Caribbean island. In 1700 a visitor to Virginia observed that the pigs "swarm like vermin upon the Earth. . . . The Hogs run where they want and find their own Support in the Woods without any Care of the Owners." The roaming livestock often escaped from the control of their owners to compose feral herds that defied recapture.

Ranging cattle and pigs wreaked havoc on an American environment that the Indians depended upon. In the Caribbean islands, Spanish pigs consumed the manioc tubers, sweet potatoes, guavas, and pineapples that the Taino Indians cultivated. In New England, the rooting swine thrived on the intertidal shellfish that the Indians gathered for their own subsistence. The pigs and cattle also invaded native crop fields to consume the precious maize, beans, and squash. When Indians killed and ate trespassing livestock, the colonists howled in protest and demanded compensation for their lost property. When denied, angry colonists sought a disproportionate revenge by raiding and burning Indian villages.

Other European animals hitched along to the Americas despite the colonizers' best efforts to prevent it. These included the European rats, which were larger and more aggressive than their North American counterparts. Hated parasites on crops and granaries, the rats were skilled stowaways in almost every wooden ship. Once ashore, they rapidly reproduced and spread, afflicting the colonists but especially the Indians, whose storage pits proved woefully inadequate to repel such novel, voracious, numerous, and resourceful pests.

The colonists also unintentionally imported disagreeable plants known as weeds: fast-growing and hardy plants that compete with the edible domesticated plants preferred by people. The nineteenth-century naturalist Susan Fenimore Cooper described weeds as plants with "a habit of shoving themselves forward upon ground where they are not needed, rooting themselves in soil intended for better things, for plants more useful, more fragrant, or more beautiful." Weeds reproduce and grow rapidly, filling any piece of open, disturbed ground. Tough and combative weeds endure exceptional abuse to push up and around rival plants.

Prior to the colonial invasion, Indian farmers certainly had to cope with their own weeds, such as ragweed, goldenrod, and milkweed. But the indigenous weeds were not as tough as those that came from Europe, which included dandelions, thistles, plantain, nettles, nightshade, and sedge. Just as the Europeans had acquired more virulent strains of microbes, they had also developed more persistent and hardy weeds. In large part, the more formidable weeds and the more dangerous microbes of Europe had a common cause. Over the centuries, both had adapted to life amid the large domesticated mammals kept by peasants and herders. European weeds had evolved to endure the heavy trampling and voracious grazing of cattle, sheep, goats, pigs, and horses. Hardy opportunists, the Old World weeds also benefited from the earth exposed to the sun by animal-drawn plows.

Weeds spread and colonized as rapidly as the European rats and pigs. Mixed in the hay and grain brought in European ships to subsist their imported livestock, the weed seeds passed through digestion for deposit with manure wherever the animals roamed. In 1672 the naturalist John Josslyn identified twenty-two weeds as already "sprung up since the English planted and kept cattle in New England." One of the newcomers was the plantain that northeastern American Indians named "Englishman's foot" because it seemed to sprout wherever the colonists walked. Today botanists estimate that 258 of the approximately 500 weed species in the United States originated in the Old World.

Colonists and their livestock unwittingly facilitated the spread of their weeds by disrupting the native plants and by exposing great swaths of soil to the sun, wind, and rain. The newcomers hacked down the forests to procure lumber and to make farms, where grazing and plowing exposed the soil to erosion and desiccation. Especially well adapted to Europeans and their livestock, Old World weeds outdid their American cousins in reclaiming the bare and battered ground. Unlike their New World counterparts, the newly arrived weeds had abundant experience filling in where plows, hooves, and grazing mouths opened up gaping holes in the wild biota. Although unappreciated by farmers, the imported weeds helped stabilize the environmental shock wrought by colonization.

The European invasion effected an ecological revolution—an abrupt break with the interplay of nature and humanity that had previously characterized life in the Americas. Never before in human history had so much of the world's flora and fauna, large and small, been so thoroughly and so abruptly mixed and altered. This is certainly not to say that the native peoples previously had lived in nature without affecting it, for every human group affects its setting. Indeed, by fishing and hunting, by burning forests and clearing fields, and by domesticating and cultivating a few favored plants, Native Americans had selectively shaped their nature. This impact was greatest where Indians were most numerous, especially in central Mexico and the great Mississippi Valley. But the Europeans and their associated biota placed new and unprecedented demands upon the American nature. By a mix of design and accident, the newcomers triggered a cascade of processes that alienated the land, literally and figuratively, from its indigenous people.

In sum, native peoples and their nature experienced an invasion not just of foreign people but also of their associated livestock, microbes, vermin, and weeds. These worked in both synergy and competition to transform the environment, shaking and altering the nature previously known and made by the natives. When in the most isolated and least developed pockets of North America today, we like to think that we have rediscovered a timeless "wilderness" and that we experience there the nature known by Native Americans before 1492. In fact, everywhere we see an altered nature profoundly affected by all the plants and animals that tagged along with the colonists to remake this continent.

Although the demographic disaster and ecological imperialism undermined the Indians' ability to defend their lands and autonomy, they remained sufficiently numerous and resourceful to hinder and compromise the colonial conquest. Despite the depopulation, nowhere did the colonizers find a truly empty land. Although the population collapse made it possible (even probable) that European colonists and their slaves would eventually swarm over the continent and subdue the native peoples, that process took nearly four centuries to complete.

Although shrunken in number and shaken by catastrophe, the native peoples proved remarkably resilient and resourceful in adapting to their difficult new circumstances. Sometimes natives seized upon the new plants and animals for their own advantage. For example, on the Great Plains during the eighteenth century, the Indians acquired large herds of horses that endowed the natives with a new mobility and prowess as buffalo hunters and mounted warriors. Better fed, clothed, and equipped than ever before, the mounted Indians could defy colonial intrusions and even roll back some of their settlements along the margins of the Great Plains. Similarly, the Navajo people of the American southwest became newly rich by appropriating European sheep and looms to their own ends, producing distinctive and beautiful wool cloth. Acquiring horses and firearms, the Navajo also defended their canyons with enhanced vigor and plundered their Indian and Hispanic enemies with a new verve.

Because of their resilience, Indians became indispensable to the European contenders for North American empire. On their contested frontiers, each empire desperately needed Indians as trading partners, guides, religious converts, and military allies. By the late seventeenth century, the imperial contests were primarily struggles to construct networks of Indian allies and to unravel those of rival powers. Indian relations were central to the development of every colonial region.

3

New Spain

★

1500–1600

A European Catholic vision of the conquest of America as divine duty. Inspired by a vision of the Virgin Mary and the baby Jesus, Spanish conquistadores conquer Indians as an act of revenge on Indians who martyr priests in the act of disrupting the idolatrous worship of the devil. An engraving from Caspar Plautius, Nova Typis Transacta Navigatio *(n.p., 1621).*

The benign consequences of colonization as imagined by a champion of the Spanish empire. The violence of the conquest appears fully justified as priests instruct Indians (who have discarded their weapons) in Christianity and the arts of constructing civilization. While the Indians receive the gospel at their leisure, the priests appear to do all the hard work of construction. European vessels and a fortified colonial town fill in the background. An engraving from Caspar Plautius, Nova Typis Transacta Navigatio *(n.p., 1621).*

DURING THE SIXTEENTH CENTURY, the Spanish created the most formidable empire in European history by conquering and colonizing vast stretches of the Americas. By 1550, Spain dominated the lands and peoples around the Caribbean and deep into both North and South America: a domain more than ten times larger than Spain. The approximately twenty million (but shrinking) new Indian subjects dwarfed the seven million Spaniards at home. In extent and population (and cultural diversity), the Spanish empire in the Americas exceeded even the ancient Roman, previously the standard of imperial power. Extolling the Spanish king, a priest exulted, "If the Romans were able to rule the world simply by ruling the Mediterranean, what of the man who rules the Atlantic and Pacific oceans, since they surround the world?"

The sixteenth-century Spanish empire terrified its European rivals, which felt vulnerable to Spanish domination. In both greed and self-defense, the French, Portuguese, English, and Dutch sought American plunder and colonies by robbing the Spanish. To justify their own imperialism, the rival Europeans elaborated upon some very real Spanish atrocities to craft the notorious and persistent "Black Legend": that the Spanish were uniquely cruel and far more brutal and destructive than other Europeans in their treatment of the Indians. In fact, all sixteenth-century European colonizers behaved with similar arrogance and cruelty, whenever and wherever superior power enabled them to dominate and exploit native peoples. By virtue of their head start in New World exploration, the Spanish simply had a far wider opportunity to conquer greater numbers of Indians at their most vulnerable moment. And on the other side of the coin, in addition to producing consummate conquerors, sixteenth-century Spain provided the earliest and most eloquent critics of colonial violence, especially Bartolomé de Las Casas. But, while steering clear of the Black Legend, we should avoid substituting a "White Legend" that whitewashes the immense human costs exacted by Spanish colonization.

CONQUESTS

At the start of the sixteenth century, as the Taino of Cuba and Hispaniola dwindled from disease and exploitation, the Spanish desperately needed replacements to work their gold mines, cattle ranches, and sugar plantations. To provide new slaves, Spanish military entrepreneurs raided the mainland of Central America, grabbing Indians for profitable sale to the miners and planters of the islands. Because the new slaves proved just as short-lived as the Taino, the demand for slave raiding widened, devastating the native villages around the Gulf of Mexico from Venezuela to Florida and up the Atlantic coast as far as present-day South Carolina.

From their captives, the Spanish learned of the rich and populous Aztec empire in central Mexico, which had cities with stone temples and palaces and an immense population sustained by vast fields of maize, squashes, and beans. The Aztecs exacted tribute and labor from subject peoples over several hundred square miles. The tribute included a steady supply of victims for sacrifice to their gods, for the Aztecs believed that only regular, ritual effusions of blood could maintain the divine favor to sustain their rule and to ensure the life-nourishing crops.

Allured by the reports of great wealth, and appalled by accounts of pagan sacrifices, ambitious Spaniards prepared to invade and conquer the Aztecs. In 1519 the brilliant, ruthless, and charismatic Hernán Cortés led an unauthorized expedition of six hundred armed volunteers from Cuba to the coast of Mexico and into the interior, pushing through the hills to the great central valley. A younger son born into the *hidalgo* class in 1485, Cortés had university training as a lawyer. Frustrated in Spain, he left in 1504 to try his luck in the New World. A subordinate commander in the conquest of Cuba, Cortés acquired plantations, gold mines, and a burning ambition for more power and wealth. Invading the Aztec empire on his own authority, Cortés defied his superior, the governor of Cuba, who wanted the plunder and the conquest for himself.

Alternating brutal force with shrewd diplomacy, Cortés won support from the native peoples subordinated by the Aztecs. The tributary Indians did not anticipate that the newcomers would eventually prove even more demanding masters than the hated Aztecs. The approach of Cortés's army with its strange new apparatus—cannon, muskets, steel armor, swords, and horses—alarmed the Aztec emperor, Moctezuma. Although there are good grounds to doubt the old legend that Moctezuma mistook Cortés for a returning god, the emperor certainly suspected that the invader possessed some peculiar spiritual prowess. Hoping to buy off the invaders or overawe them with his own supernatural powers, the great Aztec invited the Spanish into the midst of his city as honored guests.

By far the largest city in the Americas, Tenochtitlán occupied a cluster of islands in a large lake. Interwoven with canals, the city reached the mainland by three long and narrow causeways. Fresh water arrived by a stone aqueduct. Most of the whitewashed adobe buildings were small and humble, but some lofty aristocratic houses embraced internal courtyards and gardens. Above all, the Spanish marveled at the immense palace of Moctezuma. Cortés declared, "In Spain there is nothing to compare with it." The city's central plaza of tall stone pyramid-temples also dazzled with a combination of red, blue, and ocher stucco. Dedicated to both Huitzilopochtli, the Aztecs' god of war, and Tlaloc, their god of rain, the largest pyramid stood sixty meters tall. Every year it hosted public ritual human sacrifices of captured people, their chests cut open and their still-beating hearts held up to the sun.

The population of about 200,000 dwarfed the largest city in Spain, Seville, which had only 70,000 inhabitants. Accustomed to the din, clutter, and filth of European cities, Spaniards marveled at the relative cleanliness and order of the Aztec metropolis. The soldier Bernal Díaz del Castillo recalled, "These great towns and pyramids and buildings arising from the water, all made of stone, seemed like an enchanted vision from the tale of Amadis. Indeed, some of our soldiers asked whether it was not all a dream."

Instead of humbling the Spanish, the city's wealth inflamed their desire to conquer, plunder, and enslave. They saw justification in the religious idols and human sacrifices that so horrified them. The Spanish quickly turned Moctezuma into a shackled hostage and ultimately a corpse, as they provoked bloody street fighting that, for a time, ousted them from the city. Returning with reinforcements, both Spanish and Indian, Cortés besieged Tenochtitlán. In August 1521, after four months of fighting, the Spanish and their native allies reduced the city to a bloody rubble. Recalling his first, dazzled vision of Tenochtizlán, Díaz del Castillo sadly concluded, "But today all that I then saw is overthrown and destroyed; nothing is left standing." Even greater than the Spanish disappointment was the Aztecs' grief and pain, recalled in their poem:

> Broken spears lie in the roads;
> we have torn our hair in our grief.

The houses are roofless now, and their walls
are red with blood.

Worms are swarming in the streets and plazas,
and the walls are splattered with gore.
The water has turned red, as if it were dyed,
and when we drink it,
it has the taste of brine.

We have pounded our hands in despair
against the adobe walls,
for our inheritance, our city, is lost and dead.
The shields of our warriors were its defense,
but they could not save it.

Vindictive in victory, the Spanish threw the captured Aztec priests to the war dogs to be torn apart. The victors also tortured Aztec nobles to obtain their hidden gold, later executing many as "traitors" to their new king. Branded on the face or the lip as possessions, thousands of common captives were set to work raising a Spanish capital, Mexico City, on the ruins of their own. The slaves reworked the stones from the great pyramids into a Christian cathedral and the remains of Moctezuma's palace into a residence for Cortés.

As Cortés had cynically anticipated, victory legitimized his unauthorized expedition, conducted in defiance of his superior, the governor of Cuba. Grateful for the stunning conquest and a share in the immense plunder, the Spanish ruler, Carlos V, appointed Cortés to govern Mexico and awarded him a coveted title of high nobility *(marquise)*. By his death in 1547, Cortés ranked as the wealthiest man in Spain, thanks to the revenues from his Mexican estates. As a New World conqueror, he had enjoyed the most spectacular social mobility of his century.

Beginning with Cortés's critical conquest of Mexico, Spain won its great American empire on the mainland between 1519 and 1550. During the 1530s, Francisco Pizarro with a mere 180 men conquered the Inca empire of Peru, practicing a ruthless brutality that might have shamed even Cortés. During the 1540s, Spanish forces gradually and painfully subdued the Mayan peoples of Central America. How could a few hundred Spanish adventurers—known as the conquistadores—so quickly and thoroughly overwhelm such formidable Indian empires?

The conquistadores certainly benefited from the technological superiority of Spanish weaponry. Because sixteenth-century guns, known as arquebuses, were crude, heavy, inaccurate, and slow to reload, only a few conquistadores carried them (Cortés's force of six hundred men had only

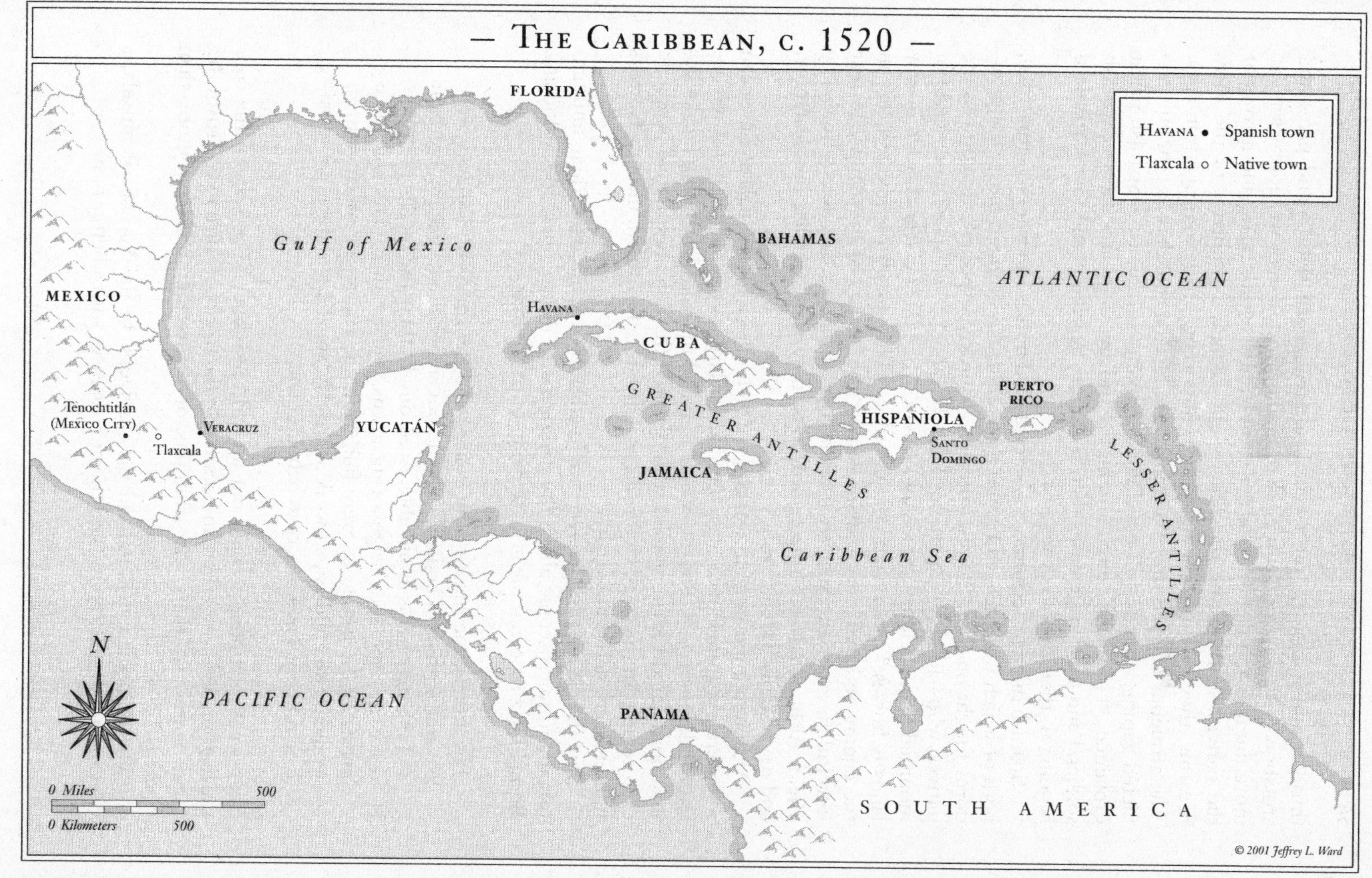
— The Caribbean, c. 1520 —
Havana • Spanish town
Tlaxcala ○ Native town
FLORIDA
Gulf of Mexico
BAHAMAS
ATLANTIC OCEAN
MEXICO
Havana
CUBA
GREATER ANTILLES
PUERTO RICO
HISPANIOLA
Santo Domingo
Tenochtitlán (Mexico City)
Tlaxcala
Veracruz
YUCATÁN
JAMAICA
LESSER ANTILLES
Caribbean Sea
N
PACIFIC OCEAN
PANAMA
0 Miles 500
0 Kilometers 500
SOUTH AMERICA
© 2001 Jeffrey L. Ward

thirteen guns). Instead, most relied on steel-edged swords and pikes and crossbows. Although essentially late-medieval, this steel weaponry was far more durable and deadly than the stone-edged swords, axes, and arrows of the natives. And despite the paucity and technical problems of the early firearms, they gave the conquistadores important psychological advantages. The arquebus belched fire and smoke, produced a thunderous roar, and inflicted gaping wounds—all novel and terrifying to Indians. A Spanish priest explained, "God hath caused among the Indians so great a fear of [Spanish soldiers] and their arquebuses that, with only hearing it said that a Spaniard is going to their pueblos, they flee."

Spanish military technology also exploited horses and war dogs (mastiffs), both of which were new and stunning to Indians. Although most conquistadores fought on foot, the few with horses proved especially dreadful to the natives, who had never experienced the shocking power, speed, and height of mounted men wielding swords and lances. "The most essential thing in new lands is horses," observed a conquistador. "They instill the greatest fear in the enemy and make the Indians respect the leaders of the army." To tear into Indian ranks, the Spanish also employed trained attack dogs with deadly effect. Although Indians possessed dogs, they were smaller, less fearsome, and never applied to warfare.

Although important advantages, the technology and animals of European war were not sufficient to overcome the far larger numbers of proud and defiant Indian warriors. But the Spanish evened the odds by finding local allies in subordinated Indian peoples who resented the dominant native people in each region. In the final, victorious assault on Tenochtitlán, most of Cortés's fighters were native auxiliaries.

But the Spaniards' greatest single advantage came from their unintentional and microscopic allies: the pathogens of diseases new to the Indians. Bernal Díaz reported the grim scene in one captured city:

> The streets, the squares, the houses, and the courts of Talteluco were covered with dead bodies: we could not step without treading on them and the stench was intolerable. Accordingly, they (the Indians) were ordered to remove to neighboring towns, and for three days and three nights all the causeways were full, from one end to the other, of men, women, and children, so weak and sickly, squalid and dirty, and pestilential that it was a misery to behold them.

Such weakened people could put up little resistance. The feats of the conquistadores seem superhuman because, in the words of Alfred W. Crosby, Jr., "they were just that—the triumphs of teams that included more than humans."

The epidemics demoralized the survivors. In the Yucatán Peninsula, a Mayan Indian sadly contrasted the new diseases with a better past:

> There was then no sickness; they had no aching bones; they had then no high fever; they had then no smallpox; they had then no burning chest; they had then no abdominal pain; they had then no consumption; they had then no headache. At that time the course of humanity was orderly. The foreigners made it otherwise.

The natives had to wonder if the newcomers did not know some powerful supernatural secret that spread death. Perhaps the safest course was to submit to their rule and their god in the desperate hope of some relief. A stunned acquiescence to the newcomers seized the native peoples most severely afflicted by the new diseases.

At the same time, the conquistadores took heart from the epidemics as a confirmation that God favored their triumph. Bernal Díaz observed, "When the Christians were exhausted from war, God saw fit to send the Indians smallpox, and there was a great pestilence in the city [of Tenochtitlán]." Men who believe in the providential inevitability of their conquest had an immense advantage in combat with a people who felt deserted by their gods.

CONQUISTADORES

The conquistador expeditions were private enterprises led by independent military contractors in pursuit of profit. The commander ordinarily obtained a license from the crown, which reserved a fifth of the plunder and claimed sovereign jurisdiction over any conquered lands. Known as an *adelantado*, the holder of a crown license recruited and financed his own expedition, with the help of investors who expected shares in the plunder. Developed in the course of the *reconquista* and applied to the Canaries, the *adelantado* system reflected the crown's chronic shortage of men and money.

Cortés and the other officers came from the Spanish gentry—the *hidalgos*—rather than the upper nobility, while the rank-and-file soldiers were restless young single men from the commercial towns and middle ranks of Spanish society. Receiving no wages, they fought on speculation, gambling for a big share in plunder and slaves. In the meantime, they had to supply their own weapons and provisions, often by borrowing money from investors, who expected a share in their booty. At the end of an expedition, every member, after collecting his share and paying his debts, was free to retire or to embark on a new expedition.

In addition to reaping plunder and slaves, the victorious commanders obtained tribute paid annually by conquered Indian villages. Grants known as *encomiendas* endowed the holder, the *encomendero*, with a share in the forced labor and annual produce of the inhabitants of several Indian pueblos (villages). In the largest, Cortés appropriated tribute from 23,000 families, the entire population of the large and fertile valley of Oaxaca. As quasi-feudal lords, *encomenderos* were supposed to defend the inhabitants against other Indians and to promote their conversion to Christianity by supporting a priest and building a church. Because only superior officers obtained *encomiendas*, ambitious subordinates longed for higher command in some new expedition in search of their own Aztec empire. Such dissatisfied adventurers expanded the frontiers of conquest, into northern Mexico and beyond to the Rio Grande.

Greed was a prerequisite for pursuing the hard life of a conquistador. Cortés meant to be disingenuous when he assured the Aztecs, "I and my companions suffer from a disease of the heart which can be cured only with gold." Of course, he was more profoundly right than he realized. According to the Aztecs, when given presents by Moctezuma, the Spanish "picked up the gold and fingered it like monkeys; they seemed to be transported by joy, as if their hearts were illumined and made new. . . . Their bodies swelled with greed, and their hunger was ravenous. They hungered like pigs for that gold."

But the conquistadores held that their greed served other, nobler motives: to extend the realm of their monarch and to expand the church of their God. They reasoned that riches were wasted on pagans and more properly bestowed upon Christian subjects of the Spanish king. Bernal Díaz concisely summarized his motives as "to serve God and His Majesty, to give light to those who were in darkness, and to grow rich, as all men desire to do."

The conquistadores regarded plunder, slaves, and tribute as the just deserts for men who forced pagans to accept Christianity and Spanish rule. After all, the conquistadores scrupulously adhered to the Spanish law of conquest by reading the *requerimiento*, which ordered defiant Indians immediately to accept Spanish rule and Christian conversion. If the Indians ignored this order, they deserved the harsh punishments of a "just war." The *requerimiento* announced, "The resultant deaths and damages shall be your fault, and not the monarch's or mine or the soldiers." Attending witnesses and a notary certified in writing that the *requerimiento* had been read and ignored, justifying all the deaths and destruction that followed. The cruel absurdity of reading the *requerimiento* in a language alien to Indians was apparent to many Spanish priests if not to the conquistadores.

Proud and prickly men, the conquistadores ultimately lusted for power over others that they might escape dependence upon a superior. This was an especially alluring dream in European societies premised upon a strict hierarchy of power that obliged almost everyone to submit to a superior. A Franciscan friar in New Spain observed, "All the Spaniards, even the most miserable and unfortunate, want to be señores and live for themselves, not as servants of anyone, but with servants of their own."

CONSOLIDATION

The dream of autonomy through power over Indians soon brought the conquistadores into conflict with the Spanish crown. Imperial officials feared that the *encomenderos* meant to rule New Spain with a high hand, giving only token allegiance to their sovereign. Having expended considerable blood and treasure at home to subdue the great lords of Spain, the crown was not about to tolerate the emergence of a new feudal aristocracy overseas. With good cause, the monarchs also worried that the conquistadores killed or enslaved too many Indians, who might otherwise have become Christian converts and taxpaying subjects.

The Spanish crown longed to consolidate an empire in a New World where almost everything was in violent flux. Ruthless, tireless, and resourceful soldiers, the conquistadores were abysmal administrators ill suited to govern their gains. Their smash-and-grab victories were no guarantee of enduring loyalty and substantial revenue from the conquered Indians. Indeed, Spanish greed, violence, and diseases depopulated and disrupted native communities that the crown wanted to stabilize, control, and tax—and that missionaries sought to convert and manage. Crushing native rulers was but the first, modest step in a true conquest, which required remaking the native culture, introducing Spanish institutions, and integrating the new lands and peoples into the transatlantic rule and commerce of Spain.

Appalled by the violence practiced by the conquistadores, the missionary friars argued that peaceful persuasion would more certainly convert the natives to Christianity and Hispanic civilization. This argument originated on Hispaniola in 1511 when a Dominican friar outraged his congregation by demanding: "Are these Indians not men? Do they not have rational souls? Are you not obliged to love them as you love yourselves?" The sermon did profoundly touch one *encomendero* in the congregation, Bartolomé de Las Casas, who renounced his *encomienda*, entered the Dominican order, and became the most eloquent and vociferous critic of the American conquest.

Although less exploitative than the *encomenderos*, the friars offered the Indians a demanding alternative: that they entirely surrender their traditional cultures to adopt, instead, the strange and uncompromising ways and beliefs of their conquerors. Priests oversaw the destruction of native temples, prohibited most traditional dances, and obliged natives to build new churches and adopt the rituals of the Catholic faith. Many Indians adopted the new faith with apparent enthusiasm but continued to venerate their old idols in secret.

To sustain a measure of psychological autonomy, Mexican Indians privately nurtured a mythic understanding of the Spanish conquest as cosmically insignificant and ephemeral: of no more enduring significance than the many previous cycles of rising and falling native powers. Having experienced the Aztecs, and the Toltecs before them, the natives of Mexico expected to outlast their Spanish masters. From our own vantage point on the radical transformation of Indian lives under the onslaught of colonization, this native myth seems far from "true." But the Indians preserved much of their own cultural identity within that transformation, rendering the myth real in their thoughts.

Because of the internal nature of native resistance, the friars could achieve no more than a compromise in matters of faith and practice. They ultimately had to tolerate a vibrant religious syncretism in which the new Catholic forms absorbed native content. The cult of the Virgin assumed a special importance as it came to resemble the former celebration of the maternal spirits of the maize, the "corn mothers."

During the 1530s the leading conquistadores either died fighting one another over the spoils of conquest, as did Pizarro in Peru, or were forced into retirement by the crown, which was the fate of Cortés in 1535. Although displaced from command, the surviving *encomenderos* usually retained their *encomienda* rights and persisted as a wealthy and influential local elite. Administration of the colonies passed to lawyers, bureaucrats, and clerics.

Responding to the missionaries' complaints, the Spanish crown also enacted reform legislation meant to protect the Indians from the most extreme forms of *encomendero* exploitation. But these reforms were indifferently enforced by colonial officials, who balked at angering the *encomendero* class. The officials also understood that the king did not expect humanitarianism to interfere with the homeward flow of his American revenues, which ultimately depended upon keeping the Indians at work on estates, in mines, and in urban workshops.

Labor conscription concentrated overworked Indians in unsanitary camps and urban *barrios*, increasing their exposure to infectious diseases and weakening their resistance. And hunger afflicted the Indians who remained in their rural villages as ranging and voracious cattle, pigs, and sheep invaded their fields, consuming the crops. Exceeding the carrying capacity of the land, the introduced herds of new livestock also provoked widespread erosion and even desiccation, to the detriment of native hunting, gathering, and irrigation.

Hungry, overworked, and dislocated, the natives of Mexico were especially vulnerable to disease. The native population dwindled from a preconquest ten million natives to about one million by 1620. As the Indians dwindled, Spanish enterprises seized direct ownership of the land in Mexico. To reward their friends and reap fees, the viceroys granted large rural estates, known as *haciendas*, to wealthy colonists. Most of the surviving Indians labored for wages or crop shares on the *haciendas*, which, during the seventeenth century, supplanted the *encomiendas* as the chief institution for exploiting the land and people of rural Mexico.

COLONISTS

During the sixteenth century, the New World drew about 250,000 Spanish emigrants to the Americas. Most originated in Castile and emigrated through the port of Seville, which monopolized Spanish trade to the Americas. All social classes participated, but people of middling property, especially skilled artisans from the market towns, predominated. Both push and pull motivated their movement. Fearing a decline into poverty if they remained in Spain, ambitious but middling folk looked to New Spain for opportunities to get ahead. In 1564 the tailor Diego de San Lorente exhorted his wife to join him in Mexico: "Here we can live according to our pleasure, and you will be very contented, and with you beside me I shall soon be rich."

If she did join him, the tailor was unusually fortunate. Early in the sixteenth century almost all the emigrants were young single men, for the dangers and hardships of transatlantic emigration deterred women. By the 1570s the number of emigrant women had increased but remained less than a third of the total. As a result, the male emigrants usually took wives and concubines among the Indians, producing mixed offspring known as mestizos. Proliferating and intermarrying over the generations, the mestizos became a middling caste especially numerous in the cities and towns of New Spain, eclipsing Mexico's purely Indian population by the start of the eighteenth century. In the tropical lowlands of the Caribbean coast, the Indians were replaced primarily by imported African slaves and their offspring, including mulattoes sired by Hispanic masters.

The increasing racial and cultural complexity of New Spain challenged the stark and simple dualities of the conquest: Spaniard and Indian, Christian and pagan, conqueror and conquered. In place of the old polarities, the colonial authorities developed a complex new racial hierarchy known as the *castas*, which ranked people from the pure African and Indian at the bottom through multiple gradations of mixture to the pure Spaniard imagined at the pinnacle. The higher *castas* enjoyed greater legal privileges at the expense of the lower.

Of all the European empires in the Americas, the Spanish developed the largest number of urban centers and the greatest density of cosmopolitan institutions. By 1574 the Spanish had chartered 121 towns in the Americas, and another 210 followed by 1628. Modeled on Spanish precedents, the charters entrusted local power to *cabildos:* town councils composed of self-perpetuating oligarchies derived from the wealthiest and most prestigious citizens. Carefully planned, the towns possessed a spacious gridiron pattern of streets with the public buildings—principally a town hall and a church—arranged around a central plaza. The families of the wealthiest citizens, including the members of the *cabildo*, dwelled near the central plaza, with the people of lower status and lesser property (and darker complexion) living on the peripheries.

EMPIRE

At mid-century, Mexico and Peru became the two great centers of the Spanish empire, eclipsing the older Spanish colonies in the Caribbean. Larger in size, richer in minerals, and retaining larger Indian populations than the island colonies, Mexico and Peru attracted most of the Spanish capital and emigrants sent to the New World after 1525. Cuba and Hispaniola diminished in importance to way stations between Spain and the two great American mainland colonies of the empire.

The Spanish crown divided the American empire into two immense administrative regions, known as viceroyalties, each governed primarily by a viceroy appointed by the king. In the mid-sixteenth century the viceroyalty of New Spain consisted of Mexico, Central America, and the Caribbean islands, while the viceroyalty of Peru included all of South America except Portuguese Brazil. Ever fearful of losing control over the rich and distant empire, the Spanish crown structured colonial authority to prevent the viceroys from accumulating too much power. In particular, the crown established a council known as an *audiencia*. Combining the functions of legislature, executive cabinet, and supreme court, the *audiencia* drafted laws, advised the viceroy, and conducted major trials. Unlike the later English colonies, the viceroyalties had no elective assemblies; the Spanish permitted none in their New World. Each viceroyalty also had an archbishop appointed by the monarch (by subcontract from the pope) to supervise the clergy, convents, and churches. As a further check on the viceroy, *audiencias*, and archbishop, the crown periodically subjected all three to a probing audit and investigation known as a *visita* conducted by special deputies sent from Spain. One investigative report on a viceroy of Peru ran to 49,555 pages.

The leaders of both the archbishopric and the *audiencia* were, like the viceroys, proud and ambitious aristocrats jealous of their privileges and perquisites. Inevitably, they sparred over their proper shares of colonial wealth and power. Although fatal to administrative efficiency, the frictions perpetuated the ultimate control of the monarchy in distant Madrid. Competing vigorously for the crown's favor, all three sets of leaders reported (or invented) the malfeasance of their rivals. The empire became clogged with paperwork as the clashing interests generated reams of reports and counter-reports that encouraged almost endless dispute and indecision. Multiple appeals and counterappeals from rival officials delayed action for years, often till long after the protagonists had died.

The immense size of the American empire, its distance from Spain, and the crown's obsession with control combined to render Spanish colonial administration highly bureaucratic, inefficient, and slow. Distrusting its colonial officials, the crown reserved authority over all important decisions and many minor ones. Unfortunately, any colonial request for crown instructions required at least a year for an answer, given the slow pace of transatlantic shipping and the bureaucratic inertia in Spain. One despairing viceroy complained, "If death came from Madrid, we should all live to a very old age."

On the other hand, the complex system also enabled colonial authorities to delay or frustrate any especially distasteful order from the crown. In the cynical phrase of their time, the officials resolved to "observe but not obey" any dictates that seemed unrealistic or inconvenient. Although all-pervasive, the imperial state was not all-powerful. The Spanish crown affected every aspect of public life in the colonies, but the monarchy could never achieve its aspirations to total control.

GOLD AND SILVER

At its core in central Mexico and Peru, the Spanish empire was phenomenally rich, especially in the mining of precious metals. Between 1500 and 1650 the Spanish shipped from America to Europe about 181 tons of gold and 16,000 tons of silver. The bullion primarily paid private debts for imported goods, but a fifth went in tax to the crown. By 1585 American bullion amounted to 25 percent of the crown's total revenue. The acquisition of so much gold and silver rescued the Spanish (and by extension, all of Europe) from their previous imbalance of trade with Asia, enabling the purchase of unprecedented quantities of Far Eastern spices and cloth.

But the gold and silver sent homeward was a mixed blessing. The infusion expanded the money supply faster than the growth of goods and services, contributing to a dramatic inflation of prices that spilled over into the rest of Europe. After the relative price stability of the fifteenth century, Europeans experienced a fivefold rise in prices during the sixteenth century. Laboring people especially suffered from the inflation, because the cost of living rose faster than their wages. In Spain, the real value of wages, relative to prices, declined by a fifth. The American bullion may have made the Spanish nation rich, in the aggregate, but it worsened the already hard lot of the peasants and laborers—together the great majority of the population.

The American bullion also weakened manufacturing in Spain, by inflating the prices of Spanish-made goods. This encouraged cheaper imports from the rest of Europe while rendering Spanish manufactures too expensive to compete in export markets. The Spanish loss benefited manufacturers elsewhere in Europe, especially the Dutch, who increased their exports to Spain. Offering little attraction to investors, Spanish manufacturing lagged behind the rest of western Europe in quantity, quality, and technological innovation. That lag would, in turn, greatly weaken the Spanish empire in the

Americas, as Indian and Hispanic consumers increasingly turned to Dutch, English, and French traders to procure cloth and metal goods.

The gold and silver revenue also encouraged the crown to pursue an aggressive and costly policy of military intervention in North Africa, Italy, and the Netherlands. Drained by foreign wars, the Spanish military and economy decayed dramatically during the seventeenth century. Before that unexpected decline, however, neither the Spanish nor their many enemies could see the ruinous consequences of the American gold and silver.

The sixteenth-century rulers of Spain felt entrusted with a divine mission to convert and command the peoples of the world. These convictions rendered Spanish policy uncompromising, especially during the long reign of King Philip II (1556–98). A devout and rigid Catholic, Philip regarded Protestantism as a rank heresy, which he meant to destroy. In 1573 the king assured a military commander, "You are engaged in God's service and in mine—which is the same thing." Emboldened by the easy destruction of Indian empires, Philip treated European opponents with contempt. In 1570 he announced, "These Italians, although they are not Indians, have to be treated as such, so that they will understand that we are in charge of them and not they in charge of us." This attitude understandably alarmed other Europeans, who read with grim interest the lurid accounts of Spanish atrocities in the New World.

European alarm grew in 1580–81, when Spanish power seemed to make another quantum leap as Philip completed the unification of the Iberian Peninsula by adding Portugal to his realm. The union also combined the far-flung and wealthy Portuguese colonies with the already immense Spanish empire. Those colonial acquisitions included the Atlantic islands of the Azores and Madeiras, the wealthy sugar colony of Brazil in South America, and lucrative entrepots on the coasts of Africa, India, and the East Indies: the sources of valuable slaves and spices.

Without their own share in the overseas riches, other Europeans dreaded that they would fall under domination by Spain. The greatest English promoter of overseas expansion, Sir Walter Ralegh, warned of the Spanish king: "It is his Indian Gold that . . . endangereth and disturbeth all the nations of Europe."

The quickest way to obtain American wealth was to steal it on the high seas after the Spanish had conveniently mined and packaged the gold and silver and loaded it onto ships. Lacking substantial navies, the Dutch, English, and French encouraged private investors to send armed ships to attack and plunder the Spanish shipping. In 1523 much of the gold stolen by Cortés from the Aztecs and shipped homeward was restolen by French pirates in the Atlantic. During the 1550s, French pirates extended their raids into the Caribbean, capturing, plundering, and burning Havana, the great port of Cuba.

In response, the Spanish organized a grand annual convoy of sixty to seventy large ships protected by a royal fleet. No longer relying upon the small, lightly armed caravels of the late fifteenth century, the Spanish had developed large vessels known as galleons, each studded with heavy cannon. Drawn from Veracruz and Panama and laden with the gold and silver of Mexico and Peru, the return convoy gathered at Havana for the run home via the Gulf Stream during the early autumn. Although the convoy system enabled the shipping to get through, the cargoes were heavily taxed to recoup the high costs.

The expense of the official convoy trade—and the long intervals between the arrivals of shipments in the New World—put Spanish merchants at a disadvantage. They faced increasing competition from foreign interlopers who, as smugglers, garnered a growing share of the Hispanic market in the Americas. Because the smugglers paid no Spanish taxes and obeyed no Spanish convoy regulations, they could more readily and cheaply provide manufactured goods to Hispanic consumers in the Americas. Often the smugglers were the pirates in another guise.

During the 1580s and 1590s, the English succeeded the French as the leading predators upon the ships and seaports of New Spain. The greatest English mariner, Francis Drake, ravaged the Caribbean coast and even broke into the Pacific Ocean to devastate Spanish shipping along the Peruvian and Mexican coasts, before heading west to circumnavigate the globe. These bold raids endeared Drake to the English monarch, Queen Elizabeth I, who took a cut of his profits and rewarded him with a knighthood. His patron, Sir Walter Ralegh, said that Drake was more than a pirate because of the immense scale of his theft: "Did you ever knowe of any that were pyratts for millions? Only they that risk for small things are pyratts."

English piracy and aid for Protestant rebels in the Netherlands infuriated King Philip II. In 1588 he sent an armada of warships to seize control of the English Channel and so permit an invasion of England by the Spanish troops posted in the Netherlands. When a subordinate warned of dangerous storms, the king serenely replied, "We are fully aware of the risk . . . but . . . since it is all for His cause, God will send good weather." The Armada consisted of 130 warships carrying 2,431 cannon and 22,000 sailors and soldiers. The English warships were fewer and smaller but also faster, more mobile, and mounted with longer-range cannon. They broke up the Armada, which in retreat homeward was battered by storms in the North Sea and Irish Sea that destroyed or crippled most of the Spanish vessels.

The debacle saved England from invasion and wounded Spanish prestige, which emboldened the English to escalate their maritime predation. Unable to invade England, Spain had to settle for bolstering its defenses in New Spain by constructing immense and expensive stone fortifications to guard the major seaports. Although effective in frustrating pirate attack, these expenditures consumed much of the American bullion, reducing the share shipped homeward. In 1620, Spanish crown receipts of American silver fell to less than a third of their 1590s level, producing a financial crisis. In 1631 the Spanish king's prime minister vented his frustration aloud at a cabinet meeting, wondering whether the burdens of American empire had not "reduced this monarchy to such a miserable state that it might fairly be said that it would have been more powerful without the New World."

Possessing no such doubts, the French, Dutch, and English escalated their attempts to construct their own empires in the Americas. The rival nations gradually recognized that raiding was only a hit-or-miss means to capture the benefits of overseas empire. To obtain a more regular and predictable flow of wealth, the European rivals needed their own colonies, where they might harvest precious minerals and tropical and semitropical crops—sugar, cacao, and tobacco—that had a high market value because they would not grow in temperate Europe.

However, it was not easy to shift from state-sponsored piracy to the development of mining and plantation colonies. On the one hand, the profits of piracy stimulated shipbuilding, improved naval technology, and trained mariners in transatlantic navigation. On the other hand, piracy soaked up ships and investment capital, to the detriment of other overseas enterprises that required more time to become profitable.

The rival empires could acquire colonies by seizing them from the Spanish, but this was dangerous and expensive. An alternative approach was slower but safer: to find some American coast unsettled by the Spanish for colonial settlement. During the sixteenth century, English, French, and Dutch mariners probed the unguarded Atlantic seaboard of North America seeking bases for both piracy and plantations. Those probes alarmed the Spanish, reigniting their interest in exploring and colonizing the vast mainland north of the Gulf of Mexico to fend off their enemies.

4

The Spanish Frontier

1530–1700

The burial ceremonies for a Timucuan chief in Florida. The bereaved people gather around a grave demarcated by the chief's arrows and surmounted by the shell he used as a drinking cup. The women have cropped their hair short in mourning, and in the lower left a warrior is about to have his head shorn. In the background the chief's temple and house, within the palisade, have been set ablaze to mark the break in village leadership. From Johann Theodor de Bry, Great Voyages *(Frankfurt, 1590).*

SPANISH EXPANSION SLOWED beyond the core regions of central Mexico and Peru, where sedentary agriculture and large, permanent native villages prevailed. Because conquistadores lived as parasites off the native produce of the invaded regions, they could not linger where the Indians did not practice horticulture. Fields of maize attracted conquistadores, and their absence deterred them. On the frontiers, the Spanish also faced more effective resistance from more dispersed, more mobile, and less prosperous Indians, like the Chichimeca of northern Mexico. Indeed, the nomadic Indians adapted to the colonial intrusion by raiding isolated mining camps, ranches, and mule trains to obtain animals, captives, provisions, and weapons. The horticultural Indians of the core were the foundation of the Hispanic empire, but the nomadic Indians of the peripheries were formidable obstacles to further expansion. Lacking maize, cities, and gold, the Indians of the peripheries seemed hardly worth the greater effort needed to conquer them.

The Spanish, however, persistently hoped that other core regions of civilized, rich, and vulnerable Indians lurked out in the great beyond. After all, Cortés had penetrated a relatively impoverished coastal district to conquer the wealthy and populous Aztec empire. His phenomenal success inspired emulators primed to believe the most glowing rumors of greater riches and wondrous sights just beyond the northern frontier of New Spain. Interest in northern expeditions especially soared after the 1536 return of a long-lost traveler named Alvar Núñez Cabeza de Vaca.

CABEZA DE VACA

In March of 1536, Spanish slave raiders in northwestern Mexico were surprised to find three Spaniards and a Moorish slave all dressed as Indians and accompanied by nearly six hundred natives. The leader among the four, Cabeza de Vaca, noted that the slave raiders were "thunderstruck to see me so strangely dressed and in the company of Indians. They went on staring at me for a long space of time, so astonished that they could neither speak to me nor manage to ask me anything." About forty-five years old, Cabeza de Vaca had been missing for eight years. He and his companions had trekked across much of North America, from the swamps of Florida to the coast of Texas and then through the deserts, mountains, and valleys of northern Mexico. Along the way, Cabeza de Vaca endured a searing double transformation, first from conquistador to slave, and then from slave to sacred healer.

His long, hard journey had begun in 1528 on Tampa Bay in Florida, as the second-in-command over an expedition of three hundred conquistadores. His superior, Panfilo de Narváez, was an unfortunate incompetent who had lost an eye in a failed attempt to wrest Mexico away from Cortés. Pressing into the northern interior of Florida, the conquistadores found little gold but many debilitating attacks from the Apalachee Indians. Retreating to the coast, the Spanish constructed five barges to attempt an escape by coasting around the Gulf of Mexico, but the barges broke apart off the coast of Texas, drowning most of the men, including Narváez. The shipwreck stripped the survivors of their intimidating apparatus as conquistadores: their horses, gunpowder, and steel armor and weapons. Most of the remaining Spanish soon died of disease, exposure, and malnutrition. The surviving few became scattered among several Karankawa Indian bands, where they suffered hunger and hard labor. In a reversal of roles, Spaniards, who had come to enslave, became instead the slaves of the Karankawa.

The last four survivors included Cabeza de Vaca and a black Moorish slave named Esteban. Although lacking in medical training, they reluctantly became magical healers at the Indians' insistence. The natives apparently assumed that only the Spaniards possessed the power to cure the deadly new illnesses associated with their arrival. Cabeza de Vaca explained, "The way in which we cured was by making the sign of the cross over them and blowing on them and reciting a Pater Noster and an Ave Maria; and then we prayed as best we could to God Our Lord to give them health and inspire them to give us good treatment." Most of their patients recovered, and the four became honored men among their native hosts.

Both the natives and the Spaniards interpreted the cures as effected by supernatural power, but they differed over whether that power came from within the healers or derived from a distant God. The natives regarded the four men as especially potent shamans who could magically manipulate the supernatural. But Cabeza de Vaca insisted upon a Catholic explanation: the healers were passive conduits for the power of their God, who chose to save them from the Indians. In contrast to both of those sixteenth-century peoples, we seek a "rational" explanation: perhaps that the power of suggestion effected cures without magic or divine intervention. The passage of nearly five centuries has rendered the sixteenth-century peoples even more culturally alien from us than they were to one another.

In the fall of 1534 it was the Indians' explanation for the cures that set the four men free and in motion homeward. Word of their cures empowered the particular band that hosted them; in return for food and other gifts, one band passed the healers on to the next. In this fashion, the four men moved westward across south Texas and New Mexico into northwestern Mexico, passing through diverse native peoples now labeled Coahuiltecan, Jumano, Concho, Pima, and Opata. Those dwelling in arid south Texas led an often harsh existence as seasonally migratory hunter-gatherers, but in northwestern Mexico the four sojourners found more permanent adobe pueblos and productive fields of maize.

Unfortunately, these impressive villages were under devastating attack from slave-raiding conquistadores. Cabeza de Vaca recalled, "It made us extremely sad to see how fertile the land was, and very beautiful, and very full of springs and rivers, and to see every place deserted and burned, and the people so thin and ill, all of them fled and hidden." He was especially horrified when the commanding conquistador proposed enslaving the Indians who had guided the four travelers. The commander desisted only reluctantly and after a heated confrontation with the four sojourners, who refused to betray their benefactors.

In narrating his confrontation with the slavers, Cabeza de Vaca expressed a new perspective more like that of a friar who had taken a vow of poverty: "We healed the sick, they killed the sound; we came naked and barefoot, they clothed, horsed, and lanced; we coveted nothing but gave whatever we were given, while they robbed whomever they found." The "they" described his own past as well as the immediate slavers, for in them he saw what he had been eight years before in Florida with a sword in hand, destroying Apalachee villages.

Cabeza de Vaca's long, harsh, and unsettling experience had chastened and transformed the former conquistador. Stripped of the power to coerce Indians, he had to learn their ways to survive. Deprived of his shell, psychological as well as physical, as a conquistador, Cabeza de Vaca obtained an unprecedented insight into the complex cultures of his Indian hosts. Once back among the Spanish, he struggled to readjust. At first he could neither abide European clothing nor sleep on a bed, preferring the floor.

But Cabeza de Vaca had to reenter a society that valued what he had learned only as a means to further conquest. Still ultimately committed to the Catholic faith and Hispanic civilization, he hoped to reconcile their triumph with his new empathy for Indians. In his report to the Spanish crown, Cabeza de Vaca preached a policy of pacification, more akin to Las Casas than to Cortés: "All these [native] people, if they are to be brought to be Christians and into obedience of Your Imperial Majesty, must be led by good treatment, and . . . this is a very sure way, and no other will suffice."

Cabeza de Vaca helped shift official Spanish policy away from unregulated conquest toward a greater emphasis on winning a measure of native consent. The Spanish continued, ultimately, to rely on their military might for expansion, but the crown insisted that commanders minimize Indian casualties and avoid enslaving natives. The monarchy also paid for missionary friars to accompany and advise the conquistadores. This shift in emphasis from conquest to "pacification," however, was slow and incomplete, especially in the expeditions immediately inspired by Cabeza de Vaca's return.

SOTO

Although Cabeza de Vaca reported little or no precious metals among his hosts, he vaguely referred to rumors of richer peoples to their north. That sufficed to arouse the aspiring conquistadores of New Spain, who gave to his report an imaginative gloss that reflected their own fantasies. Surely, they

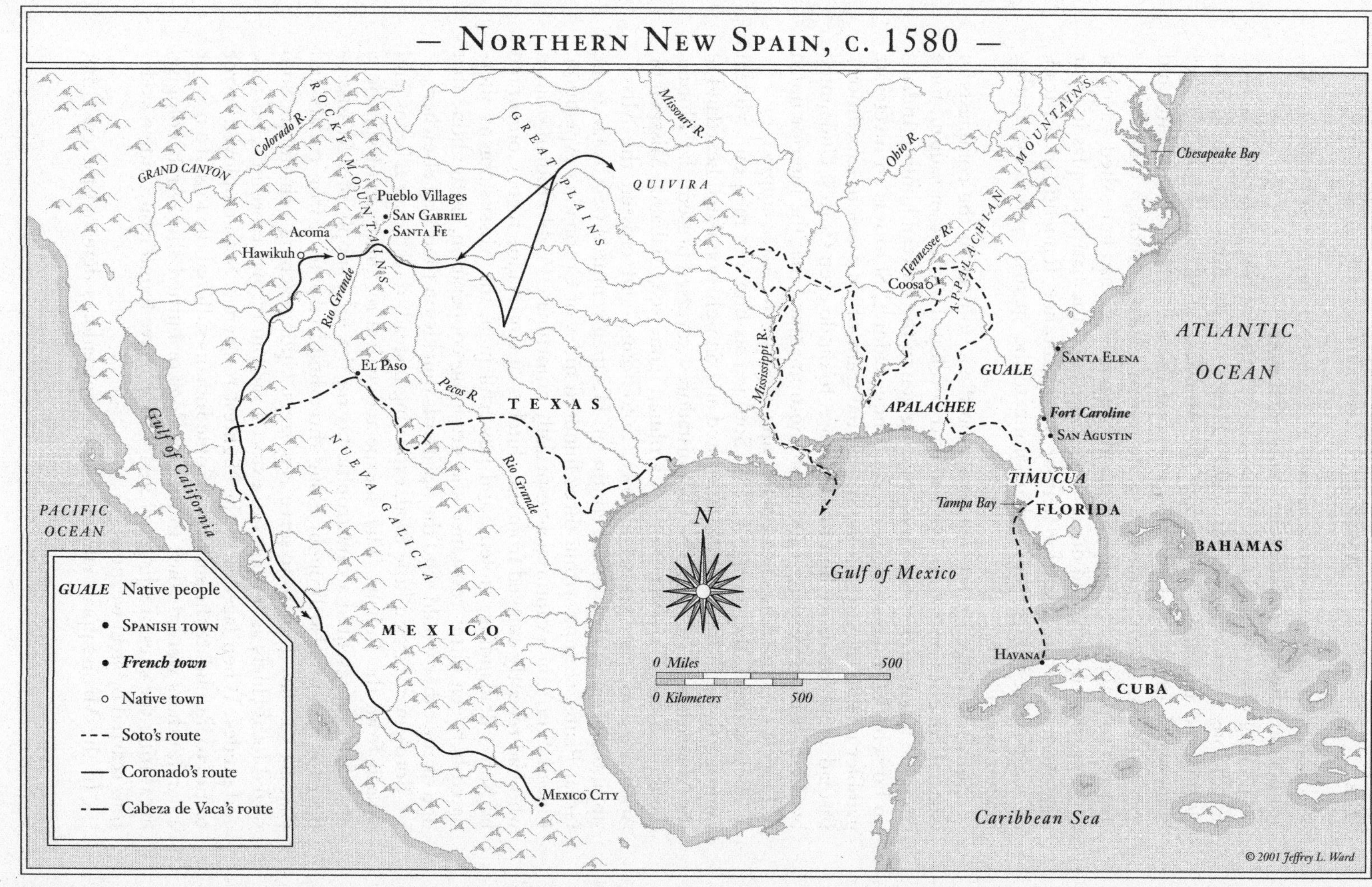
— Northern New Spain, c. 1580 —
ROCKY MOUNTAINS
Colorado R.
GRAND CANYON
GREAT PLAINS
Missouri R.
QUIVIRA
Ohio R.
APPALACHIAN MOUNTAINS
Chesapeake Bay
Pueblo Villages
San Gabriel
Santa Fe
Acoma
Hawikuh
Rio Grande
Tennessee R.
Coosa
El Paso
Pecos R.
TEXAS
Mississippi R.
APALACHEE
GUALE
Santa Elena
ATLANTIC OCEAN
Fort Caroline
San Agustin
TIMUCUA
Tampa Bay
FLORIDA
BAHAMAS
Gulf of California
PACIFIC OCEAN
NUEVA GALICIA
Rio Grande
N
Gulf of Mexico
MEXICO
0 Miles 500
0 Kilometers 500
Havana
CUBA
Mexico City
Caribbean Sea
GUALE Native people
Spanish town
French town
Native town
Soto's route
Coronado's route
Cabeza de Vaca's route
© 2001 Jeffrey L. Ward

reasoned, other native empires, as rich as the Aztecs, must exist farther north, just beyond the route of the four sojourners.

During the years 1539–43, Vaca's report inspired two great conquistador expeditions northward. From Cuba, Hernando de Soto led the first to Florida and through what is now the American southeast. From Mexico, Francisco Vásquez de Coronado marched the second expedition into and across the American southwest to the Great Plains. Although officially instructed to practice restraint, Soto and Coronado instead unleashed waves of violence, destruction, and disease that devastated the native peoples in their way. And all to no avail, for neither found another Tenochtitlán. Instead, their expensive failures set northern limits to the Spanish empire by limiting further expeditions.

Soto had reaped a fortune as a subordinate officer in the conquests of Central America and Peru. He had also developed a streak of sadism, for a comrade reported that Soto was "much given to the sport of hunting Indians on horseback." Like so many of the conquistadores, Soto was an inveterate gambler unable to retire on the substantial fruits of his previous expeditions. Instead, ambition drove him to seek more, to outdo even Cortés. Undaunted by the disastrous Narváez expedition, Soto imagined that the interior north of Florida contained his own golden equivalent of the Aztec empire.

Beginning in the spring of 1539, Soto led six hundred men on a violent rampage through the carefully cultivated and densely populated heartland of the Mississippian culture. The conquistadores traversed present-day Florida, Georgia, South Carolina, North Carolina, Tennessee, Alabama, Mississippi, Arkansas, and east Texas. In 1541, Soto found and crossed the Mississippi, the greatest river in the continent. His men ventured west as far as the Great Plains, coming within three hundred miles of Coronado's expedition. Indeed, Soto's men captured an especially unfortunate Pueblo Indian woman who had recently escaped from the clutches of Coronado's men. Confronted by Soto's demanding, violent, and powerful men, the Mississippians alternated between bitter resistance and grudging cooperation, in the hope that one or the other would send the Spaniards quickly on their way elsewhere.

Soto's men carried little food, expecting instead to take maize, beans, and squash from the Indians. The unexpected arrival of hundreds of voracious Spaniards represented a catastrophic tax on the food supply of a Mississippian town. Soto also brought along three hundred sets of iron collars and chains to enslave Indians to serve as porters. Upon reaching a chiefdom, Soto seized local chiefs as hostages to extort a ransom of maize, women, porters, and guides. When faced with the slightest resistance, Soto employed terror tactics to intimidate the survivors. Some Indians suffered the loss of a nose or a hand; others were thrown to the war dogs or burned alive. Archaeologists excavating the sites of villages visited by Soto have found many Indian skeletons scarred by steel weapons.

In the Mississippian villages, the conquistadores detected the cues that they thought indicated sure wealth. Like the Aztecs, the Mississippians possessed large fields of abundant crops, ceremonial centers featuring temple mounds and substantial populations, and powerful chiefs able to mobilize hundreds of warriors. But nowhere could the Spanish find gold or silver in any quantities, despite widespread pillaging of villages and graves and the torture of Indian informants. Frustrated, and feeling betrayed, the conquistadores left a trail of corpses, mutilations, ravaged fields, emptied storehouses, and charred towns.

In May of 1542, Soto sickened and died on the banks of the Mississippi, leaving the command to Luis de Moscoso. When the local Indians suspiciously asked where Soto had gone, Moscoso replied that he had ascended into the sky. In fact, with a ballast of sand, Soto had been surreptitiously cast into the Mississippi River to hide his mortality from the Indians. The humanitarian friar Bartolomé de Las Casas observed, "We do not doubt but that he was buried in hell . . . for such wickedness." In 1543 the conquistadores gave up and fled, building boats to descend the Mississippi and sail southwest along the Gulf Coast. About half of the original force survived to reach Mexico in September of 1543.

The Mississippians were not so lucky. The Soto expedition introduced diseases that decimated the natives. Death and misery spread throughout the great valley as Indian travelers, traders, and refugees carried the diseases to distant natives who had never directly encountered Soto's men. Because epidemics disseminate most easily among dense settlements, the Mississippian towns were deathtraps. By 1600, the region's population had collapsed to a small fraction of its former numbers.

When French explorers first visited the Mississippi Valley during the 1670s, they found relatively few Indians. In an area of southern Arkansas and northeastern Louisiana where Soto had counted thirty substantial towns, the French noted only five small villages. On the upper Coosa River of Georgia and Alabama, the setting for a populous and powerful chiefdom encountered by Soto, archaeologists have found five townsites dating from the early sixteenth century but only one from the end of the century.

The population collapse devastated the Mississippian culture. Dreading both the disease and the uneasy spirits of the many dead, the survivors abandoned the great towns and dispersed into the hilly hinterland. As their societies shrank and relocated, they became less complex, diminishing the power of the chiefs. In most places there were simply no longer enough people to raise the agricultural tribute necessary to sustain a costly and elaborate elite. And the survivors must have lost faith in their ruling chiefs and priests, who had failed to stop the waves of death.

The demographic and cultural disaster profoundly disrupted the geography of power in the Mississippi watershed. At the time of Soto's expedition, the densely settled villages of the powerful chiefdoms occupied the fertile valleys. Poorer and weaker peoples dwelled in small, scattered villages in the less fertile hills, where they lacked the means to sustain a centralized chiefdom. After Soto's invasion and epidemics, the hill peoples became comparatively powerful as the valley chiefdoms collapsed. Indeed, the dispersed hill peoples suffered less severely from the microbes that fed most destructively on the human concentrations in the lowland towns. And the upland peoples absorbed refugees fleeing from the valleys to escape the epidemics.

In the depopulated valleys, forests and wildlife gradually reclaimed the abandoned maize and bean fields, while the refugees farmed the less fertile but safer hills. The resurgent wildlife included bison, common in the southeast by 1700 but never sighted by Soto's conquistadores 160 years before. Far from timeless, the southeastern forest of the eighteenth century was wrought by the destructive power of a sixteenth-century European expedition. Soto had created an illusion of a perpetual wilderness where once there had been a populous and complex civilization.

By 1700, the paramount chiefdoms encountered by Soto had collapsed, with one exception: the Natchez people dwelling along the lower Mississippi River. Elsewhere, the paramount chiefdoms gave way to loose new confederations of smaller and more autonomous villages. The new chiefs possessed little coercive power; their people built them no pyramids; and their graves contained no human sacrifices. Eighteenth-century colonists called the principal confederacies the Choctaw, Chickasaw, Creek, and Cherokee.

The new confederations exemplified the widespread process of colonial "ethnogenesis"—the emergence of new ethnic groups and identities from the consolidation of many peoples disrupted by the invasion of European peoples, animals, and microbes. Scholars used to assume that nineteenth-century Indian nations were direct and intact survivors from time immemorial in their homelands. In fact, after 1700 most North American Indian "tribes" were relatively new composite groups formed by diverse refugees coping with the massive epidemics and collective violence introduced by colonization.

CORONADO

Cabeza de Vaca's report also mobilized Spanish interest in the northern Rio Grande Valley, where he had encountered well-fed peoples who practiced sedentary agriculture, made textiles, employed pottery, and lived in permanent villages of stone and adobe brick. On the Aztec precedent, the Spanish assumed that every such Indian people also possessed gold or precious gems. The natives of the American southwest would pay dearly for this fallacy.

In 1538 the viceroy of New Spain, Antonio de Mendoza, dispatched northward a small scouting expedition led by a credulous (or mendacious) Franciscan friar, Fray Marcos de Niza, and guided by Esteban, the black member of Cabeza de Vaca's party. Proceeding ahead, Esteban won entry into a Zuni village in what is now western New Mexico. But he soon offended his hosts by abusing their women, for which he was killed. Intimidated, Fray Marcos beat a hasty retreat to Mexico, where he breathlessly reported that he had seen a city, named Cibola, larger and richer than Tenochtitlán and one of seven great cities in the Zuni region. His report seemed to confirm a popular Spanish romance that "Seven Cities of Antilia" of incomparable riches lay somewhere in the New World. Although Fray Marcos had never entered any of the Zuni pueblos (of which there were only six), he described temples sheathed in precious metals and studded with valuable gems. That misinformation had profoundly tragic consequences, as it drew hundreds of Spanish conquistadores into prolonged and severe hardships and brought destruction upon native peoples lacking any precious metals.

Eager to believe, the viceroy invested in a new, larger expedition capable of conquering the Seven Cities. He entrusted command to a protégé, thirty-year-old Francisco Vásquez de Coronado. Combining his own funds with his wife's dowry and the viceroy's investment, Coronado recruited and equipped a force of about three hundred Hispanic soldiers, six Franciscan priests, eight hundred Mexican Indian auxiliaries, and some fifteen hundred horses and pack animals.

Guided by Fray Marcos, the conquistadores crossed the deserts and mountains of northern Mexico to reach the Zuni country in July 1540. The mounted, bearded, metal-clad soldiers were hot, weary, hungry, and parched when they approached the Pueblo that the Zuni called Hawikuh. But the conquistadores expected a rich reward, for Fray Marcos insisted that the pueblo was the fabulous city of Cibola that he had sighted the year before. When denied entrance, the Spanish stormed Hawikuh, killing hundreds and expelling the survivors. The hungry victors obtained stores of beans, corn, and turkeys but none of the rumored gold and silver that had lured them across hundreds of miles of hard, dry terrain. To their dismay, "Cibola" was only a modest pueblo of multistory tenements made of sunbaked brick. The frustrated soldiers heaped insults and curses upon their hapless guide, Fray Marcos. A disgusted Coronado reported that the friar had "not told the truth in a single thing."

To recoup his heavy investment, Coronado pressed onward, pursuing the usual rumors that some other Indian people just over the horizon possessed the riches of Spanish dreams. Pressing into the Rio Grande Valley in what is now New Mexico, Coronado imposed his forces upon the various native villagers, whom he lumped together under the name Pueblo because all dwelled in compact adobe-brick villages and practiced sedentary horticulture. Those similarities masked considerable linguistic and ceremonial differences. The Pueblo did not think of themselves as a common people, for they spoke at least seven distinct languages: Keresan, Piro, Tano, Tewa, Tiwa, Tompiro, and Towa. Not even the speakers of a common language shared a political union. Instead, the Pueblo divided into at least sixty autonomous villages that were often at violent odds with one another.

They began, however, to find a new commonality in their common treatment by the Spanish invaders during the winter of 1540–41. Offended by the rape of their women and the plunder of their food, the Pueblo rebelled. The Spanish counterattack destroyed thirteen villages and killed hundreds of natives. To make a vivid and intimidating example, Coronado ordered one hundred captured warriors burned to death at the stake. None of this was what Cabeza de Vaca had intended.

Unable to defeat the Spanish, the Pueblo peoples tried to get rid of them by telling alluring stories of a wealthy kingdom named Quivira to the north and east on the far side of a great, grassy plain. In pursuit of Quivira, Coronado and his men crossed the Great Plains, a vast sea of grass without apparent landmarks. The only inhabitants were small groups of nomads who subsisted by hunting, on foot, immense herds of buffalo. After enduring weeks of hunger and thirst, crossing what are now parts of Texas, Oklahoma, and Kansas, the conquistadores reached Quivira, a modest village of beehive-shaped and grass-thatched lodges inhabited by Wichita Indians. They possessed a productive agriculture but neither gold nor silver. In frustration and fury, the Spaniards tortured and strangled their Pueblo guide, who confessed the plot to lead the Spanish astray where they might get lost and die. To the dismay of the Pueblo, the Spaniards used a compass to find their way back to the Rio Grande, where they again proved larcenous and violent guests for the winter of 1541–42.

Demoralized by repeated disappointments and a severe riding injury, Coronado cut his losses and returned to northern Mexico in April 1542. He left behind a Franciscan priest and four assistants, who soon fell victim to Pueblo revenge. Coronado never fully recovered either his health or his fortune after the long, hard, and futile expedition. He even endured the indignity of an official prosecution for his abuse of the Pueblo. Unsuccessful conquistadores enjoyed neither the riches nor the impunity that success had bought for Cortés, whose greater crimes had been obscured by his great conquest.

FLORIDA

The expensive and destructive fiascos of Soto and Coronado further discredited conquistador expeditions and dissipated Spanish interest in the northern lands. During the 1560s, however, that interest revived as a defensive measure meant to protect the treasures produced by Mexico. During the late 1550s, predation by French pirates cut in half the Spanish royal revenue from the New World. The pirates concentrated their attacks on the most vulnerable run for Spanish shipping bound from the Caribbean to Spain: the relatively narrow channel between Florida and the Bahamas. Spanish ships also suffered from the treacherous shoals and occasional storms that littered the Florida coast with shipwrecks. In an ironic reversal of the usual colonial process, the wrecks endowed a native people with gold, silver, and slaves, for the Calusa Indians scavenged the hulks for the shiny metals and enslaved the castaway sailors.

To recover the bullion, redeem the castaways, and protect shipping, the Spanish crown decided to establish a fortified colony along the Atlantic coast of Florida. The crown entrusted leadership to Pedro Menéndez de Avilés, a resourceful and ruthless naval officer. As an *adelantado*, he bore most of the costs and hoped to find in Florida the riches that had eluded Narváez and Soto. His expedition assumed a new urgency in 1565 when the Spanish learned that their French enemies had just built a small base, named Fort Caroline, in Florida at the mouth of the St. Johns River. Worse still, the French colonists were Protestants—known as Huguenots—whom the Catholic Spanish regarded as heretics.

At dawn on September 20, Menéndez and five hundred soldiers surprised and killed most of the Huguenots at their fort. A few days later the remaining French in the vicinity surrendered to the Spanish, expecting to save their lives. Menéndez promised only "that I should deal with them as Our Lord should command me." His God commanded Menéndez to tie their hands "and put them to the knife." Nearly three hundred French died in the two massacres. Reporting to his king, Menéndez explained, "It seemed to me that to chastise them in this way would serve God Our Lord, as well as Your Majesty, and that we should thus be left more free from this wicked sect." King Philip II applauded Menéndez's conduct.

To defend Florida against a French return, Menéndez founded a fortified town, named San Agustín (St. Augustine), on the coast forty miles south of the former Fort Caroline. San Agustín was the first enduring colonial town established by any Europeans within the bounds of the future United States. To intimidate the Indians and watch for pirates, Menéndez built seven other posts along the Gulf and the Atlantic coasts, principally Santa Elena at Port Royal Sound (in present-day South Carolina).

In 1570, Menéndez established a short-lived Jesuit mission far to the north on Chesapeake Bay. To avoid provoking the Indians, the priests declined Menéndez's offer to provide a company of soldiers. Instead, the Jesuits relied upon their native guide, a young man who was the son of a petty chief in the region. In 1561 he had been captured by Spanish mariners and carried to Mexico for baptism as "Luis de Velasco"—renamed in honor of the viceroy who served as his godfather. Sent to Spain, the Indian Luis de Velasco met the king and persuaded Spanish officials that he longed to return home to convert his people to Christianity.

But once back at Chesapeake Bay with the Jesuits, de Velasco promptly deserted to rejoin his people, warning them to dread and resist the newcomers. In February 1571 he led a surprise attack that massacred the eight Jesuits and destroyed their chapel. Only a Spanish boy survived as an Indian captive in 1572, when Menéndez visited Chesapeake Bay to investigate. Unable to capture Luis de Velasco, Menéndez settled for killing twenty Indians in combat and hanging another fourteen from the yardarm of a warship. He then sailed away, leaving Chesapeake Bay to the Indians. The Spanish withdrawal subsequently benefited the English, who founded their Jamestown colony near the destroyed mission.

Most of the other small Spanish posts and missions in greater Florida also soon succumbed to either French or Indian attack. In addition, Menéndez ran out of money, having failed to find any silver mines. Frustrated, Menéndez denounced the official policy of pacification, commenting, "It would greatly serve God Our Lord and your majesty if these [Indians] were dead, or given as slaves." When Menéndez died in 1574, his Florida settlements had been reduced to just two, San Agustín and Santa Elena, neither prospering.

Upon his death, the crown became responsible for the faltering colony. Fearing English attack, in 1587 the Spanish evacuated and destroyed Santa Elena, withdrawing the colonists and their property to San Agustín, which became the sole Spanish settlement in Florida. Generating virtually no revenue, San Agustín drained the Spanish crown, which paid and supplied the demoralized garrison that kept the town barely alive. In 1673 the governor of Cuba confessed, "It is hard to get anyone to go to San Agustín because of the horror with which Florida is painted. Only hoodlums and the mischievous go there from Cuba."

Unable to attract colonists to Florida, the authorities tried to compensate by transforming Indians into Hispanics through the agency of Franciscan missionaries. The Spanish hoped that missions could consolidate their control over the interior and its natives more cheaply and securely than could soldiers. During the 1590s and early 1600s, Franciscan friars established an impressive set of missions along the Atlantic coast north of San Agustín into Georgia (Guale), in north-central Florida (Timucua), and to the west in the Florida panhandle above the Gulf Coast (Apalachee).

The governor at San Agustín helped by bestowing generous gifts on Indian chiefs who welcomed the priests into their villages. The Spanish also tempted the Indians with a trade that supplied coveted knives, fishhooks, beads, hatchets, and blankets. By embracing the Spanish alliance and accepting Franciscan missionaries, some chiefs also hoped to bolster their own power at the expense of rival native villages. Finally, the inability of traditional shamans to shield their people from the devastating new diseases induced many natives, in desperation, to hope that the newcomers offered a more powerful spiritual protection.

Conversion, however, came at a cultural cost. The priests systematically ferreted out and burned the wooden idols cherished by the natives, banned their traditional ball game, and enforced Christian morality, which required marriage, monogamy, and clothing that covered female breasts. In vain, the Timucua protested that "they enjoyed their vice and therefore it must not be evil but good and just." Converts who defied the friars suffered severe whippings that bloodied their backs. When persuasion, gifts, and whippings failed, the Spanish employed military force to punish and intimidate, brutally suppressing rebellions in 1597 at Guale and 1656 at Timucua.

The priests built their missions beside the major Indian villages: dozens of round wattle-and-daub houses with dome-shaped roofs of palm thatch. A principal village had communal storehouses, a large council house, and a circular public plaza that served as a ball court. The natives supported themselves and their new priests from productive fields of corn, beans, and squash, supplemented by hunting, fishing, and gathering. With Indian labor and local materials, the friars constructed a church, a cookhouse, a residence for the missionaries, and a barracks for a few soldiers. Every mission also had a new Christian cemetery that quickly filled with the Indian victims of epidemics. In 1659 the governor reported that ten thousand mission Indians had recently died of measles. Conversion bought safety from Spanish muskets but not from Spanish microbes. Despite the losses to disease, the system grew as the priests founded new missions in additional villages. At the peak in 1675, forty friars ministered to twenty thousand native converts who worshiped in thirty-six churches. After failing to build a settlement colony, the Spanish had apparently succeeded in Florida by pursuing the Franciscan mode of pacification—with a modicum of Indian consent.

NEW MEXICO

At the same time that the Spanish were resuscitating their Florida colony, other Spaniards returned to the Rio Grande to practice a similar program of pacification led by missionaries. Franciscans favored the venture as an opportunity to save Indian souls, which the crown welcomed as a source of new subjects and taxpayers. As in Florida, the crown also supported the Rio Grande colony from an exaggerated fear that rival empires had designs on the valley as a base for attacking Mexico. Finally, some secular colonists enlisted in the persistent hope that silver mines could be found in the northern interior.

Although the Spanish continued to rely on the *adelantado* system, the crown imposed naive new restrictions. Issued in 1573, the Royal Orders for New Discoveries ruled that future expeditions were "not to be called conquests." Instead, they were explicitly renamed "pacifications." The crown directed every *adelantado* to proceed "peacefully and charitably," for there was no "excuse for the employment of force or the causing of injury to the

Indian." But this imposed a fatal contradiction, for every *adelantado* assumed large debts to organize his expedition and needed a quick and big score to satisfy his creditors, which meant conquering and exploiting Indians.

The viceroy named Don Juan de Onate the *adelantado* to pacify the Rio Grande Valley and found the colony of "New Mexico." Like his predecessors, Onate suffered from delusions of grandeur, assuring his king, "I shall give your majesty a new world, greater than New Spain." In fact, he ventured into a country of scarce resources that sorely tested his patience and the Royal Orders for New Discoveries.

At first, all went deceptively well. During the spring of 1598, Onate led about five hundred colonists, including 129 soldiers and seven Franciscan friars, into the northern Rio Grande Valley. Alternating new promises of fair treatment with traditional displays of Spanish weapons, they founded their settlement in the midst of the Pueblo peoples, who initially offered no resistance.

But strains quickly developed between the Pueblo and their uninvited guests. Rather than construct their own settlement, Onate's colonists seized a pueblo, which they renamed San Gabriel, evicting the native inhabitants. Onate's undisciplined soldiers also ranged far and wide, extorting maize, deerskins, cotton blankets, buffalo robes, firewood, and women. These demands threatened Pueblo subsistence, for the natives had little surplus to spare, especially after Spanish cattle invaded their unfenced fields, severely damaging the crops. Soldiers noted that the Indians parted with their maize "with much feeling and weeping" as if "they and all their descendants were being killed." When an Indian rebuked Onate for seizing grain, the governor threw him off the roof of his pueblo. "He fell on his back and was killed instantly, never moving hand or foot," a soldier recalled. A sympathetic friar noted that when winter began, "our men, with little consideration, took blankets away from the Indian women, leaving them naked and shivering with cold."

The crisis came in December 1598, when Onate's nephew, Captain Don Juan de Zaldívar, led a patrol to the pueblo of Acoma to extort provisions. Fed up, the native warriors killed Zaldívar and ten soldiers. Onate and his colonists suddenly felt profoundly isolated, outnumbered, and vulnerable, surrounded by thousands of vengeful Pueblo Indians. From this sense of dread and weakness, Onate resolved to make a grim example of Acoma that would preserve his colony by intimidating the other Pueblo.

In January 1599, Spanish soldiers stormed Acoma, killing eight hundred Indian men, women, and children during three days of savage hand-to-hand and house-to-house combat. The victors herded five hundred survivors eastward to the Rio Grande for trial by Onate for treason and murder. He condemned all who were over the age of twelve to serve as slaves for twenty years. Those who were male and over the age of twenty-five also suffered the severing of a foot, to discourage them from running away or resisting their masters. Onate declared innocent the captured children under the age of twelve, but he confiscated them from their families for rearing in Mexico as servants to Christian families.

The deaths and mutilations yielded a scant return on Onate's mounting debts, for the silver mines remained as elusive as ever and it was costly to supply and reinforce such a distant and isolated colony. Desperate and often irrational, Onate took flight into ill-conceived explorations, indulging in old-style fantasies of the fabulous just around the next bend. In 1601 he repeated Coronado's folly with a five-month trek across the Great Plains in search of golden Quivira and the Atlantic seaboard, finding neither. In 1604–5 Onate turned westward, seeking a route to the Pacific Ocean. With immense difficulty, he got only as far as the Colorado River.

To justify his western expedition, Onate reported as facts the fabulous hearsay of Indian informants. Onate assured the viceroy that he had nearly reached "extraordinary riches and monstrosities never heard of before." These included an Indian people with immense ears that hung to the ground; a second tribe never ate, but lived on odors, "because they lacked the natural means of discharging excrement"; and a third had men with "virile members so long that they wound them four times around the waist, and in the act of copulation the man and woman were far apart." The Indians delighted in Onate's credulity, but the viceroy was not amused. "This conquest is becoming a fairy tale," he wrote home to the king. Of course, he slipped in calling the expedition a "conquest," for official discourse required the term "pacification."

The colonists and their priests turned against Onate. The discouraged colonists bitterly complained that Onate had allured them with false promises into a harsh land where they could never prosper. By 1602 most had fled back to Mexico. Worse still, Onate alienated the Franciscan friars, who commanded the viceroy's attention. They denounced the governor for adultery and protested that his exactions ruined and alienated the Indians, undermining the friars' efforts to convert them. The friars demanded, "If we who are Christians cause so much harm and violence, why should they become Christians?" In 1607 the exasperated viceroy removed Onate and ordered his prosecution. After prolonged judicial proceedings, in 1614 the court found Onate guilty of adultery and of abusing both Indians and colonists. Fined and stripped of his titles and offices, he was ordered never to return to New Mexico.

By removing Onate, the viceroy became responsible for governing the distant and vulnerable colony. He favored abandoning New Mexico, but the Franciscan friars urged persistence under a reformed regime, insisting that more than seven thousand Pueblo Indians had been provisionally converted. If denied Spanish priests and protection, the converts would lapse from the faith and lose their claims to heaven. Unwilling to risk his soul on their damnation, the viceroy reluctantly retained New Mexico, subject to new restrictions meant to contain costs and avoid conflicts with the Indians. In 1609 the viceroy commanded the new governor, Don Pedro de Peralta, to relocate the main Spanish settlement away from the native pueblos, by founding a new town named Santa Fe. To minimize the provocative food exactions on the Pueblo, the viceroy also directed the colonists to raise their own crops. To reduce rapes, the viceroy ordered that only married men could serve as soldiers in New Mexico. To restrict expenditures, he also reduced the garrison to just fifty men and forbade further exploration into the hinterland. The ethos of pacification would be given a second try in New Mexico, at crown expense and with the Franciscan priests preeminent in directing the feeble little colony.

Distance and isolation sentenced most New Mexican colonists to hardships and poverty. To obtain imported manufactured goods, including clothing and metal tools, they depended upon a government shipment that arrived only once every three or four years. Accompanied by soldiers, this caravan of ox-drawn, iron-wheeled wagons took six months to cover the fifteen hundred miles from Mexico City, much of it across harsh deserts, over steep mountains, and vulnerable to raiding by nomadic Indians. The Hispanics aptly called the most dangerous stretch the Jornada del Muerto. Spanish policy compounded the expense by adding customs duties and internal tolls to the exorbitant prices charged for consumer goods. The prohibitive costs of overland transportation also prevented the colonists from shipping their bulky agricultural produce to market in distant Mexico. Only salt, piñon, cattle hides, buffalo robes, and Indian slaves could bear the cost of transportation to net a small profit in Mexico. These commodities derived primarily from the tribute extorted from the Pueblo peoples. Caught in a double squeeze of high costs and small income, the New Mexicans had the lowest standard of living of any colonists in North America.

Prosperity remained confined to a small elite of about thirty-five families headed by former army officers. Favored by the governors, only the elite enjoyed both substantial land grants and *encomienda* rights to the Indian tribute and labor needed to develop their new properties into farms and ranches. The common Hispanics were mestizos who possessed modest status and limited means as farmers and artisans with small landholdings. Lacking the envied *encomienda* rights, the commoners had to work for themselves. To improve their lot, they coveted opportunities to procure Indian slaves.

Seventeenth-century New Mexico attracted few colonists, primarily desperate people who lacked opportunities elsewhere or convicts sent north as conscripted soldiers. In 1692 a Hispanic soldier described New Mexico as "at the ends of the earth . . . remote beyond compare." The slow pace of settlement kept the colony underdeveloped, which perpetuated its daunting reputation as a land of poverty and danger. Never more than 1,000 during the seventeenth century, the colonists remained greatly outnumbered by the Indians, despite the epidemics that reduced Pueblo numbers from 60,000 in 1598 to 17,000 in 1680.

Hoping to isolate their Indian converts from the colonists, the Franciscans preferred that New Mexico remain thinly populated by Hispanics. Too much past experience had taught the Franciscans to regard most frontier settlers as moral dregs who set a bad example. They drank too much and committed thefts, rapes, and blasphemies that contradicted Franciscan preaching and alienated Indians. Worse still, the colonists competed with the friars to command and exploit the natives as laborers. Far better, the missionaries reasoned, for the Hispanics to remain just numerous enough to support and defend the missions, but not so many as to harass the Indians and commandeer their labor. Given a free hand with the Pueblo peoples, the Franciscans believed that they could convert them into especially tractable and pure Christians—superior to common Hispanics.

THE NEW MEXICO MISSIONS

Like their brethren in Florida, the Franciscan missionaries of New Mexico enjoyed remarkable success in the early seventeenth century. Because the Pueblo peoples already lived in permanent, compact horticultural villages, it was relatively easy to create a mission simply by adding a church, a priest or two, and a few soldiers. By 1628 the friars had founded fifty missions, spread throughout the Rio Grande Valley and the adjoining Pecos Valley. A year later they added new missions far to the west in the Acoma, Zuni, and Hopi pueblos. The priests filled these new churches with thousands of converts, each sealed by the public sacrament of baptism, a ritual sprinkling of holy water on the head. In 1630 the chief administrator of the New Mexican missions, Fray Alonso de Benavides, reported, "If we go passing along the roads, and they see us from their pueblos or fields, they all come forth to meet us with very great joy, saying Praised be our Lord Jesus Christ!" According to Benavides, miracles also demonstrated that God had blessed the New Mexican missions: baptismal waters restored a dead Acoma infant to life; a Christian cross gave sight to a blind Hopi boy; a thunderbolt struck dead a shaman at Taos Pueblo; when Indians tried to kill a priest at Picuris Pueblo, he became invisible and escaped.

The progress was especially remarkable because the Franciscans demanded so much from their converts. Christian churches obliterated and replaced the circular *kivas*, sacred structures for religious dances and ceremonies. The priests smashed, burned, or confiscated the *katsina* images sacred to the Indians, deeming them idols offensive to the true God. In addition to mastering Christianity, the Indians were supposed to dress, cook, eat, walk, and talk like Spaniards, for the friars deemed everything traditionally native to be savage and pagan. The Franciscan God demanded chastity before and monogamy within marriage. To promote a new sense of shame and modesty, the New Mexico Franciscans ordered the Indian women to cover themselves with cloth from neck to ankles. Backsliding or resistant converts suffered whipping with the lash, sometimes followed by a smearing dose of burning turpentine over the bloody back, which could prove fatal. One friar conceded that conversion had to be "reinforced by the fear and respect which the Indians have for the Spaniards."

Although the Franciscans were demanding and punitive, most Pueblo peoples decided that it was best to receive and heed them. In part, the Pueblo acted from fear of the Hispanic soldiers, who backed up the priests with their firearms, dogs, horses, whips, and gallows. Far better to ally with than to oppose such formidable men. Indeed, many Pueblo hoped that a military alliance with the Spanish would protect both from the nomadic warrior bands—Apache and Ute—of the nearby mountains and Great Plains. The tall and thick walls of the new missions made them formidable citadels for defense as well as churches for worship.

The Pueblo peoples also saw material advantages in an alliance with the Hispanics and their priests. They introduced appealing new crops, including watermelons, grapes, apples, and wheat, and metal tools superior to the traditional stone implements of the Pueblo, as well as domesticated sheep, goats, cattle, pigs, and mules, which enlarged the supply of meat and cloth or provided power for plowing and hauling. Given the manifest power of the Spanish and their impressive material culture, many Pueblo thought it best to mollify the invaders and gain some of their advantages.

The Pueblo especially longed to co-opt the supernatural powers exercised by the priests. The natives recognized the charisma and dedication that apparently rendered the priests so adept in the ways of the spirit world. Exceptional men, the Franciscans made extraordinary sacrifices and endured severe hardships. Zealous in spreading their faith, the friars embraced chastity and lived in a distant and difficult land among peoples of strange appearance and manners who periodically fulfilled the priests' longing for martyrdom. Seeking pain as a test of faith, many missionaries wore hair shirts, walked barefoot over a stony land, and periodically bloodied their own backs with sharp sticks. The priests also stood out among the other Hispanics because they rarely raped Indian women and preferred their vow of poverty to the accumulation of gold. In 1628 one friar assured the Zuni that he had come "not for the purpose of taking away their property, because he and the members of his order wished to be the poorest on earth." The friars also dazzled the natives with elaborate and novel displays of vestments, music, paintings, and sacred images all combined into the performance of elaborate processions and the ceremony of the mass. In their theatricality, celibacy, endurance of pain, and readiness to face martyrdom the priests manifested an utter conviction of the truth and power of their God.

The natives, however, wondered whether the apparent powers of the Franciscans were benevolent or malign. In particular, the deadly epidemics presented the Franciscans with both an opportunity and a test. On the one hand, the new diseases discredited as ineffectual the Pueblo's traditional spiritual guides, the shamans, which eased the Franciscans' access to the pueblos, where desperate natives sought protection in the Christian magic. On the other hand, because the Pueblo peoples associated the diseases with the newcomers, many natives suspected that the friars practiced a deadly sorcery, particularly by administering baptism. One Hopi warned his people that the priests "were nothing but impostors and that they should not allow them to sprinkle water of their heads because they would be certain to die from it."

Consequently, the priests were in a state of probation as the Pueblo tried to determine whether they benefited or suffered from the Christian power over the spirit world. No matter how successful in getting a church built and hundreds baptized, every priest lived in the shadow of violent death. If the epidemics increased, natives who had seemed docile could conclude that their priests were dangerous sorcerers who must be killed. Of the approximately one hundred Franciscans who served in New Mexico during the seventeenth century, forty died as martyrs to their faith.

Although the Franciscans had spread their message through the Pueblo peoples with remarkable speed, conversions were rarely as complete and irreversible as the priests initially believed. There was a fundamental misunderstanding between the friars and the Pueblo—a misunderstanding characteristic of every European missionary venture in North America. The Pueblo peoples were willing to add Christian beliefs and practices, as they understood them, to their own supernatural traditions. Natives had long adopted and augmented their spiritual repertoire—provided that the additions did not challenge their overall framework, in which supernatural power was regarded as diverse and woven into their natural world. But the Franciscans erroneously believed that their Pueblo converts had forsaken their pagan ways once and for all, without compromise.

In fact, most Pueblo compartmentalized their beliefs, old and new. They accepted features of Hispanic culture and the Catholic faith that they found useful or unavoidable, while covertly maintaining their traditional spiritual beliefs. While adopting elements of Hispanic culture that would help them adjust to a transformed world, most Pueblo peoples also tried to preserve a distinct identity and core culture derived from their ancestors. That compartmentalization enabled the Pueblo to reserve the inner resources needed to rebel suddenly against their new masters. If the priests and their soldiers pushed too hard while delivering too little, the Pueblo could abandon Christianity and resort entirely to their ancient spirits for help in recovering their autonomy.

THE PUEBLO REVOLT

In New Mexico, relations were especially tense between church leaders and government officials, and between the missionaries and the colonists. The Franciscans both needed and resented the Hispanic colonists. Although they provided a military reserve needed to intimidate the Indians, the colonists also competed with the friars for control over Indian labor. Each colonial group pretended to be the truer friend of the Indians, and each denounced the other as selfish exploiters.

The competition led to violent conflicts between the priests and the colonial governors—who had not come to New Mexico to keep a vow of poverty. The governors needed to recoup the sums that they had paid the viceroy to purchase their office, to reap some further profit beyond the high costs of living in their hardship post, and to set aside an additional fund to bribe their successors to keep their peculations secret. To make money, the governors established their own ranches, farms, and workshops, all of which demanded Indian workers. Consequently, the governors shared the colonists' resentment of the Franciscan success in capturing so much Indian land and labor for building up the missions.

Some governors also worried that the priests demanded too much change too fast from the Indians, demands that might provoke a rebellion that would destroy the weak colony. In the interests of security, the governors sometimes contradicted the efforts by the priests to suppress the native dances, *katsina* images, and polygamy. In 1660, Governor Mendizabel infuriated the friars by defending ceremonial dances as harmless nonsense "that signified nothing." He was wrong; their dances signified much to the Pueblo, who felt in renewed contact with their spirit world. As the priests had feared, the revival of traditional dances undercut their authority.

Inconsistent in their Indian policies, the governors treated the Pueblo more indulgently but the nomadic Indians of the hinterland more callously. Beginning during the 1620s, the governors made money by organizing slave raids against the Apache and Ute of the hinterland. The governors employed the captives on their own properties, bestowed them upon local favorites, or sold them in Mexico, where the slaves worked on *haciendas* and in the silver mines. In Indian slaves, the seventeenth-century governors discovered the profitable commodity for export that had so long eluded their predecessors. Governors justified the raids to the viceroy as part of a "just war" provoked by the nomads, who had to pay with their lives and their labor for defying Hispanic rule. Although enriching to governors and their cronies, the slave raids provoked counterattacks that devastated common settlers and the Pueblo peoples. By stealing horses and some guns from Hispanic missions and ranches, the nomads gradually became faster and more dangerous raiders, quickly striking and retreating.

Because the governors drafted Pueblo Indians to serve in the slave raids, the nomads considered them Spanish allies and the proper targets for revenge. Because hungry and bloodied Pueblo did not make for productive and dedicated converts, the Franciscan friars saw their influence decline as the nomadic raids increased. Worse still, growing numbers of Pueblo fled from their vulnerability and Franciscan dictation to seek refuge among the Apache. One friar complained that the runaways had "gone over to the heathen, believing that they enjoy greater happiness with them, since they live according to their whims, and in complete freedom."

Tracing the troubles to their source, the Franciscans denounced the governors as corrupt, vicious, and impious meddlers. The friars repeatedly appealed to the viceroys in Mexico City to recall every offending governor. The governors responded by imprisoning and humiliating Franciscans and by withholding the soldiers that the priests needed to discipline the Indians. Once begun, these conflicts festered and intensified for years, in part because the appeals of both parties to Mexico City took so long. In turn, the cautious viceroys often preferred to consult with their superiors across the Atlantic in Madrid before taking action in New Mexico. An exchange of official recriminations and investigations and counterinvestigations dragged on over the years, entangling most governors in legal webs that consumed their estates.

Unwilling simply to await the viceroy's ruling, the Franciscans sometimes took immediate action in New Mexico. At a minimum, they excommunicated the offending governor, which cut off church sacraments and consigned his soul to eternal damnation. On one occasion, the friars even tore out the governor's church pew and hurled it into the street. The missionaries also encouraged restive soldiers to imprison one governor for nine months and to assassinate a second.

These conspicuous conflicts diminished Pueblo respect for, and fear of, all Hispanics. In 1639 an Indian congregation was shocked when Governor Rosas took offense at a Franciscan sermon, stood up, and bellowed, "Shut up, Father, what you say is a lie!" For Indian audiences, Rosas also staged plays that mocked Christian ritual and clerical authority. Governor Mendizabal liked to visit pueblos to hold impromptu trials that found the local friar guilty of siring Indian children. Because Indians especially valued public harmony and serenity, the Pueblo peoples felt contempt as they witnessed the backbiting conflicts among the Hispanics.

As the Spanish divided, the disparate Pueblo peoples became more unified, in response to the Hispanic presence. Previously lacking any common language and identity, the Pueblo peoples obtained both—as Spanish became a common second language and as they developed shared grievances against a set of exploiters. Both developments improved their ability to unite against the colonizers.

During the late 1660s and 1670s a prolonged drought repeatedly undercut harvests, reducing many Pueblo to starvation. In 1669 a priest reported that after three years of failed harvests, "a great many Indians perished of hunger, lying dead along the roads, in the ravines, and in their huts." They were reduced to eating cattle hides, "preparing them for food by soaking and washing them and toasting them in the fire." Lacking surplus produce to trade, the Pueblo suffered increasing raids by the nomads, who took by force what they had previously sought through barter. The more exposed and vulnerable Pueblo communities in the Pecos Valley dissolved, and the survivors either joined their tormentors on the Great Plains or fled to the Rio Grande Valley pueblos, where the refugees compounded the strain on the scant supply of food.

The related ravages of drought and raiders rendered more oppressive the persistent Spanish demands for Indian tribute in labor and produce. Exactions that could be tolerated in good years became intolerable in hard times, especially because the Hispanics refused to reduce their demands for tribute to reflect the diminished means and shrinking numbers of the Pueblo. Afflicted by disease, famine, and violence, the Pueblo population fell from 40,000 in 1638 to 17,000 by 1680. Nonetheless, the Pueblo remained collectively responsible for the same level of tribute, so the amount of maize and blankets that every Indian had to pay more than doubled. After the uprising of 1680 a royal attorney sent from Mexico City investigated and concluded that the colonists' "many oppressions . . . have been the chief reason for the rebellion."

By 1675 it had become abundantly clear that the Christian God could not protect the Indians from epidemic diseases, drought, and nomadic raiders, much less from exploitation by the Hispanics. Led by their shamans, the Pueblo peoples revived their traditional ceremonies, hoping to restore the disrupted balance of their world. The revival terrified the Franciscans, the colonists, and the governor. In 1675 the Hispanics arrested and whipped forty-seven Pueblo shamans on charges of sorcery. Three of the prisoners also suffered death by hanging, and a fourth committed suicide. The governor meant to export and sell the other forty-three as slaves but backed off when confronted and threatened by a large and enraged force of Pueblo warriors. In two ways the episode prepared the Pueblo for mass rebellion. The brutal persecution taught them that the Hispanics would never permit an open revival of the ancient ways that the Pueblo needed to restore their collapsing world. And having intimidated the governor, the Pueblo saw, for the first time, their potential to overcome their oppressors. Pueblo leaders began to plot a massive rebellion.

The chief plotter was a charismatic shaman named Popé, who had been whipped in the witch-hunt of 1675. He preached that the Pueblo could recover their health, dignity, prosperity, and freedom by destroying the Christians and their churches. Developing contacts in most of the native pueblos, Popé cultivated a large and growing following dedicated to his message of native revival. Especially appealing to men outraged at the Franciscan attack on polygamy, Popé promised each warrior a new wife for every Hispanic he killed.

In August 1680, most of the seventeen thousand Pueblo people rose up in a well-coordinated rebellion, involving more than two dozen towns scattered over several hundred miles, all newly united by shared hardships, oppressions, and a rudimentary understanding of Spanish. Some Apache bands assisted the uprising, for they had their own scores to settle with the Hispanic slave raiders. The rebels destroyed and plundered missions, farms, and ranches, procuring horses and guns. Venting their rage at eighty years of exploitation, the rebels took special pains to desecrate churches, to smash altars, crosses, and Christian images, and to mutilate the corpses of priests.

The colonial survivors either fled south to El Paso or took refuge at Santa Fe, where they confronted a siege by two thousand rebels. When the rebels cut off the town's water supply and tightened their cordon around the palace, Governor Antonio de Otermín and the colonists evacuated Santa Fe, fighting their way to safety three hundred miles down the Rio Grande to El Paso. The rebellion killed about two hundred of the one thousand colonists in New Mexico, including twenty-one of the forty priests. In a few weeks, the Pueblo rebels had destroyed eight decades of colonial work to create Hispanic New Mexico. The Pueblo Revolt of 1680 was the greatest setback that natives ever inflicted on European expansion in North America.

Popé encouraged the Pueblo to restore their native names and to reverse their baptisms by plunging into the Rio Grande in a ceremony of purification. He declared Christian marriages dissolved and polygamy restored. To replace the churches, the Indians restored their sacred *kivas.* Popé urged forsaking everything Hispanic, including the new crops and domesticated livestock, but most Pueblo found these too useful to relinquish. Selective in adapting Hispanic culture, the Indians were equally selective in rejecting it.

The rebellion began to falter almost as soon as it triumphed. Deprived by victory of their common enemy, the Pueblo peoples revived their traditional feuds, falling out both within villages and between them. In addition, renewed drought brought famine and another rupture in trade with their Apache allies, who resumed their raiding. The troubles discredited Popé, who had promised that the rebellion would bring perpetual peace and prosperity. Losing influence, he died in obscurity sometime before 1690.

In 1691 the beleaguered Hispanic refugees at El Paso rallied under the able leadership of a new governor, Diego de Vargas, an ambitious, resourceful, and selectively ruthless Spanish nobleman. Exploiting divisions and war-weariness among the Pueblo, he reclaimed New Mexico in 1692–93, overcoming the greatest resistance at Santa Fe, which he captured by storm. In 1696 he suppressed a renewed but smaller rebellion that killed five priests and twenty-one colonists and soldiers. But to the west, the Zuni and Hopi peoples successfully defied the governor and secured their *de facto* independence, which provided a refuge for Pueblo militants fleeing from Spanish rule in the Rio Grande Valley.

The Pueblo peoples of the Rio Grande never again mounted a major rebellion against Spanish rule. Bloody and destructive to the Pueblo as well as the Spanish, the rebellions of 1680 and 1696 taught both to compromise. The Pueblo peoples accepted Spanish persistence and authority, while the Hispanics practiced greater restraint. The governor abolished the *encomienda*—the extortion of their labor and tribute that was the single greatest grievance of the Pueblo. He also guaranteed to each pueblo a substantial tract of land and appointed a public defender to protect Pueblo legal rights in disputes with colonists. The returning Franciscans also lowered their expectations, tolerating as harmless many Pueblo ceremonies that they had previously suppressed as heathen. The Rio Grande Pueblo accepted the Catholic sacramental and seasonal cycle of festivals, quietly conducting traditional ceremonies in their *kivas*—while the Franciscans wisely looked the other way. And the leading Hispanics, official and religious, kept their feuding within new bounds, avoiding the overt ruptures that had so discredited them in Pueblo eyes during the seventeenth century.

After 1696 the Hispanic and Pueblo peoples of New Mexico also needed one another for mutual protection against the nomadic warrior peoples of the Great Plains and the Rocky Mountains. As the dominant party, the Hispanics led the alliance, but they depended upon Pueblo warriors. Together they sustained the colony—but at the heavy cost of chronic warfare with the nomads.

5

Canada and Iroquoia

1500–1660

A French engraving of the 1609 battle in which Samuel de Champlain and two other French musketeers helped their Indian allies defeat Iroquois warriors beside Lake Champlain. The advent of firearms revolutionized Indian warfare, discouraging the use of the mass formations and wooden shields depicted here. From Samuel de Champlain, Les Voyages de Champlain *(Paris, 1613).*

DURING THE SIXTEENTH CENTURY, English, French, and Dutch mariners intermittently crossed the Atlantic to plunder Spanish shipping and colonial towns or to conduct a smuggling trade. But to enjoy a steady and enduring share in the trade riches of the Americas, Spain's rivals needed their own colonies. Settling in or near the Caribbean, close to New Spain, had its temptations: proximity facilitated piracy on Spanish ships and ports, and the subtropical climate would permit the development of valuable sugar plantations. But, as the French discovered in Florida during the 1560s, the Spanish were a powerful foe, able to destroy any hostile colony within easy reach.

Distant from Spanish power, the northern latitudes of North America offered a safer setting for a French colony, but smaller prospects of profit. Despite repeated efforts, French and English explorers had failed to find either precious metals or a "Northwest Passage" through or around northern North America to the Pacific and the trade riches of Asia. And because of long winters and short growing seasons, the northern lands could not produce the tropical crops so cherished in Europe. In 1541 the Spanish emperor declined to block a French expedition to colonize along the St. Lawrence River in Canada. The emperor explained, "As regards settling in the Northern Sea, there is nothing to envy in this; for it is of no value, and if the French take it, necessity will compel them to abandon it." As predicted, that French settlement, led by Jacques Cartier, was defeated by the bitter cold, the ravages of scurvy, and the hostility of Indians provoked by French thefts and threats.

With nothing but corpses to show for the expensive effort, the French abandoned further attempts at permanently colonizing the St. Lawrence Valley until the next century. In the meantime, French voyagers developed a profitable and semipermanent presence at the river's broad mouth in the Gulf of St. Lawrence. Along with English, Basque, and Portuguese mariners, the French discovered two profitable commodities that made northern colonization possible: fish and furs. But those commodities and the cold climate limited the numbers of fur traders and the seasonal stay of fishermen.

The fur trade deeply implicated Europeans and natives in mutual dependency. The concept of Indian trade "dependency" has become controversial. Some historians believe that dependency was early, addictive, irreversible, and quickly destructive to natives, while endowing European traders with almost complete mastery. At the other extreme, critics of "dependency theory" insist that trade remained limited and natives retained the upper hand because they could readily return to stone tools and weapons and animal-skin attire.

Both positions miss the deepening *mutuality* of dependency, binding Europeans and Indians together in an uneasy embrace. As Indians became dependent upon European metals, cloth, and alcohol, the traders and their empires became hostage to Indian demand. Because a cutoff of trade increasingly threatened the Indians with hunger and destitution, they considered it an act of war. Needing Indians as allies and hunters, the northern traders could not afford them as enemies. Rather than risk a breakdown in trade, the traders grudgingly accepted Indian trade protocols, restrained their prices, and cultivated alliances. Entangled in alliances with Indians, European traders often felt compelled to assist native wars that complicated and slowed their pursuit of profit. From the Indian perspective, the French came, in the words of historian Allan Greer, "not as conquering invaders, but as a new tribe negotiating a place for itself in the diplomatic webs of Native North America." In those webs, the Indians negotiated from a position of strength.

In their cultures and languages, the Indians of northeastern North America divided into Algonquian and Iroquoian peoples. Centrally located, the Iroquoian peoples clustered around Lake Ontario and along the St. Lawrence Valley, to the east, or the Susquehanna Valley, to the south. The Iroquoians were surrounded by an even larger and more diverse array of Algonquian speakers, who occupied the Atlantic seaboard from Labrador to North Carolina and along the northern and western margins of Iroquoia to Lake Superior.

The Iroquoians practiced a mixed economy in which hunting and gathering supplemented a highly productive horticulture that sustained many large and permanent villages. A similar way of life prevailed among the more southern Algonquians, along the coast from New England to North Carolina. The northern Algonquians, however, lacked horticulture and were more mobile and dispersed, relying on a seasonally shifting round of fishing, hunting, and gathering over broad, cold territories.

During the late sixteenth century, the French took an early lead in the fur trade by establishing a summer presence at Tadoussac, on the northern shore and near the mouth of the St. Lawrence River. The French traders developed alliances with the northern Algonquians, especially the Micmac, Montagnais, and Algonkin. Through their nexus, during the early seventeenth century, the French became drawn up the St. Lawrence Valley to the Great Lakes, where they contacted the Huron, an especially numerous and prosperous people with an Iroquoian culture. By allying with the northern Algonquians and the French, the Huron broke with their fellow Iroquoians, the Five Nations, who dwelled south of Lake Ontario.

In 1610 the French choice of allies (and enemies) seemed astute, for the Five Nation Iroquois, by virtue of their more southern setting, were inferior hunters and indifferent traders. But they were formidable warriors who, after 1610, obtained metal weapons from their own European suppliers, the Dutch, who colonized the Hudson Valley. As they became better armed than their enemies, the Five Nation Iroquois violently disrupted the northern trade alliance and imperiled the small French colony on the St. Lawrence. Drawn deep into North America by the fur trade and its native alliances, the French had made especially dangerous enemies.

THE FUR TRADE

By 1580, around Newfoundland and in the Gulf of St. Lawrence, the fisheries and the whale and seal hunts employed at least four hundred vessels and some twelve thousand men. No nation controlled the fisheries, which attracted a mix of French, Basque, Portuguese, and English. In 1583, Sir Humphrey Gilbert visited and proclaimed his authority under the English queen to govern the fishing camps at Newfoundland, but no one heeded this pompous declaration after he departed a few weeks later and drowned on his return homeward.

To obtain firewood, fresh water, and room to sun-dry their fish or to render whales into oil, the fishermen and whalers established temporary camps on shore in sheltered coves. The shore camps brought the mariners into contact with Indian hunters wearing attractive furs: beaver, fox, otter, lynx, and martin. By offering European manufactured goods—especially beads, kettles, and knives—the mariners purchased furs from eager Indians. In 1534 along the coast of Acadia (now Nova Scotia), Jacques Cartier found Micmac waving furs on sticks as an invitation to land and trade. Offering high value per volume, furs were an ideal colonial commodity, one that (like gold and silver) could more than pay for its transatlantic transportation. Rendered scarce in Europe by overhunting, furs commanded high prices for making hats and for trimming fine clothes. Because Indians voluntarily performed the hard work of hunting the animals and treating their furs, traders could immediately profit in America without the time, trouble, expense, and violence of conquering Indians to reorganize their labor in mines and plantations.

At first, the Indians pursued the trade within their own cultural parameters. Living within an animistic conception of the cosmos (rather than a capitalist notion of an economy), the Indians thought of all objects, material as well as living (stones as well as beavers), as possessed of some spiritual power, which the Algonquian speakers called *manitou*. Detecting *manitou* concentrated in especially bright and shiny objects, the northeastern Indians traditionally cherished copper ornaments brought from Lake Superior or polished seashell beads, known as wampum, from Long Island Sound. They discerned the same beauty and spiritual power in the colorful glass beads and shiny metals brought by European mariners and traders. Displayed on the body or carried into the grave, the new trade goods demonstrated high status and access to *manitou*. Adapting the shiny new materials to traditional uses, Indians broke up brass kettles for reworking into arrowheads, necklaces, earrings, finger rings, and armbands.

The natives also adapted alcohol to their own purposes. At first, they balked at the novel taste and disorienting effect, but eventually they developed a craving. Drinking as much and as rapidly as they could, the Indians

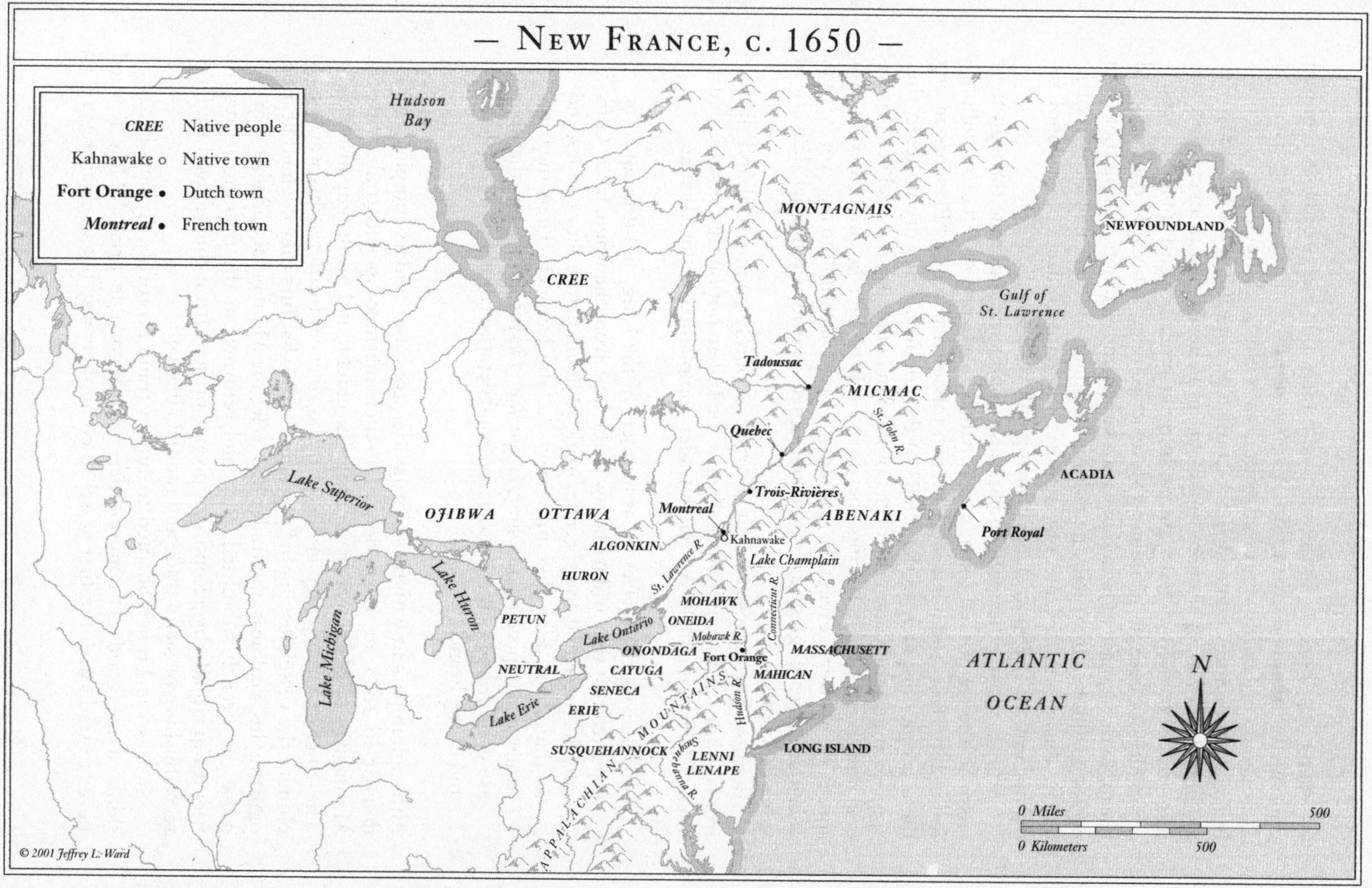
— New France, c. 1650 —
CREE Native people
Kahnawake ○ Native town
Fort Orange • Dutch town
Montreal • French town
Hudson Bay
CREE
MONTAGNAIS
NEWFOUNDLAND
Gulf of St. Lawrence
Tadoussac
MICMAC
St. John R.
Quebec
ACADIA
Trois-Rivières
Montreal
ABENAKI
Port Royal
OJIBWA
OTTAWA
Kahnawake
ALGONKIN
Lake Champlain
Lake Superior
HURON
St. Lawrence R.
Lake Huron
MOHAWK
Connecticut R.
PETUN
Lake Ontario
ONEIDA
Mohawk R.
Lake Michigan
ONONDAGA
Fort Orange
MASSACHUSETT
NEUTRAL
CAYUGA
MAHICAN
ATLANTIC OCEAN
N
SENECA
Lake Erie
ERIE
Hudson R.
MOUNTAINS
SUSQUEHANNOCK
Susquehanna R.
LENNI LENAPE
LONG ISLAND
APPALACHIAN
0 Miles 500
0 Kilometers 500
© 2001 Jeffrey L. Ward

got drunk as a short cut to the spiritual trances that had previously required prolonged fasting and exhaustion. Alcohol also offered a tempting release of aggressions, ordinarily repressed with great effort and much stress, because Indian communities demanded the consistent appearance of harmony. Regarding alcohol as an animate force, natives believed that drinkers were not responsible for their violent actions. Initially appealing and apparently liberating, alcohol became profoundly destructive once it became common and cheap. In drink, natives lashed out with knives and hatchets, killing their own people far more often than the colonial suppliers of their new drug. Fortunately, during the seventeenth century, the natives' access to alcohol remained limited and sporadic, permitting only occasional binges.

At first, the northeastern Indians also conducted the trade through their chiefs in the traditional form: as a ritualized exchange of gifts to symbolize friendship, trust, and alliance. A French missionary noted, "Presents among these peoples dispatch all the affairs of the country. They dry up tears; they appease anger; they open the doors of foreign countries; they deliver prisoners; they [symbolically] bring the dead back to life; [a chief] hardly ever speaks or answers, except by presents." In Indian diplomacy, words were cheap and meaningless unless accompanied by the ceremonial delivery of valued presents.

Because Europeans thought of trade as purely commercial and distinct from diplomacy, they initially balked at the Indian notion that trade sealed an alliance between equals. A French trader complained of the Micmac:

> And they set themselves up as brothers of the King, and it is not to be expected that they will withdraw in the least from the whole farce. Gifts must be presented and speeches made to them, before they condescend to trade; this done they must have . . . the banquet. Then they will dance, make speeches and sing *Adesquidex*, *Adesquidex*. That is, that they are good friends, allies, associates, confederates, comrades of the King and of the French.

Although impatient with these formalities, the wiser traders complied. At Tadoussac in 1623 an inexperienced French mariner opened trade with the Montagnais by offering a present that the chief found insultingly insufficient. The chief cast the paltry goods into the river and ordered his warriors to plunder the vessel, leaving in "payment" only what furs they deemed fit. Recognizing his weakness, the trader had to let the Montagnais rifle his ship. Because the French submitted, the chief returned in the evening to restore friendship ritually by accepting a proper present from the relieved trader—reestablishing peaceful trade and mutual alliance.

Just as the French adapted to Indian trade protocols, Indians began to think of the goods as commodities with negotiable prices. They learned never to trade with the first vessel to come their way but to await several to compete for their furs. The natives became adept at driving a hard bargain, to the dismay of the Europeans, who preferred to think of Indians as perpetual children. An English trader complained, "They are marvailous subtle in their bargaines to save a penny. . . . They will beate all markets and try all places, and runne twenty, thirty, yea forty mile[s], and more, and lodge in the Woods, to save six pence." Proud of their triumphs in trade, Indians defied stereotype to regard many Europeans as naive and easy marks. A Montagnais boasted to a Frenchman, "The English have no sense; they give us twenty knives like this for one Beaver skin." But their canny bargains meant no conversion to capitalist thinking. Indeed, European traders noted that the Indians sought higher prices for their furs so that they could reduce their work, preferring leisure once their basic desires had been met.

As coastal traders proliferated, their goods became cheaper, more ubiquitous, and demystified. Indians came to value the trade goods more for their utility than for their shine. Natives appreciated the superior strength and cutting edge of metal arrowheads, axes, knives, and hatchets—all useful as both tools and weapons. Iron or brass kettles facilitated cooking, and metal hoes eased the work of tilling maize, beans, and squash. All these items eased the strain and reduced the duration of native work.

Occasionally the more ruthless mariners interrupted trade to kidnap Indians as human commodities. Taken to Europe, they were put on profitable display as curiosities and trained to assist future voyages as interpreters. Eager for a voyage home, the captives shrewdly told their captors what they wanted to hear, promising to reveal gold and silver and friendly Indians eager for Christianity. Unfortunately, European diseases consigned most of the captives to European graves before European fantasies could take them home.

In some regions, the kidnapping soured relations between the natives and mariners. When Giovanni da Verrazzano, an Italian mariner in the French service, visited the coast of Maine to trade with the Abenaki Indians, he discovered:

> If we wanted to trade with them for some of their things, they would come to the seashore on some rocks where the breakers were most violent, while we remained on the little boat, and they sent us what they wanted to give on [a] rope, continually shouting to us not to approach the land; they gave us the barter quickly, and would take in exchange only knives, hooks for fishing, and sharp metal. We found no courtesy in them, and when we had nothing more to exchange and left them, they made all the signs of scorn and shame that any brute creature would make, such as showing their buttocks and laughing.

Although the Abenaki had learned fear of, and contempt for, the mariners, they did not wish to stop trading, for the new metal goods had become too useful to do without.

Unable to make the wonderful new things themselves, the Indians could get them by increasing their hunting. The northern Algonquian peoples began to hunt throughout the year. A Montagnais explained, "The Beaver does everything perfectly well, it makes kettles, hatchets, swords, knives, bread; in short, it makes everything." By the mid-seventeenth century, the trade goods were sufficiently common that the northeastern Algonquian peoples had forsaken their stone tools and weapons—and the craft skills needed to produce them. If cut off from trade, natives faced deprivation, hunger, and destruction by their enemies.

By enhancing the Indians' needs, trade increased their demands upon the environment. No longer hunting only to feed and clothe themselves but also to supply an external market, the Indians had to kill more animals, especially beaver. As market incentives overwhelmed the inhibitions of animism, the Indian hunters killed animals at an unprecedented rate that depleted their numbers. During the 1630s a French Jesuit reported that the Montagnais broke open beaver lodges to "kill all, great and small, male and female." He worried that they would soon "exterminate the species in this Region, as has happened among the Hurons, who have not a single Beaver."

Upon depleting their local beaver, Indians extended their hunting into the territories of their neighbors, provoking new and more desperate conflicts. Exploiting their edge, the trading natives raided poorly armed neighbors who lacked regular access to transatlantic commerce. For example, from French traders the Micmac obtained metal weapons and small sailboats, which they employed to attack the Indians of New England, taking scalps and captives. The raids also compelled the New England Indians to stick closer to home, opening up beaver territories for Micmac hunters.

Initially luxuries, the trade goods became necessities of survival in a more violent world, as the new weapons increased the stakes of warfare. Indians had long conducted sporadic and limited wars, inflicting a few casualties every year. The new weapons, however, enabled the well-armed to destroy their trade-poor neighbors. In addition to providing enlarged hunting grounds, such conquests endowed victors with captive women and children to replace the hundreds lost to the new diseases introduced by the traders. A people who lost captives and hunting territory faced obliteration, for want of the means to reproduce and to attract the traders needed to stage a comeback with their own weapons.

Although the fur trade pitted the Indians against one another in destructive competition, no people could opt out of the intertwined violence and commerce. As a matter of life and death, every native people tried to attract European traders and worked to keep them away from their Indian enemies. The more vulnerable and distant Indians felt compelled to break through to the European traders, who were game for recruiting new customers. As competitors in a capitalist market, the traders always needed additional hunters and more pelts. Indeed, distant and desperate peoples gave more furs for fewer trade goods, assuring larger profits to the trader. Consequently, the coastal Micmac and Montagnais found it increasingly difficult to keep their European suppliers away from their native enemies to the south and west.

While the best-positioned natives sought to control the supply of furs, they also worked against comparable efforts by Europeans to monopolize their end of the trade. Just as the Indians employed violence to constrain the trade for their own benefit, Dutch, English, and French traders exploited their national enmity toward one another. The violent competition also divided traders of the same nation, primarily pitting official monopolies against smaller rivals.

CANADA

The fur trading companies felt ambivalent about establishing permanent posts within their trading territory. On the one hand, posts attracted Indians more surely than did seasonal vessels. Moreover, if fortified and armed with cannon, a post might scare away other traders. On the other hand, fortified posts also attracted growing numbers of colonists, who might plunge into the fur trade on their own account. Wanting no new competitors, the companies preferred to keep their posts small and inhabited exclusively by their own dependents.

At the turn of the sixteenth century into the seventeenth, French fur traders focused their efforts around Tadoussac, on the Gulf of St. Lawrence, and along the peninsula they called Acadia (now Nova Scotia). To enforce a monopoly in Acadia, the official French trading company (which shifted over the years as one company succeeded another in royal favor) founded a succession of small, all-male, and short-lived settlements at Sable Island (1598–1603), St. Croix River (1604–5), and Port Royal (1605–7 and 1610–13). All failed to deter interloping traders, who found many unguarded coves and harbors on the long Acadian coast. Moreover, harsh and scurvy winters annually killed most of the colonists and demoralized the survivors. In 1613 an English pirate destroyed Port Royal, asserting his nation's counterclaim to the region.

By then the French had shifted their focus northward to reclaim the St. Lawrence Valley, formerly probed by Jacques Cartier. Known as Canada, the St. Lawrence Valley was a poor location for an agricultural colony. The growing season was short and the winters long. The French, however, initially did not come to farm. For their prime purpose, securing the fur trade, the St. Lawrence was ideal for five reasons. First, the valley was safely distant from Spanish power. Second, the northern location meant especially thick and valuable furs. Third, the resident Montagnais and Algonkin were especially skilled hunters, more so than more southern peoples. A more southern setting would have entailed a better growing season, but at the expense of inferior animal pelts and less skilled hunters (and greater risk of Spanish enmity).

Fourth, the long St. Lawrence offered the deepest access westward into the continent of any river that flowed into the North Atlantic. Cartier had demonstrated that European ships could ascend a thousand miles to meet Indians, who could come even greater distances by canoe from the vast Great Lakes country, where beaver abounded. The St. Lawrence promised the French a more extensive fur trade with many more northern Indian peoples than any other river system in the continent could provide. Fifth, at a place the French called Quebec, the river narrowed to provide both a good harbor for ships and high ground ideal for a fortified post bristling with cannon to keep out the vessels of competitors. Frustrated by Acadia's open access, the official French company delighted in the prospect of a vast northern interior rich in furs—and with a single point of entry.

The shrewd and resourceful Samuel de Champlain led the renewed French bid to found the colony of New France on the St. Lawrence River. Combining the talents of trader, soldier, cartographer, explorer, and diplomat, Champlain recognized that French success in Canada depended upon building an alliance with a network of native peoples. During the summer of 1608, Champlain built a small fortified trading post at Quebec. In 1627, after nearly two decades of colonization, New France still had only eighty-five colonists, all of them men and all at Quebec. Cultivating a mere seventeen acres, the colonists relied upon French supply ships for much of their food. And they depended upon Indian goodwill for their survival and prosperity.

The valley's Montagnais and Algonkin bands allowed their Huron allies access to the French traders at Quebec. The Huron were welcome allies primarily because their villages lay at the strategic portage between Lake Huron and the Ottawa River, a northwestern tributary of the St. Lawrence that was the trade gateway to the western Great Lakes. Consequently, the Huron could broker the flow eastward of copper and furs from around Lake Superior and the return circulation of European trade goods headed westward.

The most tightly clustered people in the northeast, the twenty thousand Huron lived in about twenty fortified towns set among extensive fields of corn, squash, and beans. Because their large numbers quickly overhunted the nearby animals, including the beaver, the Huron could not contribute much to the fur trade as hunters. Instead, they staked out a role as provisioners and middlemen in the west-to-east trade network of the north country. The Huron traded their agricultural surplus to more northern and western Indian hunters—the Algonkin, Nipissing, Ottawa, and Ojibwa—in return for their furs. The Huron then carried the pelts eastward via the Ottawa River in canoes to trade to the French at Quebec. In exchange, the Huron obtained manufactured goods both for themselves and to trade, at inflated prices, to their Indian clients for more furs. During the 1620s, the Huron annually supplied ten to twelve thousand pelts, nearly two-thirds of all the furs obtained in New France, although very few derived from animals killed by Huron hunters.

By framing an alliance to control the east-west trade, the Montagnais, Algonkin, and Huron excluded and alienated the Five Nation Iroquois. Dwelling to the south in what is now upstate New York (west of the Hudson, south of Lake Ontario, and east of Lake Erie), the Five Nations were, from east to west, the Mohawk, Oneida, Onondaga, Cayuga, and Seneca. Determined to take trade goods, captives, and revenge, the Five Nation Iroquois frequently raided northward to afflict the Montagnais, Algonkin, and Huron—which hurt the French trade.

Few in number and dependent on the fur trade, the French at Quebec needed good relations with their suppliers and hosts, the Montagnais, Algonkin, and Huron. The Canadian French could not afford to bully, dispossess, or enslave the Indians, needing them instead to persist as suppliers of furs—a role the natives were eager to perform. Coming in small numbers, the French needed relatively little land, putting slight pressure on Canada's natives, who had more territory than they needed after the epidemics of the sixteenth century.

In making Indian friends, however, Europeans almost invariably made other Indians their enemies. As their price of business and protection, the Montagnais, Algonkin, and Huron expected the French to help them fight the Five Nation Iroquois. Compelled to choose, the French embraced the northern alliance and made southern enemies.

In June 1609, Champlain and nine French soldiers joined a large allied war party that ventured south to attack the Iroquois. Reaching the lake subsequently named Champlain, the French and their allies found a fortified encampment of two hundred Iroquois, probably Mohawks. After both sides spent the night singing and shouting insults, the Iroquois sallied out from their barricade at dawn. Expecting a traditional Indian battle, rich in display and light in casualties, they formed up in a mass, relying on wooden shields, helmets, and breastplates for protection from arrows. Three Iroquois war chiefs led their advance. Springing from hiding in the bush, Champlain and his soldiers stepped forward and discharged their guns, mortally wounding all three chiefs. Astonished, the other Iroquois broke and fled, suffering additional casualties from the pursuit by their Indian enemies. A year later, the French and their firearms helped their allies win a second and even bloodier battle near the site of the first.

The introduction of firearms revolutionized Indian warfare as the natives recognized the uselessness of wooden armor and the folly of massed formations. Throughout the northeast, the Indians shifted to hit-and-run raids and relied on trees for cover from gunfire. They also clamored, with increasing success, for their own guns as the price of trade. Previously, colonial officials of all empires had forbidden the sale of guns to Indians, even if allies, but as the fur trade grew more competitive, traders recognized the immense profits in selling what the Indians wanted most. Eager for weapons to even scores against their enemies to the north, the Iroquois paid up to 120 florins for a gun that cost Dutch traders only 6 florins.

As a second consequence of the battles, the Iroquois identified the French with their enemies and saw the importance of disrupting their fur trade. Otherwise, the Huron, Algonkin, and Montagnais would grow ever more powerful with metal weapons. The Iroquois sought their own weapons by waylaying and plundering Huron, Algonkin, and Montagnais canoes.

THE FIVE NATIONS

Unfortunately for the French, the Five Nation Iroquois were especially formidable enemies dwelling in large, fortified hilltop villages. The women cultivated large and productive fields of maize, beans, and squash, producing an abundant surplus that freed their young men to pursue war. More than any other northeastern people, the Five Nation Iroquois could sustain long-distance and large-scale raids against multiple enemies. The Huron could nearly match the horticultural surplus and devotion to war, but the Montagnais and Algonkin were hunter-gatherers who could not.

Success in war boosted male prestige and influence, creating powerful incentives for young men to prove themselves against outsiders. Plunder and increased hunting territories were important but secondary benefits in wars meant primarily to obtain scalps and prisoners from the enemy. By adopting or by torturing prisoners, warriors maintained the power of their people, which was understood to be both spiritual and numeric.

Any individual's death diminished the collective power of his or her lineage, clan, village, and nation, provoking powerful and angry bursts of grief, especially by female relatives. Natives feared that their dead would linger about the village, inflicting disease and misfortune unless appeased with loud and expressive mourning. To draw the bereaved out of their agony and to encourage dead spirits to proceed to their afterlife, neighbors staged condolence rituals with feasts and presents. The best present of all was a war captive meant to replace the dead.

To appease grief, to restore power, and to build their own status, Iroquois warriors conducted "mourning wars" in which they sought prisoners from their enemies. The chiefs distributed the prisoners to grieving matrilineages, whose elder women decided their fate: adoption or death. The matrons usually adopted women and children, who were more readily assimilated. Captive men more often faced death by torture, especially if they had received some crippling wound. Inflicting death as slowly and painfully as possible, the Iroquois tied their victim to a stake, and villagers of both genders and all ages took turns wielding knives, torches, and red-hot pokers systematically to torment and burn him to death. The ceremony was a contest between the skills of the torturers and the stoic endurance of the victim, who manifested his own power, and that of his people, by insulting his captors and boasting of his accomplishments in war. After the victim died, the women butchered his remains, cast them into cooking kettles, and served the stew to the entire village, so that all could be bound together in absorbing the captive's power. By practicing ceremonial torture and cannibalism, the Iroquois promoted group cohesion, hardened their adolescent boys for the cruelties of war, and dramatized their contempt for outsiders.

A captive chosen for adoption usually endured the early, less crippling stages of torture before being rescued and suddenly lavished with care and affection. That sudden alteration served psychologically to bond the relieved captive with the captors. Given the name of a recently deceased Iroquois, the adoptee had to embrace that identity. The successful could enjoy considerable prestige and even become, in time, honored chiefs or matrons. The resistant reaped the dishonor of a sudden and unceremonious death blow from a hatchet.

Probably introduced by the Iroquois peoples, the rituals of torture and adoption had spread to their Algonquian neighbors to become common throughout the northeast long before the European invasion. Although horrifying to European witnesses, the torments of northeastern torture had their counterparts in early modern Europe, where thousands of suspected heretics, witches, and rebels were publicly tortured to death: burned at the stake, slowly broken on a wheel, or pulled apart by horses. The seventeenth century was a merciless time for the defeated on either side of the Atlantic.

During the fifteenth century, the Five Nation Iroquois had waged ferocious wars upon one another. For safety, they congregated in fewer but more crowded villages surrounded by wooden palisades and located on defensible hilltops. The broken and randomly discarded human bones of apparently tortured and executed prisoners proliferated in the refuse middens of Iroquois villages. Their oral tradition later recalled, "Everywhere there was peril and everywhere mourning. Feuds with outer nations, feuds with brother nations, feuds of sister towns and feuds of families and of clans made every warrior a stealthy man who liked to kill." The internal violence threatened to destroy the Five Nations.

During the early sixteenth century, a prophet named Deganawida and his chief disciple, Hiawatha, preached a new message of unity and peace meant to stem the violent feuding between the Iroquois nations. Deganawida and Hiawatha persuaded the Five Nations to form a Great League of Peace and Power. They periodically sent chiefs to the main village of the central nation, the Onondaga, to hold condolence ceremonies as an alternative to the further killing of the mourning war. In these ceremonies, the chiefs presided as the kinfolk of a killer gave presents to the relatives of the victim. Delivery and acceptance restored peace and broke the cycle of revenge killings. Right thinking restored, the chiefs returned home.

The Great League was not a European-style nation-state. Unlike the kingdoms of France, England, and Spain, the Iroquois Great League possessed no central political authority to devise collective policies or to coerce its own people into obedience. Indeed, the various villages preserved their autonomy, all free to go their own way, provided they relied on the condolence ceremonies to keep the peace with their fellow confederates. The Great League was primarily a ceremonial and religious forum for promoting calm and peaceful thinking in a world where grief, rage, and war prevailed. For the Iroquois, peace and war were primarily states of mind. Only through periodic public, oral, and ritual reiteration could peace have a chance to compete on an equal footing with the anger of warriors.

But the Great League did have political, diplomatic, and military consequences. By performing its spiritual ceremonies effectively, the Great League kept the Five Nations at peace. In effect, the Great League functioned as a pact of mutual nonaggression. And peace within rendered the Five Nation Iroquois more formidable external foes.

The Iroquois thought of themselves as especially devoted to peace, but others knew them as particularly fearsome in war. To appease mourning, exercise rage, and test young men as warriors, Iroquois culture required enemies, if not nearby, then farther away. Consequently, internal peace refocused Iroquois warfare outward, to the detriment of the many peoples living beyond the Great League. Many of their enemies were Algonquian-speakers, including the Montagnais and the Algonkin to the north in Canada; the Abenaki, Mahican, Mohegan, Nipmuck, Massachusett, and Wampanoag to the east in New England; and the Lenni Lenape to the southeast in the Delaware Valley.

But the Great League ideology led the Five Nation Iroquois especially to focus their hostility on the many Iroquoian-speaking nations that rejected pointed invitations to join. In 1600 the Five Nations of the Great League included only about 22,000 of the 95,000 northeastern Iroquoians. Those living beyond the Great League included the Huron and Petun to the north, the Erie, Wenro, and Neutral to the west, and the Susquehannock to the south. Other Iroquoians were also especially favored war victims, because their linguistic and cultural similarities facilitated their incorporation as captives into Five Nation villages.

During the seventeenth century, the Five Nations needed ever more captives as they coped with an increased death rate wrought primarily by new diseases and secondarily by a more violent warfare featuring metal weapons and guns. In 1633–35, smallpox and measles epidemics killed half of the Iroquois, plunging their nations into grief. The angry survivors suspected sorcery by an enemy people, such as the Huron, which demanded revenge and captives. Young men, eager to prove themselves, responded to clan mothers clamoring for new adopted relatives to appease their grief and for the ritual execution of enemies to vent their rage. Captives renewed Iroquois power while weakening an enemy. But a mourning war was a vicious circle, for almost every war party suffered casualties, which demanded more captives and more torture. And every war party provoked a counterraid from the enemy, carrying death into an Iroquois village and carrying away captives—which of course demanded a further escalation.

THE DUTCH TRADE

Unfortunately for the French and their native allies, in August 1609, just five weeks after Champlain helped defeat the Iroquois, Henry Hudson, an English mariner in Dutch employ, ascended the river later named for him to initiate a fur trade with the Mohawks. In 1614 a Dutch company established a year-round trading post on the upper Hudson near present-day Albany. Initially called Fort Nassau and later (after 1624) Fort Orange, this fortified post on the Hudson River was the Dutch equivalent of French Quebec on the St. Lawrence. Although much shorter than the St. Lawrence, the Hudson partially compensated by offering a more southern outlet that usually remained ice-free and open to shipping year-round. By occupying two adjacent river systems, the French and the Dutch drew the battle lines of European commerce and empire along the preceding fault line of native rivalry—and they raised the stakes.

Formerly at a geographic disadvantage in seeking access to the trade goods of the St. Lawrence, the Iroquois suddenly enjoyed immediate proximity on the Hudson to the Dutch, Europe's premier manufacturers and traders. Understanding the newcomers primarily as purveyors of new and valuable goods, the Mohawks named the Dutch *Kristoni*, which meant "metal-making people." Indeed, the Dutch could supply better-quality metal goods at a lower cost than could the French. Moreover, the Dutch at Fort Orange more quickly offered guns to their Indian customers than did the French at Quebec.

During the late 1620s the easternmost Iroquois nation, the Mohawk, improved their access to Fort Orange by displacing the Algonquian-speaking Mahican, who had lived around the post and had tried to control the trade. Routed and driven eastward, the Mahican left the west bank of the Hudson to the Mohawk, who shared the Dutch trade with their Iroquois confederates to the west. Hoping to tap the northern trade connections of the Mahican, the Dutch had tried, in vain, to stem the Mohawk assault, suffering three dead colonists for their pains. Rather than risk profits in avenging the loss, the pragmatic traders accepted the Mohawk victory, recognizing the Iroquois as their primary trading partners. Although occupied by the Dutch, Fort Orange functioned as an asset, and almost a possession, of the Iroquois, who acquired growing quantities of European weaponry.

Become much better armed than their Algonkin, Montagnais, and Huron enemies, the Iroquois escalated their northern raids. At first, the Iroquois primarily attacked canoe convoys on the Ottawa and St. Lawrence rivers. From the westbound convoys the Iroquois seized French trade goods to supplement their Dutch supplies; from the eastbound convoys they stole pelts to take south to trade to the Dutch at Fort Orange.

To protect the fur trade, the French extended their fortified trading posts westward up the St. Lawrence, founding Trois-Rivières in 1634 and Montreal in 1642, but both posts remained small and weak. In 1644 the Iroquois raiding led a French priest to despair:

> It is almost impossible to make either peace or war with these barbarians; not peace because war is their life, their amusement, and their source of profit all in one; not war because they make themselves invisible to those who seek them and only show themselves when they have heavy odds in their favor. Go to hunt them in their villages and they fade into the forest. Short of leveling all the forests in the country, it is impossible to trap them or to halt the destruction of these thieves. . . . It is not that these thieves are always all around us, but that one is never sure either that they are there, or that they are not, hence we have to beware of them all the time. Were it not that we hope God will eventually deliver us, the country would have to be abandoned, for we are well aware that human strength and wisdom alone cannot save us.

Ironically, the French also came to depend upon Iroquois hostility as a barrier that kept the northern Indians from traveling south to trade with the Dutch. The French recognized that they could not compete with the quality, quantity, or price of the Dutch trade goods. Therefore, a prolonged peace with the Iroquois would tempt northern Indians to carry their furs to Fort Orange for shipment to Amsterdam—to the detriment of Quebec and Paris. The French could ill afford friendship with the Iroquois, although they paid a heavy price in death and destruction for their enmity.

The Five Nation Iroquois became equally ambivalent about peace with the French. The Iroquois usually preferred to steal furs from their northern enemies to take to Fort Orange, rather than permit them as friends a free passage to the Dutch traders. Because the northern Indians possessed better furs, they would, in the event of peace, become the preferred clients and customers of the Dutch, to the detriment of the Iroquois. As inferior suppliers of furs, the Iroquois had a perverse common interest with the French, an inferior source of manufactured goods. They both tacitly worked to keep apart the best suppliers of furs (the northern Indians) and of manufactures (the Dutch).

In effect, during most of the seventeenth century, the Iroquois and the French needed one another as enemies. Although tempted by anger to obliterate each other, neither could do so, and cooler heads in both camps recognized a certain mutual interest in the survival of the other. Indeed, as a trade magnet that drew the Huron and Algonkins into Iroquois ambushes, the New French trading posts were better harassed than destroyed.

JESUITS

The fur trade launched New France, but the colony was sustained by a Catholic bid to convert the Indians. The two pursuits were overlapping but not identical. By converting the Indians to Catholicism, French leaders hoped to make the natives more dependent and dependable as allies and trading partners. The French colonizers drew inspiration from the Spanish success in building Franciscan mission systems to consolidate apparent control in Florida and New Mexico. The Spanish success seemed especially germane because New France, like Florida and New Mexico, needed to compensate for a small colonial population. But the mission system was not perfectly compatible with the fur trade, which was conducted primarily by rough characters with little interest in religion. The French priests frequently denounced the fur traders as moral reprobates who set a vicious example to the Indians, while the traders often resented the missionaries as unrealistic meddlers who ruined the natives as hunters and warriors. Consequently, French officials had to balance the interests of the fur trade and the missions in hopes of preserving the Indian alliance and the colony of New France. Those officials also had to mollify Indians who wanted trade more than missionaries.

The French missionaries manifested the Counter-Reformation, a reform movement meant to stem and reverse the growth of Protestantism by bringing a new rigor and zeal to Catholic institutions. The missionaries meant to steal a march on the Protestant heretics by converting the world's heathen peoples to Catholicism. The missionaries also worried that thousands of Indians faced an eternity in hell for want of Christianity. These concerns loosened the purse strings of devout and wealthy French men and women, who funded missions and convents in New France.

Seventeenth-century Europeans regarded non-Europeans as socially and culturally inferior—but not as racially incapable of equality. Lacking a biological concept of race, seventeenth-century Europeans did not yet believe that all people with a white skin were innately superior to all of another color. European elites primarily perceived peoples in terms of social rank rather than pigmentation. Elites (including missionaries) possessed a powerful caste consciousness of their immense superiority over the common people of their own nation, whom they readily disciplined with pain and treated with contempt. Seventeenth-century colonial leaders ordinarily considered the common peasants and laborers of Europe as little better than Indians. And the elite deemed Indians fully capable of forsaking their backward culture in favor of a superior one. Once assimilated to French culture and religion, Indians were entitled to equality with common colonists. Of course, assimilation to the bottom ranks of a European social hierarchy was not an especially appealing prospect.

In 1615 the French launched their first effort to evangelize the Indians of Canada, sending four priests of the Recollet order (the French branch of the Franciscans) to convert the Montagnais. But the Recollets faced grave difficulties in attending to far-flung and highly mobile northern Indians. Unlike the Indians of New Mexico and Florida, the Canadian Indians enjoyed the upper hand in their alliance and could safely treat priests with indifference or contempt. The missionaries had to endure muscle-numbing days paddling canoes or portaging them through clouds of mosquitoes and blackflies. The priests could not decide which was worse, the prolonged spells of hunger or consuming the Indian stews bubbling with strange plants, animals, and insects. The priests also spent restless nights in bark lodges, filled with bodies, fleas, dogs, and smoke. Overmatched by the hardships, the distances, and the indifference of the Montagnais, the four Recollet priests managed, in ten years, to baptize only fifty natives, almost all on their deathbeds and hedging their eternal bets.

The missionary cause obtained critical reinforcements in 1625–26 with the arrival of eight priests of the Jesuit order. Wearing long dark robes, the Jesuits became known to the Indians as the Black Robes. Better organized, financed, and trained for missionary service, the Jesuits took the lead in Canada as the Recollets faded. Instead of pursuing the poor and mobile Montagnais near Quebec, the Jesuits proceeded farther west to target the more prosperous and settled Huron. In 1636, Father Charles Garnier explained, "If Canada in my view is a holy and sacred temple built by God, the country of the Hurons is the *sanctum sanctorum* . . . because they are a stable nation and not vagabonds like most of the others." In Huron country, the Jesuits established four satellite missions around a formidable central mission, Sainte-Marie, which had a palisade, stone bastions, and a chapel, hospital, forge, mill, and stables. By 1647 the Huron missions employed eighteen priests and twenty-four lay assistants.

The Jesuits also benefited from the growing French influence over the Huron. As they became more dependent on trade, the Huron became more susceptible to French pressure. In 1609 the Huron had compelled Champlain to help them fight the Iroquois as the price of trade. In 1634, Champlain obliged the reluctant Huron to accept Jesuit priests as his price for continued trade. The Huron did not dare call Champlain's bluff, although he probably would have backed down, for trade was at least as critical to the French as to the Huron. Trade dependency ran both ways in New France.

Like their Spanish counterparts, the French Jesuits devoutly believed that everything in this life was inconsequential except as a preparation for the next. The salvation of souls for an eternal afterlife in heaven was all that truly mattered. One Jesuit exulted, "The joy that one feels when he has baptized an Indian who dies soon afterwards and flies directly to Heaven to become an Angel certainly is a joy that surpassed anything that can be imagined." The missionaries also advanced their own claims to heaven by the degree to which they suffered to save the souls of others. Above all, those who suffered martyrdom for their faith won an immediate and honored place in heaven next to God.

Compared with other European missionaries, including the Recollets, the Jesuits proceeded more patiently in converting the Indians. In 1642 a Jesuit explained:

> To make a Christian out of a Barbarian is not the work of a day. . . . A great step is gained when one has learned to know those with whom he has to deal; has penetrated their thoughts; has adapted himself to their language, their customs, and their manner of living; and when necessary, has been a Barbarian with them, in order to win them over to Jesus Christ.

Rather than compel Indians to learn French and relocate into new mission towns, the Jesuits mastered the native languages and went into their villages to build churches.

Most Jesuits also astonished the natives by their single-minded dedication, by their lack of interest in the land, furs, and women that other Europeans coveted. One priest returned to the Huron after having survived capture and torture by the Iroquois, losing most of his fingers. Because the Huron cherished stoicism under torture as the ultimate test of manhood, they honored this priest. One Huron remarked, "I can neither read nor write, but those fingers which I see cut off are the answer to all my doubts."

Despite their patience and zeal, the Jesuits still had to bridge a cultural chasm. In contrast to the religious absolutism of the Christian missionaries, the natives insisted that there were multiple and relative supernatural truths—some intended for Europeans and others for Indians. Committed to consensus, the natives also disliked the disputation and dogmatism of the missionaries. In turn, the natives' bland equanimity in reply especially infuriated the priests. A frustrated Jesuit reported that the Indians listened patiently but ultimately replied, "You can have your way and we will have ours." He added, "If we reply that what they say is not true, they answer that they have not disputed what we have told them and that it is rude to interrupt a man when he is speaking and tell him he is lying." Another impatient missionary remarked, "What can one do with those who in word give agreement and assent to everything, but in reality give none?"

The natives did not believe in a starkly dichotomized afterlife of heaven and hell. Instead the Indian dead passed into a dreamworld where they lived much as they had in this life, employing items cast into their graves. In 1637 a missionary complained, "You find some of them who renounce [the Christian] Heaven when you tell them there are no fields and no corn there; that people do not go trading nor fishing there; and that they do not marry." The Indians also had spiritual experts, known as shamans, who manipulated the spirits, sometimes inflicting and sometimes curing disease. Because their spiritual power was double-edged, capable of harming as well as hurting, the shamans were both feared and respected. Naturally, they proved to be the greatest enemies of the missionaries.

As Catholics, the priests could practice their own divine magic that made them effective competitors with the shamans. Unlike Protestant ministers, the Jesuit priests believed that their rituals—especially the mass—could induce God to provide immediate relief: needed rain, abundant game, or the destruction of a crop pest. And, as Catholics, the Jesuits had sacred items—crucifixes, rosaries, Agnus Dei medals, and saints' relics that could replace the stone charms kept in pouches by Indians as sources of spiritual power. Indeed, the missionaries exploited the ceremonial complexity and sacred objects of Catholic worship to impress the natives. A Jesuit explained:

> The outward splendor with which we endeavor to surround the Ceremonies of the Church . . . the Masses, Sermons, Vespers, Processions, and Benedictions of the Blessed Sacrament . . . with a magnificence surpassing anything that the eyes of our savages have ever beheld—all these things produce an impression on their minds, and give them an idea of the Majesty of God.

Initially, like other Indians elsewhere, the Huron were drawn to the apparent magical prowess of the Jesuits rather than to their abstract Christian message.

But by competing with the shaman as divine magician, the priest inherited his obligation to preserve the people from disease and famine. A Jesuit lamented, "And then you are responsible for the sterility or fecundity of the earth, under penalty of your life; you are the cause of droughts; if you cannot make rain, they speak of nothing less than making away with you." The missionary reaped the shaman's ambivalent reputation as a powerful source of both menace and relief.

The lethal diseases that accompanied the Jesuits from Europe especially complicated their mission. During the 1630s, epidemics killed half of the Huron, reducing their number to ten thousand. A Huron mourned, "The plague has entered every lodge in the village, and has so reduced my family that today there are but two of us left, and who can say whether we two will survive?" The survivors wondered why they died in such great numbers shortly after the priests came among them, and why the diseases killed Indians while sparing the priests. Many Huron suspected that the priests were deadly sorcerers—especially given the Jesuit eagerness to hover over the terminally ill to administer the rite of baptism. Although the Jesuits insisted that baptism secured salvation for the next world, Indians suspected a water sorcery that terminated lives in this world. A Jesuit conceded, "For it has happened very often . . . that where we were most welcome, where we baptized most people, there it was in fact where they died the most."

Ties of kin and clan held Indian villages together and served as the bonds that either resisted or disseminated the Jesuit message. Because the priests ruled that Christian converts could marry only fellow converts, many Indians initially balked at converting for fear they would not find a husband or wife. Because the Jesuits preached that Christians and non-Christians went to separate afterlives, Indians also dreaded eternal separation from their ancestors and relatives. One Huron protested, "For my part, I have no desire to go to heaven, I have no acquaintances there." The Jesuits needed to persuade entire lineages to convert together. But once the Jesuits achieved a certain critical mass of converts, the process rapidly snowballed. The consideration that had held people back then became an incentive to convert, so that entire lineages could be reunited after death in the Christian heaven.

As the Jesuits gathered a following, they demanded more cultural concessions from their Huron converts. The Jesuits denounced torture and ritual cannibalism, premarital sex, divorce, polygamy, and the traditional games, feasts, and dances. An exasperated Huron chief complained to a priest, "My nephew, we have been greatly deceived; we thought God was to be satisfied with a Chapel, but according to what I see he asks a great deal more." Another Huron concluded, "God does not love us, since he gives us commandments that we cannot keep."

The growing numbers of Christian converts and the escalating demands of the priests undermined the unity and morale of the Huron villages. Some traditionalists argued for breaking with the French, killing the priests, and making peace with the Five Nation Iroquois. But most Huron felt that they could not live without trade and alliance with the French. To retain both, the Huron had to keep hosting the dangerous and divisive Jesuits. Their decision attracted mounting attacks from the Five Nations, well armed with Dutch muskets.

DESTRUCTION

In the mid-seventeenth century, Iroquois warfare dramatically escalated to nearly genocidal proportions, devastating their native enemies and imperiling the French colony. In 1643 a Jesuit feared that the Iroquois meant "to ravage everything and become masters everywhere." Never before had native peoples attacked and killed each other on the scale and with the ferocity of the Iroquois during the 1640s and 1650s. European trade and diseases combined both to empower and to distort the Iroquois way of war, ultimately to their own detriment, as well as to the misery of their many enemies. Dutch guns enabled the Iroquois to take the offensive, while Dutch-introduced pathogens increased deaths, escalating the frequency, distance, bloodshed, and captive-taking of mourning wars as the Iroquois desperately tried to restore numbers and spiritual power, lest both ebb and their enemies triumph.

Historians usually characterize the Iroquois attacks as a "beaver war," as an Iroquois drive to destroy the Huron as competitors in the fur trade. There are some grounds for that interpretation. The fur trade did reinforce the Huron and Iroquois place in competing alliances, and the commerce did provide the metal hatchets and firearms that made possible the Iroquois victory. But the Iroquois assault on the Huron was primarily a mourning war and only secondarily a beaver war. The Five Nations especially targeted the Huron to obtain captives for adoption into Iroquois families and villages, reeling from their recent losses to disease and war.

Assailing the Huron also served the ideology of the Great League of Peace and Power. Because the Huron had repeatedly rejected invitations to join the confederacy, the Iroquois felt duty-bound to destroy their independence and absorb them as adopted captives, or as consumed victims, into the Great League. A Jesuit noted, "So far as I can divine, it is the design of the Iroquois to capture all the Hurons, if it is possible; to put the chiefs and a great part of the [men] to death, and with the rest to form one nation and one country."

In 1648 and 1649, Iroquois warriors stormed the Huron villages, killing and capturing hundreds. During the assaults, Jesuit priests hurriedly baptized all they could reach before they too were hacked or burned to death. By 1650 the Huron villages had all been destroyed or abandoned. The surviving Jesuits tried to find some divine purpose in the massive destruction by pagans of a people who had begun to convert to Catholicism. One priest concluded, "Let them be killed, massacred, burnt, roasted, broiled, and eaten alive—patience! that matters not, so long as the Gospel takes its course, and God is known and souls saved."

The Iroquois eliminated the Huron villages to deter their thousands of captives from running away home. Indeed, the Iroquois systematically hunted down for death or capture groups of Huron refugees, no matter how far they ran. Several hundred Huron survivors fled eastward to live as refugees at Lorette near Quebec. Many more headed west beyond Lake Michigan, where they gradually amalgamated with other Iroquoian-speaking refugees, the Petun, to make up a new, composite people known as the Wyandot. But the great majority of the Huron survived only as adopted captives among the Iroquois. In 1650 a stray Huron surrendered to the Mohawk, explaining, "The country of the Hurons is no longer where it was,—you have transported it into your own. It is there that I was going, to join my relatives and compatriots, who are now but one people with yourselves."

During the 1650s, the Iroquois ravaged the three independent Iroquoian peoples living along Lake Erie and Lake Huron: the Erie, Petun, and Neutral. As with the Huron, the victors killed most of the defeated warriors, captured their women and children for adoption, and burned the villages to discourage their flight homeward. The massive influx of captives barely covered the continuing Five Nation losses to disease and war. In 1657 a French priest visited the Iroquois and concluded that adopted captives had become a majority. By 1660, through conquest, the Great League of Peace and Power seemed at last to have absorbed almost all of the Iroquoians—but at a very heavy cost in bloodshed and destruction.

From the perspective of their enemies, the Iroquois appeared relentlessly united, purposeful, and invincible. Yet, viewed from within Iroquoia, their wars seem more desperate than calculated, and more internally corrosive than securely triumphant. By winning such massive victories and taking more captives than they could assimilate, the Iroquois provoked new dissensions and divisions within their own nations. The adopted captives often clung to their previous identity and ideas. Many Huron exhorted their new kin to embrace Catholicism and a French alliance. During the 1670s, they persuaded about four hundred Mohawk to secede and emigrate northward to settle at Kahnawake, near Montreal, to benefit from French trade and a French mission. Their secession weakened the Five Nation Iroquois as it strengthened New France with new Indian allies.

But nothing was ever quite that clear-cut in the paradoxical complexities of the colonial world. By maintaining kinship and trade ties with the Mohawk Valley, the Kahnawake Mohawk compromised French imperial interests. They discouraged French attacks on their southern kin, shared sensitive military information, and smuggled Canadian furs to Albany (the former Fort Orange), where the merchants paid higher prices. Just as the destruction of the Huron did not ruin the French interest (or entirely benefit the Iroquois), so too the defection to Kahnawake proved a mixed blessing for New France. Fundamentally, natives pursued their own interests and manipulated the wishful thinking of the colonizers.

Trade, alliance, and war entangled colonizers and natives in ways that they could not have predicted, could rarely control, and might not have chosen—had they had that luxury. New France proved far more violent and precarious and much less profitable than Champlain had hoped. In pursuit of fur-trade profits, the French had been drawn into a complex world of native alliances and enmities that compelled unanticipated investments of lives and money. Colonial empires never fulfilled the European fantasies of command and control, although they unleashed powerful forces of disease, trade, and war that, although beyond European control, fundamentally disordered far-flung and diverse native peoples.

Part II

COLONIES

6

Virginia

1570–1650

The Countrey wee now call Virginia beginneth at Cape Henry distant from Roanoack 60 miles, where was S.r Walter Raleigh's plantation. and because the people differ very little from them of Powhatan in any thing, I have inserted those figures in this place because of the conveniency.

King Powhatan comands C.Smith to be slayne, his daughter Pokahontas beggs his life his thankfullness and how he Subiected 39 of their kings reade ÿ history

Pocahontas intercedes to save Captain John Smith from execution within the council house of her father, the paramount chief Powhatan, who looms large in the right background. Pocahontas probably played a scripted part in an adoption ceremony that Smith misunderstood. From John Smith, Generall Historie of Virginia *(London, 1624).*

DURING THE SIXTEENTH CENTURY, Spanish and French mariners explored the long coast north of Florida and south of Acadia (Nova Scotia) but deemed the temperate region of little value for colonies: too cool for tropical crops but too warm for the best furs. Foiled in Florida during the 1560s, the French thereafter kept to the north, exploiting the fish and furs of Acadia and Canada. After retaking Florida, the Spanish established undermanned missions as far north as Chesapeake Bay (in present Virginia), but native resistance compelled their retreat in 1572. Thereafter, the Spanish concluded that Florida adequately protected the precious heartland of their empire to the south in Mexico and the Caribbean.

Neglected by the Spanish and French, the mid-Atlantic seaboard remained open to English colonization during the 1580s. Previously, English mariners had explored the frigid waters and barren coasts north of Labrador, in a vain search for gold and the Northwest Passage to China. More successfully, fishermen from southwestern England seasonally exploited the abundant cod in the waters around Newfoundland. But English leaders considered Newfoundland too cold and barren for year-round inhabitation by colonists. Moreover, during the mid-sixteenth century, the English were preoccupied with the conquest and colonization of Ireland.

Later in the century, success in Ireland emboldened English leaders to extend their colonial ambitions across the Atlantic to the region they called Virginia, named in honor of their queen, Elizabeth I, a supposed virgin. Between 1580 and 1620 the English applied the name to the entire mid-Atlantic coast between Florida and Acadia. Initially, the English colonizers pursued get-rich-quick schemes: a search for gold mines on land and for Spanish treasure ships by sea. When those schemes proved expensive and deadly failures, the colonizers gradually turned to the slower and more laborious development of plantations. In 1616, the colonists belatedly discovered their prime commodity in tobacco, which permitted an explosive growth in population, territory, and wealth. That expansion escalated to a crisis of confrontation between the English colonists and the Algonquian Indians, who defended their lands and culture against the intruders.

PROMOTERS

Possessed of a relatively small and poor realm, the English queen lacked the means to finance and govern an overseas colony, especially after a full-scale war erupted with Spain in 1585. Obliged to play defense in the nearby Netherlands and English Channel, the English crown lacked the men and ships for risky ventures far from home. Instead, following French and Spanish precedent, the crown subcontracted colonization by issuing licenses and monopolies to private adventurers, who assumed the risks in speculative pursuit of profits.

Because sober merchants wisely sought safer investments in trade routes closer to home, the earliest English colonial promoters were dreamers and gamblers driven by their visionary imagination. The prime movers were politically well-connected gentlemen from the southwestern counties of England, where ambitious people looked westward toward Ireland and beyond for opportunities. Known as the "West Country men," the promoters included Sir Francis Drake, Sir Richard Grenville, Sir John Hawkins, Sir Walter Ralegh, and Sir Humphrey Gilbert. In London, they retained as publicists two cousins both named Richard Hakluyt, the elder a prominent lawyer and the younger a clergyman.

Zealous English patriots and devout Protestants, the West Country men yearned to advance their fortunes and consolidate their political influence at the royal court. In addition to leading the English conquest of Ireland, the West Country men designed the English assault on the Spanish empire, for they regarded colonial trade as the key to imperial power. Ralegh preached, "That hee that commaunds the sea, commaunds the trade, and hee that is Lord of the Trade of the world is lord of the wealth of the worlde." The elder Hakluyt succinctly summarized their goals: "1. To plant Christian religion. 2. To trafficke. 3. To conquer."

In wooing investors and the crown, the West Country promoters also addressed a pervasive anxiety over the proliferation of poverty, vagrancy, and crime in sixteenth-century England. They pitched a radical program of overseas colonization by appealing to a conservative fear that the hierarchical society of England was eroding. In their view, England needed to expand outward lest it collapse from within.

Sixteenth-century England concentrated wealth and power at the narrow top of the steep social pyramid, in the hands of a monarch, an aristocracy, and a lesser aristocracy known as the gentry. Less than 5 percent of the population, the elite displayed their wealth and power in elaborate city palaces, great country estates, silk clothing, gilded carriages, and numerous servants. Below them on the social scale lived the common people, about 95 percent of the population. A diverse lot, those with some property ranged from a few wealthy urban merchants to the far more numerous "middling sort of people": a mix of farmers, artisans, and shopkeepers. But most commoners lacked property and belonged to "the lower sort": a combination of the working poor (rural peasants and urban laborers) and beggars without work. In years of reduced trade and poor harvests, displaced peasants and unemployed laborers swelled the ranks of the starving. Claiming a monopoly on honor and power, the elite with great property ruled the majority with little or none. In 1565, Sir Thomas Smith noted the obvious: "Day labourers have no voice nor authority in our commonwealth, and no account is made of them but only to be ruled."

The executive power belonged to the monarch, ordinarily a king, but sometimes, for want of a male heir, a queen, as in the late sixteenth century.

The realm included the distinct kingdoms of England, Wales, and Ireland and, after 1603, Scotland as well. As the wealthiest and most populous kingdom, England dominated the whole, from the capital in London. Unlike the authoritarian kings of France and Spain, Queen Elizabeth had to share national power with the aristocracy and gentry, who composed the bicameral national legislature known as Parliament. By birthright, the aristocracy filled the House of Lords, while the gentry dominated the House of Commons by winning elections to represent an electorate of the middling sort of men. Only about 25 percent of the adult men owned enough property to qualify for the vote—and only for one house of Parliament. Of course, the structure of power also disenfranchised all women. Although a narrow system of government by our standards, the English constitution was extraordinarily open and libertarian when compared with the absolute monarchies then developing in the rest of Europe. Consequently, it mattered greatly to the later political culture of the United States that England, rather than Spain or France, eventually dominated colonization north of Florida.

During the later sixteenth century, the English "lower sort" grew in number and deteriorated in circumstances. Economic growth failed to keep pace with a population that surged from about three million in 1500 to four million in 1600 and five million by 1650. At the same time, the kingdom's leading manufacturing sector, the cloth trade, stagnated as English makers lost market share on the European continent. In 1618, Robert Reyce remarked, "Where the clothiers do dwell or have dwelt, there are found the greatest number of the poor."

Most English folk, perhaps 80 percent, lived in country villages and tended livestock or cultivated grains. During the late sixteenth and early seventeenth centuries, the rural people suffered increasing displacement and unemployment as their aristocratic landlords adopted a program known as enclosure. Meant to increase profits by rationalizing estates, enclosure fenced in large tracts of land and fenced out most of their former inhabitants. On enclosed estates, flocks of sheep, teams of hired laborers, and a few tenants replaced a larger number of peasant smallholders. The landlords also enclosed common lands formerly used by the peasants to pasture livestock and to gather fuel, herbs, roots, fish, and rabbits. In the long term, the enclosure movement increased agricultural productivity and national wealth. In the short term, enclosure rendered redundant, homeless, and miserable thousands of peasants and laborers. Probably about half the rural peasantry lost their lands between 1530 and 1630.

Known as "sturdy beggars" (to distinguish them from the traditional sort of paupers crippled by some injury or ailment), the evicted and unemployed joined the swelling ranks of vagrants who roamed the land in search of work and charity. As a last resort, they stole, which brought growing numbers to the gallows, for theft was a capital crime. The new poor gravitated from the rural villages to the market towns and seaport cities, especially London,

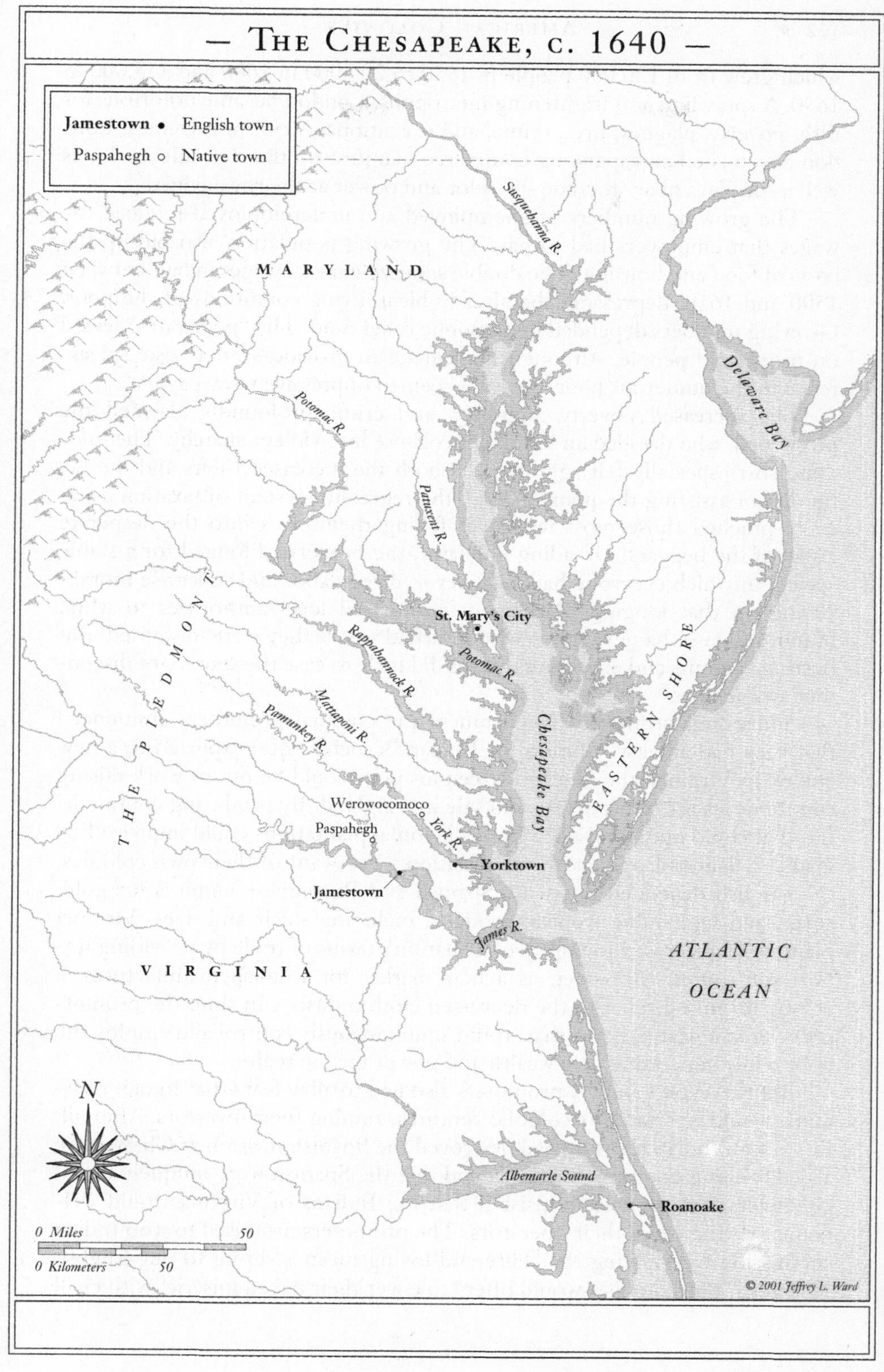
— The Chesapeake, c. 1640 —
Jamestown • English town
Paspahegh ○ Native town
MARYLAND
Susquehanna R.
Delaware Bay
Potomac R.
Patuxent R.
THE PIEDMONT
St. Mary's City
Rappahannock R.
Potomac R.
Mattaponi R.
Pamunkey R.
Chesapeake Bay
EASTERN SHORE
Werowocomoco
York R.
Paspahegh
Yorktown
Jamestown
James R.
ATLANTIC OCEAN
VIRGINIA
N
Albemarle Sound
Roanoake
0 Miles 50
0 Kilometers 50
© 2001 Jeffrey L. Ward

which grew from 120,000 people in 1550 to 200,000 in 1600 and 375,000 in 1650. A sprawling and frightening metropolis, London became notorious for filth, poverty, plagues, fires, crime, and executions. A city of extremes, London also hosted an expanding commerce manifest on the riverside docks, as well as displays of aristocratic splendor and power at the royal court.

The growing numbers of unemployed and underemployed reduced the wages that employers had to pay. The growing population also bid up the costs of food and housing. The double squeeze cut real wages in half between 1500 and 1650, depressing the already bleak living conditions of the poor. Growing numbers depended upon public relief funded by "poor rates" levied on propertied people. Although inadequate to provide even a basic subsistence to the numerous poor, the rates seemed oppressive to taxpayers.

The increased poverty, vagrancy, and crime profoundly alarmed the propertied, who dreaded an imminent collapse into violent anarchy. The middling sort especially felt aggrieved by both the increased thefts and the tax burden of assisting the poor. Indeed, the regressive system of taxation especially pinched those most fearful of falling themselves into the desperate ranks of the beggars. Dreading upheaval, the propertied longed for a stable society in which everyone had a master to direct labor and supervise morals. Acting on that longing, Parliament authorized local authorities to whip, brand, and even hang vagrants who returned where they were unwanted. But ousting vagrants and executing thieves did little to ease the sources of discontent and anxiety.

Addressing propertied Englishmen, the colonial promoters announced that they had an easy solution for England's social woes: exported to a new colony in Virginia, the idle and larcenous poor could be put to work raising commodities for transport to, and sale in, England. By producing commodities that could not be raised at home, colonial plantations could improve England's balance of trade with other nations. For want of their own colonies, the English depended upon the Spanish and Portuguese empires for gold, silver, and high-value tropical produce, including sugar and dyes. Virginia plantations promised to improve the nation's terms of trade by providing import substitutes. Moreover, as a new market for English manufactures, a colony promised relief to the depressed cloth industry. In sum, the promoters offered a neat package that would simultaneously control and employ the poor while generating new wealth and power for the realm.

But the West Country promoters also had to allay fears that Indian resistance would frustrate the colonial ventures, ruining their investors. After all, in 1571 an Indian uprising had destroyed the Spanish mission at Chesapeake Bay. Dwelling upon the Black Legend that the Spanish were uniquely brutal colonizers, the promoters insisted that the Indians of Virginia would welcome the English as their liberators. The promoters promised to woo Indian submission by applying the "faire and loving meanes suting to our English Natures." The colonists would offer "to cover their naked miserie, with civill use of foode, and cloathing, and to traine them by gentle meanes, to those manuall artes and skill, which they so much affect, and doe admire to see in us." The promoters could not conceive that the native peoples might prefer no colonial masters and no new system of labor. Satisfied with their own ways, the Indians wished little change, except to procure by trade the metals and cloths of the Europeans.

The sixteenth-century conquest of Ireland contradicted the English pretensions to "faire and loving meanes" as colonizers. Indeed, the illusions of the English lowered their threshold for brutal violence when frustrated. Convinced of their own benign intentions and superior civilization, the English regarded Irish resistance as rank ingratitude by stubborn barbarians. One West Country leader concluded that "nothing but fear and force can teach duty and obedience to such rebellious people." Treating the Irish as treacherous beasts, the English waged a war of terror and intimidation, executing prisoners by the hundred, including women and children. The English commander Sir Humphrey Gilbert decorated the path leading to his tent with human heads. His publicist boasted that the scene brought "greate terrour to the people when they saw the heads of their dead fathers, brothers, children, kinsfolke, and friends, lye on the grounde before their faces, as they came to speak with the colonel." Dispossessing many of the Irish, the victors obtained great estates that they colonized with Protestant settlers from England and Scotland.

Contrary to the Black Legend, the English treated the Irish no better than the Spanish treated the Guanche, and they offered no prospect of fairer play for the Indians of Virginia. Indeed, the conquest and colonization of Ireland served as the English school for overseas empire, the English equivalent of the Spanish invasion of the Canaries. In Ireland, the English developed both the techniques and the rhetoric of colonial conquest. In Ireland, the English learned to consider resisting peoples as dirty, lazy, treacherous, murderous, and pagan savages, little if any better than wild animals, and to treat them accordingly. In Virginia, the English employed the same language and meted out the same treatment whenever Indians violated the initial role cast for them: grateful innocents eager to submit to their superior benefactors. Unwilling to play along, Indians faced the formidable fury of their uninvited guests.

ROANOKE

In 1585, Sir Walter Ralegh sent about one hundred colonists, all of them men, across the Atlantic to settle on Roanoke, a small island on the North Carolina coast (then part of "Virginia"). Buffered by dangerous shoals and long sandbanks, the location promised obscurity from Spanish discovery and attack, but the colonists paid a high price for this measure of security. The shoals and sands made it difficult for English ships to land supplies or to load commodities, and the sandy, infertile soil produced scanty crops. The poor location virtually doomed Roanoke to failure.

The island's paltry potential for agriculture did not initially bother the colonists, who expected to be fed by the local Algonquian Indians. Commanded by Ralph Lane, a hardened veteran of the grim war in Ireland, the colonists behaved no better than conquistadores. Initially hospitable, the Indians ran out of patience as the English persisted through the winter, demanding ever more maize while the native supply ran perilously low. In the early spring of 1586, the local chieftain, Wingina, refused to provide any more food. In a sudden surprise attack, Lane killed Wingina and his deputy chiefs. Meant to secure maize by terrifying the survivors, Lane's atrocities instead put the Indians to flight, blighting prospects for a new crop to feed the improvident colonists. The starving colonists eagerly abandoned Roanoke later that spring, when English ships stopped by en route home from raiding the Spanish Caribbean.

Trying again in 1587, Sir Walter Ralegh and his associates dispatched a second set of colonists with a new civilian leader named John White. The ninety-four colonists included seventeen women and nine children: the first English families to settle in the Americas. Ralegh and White planned to locate the colony at Chesapeake Bay, to the north, where the land was more fertile and the natives less alienated. But the impatient mariners dumped the colonists at Roanoke before hastening on to the Caribbean to attack Spanish ships.

Seeking supplies and reinforcements, White soon returned home, where he had to linger while the struggle against the Spanish Armada preoccupied English shipping during 1588 and 1589. At last, in August 1590, White returned to Roanoke with a relief expedition to find the settlement mysteriously abandoned with no signs of attack by either the Indians or the Spanish. The lone clue was carved into a tree—the word "Croatoan," the name of a nearby island. But the fearful and impatient English mariners refused to venture through the dangerously shallow waters to Croatoan to investigate. Sailing away in pursuit of Spanish treasure ships, the mariners abandoned any surviving colonists to their still mysterious fate.

After retreating to Croatoan and failing to contact a passing ship, the surviving colonists probably headed north to Chesapeake Bay to execute their original plan. They apparently found haven in an Indian village. In 1607, when English colonists reached Chesapeake Bay, some Indians reported that white people had recently lived nearby as refugees in a native village. Unfortunately, the village had run afoul of a powerful chieftain, Powhatan, who killed all the refugees.

The English colonial promoters had insisted that the diverse attractions of colonization would all work together in perfect harmony. In fact, Roanoke demonstrated that the distracting pursuit of immediate wealth worked against the laborious and patient development of a plantation colony. Why cultivate corn when an overland exploration might yield a gold mine or sea raiding might capture Spanish bullion? Eager to search for Spanish ships, the English mariners dumped colonists and their supplies with an indecent, wasteful haste, or they bypassed Roanoke altogether. The poor location reinforced their aversion, for mariners dreaded the shoal waters and adverse winds as a graveyard for ships and sailors. For months on end, the colonists lacked supplies from and contact with England. Naturally, they begged to be taken away on the rare occasions when ships did happen by.

POWHATAN

In 1607 the English tried again, this time at Chesapeake Bay, which offered better harbors, navigable rivers, and a more fertile land. About two hundred miles long and twenty wide, the bay was a complex system of waterways, an environmental meeting place of tidewater estuaries and freshwater rivers that abounded in fish, shellfish, edible plants, and game animals. On the western shore, four major rivers, with many tributaries, flowed from northwest to southeast into the bay, dividing the land into a series of long, fertile peninsulas. From south to north, the English called these wide, deep, and muddy rivers the James, York, Rappahannock, and Potomac. The rivers offered ready navigation about one hundred miles upstream until interrupted by waterfalls, where the coastal plain gave way to the rolling hills of the Piedmont.

The broad coastal plain sustained about 24,000 Indians divided into thirty tribes but united by an Algonquian language and the rule of a paramount chief named Powhatan. They lived by a mix of horticulture, fishing, hunting, and gathering. During the winter, the natives dwelled in many villages consisting of one to two hundred inhabitants, occupying twenty to thirty houses. In the spring, they dispersed into still smaller and scattered encampments to fish and gather shellfish and aquatic tubers from the rivers, marshes, and bay. During the summer they returned to their village to cultivate fields of beans, maize, and squashes. In the fall, they scattered again to hunt for waterfowl in the wetlands and for deer in the broad forest of immense deciduous trees, while the women and children gathered edible nuts, roots, and berries. Employing dugout canoes paddled or poled by hand, the natives exploited the river system to conduct a small-scale but long-distance trade with the Indians of the interior, exchanging maize and seashells for the freshwater pearls and copper of the hinterland.

Because this mobile way of life generated a scant surplus, the Virginia natives annually experienced lean periods, especially in the late spring and early summer after exhausting the previous year's harvest. Living close to the bone, the Indians had precious little to tide them over in case of some unanticipated shortfall like an infestation of worms in the corn or the arrival of hungry and well-armed colonists.

The Indians' seasonal mobility discouraged the accumulation of property beyond seashell jewelry and wood and stone tools. They lived in simple but ingenious lodges constructed by placing mats and bark over an oval framework of poles set atop an earthen floor. Smoke from the central hearth escaped through a hole at the top. Quick to build and easy to take down, these lodges facilitated mobility. Expressing both admiration and discomfort, the English colonist Captain John Smith described the tight and crowded lodges as "warme as stoves, but very smoaky." Smith found none of the furniture of an English house—no tables, chairs, or chests—only raised wooden platforms for beds made of animal pelts. Neither house nor furnishings provided opportunities for the conspicuous consumption that helped determine status in England.

In contrast to the occupational specialization and class stratification in England, the Virginia Indians divided tasks almost exclusively along gender lines. Women cultivated crops, gathered nuts and fruits, and tended the village or camp, putting up the lodges and preparing the skins to make clothing. Men hunted, fished, cleared land for crops, and made dugout canoes. The only specialists were a few shamans. Set apart by their supernatural knowledge, they combined the roles of healer, conjurer, and priest. The shamans tended temples, constructed like regular houses, but substantially larger—twenty feet wide and one hundred long—and elaborately decorated with carved wooden corner posts. The temples housed the bundled bones of dead chiefs, the tribute paid to the living chief, and a wooden statue representing an especially powerful and vengeful spirit known as Okeus. Polytheistic and pragmatic, the Virginia Indians especially honored Okeus to disarm his formidable capacity to inflict harm.

Their ruler, Powhatan, led the largest and most powerful chiefdom that the English found along the Atlantic seaboard during the seventeenth century. In his sixties in 1607, Powhatan impressed the English colonists with his powerful build, dignified demeanor, and "subtle understanding." During the late sixteenth century he inherited power over six tribes, which he increased to thirty through a shrewd combination of diplomacy, intimidation, and war. This was not quite a Mississippian chiefdom, for his people built no pyramids and lived in relatively small towns, but Powhatan exercised a power of life and death over his people and received their public obeisance. From his especially large lodge in the village of Werowocomoco on the York River, Powhatan displayed a large entourage of servants, forty bodyguards, and one hundred wives, all supported from the tribute in maize and deerskins collected from the subordinated villages. A council of veteran warriors and shamans advised the paramount chief.

Unlike a nation-state, which relies upon bureaucratic institutions and a national identity to maintain obedience and collect taxes, a paramount chiefdom was an elaborate kinship network that gathered and redistributed tribute. Sometimes Powhatan retained and adopted the village chiefs he defeated and subordinated, taking their daughters as wives. Other chiefs he replaced with blood relatives: sons, brothers, and occasionally his sisters. Consequently, his polygamy united his chiefdom in two ways, by taking the wives of subordinated chiefs into his own family and by producing numerous children to direct other villages. Powhatan usually left the subordinate chiefs alone to govern their villages, as long as they paid their tribute and cooperated with his war parties. Powhatan employed the tribute to stage feasts, to sustain the shamans, to support his wives, to reward his warriors, and to trade with outsiders.

In addition to cycling tribute through his hands to dependents, Powhatan united his chiefdom by channeling outward the energy of warriors, discouraging the fighting that had previously divided the coastal tribes. Every winter Powhatan organized large-scale hunts in the Piedmont to procure deer and to provoke the hinterland peoples, Siouan-speakers known as the Monacan and Manahoac. These regular clashes unified his own warriors and distracted them from reviving old feuds between the Algonquian villages.

Lacking property to plunder, the Indians primarily fought for scalps or captives, both to boost their own honor and to degrade that of their enemies. The English captain John Smith observed, "They seldome make warre for landes or goodes, but for women and Children, and principally for revendge, so vindicative and jelous they be, to be made a derision of, and to be insulted upon by an enemy." Although chronic, Algonquian warfare killed relatively few people by English standards. The natives waged short raids intended to kill a few warriors, take some captives, and humiliate a rival, then beat a hasty retreat homeward to celebrate.

Lacking state institutions and professional armies, the Indians could not sustain protracted and distant campaigns like those of the English in Ireland. To conquer a land, Europeans fought for years and even decades, with the massacre of entire villages and cities a standard technique meant to intimidate others into surrender. In Virginia, veteran English commanders initially felt contemptuous of the Indian way of war as cowardly and ineffective. In turn, the English mode of total war introduced by the colonists shocked the Indians of Virginia as pointless and wasteful.

ENCOUNTER

Initially, the Powhatan Indians regarded the English colonists with considerable ambivalence. On the one hand, the natives were intrigued by the technology of the visitors, especially their metal tools and weapons, which were far sharper, stronger, and more durable than stone implements. Rather than fight such dangerous people, perhaps they could be turned to advantage, co-opted as allies for use against the Monacan and Manahoac. On the other hand, the Algonquians had learned to distrust Europeans from their previous abusive visits in ships. Putting into Chesapeake Bay to procure fresh water and firewood and to trade for deerskins and maize, Spanish and English mariners sometimes kidnapped or killed natives. Apart from the metal goods and firearms, the Indians saw little in European culture that appealed to them.

The challenge confronting Powhatan and his people in 1607 was to turn the English newcomers to advantage. Instead of trying to crush the newcomers and risk heavy casualties, Powhatan hoped to contain them, subject them to his power, enlist them as subordinate allies against his own enemies, and secure through trade their metals, including weapons. Unable to predict the future, the Algonquians did not know that the initial few colonists were the opening wedge for thousands to follow, bent upon transforming the land and destroying the Indian world.

For their part, the ethnocentric English were poorly prepared to understand and accept a culture so different from their own. Coming from a more property-ridden and laborious culture, the English considered the Indians lazy and benighted. In 1612, William Simmonds lamented that in Virginia "we found only an idle, improvident, scattered people, ignorant of the knowledge of gold, or silver, or any commodities; and careless of anything but [living] from hand to mouth." Because the English expected men to cultivate crops and women to tend permanent homes, they regarded the native women as drudges and the men as lazy exploiters. Because the English encased themselves in heavy clothing, they defined as savage any people as scantily clad as the Indians. Because the English worshiped a single omnipotent God, they disdained the native pantheism as paganism at best and devil-worship at worst.

The colonial leaders also suspected that their own laborers hated civilized discipline and longed to run away to join the Indians to live in greater ease and equality. Experienced in the Irish conquest, the colonial promoter Sir William Herbert warned:

> Colonies degenerate assuredly when the colonists imitate and embrace the habits, customs, and practices of the natives. There is no better way to remedy this evil than to do away with and destroy completely the habits and practices of the natives.

The colonizers felt obliged to subvert the native culture and transform the Indians into lower-sort English men and women—lest the lower-sort colonists turn Indian and turn against the colony.

Initially, the colonists sought not to exterminate the Indians but, instead, to assimilate them as menials. In 1612 the secretary for the Virginia colony explained that the proper Indian policy was "by degrees [to] chaung their barbarous natures, make them ashamed the sooner of their savadge nakednes, informe them of the true god, and of the waie to their salvation, and fynally teach them obedience to the king's Majestie and to his Governours in those parts." But the Algonquians recoiled in horror at the prospect of adopting a European way of life that would obligate their men to forsake war and, instead, adopt the female role of agricultural laborer.

Unlike the Spanish in Florida and the French in Canada, the English sent no missionaries to convert the Indians of Virginia. More thoroughly commercial, the English meant to Christianize the Indians by first absorbing them as economic subordinates. Indian laborers could then be indoctrinated in Protestant Christianity by the regular church services of the colonists. In 1619, Virginia promoters concisely bundled their motives as "to settle and plant our men and diverse other inhabitants there, to the honour of Almighty God, the enlarging of Christian religion, and to the augmentation and revenue of the general plantation in that country, and the particular good and profit of ourselves." English colonizers had a peculiar confidence that their economic self-interest served God.

Of course, by subordinating and converting the Indians, the Virginia promoters meant to free up most of their lands for the settlement of English plantations. In a 1609 sermon blessing the Virginia colony, the Reverend Robert Gray asked a pointed question: "The first objection is, by what right or warrant we can enter into the land of these Savages, take away their rightful inheritance from them, and plant ourselves in their places, being unwronged or unprovoked by them." He answered, to the complete satisfaction of the promoters, that savages had no right to keep any land that they did not exploit to its fullest potential. The colonizers refused to see that the Indians did occupy, use, and shape their land. Overlooking the many native villages and extensive fields of maize, Captain John Smith described Virginia as "overgrowne with trees and weedes, being a plaine wildernes as God first made it." The English insisted that God required them to improve the wilderness into productive farmland, subduing the Indians in the process.

Indeed, the English held that their changes would benefit the Indians, who had, therefore, no right to resist. A promoter predicted, "Our intrusion into their possession shall tend to their great good, and no way to their hurt, unlesse as unbridled beastes, they procure it to themselves." Indians who resisted the bridle of English rule could expect to be treated like wild and dangerous beasts. In Virginia as in Ireland, the colonial leaders sustained an overwhelming sense of cultural superiority that was impervious to the mounting evidence of their own follies in a land long mastered by the Indians.

JAMESTOWN

In 1604 a peace treaty with Spain reduced (but did not eliminate) the danger of Spanish attack on a new colony. Peace also freed up capital, shipping, and sailors previously employed in attacking the Spanish. No longer able to invest in privateers, the great merchants and lawyers of London took a new interest in colonizing Virginia. They supplanted the West Country men (including Ralegh), who had lost their influence at the royal court, after the new king, James I, succeeded Queen Elizabeth in 1603. In 1606, London investors incorporated the Virginia Company and King James granted them a charter to colonize and govern Virginia.

In December 1606, three vessels left England for Virginia, taking the standard circle route southwest via the trade winds to the Canaries, westward to the West Indies, and then north with the Gulf Stream to Virginia. They reached Chesapeake Bay on April 26, 1607. Seeking some security from Spanish discovery and attack, the colonists ascended the broad James River about sixty miles, to establish their settlement, Jamestown, beside a marsh on the north bank. They named both river and town to flatter their new king. For further protection, the colonists surrounded their wooden shelters with a triangular stockade mounted with cannon at the corners.

The Virginia Company naively instructed the colonial leaders never to allow the Indians to see any English die, lest the natives learn that the colonists were "but common men" rather than immortals. This instruction quickly proved impossible to follow, as the colonists died in droves from disease and hunger. Of the initial 104, only 38 were alive nine months later. Despite shipping hundreds of reinforcements annually, the Virginia Company barely kept ahead of the continuing deaths at Jamestown. In December 1609 there were 220 colonists; after an especially deadly winter, only 60 remained alive by the next spring. One starving colonist killed and ate his wife, for which he was tried, convicted, and burned at the stake. In despair, the survivors abandoned Jamestown, putting off down the river in June 1610. But near the river's mouth they were intercepted by three ships from England bearing 300 new colonists, which compelled the reoccupation of Jamestown, where disease and hunger continued to kill the English by the hundreds. Between 1607 and 1622 the Virginia Company transported some 10,000 people to the colony, but only 20 percent were still alive there in 1622. An English critic belatedly remarked, "Instead of a plantacion, Virginia will shortly get the name of a slaughterhouse."

Jamestown lay beside a broad swamp, which was good for defense against Spanish or Indian attack but bad for the health of the colonists. In the hot and humid summer, the swamp bred millions of mosquitoes, carriers of malaria. In addition, the shallow wells were contaminated by brackish water, exposing the inhabitants to salt poisoning, especially during the summer when the river ran low. The stagnant river waters of summer and early fall also retained the garbage and excrement generated by the colonists, promoting the pathogenic microbes of dysentery and typhoid fever. A colonist recalled, "Our drinke [was] cold water taken out of the River, which was at floud [tide] verie salt[y], at a low tide full of slime and filth, which was the destruction of many of our men." The salt poisoning and the debilitating diseases killed many and often rendered the rest too weak and apathetic to work. Unable to cultivate enough corn in summer, they starved during the winter and spring.

Even when healthy, many colonists refused to work diligently at raising corn to feed themselves. They were an unstable and fractious mix of gentlemen-adventurers in command and poor vagrants rounded up from the streets of London and forcibly sent to Virginia. Neither group had much prior experience with work. In England, birth and wealth had screened the gentlemen from manual labor, while the vagrants, for want of employment, had learned to survive by begging and stealing. The president of the Virginia Company complained of the settlers: "A more damned crew hell never vomited." Unfamiliar with the new territory, they all lacked the Indians' skills at fishing, hunting, and raising maize.

For a time in 1608–9, Captain John Smith commanded the colony and forced the colonists to work six hours a day in the fields. For this he reaped bitter complaints and was hounded from the colony, never to return. It is no coincidence that the great starving winter followed his departure in October 1609. When a new governor arrived in May 1611, he was shocked to find that the colonists again had neglected to plant sufficient crops. Instead, he found them at "their daily and usuall workes, bowling in the streetes."

Rather than cultivate corn, the first colonists preferred to search for precious metals, in emulation of the Spanish conquistadores. Over Captain Smith's protests, the colonists greedily gathered the local mica, persuaded that it was an ore rich in gold. Smith marveled, "There was no talke, no hope, nor worke, but dig gold, wash gold, [and] refine gold." For a time, the colonists worked hard to load a ship with the mica of their golden dreams, which proved worthless upon arrival and examination in England. Arriving with alluring misconceptions of a rich and easy land, the colonists experienced the hard realities as a demoralizing shock from which many never recovered.

VIOLENCE

Preferring to explore for gold, the colonists expected the Indians to feed them. After all, the promoters had promised that the natives would welcome the English with generosity and submission. And what was the purpose of being civilized Christians with superior arms and armor if not to command the weaker heathen peoples of new lands? The colonists did not understand that the local Indians had scant surplus to spare, raising little more than they needed every year. If pressed too hard for food, the Indians lashed out. When seventeen colonists imposed themselves on one village, the natives killed them, stuffed their dead mouths with maize as a sign of contempt, and left the corpses for their countrymen to discover.

Noting the Spanish success at conquering Indians by capturing their paramount chiefs, the English hoped to trick and seize Powhatan, but he shrewdly declined their invitations to visit Jamestown. Instead of capturing Powhatan, Captain John Smith became his captive after stumbling into an ambush in the woods. Powhatan seized the opportunity ritually to adopt Smith as a subordinate chief. Staged as a mock execution interrupted by Pocahontas, the daughter of Powhatan, the ritual was supposed to render Smith's people tributary. Powhatan misunderstood Smith's gratitude at survival for consent to his terms, and Smith misunderstood the ritual as no more than an execution stopped by Powhatan's chivalrous daughter. Upon his release and return to Jamestown, the obtuse captain resumed bullying the Indians to obtain corn.

Pursuing a policy of containment rather than total war, Powhatan relied upon the tribe closest to Jamestown, the Paspahegh, to observe and harass the colonists. The strategy was more deadly than Powhatan had anticipated, for it kept the colonists in disease-ridden Jamestown and away from healthier and more fertile places at a distance. Meanwhile, Powhatan continued to trade with Jamestown, disingenuously disavowing the attacks as the work of a few malcontents beyond his control.

Frustrated, the English made violent and terrifying examples of resisting Indians. In August 1610, Captain George Percy surprised and attacked a Paspahegh village, killing at least sixty-five inhabitants and destroying with fire their homes and fields of growing corn. Taking prisoner the wife and children of the local chieftain, the colonists headed back to Jamestown by boat. En route, as a sport, they threw the children overboard and shot them in the water as they tried to swim for shore. Back at Jamestown the governor rebuked the captain, not for his brutality, but instead for sparing the woman's life. The governor promptly had her executed, run through with a sword. This raid seems peculiarly perverse as well as ruthless. Why would starving colonists burn a field of growing corn? The colony's leaders believed that they would get far more corn from the other Indians by making one especially horrifying example of those who failed to obey English orders.

The colonial leaders applied the same brutal logic to their own colonists, in the conviction that only pain and terror could motivate the poor. Convicting a laborer of stealing two pints of oatmeal to allay his hunger, the leaders had a long needle thrust through his tongue, to keep him from ever eating again. Chained to a tree, the convict slowly starved to death, a vivid and lingering example to terrify his fellow colonists.

The leaders were especially dismayed when several dozen colonists ran away to join the Indians. Evidently disgusted by the hunger, hardships, danger, and brutality of colonial life under domineering leaders, the runaways sought an easier lot among the natives. The Indians killed those who brought nothing but welcomed those bearing steel weapons, including a few guns. With good cause, the colonial leaders dreaded the slow attrition of colonists and the new strength they gave to the Algonquians. In the spring of 1612, the governor recaptured most of the fugitives and, to deter further runaways, made painful and conspicuous examples of them. The lucky were hanged or shot. The unlucky were burned at the stake or had their backs slowly broken on the wheel.

The simmering conflict between the colonists and the Algonquians remained stalemated until 1613, when the English captured Powhatan's favorite daughter, the teenage Pocahontas. Held in Jamestown and indoctrinated by the English, she accepted Christian conversion, took the name Rebecca, and married a colonist, John Rolfe, in 1614. Weary with war, Powhatan reluctantly made peace with the English. Seizing the promotional opportunity, the Virginia Company brought Rolfe and Pocahontas to England to drum up greater investment and crown support for the colony. Dressed in fine English clothing, the lovely Pocahontas suggested the ease of assimilating the natives, but looks proved deceiving. She died of disease in England in March 1617 at the age of about twenty-one. Powhatan expired a year later, and power passed to his brother Opechancanough, who from long and bitter experience despised the invaders.

TOBACCO

By 1616 the Virginia Company had transported more than seventeen hundred people to the Chesapeake and spent well over £50,000—an immense amount for that century—yet all it had to show for the investment was an unprofitable town of 350 diseased and hungry colonists. The settlers had gathered or made and shipped homeward a variety of commodities—glass, pitch, tar, potash, clapboards, sassafras, and iron—but in London these sold for small prices far below the company's immense costs for shipping people, equipment, and provisions across the Atlantic. Deeply in debt, the Virginia Company teetered toward bankruptcy.

During the later 1610s, however, the company and the colonists made two great adjustments. First, the company gave up trying directly to control the land and the laborers and instead permitted the colonists to own and work land as their private property. Indeed, the company adopted a "headright system" that awarded land freely to men with the means to pay for their own passage (and that of others) across the Atlantic. Such emigrants received fifty acres apiece, and another fifty acres for every servant or relative brought at their own expense. Servants were also entitled to fifty acres each, if and when they survived their terms of indenture—which afforded them new incentive to emigrate. As private property owners, rather than company employees, the colonists showed much greater initiative and effort in cultivating the corn, squash, and beans that ensured their subsistence. But to prosper, they still needed a commercial crop to market in England.

Led by John Rolfe, the planters learned how to raise tobacco in 1616. A New World plant long cultivated in the West Indies, tobacco had become popular for smoking in much of England and Europe. Ahead of his time, King James fought a losing battle when he denounced smoking as "a custom loathsome to the eye, hateful to the nose, harmful to the brain, [and] dangerous to the lungs." Eventually he learned to love the large revenues that the crown derived from taxing tobacco imports. Laden with addictive nicotine, tobacco was an ideal colonial commodity, for consumers would pay high prices to satisfy their craving. Because tobacco plants prefer a long, hot, and humid growing season, the crop thrived in Virginia but not in England, giving the colonial farmers a comparative advantage. Blessed with numerous harbors and an extensive river system, the Chesapeake also welcomed the shipping needed to carry tobacco in bulk across the Atlantic to European consumers. Virginia's tobacco production surged from 200,000 pounds in 1624 to 3,000,000 pounds in 1638, as the Chesapeake outstripped the West Indies to become the principal supplier of tobacco to Europe.

During the 1620s, tobacco sold in England for about five to ten times as much as it cost to produce in the Chesapeake. That meant that if a planter could obtain land and a few laborers and keep them alive and working, he could make more in a year than in a decade spent in England. Tobacco's profits increased the value of indentured servants, which stimulated the flow of emigrants to Virginia. From only 350 in 1616 the colonial population in the Chesapeake surged to about 13,000 by 1650. Increased immigration, rather than natural increase, drove this population growth, for the annual mortality rate remained about 25 percent until mid-century. In 1638, proposed English legislation to limit emigration alarmed the Virginians, who complained that their colony would "in [a] short time melt to nothing for want of supplyes of people."

As tobacco cultivation expanded and the population grew, the planters needed more land, which they obtained at the Indians' expense. The expanding English plantations brought voracious and far-ranging cattle and pigs into the vicinity of Indian villages, with devastating consequences for native cornfields. The Indians also seethed at the contempt the English displayed toward them as supposed "savages." One unusual Virginian, George Thorpe, confessed:

> There is scarce any man amongst us that doth soe much as afforde them a good thought in his hart, and most men with their mouthes give them nothing but maledictions and bitter execrations. . . . If there bee wronge on any side, it is on ours who are not soe charitable to them as Christians ought to bee.

Indeed, the colonial minister, the Reverend Jonas Stockham, denounced the Indians, insisting that "till their Priests and Ancients have their throats cut, there is no hope to bring them to conversion."

For a time, the new paramount chief, Opechancanough, shrewdly kept hidden his bitter resentment. Indeed, he insinuated that he meant to convert to Christianity, and he invited the colonists to spread out and settle on any lands not occupied by Indian villages, lulling their suspicion and encouraging their vulnerable dispersion. On March 22, 1622, in a well-coordinated surprise attack, the Indians destroyed the outlying plantations, killing 347 men, women, and children—nearly a third of the colonists in Virginia. The dead included George Thorpe, perhaps the only colonist with a good word for the Algonquians. The survivors rallied at Jamestown and a few other fortified settlements, while the Indians killed livestock and burned plantations.

After the initial shock and horror, the colonial leaders felt delighted by the opportunity to dispossess and exterminate the Indians. The governor, Sir Francis Wyatt, declared, "Our first worke is expulsion of the Salvages to gain the free range of the countrey for encrease of Cattle, swine &c . . . for it is infinitely better to have no heathen among us, who at best were but thornes in our sides, than to be at peace and league with them." Back in England, Captain John Smith rejoiced at news of the massacre as "good for the plantation because now we have just cause to destroy them by all means possible."

The Virginians developed the strategy, practiced in subsequent colonial wars, of waiting until just before corn harvest to attack and destroy the Indian villages and their crops, consigning the natives to a winter and spring of exposure and starvation. In May 1623, when the Indians' hunger was greatest, the English pretended that they were ready to make peace. At the conclusion of the negotiations, the English invited the 250 attending Indians to drink a toast of alcohol. The Indians' share was poisoned. Drugged and incapacitated, the victims were easily finished off by the swords of the vengeful English.

But Opechancanough had not attended the treaty, and he persisted in resistance until 1632, when the English at last offered a real peace. They extorted massive land concessions, which permitted their settlements to spread northward up Chesapeake Bay and the Rappahannock and Potomac rivers. On April 18, 1644, Opechancanough staged a second and even deadlier surprise attack, killing more than four hundred colonists. But this was a smaller proportion of a much larger colonial population, ten thousand, which had come to outnumber the local Indians, who were much diminished by disease and war. English counterattacks destroyed most of the Indian towns along the rivers, dispersing the survivors into the hinterland. In 1646 the English captured Opechancanough, who was about one hundred years old, nearly blind, and so crippled that he had to be carried on a litter. The governor put his trophy prisoner on display in Jamestown, but an angry soldier shot

Opechancanough dead, terminating the paramount chiefdom built by Powhatan.

Disease and war reduced the Virginia Algonquians from 24,000 in 1607 to only 2,000 by 1669. Losing almost all of their lands, the survivors became confined on small reservations, surrounded by colonial settlements. Restricting the surviving Indians as a security risk, Virginia law invited landholders to shoot any native caught trespassing on their plantations. The law showed far less concern for the Indian cornfields invaded by colonial livestock. Beleaguered Indians begged the colonial leaders, "Your Hogs & Cattle injure Us. We Can fly no farther. Let us know where to live & how to be secured for the future from the Hogs & Cattle." Of course, other Indian peoples remained numerous and autonomous to the north, west, and south of the Virginia colony. In particular, the formidable Susquehannock, an Iroquoian people, dwelled north of the Potomac.

While the Indians' presence and power dwindled on the coastal plain, the colonials' numbers and prosperity surged, especially during the 1650s and 1660s as they occupied the fertile lands recently wrested from the natives. Responding to colonial opportunity, emigration from England to the Chesapeake more than doubled from about 8,000 per decade during the 1630s and 1640s to 18,000 per decade during the 1650s and 1660s. The Chesapeake colonial population grew from 13,000 in 1650 to 41,000 in 1670.

The newcomers cleared new fields for expanding crops of tobacco. By the end of the 1660s, the colonists annually shipped ten million pounds of tobacco to England—up from about three million pounds in 1638. The increased production drove down the price of tobacco from about two shillings per pound during the boom years of the 1620s to about two pence per pound in the late 1650s, but most planters continued to profit because they substantially lowered their costs (especially for shipping) and increased the productivity of their labor. The growth in production and productivity rendered tobacco cheaper, opening a much larger market in England.

The Chesapeake tobacco boom came too late to save the teetering Virginia Company from bankruptcy and foreclosure. Already encumbered with debt, the company could not cope with the losses suffered from Opechancanough's destructive first rebellion. In 1624 the impatient crown terminated the company charter, taking control of Virginia as the first royal colony in the new English empire. The crown acted to secure the growing revenue generated by the tobacco trade. Paying an especially heavy tax, tobacco generated 25 percent of the customs revenue collected by the crown in England during the 1660s.

In 1632 the crown set aside about twelve million acres of land at the northern head of Chesapeake Bay as a second colony, named Maryland after the queen of the new monarch, Charles I (son of James). The king gave the new colony to a favorite aristocrat and political ally, Cecilius Calvert, the second Lord Baltimore, to own and govern as a "proprietary colony." During the seventeenth century, the English developed two types of colonial governments: royal and proprietary. Relatively few until the eighteenth century, the royal colonies belonged to the crown. Initially more numerous, the proprietary colonies belonged to private interests.

By owning and governing a colony, Lord Baltimore sought to gain additional wealth and to provide refuge for his fellow Catholics. Harassed in England by the Protestant majority, some Catholics contemplated emigration to an American colony. As a Catholic sympathizer, King Charles I favored Lord Baltimore's plan to demonstrate that a policy of religious toleration could permit Protestants and Catholics to live together in harmony. Tending to his estates and political interest, Lord Baltimore remained in England and entrusted the governorship of Maryland to his younger brother, Leonard Calvert. In 1634 the new governor led two ships laden with colonists, both Protestant and Catholic, across the Atlantic to Chesapeake Bay. On a tributary of the Potomac River, Calvert established the first settlement and colonial capital at St. Mary's City.

Contrary to Lord Baltimore's hopes, relatively few Catholics emigrated to Maryland. Instead, most of his colonists were Protestants, primarily relocating Virginians. Many were especially radical Protestants, known as Puritans and Quakers, wearied by Virginia's sporadic efforts to enforce adherence to the official Church of England. Eager to attract settlers of any Christian faith, the proprietor adopted an especially generous headright system that granted one hundred acres for every adult (free or servant) transported to Maryland, plus fifty acres for every child less than sixteen years old. The recipients paid nothing down and thereafter only a modest annual quitrent of two shillings per hundred acres. As a frontier colony, Maryland offered greater opportunities to ambitious men of modest means than did older, more crowded, and increasingly competitive Virginia. By attracting experienced colonists, Maryland benefited from the expertise garnered by hard trials and many errors in the older colony of Virginia. Suffering fewer and shorter growing pains, Maryland rapidly prospered as a tobacco colony.

After an immense cost in lives—native and colonist—the English had secured a lucrative, dynamic, and expansive base on the North American continent. Their once tenuous beachhead had become two thriving provinces and a dynamo for further expansion. As the West Country promoters had hoped, Virginia and Maryland consumed English manufactures and produced an agricultural staple that replaced an import, improving the nation's balance of trade. And, as the promoters had predicted, the Chesapeake absorbed thousands of poor laborers considered redundant and dangerous in England. From the perspective of the Indians, however, the English had metastasized an especially malignant and voracious tumor that spread with destructive rapidity, imperiling the native world.

7

Chesapeake Colonies

★

1650–1750

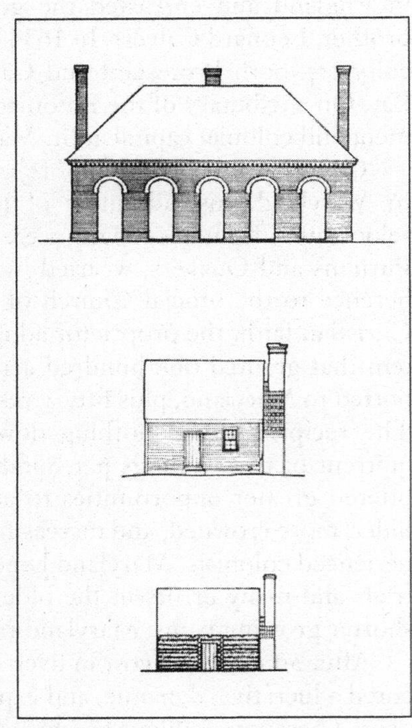

These drawings by Cary Carson and Benjamin Hillier represent the social hierarchy in the built landscape of eighteenth-century Virginia. The relative size and permanence of the structures vividly conveyed and reinforced the system of unequal wealth, power, and status. The grandest structure, built of brick and stone, was Sabine Hall (top left), *the mansion of a great planter (two stories, 60 by 42 feet). Next in social priority came an Anglican parish church* (bottom left), *also built of brick (71 by 69 feet), and the brick courthouse of King William County* (top right; *50 by 49 feet). The common white planters lived in far smaller, humbler, and less permanent framed wood structures* (middle right; *about 21 by 16 feet). And the most miserable housing and lowest status belonged to the enslaved Africans, who generally lived in windowless log cabins* (bottom right; *about 18 by 17 feet). From Rhys Isaac,* The Transformation of Virginia, 1740–1790 *(1982), 66–67.*

THERE WAS LITTLE MISTAKING who ruled in England, where an aristocracy and gentry combined noble birth, a classical education, refined manners, extensive lands, and conspicuous wealth. But Virginia and Maryland attracted few aristocrats or gentry, except as occasional governors who soon returned home. Instead, hard-driving merchants and planters of middling origins created the greatest fortunes and claimed the highest offices. As a rule, their education and manners lagged far behind their acquisition of land, servants, and political influence. That lag encouraged grumbling and disobedience by laboring people who refused deference to officials wanting in the gentility and high birth demanded by political tradition.

During the seventeenth century, the Chesapeake's leading men lacked the mystique of a traditional ruling class. Competitive, ruthless, avaricious, crude, callous, and insecure, they were very touchy about their origins, qualifications, and conduct. When Richard Crocker accurately but recklessly denounced two Virginia councillors as extortioners, the council put him into the public pillory with his ears nailed to the wooden frame. More commonly, the judges, assemblymen, and councillors sentenced their defamers to a bloody bout at the whipping post followed by a stiff fine paid in many pounds of tobacco. Such brutality silenced overt protest without building public respect for the bullying and blustering leaders.

The colonists grudgingly accepted such leaders so long as prosperity prevailed, as it did during the tobacco boom of the 1640s and 1650s. That boom primarily benefited the common planters: former indentured servants who acquired fifty to three hundred acres of land. The ownership of productive land endowed men with the coveted condition of "independence," free at last from the dictates of a master. Their new independence enabled many to acquire their own dependents: wives, children, and servants. In a world where dependence was the norm, independence was an especially cherished and vulnerable status. Dreading a relapse into dependence upon a master, the small planters chronically feared the loss of their land to mounting debts, bad harvests, a poor market, Indian raids, heavy taxes, or corrupt rulers.

They had good cause to fear when the mid-century age of opportunity faded during the 1660s and 1670s as tobacco prices fell and good land became scarce. The proportion of landowners constricted as the more successful planters consolidated larger plantations at the expense of smaller, less profitable farms. Newly freed servants had to accept tenancy or move to the frontier, where they provoked new conflicts with the Indians.

In 1676, Virginia erupted in rebellion when the frustrated servants and freedmen blamed their plight on an insensitive, exploitative, and unqualified class of ruling planters. Led by Nathaniel Bacon, the ill-fated rebellion invited increased crown intervention in Virginia's government. To stem that encroachment and defend their power, the leading Virginians created a more popular mode of politics, which required an alliance between common and great planters. At the same time, the passage of time and increased fortunes permitted the planter elite to perfect a genteel style that commanded greater respect from the common planters. Their alliance became both easier and more essential at the turn of the century, when the great planters switched their labor force from white indentured servants to enslaved Africans. Class differences seemed less threatening as both the common and great planters became obsessed with preserving their newly shared sense of racial superiority over the African slaves. As the historian Edmund S. Morgan has aptly argued, the colonial Virginians developed the American interdependence of elite rule, popular politics, and white racial supremacy. That distinctive combination increasingly set the colonies apart from both their English origins and the colonies of other empires.

COMMONWEALTHS

In both Chesapeake colonies, the distant crown (for Virginia) or lord proprietor (for Maryland) had to share power with the wealthiest and most ambitious colonists. They refused to pay taxes unless authorized by their own elected representatives in a colonial assembly. Governors who defied the local elite faced obstruction and risked rebellion. In 1635 the Virginia assembly and council arrested and shipped homeward a confrontational governor. By appointing a more cooperative replacement, the crown accepted the claims of the planter elite to a share in colonial power. This decentralization of power stood in marked contrast to the Spanish and the French colonies, which permitted neither elected assemblies nor individual liberties. Of course, the English colonial system restricted power and liberties to the free men who owned land, denying them to indentured servants, the landless freedmen, and all women. Conclaves of local magnates, the assemblies were oligarchical rather than democratic.

The wealthiest planters also dominated the county system of local government. Because tobacco cultivation and the river system encouraged dispersed plantations, the Chesapeake had only two towns, both small: the colonial capitals of Jamestown and St. Mary's City. Neither possessed even five hundred inhabitants. Lacking towns, the colonists relied upon larger territorial units, the counties, for their local governments. The county courts held trials, executed sentences, licensed taverns and ferries, established and maintained roads, set and collected local taxes, supervised the county militia, conducted elections to the assembly, and enforced provincial legislation. On the advice of the assembly, the governor appointed the judges, sheriff, and county clerk, who all came from the local elite.

In Virginia, the county usually doubled as an Anglican parish, and the leading planters composed the parish vestry: a board responsible for building and maintaining churches, hiring parsons, and providing poor relief. Headed by the king, the Church of England was the lone official church entitled to support from taxes levied on all inhabitants. Most English men and women believed that social order and stability depended upon interlocking the institutions of church and state to link political obedience and religious devotion. By 1668, Virginia had sixty-two Anglican churches—belying its notorious but overstated reputation as a godless land.

In theory, the Chesapeake colonists lived in a political hierarchy with four tiers. At the top was the distant king, governing the realm in collaboration with Parliament. Closer to home, the colonist answered to the provincial government: the governor, council, and assembly meeting in Jamestown or St. Mary's City. The county court and parish vestry followed next down the political ladder and closer to the common colonist. The fourth and most intimate tier of government was the family household, which the English called a "little commonwealth." Including servants as well as kin, every little commonwealth had a petty monarch, ordinarily a married man, more rarely a widow. Indeed, widows were few and their status brief in colonies where women were in such short supply and in such great demand for remarriage. By the law of "coverture," married women had neither legal nor political existence, but depended upon their husbands to represent the household to the outside society. The husband also supervised and disciplined his dependents: wife, children, and servants. If a servant, child, or wife killed his or her master, the law considered the culprit guilty of "Petit Treason" as well as murder.

The political culture assumed that the health and survival of the larger commonwealths of county, colony, and realm all depended upon the order, morality, and allegiance maintained in the many little commonwealths. Consequently, the higher authorities vested patriarchal power in the male heads of household. By law only the head of the household could own land and make contracts and only male heads could vote, serve on juries, or hold political office. But the authorities also held the patriarchs responsible for the misconduct of their dependents. In 1663, a Virginia county court rebuked and punished both a maidservant, for public insolence, and her master, for failing to control her "scolding." The court reasoned that the master "hath degenerated so much from a man, as neither to beare Rule over his woman Servant nor [to] govern his house."

Because of the Chesapeake's skewed sex ratio, many men never found the wives they needed to form family households. In 1625, men composed 74 percent of Virginia's population; only 10 percent were women; the remaining 16 percent were children. The gender gap later diminished, but throughout the seventeenth century, men greatly outnumbered women in the Chesapeake. The prevalence of single men deprived the Chesapeake colonies of a stable foundation of little commonwealths, increasing the social volatility.

LABOR

In contrast to England, where there was too little work for too many people, the Chesapeake demanded too much labor from too few colonists. During nine months of the year, from early spring to late fall, tobacco required attention and diligence to sow, transplant, weed, trim, eliminate worms, cut, cure, pack, and ship. The planters also needed regularly to clear new fields with axes, for after three years of cropping, the cultivated lands lost their fertility, and the planter had to clear another field to allow the old to lie fallow.

As a result, the replication and expansion of profitable tobacco fields demanded more laborers who could be driven to work under harsh conditions. Efforts to enslave the Algonquians failed because they too quickly escaped into the forest or too soon died of disease. Beginning in 1619, some planters bought a few slaves imported from Africa, but slavery was not yet economical because slaves were too expensive to risk where few newcomers, either black or white, survived more than five years. Given the short life expectancy of all Chesapeake laborers, planters wisely preferred to buy English indentured servants for four or five years rather than purchase the more expensive lifelong slaves from Africa. In 1650 enslaved Africans numbered only three hundred, a mere 2 percent of the Chesapeake population.

English servants composed at least three-quarters of the emigrants to the Chesapeake during the seventeenth century: about 90,000 of the 120,000 total. Too poor to afford the £6 cost of a transatlantic passage, the servants mortgaged four to seven years of their lives to a ship captain or merchant, who carried them to the Chesapeake for sale to tobacco planters. Unpaid during their terms, the servants received basic food, clothing, and shelter—generally just sufficient to keep them alive and working. At the conclusion of a term, the master was supposed to endow his servant with "freedom dues": a new set of clothes, tools, and food. During the first half of the seventeenth century, Virginia and Maryland also provided each "freedman" with fifty acres of land. Given that a sturdy beggar could never anticipate obtaining land in England, the colony offered an opportunity unavailable at home. Of course, that opportunity required men and women to gamble their lives in a dangerous land of hard work and deadly diseases.

Before 1620, most of Virginia's indentured servants were forcibly transported either as unwanted orphans or as criminals punished for vagrancy and petty theft. After 1620 the great majority were technically volunteers—but their poverty in England constrained their exercise of free choice. The push of unemployment and hunger in England combined with the pull of Virginia opportunity to draw servants to the Chesapeake. The annual flow of servants fluctuated positively with the price of tobacco and inversely with the level of real wages in England. When tobacco sold low and English wages rose, servant emigration declined. When tobacco was high and English wages were especially depressed, emigration surged. Emigration peaked between 1630 and 1660, which were especially hard years for laboring people in England but an especially promising period for tobacco cultivation.

As a rule, Chesapeake emigrants were a subset of the many poor people moving around England in search of food and work. Usually born in a country village, the future servant first moved to a town and then on to a larger seaport in pursuit of employment. Failing to find work, the desperate signed (usually with an X) an indenture for service in the Chesapeake. Hungry and homeless people who were reasonably healthy and young could find immediate food and shelter on board a vessel loading for the Chesapeake. In the short term, this seemed a great improvement over starving and shivering in the streets of Bristol or London. As a longer-term incentive, the shipper also promised eventual "freedom dues," including land from the colony—if the servant survived his or her term.

According to registers kept at the English seaports, most servants were laborers, who owned nothing, or journeyman artisans, who possessed a skill and some tools but no shop. The great majority were young, in their late teens or early twenties, and unmarried. The shippers primarily enlisted men, who were in the greatest demand as tobacco hands. Females constituted only 14 percent of the 2,010 emigrants bound to the Chesapeake from London in 1635 (the best-documented port and year in the surviving records). In the colonies, the female servants primarily worked as housekeepers and maidservants rather than as field hands. Although provided no land at the end of her indenture, the female servant had better prospects in the Chesapeake than in England of marrying a man with a productive farm.

Before 1640, most indentured servants endured harsh but short lives in the Chesapeake. Having staked their health in pursuit of farms, most lost their gamble, finding graves before their terms expired. Despite the importation of fifteen thousand indentured servants between 1625 and 1640, Virginia's population increased by only seven thousand. The servants died from the combination of diseases and overwork as the extremes of the Chesapeake environment shocked English bodies used to the milder pathogens, insects, and climate of their rainy and temperate homeland. The intense labor of tobacco cultivation peaked with the blistering sun, soaring temperatures, thick humidity, and voracious mosquitoes of the long, hot Chesapeake summer.

If it was in the planter's interest to keep his human chattel alive, it was also in his interest to extract as much work as possible before terms expired. Planters readily resorted to the whip, convinced that only fear and pain could motivate servants, whom they considered "loose, vagrant People, vicious and destitute of a means to live at home." Until their terms expired, the servants were fundamentally property rather than people. Masters readily bought and sold the contracts of their servants. Some masters even transferred servants to pay gambling debts.

In the Chesapeake, the county courts regulated indentured servitude on behalf of the master class. Themselves wealthy planters, the judges almost always sided with masters accused of denying food and clothing to their servants or of inflicting especially brutal punishments. Even when servants died, the court preferred to exonerate the master. In 1624, Elizabeth Abbott succumbed to beatings inflicted by her master. A witness saw Abbott's "body full of sores and holes very dangerously raunckled and putrified both above her wa[i]st and uppon her hips and thighes." Deeming the beatings necessary, the court dismissed the case, although her master had previously killed another servant with a rake and with impunity.

Instead of punishing abusive masters, the courts disciplined defiant servants by extending their indenture time. Running away was widespread, but when apprehended, runaways had their servitude extended by at least double the length of their absence and sometimes by five times. In another common form of resistance, servants covertly killed their masters' hogs to hold feasts in the woods. If caught, the servant suffered an additional year or two of service for every hog slain. A maidservant who bore a child had to compensate her master for medical expenses and lost worktime by serving another two years.

The Chesapeake also received a minority of free emigrants with the means to pay their own passage and to obtain land immediately. About one-quarter of the seventeenth-century emigrants, the free arrivals were a diverse lot, ranging from skilled artisans, farmers, and petty traders to wealthy merchants and gentlemen. Most were single men in their twenties from London, Bristol, Liverpool, and their respective hinterlands, drawn across the Atlantic primarily to obtain the land and labor to raise tobacco or to manage the tobacco trade as merchants. Although a minority, the free emigrants dominated the economic and political life of the Chesapeake. Endowed with head start in the race for wealth and political influence, the free emigrants became the councillors, assemblymen, and justices.

PROSPERITY

At mid-century, the Chesapeake became a bit healthier and many more servants lived long enough to claim their freedom and farms. In 1648 a Virginian marveled that only one in nine immigrants died during their first year, compared with one in four during the preceding generation. In part, health improved as many new plantations expanded upstream into locales with fresh running streams, away from the stagnant lowlands, which favored malaria, dysentery, and typhoid fever. Gradually, the Chesapeake farms also developed apple orchards, and cider was healthier than well water tainted with salt or bacteria. In addition, over time, a growing proportion of the population became "seasoned" by surviving bouts with the local diseases. The "seasoned" acquired a higher level of immunity, which they passed on to their offspring. But the overall improvement was only modest; the Chesapeake colonists continued to die sooner than did their counterparts in England.

At mid-century, freed servants more easily obtained farms because the 1646 victory over the Indians provided fertile land conveniently located beside navigable streams and rivers. With land abundant and tobacco profitable, most new producers prospered. The entry costs of tobacco planting were modest: a set of hand tools, a year's provisions, a few head of cattle and pigs, some seed, and about fifty acres of land. The servants acquired part of these essentials as their freedom dues and the rest on credit from merchants eager to procure more tobacco during the boom. The most fortunate new planters eventually acquired their own servants, which immensely eased their labor and permitted expanded cultivation.

The frontier conditions enabled labor to create new income and assets at a prodigious rate for a preindustrial economy. The planters prospered by "farm-building": by clearing and cultivating new fields and by constructing new fences and buildings. Some farmers chopped the trees with axes, burned the debris, and planted and hoed their corn and tobacco between the blackened stumps. Other farmers quickly and cheaply killed the trees by "girdling": cutting a strip of bark around each tree to curtail its circulation. Girdled trees persisted as ugly hulks deprived of their leaves, permitting the sun to reach plants cultivated around their dead roots. At any given time, a planter cultivated only about a tenth of his farm, leaving most of his domain heavily forested. The uncleared land served as a pasture for free-ranging cattle, as a source of wood for rails, building, and firewood, and as future cropland to replace exhausted fields. The planters raised tobacco for export as well as maize, chickens, and hogs to feed themselves and their laborers.

The Chesapeake farms did not impress English visitors, who saw a wasteful landscape of straggling farms, girdled trees, rotting stumps, flimsy and unpainted houses, impermanent fences, weedy fields, and scrawny, neglected livestock. Although at odds with the English ideal of carefully tending scarce land, the new frontier farms efficiently conserved the scarcest factors of production in the colonies, capital and labor, by clearing land quickly to shift fields as each lost its nutrients after a few years of cropping.

The common planters' economic success came at a heavy cost. The Indians unwillingly paid the highest price by losing their lives and domain to provide the lands essential to farm-building. But the Chesapeake colonists also made heavy sacrifices, accepting shorter life expectancy, poor prospects for marriage and children, and a harder work regimen. They also endured a more extreme climate in hastily built houses made of unpainted, riven clapboards nailed onto a timber frame and roofed with shingles, all over a floor of beaten dirt. Lacking windows, such a house admitted light only through the opened door and cracks between the clapboards. For want of stone and bricks, the house relied on a dangerously flammable wattle-and-daub chimney to carry off the smoke from the lone hearth at one gable end. Usually only sixteen feet wide by twenty feet long, Chesapeake houses offered a cramped interior with an upstairs sleeping loft under the eaves and two small rooms on the ground floor: a kitchen and a multipurpose room for eating, sitting, sleeping, and working. Quickly built without sills or foundation, the houses usually rotted within twenty years. Only five exceptional structures survive from seventeenth-century Virginia, all of them built of brick by wealthy colonists.

According to probate inventories, the common houses contained little furniture, usually only a bed, a table, a few benches, and a chest or two for clothing. The common people ate with their fingers, sharing a bowl and drinking from a common tankard, both passed around the table. They usually ate a boiled porridge of corn, beans, peas, and pork, washed down with water or cider. Most colonists had plenty to eat, in contrast to their past in both England and the early years of the colony. By moving to the Chesapeake, the common colonist sacrificed comfort and life expectancy for an improved diet and the pride and autonomy of owning land.

The mid-century age of opportunity for common planters was brief. Restricted to the frontier stage of development, social mobility quickly faded in the Chesapeake after 1665. The swelling number of producers and their increased productivity glutted the English market, depressing the price of tobacco below the costs of production. With one penny per pound the minimum tobacco price for breaking even, planters faced ruin during the late 1660s and early 1670s, when the price plummeted to only half a penny per pound. Failing in his schemes to promote economic diversity, Governor William Berkeley raged against Virginia's economic addiction to the "vicious, ruinous plant of Tobacco."

Moreover, by 1665 the planters had occupied all of the best tobacco lands along navigable waters, which pushed new freedmen onto inferior lands with higher transportation costs to market. The more competitive tobacco and land markets gave an edge to the wealthiest planters, who could ride out hard times and continue to buy up property and workers. In contrast with those of the preceding generation, the servants who became free during the 1670s enjoyed little economic success. Less than half became landowners and none achieved wealth and high status. Instead of establishing an enduring land of opportunity, the Chesapeake's brief age of social mobility led to a plantation society of great wealth and increasing poverty.

REBELLION

Hard times came to Virginia after 1665 as common planters became squeezed between their declining incomes and their heavy taxes paid to an especially callous and exploitative colonial government. During the 1660s, new imperial regulations worsened the tobacco glut by requiring colonists to ship their tobacco exclusively to England in English ships. Designed to drive Dutch merchants from their predominance in the tobacco trade, the new regulations (known as the Navigation Acts) doubly hurt the colonial planters by reducing the number of shippers competing for the tobacco trade and by saturating the English market with tobacco. The new imperial regulations also provoked wars with the Dutch, who returned to Chesapeake Bay in 1667 and 1673 with warships to capture and burn dozens of English tobacco ships, compounding the economic distress. In 1673, Governor Berkeley worried: "A large part of the people are so desperately poor, that they may reasonably be expected upon any small advantage of the enemy to revolt to them in hopes of bettering their condition by sharing the plunder of the colony with them."

Appointed in 1641 by the crown, Berkeley governed Virginia for most of the following thirty-five years. An elitist, Berkeley did not truck with radical notions like freedom of the press or public education for common people. In 1671 he declared, "I thank God, there are no free schools nor printing [in Virginia], and I hope we shall not have these [for a] hundred years; for learning has brought disobedience and heresy . . . into the world, and printing has divulged them, and libels against the best government. God keep us from both!"

Berkeley cultivated a following among the wealthiest and most ambitious planters. His favorites monopolized the major and lucrative public offices, and they received a disproportionate share in the grants of frontier land and of licenses to trade with the Indians for deerskins. For fifteen years, beginning in 1661, Berkeley refused to allow any new election to the assembly, instead perpetuating his cronies in power. By helping them, he helped himself.

Unresponsive to their constituents, the assemblymen levied heavy and inequitable taxes to sustain an especially expensive colonial government that benefited the official elite. An assemblyman received 150 pounds of tobacco in pay per day in session—about five times in value what was paid to his counterpart and contemporary in colonial Massachusetts. Governor Berkeley annually collected a salary of £1,000. To put that in perspective, most emigrants mortgaged at least four years of their working lives to pay the £6 cost of a transatlantic passage, and a small planter was fortunate to clear £3 annually over and above expenses.

The pay lavished on the elite came from taxes heaped upon the common planter, who paid on average 150 pounds of tobacco, or about a tenth of his annual crop. The common man could bear this burden more easily in the good times of the 1650s than in the hard times of the 1670s. While reaping large incomes from the public revenues, the official elite exempted themselves from the onerous poll tax and minimized the tax on large landholdings. In 1677 a crown official investigated Virginia and reported, "A poor man who has only his labour to maintain himself and his family pays as much as a man who has 20,000 acres."

Because Berkeley granted the best public lands in large tracts to his favorites, freedmen could rarely obtain their own farms after 1665. Instead, most had to rent land from the wealthiest planters at the rate of 10 to 25 percent of their tobacco crop. Such tenants composed about a third of Virginia's population by 1675. A crown investigation reported that land-hoarding was "one of the most apparent causes of the misery and mischiefs that attend this colony by occasioning the Planters to straggle to such remote distances when they cannot find land nearer to seat themselves but by being Tenants, which in a Continent they think hard."

Frustrated in their dreams of landowning independence, the freedmen felt angry and aggrieved. In one petition they protested, "Wee confess a great many of us came in servants to others, but wee adventured owr lives for it, and got owr poore living with hard labour out of the ground in a terrible Willdernis." Mostly unmarried and often armed with guns, the frustrated freedmen were restive and dangerous. In pity for himself, Governor Berkeley complained, "How miserable that man is that Governes a People wher[e] six parts of seaven at least are Poore, Endebted, Discontented, and Armed."

Rather than pay rent, many freedmen moved to the frontier, where they violently competed with the Indians. A crown official later noted:

> The English [settler] would ordinarily either frighten or delude [the Indians] into a bargaine and for a trifle get away the ground. . . . Then he comes and settles himselfe there and with his cattle and hoggs destroyes all the corn of the other Indians of the towne. . . . This was the great cause of the last warr, and most of those who had thus intruded and were consequently the principal cause of it were . . . the forwardest in the rebellion and complained the most of grievances.

In 1675, war erupted between the settlers and the Susquehannock, an Iroquoian-speaking people who dwelled north of the Potomac River. The war escalated as the settlers murdered chiefs who tried to negotiate for peace. Although relatively few, the Susquehannock were adept at hit-and-run raids that killed the families on dispersed and vulnerable frontier farms. Infuriated settlers demanded permission from the governor to exterminate all the natives on the frontier, the ostensibly peaceable as well as the openly hostile.

Governor Berkeley firmly opposed the genocidal proposal, for he and his friends cherished their profitable deerskin trade with the more peaceable Algonquian Indians. Berkeley also understood that a controlled, gradual frontier expansion better served the interests of the wealthiest planters, who wanted to retain common men as laborers and tenants rather than permit their dispersion to an open frontier as settlers. Used to governing with a high hand, Berkeley was also reluctant to concede his command over Indian policy to frontier leaders. Instead of authorizing offensive genocide, Berkeley insisted upon a defensive strategy that required an expensive system of nine new forts. That insistence outraged the frontier settlers, who regarded the forts as ineffective and wasteful follies that added to their tax burden while further enriching the governor and his cronies, who reaped the construction contracts.

The disgruntled Virginians found a leader in Nathaniel Bacon, a young (twenty-nine years old), charismatic, and prestigious newcomer. Raised in an English gentry family, Bacon had a better pedigree than any other colonist except his cousin by marriage, Governor Berkeley. Although Berkeley had rewarded him with a seat on the governor's council, Bacon was an impetuous and ambitious man willing to turn against his patron, who seemed weakened by age. Banking on his own prestige in an elitist culture, Bacon could more readily rally common planters to challenge a royal governor and his cabal.

To popular acclaim, Bacon led indiscriminate attacks on the Indians, in open defiance of the governor. Bacon demanded that the colonists destroy "all Indians in generall for . . . they were all Enemies." Because friendly Algonquians were closer and easier to catch, they died in greater numbers than did the hostile and elusive Susquehannock. In early 1676, Berkeley declared Bacon guilty of treason, which led Bacon to march his armed followers against the governor in Jamestown.

In part, "Bacon's Rebellion" represented a division within the planter elite, a split between a cabal allied with the royal governor and a rival set of ambitious but frustrated planters who resented their relative lack of offices and other rewards. Bacon and two partners felt especially aggrieved that Berkeley monopolized the Indian trade and denied their bid to purchase an interest. Determined to enjoy the perquisites and rewards of a hierarchical society, Bacon and his lieutenants intended no egalitarian revolution. Bacon depicted Berkeley's supporters as crass upstarts and unworthy leaders: "Let us observe the sudden Rise of their Estates [compared] with the Quality in which they first entered this Country . . . and lett us see wither their extractions and Education have not bin vile." Bacon denounced the Berkeley faction as "unworthy Favourites and juggling Parasites whose tottering Fortunes have been repaired and supported at the Publique chardge."

To defeat Berkeley, however, the rebel leaders needed to recruit armed support among the common planters and servants by promising redress for their many grievances. In his most radical measure, Bacon promised immediate freedom to servants who deserted Berkeley's friends to join the rebellion. In his public manifesto, the rebel commander also appealed to class resentments: "The poverty of the Country is such that all the power and sway is got into the hands of the rich, who by extorti[on]ous advantages, having the common people in their debt, have always curbed and oppressed them in all manner of wayes." Bacon implied that he would lower taxes and provide more and better lands to the freedmen. He also invited poor men to plunder the plantations of Berkeley's supporters.

In September 1676, Bacon's men drove the governor and his supporters out of Jamestown and across Chesapeake Bay to refuge on the eastern shore. To discourage their return, Bacon burned Jamestown to the ground. A month later, however, Bacon suddenly died of dysentery, leaving his movement leaderless and divided. Assisted by armed merchant ships newly arrived from England, Berkeley returned to the western shore to reassert his authority. In December and January, the rebellion collapsed. The vindictive governor hanged twenty-three rebel leaders and unleashed his men to plunder Bacon's supporters.

Although Bacon attacked a royal governor, he did not seek independence from England. In 1676 no Virginian imagined that independence was feasible or desirable. Considering themselves English people who happened to live in America, the Virginians knew that their economically dependent colony could not survive in a world of hostile empires—Dutch, French, and Spanish—without protection from England and without access to the English market. Proclaiming their loyalty to England, Bacon and his supporters insisted that they acted only against a corrupt governor who had betrayed the king by mistreating his loyal subjects.

In London, the crown authorities suspected that Berkeley and his friends had caused the troubles in Virginia by pushing the common planters too hard. Because the tobacco trade generated a crown revenue of about £5 to £10 per laboring man, King Charles II wanted no rebellion to distract the colonists from raising the crop. The king denounced Berkeley as an "old fool" and dispatched an army to restore order in Virginia. The monarch agreed with Nathaniel Bacon on one thing: the newly rich Virginia elite was unworthy of its power. Determined to maximize the crown's share in the profits of tobacco, the king disapproved of the competing exactions by the planter elite.

GREAT PLANTERS

The crown authorities seized upon Bacon's Rebellion as an opportunity to strengthen imperial control over the valuable colony of Virginia. At considerable expense, they dispatched six warships and eight transports bearing eleven hundred troops: an unprecedented intervention by royal troops in the Chesapeake. Arriving in early 1677, after the rebellion had collapsed, the English commander, Sir Herbert Jeffreys, instead restrained the vengeful Berkeley. Alarmed by Berkeley's executions and confiscations, Jeffreys feared that the defeated and aggrieved rebels might, in protest, "only make Corne, instead of Tobacco, and soe sullenly sitt downe—careless of what becomes of their owne Estates or the King's Customes."

Taking charge as governor, Jeffreys sent an embittered Berkeley back to England, where he died within a year. By wooing the common planters, Jeffreys hoped to strengthen crown power at the expense of the great planters. A Berkeley supporter denounced Jeffreys as a "worse Rebel than Bacon." Fortunately for the great planters, the crown initiative weakened in 1678 with the deaths of Jeffreys and most of the royal troops from disease. To save money, the crown discharged the two hundred remaining troops in 1682, freeing Virginia from military occupation.

In Bacon's Rebellion and the crown intervention, the great planters had received a double scare. Fearing a future reassertion of crown power, the great planters felt compelled to build a more popular political base by becoming more solicitous of the smaller planters. The leading Virginians bolstered their own authority by solidifying their claim to represent all free, white Virginians against innovative intrusions of crown power.

Seeking popularity, the assembly dramatically reduced the poll tax, the most burdensome levy borne by the poor planter. During the 1690s that tax fell to about a quarter of its 1670s level and then declined to a tenth in the early eighteenth century. In stark contrast to those of Berkeley's day, Virginia's eighteenth-century assemblymen cultivated popularity by conspicuously opposing taxes, infuriating a succession of royal governors with instructions to secure a revenue for imperial defense. In 1711, Governor Alexander Spotswood denounced the assemblymen for striving "to recommend themselves to the populace upon a received opinion among them, that he is the best Patriot that most violently opposes all Overtures for raising money."

By reducing taxes, the Virginia gentry reinvented themselves and Virginia politics, transferring the odium of parasitism and tyranny to the royal governor. This dramatically reversed the role that the crown had claimed in 1677 as the putative defender of the common planter. Relations between small and great planters also improved at the turn of the century as a surge in European demand for tobacco improved its price and so the income of all planters. Less burdened by taxes and enjoying greater prosperity, eighteenth-century common planters began to regard their wealthy neighbors as powerful protectors of their common interests.

The Virginia elite also recognized the continuing popularity of Bacon's Indian policy. To maintain their political ascendancy, the great planters needed to lead, rather than oppose, wars meant to dispossess and destroy frontier Indians. Such wars united the free whites by providing convenient external, alien scapegoats for internal frustrations and inequalities—and by providing farms for the next generation of common planters. In 1720, Governor Spotswood explained:

> A Governour of Virginia has to steer between Scylla and Charybdis, either an Indian or a Civil War. . . . Bacon's Rebellion was occasioned purely by the Governour and Council refusing to let the People go out against the Indians who at that time annoyed the Frontier.

To give servants greater hope for the future, in 1705 the assembly revived the headright system by promising each freedman fifty acres of land, a promise that obliged the government to continue taking land from the Indians. Frontier wars urged poor whites to see a better future in the dispossession of Indians rather than in rebellion against their colonial elite. In eighteenth-century Virginia, the path of least resistance was expansion outward rather than rebellion within.

The eighteenth-century planter elite also enjoyed more respect and deference as the passage of time, better education, and intermarriage gradually obscured the middling origins and rough reputations of their grandfathers. To monumentalize their enhanced status and authority, the wealthiest planters erected conspicuous brick mansions, each overlooking a plantation village of wooden (sometimes brick) sheds, shops, and slave quarters. The tutor Philip Fithian noted that the great house of Robert "King" Carter was seventy-six feet long, forty-four feet wide, forty feet high, and visible "at the Distance of six Miles."

Renowned for their generosity and hospitality, the great planters delighted in entertaining one another and genteel travelers. Hospitality provided access to news and knitted together far-flung networks of gentility. Living large, the planters delighted in drinking, gambling, fiddling, dancing, and horse racing. Combining conviviality with competition, generosity with boasting, the genteel planters measured their worth and assessed their visitors. An Englishman warned a prospective visitor that "those Virginians are a very gentle, well dressed people—and look perhaps more at a man's outside than his inside. For these and other reasons go very clean, neat, and handsomely dressed." Almost all visitors considered the eighteenth-century Virginians both exceptionally hospitable and genial but shallow and materialistic.

The eighteenth-century Virginia gentry displayed themselves in expensive clothes and with refined manners before common audiences at churches, taverns, cotillions, courthouses, and elections, creating a new aura of true gentility. In a body, the gentle folk conspicuously trooped into church just after services began, and then marched out together just before the service ended, while the common people watched and waited. Both entrance and exit enabled the commoners to see and know the few who enjoyed high status and authority.

The great planters also earned deference by mastering the genteel public style known as "condescension": a gentleman's ability to treat common people affably without sacrificing his sense of superiority. More confident in their birth, wealth, manners, and education, the eighteenth-century great planters treated common whites with a graciousness foreign to the cruder, newer leaders of the seventeenth century. The eighteenth-century lawyer and jurist St. George Tucker recalled, "The rich rode in Coaches, or Chariots, or on fine horses, but they never failed to pull off their hats to a poor man whom they met, & generally, appear'd to me to shake hands with every man in a Court-yard, or a Church-yard."

Ambitious gentlemen were especially solicitous during elections to the assembly, for about 60 percent of the white men met the property requirement to vote (a house and at least twenty-five acres). The genteel friends of a candidate "treated" the common voters to generous helpings of food, alcohol, and condescension. "Treating" flattered common men with attention from gentlemen of wealth and standing, but the expense ensured that only great planters (or wealthy merchants) could run for the assembly. Held at the county courthouse, the election was public, with each voter individually stepping forward to voice his vote, for recording by a clerk. By such performances, common voters showed gratitude for past favors and solicited future goodwill from their favored gentleman. Upon receiving a vote, the candidate politely thanked the voter, displaying the condescending gratitude of a true gentleman worthy of high office.

SLAVES

At the end of the seventeenth century, tensions between the common whites and the great planters also diminished as the numbers of indentured servants and new freedmen dwindled. English emigration to the Chesapeake declined from 18,000 during the 1660s to 13,000 during the 1680s. Economic growth in England pushed up real wages at the same time that bad economic news from the Chesapeake discouraged potential emigrants. Better able to feed, clothe, and house themselves in England, more poor folk decided against colonial emigration. During the 1680s and 1690s, those who did emigrate preferred other, newer colonies—Jamaica, Carolina, and Pennsylvania—that offered the sort of frontier opportunities that had dissipated in the Chesapeake. As a consequence of the diminished emigration, servants had vanished from most Chesapeake households by 1700. During the 1660s the average York County household had two servants. By the 1690s the county averaged only two servants for every ten plantations.

Faced with a declining supply of white laborers, the Chesapeake planters increasingly turned to African slaves for their plantation labor. At the end of the seventeenth century, slaves became a better investment, as servants became scarcer and more expensive: £25 to £30 for a lifelong slave compared well with £15 to purchase just four years of a servant's time. In addition, the moderating virulence of the local diseases increased life expectancy, which made planters more confident that their slaves would live and work long enough to repay their extra cost. It also helped that slave traders began to visit the Chesapeake in growing numbers, increasing the supply of slaves at stable prices, despite the growing demand. In 1698, Parliament lifted the monopoly slave trade conducted by the Royal African Company, permitting an influx of smaller competitors who sought out new markets, including the Chesapeake. The slave numbers surged from a mere 300 in 1650 to 13,000 by 1700, when Africans constituted 13 percent of the Chesapeake population. During the early eighteenth century, their numbers and proportion continued to grow, reaching 150,000 people and 40 percent by 1750.

The planters shifted from servants to slaves for economic reasons, but that change incidentally improved their security against another rebellion by angry freedmen. During the 1660s and 1670s, the system of indentured servitude had annually unleashed a host of new freedmen into a society of diminishing opportunity. Frustrated and armed, they had rebelled in 1676. Thereafter, fewer servants meant fewer new freedmen who might stew in their frustration and rally to another rebel commander. Bacon's Rebellion did not cause the switch from servants to slaves, but that shift did discourage poor whites from rebelling in the eighteenth century.

While they no longer feared their poorer white neighbors, the planter elite developed a new dread of their enslaved Africans. Taking advantage of their numbers, blacks might surprise and massacre their masters with knives and hatchets, to seize the guns needed to expand their rebellion. To keep the slaves intimidated, the great planters needed a colonial militia drawn from the common farmers. Consequently, in shifting to African slaves, the great planters acquired yet another reason to cultivate the common white men. Instead of a threat to social order, the armed whites became essential to its defense against slave rebellion.

Before 1670, planters developed no systematic legal code to regulate slaves, because they were so few. Early in the century Chesapeake slavery was relatively amorphous and fluid. Some early planters apparently treated their Africans like indentured servants, freeing the survivors after a few years of hard labor. More commonly, masters permitted slaves to acquire and manage their own property, primarily a few chickens, hogs, cattle, and small garden plots of maize and tobacco. By accumulating and selling property, dozens of early slaves purchased their freedom and obtained the tools, clothing, and land to become common planters. Because the colonial laws did not yet forbid black progress, the black freedmen and women could move as they pleased, baptize their children, procure firearms, testify in court, buy and sell property, and even vote. Some black men married white women, which was especially remarkable given their scarcity and high demand as wives for white men. A few black women took white husbands.

The most successful and conspicuous black freedman, Anthony Johnson, acquired a 250-acre tobacco plantation and at least one slave. With apparent impunity, Johnson boldly spoke his own mind to his white neighbors, telling one meddler: "I know myne owne ground and I will worke when I please and play when I please." When white neighbors lured away his slave, Johnson went to court, winning damages and the return of his property. That the authorities supported an African against whites and upheld his right to own slaves reveals that slavery and racism had not yet become inseparably intertwined in the Chesapeake. That a black man would own a slave also indicates that getting ahead in planter society was more important to Johnson than any sense of racial solidarity with his fellow Africans in Virginia.

During the late seventeenth century, the Chesapeake masters more strictly defined slavery and more severely restricted both slaves and free blacks. As Africans surged in number, they more readily sustained their own culture. African languages, prayers, funerals, ritual scars, filed teeth, and drumming became more conspicuous, alarming their masters. Fearful planters demanded new laws restricting movement and trading by blacks, lest they encourage theft and plots to rebel. No more than four slaves could assemble beyond their plantation, and none could leave it without a written pass from the master. Militia squads patrolled the roads to demand passes from traveling blacks. The militiamen also inspected slave quarters to search for weapons and to break up gatherings of visiting blacks. The courts severely fined lax planters who allowed their slaves to roam.

The masters also forced slaves to work longer days under stricter supervision. Saturday became a full workday, and some slaves labored even on Sunday. After devoting the daylight to tending the tobacco and maize, they often had to work late into the night pounding corn by hand. Although slaves continued to tend small gardens for subsistence, they rarely had the time or energy to raise a surplus to market on their own account, which precluded their purchase of freedom. Moreover, their masters virtually abolished such purchases from a new resolve to retain all of their slaves for life. The planters also afforded the Africans even less food, poorer housing, and less medical attention than servants had received.

As slaves became more numerous and more conspicuously African, masters became convinced that only pain and fear could motivate them. In self-pity the planter William Byrd lamented that one "unhappy effect of owning many Negroes is the necessity of being severe. Numbers make them insolent, and then foul means must do, what fair will not." Unlike servants, slaves could not be punished with added years of service. Instead, they had to feel the lash and suffer other torments. Chronic runaways had their toes chopped off or suffered castration. The colonial authorities held no master liable for the death of his slave from excessive punishment.

The planters rationalized their increased brutality by thinking of the Africans as stupid brutes. An English visitor noted, "The planters do not want to be told that their Negroes are human creatures. If they believe them to be of human kind, they cannot regard them . . . as no better than dogs or horses." The brutality failed to break most slaves, who subtly resisted by working as slowly and indifferently as possible. The great planter Landon Carter complained that "the more particular we are in our charges and the fonder we show ourselves of anything, the more careless will our slaves be." Pretending to the stubborn stupidity projected upon them by their masters, slaves slyly frustrated their masters. But it was always a dangerous contest.

Alarmed for their own security, the great planters needed the common whites to identify with them and against the African slaves. New legislation promoted racial solidarity by all whites across their class lines. In 1680, Virginia prescribed thirty lashes on the bare back of any black slave who threatened or struck any white person, which invited poor whites to bully slaves with impunity, creating a common sense of white mastery over all blacks. In another measure crassly calculated to drive a wedge between poor whites and enslaved blacks, in 1705 the assembly empowered parish vestries to seize all livestock that belonged to slaves for sale to benefit the white poor. This law invited poor whites to get ahead by informing on blacks, thereby preventing slaves from ameliorating their own lot.

The Virginia assembly also worked to divide the races by forbidding interracial marriage and by criminalizing interracial sex when the woman was white. Of course, the assembly passed in silence over the far more numerous cases in which white masters procreated with enslaved women. Raping a slave was not a crime but marrying her was. In 1705 the law subjected any minister who conducted an interracial marriage to a fine of ten thousand pounds of tobacco. A white man who married a free black or a white woman who slept with any black man faced six months in prison and a £10 fine. A free white woman who bore a mulatto baby risked a five-year sentence of indentured servitude. The child fared even worse, consigned to service until age thirty-one. Indeed, if that child was female and bore her own children before her sentence expired, they suffered their own thirty-one years as property. But the great planters could neither acknowledge nor prevent their own covert role in creating many more mixed-race children than did all of the free white women in the colony. By indulging themselves with virtually unlimited power over the bodies of their slaves, the masters contradicted their own fantasy of perfecting a distinction between the races. And they sentenced themselves to lives of public denial.

Newly suspicious of free blacks, the assemblymen worked to shrink their numbers and autonomy by rendering their status closer to slavery. After 1691 no Virginia planter could free slaves unless he paid for their transportation beyond the colony. In 1723 the governor declared that only by fixing "a perpetual Brand upon Free-Negroes & Mulattos by excluding them from that great Priviledge of a Freeman" could they be taught "that a distinction ought to be made between their offspring and the Descendants of an Englishman, with whom they never were to be Accounted Equal." Free blacks lost the right to bear arms, hold office, vote, and employ white servants. They had to pay higher taxes, and the courts inflicted stricter penalties on free blacks than whites convicted for the same crimes. Unscrupulous slave traders kidnapped free blacks, spiriting them away for resale elsewhere. Dreading reenslavement, the descendants of Anthony Johnson fled from Virginia, where their grandfather had been a respected freeholder able to defeat whites in lawsuits.

As the great planters created a racial system of slavery, Virginia became both more stable and more distinctive from England. The common and the great planters found a new, shared identity in the psychology of race that held every white man superior to every black. A dark skin became synonymous with slavery, just as freedom became equated with whiteness. In the eighteenth-century Chesapeake colonies almost all blacks were slaves and almost every slave was black (with the exception of occasional captive Indians). A Virginian remarked, "These two words Negro and Slave have, by custom, grown Homogeneous and Convertible."

As skin color became the key marker of identity, race obscured the persistent power of class distinctions between the common planters and the great planters. About three-fifths of white Virginians belonged to a broad middling class that owned substantial farms, while the top twentieth of the population possessed growing wealth. The bottom third of the whites owned no land and verged on destitution. Over time, the gap steadily widened between the wealthiest and the poorest whites. For example, in 1700 in Virginia's Middlesex County the richest 5 percent of the white families owned more than half of the property. In sharp contrast, the poorest third of the whites owned only 2 percent of the wealth. Fifty years later, the concentration of property in the hands of the wealthiest had more than doubled.

Newly obsessed with racial difference, Chesapeake whites *felt* more equal despite the growing inequality of their economic circumstances. The new sense of racial solidarity rendered white Virginians indifferent to the continuing concentration of most property and real power in the hands of the planter elite. By increasing the capital requirements for tobacco cultivation, slavery gave competitive advantage to the already wealthy planters, discouraging the smaller planters, who had to rely on the labor of their own families. The more restless and ambitious young commoners moved westward or southward in search of the frontier opportunity to build farms out of the forest. The less ambitious remained behind in the older counties, determined primarily to minimize their manual labor. William Byrd explained that the blacks "blow up the pride and ruin the industry of our white people, who seeing a rank of poor creatures below them, detest work for fear it should make them look like slaves."

8

New England

★

1600–1700

Richard Mather, a Puritan minister, with his open Bible and spectacles. A participant in the Great Migration, he founded a dynasty of Puritan divines that included his grandson Cotton Mather. An engraving by John Foster.

DURING THE SEVENTEENTH CENTURY, the social and economic pressures within England that generated the Chesapeake colonies also spawned the colonization of a region to the north named New England. But the New English colonists differed markedly from their Chesapeake contemporaries. Where most Chesapeake settlers were poor and short-lived indentured servants, New England attracted primarily "middling sorts" who preserved their freedom because they could pay their own way across the Atlantic. And most of the New English espoused a more demanding faith than the Anglicanism practiced in the Chesapeake. Known as Puritans, they meant to purify the Protestant faith, in England if possible, in a New England if necessary.

This different set of colonists adapted to a colder, less abundant, but far healthier environment. A northern and hilly land of dense forests, sharp slopes, stony soils, and a short growing season, New England demanded hard labor to make a farm and offered little prospect of getting rich. A critic insisted that in New England, "the air of the country is sharp, the rocks many, the trees innumerable, the grass little, the winter cold, the summer hot, the gnats in summer biting, [and] the wolves at midnight howling." But in classic Puritan fashion, the New English thanked their God for leading them to a land where they had to work hard. One explained:

> If men desire to have a people degenerate speedily, and to corrupt their mindes and bodies too . . . let them se[e]cke a rich soile, that brings in much with little labour; but if they desire that Piety and Godlinesse should prosper . . . let them choose a Country such as [New England] which may yield sufficiency with hard labour and industry.

Emigrants who preferred a chance to get rich could head farther south to the Chesapeake.

Puritan values helped the colonists prosper in a demanding land. In the process, they developed a culture that was both the most entrepreneurial and the most vociferously pious in Anglo-America. Contrary to the declension model promoted by some historians, the increasing commercialism of New England life at the end of the seventeenth century *derived from* Puritan values rather than manifested their decay. As Max Weber later noted, the Puritans worked with a special zeal to honor their God and to seek rewards that offered reassurance that God approved of their efforts. New England farms, workshops, counting houses, and gristmills—as well as churches and schools—constituted the Puritans' effort to glorify God.

In crowded England, labor was plentiful and cheap, but land was scarce and expensive. New England reversed that relationship, offering abundant land but precious little labor to develop those tracts into productive farms. Where England provided too little employment for too many people, the New England colonies had too much work for too few colonists. Most New

England farmers had to rely on their own families for the labor to build their especially demanding farms. That reliance on family labor kept New England more egalitarian in the distribution of property and power than was the case in the richer Chesapeake, where an elite of great planters exploited the labor of servants and slaves.

ENGLISH PURITANS

Church and state were united in early modern England. Law demanded that everyone support the official Church of England with taxes and regular attendance. A seventeenth-century aristocrat noted that "the ecclesiastical and civil state" were so "interwoven together, and in truth so incorporated in each other, that like Hippocrates' twins they cannot but laugh and cry together." During the 1530s, Queen Elizabeth's father, King Henry VIII, had rejected the Catholic pope to become the head of an independent Church of England. Thereafter, the English monarch appointed and commanded a hierarchy of two archbishops, twenty-six bishops, and approximately 8,600 parish clergy in England and Wales. Because the monarch led the official church, religious dissent smacked of treason as well as heresy. One clergyman preached that "no subject may, without hazard of his own damnation in rebelling against God, question or disobey the will and pleasure of his sovereign." King James I pithily declared that the entire social order hinged upon the preservation of the church hierarchy: "No Bishop, no King, no nobility."

The crown employed the Anglican Church to promote political as well as religious conformity. A system of church courts (without juries) gave the crown a vehicle to extort revenue and to punish dissidents. The monarch also frequently ordered the bishops to instruct the parish ministers to preach in support of particular policies. In 1620, King James I demanded sermons against "the insolency of our women and their wearing of broad-brimmed hats, pointed doublets, their hair cut short or shorn." In 1626 his son and successor, King Charles I, dictated that the clergy preach that Parliament sinned when it denied new taxes demanded by the monarch. Charles noted, "People are governed by the pulpit more than the sword in time of peace."

The merger of church and state in service to a hierarchical social order gave political significance to every religious issue. The combination obliged dissidents to express their social and political grievances in religious rhetoric, and it made social and political critics of those seeking religious purity. Especially devout reformers, known as Puritans, wanted to change both the Church of England and the larger society.

Begun as an epithet, "Puritan" persists in scholarship to name the broad movement of diverse people who shared a conviction that the Protestant Reformation remained incomplete in England. Because the monarchs favored religious compromise and inclusion, the Anglican Church was, in the horrified words of one Puritan, "a mingle-mangle" of Protestant and Catholic doctrines and ceremonies. The ecclesiastical structure of bishops and archbishops remained Catholic except for the substitution at the top of the king for the pope.

In seeking reform, Puritans divided over the details. Most remained within the Anglican Church, seeking to capture and reform it, preserving the link between church and state. The more radical Puritans, however, became "Separatists," determined immediately to withdraw into their own independent congregations. Without any larger authority to enforce orthodoxy, the many autonomous Separatist congregations steadily splintered in their beliefs and practices, forming many distinct sects.

Disdaining the legacy of medieval Catholicism, the Puritans sought to recover the original, pure, and simple church of Jesus Christ and his apostles. In a "Reformed Church" individual souls could nurture a more direct relationship with God. Rejecting the intercession of priests administering ceremonial sacraments, the Puritans instead urged every believer to seek God by reading the Bible, forming prayer groups, and heeding learned and zealous ministers who delivered evangelical sermons. Puritans wished to strip away church ceremony and formulaic prayers as legacies of papacy. They also wanted to eliminate or reduce the authority of the bishops by increasing the authority of local congregations.

Puritans longed to experience the "New Birth": a transforming infusion of divine grace that liberated people from profound anxiety over their spiritual worthlessness and eternal fate. By moral living, devout prayer, reading the Bible, and heeding sermons, the hopeful Puritan prepared for the possibility of God's saving grace. But not even the most devout could claim conversion and salvation as a right and a certainty, for God alone determined. He saved selectively and arbitrarily, rather than universally or as a reward for good behavior. In this belief in God's complete power over grace and salvation, the Puritans elaborated upon the "Calvinist" doctrines of the sixteenth-century Swiss theologian Jean Calvin.

Nonetheless, Puritans were incorrigible doers, seeking out the preached word, reading the Scriptures, perfecting their morality, and proposing radical schemes for improving society and disciplining the unruly and indolent. To satirize Puritanism, the seventeenth-century dramatist Ben Jonson aptly named a Puritan character Zeal-of-the-Land Busy. Their prodigious energy expressed their conviction that godly doing manifested itself in those God had elected for salvation. One Puritan subtly explained, "We teach that only Doers shall be saved, and by their doing though not for their doing." Because diligence and discipline honored God, Puritans labored ever harder to perfect their morality and worship—and to extend both to others.

The Puritan movement especially appealed to residents of the most commercialized area in England: the southeast, particularly London, East Anglia, and Sussex. Puritans came from all ranks of English society, including a few aristocrats, but most belonged to the "middling sort" of small property holders: farmers, shopkeepers, and skilled artisans. The Puritan tended to be the self-employed head of a household, of whom Robert Reyce said that "though hee thriveth ordinarily well, yett he laboreth much." Their own modest property put them a leg up on the impoverished and underemployed half of the English population.

Puritanism reinforced the values of thrift, diligence, and delayed gratification that were essential to the well-being of the middling sort. Puritans held that men honored God and proved their own salvation by working hard in their occupation—which they deemed a "calling" bestowed by God. A Puritan explained, "God sent you unto this world as unto a Workhouse, not a Playhouse." Offering a strict code of personal discipline and morality, Puritanism helped thousands of ordinary people cope with the economic and social turmoil that afflicted England during the early seventeenth century. Puritanism liberated people from a sense of helplessness by encouraging effort, persistence, study, and purpose.

Taking on a demanding tension, the Puritans strove to live in the world, without succumbing to worldliness. On the one hand, Puritans hinted that God would reward the diligent and godly with prosperity. On the other hand, they cautioned that wealth must not be an end unto itself lest carnal temptations overwhelm the ultimate purpose of human life: preparation for salvation in the next world. Puritans denounced conspicuous consumption and covetousness and urged generous donations to spread the Gospel. But the godly could never escape worldly temptation, because Puritan virtues helped them to accumulate money.

Puritans felt sorely afflicted by the many English people who possessed neither their virtues nor their zeal. Puritan rhetoric depicted England as awash in thieves, drunks, idlers, prostitutes, and blasphemers. The godly blamed the unruly and the indolent—and indulgent authorities—for all the social and economic troubles of the realm. Puritans advanced the radical notion that England could be cleansed of poverty and crime if godly men and women united to take charge of their churches and local governments, introducing moral rigor to both.

This Puritan vision appealed to many pious and propertied people weary of the economic upheaval, crime, and poverty of the late sixteenth and early seventeenth centuries. Puritan magistrates strictly enforced the long-neglected laws against gambling, blasphemy, adultery, public drunkenness, and Sabbath-breaking. And Puritans longed to purify the churches by ousting all conspicuous sinners and by inviting members to monitor one another for consistent morality and sound theology. This zeal, however, dismayed most English people, who preferred Anglicanism and the traditional culture characterized by church ales, Sunday diversions, ceremonial services, inclusive churches, and deference to the monarch.

The Puritan rigor also alarmed the seventeenth-century kings, who

— New England, c. 1650 —

ABENAKI	Native people
Natick ○	Native town
Boston •	English or Dutch town
Montreal •	French town

Montreal

N

Lake Champlain

MAINE

Kennebec R.

Androscoggin R.

© 2001 Jeffrey L. Ward

ABENAKI

Saco R.

NEW HAMPSHIRE

Connecticut R.

Merrimack R.

Piscataqua R.

York

Portsmouth

Hudson R.

Mohawk R.

Fort Orange

PENNACOOK

Gloucester

MASSACHUSETT

Salem

MASSACHUSETTS

Boston

Natick

NIPMUCK

POKANOKET

CAPE COD

Plymouth

NARRAGANSETT

PLYMOUTH

Hartford

Providence

NEW NETHERLAND (NEW YORK)

CONNECTICUT

RHODE ISLAND

WAMPANOAG

MOHEGAN

Housatonic R.

Thames R.

Mystic R.

PEQUOT

Newport

New Haven

Narragansett Bay

MARTHA'S VINYARD

NANTUCKET

Long Island Sound

Hudson R.

ATLANTIC OCEAN

LONG ISLAND

New Amsterdam

0 Miles 50 100

0 Kilometers 100

wanted a united and quiet realm of unquestioning loyalty. They recognized the subversive potential in Puritanism's insistence on the spiritual equality of all godly men and on their superiority to all ungodly men—who, in Puritan eyes, included most of the king's bishops. In 1604, King James I declared that Puritanism "as well agreeth with a monarchy as God and the devil. Then Jack and Tom and Will and Dick shall meet, and at their pleasures censure me and my council and all our proceedings." If the Puritans did not conform to his authority and church, he threatened to "harry them out of the land."

They indifferently conformed, and James reluctantly tolerated their persistence within the realm. Indeed, during his reign dozens of Puritan ministers continued to serve Anglican parishes, and hundreds of lay Puritans retained royal commissions as local magistrates. Purging the pulpits and courts of Puritans was difficult, for the crown depended upon propertied and educated men to keep and preach order in the counties, and such men were often Puritans.

That grudging accommodation between Puritans and most church hierarchy eroded late in James's reign and collapsed in 1625 upon the accession of his son as King Charles I. Married to a Catholic princess, Charles hoped to reconcile English Catholics by restoring some church ceremonies previously suspended to mollify the Puritans. Charles elevated William Laud, the greatest champion of ceremonies, to bishop in 1628 and to archbishop in 1633. In return, Laud and his allies preached the Christian duty of Parliament and taxpayers to submit to the king.

During the late 1620s and early 1630s, Laud and most other bishops enforced the new Anglican orthodoxy, dismissing Puritan ministers who balked at conducting the high church liturgy. Church courts also prosecuted growing numbers of Puritan laypeople. Laud strictly censored Puritan tracts and had pilloried, mutilated, and branded three Puritans who illegally published their ideas. Puritan hopes of securing redress dissipated after 1629, when Charles I dissolved Parliament and proceeded to rule arbitrarily for the next eleven years. Faced with the growing power of the king and his bishops, some despairing Puritans considered emigrating across the Atlantic to a New England.

THE GREAT MIGRATION

The Puritan emigrants followed French and English mariners, fishermen, and fur traders who had visited the New England coast during the summers. In 1607 English West Country promoters established a small settlement at the mouth of the Kennebec River on the coast of Maine. But Indian hostility and the hard winter demoralized the colonists, who eagerly sailed home in the spring of 1608. Their failure saddled the region with a daunting reputation as frigid and hostile. Determined to improve that reputation, Captain

John Smith (of Jamestown fame) explored the coast in 1614 and named it New England because, he claimed, the climate and soil replicated the mother country. Smith published promotional literature, including an appealing map, which greatly intrigued Puritans disgruntled with their Anglican rulers.

The first Puritan emigrants consisted of 102 Separatists, subsequently called the Pilgrims. In 1620 they crossed the Atlantic in the ship *Mayflower* to found a town named Plymouth on the south shore of Massachusetts Bay. Beneficiaries of a devastating epidemic that had recently decimated the coastal Indians, the Plymouth colonists occupied an abandoned village with conveniently cleared fields. In 1620–21, a long, hard, starving winter killed half of the newcomers, but thereafter good crops and more emigrants from England stabilized and strengthened the colony. By 1630 about fifteen hundred English dwelled in the Plymouth colony.

In 1630 a much larger Puritan emigration, subsequently called the "Great Migration," began under the leadership of John Winthrop. A genteel lawyer, Winthrop represented a syndicate of wealthy Puritans who obtained a royal charter as the Massachusetts Bay Company. Unlike those of its unfortunate predecessor, the Virginia Company, the leaders of the Massachusetts Bay Company quickly relocated themselves, with their capital, charter, and records, to New England. In effect, they converted their commercial charter into a self-governing colony three thousand miles away from bishops and king. Once in Massachusetts, the company leaders established the most radical government in the European world: a republic, where the Puritan men elected their governor, deputy governor, and legislature (known as the General Court). Until his death in 1649, John Winthrop almost always won annual reelection as governor.

Beginning with a settlement named Boston, Winthrop's Puritans established the Massachusetts Bay colony on the coast north of Plymouth. After a hungry winter in 1630–31, the Massachusetts colonists raised enough food to sustain themselves and numerous new emigrants, who followed throughout the decade. In New England, the starving time of adjustment proved far shorter and less deadly than in the Chesapeake.

From the coastal towns, the colonists expanded into the interior during the 1630s and 1640s. The expansion troubled colonial leaders who preferred consolidated settlement as more secure from Indian attack and more convenient to sustain schools and churches. But the colonists could not resist the allure of spreading out in search of larger tracts of land for farming. And the colonial Puritans were discovering their disagreements over the proper rules to govern their new towns and churches. Often with a push from local majorities, the disgruntled minority factions bolted for new locations where they hoped to enforce their own rules and obtain better lands.

By 1640 the expanding settlements spawned new colonies. To the northeast, some Puritans settled along the coasts of New Hampshire and Maine, where they mingled uneasily with fishing folk, nominal Anglicans who came from the English West Country. Southeastern New England became a haven for especially radical Puritan Separatists who settled around Narragansett Bay in independent towns that eventually made up the colony of Rhode Island. At the other religious extreme, some particularly conservative and ambitious Puritans found Massachusetts too lax in religion and too stingy in land grants. They proceeded southwest to found the colonies of Connecticut and New Haven along the Connecticut River and Long Island Sound. With 20,000 of the region's 33,000 inhabitants in 1660, Massachusetts remained the most populous, influential, and powerful of the New England colonies.

Later in the century, Rhode Island, Connecticut, and New Hampshire secured their own charters of government from the crown. Maine, New Haven, and Plymouth were less fortunate. In 1652, Maine's poor and vulnerable settlements accepted rule and protection by Massachusetts. In 1665, Connecticut absorbed the New Haven colony. In 1691, the crown issued a new charter for Massachusetts, extending its jurisdiction over Plymouth. That left four colonies in New England: Massachusetts, Connecticut, Rhode Island, and New Hampshire.

RELIGION AND PROFIT

Historians have long debated whether the Puritan faith or economic aspirations took precedence in mobilizing migration from England to New England. In fact, the religious and the economic were interdependent in the lives of people who saw piety and property as mutually reinforcing. A leading Puritan said that New England should belong to those in whom "religion and profit jump together." Another Puritan characteristically gave two reasons for urging immediate emigration: "First, if you linger too long, the passages of Jordan through the malice of Satan may be stopped, that you cannot come if you would. Secondly, those that come first speed best here and have the privilege of choosing choice places of habitations." Because the Puritans prepared for the next world by their moral life in this one, their rhetoric yoked together material aspiration and the pursuit of salvation. It is anachronistic for us to separate the two.

During the 1620s and 1630s the English middling sort had economic cause to consider emigrating across the Atlantic. Alarmed by the worsening conditions of the laboring poor, the small property holders feared that they would next feel the pinch. Nothing frightened the middling sort more than the prospect of slipping into the ranks of the sturdy beggars. The push factor grew more powerful in the late 1620s when harvests failed, food prices soared, and famine killed many poor people. At the same time, the depression of the cloth industry deepened, threatening to ruin hundreds of Puritan cloth-makers. The middling sort also felt burdened by increasing crime and by escalating taxes both to feed the poor and to fund the government of an arbitrary king.

Meanwhile, New England began to exercise a new pull on Puritan minds. Fearing worse to come at home, many Puritans took a new interest in Captain John Smith's alluring description of New England: "Here every man may be master of his own labour and land . . . and by industry grow rich." By emigrating and acquiring substantial farms, middling folk hoped to escape the threat of poverty in England and to secure a prosperous future for their children in a New England. By emigrating to a new land, they sought to ensure their "independence" as small producers working on their own property.

Purely economic motives, however, would have dispatched few people to cold, distant, and rocky New England. English people could more cheaply, easily, and certainly improve their material circumstances by moving to the nearby and booming Netherlands, which welcomed skilled immigrants. Because shipboard capacity was limited and expensive, the transatlantic emigrants also had to divest themselves of much of the property that they had so painstakingly accumulated: of course their land and buildings, but also much of their livestock, furniture, and household goods. For a people who cherished property as their security, divesting was painful. Those who made such sacrifices to leap into the New England unknown went primarily in groups that shared a Puritan zeal and a dread over the worsening state of the English church and state.

The Puritans understood in spiritual terms many causes that we might define as "economic." They interpreted the wandering beggars, increased crime, cloth trade depression, and famines as divine afflictions meant to punish a guilty land that wallowed in sin. Even more than Archbishop Laud's direct persecution (which was inconsistent and inefficient), Puritans suffered psychologically from a growing despair that England's crown and bishops were retreating from the Protestant Reformation, moving the nation into an overt hostility toward God that would inevitably reap divine punishment in mounting disasters.

To redeem their hope for a brighter future, many Puritans sought a distant refuge, where they could live apart from sinners and far from the supervision of persecuting bishops. In a New England, the Puritans could purify their churches, supervise one another, and enact a code of laws derived from the Bible. At a minimum, withdrawal across the Atlantic might save the godly from the divine punishments gathering against the wicked English nation. John Winthrop concluded that God had designated New England as "a refuge for manye, whome he meant to save out of the general destruction." But some Puritans hoped that New England could be much more than a refuge. Perhaps by prospering morally and economically, the Puritan colonists could inspire their countryman in England to reform and save the nation. John Winthrop exhorted his fellow colonists to make Massachusetts a

"City upon a Hill," an inspirational set of reformed churches conspicuous to the mother country.

But by no means was there a consensus among the English Puritans in favor of colonial emigration, given its high costs, grave dangers, and uncertain consequences. After all, as of 1630 most of the English who had migrated across the Atlantic were already dead in Chesapeake or West Indian graves, and the worldly societies established in those colonies were a Puritan's despair. In 1630 no one could be sure that New England would turn out any better. As a result, most English Puritans regarded the migration as premature and dangerous, a foolish weakening of the reform cause at home. Robert Reyce warned his friend John Winthrop, "The Church and Commonwelthe heere at home hath more needs of your best abillitie in these dangerous tymes, than any remote plantation."

Emigration across the Atlantic in a small and crowded wooden ship was also a daunting prospect. Battling the prevailing Atlantic winds and currents, the slow-moving vessels usually took eight to twelve weeks to cross. Few of the Puritans, who were mostly artisans and farmers, or their wives and children had traveled by ship. On board the standard vessel, about one hundred passengers shared the cold, damp, and cramped hold with their property, including some noisy and rank livestock. The emigrants consumed barreled water, salt meat, and hard bread, a fare that worsened as the voyage proceeded: the food spoiled, worms proliferated, and the water turned foul. Only in relatively calm weather, and only for a few hours a day, could the passengers partake of the fresh air and distant views from the deck. Most of the time they huddled below as the pitching vessel churned through the cold and stormy waters.

The darkness, uncertainty, and violent motion played havoc with unprepared stomachs and jangled nerves. Francis Higginson recalled one "sore & terrible storme; for the wind blew mightily, the rayne fell vehemently, the sea roared & the waves tossed us horribly; besides it was fearfull darke & the mariners . . . was afraid." William Bradford recalled that upon reaching New England, the Plymouth colonists "fell upon their knees and blessed the God of Heaven, who had brought them over the vast and furious ocean, and delivered them from all the perils and miseries thereof, again to set their feet on the firm and stable earth, their proper element."

Their God was remarkably merciful. During the 1630s, of 198 recorded voyages bearing passengers to New England, only one sank, and the mortality from disease was less than 5 percent, far lower than what indentured servants experienced on a voyage to the West Indies or the Chesapeake—to say nothing of the African slaves bound to the New World.

Remembered for the rest of their days, the ocean passage was an especially powerful and pivotal experience, akin to their New Birth. Close quarters and proximity to death gave a new intensity to the daily prayers and other religious exercises that kept up the spirits of the passengers. A literal rite of passage, the shared hardships, fears, and services strengthened the religious purpose and the common bonds of the emigrants. In the new land, their ministers often recalled the crossing as a searing test that they had weathered together—but it was an experience that few wished to repeat. Most had come to New England to stay.

About fourteen thousand English Puritans participated in the Great Migration of the 1630s. Although certainly great in its consequences for New England, this migration had three important limits. First, most English Puritans persisted at home, waiting to see how God would treat both the mother country and the New England experiment. Second, the New England emigration represented only 30 percent of all the English who crossed the Atlantic to the various colonies during the 1630s. Many more people emigrated to the Chesapeake and the West Indies. Third, the Great Migration was brief, for emigration declined to a trickle after 1640, amounting to only seven thousand for the rest of the century. Consequently, colonial New England became peopled primarily by the descendants of the one great surge of emigrants during the 1630s.

By colonial standards, New England attracted an unusual set of emigrants: the sort of skilled and prosperous people who ordinarily stayed at home rather than risk the rigors of a transatlantic crossing and the uncertainties of colonial life. Most seventeenth-century English emigrants were poor young single men who lacked prospects in the mother country. Seeking regular meals in the short term and a farm in the long, they gambled their lives as indentured servants in the Chesapeake or the West Indies. In sharp contrast, most of the New England colonists could pay their own way and emigrated as family groups. In 1631 a Puritan boasted that the emigrants were "endowed with grace and furnished with means." They also enjoyed a more even balance between the sexes. At mid-century, the New England sex ratio was six males for every four females, compared with four males for every female in the Chesapeake. Greater balance encouraged a more stable society and a faster population growth.

New England lacked a profitable plantation crop that would both demand and finance the importation of indentured servants. During the 1630s, indentured servants constituted less than a fifth of the New England emigrants. And in contrast to the Chesapeake and West Indies, where servants came in large numbers for sale upon arrival to new masters, almost all of the New England servants came with the emigrant families, generally one or two per family. Over time, the servant numbers declined as their terms expired and they acquired their own land, for most New Englanders could not afford to buy replacements. By the end of the century, servants amounted to less than 5 percent of the New English population.

Nor could the New Englanders afford to buy Africans. In 1700 less than 2 percent of New England's inhabitants were slaves, compared with 13 percent for Virginia and 78 percent for the English West Indies. Compared with the rest of the empire, New England possessed an unusually homogeneous colonial population and culture: free, white, and transplanted English.

Relative to the Chesapeake, the New England environment demanded more labor and provided smaller rewards, but it also permitted longer and healthier lives. In contrast to the Chesapeake tidewater with its long, hot, and humid summers and low topography, New England was a northern and hilly land with a short growing season and faster-flowing rivers and streams, which discouraged the malaria and dysentery that afflicted southern planters. In New England, people who survived childhood could expect to live to about seventy; in the Chesapeake, only a minority survived beyond forty-five. Francis Higginson boasted that for "a healing nature . . . a sup of New England's air is better than a whole draught of old England's ale."

This healthier, longer-lived, and more sex-balanced population sustained a rapid growth through natural increase, whereas in the Chesapeake and West Indies, only continued human imports sustained growth. During the seventeenth century, New England received only 21,000 emigrants—a fraction of the 120,000 transported to the Chesapeake, not to mention the 190,000 who colonized the West Indies. Yet in 1700, New England's colonial population of 91,000 exceeded the 85,000 whites in the Chesapeake and the 33,000 whites in the West Indies. Although not the wealthiest English colonial region, New England was the healthiest, the most populous, and the most egalitarian in the distribution of property.

LAND AND LABOR

The New England colonies granted lands to men who banded together as a corporate group to found a town. This town system contrasted with the Chesapeake colonies, where the leaders allocated land directly to individuals and usually in large tracts to the wealthy and well-connected. The Chesapeake practice dispersed settlement, which rendered it more difficult to sustain schools and churches and to repel Indian attacks. New English leaders favored relatively compact settlement in towns to concentrate people sufficiently for defense, to support public schools, to promote mutual supervision of morality, and, above all, to sustain a convenient and well-attended local church.

The colonial legislature defined the town boundaries but left to each town corporation the allocation of land for household farms and the location of a village center with church and school. More than simply a tract of land, the town was also a local government, fundamental to New England politics—in contrast to the Chesapeake colonies, which relied on the larger county. Gathered in town meeting, the male property holders elected their local officials, principally a board of selectmen.

Favoring a gradual and modest distribution of land, the town founders initially awarded each household only ten to fifty acres (depending upon social status). Eventually, however, most seventeenth-century families acquired between one hundred and two hundred acres of farmland. Although about half the size of most Chesapeake plantations, the average New England farm was significantly larger than most landholdings in England, where few farmers owned so many as fifty acres and where over half the men possessed no land. And in New England almost all farmers enjoyed complete ownership, known as a freehold, in contrast to the leaseholds that prevailed in England. Freehold lands offered security from the rising rents charged by English landlords or Chesapeake great planters. The New English also avoided paying the quitrents charged by the lords proprietor or the crown in more southern colonies. A Puritan emigrant to New Jersey "swore—godzooks, he would have nothing to do with land as payed quitrents, for they paid none in New England."

To make farms, the colonists had to cut clearings in the forest, chop firewood, erect fences, build barns and houses, plow and plant fields, harvest crops, and construct mills—all from scratch by hand labor. This work was more demanding in cold and rocky New England than in the flatter, warmer, and fertile Chesapeake. And while demanding more labor to build, the New England farm generated smaller profits than the Chesapeake plantation. The shorter growing season and rougher land precluded the cultivation of the colonial staples in greatest European demand, tobacco and sugar. Instead, the New English farmers raised a northern medley of small crops—wheat, rye, maize, potatoes, beans, and garden plants. None could be profitably shipped for sale in England, where a similar climate permitted the same crops.

The New England farm family also tended a modest but critical herd of livestock—commonly two oxen, five other cattle, a horse, two sheep, and six pigs. Because livestock needed more land than grains, the New England farm had large pastures and hayfields but relatively small fields of grain. The farm families consumed most of their own crops and butchered animals or traded them for the goods and services of local artisans, principally carpenters, blacksmiths, and shoemakers. New England's diversified farms were less prone to disruption by the boom-and-bust price cycle than were the southern plantations specializing in a staple crop for an external market.

Unable to afford servants or slaves, the New English instead relied upon the family labor of their sons and daughters. A seventeenth-century Englishman reported, "Virginia thrives by keeping many servants, and these in strict obedience. New England [conceives that] they and their Children can doe enough, and soe [they] have rarely above one Servant." The healthy climate and good diet enabled parents to raise six or seven children to maturity. By age ten, boys worked with their fathers in the fields and barn, while daughters assisted their mothers in the house and garden. Most sons remained unmarried and working on the paternal farm until their middle or late twenties, retained by the prospect that their father could eventually provide each with a farm from the family rights in the town lands.

Diligent and realistic, most New England families sought an "independent competency." "Independence" meant owning enough property—a farm or a shop—to employ a family, without having to work for someone else as a hired hand or servant. A "competency" meant a sufficiency, but not an abundance, of worldly goods: enough to eat, adequate if simple clothing, a roof over their heads, some consumer goods, and an ability to transmit this standard of living to many children. Although no land of riches, New England provided many independent farms and a secure household competency to hard and persistent labor. Edward Johnson of Massachusetts noted that even "the poorest person . . . hath a house and land of his own, and bread of his own growing, if not some cattel." Puritans regarded such a broad-based prosperity as more compatible with a godly life than the extremes of wealth and poverty found in England, the Chesapeake, and the West Indies. The Puritan minister John White observed, "Nothing sorts better with Piety than Competency."

Compared with those in the Chesapeake or West Indies, social gradations were subtle among the New English, who overwhelmingly belonged to the middling sort. Their modest and diversified farms produced less wealth than did the staple plantations of the Chesapeake and the West Indies, but the New England economy distributed its rewards more equitably among many farmers and tradesmen. In New English country towns the leading men were substantial farmers, who worked with their hands on properties only two or three times larger than the local average. And the leading rural men possessed few if any imported servants or slaves. The largest seaports—Boston, Salem, and Newport—did host a wealthy elite of merchants, lawyers, and land speculators. But they enjoyed less collective power than did the great planters in the Chesapeake and West Indies, because the New England system of many nearly autonomous towns dispersed political power in the countryside. Because New England had the most decentralized and popularly responsive form of government in the English empire, royalists despised the region as a hotbed of "republicanism."

FAMILY LIFE

It took a family to cope with the diverse and constant demands of building and maintaining a farm in New England. English culture expected all adults to marry and divided their labors into male and female responsibilities. Men conducted the heaviest work, including clearing, constructing, tending the livestock, harvesting the hay, and cultivating the grain crops. Women maintained the home and its nearby garden, cared for the numerous children, made clothing and soap, and prepared and preserved foods, including butter, eggs, and cheese. But when a husband was away or incapacitated, the wife also had to assume his labors, taking on the role of "deputy husband" until he returned or recovered.

The New English understood marriage as both romantic and economic. Husband and wife were supposed to be both temperamentally and financially compatible, able to work together as a loving couple and provident parents for the rest of their days. Puritan parents rarely dictated marriage partners to their children, but they could veto choices that seemed unwise. In general, a young couple developed an attraction and proposed their marriage to parents for approval. If amenable, the two sets of parents negotiated a property settlement to provide the new couple with the land, tools, and livestock to commence a farm or a trade. In seeking a balance between young choice and parental authority, and between romance and property, New England Puritans were somewhat more indulgent than was traditional in the old country.

As in the mother country, New English men monopolized legal authority, landownership, and political rights. As patriarchs, they expected to govern their families as so many "little commonwealths"—the essential components of the social order. The minister John Cotton asserted that God meant civilized people "to live in Societies, first of Family, Secondly Church, and Thirdly, Common-wealth." Because the seventeenth-century English understood all three to interlock in mutual support, disorderly families threatened to dissolve society into violent anarchy. Understanding every commonwealth, small and large, as needing an ultimate ruler, the English expected husbands to govern their families as petty monarchs. By the law of "coverture," wives were subsumed within the name and the legal identity of their husbands. Only widows who had not remarried could own property, enter contracts, and resort to the courts in property disputes. No women, not even widows, could vote or hold public office or aspire to the ministry.

In all of this, New England simply replicated the gender hierarchy of the mother country. More noteworthy are the modest ways in which the Puritan faith provided a bit more authority, protection, and respect for women in New England than they enjoyed in the Chesapeake or old England. Although Puritan ministers dwelled on the wife's duty to submit to her husband, they took equal pains to uphold his duties to behave kindly and generously. Above all, Puritanism preached the importance of love and mutual respect as the foundations for Christian marriage. In contrast to their counterparts in England and the Chesapeake, where authorities rarely intervened in domestic disputes, New England magistrates and church congregations routinely protected women from insult and abuse. (Sometimes they had to protect husbands.) New England women could also more easily obtain divorce when abandoned or sexually betrayed by their husbands. Historian Cornelia Dayton concludes that the effort "to create the most God-fearing society" tended "to reduce the near-absolute power that English men by law wielded over their wives."

Puritanism regarded women and men as spiritual equals. Indeed, after 1650, women seemed spiritually superior, as they outnumbered men as full church members. In 1692 the Boston minister Cotton Mather acknowledged:

> There are far more *Godly Women* in the World than there are *Godly Men*. . . . I have seen it without going a Mile from home, That in a Church of between *Three* and *Four* Hundred *Communicants*, there are but few more than *One* Hundred *Men;* all the Rest are Women.

Although church membership afforded women considerable public honor, that did not stop Puritan men from continuing to monopolize the government of church affairs, including the hiring and firing of ministers.

Thanks to the more even gender balance and the tighter communities of denser settlement, larger numbers of New English women lived in closer proximity than did their Chesapeake sisters. In New England, women could more readily and routinely visit to borrow, lend, help, and talk. Female mutuality was strongest and most conspicuous at the most important, perilous, and joyful occasion in their lives: childbirth. Men were excluded from the birthing chamber as the neighboring women gathered to pray and to assist. In the early stage of labor, the mother served refreshments of beer and cake. As her pains increased, the guests assisted the midwife in conducting the birth, supporting the squatting mother in their arms.

Through their female networks, women exercised considerable informal influence, especially in regulating the all-important reputations of individuals. Women played a leading role in the oral circulation of news and opinion that determined the standing of men, as well as fellow women, in the community. Anyone, even a minister, who ran afoul of female opinion lost credit and faced court or church inquiry. Recognizing women's oral power over reputation, New English men frequently haled women into court for slander.

Indeed, women routinely appeared as plaintiffs, defendants, and witnesses in seventeenth-century New England courts. The central concerns of Puritan law reinforced the female role in maintaining neighborly harmony, ensuring fair trading in the marketplace, and regulating sexual conduct. Women appeared less frequently in the eighteenth century, when the courts became reoriented to regulate the increasingly extensive credit networks of expanding commerce: the realm of propertied men.

COMMERCE

During the late 1630s, New England thrived primarily from the regular infusion of newcomers, who brought currency and other capital and consumed, at enhanced prices, the crops produced by the first-comers. Consequently, termination of the Great Migration in 1640 produced an economic depression. Repeating conventional wisdom, Oliver Cromwell wrote off New England as "poore, cold, and useless." During the 1640s however, the New English innovated, developing a complex and profitable place within the Atlantic networks of commerce.

The process began with the creation of a fishing trade based in the northeastern coastal towns of Maine, New Hampshire, and Essex County, Massachusetts (principally the towns of Marblehead and Gloucester). The fishermen primarily pursued cod in the nearby Georges Bank or in the more distant but larger Grand Banks near Newfoundland. The New England fishermen exploited the disruption wrought during the 1640s by civil war in England, which often prevented English fishing boats from venturing across the Atlantic. New England entrepreneurs rushed their boats into the gap, securing the leading share in a valuable staple. In 1641 the New English caught and marketed 600,000 pounds of fish, a catch that grew tenfold to six million pounds in 1675, when the New England fisheries employed 440 boats and more than a thousand men. The New English shipped the better-quality fish to Spain and Portugal and their Atlantic islands (the Azores, Madeira, and the Canaries). The inferior grades of fish went to the West Indies to feed the slaves working on sugar plantations.

Especially hard, cold, dirty, dangerous, and poorly paid work, fishing had little appeal to middling-sort Puritans, especially in a region that offered substantial farms. In New England, as in old England, fishing employed hard-drinking and hard-swearing men with scant property and little reputation to lose. In contrast to the Puritans, who came primarily from southeastern England, most fishing folk originated in the English West Country and came to New England with previous experience in the waters around Newfoundland.

By developing the fishing trade, the Puritans rescued the region's economy, but at the cost of accepting the presence, albeit limited, of the sort of rowdy and defiant folk whom they had hoped to leave behind in England. Loud and smoky waterfront taverns abounded in Marblehead, but the inhabitants lacked a church until 1684. When obliged to choose a faith, most fishermen preferred a relaxed Anglicanism with its ceremonies to an intense Puritanism with its strict morality and long sermons. A horrified Cotton Mather reported that a fellow minister had visited a northern fishing village to rebuke the people for neglecting "the main end of planting this wilderness": a dedication to religion. A defiant fisherman retorted, "Sir, you think you are preaching to the people at the [Massachusetts] Bay; our main end was to catch fish." Fishermen disproportionately appeared in the Puritan courts, charged with public drunkenness, assault and battery, blasphemy, Sabbath-breaking, and fornication. The fishermen scandalized a 1664 official investigation that concluded, "Some here are of the opinion that as many men may share a woman as they do a boat, and some have done so."

Although important to the New England economy, the codfish never dominated the region in quite the way that tobacco determined prosperity or ruin in the Chesapeake. In New England exports, cod was but the first among a diverse set of equals. Edward Johnson explained, "Every thing in the country proved a staple-commodity, wheat, rye, oats, peas, barley, beef, pork, fish, butter, cheese, timber, mast, tar, sope, plankboard, frames of houses, clapboard, and pipestaves." Although New England farmers raised crops primarily for family and local consumption, they also generated small surpluses, which they sold to merchants to obtain West Indian and Chesapeake produce as well as manufactured goods imported from England. No family wished to live by subsistence farming alone, without the comforts of sugar, rum, tobacco, cloth, and tools. Paradoxically, because New Englanders generated many small surplus crops, each of modest value, rather than a single especially valuable staple, the region became the most pervasively commercialized within the empire. Indeed, the New English became notorious for their commercial acumen and cunning, their wheeling and dealing to obtain small advantages.

Seaport merchants packed and exported the agricultural surplus, along with lumber and fish, to the West Indies to help feed and house the indentured servants and slaves working there. In exchange, the merchants procured molasses, rum, and sugar, some for New English consumption but most for carrying to other markets in the Chesapeake and Europe. The New English exported more to the West Indies than to the mother country, which did not need what New England could produce (but did demand the West Indian produce that the New English could convey to England in their own ships). During the 1680s about half of the ships that served the English Caribbean came from New England.

Although few New Englanders owned slaves, their region's prosperity depended upon a trading system that serviced the wealthier slave-based economy of the West Indies. The royal official Edward Randolph concluded, "It is then, in a great part, by means of New England, that the other plantations are made prosperous and beneficial." But it was also commerce with the West Indian plantations that enabled New England to prosper. If we combine the population figures of New England and the West Indies, we obtain a commonwealth that, in its proportions of black and white, slave and free, looks much like the Chesapeake, which was a region that sustained both farming and plantation agriculture. In effect, seventeenth-century New England and the English West Indies developed in tandem as mutually sustaining parts of a common economic system. Each was incomplete without the other. New English freedom depended on West Indian slavery.

New England's fisheries and the carrying trade to the West Indies demanded ships. By the end of the seventeenth century, the New English were building almost all of the vessels they employed, as well as growing numbers for English merchants. New England shipbuilders exploited the abundant and cheap supplies of high-quality timber harvested from the dense forests of

New Hampshire and Maine. The low price of wood more than compensated for the higher cost of colonial labor, enabling New England to produce ships at half the cost of London shipyards. Between 1674 and 1714, New Englanders built more than twelve hundred ships, totaling at least 75,000 tons. By 1700, Boston alone had fifteen shipyards, which produced more ships than the rest of the English colonies combined. Indeed, Boston ranked second only to London as a shipbuilding center in the empire.

Shipbuilding was a powerful engine of economic development and diversification. To construct a 150-ton merchant ship required up to two hundred workers, most of them skilled artisans. Shipyards also stimulated an array of associated enterprises: sawmills, sail lofts, smithies, iron foundries, ropewalks, barrel shops, and taverns. In addition, New England farmers benefited from feeding the artisans, victualing the ships, and providing the timber to build them.

Endowed with good ships and skilled mariners, New England merchants developed profitable and far-flung transatlantic trading networks of growing complexity. New English shippers insinuated their vessels throughout the shipping lanes of the empire, earning freight charges for goods neither produced nor consumed in New England. By 1700, Boston was the third city in the empire in shipping, lagging behind only London and Bristol. Economic historians estimate that the carrying trade was worth more to colonial New England than all of its own exported produce.

Although overseas trade certainly enriched a class of seaport merchants, the transatlantic commerce also attracted and benefited a broad array of small investors, primarily master mariners, shipwrights, and other skilled artisans. Boston's shipping register for 1697–1714 reveals that over a quarter of the town's adult males owned shares in at least one ship. In sum, New England shipping and shipbuilding generated powerful "linkages," in contrast to a plantation staple, which discouraged collateral diversification and development. Ironically, for want of a plantation staple like tobacco or sugar, New England avoided the trap of a plantation economy: the highly uneven distribution of skill and income as a labor-intensive crop polarized the population into large numbers of unskilled workers exploited by a smaller, wealthier elite.

Built more on human frugality, labor, and ingenuity than upon material abundance, New England's surprising economic success generated more envy than admiration elsewhere in the English empire. Too much like the old country in climate, resources, and people, New England did not perform the preferred colonial function of producing high-value, warm-climate agricultural staples for the homeland. During the 1670s an imperial official declared that Massachusetts was "one of the smallest and poorest tracts of land and produces least of any of the other colonies for exportation." Worse yet, New England conducted fisheries, the carrying trade, and shipbuilding, rendering the region a competitor rather than a complement to the economy of the mother country. English fishermen, merchants, and shipbuilders cried foul as they lost markets to the New English. Sir Josiah Child warned:

> Of all the American Plantations his Majesty has, none are so apt for the building of Shipping as New-England, nor none more comparably so qualified for the breeding of Seamen, not only by reason of the natural industry of that people, but principally by reason of their Cod and Mackeral Fisheries: and in my poor opinion, there is nothing more prejudicial, and in prospect more dangerous to any Mother-Kingdom, than the increase of Shipping in her Colonies, Plantations, or Provinces.

Seizing upon New England's reputation in the mother country as a den of Puritan heretics and hypocrites, English economic interests called for an end to New England's virtual autonomy within the empire.

BIBLE COMMONWEALTH

More than the colonists in any other region, the orthodox New English maintained that they had a divine mission to create a model society in America: a Bible Commonwealth dedicated to the proper worship of God and to the rules of a godly society. As Calvinists, the Puritans did not believe that publicly mandated good behavior would lead people to heaven, but they hoped that a moral society would abate God's wrath in this world, sparing New England from famines, epidemics, wars, and other collective afflictions.

The Puritans believed that God held them to far higher standards than other, less godly people, that they reaped precious benefits and bore extraordinary burdens in New England because they had entered into a close and particular contract, a "covenant," with God. As God's favored people, they considered themselves the heirs to the ancient Israelites of the Old Testament. If they honored his wishes, God would bestow health and abundance upon them in this world. But should they deviate from his will in any way, God would punish them as rebels—more severely than he chastised common pagans, like the Indians.

Consequently, any hardship or setback called for a collective reassessment, and much individual soul-searching, to determine how they had disappointed God. And hardships and setbacks were frequent in the hard business of making new farms and new towns in a frontier setting an ocean removed from the hearth of their civilization. Profoundly insecure throughout the seventeenth century, the Puritans recurrently tried to recover the protective purity that they imagined had characterized their founding moment.

Moreover, as God's stronghold, Puritan New England invited relentless attack from Satan, who meant to destroy the Bible Commonwealth. Embroiled in the cosmic struggle between God's will and Satan's wiles, New England was a pivotal battleground for the eternal fate of all mankind. Puritans did not doubt the ultimate power and eventual triumph of God, but they also knew that, to castigate unwary humans, God permitted Satan to wax powerful on earth in the short term. No distant abstraction, the battle raged in every act and event that affected human life. Consequently, the Puritan authorities felt compelled to punish or exile people who seemed bent on the devil's work of destroying New England: sinners, dissidents, and witches. Otherwise, God would withdraw his favor and permit Satan the temporary triumph of destroying New England.

Designed to please God, Puritan New England was a selective distillation from the more complex and conflicted culture of seventeenth-century England. The New English left behind many traditional customs and institutions that they believed offended God in England. By design, New England lacked church courts and tithes, bishops and archbishops, church weddings and ales, Sunday sports and maypoles, saint's days and Christmas. And except in rhetorical allegiance, there was no king. Rejecting much that was traditional to England, the Puritans promoted a Reformed culture that emphasized literacy and lay participation in governing congregations.

Puritans cherished direct access to holy and printed texts as fundamental to their liberty and identity as English and Protestant folk. They insisted that every individual should read the Bible, rather than rely exclusively upon a priesthood for sacred knowledge. Almost every New England town sustained a public grammar school, and most women and almost all men could read—which was not the case in the mother country or in any other colonial region. And book ownership, primarily of Bibles and religious tracts, was more widespread in New England than anywhere else in the world. The New English imported most of their books from London, but they also established a press, the first in English America, at Cambridge, Massachusetts, in 1640. Possessed of print and the ability to read it, the common people of New England were far from passive recipients of religious instruction. Instead, they were demanding participants, active in the Christian discourse of their culture—often challenging and criticizing their ministers.

New England Puritans also had far more regular access to preaching than did any other English colonists. In 1650, Massachusetts had one minister for every 415 persons, compared with one per 3,239 persons in Virginia. By law every town had to sustain a church, supported by taxes levied on all the householders, whether members or not. And law required all inhabitants to attend midweek religious "lectures" and Sunday services, both morning and afternoon, each about two hours long. Puritan worship featured the minister's learned and forceful sermon based on a particular text of scripture. The average New English churchgoer heard about seven thousand sermons in the course of his or her lifetime. To train an orthodox Puritan ministry for so many churches, Massachusetts founded Harvard College in 1636—the first such institution in English America (the Spanish had already established several universities in their colonies). At mid-century, Harvard graduates began to replace the founding generation of English-born ministers.

At first, the New English restricted full, formal church membership to the "visible saints": to those who could publicly and persuasively recount a New Birth experience, a personal journey from a despairing sense of utter worthlessness to joyous union with Christ. While everyone in the community had to attend church, only full members could receive the critical sacrament of communion. And only members who were both full and male could govern the church. In effect, the full members composed a smaller, elite church within the larger church of all who attended services in eventual (but often futile) hope of receiving divine grace. By insisting upon an exclusive church of grace, the New England Puritans broke with their more moderate and inclusive English counterparts, who defended the traditional parish structure that allowed all but the conspicuously sinful to receive membership and communion.

The New English soon discovered that they could not sustain such purity and exclusivity. During the first generation of New England colonization, full members were a strong majority of the adults, but they became a minority after 1650 as fewer people—especially fewer men—felt comfortable publicly relating their spiritual experiences. Thereafter, most New English adults were partial members who had received, as infants, the sacrament of baptism, but who were not yet sufficiently confident in their conversion to seek full membership.

The declining proportion of full members does not necessarily mean an ebbing of Puritan commitment in New England. On the contrary, the laity became inhibited by their more scrupulous standard for presenting themselves as truly saved. To the dismay of their ministers, devout laypeople set, and then could not meet, a dauntingly high standard for a dramatic conversion experience. All too well, ministers had taught their congregations to dread the perils of seeking membership without an assurance of grace. Lay Puritans dreaded the grim penalties of the Biblical warnings. "For he that eateth and drinketh unworthily, eateth and drinketh damnation to himself, not discerning the Lord's body" (I Corinthians 11:29). More scrupulous than its ministers, this devout laity contradicts the myth of a Puritan theocracy lording it over religiously indifferent common people.

By 1660 the declining proportion of full members threatened to restrict baptism to a minority of the infants, because churches customarily limited that sacrament to the offspring of full members. In 1662 the Massachusetts clergy proposed a compromise known as the Half-Way Covenant: the children of partial members could receive baptism. Although this was a modest reform favored by most of the clergy, the full members in many churches initially balked and voted down the Half-Way Covenant, dreading any compromise in purity. But that scrupulous opposition gradually declined, and by the end of the century the Half-Way Covenant prevailed. The remaining sticklers for the old purity bolted to join the Baptists, a Separatist denomination that rejected infant baptism in favor of adult baptism as an initiation to full membership.

The Puritans felt a compelling duty to employ government to punish sinners, lest the colonists provoke God by tolerating sin in their midst. Drawing upon the Old Testament as well as the English common law, the Puritan colonies criminalized immorality, including breaking the Sabbath, worshiping idols, blaspheming the name of God, and practicing magic. The most sensational cases involved male sex with animals. In 1642 the New Haven authorities suspected George Spencer of bestiality when a sow bore a piglet that carried his resemblance. He confessed and they hanged both Spencer and the unfortunate sow. New Haven also tried, convicted, and executed the unfortunately named Thomas Hogg for the same crime.

Although a strong majority in New England, the Puritans never entirely succeeded in keeping out interlopers who did not share their middling-sort faith and morality. In 1621, William Bradford of Plymouth confessed, "It is our calamity that we are, beyond expectation, yoked with some ill-conditioned people, who will never do good, but corrupt and abuse others." Most of the undisciplined came as sailors, fishermen, or indentured servants.

The Puritans were even more dismayed by people who publicly promoted an alternative form of Protestanism. The Puritans emigrated to New England to realize their own ideal of a uniform society—and certainly not to champion religious toleration and pluralism. A leading New Englander denounced "the lawlessnesse of liberty of conscience" as an invitation to heresy and anarchy, and ultimately to divine anger and punishment. No Catholics, Anglicans, Baptists, or Quakers need come to New England (except to exceptional Rhode Island). All dissenters were given, in the words of one Massachusetts Puritan, "free Liberty to keep away from us." In Connecticut and Massachusetts, the Puritans prosecuted, tried, convicted, and exiled religious dissenters. Exiles who returned risked execution—the fate of four Quakers in Massachusetts between 1659 and 1661. The Massachusetts authorities also followed English precedent and established a board of censors to ensure that only orthodox Puritanism appeared in local print. And they ordered the destruction of Quaker tracts brought into the colony.

But the greatest disputes and discontent derived from within the Puritan ranks, as they struggled to balance consensus with their intense pursuit of perfection. Without bishops and crown to struggle against, Puritans quickly discovered their many disagreements. Puritans agreed that the Bible was fundamental to their social order and that every individual must seek its sacred truths, but, differing in their interpretations, they argued over the proper shape and policies of a Bible Commonwealth. Determined men and women who had suffered so much for their faith, the New English did not easily compromise their powerful convictions. Given the cosmic stakes that they invested in their colony, leading Puritans feared that compromise would sacrifice their souls and their commonwealth to divine wrath.

During the early 1630s the Salem minister Roger Williams sorely provoked the Massachusetts authorities by insisting that they had not gone far enough in separating themselves from the Church of England and the king. To evade arrest and deportation back to England, Williams fled southward with his followers to found Providence, the first settlement in what became Rhode Island.

Later in the 1630s the charismatic Anne Hutchinson sparked an even more serious and divisive controversy in Massachusetts. Claiming the powers of prophecy, Hutchinson led prayer meetings in her Boston home, attracting hundreds of followers. She suggested that most of the ministers and magistrates of the colony were godless hypocrites dangerous to the souls of their congregants and the survival of the colony. A Puritan minister described Hutchinson as "a woman of haughty and fierce carriage, of a nimble wit, and active spirit and a very voluble tongue, more bold than a man." Considering Hutchinson a threat to social order and especially to the subordination of women to men, Winthrop and his council rebuked her, "You have stepped out of your place, you have rather been a husband than a wife, and a preacher than a hearer, and a magistrate than a subject."

In 1637 the leaders of Massachusetts expelled Hutchinson, and she took refuge, with some of her followers, in Rhode Island, which orthodox Puritans considered a den of radical heretics. By drawing dissidents out of Massachusetts and Connecticut, the Rhode Island settlements helped to maintain orthodoxy in the two major Puritan colonies. Although the orthodox leaders of Massachusetts and Connecticut despised Rhode Island, they benefited from it as a safety valve for discontents who would otherwise fester in their midst. The theological diversity of Rhode Island led the colonists there to adopt a policy of religious toleration that was unique in the English world and that attracted Baptists, Quakers, and even Jews. The Rhode Islanders also sought a separation of state and church from a conviction that any mingling corrupted religion.

The leaders of Massachusetts dreaded that the criticism of dissidents would ruin the colony's reputation at home in England. News of such suppression, however, played into the hands of English critics who denounced New England as a land of religious hypocrites, seditious Separatists, and petty despots. In 1652 an English Puritan cautioned his colonial friends, "It doth not a little grieve my spirit to hear what sad things are reported daily of your tyranny and persecutions in New England. . . . These rigid ways have laid you very low in the hearts of the saints, while the enemies of the lord were gloating." Such criticism from English Puritans surprised and dismayed the New English. Indeed, at mid-century a strain developed in the transatlantic relationship as the English Puritans began to favor religious toleration for all Protestants.

In addition to fearing worldly sinners and religious dissidents, the orthodox New English periodically felt imperiled by Satan's most direct recruits: witches. A rebellious and fallen angel, Satan recruited humans to sign their names in blood in his book. The signers obtained magical power to harm and kill, in return for their eternal souls. Whenever cattle and children sickened and died, the New English suspected that some in their midst practiced satanic magic. For the safety of the community, witches had to be identified, prosecuted, and neutralized. The authorities pardoned witches who confessed and testified against others, but persistent denial consigned the convicted witch to public execution by hanging. Contrary to popular myth and previous European practice, the New English did not burn witches at the stake.

Like all seventeenth-century peoples, the New England Puritans did not dwell in the disenchanted universe of pure reason. Instead, they regularly saw and heard wondrous signs of God's purpose or the devil's menace. These included strange lights in the sky, prophetic dreams, multiple suns, eclipses, comets, deformed births (of humans or livestock), speaking infants, poltergeists, unseen and portentous voices, eerie coincidences, apparitions of warring armies or ships in the sky, and cases of blasphemers and Sabbath-breakers suddenly struck dead. Given God's omnipotence and Satan's malignity, all such "remarkable providences" seemed pregnant with a divine meaning that the godly struggled to decipher.

A belief in magic and witches made perfect sense to a premodern people who felt vulnerable to an unpredictable and often deadly natural world beyond their control. Seventeenth-century life was rife with sudden fires, floods, windstorms, droughts, crop blights, and livestock diseases. And although New England was remarkably healthy compared with the rest of the English-speaking world, the advantage was only relative. Especially after 1650, New Englanders experienced periodic epidemics of measles, influenza, and smallpox that proved especially fatal to children. These unpredictable afflictions called out for explanation, some attribution of cause, that might protect people from further suffering, or at least console them with resignation to God's will. No Puritan wished to believe that misfortune was purely random and without supernatural meaning, for that would confirm their helplessness and isolation in a world without God.

Witchcraft was also plausible because some colonists did dabble in the occult to tell fortunes and to cure, or inflict, ills (but there is little reason to believe that such "cunning folk" worshiped Satan). Moreover, occult beliefs are self-fulfilling. Anthropologists have repeatedly found that people who think themselves bewitched become distracted with fear, vulnerable to accident, and prone to wasting and deadly illness. In seventeenth-century New

England a local reputation as a magical adept could secure some wary circumspection from neighbors—and perhaps earn a few pence to help find lost property, to predict the future, or to counteract the spell of another practitioner. But pity the occultist who antagonized local consensus, including minister and magistrate.

The supposed victims of malign magic blamed particular neighbors who seemed to bear them ill will. The accused tended to be aggressive and contentious individuals—particularly poorer folk who acted with an assertion deemed beyond their proper station and who seemed to know too much about the occult. Communities and authorities disproportionately detected witchcraft in women who seemed angry and abrasive, violating the cultural norm celebrating female modesty. Women constituted both the majority of the accusers and 80 percent of the accused. While attesting that the words of women had power in Puritan communities, their disproportionate prosecution also demonstrated the considerable unease generated by that power.

An escalation of local gossip and grudges into formal and deadly action occurred only in the most troubled communities at especially difficult moments. Rather than rush to judgment, the authorities scrupulously followed legal procedures in gathering evidence and hearing witnesses. Because it was no easy matter to prove witchcraft, juries usually found innocence. The New English prosecuted ninety-three witches but executed only sixteen—until 1692, when a peculiar mania at Salem dramatically inflated the numbers.

Puritan New England, however, was certainly more anxious about witches than the other English colonies, which hosted very few trials and probably no executions. For example, Virginia tried only nine cases, convicting but one suspect, and sentencing him to whipping and banishment. The number of witch trials and executions in New England was about on a par with the pace previously set in the mother country during the late sixteenth and early seventeenth centuries. New England's chief distinction was that the Puritans continued to prosecute and execute witches after 1650, when such proceedings virtually stopped in old England. Puritanism kept New England behind the times in supernatural belief.

The most spectacular and exceptional cluster of accusations, trials, and executions occurred in and around Salem, in Essex County, Massachusetts, in 1692, when several girls and young women accused hundreds. Salem was an especially troubled town, bitterly divided between the rural Salem Village (now Danvers) and the more commercialized seaport of Salem Town. At first the accusers were girls and young women who dwelled in the village and primarily accused mature women who lived near or in the town. The legal authorities tried, convicted, and hanged eighteen suspected witches. A nineteenth—an older man—was crushed to death with heavy stones for refusing to plea in court.

Widespread anxiety, particularly over a new war with the Indians, spread the accusations and arrests into the rest of Essex County and implicated far more than the usual poor and female suspects. When the accusations targeted members of prestigious families, including the governor's wife, the legal authorities suppressed further trials in the fall of 1692. Reassessed as a fiasco, the Salem mania became a spectacular flameout that halted the prosecution of witches in New England. Witchcraft beliefs persisted among rustic people well into the nineteenth century. But the common believers could no longer enlist the support of their ministers and magistrates, who felt chastened by the debacle at Salem.

DECLENSION?

New England ultimately failed as a "City upon a Hill," because the intended audience, the English, failed to pay attention. To most people at home, the Puritan experiment seemed at best strange and at worst seditious. New England appeared especially irrelevant after the triumphant restoration of the monarchy in 1660. The Restoration terminated and discredited the short-lived revolutionary regime led by English Puritans during the 1640s and 1650s. After the Restoration, English Puritans dwindled in number, prominence, and ambition. Most of the persistent made their peace with life as a quiet minority within an Anglican society. They dismissed New England as a distant and parochial backwater. In 1683 an English correspondent confessed to Cotton Mather, "I have often heard of New England, and long ago, but never took no great heed to it, only as persons do often discourse of things remote and at random."

New England Puritans blamed themselves for failing to inspire the mother country. During the later seventeenth century the New England clergy specialized in a genre of sermon known as the "jeremiad," named after the grim Old Testament prophet Jeremiah. A jeremiad catalogued the sufferings and sins of New England: the prevalence of Indian war, earthquakes, fires, and storms sent to punish a region wallowing in immorality and irreligion. Finding the present generation wanting, a jeremiad exhorted listeners to reclaim the lofty standards and pure morality ascribed to the founders of New England. Paradoxically, the popularity of the genre attested to the persistence, rather than the decline, of Puritan ideals in New England. Determined to live better, the laity longed for the cathartic castigation of the jeremiad. And the ministry complied with eloquence and zeal. But English Puritans often took the jeremiads at face value, confirming their unduly low estimation of New England.

In this literalism, those readers anticipated historians who reiterate the myth of a New England "declension" during the late seventeenth century. In fact, the overstated disappointment of the jeremiad was defined against an unrealistic and utopian depiction of the founders. The founding generation was, of course, far less perfect and united than it appeared in the mythic memory of the later generations. Naturally and necessarily, the orthodox New English culture and society *evolved* over the seventeenth century and into the eighteenth, but the core principles persisted, especially the commitment to a moral, educated, commercial, and homogeneous people. The formula of the jeremiad masked the prodigious long-term accomplishments of the New England colonists in substantiating their faith in dozens of churches, each with a college-educated minister committed to Puritan ideals. The expensive construction and maintenance of so many churches and the long education of so many ministers—a commitment unmatched anywhere else in the English colonies—attested that the New English continued to yoke their economic achievements to their public faith. That the late-seventeenth-century New Englanders refused to take comfort or find reassurance in those accomplishments manifests how thoroughly Puritan they remained.

The myth of declension also obscures the prodigious and enduring Puritan legacy for English-speaking America. Compared with other colonial regions, New England was a land of relative equality, broad (albeit moderate) opportunity, and thrifty, industrious, and entrepreneurial habits that sustained an especially diverse and complex economy. The region's large, healthy families, nearly even gender ratio, and long life spans promoted social stability, the steady accumulation of family property, and its orderly transfer from one generation to the next. And nowhere else in colonial America did colonists enjoy readier access to public worship and nearly universal education. That those ideals remain powerful in our own culture attests to the enduring importance of the Puritan legacy. But those accomplishments also had a dark side, especially the intolerance for dissenters and suspected witches. And, as the next chapter will argue, the pursuit of Puritan ideals and Puritan prosperity depended upon dispossessing the Indians and transforming their land.

9

Puritans and Indians

1600–1700

The destruction of the Pequot village on the Mystic River in 1637 by the New English (armed with guns in the inner circle of the attackers) and their Mohegan and Narraganset allies (shooting their bows in the outer circle). From John Underhill, Newes from America *(London, 1638).*

INSTEAD OF VIEWING the precolonial landscape as beautiful, the leading Puritans perceived, in William Bradford's phrase, "a hideous and desolate wilderness full of wild beasts and wild men." The New English saw the Indians as their opposite—as pagan peoples who had surrendered to their worst instincts to live within the wild, instead of laboring hard to conquer and transcend nature. Suspecting that the wilderness was seductive as well as evil, Puritan leaders also feared that their own people would degenerate into Indians from prolonged contact with native ways and the native land. In search of larger farms on the best land, colonists dispersed, sometimes living far from the oversight of ministers and magistrates. In 1632, Governor William Bradford of Plymouth complained that "no man now thought he could live except he had cattle and a great deal of ground to keep them." In 1679 the Boston synod of ministers denounced frontier settlers who succumbed to "an insatiable desire after Land and worldly Accommodations, yea, so as to forsake Churches and Ordinances, and to live like Heathen, only that so they might have Elbow-room enough in the world."

A proponent of Puritan emigration had predicted that in New England, "religion and profit [would] jump together." But as the colonists spread over the land to make farms, Puritan leaders worried that profit and religion were jumping apart. Economic interest encouraged colonists to spread out, to acquire large and dispersed farms. But this contradicted their religious desire to live in tight communities of near neighbors, watching over one another's morals and meeting frequently for worship.

In two ways, the New English labored to reassure themselves that they remained civilized Christians and resisted the temptations of an Indian life: by changing the land and by converting the Indians. The colonists diligently reworked the landscape to resemble England, which they regarded as God's blueprint for a proper nature "improved" by human labor. They cleared and fenced fields for cultivation in the English fashion; built English-style fences, houses, barns, mills, and churches; and exterminated wild animals, especially the wolves and bears that preyed on livestock. The Puritans also worked to subdue, convert, and transform the Indians into replicas of English Christians. In sum, both to benefit and to reassure themselves, the New English worked to dominate the external world of the forest, its wild animals, and its Indians.

NATIVES

The southern New England Indians possessed cultural, and especially linguistic, affinities, but lacked political unity. The natives spoke related Algonquian languages, similar to those of the Virginia Indians, but they certainly had nothing like the paramount chiefdom of Powhatan. Their many "tribes" were primarily linguistic and ethnic groups. In southeastern New England the leading tribes were the Mohegan and Pequot of Connecticut, the Narragansett of Rhode Island, the Patuxet and Wampanoag of the Plymouth colony, and the Nipmuck, Massachusett, and Pennacook of the Massachusetts Bay colony. The tribes were subdivided into many local bands, each consisting of a few hundred people sharing a settled village for part of the year and a common hunting and gathering territory for the rest. These bands were porous, because extensive kin connections reached, through marriage, into adjoining groups. Discontented individuals or families could depart one band to find entrance, through their relatives, into another.

Each band had a leading sachem, assisted by a council of lesser sachems, shamans, and especially prestigious warriors. In consultation with his council, the chief sachem assigned cornfields, mediated disputes, and supervised trade, diplomacy, and war with outsiders. Bands and their sachems competed by waging wars meant to humiliate the defeated into paying a tribute in deerskins and wampum: strings and belts of white and purple beads made from seashells and highly coveted as symbols of spiritual power and political authority. Although chronic, these conflicts were brief and limited, producing a few casualties and captives rather than the destruction of an entire band. The sachem obtained his status and position by inheritance in the male line within a privileged family, but he could be set aside if he lost the respect of his band. Dependent upon consensus and consent, the sachem built his influence on persuasion, example, and generous gift-giving rather than on coercion.

The natives' highly productive horticulture supplied most of their diet and belied the English insistence that all Indians were nothing more than hunters. An Indian field consisted of many small hillocks with maize in the center and squashes, pumpkins, and beans tumbling down the sides. The mix of plants did not seem like proper agriculture to the English, who segregated their various crops in distinct fields. In fact, Indian cultivation was more efficient, producing substantial yields from relatively small amounts of land and labor. The squashes and pumpkins spread out along the ground, discouraging the appearance of weeds between the maize plants and preserving moisture by shielding the earth from the sun. The interwoven roots strengthened the plants against the winds, and the cornstalks provided convenient poles for the climbing bean vines. In return, beans drew nitrogen from the air for fixing in the soil, partially compensating for the maize, which was nitrogen-depleting. The combination of plants also provided a balanced diet, because the beans offered protein and an amino acid, lysine, that when eaten with corn releases the corn's protein.

To facilitate their hunting and gathering, the Indians also set fire to the forest beyond their fields. The aboriginal fires were less intense and destructive than the American forest fires of the present day. Because our own society suppresses fire, contemporary forests accumulate, over the years, large quantities of deadwood and dry brush. When a fire does ignite and escapes control, it is explosive, spreading rapidly and destructively up into the forest canopy to consume mature trees. The seventeenth-century Indians managed more modest fires. Because their fires were kindled twice a year, in both spring and fall, they found only the limited amount of deadwood and brush that had accumulated in the interim. Such fires spared the tall and thick mature trees with a dense bark, shaping a relatively open forest of many large trees and few small ones. Noting the effect, if not always the cause, colonists marveled at their ability to ride freely between immense trees through long stretches of the forest.

With fire the Indians shaped and sustained a forest that suited their needs. Regular burning favored large hardwoods, many of which yielded edible nuts. The relatively open forest also made it easier for hunters to see and pursue game. The regular burning diminished mice, fleas, and parasites that troubled people or the game that they ate. The fires also fertilized the forest floor and opened patches of sunlight. Both effects promoted ground-hugging plants, especially grasses and berries, which sustained a larger deer herd, to the ultimate benefit of their human hunters.

As in Virginia and Iroquoia, the Algonquian division of labor ran along gender rather than class lines. Each gender considered it shameful to take on the activities assigned by culture to the other. Men assumed the tasks that involved travel away from the village or encampment: hunting, fishing, warfare, and making their tools and weapons, including bows, arrows, spears, nets, snowshoes, and canoes. Men's work alternated between bursts of intense exertion, especially in fall and winter hunting, and periods of relative ease, particularly in summer. Women assumed the work compatible with the supervision and care of young children: repetitive tasks that usually kept them in or near villages and hunting camps. In contrast to the sharp polarities of male exertion and ease, women worked more steadily through the day and the year. They built and maintained their homes, known as wigwams. These were oval frames, ten to sixteen feet in diameter, made of saplings and covered with bark sheets or woven nuts. The covering left a smoke hole at the top over the central hearth. From bulrush, women wove baskets, to store food and tools, and mats, for sleeping and to cover the wigwams. They gathered firewood, tended the fires, butchered and stored the animals and fish that the men brought in, and prepared meals. Women and children also did most of the gathering of shellfish, berries, roots, and herbs.

In contrast to the colonists, who assigned most outside farmwork to men, Indian women planted, weeded, tended, and harvested the crops. Because the sight of women laboring in the fields struck the colonists as strange, they depicted native women as drudges. Because colonists ordinarily saw Indian men at their leisure in their villages in the warm months, the colonists dismissed them as lazy exploiters of their hardworking women. In fact, the labor of Indian women, although certainly considerable, was less time-consuming and exhausting than the chores of colonial women, who tended larger and more complex houses. Indian women also took pleasure in their practice of working the fields cooperatively in festive groups.

As a consequence of their mobile way of life, Indians acquired few material possessions, and they shared what they had. They owned only what they could readily carry through their annual cycle of shifting encampments: some clothing and their wooden and stone tools. Their culture also cherished leisure and generosity more than the laborious accumulation of individual property for display. Honor and influence accrued to chiefs who gave away food and deerskins rather than to those who hoarded all that they could acquire. Chiefs also bore the burden of generously entertaining official visitors, both Indian and colonial. Because hospitality and generosity were fundamental duties, violators reaped shame and ridicule. No one went hungry in an Indian village unless all starved. With so little to steal and so little need to, theft was virtually unknown and no one locked a wigwam. Here too they contrasted sharply with the English, who felt besieged by theft and took elaborate precautions to protect their property and to punish thieves. But because Indians accumulated only small caches of maize and beans, they periodically suffered from hunger, especially in the spring.

In contrast to the Indians' seasonal mobility and limited possessions, the New English lived and worked on fixed and substantial properties, primarily frame houses and barns set amid fenced fields grazed by privately owned animals. The Indians regarded most colonists as mean and stingy, enslaved by their property and their longings for more. Roger Williams conceded, "It is a strange truth, that a man shall generally finde more free entertainment and refreshing amongst these Barbarians, than amongst thousands that call themselves Christians."

Compared with the colonists, the Indians demanded less from their nature, investing less labor in, and extracting less energy and matter from, their environment. The Algonquians possessed neither the market institutions nor the mentality of capitalism. There was no market in labor, for Indians did not hire one another to work for wages. Nor did they have the concept of "capital"—much less a market for exchanging it. The Algonquians also did not own particular parcels of land as exclusive, perpetual, and private property. Instead, the sachems annually assigned garden plots and hunting territories to particular families or clans, depending upon their numbers, needs, and abilities. Indians preserved most of their domain as a commons for hunting and gathering, but responded violently to intruding hunters from any rival tribe. Because land was not a commodity for them, the Indians neither bought nor sold portions of their domain—until induced or compelled to it by colonists.

PROPERTY

Coming from a more crowded, competitive, and capitalist land where about half the population lacked sufficient food, shelter, and clothing, the colonists marveled at the apparent abundance of nature, the vast numbers of fish, birds, trees, and deer. Comparing New England with deforested and over-hunted England, a colonist marveled, "A poor servant here that is to possess but 50 acres of land, may afford to give more wood for timber and fire as good as the world yields, than many noble men in England can afford to do." In English society, men got high status by accumulating property through market transactions, rather than by redistributing property as did the Indian chiefs. In the wild plants and animals of New England, the colonists saw potential commodities as particular items that could be harvested, processed, shipped, and sold to make a profit. Consequently, the New English disdained the Indians as "Lazy Drones [who] love Idleness Exceedingly" for failing to create more property from their abundant nature. Indeed, ignoring the Indians' horticulture, the colonists dismissed the Indians as little better than wild animals who made no changes in their environment. A Puritan minister commented, "Their land is spacious and void, and they are few and do but run over the grass, as do also the foxes and wild beasts."

Puritans insisted that the Christian God meant for them to enjoy the land, in reward for their godly industry and to punish the Indians for their pagan indolence. John Winthrop explained, "As for the Natives in New England, they inclose noe Land, neither have any setled habytation, nor any tame Cattle to improve the Land by, and soe have noe other but a Naturall Right to those Countries, soe as if we leave them sufficient for their use, we may lawfully take the rest." The colonists appointed themselves to judge how much land the Indians needed, which shrank with every passing year. The resolves of the town of Milford in Connecticut in 1640 were especially blunt: "Voted that the earth is the Lord's and the fulness thereof; voted, that the earth is given to the Saints; voted, we are the Saints."

Nonetheless, to perfect their land titles, the leading colonists usually tried to buy tracts of the Indians' land, offering trade goods in return for their marks on paper documents called deeds. The New English and the Indians did not understand the deeds in the same way, for the natives did not share the European notion of private property. The colonists maintained that by signing deeds, the Indians gave up every right to the land and had to move out, in favor of the purchasers, who obtained exclusive possession. The Indians, however, regarded their deed as an offer to share the land with the colonists. The natives expected to persist in hunting and fishing where they wished as they pursued their annual cycle of mobility. Consequently, the Indians were surprised and offended when colonists abused or arrested natives as trespassers. When the Indians lashed out against this treatment, the colonists saw themselves as unoffending victims obliged to protect themselves against dangerous brutes who could not keep their bargains.

The Indians were also astonished that the colonists so rapidly cleared the forest. With steel axes, the colonists attacked the trees, making pastures for livestock and fields for grain. The colonists needed much more cleared land primarily because they kept domesticated cattle, pigs, and sheep, in contrast to the Indians, who relied on wild fish and game for their meat. Colonists also cultivated larger fields of grain to yield a surplus for export to the West Indies, unlike Indians, who raised only what they needed to eat. And the colonists deforested land to obtain lumber and timber for their buildings, fences, and ships. Instead of semipermanent villages shifting with the seasons, the colonists constructed larger and more permanent wooden structures: barns, homes, sheds, churches, stores, taverns, and workshops. Property lines subdivided the landscape into thousands of privately held farms that could be bought and sold.

As the colonists made the land more familiar and profitable to themselves, they rendered it more alien and hostile to the Indians. By clearing the forest, the colonists steadily eliminated the habitat for the wild animals and plants critical to the Indians' diet and clothing. The settlers also introduced pigs and cattle that ranged far and wide, beyond settler properties, into the forest and the Indian cornfields. In 1642 the Narragansett chief Miantonomi complained:

> You know our fathers had plenty of deer . . . and our coves [were] full of fish and fowl. But these English have gotten our land, they with scythes cut down the grass, and with axes fell the trees; their cows and horses eat the grass, and their hogs spoil our clam banks, and we shall be starved.

When Indians reacted by killing and eating the offending livestock, the colonists demanded that the culprits stand trial in their courts for theft. Insistent on their own property rights in animals, the New English were indifferent to the Indians' property rights in their growing corn.

TRIBUTE

In the early seventeenth century, the arrival of colonial goods, diseases, and people shook up the power relations between rival Indian groups. Welcoming opportunities to trade, the Indians competed to co-opt the newcomers to acquire and employ their power against native enemies. For example, during the early 1620s the Wampanoag Indians hoped to incorporate the Plymouth colonists into a mutually beneficial network of exchange and alliance.

To the surprise and dismay of the Wampanoag, as the Plymouth colonists grew in number and strength, they expanded their settlements and openly treated the Indians as inferiors. Rejecting the Wampanoag interpretation of reciprocity, the Pilgrims regarded their treaty as Indian submission to English dominion. Contrary to the first Thanksgiving myth of mutual trust, the Plymouth colonists regarded the Indians as, in Bradford's words, "savage people, who are cruel, barbarous, and most treacherous." Especially after they learned of the great Indian uprising of 1622 in Virginia, the Plymouth colonists concluded that their own survival depended upon violence and treachery against the Indians. In 1623 the Plymouth colonists made a grim example of a band of Massachusetts Indians, their neighbors to the north. On flimsy grounds, the colonists charged the band with plotting an attack. Feigning friendship, they lured their victims into a trap, killing seven, including a sachem. The colonists displayed his head atop their fort at Plymouth as a warning to other Indians.

During the 1630s, the Great Migration augmented colonial strength by establishing the populous and powerful Massachusetts colony. In alliance, Massachusetts and Plymouth openly bullied the various Indian bands, demanding their formal submission and the payment of a tribute in wampum. That tribute partially solved a major economic problem confronting the early New English. They needed a commodity for export to England to recoup their heavy debts for transportation and supplies. Although wampum had little or no value in England, it was coveted by the Abenaki Indians of Maine, who lived beyond ready access to the cherished seashells of Long Island Sound that could be made into wampum. In return, the Abenaki offered beaver pelts, which were more abundant in northern than in southern New England. The colonists extorted wampum from the southern New England Indians and then shipped it to Maine to procure furs for shipment to England. In great and growing English demand, the furs helped finance the New English debts.

In effect, the Puritan colonies ran a protection racket that compelled native bands to purchase peace with wampum. The colonists also collected wampum as court fines levied upon individual Indians convicted by colonial courts of crimes such as killing pigs that had broken into native crops. Between 1634 and 1664 the New English extorted more than 21,000 fathoms of Indian wampum (nearly seven million beads), worth between £5,000 and £10,000 once converted to furs. This racket financed the steady expansion of the settlements that dispossessed the natives of their lands.

PEQUOT WAR

The first major conflict between the New English and the Indians erupted in 1636. Determined to extend their authority into the Mystic River Valley of southeastern Connecticut, the colonial leaders demanded that the resident

Pequot pay a heavy tribute in wampum, give up several of their children as hostages, and surrender suspects accused of killing a trader. Rebuffed, the Connecticut, Plymouth, and Massachusetts colonies declared war and pressured the Narragansett and Mohegan peoples to help fight the Pequot. The Narragansett and Mohegan consented, in part from long rivalry with the Pequot and in part from a preference for joining the side likely to win. As their reward, the Indian allies meant to strengthen their numbers with Pequot prisoners.

In May 1637, Narragansett and Mohegan warriors guided the Puritan forces deep into the Pequot territory to surprise a palisaded village beside the Mystic River. The village contained about seventy wigwams and four hundred inhabitants, mostly women, children, and old men. Commanded by Captain John Mason and Captain John Underhill, the New English and their Indian allies surrounded the sleeping village and set it ablaze shortly before dawn. The Pequot died either in the flames or in flight from the inferno as they ran into the gunfire and onto the swords of their enemies. Captain Mason exulted, "God was above them, who laughed his Enemies and the Enemies of his People to Scorn, making them as a fiery Oven . . . [and] filling the Place with Dead Bodies!" Only about five inhabitants survived by breaking through the surrounding circle of their enemies.

The indiscriminate slaughter contradicted Indian custom and shocked the Narragansett and Mohegan allies, who had expected to capture and adopt the women and children. They bitterly complained that the New English mode of war was "too furious and slays too many people." A veteran of warfare in Europe, Captain Underhill dismissed the more limited Indian mode of war as "more for pastime than to conquer and subdue enemies." He sarcastically noted that "they might fight for seven years and not kill seven men." If so, on a single day, Underhill helped to destroy the equivalent of nearly four hundred years of Indian warfare.

Many Puritans in England also criticized the New English for overkill. Feeling defensive, leading colonists insisted that they had done God's bidding. Captain Underhill conceded, "It may be demanded, Why should you be so furious? (as some have said). Should not Christians have more mercy and compassion?" But he retorted, "Sometimes the Scripture declareth [that] women and children must perish with their parents. . . . We had sufficient light from the Word of God for our proceedings." Similarly, Governor William Bradford recalled:

> It was a fearful sight to see them thus frying in the fire and the streams of blood quenching the same, and horrible was the stink and scent thereof, but the victory seemed a sweet sacrifice, and they gave the praise thereof to God, who had wrought so wonderfully for them, thus to enclose their enemies in their hands and given them so speedy a victory over so proud and insulting an enemy.

Regarding war as a test of their godliness, the Puritans interpreted their especially bloody victory as compelling proof that God had found them worthy.

During the rest of 1637, mop-up expeditions killed or captured most of the remaining Pequot. The victors executed some captives and enslaved others for their own use or for profitable sale in the West Indies. But they bartered most of their captives—principally women and children—to their native allies in return for wampum. Only about half of the three thousand prewar Pequot survived the war, almost all as subjects of the Mohegan or Narragansett. The colonial leaders formally declared the Pequot nation dissolved. A generation later, however, the colonial leaders decided to weaken the Narragansett by encouraging the Pequot to secede and reconstitute themselves on part of their former homeland, but in strict subordination to Connecticut. In the next big war, in 1675–76, the Pequot helped the colonists to attack the Narragansett.

Lacking a collective identity as "Indians," the natives continued to think of themselves as members of particular bands and tribes—which rendered them all vulnerable to colonial manipulation and domination. Despite the colonists' many contentions over lands, boundaries, and theology, the New English fundamentally considered themselves a common people sharply distinguished from all Indians. When push came to shove, colonists usually set aside their squabbles to unite in war against Indians. Noting the power of colonial solidarity, in 1642 the Narragansett sachem Miantonomi urged a radical new idea: a common Indian identity in union against the invaders. He argued, "For so are we all Indians as the English are, and say brother to one another, so must we be one as they are, otherwise we shall all be gone shortly."

But Miantonomi's Pan-Indian proposal foundered against the short-term interest of rival sachems who curried favor with the powerful New English. In particular, the opportunistic Mohegan sachem Uncas built the power of his relatively small band by assisting the colonists. When the Puritans first settled in the Connecticut Valley, the Mohegan were paying tribute to the Pequot. To secure Mohegan independence, Uncas helped the colonists to smash the Pequot in 1637. In 1640, Uncas formally submitted his territory and people to Connecticut, affording that colony a legal basis for claiming independence from Massachusetts. The grateful rulers of Connecticut bestowed further presents upon Uncas, treating him as their honored viceroy responsible for controlling the other, weaker Indian bands within their boundaries. Favored by Connecticut, Uncas had no desire to help the Narragansett fight his colonial patrons.

In 1643, Uncas seized Miantonomi and surrendered him to the Connecticut authorities. Wishing him dead but washing their hands of his blood, the Puritans returned Miantonomi to Uncas for execution, piously instructing that "in the manner of his death all mercy and moderation be shewed."

Watched by Puritan deputies, Uncas's brother buried his hatchet in Miantonomi's skull. His death confirmed the long odds facing Indian visionaries who sought to transcend traditional enmities in favor of a new union against the newcomers.

Unable to unite, the various Indian bands became shrinking minorities in a land dominated by the rapidly growing colonial population. In 1670 the 52,000 New England colonists outnumbered the Indians of southern New England by nearly three to one. Many Indian bands divided over how best to deal with the powerful and demanding colonists. Should they fight to remain autonomous Indians or accept subordination as wards of the New English? Did safety lie in resistance or submission?

PRAYING TOWNS

During the 1620s and 1630s, the Puritan settlers did little to missionize the Indians, focusing instead on expanding their towns and farms. By letter from England, the Reverend John Robinson rebuked his former parishioners in the Plymouth colony for "the killing of those poor Indians. . . . Oh, how happy a thing it had been, if you had converted some before you had killed any!" He added, "It is . . . a thing more glorious, in men's eyes, than pleasing in God's, or convenient for Christmas, to be a terror to poor barbarous people."

Stung by rebukes from their godly friends at home, especially over the Pequot slaughter, some of the New English belatedly turned their attention to evangelizing the Indians. Beginning in the late 1640s, the Reverend John Eliot took the lead, often over the opposition of his fellow colonists, who preferred simply to sweep the Indians away. The missionaries sincerely wished to rescue Indians' lives from the colonists as well as to save their souls from hell, but the missionary effort demanded that Indians surrender their own culture as the price of physical survival. Because the English could not conceive of permitting the Indians to remain independent and culturally autonomous peoples, they had to convert or die.

Like the Franciscans of New Spain, the Puritan missionaries of New England believed that the first and essential step was to oblige the mobile Indians to settle down in permanent and delimited communities. John Eliot warned the Indians that they were doomed if they remained in "so unfixed, confused, and ungoverned a life, uncivilized and unsubdued to labor and order." In permanent, compact "praying towns" the Indians could be kept under closer surveillance and under more constant pressure to change their behavior and appearance. In praying towns they could also be removed from friends and relatives who refused to change their traditional ways. And, not incidentally, restricting Indians to fixed towns freed up additional lands for colonial settlements. Because the other New England colonies showed little or no interest in the missionary program, the praying towns were largely confined to Massachusetts, which hosted fourteen, with sixteen hundred inhabitants at their peak in 1674. Although less impressive than the Spanish Franciscan or French Jesuit missions, the Puritan praying towns at least improved upon the negligible effort in the Chesapeake.

The Puritan missionaries sought from the Indians a thorough conversion, manifest in virtually every behavior. They had to abandon their Algonquian names and take new English names, and they had to give up wearing body grease, playing traditional sports, and killing lice with their teeth. The missionaries compelled Indian men to cut their hair very short, in the Puritan fashion, for the New English regarded long hair as a sign of pride and vanity, sins they were quicker to detect in others than in themselves. Short hair and English attire also set the praying Indians apart from their traditionalist brethren.

Above all, the missionaries exhorted the Indians to adopt the Puritan pace and mode of work, which meant long days of agricultural labor. Insisting upon the gendered division of labor favored by the English, the missionaries urged the Indian men to forsake hunting and fishing in favor of farming. The Indian women were supposed to withdraw from the cornfields to tend the home and to spin and weave cloth, just as New English women did. Obliged to work hard six days a week, the praying Indians had to rest and worship on the seventh day, the Sabbath.

Praying towns did not appeal to those Indians who belonged to the largest and most autonomous bands, principally the Narragansett, Mohegan, and Wampanoag. Although the Wampanoag sachem Massasoit and the Mohegan sachem Uncas both cooperated in politics with the colonists, they forcefully rejected missionaries as a threat to their authority. Comfortable in their own culture, most Indians balked at converting to English ways and beliefs. One native pointedly asked why his people should convert when "our corn is as good as yours, and we take more pleasure than you." A colonist conceded that autonomous Indians avoided the praying towns because "they can live with less labour, and more pleasure and plenty, as Indians, than they can with us."

But the praying towns did appeal to small and weak bands, like the Massachusett, Nipmuck, and Pennacook, which had been especially devastated by the colonial invasion. Diminished by disease, environmental disruption, and the settler intrusion, they hoped to find in Christianity a way to make sense of their recent catastrophes. They worked to stabilize their world by seeking new supernatural guides superior to their shamans, who had failed to stem the epidemics, cattle, and settlers. In the impressive technology and apparent disease immunities of the English, these Indians detected a superior form of supernatural power that they desperately hoped to tap for their own use, seeking in the new faith a capacity to recover their numbers and power.

The weak bands saw the praying towns as their last hope for preserving their group identity on a part of their homeland. Natives worked within their confines to render the praying towns serviceable for their own needs. The syncretic nature of the praying town was evident at death, when the Indians held a Christian service but continued to bury the corpse with grave goods to carry to the next life. Eliot suspected that many of the Indians joined a praying town "not for the love of God but for the love of the place." The praying towns bore Algonquian rather than English names. Significantly, the largest and most successful community, Natick, derived its name from an Algonquian word meaning "my land."

Keenly listening to sermons and learning to read the Bible translated into their own language, some converts became close critics of colonial culture. Making the Bible their own, these praying Indians put their missionaries on the defensive by noting the many deviations of colonial behavior from Christian injunctions. One weary missionary, John Cotton, Jr., recorded 470 queries from Indians on Martha's Vineyard. Cotton had become a missionary as an act of atonement when caught in adultery with a colonial woman. Was it then simply an innocent question when an Indian asked him "whether any man that hath committed Adultery may go to heaven"? Cotton did not record his answer.

In general, the missionaries were pleased with the progress of their converts. In 1674, Daniel Gookin praised the Natick Indians for worshiping "with reverence, attention, modesty, and solemnity; the menkind sitting by themselves and the womenkind by themselves, according to their age, quality, and degree, in a comely manner." But most lay Puritans continued to distrust the praying Indians as treacherous savages with a dangerous veneer of insincere Christianity. In 1675–76 a brutal war would put to the test the sincerity of both Indians and Puritans.

KING PHILIP'S WAR

The New English called the bloodiest Indian war in their history King Philip's War, after the Wampanoag sachem named Metacom but known to the New English as King Philip. Massasoit's son, Metacom, quietly prepared for a war that he considered inevitable. In the spring of 1675 the Plymouth colonists provoked the confrontation by seizing, trying, and hanging three Wampanoag for murdering a praying town Indian who had served as a colonial informant. The executions infuriated the young Wampanoag warriors, who struck out on their own, attacking isolated colonial homesteads, looting, and burning.

The uprising spread with deadly effect during the summer and fall as the initial Wampanoag victories emboldened other bands with their own grievances. Indiscriminate Puritan counterattacks on neutral bands created additional enemies, including the Narragansett. Numbering about four thousand, the Narragansett were the largest and most powerful native people in the region. Although the Puritans imagined that Metacom was the evil mastermind of rebellion, in fact every band fought under its own leaders. Far from being any masterful plot by Metacom, the growing uprising was primarily a consequence of blundering Puritans turning their suspects into enemies.

Over the years, the Indians had gradually acquired flintlock muskets from traders, who profitably ignored New English laws against selling arms to the natives. Lighter, more accurate, and more reliable than the old arquebus, the newer flintlock musket was the primary weapon employed by both sides in King Philip's War. The Indians' mastery of the flintlock deprived the colonists of the technological edge they had enjoyed in the Pequot War.

During the summer and fall of 1675 the Indian rebels assailed fifty-two of the region's ninety towns, destroying twelve. Drawing upon the grim lesson in total war taught by the colonists in the Pequot War, the Indians often killed entire colonial families, including women and children. When the colonists counterattacked, the Indians took refuge in swamps and repelled their foes, inflicting heavy losses. Or they surprised and ambushed retreating colonists unfamiliar with the paths through the forests. The Indian victories bolstered their confidence while shocking and demoralizing the New English. Growing numbers of colonial refugees fled from the frontier to burden the resources of the coastal towns. And it became increasingly difficult to recruit colonial soldiers for the grim business of losing an Indian war.

For decades the colonists had labored to remake the New England landscape by constructing churches, houses, fences, and barns and by unleashing their livestock. To reverse the alienation of their land, the Indian rebels systematically burned, killed, mutilated, and desecrated all of those marks of English civilization. The rebels regarded every dying colonist, every burning house, every desecrated church as accumulating evidence that the English God was no match for their own returning spiritual power. The Narragansett infuriated Roger Williams by boasting that "God was [with] them and Had forsaken us for they had so prospered in Killing and Burning us far beyond What we did against them."

As the Puritans saw it, their Bible Commonwealth was failing, consigned by God to a scourging by the forces of Satan as a punishment for the sins of New England. To vindicate their God and prove their own worthiness, the Puritans felt compelled to destroy their Indian enemies. Every dead Indian and burned wigwam manifested the resurgent power of the Puritan God and his renewed approval of his chosen people, the New English. Outraged by the Narragansett boasting, Roger Williams retorted, "God had prospered *us* so that wee had driven the Wampanoogs with Phillip out of his Countrie and the Nahigonsiks out of their Countrie, and had destroyed Multitudes of them in Fighting and Flying, in Hung[e]r and Cold, etc.: and that God would help us to Consume them." In this grim equation, destruction to the other measured God's favor.

During 1675 the colonists could rarely find and attack their more mobile and elusive foes. As a result, many settlers succumbed to the temptation to attack, plunder, and kill those Indians they could easily locate: the praying town Indians. Angry colonists regarded all Indians as their enemies and considered the praying town Indians to be insidious spies and covert raiders. John Eliot sadly noted, "The prophane Indians p[ro]ve a sharp rod to the English, & the English p[ro]ve a very sharp rod to the praying Indians." To secure the praying Indians from genocide and from joining the enemy, the colonial authorities removed them to two cold and barren islands in Boston Harbor, where hundreds died from exposure, malnutrition, and disease (or were stolen by slavers) during the hard winter of 1675–76.

In early 1676 the desperate colonial leaders recognized that they could not win without the assistance of Indian allies, principally the Pequot and Mohegan. The Puritans also enlisted praying town Indians but required each to prove his loyalty and zeal by bringing in two scalps or heads taken from the enemy. Because about a third of the natives in southern New England assisted the colonists, King Philip's War became a civil war among the Indians.

During the spring and summer of 1676, the Indian allies helped turn the tide of war in favor of the colonists. The allies taught the colonists how to avoid ambushes and how to track down and destroy the rebels in their refuges. The best colonial commanders abandoned European military tactics, based upon masses of men engaged in complicated maneuvers to deliver volleys of gunfire. Instead, they adopted the Indian tactics of dispersion, stealth, ambush, and individual marksmanship. Recalling the military changes since the Pequot War, John Eliot remarked, "In our first war with the Indians, God pleased to show us the vanity of our military skill, in managing our arms, after the European mode, [but] now we are glad to learn the skulking way of war."

In spring of 1676 the Indian rebels ran out of food and ammunition, just when they faced increasing attacks from their more numerous and improved foes. Driven from their villages and fields, the rebels were on the run, desperately hungry, and often sick. Unable to make guns and gunpowder, they became vulnerable because the war cut off their access to colonial traders. The New English also exploited their alliance with the powerful Mohawk Indians (one of the Iroquois Five Nations), who lived to the west. In return for colonists' presents, the Mohawk escalated their destructive raids on their old enemies the New England Algonquians.

During the summer of 1676, the Indian resistance collapsed, as one demoralized group after another surrendered. In August, Metacom died in battle, shot down by a praying town Indian who served with the New English. The victors cut off his head for display on a post atop a brick watchtower in

Plymouth. In the late seventeenth century, tourists did not visit Plymouth to see the now celebrated rock (which was then unidentified). Instead, they gaped at Metacom's skull. One visitor, the famous minister Cotton Mather, angrily wrenched off and took away Metacom's jawbone, completing his silencing.

The bitter and bloody war devastated the Puritan settlements but especially the Indian villages. The conflict killed at least a thousand English colonists and about three thousand Indians, a quarter of their population in southern New England. The colonists suffered most of their casualties during the first year of the war, while the Indians endured their heaviest losses during the spring and summer of 1676, when their ammunition, food, morale, and numbers flagged.

VICTORY AND DEFEAT

Rather than treat their captives as prisoners of war, the Puritan victors defined the Indians as traitors, executing the chiefs and enslaving others for sale in the West Indies or the Mediterranean. For several weeks, leading Puritan ministers debated whether Metacom's nine-year-old son should be executed for his father's rebellion. Opting for what they considered mercy, the Puritans sold the boy and his mother into slavery. In his published account of the war, the Reverend William Hubbard warned readers to waste no sympathy on the dead or enslaved Indian children: "Being all young Serpents of the same Brood, the subduing or taking [of] so many ought to be acknowledged as another signal Victory, and Pledg[e] of Divine Favour to the English." Only a few Puritans, primarily missionaries, protested against the executions and enslavements, which affected even some of the Indian allies. Receiving death threats, John Eliot and his colleagues fell silent.

Most leading Puritans insisted that the colonists needed to shed blood to alienate themselves from Indian ways, thoughts, and bodies. The Reverend Increase Mather (Cotton's father) attributed the war to a just and angry God provoked by the Puritans' prewar degeneracy: "Christians in this Land have become too like unto the Indians, and then we need not wonder if the Lord hath afflicted us by them." The victors made an especially brutal example of Joshua Tift, a colonist who had married an Indian and joined her people. Colonial soldiers captured Tift when they stormed a Narragansett village. Tried and convicted, Tift suffered a traitor's painful death, pulled apart by horses.

Some of the defeated Indians escaped northward to take refuge among the Abenaki in northern New England and New France. The refugees carried with them a bitter hatred of the New English. In a long series of wars, between 1689 and 1760, the refugees and their descendants guided French raids that repeatedly devastated the frontier settlements of New England.

The Puritans' Indian allies persisted in southern New England as small minorities, dwelling on a few shrinking reservations surrounded by the colonial victors. Assigned to the lowest rungs of colonial society, the natives labored for small wages on farms and sailing ships. Others earned a humble living by making brooms, splint baskets, and herbal remedies and peddling them to the colonists. An eighteenth-century missionary at Natick sadly observed that the Indians "are generally considered by white people, and placed, as if by common consent, in an inferiour and degraded situation, and treated accordingly." The colonists "took every advantage of [the Indians] that they could . . . to dishearten and depress them."

During the eighteenth-century wars with the French and northern Indians, the New English pressured their Indians into service with colonial forces. Most did not survive the camp diseases and battle wounds, further depressing the native population in southern New England. During the eighteenth century, colonial neighbors also cheated the survivors out of most of their lands. Living on the social margins of New England towns, Indians became largely invisible to nineteenth-century New Englanders, who prematurely declared the natives extinct. Only in the twentieth century did New England Indians gain a measure of recognition that they had persisted through a long ordeal.

During the late 1670s, Puritan settlers returned to rebuild their burned and ravaged homes, while newcomers flocked into the lands left vacant by the death and exile of the defeated Indians. Despite the war, New England's colonial population surged from 52,000 in 1670 to 92,000 in 1700. By remaking the land, settlers destroyed the resources that Indians needed to preserve their autonomy, rendering it progressively more difficult for natives to reverse their dispossession. In 1789 the Mohegan lamented:

> The times are Exceedingly Alter'd, Yea the times have turn'd everything upside down, or rather we have Chang'd the good Times, Chiefly by the help of the White People, for in Times past, our Fore-Fathers . . . had everything in Great plenty. . . . But alas, it is not so now, all our Fishing, Hunting and Fowling is entirely gone.

By 1789 every native people along the Atlantic seaboard shared the Mohegan fate of living as a small minority on a changed land among invaders.

10

The West Indies

★

1600–1700

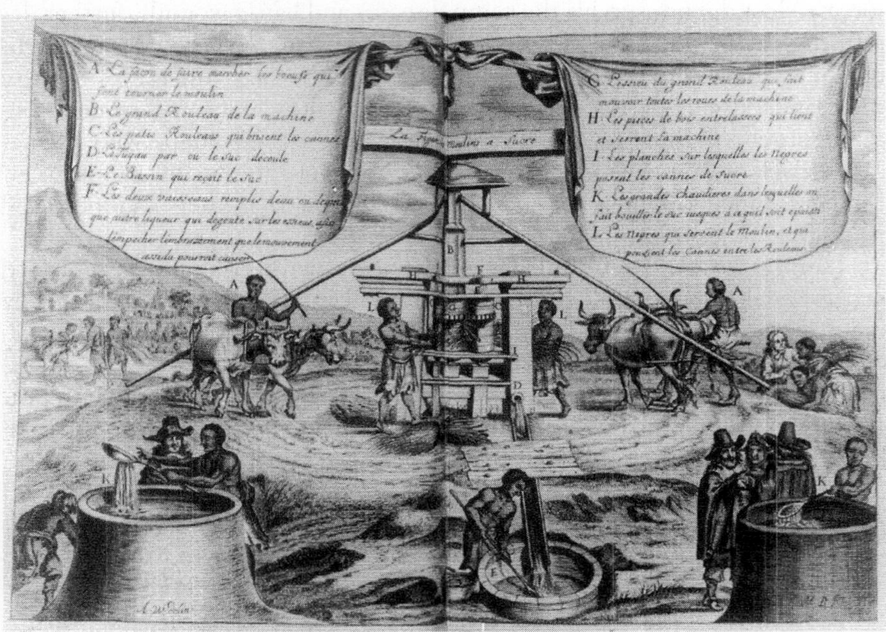

A seventeenth-century sugar mill powered by cattle. Slaves feed the cane into the rollers (L), which crush out the juice, which flows into a tank (E) for ladling into coppers (K) for subsequent boiling. During the late seventeenth and early eighteenth centuries, most planters switched to windmills. From Charles de Rochefort, Histoire Naturelle et Morale des Îles Antilles de l'Amerique *(Rotterdam, 1665).*

During the mid-seventeenth century, several small but fertile subtropical islands in the West Indies became the crown jewels of the English colonial empire. The West Indies were an arc of volcanic peaks rising from the ocean and sweeping northward from South America and then westward beneath Florida to frame the Caribbean Sea to the southwest. Most West Indian islands were lushly vegetated with tropical rain forests, appearing dark green to the sailor's eye—until the lighter green of ubiquitous sugarcane later replaced the trees.

By producing lucrative sugar, the West Indies rapidly grew to overtake the Chesapeake as the most valuable set of English colonies. In 1686, London imported West Indian produce worth £674,518, compared with £207,131 obtained from all the North American mainland colonies. Sugar constituted £586,528 of the West Indian total, while tobacco accounted for £141,600 of the mainland produce. Tobacco was valuable to the empire—indeed, more precious than all other mainland produce combined—but sugar was king. Sugar could bear the costs of long-distance transportation (and the purchase of slaves by the thousand) because it was in great and growing European demand to sweeten food and drink.

The pursuit of profits drew English colonists to an alien and dangerous setting. Risking tropical diseases and hurricanes, the West Indian colonists gambled their lives to obtain their own land and, perhaps, even a great fortune. Some succeeded, but most ultimately failed. Indeed, after a brief initial boom of abundant opportunity, the West Indian colonies became starkly stratified even by the standards of the hierarchical mother country. Although the West Indies frustrated the aspirations of most of their own colonists, the sugar islands promoted prosperity on the mainland of North America, where farmers produced lumber, fish, livestock, and grain to supply the sugar plantations. And the voracious West Indian demand for labor stimulated an explosive expansion in the English slave trade across the Atlantic. In sum, at an immense cost in human suffering, the sugar islands served as the great economic engine of the English empire.

BARBADOS

During the late sixteenth century, the English ventured to the Caribbean in armed ships determined either to plunder Spanish shipping and coastal towns or to compel the Spanish to trade on English terms. In 1604 a peace treaty between England and Spain terminated their official warfare in Europe, but unofficial pirates persisted in the Caribbean, far beyond effective constraint by any government. In the phrase of the time, there was no peace "beyond the line" of the mid-Atlantic. In a violent and exploitative age of colonial expansion, the West Indies were an especially bloody and ruthless zone.

English, French, and Dutch pirates and smugglers established semipermanent bases in the harbors of the many islands at the eastern edge of the West Indian arc. Known as the Lesser Antilles, these relatively small islands offered proximity to the Hispanic seaports and their shipping lanes. The harbors of the Lesser Antilles also provided places to repair ships, to replenish water, and to hide from Spanish pursuit. The pirates and smugglers found the Lesser Antilles conveniently unoccupied by the Spanish, who disdained the islands as too small to bother with. Overstretched, the Spanish had their hands full colonizing the four big islands at the western end of the Caribbean: Cuba, Hispaniola, Jamaica, and Puerto Rico. Moreover, the natives of the Lesser Antilles, the Caribs, were especially formidable guerrilla fighters. Lacking cities and gold but possessing a fearsome reputation, the Caribs were the sort of Indians that the Spanish had learned to avoid.

During the early seventeenth century, the temporary pirate bases in the Lesser Antilles gradually became diversified into permanent agricultural colonies. Caribs destroyed two early English attempts to colonize: at Santa Lucia in 1605 and Grenada in 1609. During the 1620s and early 1630s, however, the English founded enduring colonies on the islands of St. Christopher (1624), Barbados (1627), Nevis (1628), Montserrat (1632), and Antigua (1632).

During the seventeenth century, the French and the Dutch lagged behind the English in West Indian colonization. The Dutch focused on their profitable carrying trade and their expensive, and ultimately futile, bid to take Brazil from the Portuguese. In the West Indies, the Dutch occupied only a few especially small islands, St. Martin, St. Eustatius, Saba, and Curaçao, all better for trade than for plantations. During the late 1620s, the French uneasily shared St. Christopher (now known as St. Kitts) with the English. In 1635 the French also began to settle the fertile islands of Guadeloupe and Martinique, but Carib resistance hampered colonization for decades. During the late 1650s the French also occupied the western coast of Hispaniola, which became their colony of St. Domingue (now Haiti), but it did not prosper as a sugar colony until the eighteenth century.

During the mid-seventeenth century, the West Indies became the great magnet for English transatlantic migration. Despite their small size, the West Indies received over two-thirds of the English emigrants to the Americas between 1640 and 1660. In 1650 more white colonists lived in the West Indies (44,000) than in the Chesapeake (12,000) and New England colonies (23,000) combined. The great majority of the English West Indians dwelled on a single island, Barbados. Its relatively large population of 30,000 was especially striking because Barbados is only twenty-one miles long and fourteen wide.

Landscape, climate, location, and pigs combined to render Barbados especially attractive to English colonists. At 166 square miles, Barbados was bit larger than the other Lesser Antilles islands occupied by the English (Antigua ranked second at 108 square miles). Also less mountainous than the other islands, Barbados was easier to clear and cultivate. And Barbados no longer had any Carib inhabitants, sparing the colonists the hard fighting to displace them. Numerous in 1500, the native villages on Barbados had been depopulated by Spanish slave raiders by 1627. The absence of Carib hunters permitted wild pigs to proliferate into immense herds, the descendants of a few left in 1523 by a Portuguese navigator to colonize a meat supply for subsequent mariners. By 1627, thousands of pigs provided sport and protein for the early colonists, who destroyed and ate with a reckless, profligate abandon. In 1631, Sir Henry Colt sadly observed, "They usually kill 1500 [pigs] a week, a waste to[o] great to be continued. . . . Butt this plentifull world of theirs is now past. They needed nott to have made such a hasty distruction of them."

Located one hundred miles east of the Lesser Antilles, Barbados was also removed from the destructive wars between rival empires that repeatedly devastated the other islands. Ten of the Lesser Antilles cluster within a seventy-five-mile radius of Nevis, of which four were English, two were French, two were Dutch, one was shared uneasily by the English and French, and another was shared by the French and Dutch. Divided between English in the middle and the French on either end, St. Christopher was especially vulnerable, suffering from seven sacks in three Anglo-French wars between 1666 and 1713. A ruined planter on St. Christopher sadly concluded, "The wars here are more destructive than in any other partes of the world; for twenty yeares' peace will hardly resettle the devastation of one yeare's warre." More safely situated upwind from the fray, Barbados escaped invasion, permitting a sustained development that no other West Indian island could match during the seventeenth century.

During the late 1620s and early 1630s, colonial life on Barbados was hard, but good prospects encouraged common planters. Wielding axes and hoes, they cleared the tangle of tropical vegetation, laboring under a hot sun amid swarms of biting insects. The early plantations were small—usually five to thirty acres—and worked by their owners, assisted by a few indentured servants. Lacking sufficient capital and technical knowledge, the early colonists faltered in their experiments raising sugar. Instead, they cultivated tobacco and raised livestock for hides to export to Europe. For their own subsistence, the colonists also hunted (or tended) pigs and cultivated tropical gardens of maize, cassava, yams, plantains, and sweet potatoes.

Most early Barbadians came as indentured servants, initially from England but increasingly from Scotland and Ireland as well. As in the Chesapeake, most servants were poor, single, male, and young—in their teens and twenties. Hoping to live long enough to obtain land, they bound themselves for five years of labor to pay for their transatlantic passage. At the expiration of his term, a "freedman" obtained his "freedom dues": about £10, usually in the form of provisions, clothing, and tools. Until the mid-1630s he also received five to ten acres of land, permitting the freedman to become a small planter. But that incentive vanished as the swelling population pressed against the limited supply of land.

As positive incentives decayed after 1635, masters resorted more frequently and more brutally to punishment. They contemptuously referred to their servants as "white slaves" and applied the whip to drive and punish them—language and measures unthinkable in England. Detecting a plot by their servants to rebel in 1647, the Barbadian planters whipped dozens and executed eighteen. Richard Ligon of Barbados reported, "Truly, I have seen such cruelty there done to Servants, as I did not think one Christian could have done to another."

SUGAR

The Barbadian economy stagnated during the late 1630s as the land became crowded and the tobacco crop became unprofitable. Raising an inferior grade of tobacco that sold for a lower price, the Barbadians could not compete with the Chesapeake crop. Because of their smaller profit margin, the Barbadian planters suffered more severely from the plummeting price of tobacco as the English market became saturated with the swelling production from the Chesapeake colonies. Seeking an alternative, many Barbadian planters shifted to cotton, which proved only modestly successful. During the 1640s, however, they found their salvation in sugar.

Sugar making required costly equipment, precise timing, technical knowledge, and especially strenuous labor by a large workforce under strict supervision. By preindustrial standards, the sugar planter ran a large and complex operation that combined agriculture and manufacturing. He needed at least one mill to crush juice out of the cane, a boiling house to clarify and evaporate the juice into brown sugar crystals, a curing house to drain out the molasses and dry the sugar, a distillery to convert the molasses into rum, and a warehouse to store the barreled sugar until he could ship it to Europe.

Because cut cane spoiled unless processed within a few hours, the harvesting, milling, and boiling required close synchronization and quick work. Field gangs cut the ripe canes by hand with curved knives and carted the stalks to the mill, for prompt grinding between rollers turned by wind or cattle. Crushed from the cane, the juice had to be boiled within a few hours, before it could ferment. Boiling in a succession of copper kettles hung over a furnace evaporated the water, leaving a golden-brown sugar known as *muscovado*, which the planters packed into immense thousand-pound hogshead barrels and shipped to Europe, for further refinement there into white sugar for sale to consumers. Making *muscovado* also generated a cheap by-product, molasses, which could be rendered more valuable by distilling it into rum.

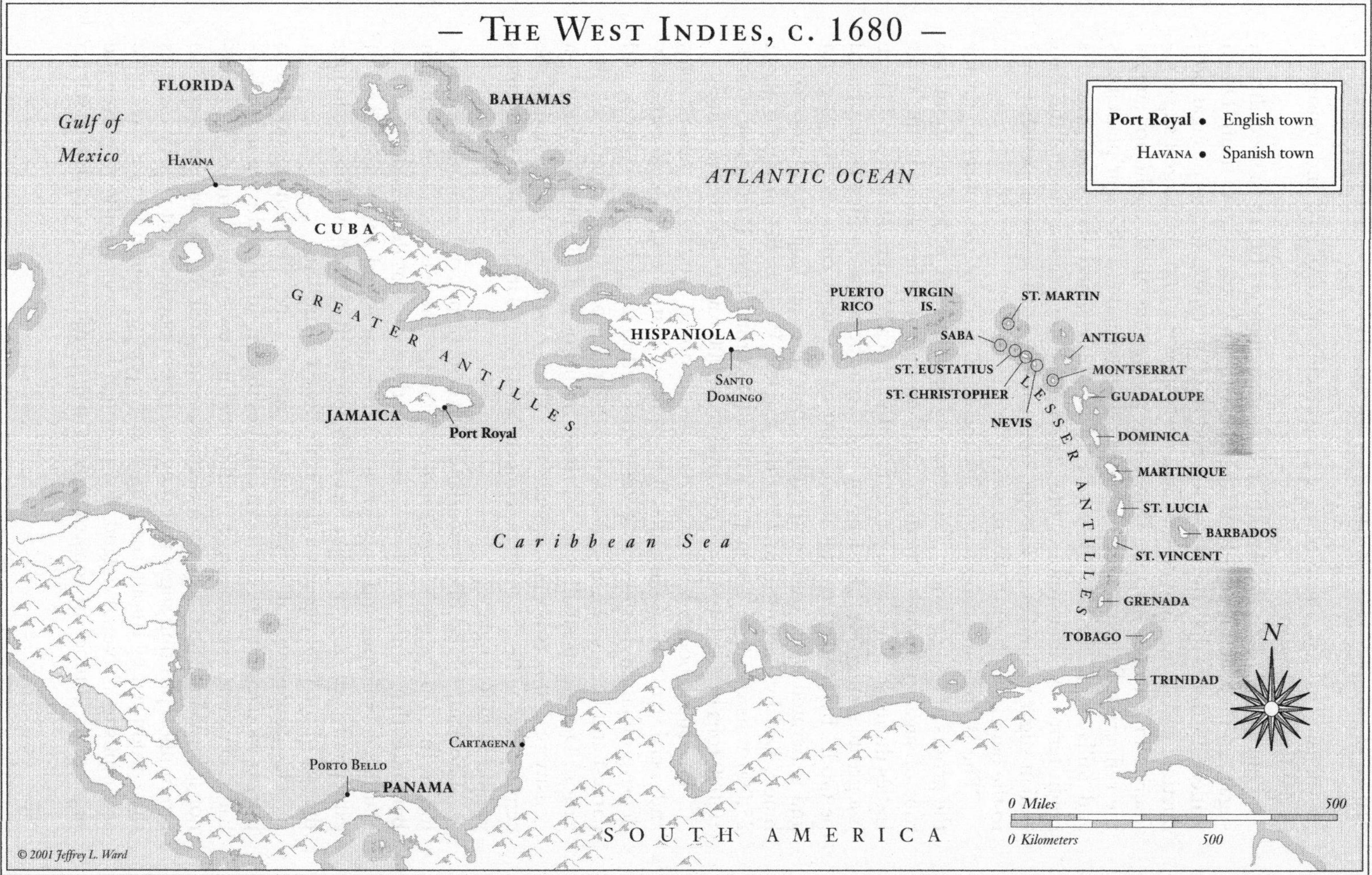
— The West Indies, c. 1680 —
FLORIDA
BAHAMAS
Gulf of Mexico
Havana
ATLANTIC OCEAN
Port Royal • English town
Havana • Spanish town
CUBA
GREATER ANTILLES
HISPANIOLA
Santo Domingo
JAMAICA
Port Royal
PUERTO RICO
VIRGIN IS.
ST. MARTIN
SABA
ANTIGUA
ST. EUSTATIUS
MONTSERRAT
ST. CHRISTOPHER
NEVIS
LESSER ANTILLES
GUADALOUPE
DOMINICA
MARTINIQUE
ST. LUCIA
BARBADOS
ST. VINCENT
GRENADA
TOBAGO
TRINIDAD
N
Caribbean Sea
Cartagena
Porto Bello
PANAMA
SOUTH AMERICA
0 Miles 500
0 Kilometers 500
© 2001 Jeffrey L. Ward

Inexpensive to make, rum became the principal alcohol sold and consumed in the English empire.

During the 1640s the wealthier Barbadian planters began to specialize in sugar as they acquired plants, equipment, and know-how from Dutch traders. In Brazil the Dutch had learned the Portuguese secrets of sugar production, and in Amsterdam they had developed the best and largest sugar refineries in Europe. Because Dutch-run plantations alone could not supply the refineries, Dutch traders financed the development of sugar plantations and mills on Barbados. They offered equipment and slaves on generous credit terms. As their reward, the Dutch profitably carried most of the Barbadian sugar to market in Europe, to the dismay of English imperialists but to the benefit of English planters.

The Barbadians happily forsook the hard times of the tobacco glut for the profits of a sugar boom. Cane thrived on Barbados, producing about two tons of sugar per acre—a better yield than on any other island in the West Indies during the seventeenth century. In 1646 a planter celebrated, "There is a greate change on this island of late, from the worse to the better, praised be God." By 1660, Barbados made most of the sugar consumed in England and generated more trade and capital than all other English colonies combined. Led by Barbados, in 1700 the English West Indies produced about 25,000 tons of sugar, compared with 20,000 tons from Portuguese Brazil, 10,000 tons by the French islands, and the 4,000 tons made by the Dutch.

The sugar boom revolutionized the economy, landscape, demography, and social structure of Barbados. The compact island developed an especially dense population, both because sugar required so much labor to cultivate and harvest and because sugar generated such large profits from an intense cultivation. Despite its small scale, by 1660 Barbados had 53,000 inhabitants—a density of 250 persons per square mile, which rose to 400 by the end of the century. In 1700 the human concentration on Barbados was four times greater than in England.

The planters also filled the island with cane plants, obliterating the native forest. In 1676 the island's governor observed, "There is not a foot of land in Barbados that is not employed, even to the very seaside." Aside from the plantation buildings and a few groves of trees, the island was a terraced sea of cane plants, which grew eight feet high at maturity. Much wildlife, including the last of the feral pigs, vanished as the forest dwindled.

Devoting almost all of their land to raising cane, the planters needed to import food from more northern colonies that could not cultivate sugar. Barbados developed an economic symbiosis with New England. In 1647, Governor John Winthrop of Massachusetts explained that the Barbadians were "so intent upon planting sugar that they had rather buy foode at very deare rates than produce it by labour, soe infinite is the profitt of sugar workes after once accomplished." New England also provided horses and cattle to power the sugar mills; lumber to construct plantations; and staves to make barrels to hold the sugar. While the expansion of sugar production on Barbados stimulated the economic development of New England, trade with New England permitted Barbados to complete its profitable specialization in sugar and slavery.

SLAVES

The sugar planters needed a large and captive body of laborers to perform especially hard, monotonous, and dangerous work in tropical conditions. During planting season, the master expected every laborer daily to dig at least sixty large holes by hand with a hoe. Each hole contained one cane plant and required the shifting of up to twelve cubic feet of earth. The critical harvest seasons further intensified the labor. Tending the mill was particularly dangerous, especially for bone-tired people working around the clock. The planter Edward Littleton warned, "If a Mill-feeder be catch't by the finger, his whole body is drawn in, and he is squeez'd to pieces."

Free people did not volunteer for such degrading and debilitating work, and it became increasingly difficult even to obtain servants. The sugar boom demanded more workers at a time when the supply of indentured Englishmen was declining. Because real wages rose in England after 1650, more laboring people could survive there without risking their lives in the West Indies. At the same time, the intense exploitation of labor associated with sugar gave Barbados a more frightful reputation. Those inclined to emigrate who exercised any choice in the matter preferred the mainland colonies on the Atlantic seaboard or the less crowded developing islands (Jamaica and Antigua) that still offered land grants as "freedom dues."

Desperate for servants, the planters accepted growing numbers of convicted criminals and political prisoners, sent to the West Indies as a punishment. Between 1645 and 1655 the English government shipped to Barbados some twelve thousand captives taken in the suppression of rebellions at home. A mix of English, Scots, and Irish Catholics, such coerced servants rebelled or ran away early and often, despite brutal punishments for those caught. Because white men could more easily escape to pass as free on another island or aboard a pirate ship, planters increasingly saw an advantage in employing only permanent slaves of a distinctive color immediately and constantly identified with slavery.

At the same time, political leaders in England developed new qualms about inflicting plantation servitude upon white men. During the early 1650s some members of Parliament embarrassed the government by challenging the shipment of political prisoners to Barbados—a practice that virtually stopped after 1655. And during the early 1660s, English courts began to prosecute unscrupulous recruiters who tricked laborers into servitude in the West Indies.

The parliamentary debate and the new prosecutions revealed the emergence of a new racial solidarity in "whiteness," which trumped even the powerful class divisions between the English. As they came to define a certain minimal dignity due to all white men, the English magnified their superiority over people of another color, especially those who seemed most different: the "black" Africans. In turn, as plantation labor became associated with enslaved Africans, it appeared doubly degrading to compel British people to suffer—even temporarily—the same labors and punishments.

At the same time that the supply of white labor dried up, a blossoming transatlantic slave trade provided planters with an alternative. As the easternmost island in the West Indies, Barbados lay closer to the West African supply of slaves. Eager to land and sell their human cargo for a quick return to Africa for more, traders gravitated to the Barbados market. The increased supply of slaves for sale lowered their average price from about £35 in 1635 to about £20 after 1645.

The price decline rendered slaves a better long-term bargain than the £12 required to purchase just four years of indentured labor. The purchaser of slaves also never had to pay the "freedom dues" owed to the laborer at the expiration of his indenture. And, in contrast to those of servants, the children of a slave woman became the property of her master, providing additional returns on the original investment. In 1655 a visitor to Barbados observed, "Our English here doth think a Negro child the first day it is born to be worth £5; they cost them nothing the bringing up, they go always naked. . . . They sell them from one to the other as we do sheep."

The planters rapidly converted their plantations from modest operations employing a handful of indentured servants to larger enterprises worked by dozens of enslaved Africans. In 1644 only about eight hundred slaves lived on Barbados, but a year later a visitor reported that the Barbadians were buying every available slave, "and the more they buy, the more they are able to buy, for in a year and a half they will earn (with God's blessing) as much as they cost."

By 1660, Barbados had become the first English colony with a black and enslaved majority: 27,000 compared with 26,000 whites. More slaves dwelled on Barbados than in all other English colonies combined. As slaves proliferated on Barbados, indentured servitude dwindled. By 1680, there were seventeen slaves for every indentured servant on Barbados.

The growing slave population depended on increased slave imports, for the Barbadian slaves died faster than they could reproduce. Although the planters brought 130,000 Africans into Barbados between 1640 and 1700, only 50,000 remained alive there at the dawn of the new century. The slaves succumbed to the deadly combination of tropical diseases, a brutal work regimen, and the inadequate diet, housing, and clothing provided by their masters. Rather than improve those conditions, the Barbadian planters found it more profitable to import more slaves.

A seventeenth-century plantation housed the slaves in a row of small, flimsy oblong huts made of cane stalks and palm leaves. The huts contained no furniture beyond mats for sleeping and no equipment except a cooking pot and calabash gourds to serve as cups. The slaves consumed a meager, starchy, and monotonous diet of plantains, corn, beans, yams, and dried fish, with occasional helpings of rum and meat. The workweek and workday varied with the seasons, but on average the slaves labored six days a week (all but Sunday), for ten or eleven hours per day. During the intense harvest, there was no day of rest and few hours for sleep.

Because English law provided no precedents for managing a system of racial slavery, the Barbadians had to develop their own slave code, which they systematized in 1661. The Barbadian slave code became the model for those adopted elsewhere in the English colonies, particularly in Jamaica (1664) and Carolina (1696), which both originated as offshoots from Barbados. The slave code began from the premise that blacks were "an heathenish, brutish and an uncertaine, dangerous kinde of people." Deemed property, such brutes had no legal or political rights, not even to venture into court when especially abused. Considered dangerous, they had to be strictly watched and brutally punished for the slightest misstep.

The slave code did set certain minimal standards meant to discourage especially negligent masters from driving their slaves to rebel, to the detriment of the planter class in general. But those standards were minimal indeed. The code required a planter annually to clothe every male with a pair of pants and a cap, every female with a petticoat and a cap. The law said nothing about shirts, shoes, diet, or working conditions. The master could drive and punish his slaves in any way he liked, for there was no penalty for whipping, torturing, maiming, castrating, or even destroying his own property. Barbadians developed the practice of "putting a man to dry": placing defiant slaves in an iron cage hung from a tree, there to die slowly of hunger and thirst as a warning to others. In 1694, for the crime of stealing a pig, judges had a black man sliced into quarters for public display. Regarding such conspicuous deaths as in the public interest, the government compensated owners for the value of their executed slaves.

The slave code also mandated strict policies of surveillance, meant to keep the slaves intimidated. No slave could leave a plantation without a written pass signed by his owner. The slaves could not "beat drums, blow horns, or use other loud instruments" lest they serve to rally rebellion. The white militia searched the slave quarters for weapons and examined passing blacks for their passes. To reward and encourage black cooperation, anyone who helped catch a fugitive received fancy new clothes decorated with "a Badge of a Red crosse on his right Arme, whereby hee may be knowne and cherished by all good people." We can only imagine what other blacks thought of a fellow bearing this badge.

No slave code could still the black longing for freedom, but it did divide the slaves, rendering it difficult to maintain the solidarity essential to plot a successful uprising. Invariably, some reckless, frightened, or greedy slave alerted a master to the impending danger. Such reports kept the planters on edge and produced brutal retribution upon the suspected. In the first major alarm, in 1675, the planters executed thirty-five suspects; at least six of them were burned alive at the stake. The slave woman who revealed the conspiracy received her freedom from the colonial government, which compensated her master.

Further executions followed every suspected plot—some of which were probably nothing more than planter paranoia apparently confirmed by confessions obtained under torture. The peak came in 1692 when the colony executed at least ninety-two suspects; fourteen others died in prison or under torture, and four slaves succumbed to botched castrations. An occasional panic and its executions served the system by keeping the planters alert and by intimidating the remaining slaves.

The planters justified slavery as the proper fate for non-Christians, especially if their skin was dark. The planters bitterly opposed efforts to evangelize the Africans, for the owners did not want clergyman muddying a convenient line by making Christians of slaves. Solicitous of planter power and patronage, the Anglican clergy dutifully refrained. This English refusal to convert slaves diverged sharply from the practice of French, Spanish, and Portuguese masters, who felt religiously and legally bound to promote the Catholic initiation of every soul, while they exploited the body. Only the Quaker minority challenged the ban at Barbados on converting the slaves. For this, they were considered dangerous radicals, and the government fined them about £7,000, executed one, and ordered their meetinghouse nailed shut. Left alone by missionaries, the slaves could retain their traditional beliefs brought from West Africa. And as the great majority of the population, the West Indian slaves more readily preserved their African languages and customs.

PLANTERS

Sugar was a rich man's crop, for small operations could not compete in the markets to acquire land, labor, and equipment. By 1650, capitalizing a hundred-acre plantation cost at least £2,000—too much for all but the rich in a century where few hired laborers made more than £10 in a year. And most planters regarded one hundred acres as barely adequate for a sugar plantation, preferring two hundred acres as optimum.

Over time, competition drove out the smaller sugar operations, concentrating large plantations in the hands of the fewer men who could afford their costs—and who reaped the profits of a larger production. During the second half of the seventeenth century, as more big operations produced more sugar, the European market became surfeited. The price of a hundred pounds of sugar fell from twenty-eight shillings in the early 1650s to ten shillings in the early 1680s. By achieving economies of scale, the big operations remained profitable, but the smaller, less efficient operations failed. The losers sold out to their better-capitalized neighbors. One great planter told a visitor that he had consolidated his eight-hundred-acre estate by purchases from forty smallholders.

Barbados became the most socially polarized colony in the English empire, as an impoverished and enslaved black majority worked primarily for a small but wealthy planter elite. By 1680 over half of the arable land on Barbados belonged to the richest 7 percent of the free colonists, the 175 big planters who possessed at least sixty slaves. A great planter commanded, on average, 115 slaves, 250 acres, and a net worth of £4,000.

Although a benefit to the wealthy few, the sugar revolution worsened conditions and prospects for the many common whites. In 1666 the planter Sir John Colleton conceded that during the preceding twenty-three years, Barbados had lost "at least 12,000 good men, formerly proprietors and tradesmen, wormed out of theire small settlements, by theire more subtle and greedy Neighbours." Colleton said that two-thirds of the remaining white Barbadians were "of noe interest or reputation, and of little innate Courage, being poor men that are just permitted to live, and a very great part Irish, derided by the Negroes, and branded with the Epithite of white slaves." Once a land of apparent promise for common tobacco planters, Barbados had become the domain of sugar grandees and their African slaves.

The elite derived from the island's minority of free immigrants, men who arrived with some capital, access to merchant credit, considerable ambition, and few scruples. By seizing the opportunity to become sugar planters, they leveraged their early advantages into substantial fortunes. During the late 1640s and early 1650s, a growing number of the great planters were wealthy newcomers, often gentry refugees from the Civil War in England, who escaped to invest their fortunes in sugar plantations.

As the richest men in English America, the Barbadian great planters lived in a lavish manner that emulated the homeland aristocracy. The great planter built a large and refined mansion on his chief plantation and another in the port of Bridgetown. He rode between town and country in an ornate carriage; wore the latest silken fashions from London; deployed numerous house servants in fine livery; imported fashionable furniture and expensive wines; and entertained lavishly. Suitably impressed, English visitors and the home authorities more readily accepted the West Indian planters as a proper elite—far superior to their cruder counterparts in the Chesapeake or New England. Between 1658 and 1700 the monarchs knighted or awarded baronetcies to seventeen Barbadians—testimony to an aristocratic standing unmatched by any other Americans.

Barbados and the other Lesser Antilles began as a "proprietary" colony, granted in 1627 by King Charles I to a favored aristocrat, the Earl of Carlisle, who named a governor and a council to administer each island. The governor and council combined all legislative, executive, and judicial authority, granting lands, passing and enforcing laws, trying and executing criminals and dissidents, levying and collecting quitrents and other taxes. This concentration of power dismayed the planters, who wanted the security to property promised by a representative assembly in control of the treasury. In 1639 the Lord Proprietor and his governor conceded to Barbados an elected assembly, which in 1643 exploited the turmoil of the Civil War at home to renounce their Lord Proprietor and to cease paying quitrents to him. In 1660 the crown supplanted the Lord Proprietor, as Barbados, the Leeward Islands, and Jamaica became distinct royal colonies, joining Virginia in that distinction. After 1660 the crown collected the quitrents, appointed the councils and governors, and accepted elected assemblies.

On Barbados, the great planters monopolized seats in the elected assembly as well as the appointed council and judiciary. Because most land belonged to a small elite, the property requirement disenfranchised about three-quarters of the white men (to say nothing of either the white women or the black majority, neither of whom had any political standing). No other English colony so tightly restricted the electoral franchise.

The planter elite also enjoyed unusual clout in Parliament and with the crown. Many English gentry families possessed investments and sons in Barbados, and many successful planters retired to England and entered the gentry class by purchasing country estates. In Parliament these gentry families combined with the great London merchants who imported sugar to compose a formidable "sugar interest"—more influential than any other colonial interest. The sugar lobby protected the planters from the nearly ruinous taxes the crown levied on Chesapeake tobacco. In 1668–69 the West Indian sugar crop sold for about £180,000 after it paid about £18,000 in customs duty—compared with the £50,000 reaped by Chesapeake planters over and above their customs duty of £75,000. The Chesapeake planter worked primarily to benefit the crown; the West Indian planter kept most of the value his slaves made.

But the Barbados planters paid some heavy psychological and physiological prices for their wealth and power. An especially ethnocentric people, the English found it particularly distasteful to dwell among Africans deemed so utterly different in complexion, speech, and culture. With good cause, the planters also suffered recurrent nightmares of slaves rising up to kill in the night. Adopting a siege mentality, the Barbadian planters walled themselves within fortified houses that kept their blacks out. After 1680, the most successful grandees sought to escape from the profitable but troubling world they had made. As quickly as possible, they aspired to make a fortune and return home, consigning their plantations to managers and overseers—

which weakened support for local institutions of religion, education, and government.

Most planters, however, died before they could get away. During the 1640s, they had increased their exposure to deadly diseases by importing slaves bearing new pathogens from Africa: principally yellow fever and malaria, which became the greatest killers of Barbadians, free and slave. The Africans also introduced and shared hookworm, yaws, guinea worm, leprosy, and elephantiasis. In 1647, Richard Ligon arrived in Barbados to find that almost all of the colonists were "new men, for few or none of them that first set foot there, were now living." Parish registers from the 1650s for the white population list four times as many deaths as marriages and three times as many deaths as baptisms. Ligon observed, "Black Ribbon for mourning is much worn there." Only new arrivals to the island sustained both planter and slave numbers.

The most thoughtful planters expressed dismay at what they had created on Barbados: a deadly materialism without higher purpose. Ligon complained that the planters' minds were "so rivited to the earth, and the profits that arise out of it, as their souls were lifted no higher." In 1710 a planter composed this acerbic acrostic:

> **B**arbadoes Isle inhabited by Slaves
> **A**nd for one honest man ten thousand knaves
> **R**eligion to thee's a Romantick storey
> **B**arbarity and ill-got wealth thy glory
> **A**ll Sodom's Sins are Centred in thy heart
> **D**eath is thy look and Death in every part
> **O**h! Glorious Isle in Vilany Excell
> **S**in to the Height—thy fate is Hell.

JAMAICA

After 1660 on Barbados the black population continued to grow, but the number of common whites declined sharply as they died or moved away in search of an opportunity to obtain land. By 1700 the free white population had fallen to 15,000 (from 26,000 in 1660) while the number of enslaved blacks had grown to 50,000 (from 27,000 in 1660). In vain the governor and assembly tried to discourage the white flight, fearing that the dwindling militia would become too weak to defend the island from either French invasion or slave rebellion. They also dreaded that the emigrants would help other English islands develop into rivals in the sugar trade. And wealthy creditors feared losing the debts owed by the emigrants. Incredibly, in 1682 the Barbados assembly blamed the white flight on "insolent" behavior by the slaves. By adding new strictures to the already draconian slave code, the assembly naively hoped to retain the common whites on an island without opportunity for them.

Squeezed out of Barbados, common whites emigrated by the thousand to the less developed West Indian islands: to the "Leeward Islands" of Nevis, St. Kitts, Montserrat, and Antigua or farther west to Jamaica, which became their principal destination. The governor of Jamaica encouraged migration by offering free land in generous quantities: thirty acres to each planter and thirty more for every additional member of his "family," including servants and slaves. In 1675 the governor of Barbados reported that former servants preferred Jamaica, "where they can hope for land, to Barbados, where there is none."

Located a thousand miles west of Barbados, Jamaica was an especially large island of 4,400 square miles, ten times bigger than the rest of the English West Indies combined. Compared with the Lesser Antilles, Jamaica was grander, lusher, hotter, wetter, stormier, more mountainous, and more susceptible to slave rebellions. To English sensibilities, that enlarged scale rendered Jamaica both the most alluring and the most disturbing place in their West Indies. Like all plantation colonies, Jamaica was conceived in violence, first wrested by the Spanish from the natives and then taken by the English. Fewer than fifteen hundred Spanish colonists and their slaves occupied part of the south coast in 1655, when their weakness attracted an English invasion and occupation.

English Jamaica had a dual economy: agriculture in the interior valleys and far-ranging piracy from the seaport of Port Royal. From the start, Jamaica attracted some great planters who procured large estates, imported gangs of slaves, and developed sugar cultivation. But most Jamaican plantations of the 1660s were small-scale operations worked by their owners, sometimes assisted by a few indentured servants. Lacking the capital and slaves for sugar, the small planters raised cattle and pigs and cultivated small fields of indigo, cotton, and cacao (as well as tropical garden crops for subsistence). Pirates also flocked to Jamaica, drawn by the island's proximity to the shipping and towns of Spanish Central America. Also known as "buccaneers," the pirates were recruited by Jamaica's royal governor, Sir Thomas Modyford, who meant both to profit from their raiding and to help secure his colony from a Spanish counterattack. Put on the defensive by devastating pirate raids, the Spanish could never mount an offensive to reclaim Jamaica.

As his partner, the governor relied upon the most successful pirate of the century, Henry Morgan. Between 1665 and 1671, Morgan's pirates plundered and burned a succession of Spanish seaports on the coasts of Nicaragua, Cuba, Panama, and Venezuela. Morgan accumulated enough plunder to acquire and develop Jamaican sugar plantations worked by more than a hundred slaves. Politically shrewd, Morgan also cultivated powerful partners and patrons in high places. In 1671, Spanish diplomatic protests at last induced King Charles II to recall Modyford as governor and to order the buccaneers suppressed. But Morgan visited London and shared enough loot with the right people to secure from the king a knighthood and appointment as Jamaica's deputy governor. In 1675, Sir Henry Morgan returned to Jamaica in triumph, and the buccaneers were back in business.

The pirates stimulated the development of Port Royal, the great seaport on the south coast of Jamaica. Located at the tip of a sand spit ten miles long, Port Royal was defended by five forts bristling with 110 cannon—the greatest stronghold in English America. Offering a superb harbor and a lively town, Port Royal became the pirates' paradise. Merchants fenced their loot, local shipyards refitted the ships for renewed predation, and taverns and brothels abounded to entertain their bodies. When buccaneers blew into town after a successful raid, Port Royal earned its reputation as the wickedest place in the English-speaking world: the Sodom of the West Indies. But paradoxical Port Royal also astonished visitors by hosting four churches (Anglican, Presbyterian, Quaker, and Catholic) and a synagogue for the more pious colonists. With 2,900 inhabitants in 1680, Port Royal was the third-largest town in English America, behind only Bridgetown on Barbados and Boston in New England.

So long as the Spanish threatened Jamaica, the planters found the buccaneers worth their considerable trouble. But as the Spanish danger receded at the end of the century, the costs of hosting the pirates became more conspicuous. The planters resented that buccaneers gave refuge and employment to runaway servants. When Spanish shipping proved elusive, the pirates were also not above plundering English vessels, which pushed up the insurance and freight rates that the planters had to pay to import their slaves and export their sugar. Worse yet, the piracy sometimes scared away shipping, depriving the planters of new slaves and clogging their warehouses with unsold sugar.

During the 1690s the crown dispatched a new governor with instructions to oust the buccaneers from Jamaica, which proved easier to accomplish in the wake of Sir Henry Morgan's death in 1688. Suffering from cirrhosis of the liver, the heavy-drinking Sir Henry sought relief from an African folk doctor. But his treatments—injections of urine and an all-body plaster of moist clay—only hastened Morgan's death.

Divine Providence also helped by destroying Port Royal with an earthquake on June 7, 1692. Within three minutes, half the town slid into the harbor and thirty feet of water swallowed up the three major streets, the chief public buildings, the wharves, and most of the merchants' shops. Hundreds of corpses floated over their former homes. A Jamaican Quaker reported:

> Ah brother! If thou didst see those great persons that are now dead upon the water, thou couldst never forget it. Great men who were so swallowed up with pride, that a man could not be admitted to speak

> with them, and women whose top-knots seemed to reach the clouds, now lie stinking upon the water, and are made meat for fish and fowls of the air.

The rotting bodies spread a malignant fever that killed most of the earthquake survivors. Throughout the English empire, preachers concluded that an angry God had punished the town for its many sins.

Rather than offend God a second time, the Jamaican authorities laid out a new port, Kingston, on firmer ground across the harbor. More closely supervised by the planter elite, Kingston was too placid for the pirates. They moved to new havens in the Bahamas, conveniently close to the Florida Channel, which funneled Caribbean shipping into the Gulf Stream. Their departure diminished the common white population on Jamaica and completed the triumph of the planter elite.

During the late 1670s and through the 1680s, the great planters consolidated most of the arable land into the largest sugar plantations in the English West Indies. Once again, the common planters found themselves unable to compete for land and labor. After 1690, white immigration to Jamaica slowed, while out-migration grew. About 10,000 in 1690, the white population declined to 7,000 by 1713. Meanwhile, slave imports surged, swelling the black population to 55,000, eight times larger than the white numbers, a ratio greater even than the three-to-one of Barbados. In 1660, Jamaica had seemed big enough for both small and great planters, but by the end of the century it became the English colony most dominated by great planters and their slaves. By 1713, Jamaica was producing more sugar than Barbados and had become the wealthiest and most important colony in the English empire.

Paradoxical Jamaica also sustained the largest population of maroons—runaway slaves living in autonomous communities—in the English West Indies. In contrast to crowded and deforested Barbados, where the runaway found scant place to hide, Jamaica offered two substantial refuges: the densely vegetated Blue Mountains of the northeast and the rugged "Cockpit Country" of the west-center. To defend themselves against pursuit and recapture, the Jamaican maroons developed formidable skills at bush fighting and plantation raiding. Frequently defeated, the colonial authorities had to seek an understanding, negotiating their first treaty in 1663. The English agreed to leave the maroons alone, provided that they left the plantations alone and returned future runaways.

In effect, the maroons became independent communities in the recesses of a colony dedicated to plantation slavery. The maroons thought of themselves as particular communities with special rights, rather than as the vanguard of a general racial uprising. Indeed, the different bands sometimes attacked one another. And as slave catchers, the maroons served as a partial barrier that kept the slave majority at work on their plantations. But the maroon example also inspired new rebellions on isolated plantations, where the slaves killed their masters, seized arms, and broke into the mountains. If they could outrun and outfight pursuit for a few years, they too could win maroon status—but maroons accounted for only one percent of Jamaica's black population.

In sum, by 1700 the West Indian colonies featured a small but rich planter elite, a marginal population of poor whites, a great majority of black slaves, and a trace element of defiant maroons. As white immigration declined, the islands grew in overall population only by a massive importation of slaves from Africa that exceeded their heavy death rate from disease and overwork. Between 1640 and 1700 the English West Indies imported about 260,000 slaves, but sustained only 100,000 alive in 1700. Although an economic success, the West Indies was a demographic failure that manifested a society in consuming pursuit of profit and with a callous disregard for life. At the end of the seventeenth century, white emigrants from the West Indies, particularly Barbados, carried the seeds of that society to the southern mainland by founding the new colony of Carolina.

11

Carolina

★

1670–1760

The Old Plantation *was painted by an unknown artist in the late eighteenth century. The setting is uncertain, but the picture was found near Charleston, South Carolina. Apparently gathered for a wedding, the slaves dance to the music of African instruments (including a banjo) while wearing their finest clothes of European manufacture. In the middle distance, slaves paddle a canoe, while a plantation featuring a great house looms in the distance.*

DURING THE 1670s, West Indian planters established a new colony on the Atlantic seaboard north of Florida but south of the Chesapeake. Called Carolina to honor King Charles II, the new colony included present-day North and South Carolina and Georgia. Carolina officially belonged to a set of English aristocrats, the Lords Proprietor—eight powerful political favorites of the king. But they remained in England, entrusting early colonization primarily to ambitious men from Barbados, led by Sir John Yeamans and his son, Major William Yeamans. Sir John Yeamans possessed his full share of the ruthless opportunism so characteristic of the great planter elite. On Barbados, he had murdered a political rival and a few weeks later married his widow. One of the lords concluded, "If to convert all things to his present private profitt be the marke of able parts, Sir John is without doubt a very judicious man."

The Lords Proprietor needed experienced colonists, which Barbados promised to provide, while Carolina offered abundant land, which appealed to the frustrated ambitions of Barbados. In contrast to the compact and mountainous West Indies, South Carolina featured a broad, fertile coastal plain meandered by many large, muddy rivers and broad swamps. Cooler in winter than the West Indies, the Carolina low country more than compensated with an especially hot, humid, and enervating summer replete with biting insects. Eliza Lucas Pinckney described the Carolina summer as "extreamly disagreeable, excessive hott, much thunder and lightening, and muskatoes and sand flies in abundance." The colonists accepted the discomfort to obtain and exploit the fertile land, which seemed so immense and alluring after the experience of crowded Barbados.

Making a plantation colony in a frontier setting, the Carolinians feared that their African slaves might combine with defiant Indians to merge slave rebellion with frontier war—a combination almost certainly fatal to the new colony. In 1741 a Carolina colonist explained, "The greater number of blacks, which a frontier has . . . the more danger she is liable to; for those are all secret enemies, and ready to join with her open ones on the first occasion." The colony needed, at a minimum, to keep the Africans and the Indians apart. Ultimately, the colonists hoped to pit the Africans against the Indians, the better to exploit both. In their treaties with native peoples, the colonists insisted upon the return of all fugitive slaves as the price of peace and trade. As a further incentive, Carolina paid bounties to Indians who captured and returned runaways, at the rate of a gun and three blankets for each. Most native peoples cooperated, preferring bounties and trade to the state of war that was the cost of welcoming runaways. In 1724 a clergyman explained that Carolinians sought "to make Indians & Negros a checque upon each other, lest by their Vastly Superior Numbers we should be crushed by one or the other."

COLONISTS

In 1670 three ships from Barbados bore two hundred colonists to the mouth of the Ashley River, where they founded Charles Town (modified to Charleston in 1783), named, like Carolina, in honor of King Charles II. Closer to Spanish San Agústin (250 miles) than to English Jamestown (500 miles), Charles Town boldly defied Spanish claims to that coast, signifying England's new confidence in its emerging imperial power as Spain grew weaker. In 1607, the English had felt obliged to hide their Jamestown colony up a distant river, but in 1670 they defiantly planted Charles Town near the coast on the very margins of Florida. The Spanish governor at San Augústin quickly sent a small flotilla north to attack the intruders, but a storm obliged the Spanish to retreat. In 1686 a Spanish attack did destroy Port Royal, a smaller English settlement even closer to Florida, but the colonists promptly returned and rebuilt.

To secure Carolina from Spanish attack and accelerate its economic development, the Lords Proprietor needed to attract more colonists quickly. The Lords offered the incentives most alluring to English settlers of the late seventeenth century: religious toleration, political representation in an assembly with power over public taxation and expenditures, a long exemption from quitrents, and large grants of land. The Lords Proprietor assured religious tolerance to everyone but atheists (who hardly existed anywhere in the seventeenth century), promising even Jews the liberty to practice their faith. To discourage violent religious disputes, the Lords forbade "any reproachful, reviling, or abusive Language" against the faith of another. Adopting an especially generous headright system, the Lords freely granted 150 acres of land for each member of a family. They also sought only a small quitrent—half a pence per acre per year—and postponed collection to 1689. The incentives worked. From 200 colonists in 1670, South Carolina grew to about 6,600 in 1700 (3,800 white and 2,800 black). The growth rendered the colonists confident that they could repel the smaller numbers of Spanish in Florida, where the population stagnated at about 1,500.

Carolina primarily attracted farmers and artisans of modest means, drawn from both the Chesapeake and the West Indies. Common colonists were essential to perform the hard work of building farms in the forest and the hard fighting of frontier warfare. At least a third of the early Carolinians began as indentured servants, procured in either Barbados or England. In 1671, Carolina's governor urged the Lords Proprietor to send more English because "wee find that one of our Servants wee brought out of England is worth 2 of the Barbadians, for they are soe much addicted to Rum, yet they will doe little but whilst the bottle is at their nose."

During the late seventeenth century, Carolina offered the frontier a combination of opportunity and danger that had been lost in Barbados and the

Chesapeake as they became more crowded and developed. In Carolina, the male servant who survived his term received the customary "freedom dues"—a set of clothes, a barrel of maize, an ax, and a hoe—from his master plus a grant of one hundred acres from the Lords Proprietor. Such land grants attracted poor people, seeking, in the words of one promotional pamphlet, "a moderate Subsistance, without the Vexation of Dependance." By selling themselves into a few years of dependence, the servants eventually sought the independence of their own land, a prospect denied them in England, the Chesapeake, and Barbados. A study of long-lived early settlers reveals that the average Carolina freedman accumulated more than 350 acres of land before death.

Although the Lords Proprietor and their Barbadian allies needed common settlers, by no means did they wish to exclude the great planters with the capital to speed development. The Lords promised that the great planter would enjoy "absolute Power and Authority over his Negro Slaves." Although the Lords favored the Christian conversion of the Africans, they promised that it would not affect the legal status of slaves. The Lords Proprietor also followed the Jamaican precedent and defined a slave as a member of a family, entitling his master to a full 150-acre headright for each one imported.

Such large land grants entranced great planters, who never rested easy with what they already possessed and who wished to provide plantations to several sons rather than see any experience downward mobility. For example, the Middleton family wanted to preserve intact its 379-acre Barbados plantation in the hands of eldest son Benjamin. Younger sons Edward and Arthur first went to Antigua to start their own sugar estates, but they became discouraged after the French raided and plundered the island in 1666. Moving on to Carolina, the brothers obtained large land grants near Charles Town along Goose Creek, the favored locale of wealthy colonists from Barbados.

Carolina also promised ambitious and wealthy men the opportunity to get in on the ground floor of a new colony. The founding families expected the perquisites and opportunities of political interest, which would increase as the colony grew in numbers, territory, and wealth. The wealthiest colonists, former West Indians, known as the Goose Creek Men, dominated the assembly and council of Carolina, generally to the dismay of the Lords Proprietor, who felt increasingly ignored and defied. Between 1680 and 1695 the Lords went through twelve administrations in a futile search for a governor capable of controlling the colonists. In exasperation, the Lords asked one overmatched governor, "Are you to govern the people, or the people you?"

Proprietary authority was especially weak in a detached cluster of settlements on Albemarle Sound, near Virginia. Founded by Virginians during the 1650s, these settlements resented their inclusion in Carolina and resisted, sometimes violently, the collection of quitrents and customs duties by proprietary officials. In 1691 the Lords Proprietor mollified the Albemarle

Sound colonists by establishing "North Carolina" as a distinct government with its own assembly and deputy governor. In 1712 the Lords completed the division by elevating their deputy in North Carolina to the status of governor.

The division left Charles Town the capital of "South Carolina," which the Goose Creek Men dominated. Arrogant and Anglican, the Goose Creek Men stifled the policy of religious toleration. In 1702, the assembly barred non-Anglicans from holding political office and established the Church of England as the colony's official, tax-supported church. The Lords Proprietor accepted the restrictive new legislation, abandoning their principal supporters in the colony, the religious dissenters. Consequently, the Lords Proprietor had few friends in South Carolina when the planter elite moved decisively in 1719 to overthrow the last vestiges of proprietary authority.

The Carolina elite regarded the Lords Proprietor as doubly maddening: meddlesome in politics but ineffectual in defending the colony in the frequent wars with the Spanish and the Indians. The colonial elite wanted direct rule by the crown to secure increased military protection from the empire. In 1719 the South Carolina assembly revolted, declaring itself "a Convention, delegated by the People, to prevent the Ruin of this Government." Seizing control of the militia, the convention chose a provisional governor and sent an agent to England with a petition requesting a crown administration to replace the proprietors.

Accepting the coup, the crown appointed royal governors for South and North Carolina and negotiated to buy out the Lords Proprietor. In 1729 the crown purchased seven of the eight proprietary shares for £22,500—a bit less than what the lords had spent administering their colonies since 1670. In both North and South Carolina, the crown obtained the authority of government, title to all ungranted lands, and rights to collect the quitrents due on improved properties. A stubborn eighth proprietor, Lord Granville, refused to sell and retained title to the lands and quitrents in the northern third of North Carolina.

The transfer consolidated the political power of the great planter elite. During the 1720s and 1730s the crown exercised little authority in South Carolina beyond appointing governors. Most appointees wisely preferred cooperation to confrontation with the assemblymen. The government primarily operated to regulate the competition of great planters for additional land grants, to promote the export of their crops, and to protect them from slave rebellions and Indian wars. Equally endangered by rebellion and war, the common planters felt bound more tightly to the rule of the great planters, who, in turn, recognized their own dependence upon the common militia. As in the Chesapeake, the common and the great planters of Carolina established a white racial solidarity that, in politics, trumped their considerable differences in wealth and power.

— The Carolinas, c. 1740 —

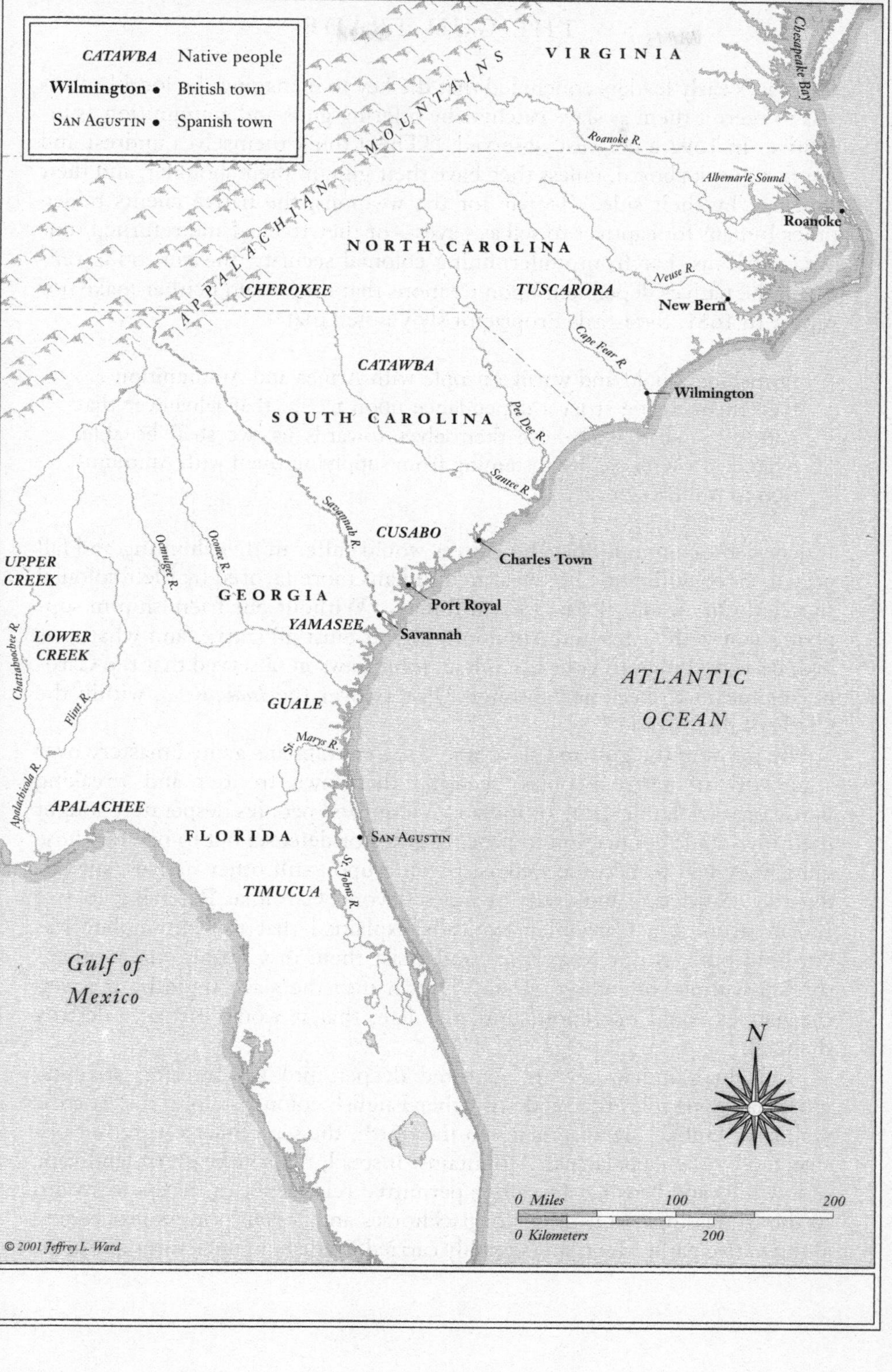

CATAWBA Native people
Wilmington • British town
San Agustin • Spanish town
VIRGINIA
APPALACHIAN MOUNTAINS
Chesapeake Bay
Roanoke R.
Albemarle Sound
Roanoke
NORTH CAROLINA
CHEROKEE
TUSCARORA
Neuse R.
New Bern
Cape Fear R.
CATAWBA
Wilmington
SOUTH CAROLINA
Pee Dee R.
Santee R.
Savannah R.
CUSABO
Charles Town
UPPER CREEK
Ocmulgee R.
Oconee R.
GEORGIA
Port Royal
YAMASEE
Savannah
LOWER CREEK
Chattahoochee R.
Flint R.
GUALE
ATLANTIC OCEAN
St. Marys R.
Apalachicola R.
APALACHEE
FLORIDA
San Agustin
St. Johns R.
TIMUCUA
Gulf of Mexico
N
0 Miles 100 200
0 Kilometers 200
© 2001 Jeffrey L. Ward

THE GUN TRADE

Carolina's early leaders concluded that the key to managing the local Indians was to recruit them as slave catchers by offering guns and ammunition as incentive. In 1692 a colonist observed, "[They] think themselves undrest and not fit to walk aboard, unless they have their gun on their shoulder, and their shot-bag by their side." To pay for the weapons, the native clients raided other Indians for captives to sell as slaves—or they tracked and returned runaway Africans. Far from undermining colonial security, the gun trade rendered the natives dependent upon weapons that they could neither make nor repair. In 1681, the Lords Proprietor slyly noted that

> furnishing a bold and warlike people with Armes and Ammunition . . . tyed them to soe strict a dependance upon us . . . that whenever that nation . . . shall misbehave themselves towards us, we shall be able, whenever we please, by abstaining from supplying them with Ammunition to ruine them.

If deprived of ammunition, the natives would suffer in their hunting and fall prey to slave-raiding by better-armed Indians more favored by their colonial supplier. One trader boasted to an Indian, "Without our friendship in supplying you with Guns and Ammunition you must all starve, and what is as bad, become a prey to your Enemies." John Lawson observed that the Carolinians meant to become "absolute Masters over the *Indians* . . . within the Circle of their Trade."

By pushing the gun and slave trade, the Carolinians gained mastery over a network of native peoples, securing their own frontier and wreaking havoc on a widening array of Indians. Victimized peoples desperately sought their own trade connection to procure guns for defense; but to pay for those guns, they had to become raiders, preying upon still other natives, spreading the destruction hundreds of miles beyond Carolina. Referring to two Indian peoples, a Carolinian cynically explained that the best policy was "to hold both as our friends . . . and assist them in Cutting one another's throats without offending either." Drawn into the slave trade by degrees, the natives could not know, until too late, that it would virtually destroy them all.

Carolina's Indian traders ventured deeper into the interior, affecting more native peoples than did any other English colonists along the Atlantic seaboard. Unlike the Virginians to the north, the Carolinians were not obstructed by the Appalachian Mountains. Instead, the southeastern landscape of low hills and broad river valleys permitted relatively easy access westward to the Mississippi. In caravans of packhorses and Indian porters proceeding along native paths, the traders readily carried English manufactures and alcohol into distant native villages. In 1707 the Carolina governor boasted, "Charles-Town Traded near 1000 Miles into the Continent."

The Carolina trader benefited from the native custom of providing wives to welcome newcomers. Unfamiliar with purely economic relationships, the natives never felt comfortable dealing with an outsider until he became an insider by adoption and marriage. In addition to its sexual pleasures, a marriage alliance endowed the trader with the protection of kinship, the advantages of inside information, and the critical labor of a woman skilled at treating deerskins. Moreover, the Indian wife and her relatives guarded the trader's stock during his absences, for their matrilineal culture regarded the property as hers. The marriage alliances also benefited the Indian family, which claimed privileged access to trade goods.

The English trader, however, usually treated his native marriage as a temporary convenience, often abandoning native wife and children for a new match in another village or for a white family in the settlements. Ultimately loyal to the competitive pursuit of profit, the Carolina trader remained an uneasy, often contentious presence among his hosts. He rarely mastered the generous reciprocity and public equanimity prized by the natives. The colonist John Lawson noted, "They say, the *Europeans* are always [w]rangling and uneasy and wonder why they do not go out of this World, since they are so uneasy and discontented in it."

Although they traded with each other, the Indians and the Carolinians did not share the same economic ethos. The trader James Adair noted, "They say we are covetous, because we do not give our poor relations such a share of our possessions as would keep them from want." By contrast, "they are very kind and liberal to every one of their own tribe, even to the last morsel of food they enjoy." John Lawson concluded that Indians were "an odd sort of People for their way of Living is so contrary to ours, that neither we nor they can fathom one another's Designs and Methods."

For example, the Creek felt insulted in the late 1740s when they discovered that the Carolina traders offered the Cherokee better prices for their deerskins. Operating from a commercial logic, the Carolinians justified their prices on the grounds that it cost them less to transport goods to the closer Cherokee Indians than to the more distant Creek. Moreover, the Cherokee provided the better-quality deerskins of their cooler country in the mountains. Such economic reasoning did not satisfy the Creek, who regarded prices as a measure of political respect. If the colonists were true to their professions of friendship, they should offer the Creek prices at least as good as those afforded the Cherokee.

Most of the time, the Carolina traders got away with their boorish behavior by offering especially prized trade goods at relatively good prices and on a generous credit. Unlike their Spanish and French rivals, the English relied almost exclusively on their economic advantage, rather than on understanding (or converting) the culture of their customers. Sheer commerce served the Carolinians well because English manufacturers and merchants had outstripped all other Europeans in the production and transatlantic shipment of the clothing, metal tools, and weapons especially desired by Indians.

In return for their cloth, knives, rum, and guns, Carolina traders sought animal hides and human slaves. Lacking the beaver of colder climes, the Carolina Indians provided the skins of deer, an animal that abounded in the warm and humid climate and an environment rich in grasses and berries (enhanced by the Indians' annual burning of the underbrush). In 1682 a Carolinian noted, "There is such infinite Herds that the whole Country seems but one continued [deer] Park." Traders shipped the treated deerskins to Europe, where they were made into bookbindings, gloves, belts, coats, work aprons, and hats. Between 1699 and 1715, South Carolina exported an average of 53,000 deerskins a year, worth about £30,000.

Indian men tracked, killed, and skinned the deer, but they depended upon women to tend the camp and butcher the carcass. Above all, women performed the long and tedious process of treating the deerskins by scraping, drying, soaking, and smoking to remove all tissue and hair. Without such treatment the hides decayed quickly from worms and maggots. By killing thousands of deer for the trade, Indian men imposed more labor upon their women.

Before the founding of Carolina, the region's Indians had hunted primarily for their own subsistence and clothing. After the advent of the trade, they killed additional animals for an export market to procure imported trade goods. The new guns enabled Indian hunters to kill many more deer than they had with their less deadly bows and arrows. By the mid-eighteenth century, the native hunter in the southeast killed about fifty to sixty dear annually, probably double the pre-trade average. The natives even abandoned their once powerful taboo against wasting an animal's body. The South Carolina surveyor William De Brahm lamented, "They make a great Carnage among the Deers, kill them for the sake of their Skins, and leave their Carcasses [to rot] in the Forrests."

The Carolina traders armed their clients with muskets to hunt people as well as deer. Indeed, the colonists paid far more for a slave than for deerskins. According to the trader Thomas Nairne, a gun cost an Indian twelve to sixteen deerhides, but a single slave "brings a Gun, ammunition, horse, hatchet, and a suit of Cloathes, which would not be procured with much tedious toil a hunting." Successful slave raids rewarded the attackers with the means to purchase additional trade goods, especially more muskets, compounding their military prowess. As a further bonus, successful slave raiding crushed and dispersed rival peoples, opening up their deer hunting grounds for exploitation by the victors.

The traders preferred women and children as captives, deeming them more adaptable to a new life as slaves. Indian men tended to die resisting attacks, or they were executed upon surrender. To mark the captives as private property, the traders branded them with hot irons on the cheek, shoulder, or arm. The Carolinians employed some captives on their own plantations, which in 1708 held 1,400 native, as well as 2,900 African, slaves. But captives too readily escaped into the nearby forest, and the Carolinians worried that contact between Indian and African slaves might embolden both to make common cause in a rebellion against their exploiters. Consequently, the Carolinians exported most of the Indian captives to the West Indies, especially Barbados, trading them for Africans, who were then brought back to work the Carolina plantations. The exchange rate of two Carolina Indian slaves for one African reflected the shorter life expectancy of the enslaved native.

The Carolinians justified enslavement as beneficial for Indians, sparing captives from execution and exposing them to Christian civilization among their English purchasers. A slave trader piously explained, "It is a more Effectual way of Civilizing and Instructing them [than] all the Efforts used by the French Missionaries." In fact, almost no religious instruction took place on a Barbados or Carolina plantation, which simply screwed as much labor as possible out of people before they died. Unlike the Spanish or the French, the Carolinians made virtually no effort to convert the Indians to Christianity. One of the few Anglican clergymen to try, the Reverend Francis Le Jau, complained, "Our Indian Traders are very much averse to see Missionaries among the Indians."

In London in 1683, the Lords Proprietor blasted the hypocrisy of the raid and trade system pursued by their colonists. By exploiting the native "Covetousness of your gunns, Powder, and Shott and other European Commodities," the Carolinians obliged them

> to ravish the wife from the Husband, Kill the father to get the Child and to burne and Destroy the habitations of these poore people into whose Country wee were Ch[e]arefully received by them, cherished and supplied when wee were weake, or at least never have done us hurt; and after wee have set them on worke to doe all these horrid, wicked things to get slaves to sell [to] the dealers in Indians [you] call it humanity to buy them and thereby keep them from being murdered.

But there was plenty of hypocrisy to go around; agents for the Lords had initiated the slave trade that they disavowed only after the Goose Creek Men had taken it over.

RAIDERS

As in early Virginia and New England, the first Carolina colonists were fortunate to find coastal natives eager for a colonial ally to provide trade goods and military assistance against Indian enemies of the interior. In 1670 the coastal Cusabo Indians were suffering from raids by the Westo, a newly arrived people who spoke an Iroquoian language and probably originated among the Erie, who had dwelled along the southern shore of Lake Erie until devastated by the Five Nation Iroquois during the early 1650s. Some of the Erie fled southward to prey upon other Indians, who called their new foes the Westo. By 1656 the Westo had reached Virginia, where they procured guns and ammunition from traders eager to recruit them as slave hunters. Migrating farther south, the Westo settled along the Savannah River and raided the Cusabo for slaves to supply the Virginia traders. In their violent displacement, new identity, and devastation of other natives, the Westo represented the power of the European intrusion to send shock waves of disruption through a succession of Indian peoples living far beyond the colonial settlements.

The Spanish in Florida claimed the Cusabo as vassals, but the Spanish failed to deliver on their promises to protect them against the Westo, for Spanish policy virtually precluded providing firearms to Indians, even their own allies. Desperate for colonial weapons, the Cusabo welcomed the English who founded Charles Town in 1670. Like the Powhatan of Virginia or the Wampanoag of Plymouth, the Cusabo initially regarded the English as *their* colonists, as a welcome alternative to the ineffectual Spanish. When the Spanish attacked Charles Town, the Cusabo helped defend the new colony.

But, to the dismay of the Cusabo, the colonists concluded that the more powerful Westo could better serve their interest. In 1674, Carolina's Indian agent, Dr. Henry Woodward, visited the Westo, opened a gun trade, and framed an alliance. The new relationship enabled the Carolinians both to freeze out the Virginia traders and to intimidate and subjugate the Cusabo, who rapidly lost their lands to the newcomers and their lives to the Westo. Instead of bringing relief to the Cusabo, the settlement of Carolina completed their destruction.

The Westo, however, soon learned that slave-raiding was a dangerous deal with the devil. In time, every client people became first debtors and then victims. The Westo dealt with an official trading company favored by Dr. Woodward and the Lords Proprietor of Carolina, who faced competition from traders beholden to the Goose Creek Men. To destroy the official monopoly, the competitors recruited a group of Shawnee known as the Savannah because they dwelled on the lower reaches of that river. Paid with alcohol and guns, during the early 1680s the Savannah crushed the Westo, converting them from slavers into slaves. The destruction of the Westo ruined the official company and opened the Indian trade to their competitors, who spread guns and slave raiding deep into the interior.

The expanded trade reached a large but loose confederation of Indians called the Creek by the English. Primarily Muskogean speakers, the 15,000 Creek included seven ethnic groups, dwelling in sixty distinct villages that formed two clusters, Lower and Upper. The Carolinians found the Lower

Creek along the Chattahoochee, Flint, and Apalachicola rivers, in what is now western Georgia and eastern Alabama. The more distant Upper Creek occupied the Coosa-Tallapoosa-Alabama river nexus in central Alabama. Especially numerous, blessed with an exceptionally fertile country, a productive horticulture, and abundant wildlife, the Creek were deemed the great prize in the contest for native trade and alliance in the colonial southeast.

The Spanish had tried to control the Lower Creek by introducing missions, but most villages rejected them. When the Spanish and their mission Indians, the Apalachee, threatened retribution, the Lower Creek sought firearms from the Carolinians. Infuriated by that overture, the Spanish and the Apalachee attacked and burned several Lower Creek villages. Rather than submit, the Lower Creek shifted eastward to get away from the Spanish and closer to their Carolina suppliers. During the late 1680s, the Lower Creek built new villages near the Ocmulgee River (in central Georgia), where they could defy the Spanish and prey upon their missions to procure the slaves needed to pay for their new weapons.

The Carolina traders encouraged the Creek raids, for the missions served the Spanish as a defensive buffer around San Agústin. The Carolinians also saw the poorly armed and conveniently clustered mission Indians—Guale, Timucua, and Apalachee—as easy pickings. During the 1680s, Savannah, Creek, and Yamasee raiders destroyed the Guale missions along the coast of Georgia. The survivors fled southward to take refuge near San Agústin. In 1702, Governor James Moore of Carolina organized a private army of about fifty Carolinians and one thousand Indians—a mix of Creek, Yamasee, and Savannah—to raid the Apalachee and Timucua missions of the Florida interior. Between 1704 and 1706 the raiders destroyed thirty-two native villages and their missions, inflicting horrific casualties and enslaving about ten thousand people. Most of the captured Spanish priests were tortured to death, and their churches went up in flames.

Relentless Creek and Yamasee warriors pursued fleeing mission Indians as far south as the Florida Keys, virtually obliterating the Guale, Apalachee, and Timucua. Florida's Indian population collapsed from about 16,000 in 1685 to 3,700 in 1715, and the missions shrank to a few in the immediate vicinity and partial security of San Agústin. In 1706, Spanish officials sadly reported, "In all these extensive dominions and provinces, the law of God and the preaching of the Holy Gospel have now ceased." The Carolina gun and slave trade had triumphed over the Spanish mission as an instrument of colonial power. Without the missions, Spanish Florida became a hollow shell, while English Carolina triumphed as the leading regional power.

After the destruction of the missions, potential captives became scarcer and the raiders fell into arrears on their debts owed to the traders. In 1707, in despair, the Savannah Indians tried to get out of the slave-raiding business by abandoning their lands to flee northward. Rather than write off the debts, the leading traders bribed the Catawba Indians to attack and enslave the fleeing Savannah. Only a minority broke through to refuge among their Shawnee kin in Pennsylvania.

The next victims were the Tuscarora, an Iroquian people living in North Carolina. Dismayed by expanding settlements, official arrogance, and slave raids, the Tuscarora lashed out, destroying colonial plantations and farms in 1711. Poor and weak, North Carolina desperately sought assistance from neighboring South Carolina, which saw an opportunity to procure new slaves. Captain James Moore, Jr., a veteran trader and the son of the former governor, commanded the South Carolina expedition, but most of his men were Indians: Cherokee, Yamasee, Creek, and Catawba. In March 1713, Moore's raiders stormed and burned the principal Tuscarora village, Nooherooka, killing hundreds. After executing 166 male captives deemed unsuitable for slavery, the raiders led 392 women and children back to Charles Town for sale. The other Tuscarora gave up the fight. Most fled northward, taking refuge among the Iroquois of New York, becoming their Sixth Nation.

Soon, the Yamasee came to regret their dangerous alliance with Carolina. Poorly paid for their Tuscarora captives, the Yamasee still owed debts worth a total of 100,000 deerskins—the equivalent of five years of hunting. Impatient traders began to seize and enslave the wives and children of the Yamasee to cover their debts. In April 1715 the Yamasee rebelled, killing traders, slaughtering cattle, and burning plantations around Port Royal. The rebels recruited the Catawba and Lower Creek, who shared their grievances. Long dependent upon a divide-and-conquer strategy, the Carolinians suddenly confronted an unexpected Indian unity along their long and vulnerable frontier. Never before in English colonial experience had so many native peoples united so effectively. During the spring and summer, the rebels killed about four hundred colonists and drove hundreds of refugees into Charles Town.

But, as in King Philip's War in New England, the Carolina Indian rebels lost momentum as they ran low on guns and gunpowder. They had counted on a continued supply from the traders in Virginia, who competed with the Carolinians. Despite that competition, during an Indian war their national and racial consciousness united them as English and white. Putting aside their rivalries, the Virginians assisted the Carolinians with weapons and troops and with an embargo on the trade in guns and gunpowder to the rebels, who discovered how painfully dependent they had become on English trade.

The Carolinians also appealed to the Six Nation Iroquois to attack the southern rebels. With their own grudges to settle, the Tuscarora guided Iroquois raiders into the Carolinas to wreak havoc on Catawba villages and cornfields during early 1716. Near starvation, the Catawba made peace with Carolina and helped to suppress and enslave the more persistent rebel peoples.

The Carolinians also enlisted the numerous and powerful Cherokee who dwelled in the southern Appalachian mountains. Initially neutral, they became worried as their longtime enemies the Yamasee and the Lower Creek devastated Carolina and its trade. After a long debate, the Cherokee decided that they wanted neither to live without trade goods nor see the Yamasee and Creek wax more powerful. Taking presents from South Carolina, the Cherokee suddenly attacked the rebels, with devastating effect. Seeking a safer distance from Carolina and the Cherokee, the Lower Creek evacuated the Ocmulgee Valley, shifting westward to their old townsites on the Chattahoochee River. The Yamasee fled southward to take refuge near San Agústin, where the pragmatic Spanish welcomed them as new allies useful for defending Florida. With critical assistance from the Iroquois and the Cherokee, the Carolinians had saved their colony.

During the early eighteenth century, John Lawson toured the Carolina interior, finding a landscape of abandoned or shrunken villages. He concluded that "there is not a sixth Savage living within two hundred Miles of all our Settlements, as there were fifty Years ago." Very little of the decline derived from direct conflict between colonists and Indians, but the population collapse had everything to do with the indirect consequences of the European intrusion into North America. The Carolina Indians dwindled from a catastrophic combination of disease epidemics, rum consumption, and slave raiding.

The depopulation reduced the slave trade but opened the Carolina interior to colonial settlement. The governor of North Carolina gave thanks that it "pleased Almighty God to send unusual sickness amongst them . . . thinning the Indians to make room for the English." In 1700, Indian numbers nearly equaled the colonists and their slaves in Carolina: 15,000 natives, compared with 16,000 colonists and Africans. By 1730 the 37,000 white colonists and 27,000 blacks in South and North Carolina had surged far beyond the local Indian population, which had declined to just 4,000.

Belatedly some Carolinians worried that the Indian depopulation had gone too far too fast, threatening their colonies in two ways. First, it created a vacuum that might be filled by maroon settlements made by runaway slaves, as had happened in Jamaica. Maroon settlements doubly threatened a colony by attracting more fugitives and by sending raiders to plunder plantations. To intercept runaways and break up incipient maroon settlements, the colonists needed *some* hinterland Indians to persist as frontier gatekeepers. A Carolina leader explained, "It can never be our Interest to extirpate [the Indians of the interior], or to force them from their Lands" for fear that "their Ground would be soon taken up by runaway *Negroes* from our Settlements, whose Numbers would daily increase, and quickly become more formidable Enemies than Indians can ever be."

Second, Indian flight westward threatened the Carolinas by drawing the refugees into the orbit of a new French colony, Louisiana, on the Gulf of

Mexico. As imperial rivals, the French and the English bitterly competed in trade and often went to war. If the refugees became French clients and allies, Carolina would lose their deerskin trade and suffer frontier raids, for without trade, Carolina lost the leverage to keep the Indians from expressing their resentments.

After winning the Yamasee War, the Carolinians regretted their success in driving the Lower Creek toward the French. Dreading French influence and Creek alienation, in 1717 the Carolinians offered a favorable peace that reopened trade. Sobered by the Yamasee War, the Carolina authorities more closely supervised the traders to restrain abuses and to redirect the trade away from slaving in favor of deerskins. The Carolinians also promised to keep their settlements east of the Savannah River, preserving a large, virtually unsettled buffer zone that facilitated deer hunting. As the commerce became less deadly to humans, it consumed the lives of growing thousands of deer. Although the Lower Creek made peace, they remained wary, adopting a neutrality policy meant to procure presents and favorable trade terms from the French, Spanish, and English.

RICE

The Carolinians knew that deerskins and Indian slaves were volatile and diminishing commodities—a flimsy economic foundation for their colony. To prosper in the long term, the colonists needed to develop a valuable agricultural staple for export. South Carolina lay too far north to grow sugar, and at a time of declining tobacco prices the colony could not compete with the efficient plantations in the Chesapeake. Instead, the Carolina planters initially competed with New England farmers to supply livestock and lumber to the English West Indies. In this trade, the Carolinians enjoyed the advantages of a shorter voyage to the West Indies and a milder winter, more favorable to raising livestock. Without the trouble and expense of erecting fences or building barns, the Carolinians simply turned their pigs and cattle loose to fend for themselves. The animals thrived in the warm and humid climate and the broad, lush coastal marshes and the nut-rich forests of hickory and oak.

Requiring little capital to begin, lumbering and cattle raising were ideal enterprises for a new frontier colony. In addition to harvesting pine trees for lumber, the Carolinians tapped their pitch for boiling to make tar, which was in great demand to waterproof ropes and caulk ships. Carolina became the leading colonial producer of tar, exporting about 44,000 barrels in 1717. Carolina also became the preeminent cattle country in the English empire, as the Carolinians pioneered many practices later perfected on a grand scale in the American West, including cattle branding, annual roundups, cow pens, and cattle drives from the interior to the market in Charles Town. Many owners entrusted the roaming cattle to the care of black slaves, who had previous experience as herdsmen in Africa. In Carolina the black herdsmen became known as "cowboys"—apparently the origin of that famous term.

During the 1670s and 1680s, slaves constituted about a quarter of the Carolina population. Frontier conditions obliged the planters to allow their slaves more autonomy than was common in either the West Indies or the Chesapeake. The early economic enterprises—woodcutting and cattle tending—dispersed slaves to work away from direct supervision. Entrusting some slaves with guns, the planters employed them to hunt game. In the frequent alarms of Spanish attack, the Carolinians also counted on armed slaves to defend, rather than attack, their masters. The colony rewarded with freedom any black who killed an enemy in time of war.

But early Carolina was no benign regime of racial harmony, for the planters also brutally punished whenever they felt their trust betrayed. In 1709 the Anglican clergyman Francis Le Jau noted, "A poor Slavewoman was barbarously burnt alive near my door without any positive proof of the Crime she was accused of, w[hi]ch was, the burning of her Master's House, and [she] protested her innocence even to my self to the last." The occasional, conspicuous, and summary infliction of public pain was essential to maintain a slave system that routinely allowed dispersion and some autonomy.

Despite their modest success as ranchers and wood purveyors, aspiring Carolinians continued to experiment with more valuable crops. During the 1690s, they developed rice as their great staple for the export market. A subtropical grain, rice thrived in the wet lowlands of Carolina, once the planters learned the proper techniques of cultivation from slaves, who had known the crop in West Africa. With slave labor, the planters reengineered the extensive tidewater swamps, diking out the tide to reserve fresh water for the rice. After planting in April and May, the planters flooded the fields during the summer to irrigate the crop and drown the weeds. Slaves harvested the grain in September and October. Removing the husk from the grain was especially laborious, requiring long hours of pounding by hand with a wooden mortar and pestle. Lasting through the fall, this process prepared the rice for shipment to market in December or January.

Carolina became the empire's great rice colony, just as the Chesapeake specialized in tobacco and the West Indies in sugar. The annual rice exports surged from 400,000 pounds in 1700 to about 43 million in 1740, when rice composed over 60 percent of the total exports from Carolina as measured by value. The English economist Arthur Young considered rice as second only to sugar in the calculus of empire: "The sugar colonies added above three millions [pounds sterling] a year to the wealth of Britain; the rice colonies near a million, and the tobacco ones almost as much."

During the 1750s, the Carolinians developed a second valuable plantation crop for export: indigo, a plant that produced a blue dye in great demand by the clothing industry in England. From a little over 63,000 pounds in 1750, South Carolina's exports surged to over 500,000 pounds by 1760. Enjoying a protected market within the empire for both rice and indigo, Carolina planters became the wealthiest colonial elite on the Atlantic seaboard—and second only to the West Indians within the empire.

The South Carolina elite became renowned as even more gracious, polite, genteel, and lavish than the gentlemen of Virginia. Competing for status, the Carolina planters vied to serve the best wines, to display fine silverware and furniture, to appear in silk clothing, and to muster servants dressed in livery. Travelers praised Carolinians for their social graces but faulted their self-discipline. One noted, "It is the doctrine here that during the warm months one should think and work little, and drink much." Another found the planters "above every occupation but eating, drinking, lolling, smoking, and sleeping, which five modes constitute the essence of their life and existence." An elite Carolinian conceded, "We eat, we drink, we play, and shall continue to until everlasting flames surprise us." Of course, this pleasure and ease depended upon the lands and hard labor forced from others. By conspicuous indolence and consumption, the planters abundantly demonstrated to onlookers that they were not slaves.

Like sugar, rice generated large profits but demanded numerous workers who could be coerced into performing intense labor under harsh conditions. A typical rice planter with 130 acres needed sixty-five laborers who could not readily desert to take another occupation elsewhere. Throughout colonial America, this combination of warm climate, fertile soil, and a profitable but laborious staple led planters to invest in African slaves.

As the planters cultivated more rice, they imported more slaves, the first both paying for and making necessary the second. Only 1,500 in 1690, the African population grew to 4,100 by 1710, when South Carolina became the first mainland colony with a black majority. By 1730, enslaved Africans outnumbered free colonists in Carolina two to one: 20,000 to 10,000. The African majority was concentrated in the rice-growing district: the hot, humid, marshy lowlands of the coastal plain. In the low country, blacks outnumbered whites by nine to one, a ratio comparable to that in Jamaica and greater than that in Barbados. As in the West Indies, the black majority preserved African traditions and languages and built their quarters in an African style. In 1737 a Swiss newcomer noted that the low country seemed "more like a negro country than like a country settled by white people." In Carolina, whites were a majority only in the newer settlements of the Piedmont, where rice did not thrive.

As in Barbados, so in Carolina, the brutal working conditions and the disease-ridden lowland environment produced a slave mortality in excess of the birthrate. In the mid-eighteenth century, a South Carolina doctor expressed a rare sympathy for the Africans in a letter to a friend in England:

> Our Staple Commodity for some years has been Rice, and Tilling, planting, Hoeing, Reaping, Threshing, Pounding have all been done merely by the poor Slaves here. Labour and the Loss of many of their Lives testified [to] the Fatigue they Underwent, in Satiating the Inexpressible Avarice of their Masters. You may easily guess what a Tedious, Laborious, and slow Method it is of Cultivating Lands to Till it all by Hand, and then to plant 100, 120 Acres of Land by Hand, but the worst comes last for after the Rice is threshed, they beat it all in the hand in large Wooden Mortars to clean it from the Husk, which is a very hard and severe operation as each Slave is tasked at Seven Mortars for One Day, and each Mortar Contains three pecks of Rice.

As in the West Indies, only continued African imports sustained the steady growth of the slave population in Carolina.

TERROR

The rice planters unwittingly paid psychological, social, and demographic costs for adopting the West Indian slave system. And they freely shared those costs with poor whites who owned no slaves. As in Barbados, the imported Africans introduced especially virulent forms of malaria and yellow fever to Carolina. The pathogens found abundant bearers, anopheles mosquitoes, in the hot and humid Carolina lowlands. Racially indifferent, the mosquitoes conveyed the deadly new diseases to white and black alike.

As in the West Indies, the planters also suffered from a haunting fear that their African majority would rise up in deadly, burning rebellion. In a desperate search for security, the Carolina planters adopted the West Indian system of strict surveillance and harsh punishment to keep the slaves intimidated and working. The new system criminalized formerly tolerated behavior, revoking the degree of trust and autonomy previously allowed most slaves in the frontier era. Slaves who traveled without a pass, congregated from a distance, kept firearms to hunt game, or learned to read a newspaper had to do so surreptitiously. Because the colonists rewarded black informants, slaves also had to distrust one another in pursuing any forbidden activity. The new rigor demanded a constant, straining vigilance from whites. Not even their Sabbath, their supposed day of rest and religious reflection, brought calm and relief. In 1724, legislation required the planters to bear firearms to church, to deter the blacks from rebelling on a Sunday. The stricter regime heightened planter terror at least as much as it intimidated the slaves. In 1720 and 1730 the colony was convulsed by rumored conspiracies to murder the planters and burn their plantations. The authorities employed torture to obtain confessions, which led to executions, sometimes by hanging but usually by burning at the stake.

On Sunday, September 9, 1739, the dread became real in a slave rebellion on the Stono River, twenty miles from Charles Town. The violence began when twenty slaves stole guns and gunpowder from a store, killing and decapitating the two storekeepers. They began to march south, hoping to reach Spanish Florida, which welcomed runaway slaves. Instead of making haste, they proceeded deliberately, displaying a makeshift flag, beating two drums, and chanting "Liberty!" They hoped methodically to gather strength in numbers by destroying plantations and recruiting more slaves to rebellion. Along the way, their number grew to at least eighty and perhaps as many as one hundred. They burned seven plantations and killed twenty whites, but showed discretion when they spared an innkeeper considered "a good Man and kind to his slaves."

Desperate to suppress the rebellion lest it succeed and inspire others, the local planters mustered their forces. Possessing horses, more guns, better training in arms, and a militia command structure, the whites could rally overwhelming power. On the second day of the uprising, about one hundred armed and mounted white militiamen surprised and routed the rebels, killing most, usually after they had surrendered. To terrify the other slaves, the victors cut off the rebels' heads and placed them on posts, one every mile, between the battlefield and Charles Town. About thirty rebels escaped into the forest, but within a month almost all were killed by a massive manhunt that included Indian bounty hunters.

Victory did not stem the planter dread. After suppressing another suspected slave conspiracy in 1740 in Charles Town, a colonist lamented, "Every one that had any Relation, . . . every one that had a Life to lose were in the most sensible Manner shocked at such Danger daily hanging over their Heads." No matter how repressively they ruled, or how cowed the Africans seemed, the masters ultimately sensed that their slaves hated them and would, if they could, kill to be free.

Masters pitied themselves that they possessed such a dangerous form of property. In 1741 the South Carolina assembly lamented, "With Regret we bewailed our peculiar Case, that we could not enjoy the Benefits of Peace like the rest of Mankind and that our own Industry should be the Means of taking from us all the Sweets of Life and of rendering us Liable to the Loss of our Lives and Fortunes." The planters thought of themselves as the innocent victims of vicious blacks and of circumstances that compelled white Carolinians to own slaves.

At the same time, the planters took great pride in their thriving plantations and their growing colony. Without any sense of irony, the assembly boasted that South Carolina had "become the land of plenty, as well as of liberty." Compartmentalizing their slaves as something other than people, the planters rendered invisible the slave majority in their political discourse.

GEORGIA

During the late 1720s, Carolina officials and British imperialists strengthened their hold on the southern frontier by founding a new colony south and west of the Savannah River. Named Georgia, in honor of King George II, the new colony appealed to a group of London philanthropists and social reformers, known as the Georgia Trustees. Led by James Oglethorpe (a landed gentleman, member of Parliament, and former army officer), the Georgia Trustees were a mix of wealthy merchants, landed gentry, and Anglican ministers. They hoped to alleviate English urban poverty by shipping "miserable wretches" and "drones" to a new southern colony, where hard work on their own farms would cure indolence. By this moral alchemy, people who drained English charity would become productive subjects working both to improve themselves and to defend the empire on a colonial frontier. In effect, the Georgia Trustees revived the scheme of the sixteenth-century West Country promoters, who had proposed Virginia as a colonial workhouse to redeem England's idle poor.

In addition to raising charitable contributions, the Georgia Trustees secured financial assistance from the crown and Parliament. Their 1732 royal charter awarded the new colony to the trustees for a period of twenty-one years, after which Georgia would become a royal colony. Until 1752, 90 percent of the colony's funding came from Parliament, making Georgia the first colony financed by British taxpayers. From 1733 to 1742 the trustees freely transported, and provided small farms to, about 1,800 charity colonists. Other colonists paid their own way, lured by the prospect of free land.

In 1733, Oglethorpe personally conducted the first colonists across the Atlantic to found the town of Savannah, on a bluff near the mouth of that river. Farther upriver he located the town of Ebenezer, as a haven for German Lutherans recently evicted from a Catholic principality. Farther south, at the mouth of the Altamaha River, he established Highland Scots, to guard the border against Spanish raids.

In 1743, Oglethorpe returned to England, where he found the trustees embattled by protests that they were stifling the economic development of their colony. In designing Georgia, the trustees had reacted against the large landholdings and slave majority that characterized South Carolina. Large plantations and many slaves reduced and dispersed the free white population needed for a militia to defend a frontier. Moreover, black slavery made manual labor seem degrading to free men, which discouraged exertion by common whites, who aspired, instead, to acquire their own slaves to do the dirty work. Consequently, slavery threatened to corrode the labor discipline that the Georgia colonists needed to redeem their characters and please the trustees.

To maximize the number of whites willing to labor and capable of bearing arms, the Georgia Trustees wanted many compact farms worked by free families, instead of larger but fewer plantations dependent upon enslaved Africans. To mandate their vision, the founders restricted most new settlers to fifty-acre tracts—about an eighth of the size of a Carolina plantation—and the trustees forbade the importation or possession of slaves. Instead of raising rice and indigo on plantations with slave labor, the Georgians were supposed to cultivate compact and high-value crops of hemp (to make rope), flax (to make linen), mulberry (to feed silkworms), and grapes (to make wine). Industrious and tightly settled, these ideal Georgians would make a formidable and numerous militia to defend the new colony on a dangerous frontier.

Georgia was the first and only British colony to reject the slave system so fundamental and profitable to the rest of the empire. Driven by concerns for military security and white moral uplift, the antislavery policy expressed neither a principled empathy for enslaved Africans nor an ambition to emancipate slaves elsewhere. During the early eighteenth century, almost all Britons, including the Georgia Trustees, accepted slavery as normative, profitable, and essential to the imperial economy as a whole. Indeed, by securing the southern frontier, Georgia could obstruct the flight of Carolina's runaway slaves to safe haven in hostile Florida. Georgia promised to strengthen slavery in Carolina by closing an escape hatch that invited both flight and rebellions.

The Georgia Trustees were powerful and distant elitists who did not trust their colonial subjects to improve themselves without strict guidelines. In addition to banning slavery and restricting landholdings, the trustees tried to prohibit rum-drinking as another deterrent to hard work and moral uplift. To discourage litigation and agitation, the founders also banned lawyers from practicing in the new colony. Permitting no elected assembly, the trustees instead appointed a court of four officials to govern the colony.

These restrictions rankled the more ambitious colonists, who increasingly resented the trustees as unrealistic, unresponsive, and dictatorial. Overestimating the Georgia environment as idyllic, the trustees underestimated the hardships of making frontier farms in a hot, humid, swampy, and densely vegetated land—just as they slighted the difficulties of turning urban paupers into colonial farmers. Frustrated and impatient, the settlers contrasted their hardships and poverty with the relative ease and prosperity of the white men on South Carolina's plantations. Seeking a quick solution, the discontented settlers became fixated on the antislavery ban as the chief obstacle to their ambitions. An official described the colonists as "stark Mad after Negroes."

During the late 1730s and early 1740s, the trustees lifted the bans on lawyers, liquor, and large landholdings—but held firm against slavery and an assembly. In 1739, Oglethorpe insisted, "If we allow Slaves, we act against the very Principles by which we associated together, which was to relieve the distressed." A colonist retorted, "Thus have you *Protected us from Our-*

selves . . . by Keeping all Earthly Comforts from us. You have afforded us . . . the Integrity of the *Primitive Times*, by intailing a more than *Primitive Poverty* on us."

The Georgia dissidents rallied behind the revealing slogan "Liberty and Property without restrictions"—which explicitly linked the liberty of white men to their right to hold blacks as property. Until they could own slaves, the white Georgians considered themselves unfree. Such reasoning made sense in an eighteenth-century empire where liberty was a privileged status that almost always depended upon the power to subordinate someone else. Under increasing pressure from a Parliament solicitous of the slave trade, in 1751 the trustees capitulated, permitting slavery and surrendering Georgia to the crown. Georgia received the usual tripartite arrangement of an elected assembly, a crown-appointed council, and a royal governor.

Rejecting the reformist vision of the trustees, Georgians soon made a plantation society that virtually replicated South Carolina. The elected assembly wrote a strict slave code modeled on South Carolina's. The new regime partially fulfilled the dissidents' hopes by stimulating an economic and demographic boom, but this ultimately vested most of the benefits in the hands of newcomers from Carolina. From about 3,000 whites and 600 blacks in 1752, Georgia's population surged to 18,000 whites and 15,000 blacks in 1775. The growth depended primarily upon emigrants from South Carolina bringing slaves to develop rice and indigo plantations along the coast and the major rivers. The experiments in wine, silk, hemp, and flax collapsed. As the trustees had feared, the introduction of plantation slavery concentrated wealth and power in a planter elite, principally former Carolinians. While producing the appearance of white equality in a shared hegemony over black slaves, the plantation system increased the real inequalities of wealth and power between white men.

CONCLUSION

By 1760 the low country of both Georgia and South Carolina had largely replicated the West Indian plantation system. A relatively small group of whites became immensely rich, leisured, and politically powerful by exploiting a large and growing population of enslaved Africans. Because Carolina society so closely resembled Barbados, English officials commonly referred to "Carolina in the West Indies." This development was ironic, for plantation society had driven from Barbados the original emigrants who became the first Carolinians. But they went to Carolina with no radical vision of an egalitarian alternative to the staple and slave system of the West Indies. On the contrary, the emigrants sought their own place to achieve the mastery and wealth of great planters.

Only a minority won that lottery, but the vast and fertile lands of

Carolina and Georgia provided more room for common opportunity than did the confined West Indies. After the great planters helped themselves to large tracts in the lowlands for rice and indigo plantations, there was still plenty of land left in the Piedmont to endow most common whites with substantial farms. And because of the open frontier with Spanish enemies and potential Indian foes, the Carolina and Georgia great planters especially needed a militia drawn from the ranks of common whites. Consequently, the common and great planters of Carolina and Georgia enjoyed a more stable relationship than had their predecessors on small and crowded Barbados.

12

Middle Colonies

★

1600–1700

A Dutch colonial couple in the foreground, with the shipping and buildings of New Amsterdam in the background, c. 1650. The image conveys the centrality of transatlantic commerce and the prominence of enslaved Africans in the Dutch colonial town. From I. N. Phelps Stokes, Iconography of Manhattan Island *(New York, 1915).*

DURING THE EARLY SEVENTEENTH CENTURY, the English developed two distinct and populous clusters of settlements along the Atlantic seaboard: the Chesapeake to the south and New England to the north. Until mid-century, the English neglected the intervening mid-Atlantic coast, despite its advantages. More fertile and temperate than New England, but far healthier than the Chesapeake, the mid-Atlantic region was especially promising for cultivating grain, raising livestock, and reproducing people. The region also boasted three navigable rivers, reaching deep into the interior: the Susquehanna, Delaware, and Hudson. The English neglect enabled the Dutch and Swedes to establish their own small colonies: New Netherland in the Hudson Valley and New Sweden in the Delaware Valley. Although the English protested, they initially lacked the power to oust their rivals, and deemed it impolitic to try, for the Dutch and Swedes were fellow Protestants and allies in the European wars of religion during the early seventeenth century.

At mid-century, however, as the English grew in power and ambition, their rulers developed a violent envy of Dutch wealth. King Charles II (1660–85) and his brother, James, the Duke of York, hoped to build the crown's clout within England by expanding the empire in America. They recognized the connection, pioneered by the Dutch, between overseas colonies, commercial expansion, and national power. By conquering New Netherland, Charles and James meant to strengthen England's commerce by weakening its principal rival, the Dutch empire. The acquisition of New Netherland (which had swallowed up New Sweden) would also close the gap between the Chesapeake and New England, promoting their mutual defense against other empires and the Indians. Finally, a conquest also promised increased crown control over its own fractious colonies.

Compared with the Spanish, French, and Dutch rulers, the English monarch exercised little power over his colonists, primarily because of the persistent reliance on a proprietary system of colonization. During the early seventeenth century, the underfunded English crown had lacked the means to launch and administer distant colonies. Instead the crown entrusted early colonization to private interests licensed by royal charters, which awarded the proprietors both title to colonial land and the right to govern the colonists—subject to royal oversight, which was sporadic at best. Most charters went to joint stock companies of merchants—for example, the Virginia Company—or to especially wealthy and ambitious aristocrats, such as Lord Baltimore, who obtained Maryland, or the Earl of Carlisle, who procured the Lesser Antilles.

The colonists compelled their distant and weak proprietors to share political power. The proprietors appointed the governor and council, but propertied colonists elected an assembly with power over finances. Throughout the empire, propertied Englishmen cherished legislative control over taxation as their most fundamental liberty. The proprietors accepted assemblies as a means to attract or retain propertied colonists, who were essential to a colony's economic development, which was critical to the proprietors' revenues.

The New England colonies were a special case. Leading Puritans formed the Massachusetts Bay Company to secure a colonial charter, which they carried across the Atlantic to establish a virtually independent colonial government. Without the benefit of any charter, Puritans or their dissidents founded the adjoining colonies of Plymouth, Connecticut, and Rhode Island. In 1663, Rhode Island and Connecticut belatedly obtained royal charters; Plymouth never so succeeded. By virtue of their especially indulgent charters, the New England colonies were virtually independent of crown authority. Answering to no external proprietors, the New English developed republican regimes where the propertied men elected their governors and councils, as well as their assemblies, and where much decision-making was dispersed to the many small towns.

The proprietary system became a liability later in the seventeenth century, as the crown developed greater imperial ambitions. Noting the growing numbers and prosperity of the colonists, imperial officials sought tighter control, the better to regulate and tax colonial commerce. The officials also worried that colonial wealth would attract predation by another empire. Divided into many distinct colonies, each jealous of the other and all internally divided by factions in their assemblies, the colonial arrangement seemed designed for many separate surrenders rather than for collective defense. In a crisis with another empire, one English colony could appeal for help from the others, but it was unlikely to receive much. Imperial bureaucrats believed that the proprietary colonies should first be converted into royal colonies and then consolidated into an overarching government like the Spanish viceroyalty of New Spain.

During the seventeenth century, crown officials gradually converted a few proprietary colonies into royal colonies. Such conversion primarily meant that the king, rather than a proprietor, appointed the governor and council, for the crown felt obliged to retain the elected assemblies. The crown acted first where the revenues were greatest, to secure control over tobacco-rich Virginia and the sugar colonies of Barbados, the Leeward Islands, and Jamaica. The crown was slower to reorganize the New England colonies because they lacked a lucrative staple critical to the royal revenue. Moreover, the numerous Puritan colonists promised to make any imperial attempt to compel their obedience expensive and difficult.

In 1664 an English naval squadron with soldiers crossed the Atlantic, bound for North America. Rumor insisted, the New English feared, and the Dutch hoped that the flotilla was bound to Boston to subdue the Puritans. Instead, the warships sailed to the Hudson to conquer New Netherland. But the crown also meant that conquest to impress a New English audience, to intimidate the colonists into a new respect for royal authority. By smiting the Dutch, the crown hoped to strengthen its own power within a more consolidated empire. The conquest also initiated the development of a new cluster of English colonies—the middle colonies, defined by their setting between New England and the Chesapeake.

THE DUTCH EMPIRE

The Dutch colony on the Hudson River was a relatively minor enterprise in an especially wealthy, ambitious, and far-flung empire that developed with remarkable rapidity. During the early seventeenth century, the Netherlands emerged as an economic and military giant, out of all proportion to its confined geography and small population of 1.5 million (compared with 5 million English and 20 million French). The Dutch exploited their prime commercial location by the mouth of the Rhine River, beside the North Sea, and near the entrance to the Baltic Sea. The Netherlands became the nexus of northern European commerce between France and England to the west, the German cities and principalities to the east, and Russia and the Scandinavian countries to the northeast. Possessing Europe's most efficient merchant marine and fishing fleet, the Dutch dominated the carrying trade of northern and western Europe, the North Seas fisheries, and Arctic whaling. In 1670 the Dutch employed 120,000 sailors on vessels totaling 568,000 tons—more than the combined shipping of Spain, France, and England. The English writer Daniel Defoe aptly explained:

> The Dutch must be understood as they really are, the Middle Persons in Trade, the Factors and Brokers of Europe. . . . They *buy* to *sell* again, *take* in to *send* out, and the greatest Part of their vast Commerce consists in being supply'd from All Parts of the World, that they may supply All the World again.

The great Dutch city of Amsterdam (and its port of Rotterdam) became the preeminent shipping, banking, insurance, printing, and textile manufacturing center, not only in the Netherlands but in all of northern Europe.

The Dutch economy also benefited from a liberal government that adopted policies of intellectual freedom and religious toleration unique in seventeenth-century Europe. While the other European states were developing authoritarian and centralized monarchies, the Dutch opted for a decentralized republic dominated by wealthy merchants and rural aristocrats. Each of the seven provinces in the Dutch confederation enjoyed domestic autonomy, but the most populous and prosperous province, Holland, usually determined the nation's military and foreign policies. Over the course of the seventeenth century, the confederation's military commander, usually a prince of the House of Orange, accumulated growing power over foreign affairs.

— The Middle Colonies, c. 1690 —

MAHICAN Native people
Kahnawake ○ Native town
Kingston • English town
Montreal • French town

Montreal
CANADA
Kahnawake
St. Lawrence R.
Lake Ontario
Lake Champlain
Lake George
Lake Oneida
FIVE NATIONS
Mohawk R.
Connecticut R.
NEW HAMPSHIRE
Schenectady
Albany (Fort Orange)
MAHICAN
NEW NETHERLAND
(NEW YORK)
MASSACHUSETTS
Hudson R.
Springfield
Kingston
Hartford
RIVER INDIANS
Housatonic R.
CONNECTICUT
New Haven
Delaware R.
PENNSYLVANIA
Long Island Sound
New York
(New Amsterdam)
LONG ISLAND
Perth Amboy
SUSQUEHANNOCK
LENNI LENAPE
NEW JERSEY
Susquehanna R.
Schuylkill R.
ATLANTIC OCEAN
Philadelphia
Burlington
Fort Christina (Wilmington)
New Castle
MARYLAND
N
Baltimore
Delaware Bay
Potomac R.
Annapolis
VIRGINIA
Chesapeake Bay
DELAWARE
LOWER
COUNTIES
0 Miles *50* *100*
0 Kilometers *100*

Seeking uniformity, most European realms persecuted religious dissidents, often expelling minorities. The Dutch welcomed those outcasts, including French Protestants and Iberian and German Jews, reaping their talents and investments. European intellectuals also gravitated to Amsterdam because the Dutch allowed greater latitude to new ideas. The great seventeenth-century philosophers René Descartes, John Locke, and Benedict de Spinoza all emigrated to escape intolerance in their own countries. A German visitor observed that the Dutch "love nothing so much as they do their freedom."

The combination of republican government, religious toleration, naval power, colonial trade, and a manufacturing boom endowed the Dutch with the greatest national wealth and the highest standard of living in Europe. Perceived as a land of opportunity, the Netherlands attracted a steady stream of ambitious immigrants, particularly from Germany and Scandinavia. Many came to serve in the "Dutch" army and navy, constituting a majority of the soldiers and sailors who extended the power of that small country.

The wealth and power of the Netherlands were especially remarkable because they had been achieved so rapidly from modest origins. Until the late sixteenth century, the Netherlands was subordinated within the Spanish empire in Europe. Largely Protestant, and specifically Calvinist, the Dutch bitterly resented Spanish economic exploitation and religious persecution. During the 1570s, the Dutch provinces rebelled and gradually secured their independence after a long, hard war.

Both to weaken their enemy and to reap profits, Dutch warships carried the conflict around the globe to prey on Spanish and Portuguese shipping and colonies and to build their own lucrative and far-flung empire. By capturing fortified entrepôts in the East Indies (Indonesia) and Ceylon (Sri Lanka), the Dutch supplanted the Portuguese as the primary carriers of the especially valuable spice and silk trade from Asia to Europe. To protect that trade route, in 1652 the Dutch founded a small colony at the Cape of Good Hope at the southern tip of Africa—the future Capetown, South Africa.

During the early and middle seventeenth century, the Dutch also stole the Portuguese primacy in the other two great, and interrelated, forms of imperial commerce conducted by Europeans: the export of sugar from American plantations and the transportation of slaves from West Africa to cultivate that sugar. In 1637 the Dutch captured Elmina Castle, the principal Portuguese fortified trading post on the west coast of Africa.

After 1640 most of the slaves sent to the Americas went in Dutch rather than Portuguese vessels, enriching the merchants of Amsterdam rather than those of Lisbon. During the 1630s, the Dutch seized the northeastern coast of Portuguese Brazil, then the preeminent sugar-producing colony in the Americas. By 1650 the Dutch were refining most of the sugar consumed in Europe. The Dutch also occupied several islands in the West Indies, including Curaçao, St. Martin, and St. Eustatius, to augment their sugar plantations and to facilitate smuggling with, and piracy upon, Spanish ports and ships in the Caribbean.

To prosecute their attacks and build their new empire, the Dutch developed the most formidable fleet of warships in Europe. A mix of public and private investment, this navy sought both national power and mercantile profit. In the single most spectacular success, a Dutch flotilla intercepted and captured the entire Spanish treasure fleet homeward bound from the Caribbean in 1628. The loss of the ships and 200,000 pounds of silver virtually bankrupted the Spanish crown and enormously enriched the Dutch investors in the attacking fleet.

The Dutch victories dismayed the Portuguese, who lost confidence in the protection of their Spanish king. Fed up with Spanish rule, the Portuguese rebelled, reasserting their independence in 1640, further weakening the once mighty Spanish empire. That decline elevated the Netherlands to preeminence in the European competition for American commerce and colonial power. By 1650 the Dutch reaped most of the profits taken in European commerce with China, India, Africa, Brazil, and the Caribbean. In turn, that commerce stimulated the further development of manufactures in Holland to supply outgoing cargoes and to build more ships for commerce and war.

However, the Dutch spread themselves perilously thin in their effort, as a small country, to maintain global trade by imperial violence. Their European rivals watched with envy and noted that commerce, colonies, naval might, and national wealth fed upon one another. By mid-century, the Dutch faced attacks from their former allies against Spain: the French and the English. Their targets included the seventeenth-century Dutch colony along the Hudson, New Netherland, which was a minor operation on the fringes of an overextended empire with wealthier assets and higher priorities to defend elsewhere in the world.

NEW NETHERLAND

Beginning with Henry Hudson in 1609, Dutch merchants annually sent ships across the Atlantic and up the Hudson River to trade for furs with the Indians. Seventeenth-century ships could ascend the river 160 miles, as far as the future Albany, a greater distance than was possible on any other river on the Atlantic seaboard. From the upper Hudson, traders could contact distant northern Indians coming in canoes via two corridors. The first proceeded northward by Lake George, Lake Champlain, and the Richelieu River to the St. Lawrence, and the second reached westward via the Mohawk River to the Great Lakes. But using either corridor required the goodwill of the Iroquois.

In 1614 Dutch traders established a year-round presence on the upper Hudson by founding Fort Nassau, later relocated and renamed Fort Orange, with an associated village called Beverwyck ("Beaver Town"). During the late 1620s, Fort Orange had only about fifty Dutch inhabitants, about half fur traders and half soldiers, all employees of the monopolistic Dutch West India Company. Fur trading operations wanted only a few colonists, to minimize the costs of supply and to discourage competitors trading on their own accounts.

The Dutch West India Company, however, recognized that it needed populous settlements to protect the mouth of the Hudson. Without strength in numbers to guard the colony's entrance, the furs at Fort Orange would tempt easy seizure by French or English warships. In the lower Hudson Valley, farms also could help the company by producing grain, cattle, and lumber to supply the fur traders at Fort Orange and to ship to the Dutch West Indies to feed the slaves on the sugar plantations. In 1625, the Dutch founded the fortified town of New Amsterdam on Manhattan Island at the mouth of the river. Possessing the finest harbor on the Atlantic seaboard, New Amsterdam served as the colony's largest town, major seaport, and government headquarters. New Amsterdam encouraged agricultural settlement in its vicinity to the east on Long Island, to the north beside the Hudson, and to the west in present-day New Jersey. New Netherlands became bifurcated between a small fur-trading post upriver and larger agricultural settlements on the lower river.

The bifurcation led to different Indian policies in the two halves of the valley. Upriver the Dutch were too few, and too dependent upon trade, to intimidate their native neighbors, the formidable Iroquois Five Nations (primarily the nearby Mohawk). Terrifying as enemies but invaluable as trading partners, the Iroquois determined the success or failure of the trading post. Fort Orange became as much a Mohawk as a Dutch asset.

The upriver respect for Iroquois power contrasted with the Dutch treatment of the Hudson River Indians, a disunited set of Algonquian-speaking bands. Compared with the Iroquois, the Algonquians of the lower Hudson contributed little to the fur trade and their warriors were fewer and less well supplied with firearms. Because the downriver Dutch came in substantial numbers to develop farms, they also regarded the Algonquians as a nuisance best removed as quickly as possible. On the lower Hudson, the Dutch could indulge in the ethnocentrism that they had to restrain on the upper river.

Come to trade or to farm, the Dutch made virtually no missionary effort, in contrast to the French, the Spanish, and even the Puritan English. In New Netherland, the ministers of the Dutch Reformed Church were few, preoccupied with the colonists, and disgusted by the Indians. The colony's preeminent clergyman declared, "As to the natives of this country, I find them entirely savage and wild, strangers to all decency, yea, uncivil and stupid as garden poles, [and] proficient to all wickedness and godlessness." For want of trying, the New Netherland clergy made only a single Indian convert, and he soon lapsed, pawning his Bible for brandy. Fundamentally commercial in outlook, the Dutch regarded missions as an unnecessary expense, if not an impediment to free trade with natives, who preferred their traditional beliefs and disliked meddling missionaries. The Dutch counted on the high quality and low prices of their goods to attract Indian trade, while the French hoped that missions would bind natives into their orbit, compensating for their economic disadvantages.

Despite the growing fur trade, the Dutch West India Company faltered toward bankruptcy. From 4,700 furs in 1624 the colony's exports surged to 16,300 in 1635 and 35,000 in 1656, but the company increasingly lost its share in the growing trade to illegal competition from private traders, who defied the official monopoly. Accepting defeat, in 1639 the company opened the fur trade on the upper Hudson to any colonist. The corporate leaders hoped to earn more by collecting a 10 percent tax on fur exports than they could by pretending to exercise a monopoly. But the company continued to lose money, for its New Netherland revenues lagged behind its expenditures as the colonists mastered tax evasion.

Although ruinous to the West India Company, the competitive fur trade benefited the Five Nation Iroquois, who took advantage of the market when it was favorable and employed intimidation when it was not. At Beverwyck in 1643 a visiting French priest noted, "Trade is free to every one, which enables the savages to obtain all things very cheaply: each of the Dutch outbidding his companion, and being satisfied, provided he can gain some little profit." During the early 1650s, when a maritime war with the English interrupted the flow of Dutch trade goods, the shortages and high prices angered the Mohawk, who promptly slaughtered the roaming cattle of the Beverwyck colonists. The local officials then wisely obliged their traders to give up their last remaining goods to bestow on the Mohawk as presents, restoring amity. Fortunately, a peace with England soon revived the trade. No sentimentalists, the Iroquois recognized that only economic interest bound them to the Dutch. In 1659 a Mohawk chief noted, "The Dutch say we are brothers and that we are joined together with chains, but that lasts only as long as we have beavers. After that we are no longer thought of."

Dutch relations with the Indians were far worse in the lower Hudson Valley, where the growing numbers of colonists clashed with the local Algonquians. Colonists' roving pigs and cattle invaded cornfields, provoking the natives to kill and eat the livestock—which, of course, outraged the settlers. In 1639 an especially heavy-handed governor, Willem Kieft, worsened relations by demanding that the Algonquians pay an annual tribute in maize or wampum. They bitterly protested that Kieft "must be a very mean fellow to come to live in this country without being invited by them, and now wish to compel them to give him their corn for nothing." Some Algonquians resisted payment and killed two colonists. Declaring the river Indians subject to Dutch law, the governor demanded the surrender of suspects for trial and execution, but the natives refused, clinging to their autonomy.

In 1643, Kieft made a bloody example of one Algonquian band that, oblivious of danger, had encamped on Manhattan Island. Kieft sent soldiers at night to surprise and butcher at least eighty Indians, mostly women and children. Outraged, the other river Indian bands attacked the scattered farms of colonial settlers, burning, looting, and killing in the rural settlements around New Amsterdam. The colonial dead included Anne Hutchinson, the famous Puritan dissident, who had moved to New Netherland after her exile to Rhode Island.

The Dutch entrusted command of their counterattacks to another notorious New Englander, Captain John Underhill, a mercenary who had helped massacre the Pequot Indians in 1637. Applying similar tactics to the Algonquians of New Netherland, Underhill's men killed more than five hundred fleeing from a burning village in 1644. A year later, the defeated Algonquians sued for peace. In three subsequent wars, in 1655, 1659–60, and 1663–64, the Dutch further devastated the Algonquians, who lost most of their lands. Although the Dutch had won, they paid a heavy price, saddling New Netherland with a dangerous reputation that deterred badly needed emigrants.

The Dutch also squandered precious resources contending with the Swedes for control of the Delaware Valley to the west. The colony of New Sweden began as a scam by renegade Dutch entrepreneurs exploiting the Swedish flag to defy the monopolistic West India Company. The renegades included Peter Minuit, a disgruntled former governor of New Netherland, who lent his considerable American expertise to the New Sweden Company, chartered in 1637. Based in the west Swedish port of Gothenberg, where Dutch émigrés dominated the merchant community, the New Sweden Company sent two ships across the Atlantic under Minuit's command. After a rough crossing, they reached the Delaware River in early 1638. At the mouth of Brandywine Creek (present-day Wilmington, Delaware), the colonists established Fort Christina, named in honor of the Swedish queen. Like Fort Orange on the Hudson, Fort Christina on the Delaware specialized in the fur trade with Indians. Customers included both the Algonquian-speaking Lenni Lenape of the Delaware valley and the Iroquoian-speaking Susquehannock, who dwelled farther west in the Susquehanna Valley.

Because the trading post lost money, the Dutch investors lost interest, selling their shares to their Swedish partners and the Swedish crown. In 1643 the reorganized company reoriented the colony by dispatching farm families to raise provisions, livestock, and tobacco. Some were Swedes, but most came from Finland, then under Swedish rule. Skilled at pioneer farming in heavily forested Sweden and Finland, the colonists adapted quickly to the New World and introduced many frontier techniques that eventually became classically "American," including the construction of log cabins.

Although highly skilled, the New Sweden colonists were too few to hold the land in a violent confrontation with their Dutch neighbors. The New Swedes numbered only about three hundred men, women, and children in

September 1655 when the Dutch governor of New Netherland, Pieter Stuyvesant, appeared with seven warships and more than three hundred armed men. Bribed by the Dutch, the Swedish commander quickly surrendered and left by ship for home. Most of the colonists persisted, accepting Dutch rule. During the next decade, the Delaware settlements grew modestly to about five hundred colonists as new Dutch settlers joined the Swedes and Finns. But the Dutch colony had become stretched too thin to hold both the Delaware and the Hudson against the English.

"DUTCH" COLONISTS

The Dutch extended their religious toleration but not their republican government to New Netherland. The West India Company appointed the governor and an advisory council of leading colonists but permitted no elected assembly. Rarely even consulting the council, the governors were contentious, arbitrary, and mostly incompetent. The ablest but angriest of them, Pieter Stuyvesant, governed effectively but autocratically from 1647 to 1664. Although run by authoritarian governors, New Netherland welcomed many religious dissenters rendered unwelcome in New England, including the unfortunate Anne Hutchinson. Officially, only the Dutch Reformed Church could hold public services, but the authorities usually looked the other way at some considerable "private" meetings for worship by the many religious dissenters in the colonies: a mix of Puritans, Quakers, Lutherans, and Jews.

A zealous Calvinist, Governor Stuyvesant joined the Dutch Reformed clergy in urging a new policy meant to keep Jews as well as other Protestants out of New Netherland. But the Dutch West India Company consistently defended tolerance as best for business, reminding Stuyvesant of "the large amount of capital which [Jews] still have invested in the shares of this company." The Jews remained, enjoying more freedom in New Netherland than in any other colony.

Thanks primarily to this religious tolerance, New Netherland became the most religiously and ethnically mixed colony in North America. Indeed, the Dutch were a minority in their own colony. In 1643 a French priest visiting New Amsterdam heard eighteen different languages—some European, some Indian, and some African. New Netherland attracted emigrants from Belgium (Flemings and Walloons), France (Huguenots), Scandinavia, and, especially, Germany. The non-Dutch whites composed nearly half of the New Netherland colonists. In general, they had migrated to live and work in Holland before making the further journey across the Atlantic to New Netherland. As in New England, the emigrants were primarily family groups of modest means and farmer or artisan status, rather than the indentured, unmarried, and young men who prevailed in the early Chesapeake and West Indies. A fifth of the New Netherland colonists were dissident Puritans who relocated from New England to settle on Long Island. And about a tenth of the inhabitants were enslaved Africans, mostly owned by the Dutch West India Company and resident in New Amsterdam, where they constructed wharves and buildings and loaded and unloaded ships. The company rewarded favored slaves with a status called "half-freedom," which permitted free movement within the colony and the rights to marry and own private property, in return for an annual payment in grain, furs, or wampum.

In New Netherland, women also enjoyed greater legal rights and economic opportunities than did their sisters in the English colonies. In contrast to English women, Dutch wives kept their maiden names, which reflected their more autonomous identity by law. Unlike the "coverture" of English common law, the Dutch legal code (derived from Roman law) did not deprive married women of their legal identity and their rights to own property. If a wife survived her husband, she received half of the property, while the other half went to their heirs—significantly better than the one-third allowed widows by English law. Most wills bestowed land or its cash value on daughters in proportions equal to sons, another marked contrast with English colonial practice, which favored males.

In New Netherland, the married couple formed an economic partnership that shared in the profits and losses. In the English colonies, men made almost all the wills and land deeds; in New Netherland, the husband and wife jointly crafted these legal documents. Although husbands usually took the lead in managing the family property, wives could make contracts, conduct commerce, and prosecute lawsuits in their own right. At New Amsterdam and Beverwyck, women ran businesses as bakers, laundresses, tavern keepers, brewers, and traders. Between 1661 and 1664, 383 women conducted or faced lawsuits in the courts at New Amsterdam. To the dismay of West India Company officials, women even aggressively participated in the fur trade. An overmatched official complained:

> It happened one day that the wife of Wolfert Gerritsz came to me with [the pelts of] two otters, for which I offered her three guilders, ten stuivers. She refused this and asked for five guilders, whereupon I let her go, this being too much. The wife of Jacob Laurissz, the smith, knowing this, went to her and offered her five guilders.

The unhappy official then paid the five guilders to secure the otter pelts for the company.

Despite an appealing location and a (relatively) tolerant society, the Dutch colony failed to attract sufficient settlers to compete with its English neighbors. In 1660 New Netherland had only 5,000 colonists—better than the 3,000 in New France, but far behind the 25,000 in the Chesapeake and the 33,000 in New England. Moreover, about a fifth of the New Netherland colonists were New English dwelling on Long Island. Far from building the security of New Netherland, the restive Long Island settlers frequently defied Dutch authority and seemed likely to help any English invasion.

Why did the colonization of New Netherland falter? In part, the colony suffered from its reputation for arbitrary government and Indian wars. In addition, the vast and rich Dutch empire provided many colonial alternatives more alluring to ambitious emigrants, especially in Ceylon, the East Indies, and Brazil. But the principal explanation is that the Netherlands had a smaller pool of potential emigrants with fewer incentives to emigrate, compared with the more numerous and more discontented English.

In mobilizing seventeenth-century emigration across the Atlantic, push was stronger than pull, and push was far stronger in England than in the Netherlands. Blessed with a booming economy and a higher standard of living, the 1.5 million Dutch had less reason to leave home than did the 5 million English, who were suffering through a painful economic transition and bitter religious strife. The Dutch lacked the masses of roaming poor who became indentured servants in the tobacco and sugar colonies established by the English in the Chesapeake and West Indies. And the tolerant Netherlands did not generate a disaffected religious minority such as the Puritans who founded New England.

The English succeeded as colonizers largely because their society was less successful at keeping people content at home. Poorer and more disaffected, the seventeenth-century English prevailed in emigrating to colonize the Atlantic seaboard of North America. But if religious conflict and economic misery sufficed to push colonial emigration, the French would have triumphed over both the English and the Dutch. The further difference was that, unlike France, England permitted its discontented freer access to its overseas colonies and greater incentives for settling there.

Thinly populated, New Netherland proved vulnerable when the Dutch and English empires came to blows. No longer united as fellow Protestants against the superior power of Spain, the English and Dutch became violent rivals in global commerce during the 1650s and 1660s. As the English aggressively pressed their own armed trading ships into the oceans around Africa and India, they rankled the Dutch. In 1658, English sea captains complained to Parliament, "The Dutch . . . refuse to sell us a hogshead of water to refresh us at sea, and call us 'English Dogs,' which doth much grieve our English spirits." The rulers of England also resented that the more efficient Dutch shippers had captured most of the lucrative trades exporting tobacco and sugar from the English colonies in the Chesapeake and West Indies. To maximize their own profits, the tobacco and sugar planters preferred Dutch shippers, who charged 33 percent less than their English competitors. To curtail the Dutch colonial carrying trade, the English Parliament adopted a provocative and imperialist program known as the Navigation Acts.

NAVIGATION ACTS

Dutch success taught the English that an expanding colonial commerce depended on naval power and that naval might hinged upon the revenues collected from overseas trade. In 1672 an English pamphleteer explained, "The undoubted Interest of England is Trade, since it is that alone which can make us either *Rich* or *Safe*, for without a powerful Navy, we should be a prey to our Neighbours, and without Trade, we could have neither sea-men [n]or Ships." To obtain more sailors, ships, and trade, Parliament enacted a protectionist system, the Navigation Acts.

Begun in 1651 and strengthened in 1660 and 1663, the Navigation Acts had three fundamental principles. First, only English ships could trade with any English colony. The acts defined as English any ship built within the empire, owned and captained by an English subject, and sailed by a crew at least three-quarters English. Because the colonists were English subjects, their ships and sailors fell within the definition. Any trade open to the merchants and mariners of the mother country was equally open to the colonists. Second, the acts specified that a few "enumerated commodities" produced in the colonies could be shipped only to the mother country. The acts enumerated those commodities that yielded the greatest profit to merchants and the highest revenues to the customs: primarily tobacco and sugar. Colonial ships were free to take their other produce where they wanted. Third, the acts stipulated that all European goods carried to the colonies had to pass through an English port, where they paid customs duties. If a Virginian wanted a bottle of French wine, it had to come via England, rather than direct from France. Violators of the acts risked the confiscation of their ships and cargos.

In sum, the Navigation Acts sought to enhance customs revenue collected in England, increase the flow of commerce enriching English merchants, stimulate English shipbuilding, and maximize the number of English sailors, swelling the reserve for the royal navy. The Navigation Acts expressed the "mercantilist" political economy that prevailed in seventeenth-century Europe. According to the mercantilist view, the government had every right, indeed the duty, to shape the economy to serve its needs for more revenue, ships, and men for use in war to drive other nations out of overseas markets. Assuming a chronic state of economic war, mercantilism considered all other nations as competing for the same limited quantity of trade.

Enforced by an expanding navy and a more diligent customs service, the Navigation Acts promoted the dramatic growth of English overseas commerce. English merchant shipping more than doubled, from 150,000 tons in 1640 to about 340,000 in 1686. In 1600, England had been an insular and agricultural nation, trading primarily with nearby northern Europe. By 1700,

England's commerce was complex and global, as London competed successfully with Amsterdam for American produce and Asian luxuries. In 1600, English trade beyond Europe was negligible; by 1700 the American and Asian trades employed over two-fifths of English tonnage. Except for the Dutch, no other European nation depended on foreign trade for such a high proportion of its employment and gross national product.

The expansion of transoceanic trade had powerful multiplier effects upon the English and colonial economies. The larger merchant marine supported at least fifteen thousand sailors, many of them colonists. Increased shipping meant more shipbuilding, which employed more skilled artisans, including shipwrights, carpenters, blacksmiths, sailmakers, rope-makers, and gunsmiths. And maritime trade stimulated the urban construction trades that built or repaired wharves, storehouses, and the offices and homes of merchants. In addition, provisioning ships for long voyages encouraged commercial agriculture, while overseas markets stimulated demand for English manufactures, especially cloth and metal goods.

CONQUEST

To defend their commercial primacy, the Dutch waged three wars against English enforcement of the Navigation Acts: in 1652–54, 1664–67, and 1672–74. Fought primarily at sea and to a draw, the wars failed to change English colonial policy, a persistence that rendered England stronger and the Dutch weaker over time.

In 1664 the English instigated the second war by sending an expedition to conquer New Netherland. King Charles II meant to eliminate New Amsterdam as a base for the Dutch shippers who traded with Virginia, to capture the valuable fur trade conducted on the upper Hudson, to intimidate the wayward New England colonies nearby, and to erase New Netherland as an obstruction between the Chesapeake and New England colonies. The king also wanted to reward his younger brother James Stuart, the Duke of York, with possession of the conquest as a proprietary colony. For a pretext, the invaders claimed that New Netherland was an intrusion on land previously explored and claimed by the English. But the blunt Duke of Albemarle urged the rest of the English cabinet to dispense with pretext: "What matters this or that reason? What we want is more of the trade the Dutch now have."

Taken by surprise in the undeclared war, New Netherland could not resist the arrival of three English warships bearing three hundred soldiers commanded by Colonel Richard Nichols. The invaders also rallied the New English militia of Long Island, who rebelled against Dutch rule and marched on New Amsterdam. Fearing the destruction of their town and property, the intimidated Dutch refused to fight, obliging the enraged Governor Stuyvesant to surrender. Nichols sent a subordinate with a smaller English force to seize the Delaware Valley. Confronting and overcoming more resistance there, the English plundered indiscriminately and sold the captured Dutch garrison into servitude in Virginia.

In a 1667 peace treaty, the Dutch formally gave New Netherland to the English. In a renewed war in 1673, the Dutch briefly recaptured their colony, but they surrendered it for good a year later. The Dutch colony of New Netherland became the English colony of New York; New Amsterdam became New York City; and Beverwyck and Fort Orange became known as Albany. Victory secured to the English the entire Atlantic seaboard between Florida and Acadia.

The generous terms of the 1664 capitulation freed the Dutch colonists from fighting against the Netherlands in any renewed war and permitted them to retain their properties, their inheritance laws, and their Dutch Reformed Church. But when some of the colonists welcomed and assisted the brief Dutch reconquest of 1673, the English voided the guarantees and ruled more arbitrarily. In 1675, Governor Edmund Andros imposed the English common law, forbade the use of Dutch in the courts, excluded Dutch colonists from his administration, and required all men to take an oath of allegiance. When eight Dutch leaders protested, Andros jailed them and confiscated their property. The protestors capitulated, taking the offensive oaths of allegiance to recover their freedom and two-thirds of their property. The Dutch also resented the English troops posted at New York, Esopus, and Albany, where undisciplined soldiers robbed and assaulted the colonists with apparent impunity.

The imposition of English common law eroded the opportunities for Dutch colonial women to hold, manage, and dispose of property. As they became legally "covered" by their husbands' identity, Dutch women dwindled as entrepreneurs, litigants, and testators. During the early 1660s about forty-six women conducted commerce in their own names at Beverwyck; none did so in the Albany of 1700. Gradually Dutch parents ceased providing land to most daughters, reserving all inheritance in real estate to their sons, as was the practice in the other English colonies. The widow's share of an inheritance also declined from the Dutch half to the English third, and she became more encumbered in her management and disposal of that share.

Except where obliged by the new legal system, the Dutch resisted assimilation to English culture. Indeed, the previously polyglot ethnic groups of New Netherland rallied around a Dutch identity and the Dutch language, strengthening support for the Dutch Reformed Church as a cultural haven from the English-dominated government. During the first decades of English rule, the colonists became more alike and more Dutch than they ever had been under direct Dutch rule. In 1699, more than thirty years after the conquest, the leading Anglicans of New York noted that the colony "seemed rather like a conquered Foreign Province held by the terrour of a Garrison, than an English Colony, possessed and settled by a people of our own Nation." Not until the mid-eighteenth century did most of the Dutch colonists begin to adopt the English language and English customs.

COVENANT CHAIN

By conquering New Netherland, the English replaced the Dutch in their alliance and trade with the Iroquois Five Nations, particularly the Mohawk, who lived nearest Albany, which became the most strategic place along the frontier of English America. A center for the fur trade and Indian diplomacy, Albany also lay at a critical juncture along the primary invasion corridor between New York and New France. A Massachusetts governor noted, "Albany is the Dam, which should it, through neglect, be broken down by the weight of the Enemy, we dread to think of the Inundation of Calamities that would quickly follow thereupon." After 1664, Albany's fur trade competition with Montreal merged into both the imperial rivalry between England and France for commercial dominance and the Iroquois' struggle to maintain their edge in a violent and disrupted world of native peoples.

At first, the English bitterly disappointed the Iroquois, who needed an active ally to counteract New France. During the 1660s and 1670s, the English crown avoided conflict with France, preferring to fight the Dutch. The English and the Dutch wars disrupted the supply, and enhanced the prices, of goods at Albany, to the Iroquois' dismay. Worse still, the Albany colonists failed to help defend the Mohawk against a destructive raid by the French and their Indian allies in 1666.

Obliged to make a humiliating peace, the Iroquois accepted French Jesuit missionaries in 1667. As with the Huron of the 1630s, the French employed the Jesuits to convert the Iroquois into French allies as well as Catholic believers. And as with the Huron, the missionaries bitterly divided the Iroquois. Traditionalists charged that the Jesuits weakened the Iroquois from within, sabotaging the warrior ethos, spiritual knowledge, ritual exercise, and political unity that together constituted Five Nation power. During the late 1670s and early 1680s the traditionalists drove the Jesuits and their converts out of Iroquoia to French Canada, where they resettled in mission villages at Kahnawake and Oka, both near Montreal.

The Iroquois traditionalists acted from a renewed confidence in Albany as a source of trade and a base for allies. After 1674, peace between the Dutch and the English permitted trade goods to reach Albany more safely and abundantly. And New York's ambitious new governor, Edmund Andros, aggressively cultivated the Five Nations and cleverly embraced their pretensions to have conquered the Ohio Valley and the Great Lakes country. By claiming authority over the Iroquois, Andros insisted that the English empire owned their western conquests by proxy—which the French, of course, bitterly disputed.

Andros also recruited the Five Nations to intimidate coastal Algonquian peoples who resisted English colonial expansion. The English and the Iroquois framed an alliance called the Covenant Chain, which invited the Five Nations to dominate the other native peoples in the northeast. In sum, the Five Nations (especially the Mohawk) and the English collaborated to build their respective power, at the expense of weaker Indians. Whenever English colonial governors wanted coastal Algonquians threatened or relocated, they lavished praise and presents on Five Nation chiefs, who then mobilized their warriors as enforcers. In addition to procuring flattery and presents, the Iroquois settled some old scores against the Algonquians and obliged many to become their dependents dwelling on the margins of Iroquoia as a security buffer. For example, in 1676 Andros persuaded Mohawk warriors to attack the New England Algonquian peoples, turning the tide of King Philip's War in favor of the colonists. The Mohawk resettled many of the defeated Algonquians northeast of Albany, to shield their frontier against renewed French attacks.

Emboldened by the ouster of the Jesuits and by the Covenant Chain alliance, during the early 1680s the Iroquois resumed their attacks on the French and their western Indian allies, especially in the Illinois country. Contrary to French suspicions, the English authorities in New York did not directly encourage the Iroquois attacks, for England remained officially at peace with France. But, as the French noted, the Iroquois could not have resumed western hostilities without confidence in their trade for guns and ammunition at Albany.

After initial success, the Iroquois war parties suffered heavy losses against stiff resistance by their well-armed western foes, especially during 1683 and 1684. Worse still, in 1687 a mixed force of French soldiers, Canadian militia, and western Indians invaded Iroquoia, looting and burning four Seneca villages. Over the smoldering ruins the French commander provocatively erected the coat of arms of his king, Louis XIV, to represent France's claim to command the Iroquois and their country. Thomas Dongan, Andros's successor as governor of New York, could only stew in frustration, for he lacked the means and the authority from his home government to fight the French. To their dismay, the Iroquois discovered that the New Yorkers honored the Covenant Chain alliance only when convenient.

NEW JERSEY

In principle, King Charles II and the Duke of York wanted to strengthen crown control over all of the English colonies, the better to tax their growing commerce. In practice, however, the Stuart brothers compounded the political complexity of the empire by awarding new proprietary colonies in New Jersey, Pennsylvania, and the Carolinas to reward English aristocrats and gentlemen, as payoffs for political favors and cash debts.

In 1664 the Duke of York granted the lands between the Hudson and the Delaware rivers as a distinct new colony called New Jersey. He awarded New Jersey to two English noblemen to further his political interests, but in 1673 and 1682 they sold out to two sets of investors, one Scottish and the other led by English Quakers. The purchasers divided New Jersey into two still smaller colonies, East and West Jersey (about 3,000 and 4,600 square miles respectively). The Scots took East Jersey, near New York, while the Quakers obtained West Jersey, along the Delaware.

Both sets of proprietors recruited farmers to clear and cultivate the land, which would enable them to pay annual quitrents. To attract colonists, the proprietors promised religious toleration to all Protestants and an elected assembly to share governance with an appointed governor and council. The incentives hastened development, pushing the population of the two Jerseys to fourteen thousand by 1700.

English Quakers primarily colonized West Jersey, while East Jersey became especially multiethnic. Some Dutch farmers had settled in East Jersey before the conquest of 1664, and more emigrated there during the 1670s and 1680s to escape oversight by the English officials in New York. East Jersey also attracted Puritans from New England, seeking larger and more fertile farms. Gathering in their own towns, the New English dwelled apart from the older Dutch settlements. The Scottish proprietors also recruited about six hundred of their countrymen as colonists. Clustering together, the Scots kept their distance from both the Dutch and the New English. The different ethnic mixes in the two Jerseys produced distinctive political polarities, but a similar contentiousness along ethnic and religious lines. In 1703 an imperial official explained, "The Contests of West Jersey have always been betwixt the Quakers and her majesty's subjects that are no Quakers. . . . The contest in East Jersey is of a different nature, whether the country shall be a Scotch settlement or an English settlement."

In 1702 the crown reunited East and West Jersey as the royal colony of New Jersey. While surrendering their rights of government, the East and West Jersey proprietors retained legal title to all frontier lands for their future sale and profit. The greedy demands of the East Jersey proprietors provoked several generations of riots by settlers determined to hold their lands by some cheaper title. Relatively small and poor, New Jersey remained economically dominated and politically overshadowed by its wealthier, more numerous, and more powerful two neighbors: New York to the northeast and Pennsylvania to the southwest.

PENNSYLVANIA

West Jersey's Quaker proprietors included William Penn (1644–1718), who developed a grand ambition to procure his own, larger colony. To cancel a debt of £16,000 owed to Penn's late father, Admiral William Penn, the king agreed in 1680 to grant the younger Penn 45,000 square miles west of the Delaware River as the colony of Pennsylvania ("Penn's Woods"). In 1682 the Duke of York also assigned to Penn the old Swedish-Finnish-Dutch settlements on the lower Delaware River (the future colony and state of Delaware).

A paradoxical man, William Penn combined an elite status with a radical religion. As Admiral Penn's son and heir, William Penn enjoyed a university education and large landed estates in Ireland and England. His annual income of £2,000 placed Penn near the top of the gentry class. He lived in a grand country house in Sussex, wore expensive clothing with silver buckles, ate and drank abundantly well, kept three coaches, and employed a staff of eight servants. In his colony, he also acquired several slaves. His genteel manners and considerable wealth afforded Penn the political influence and social privileges of a prominent and well-connected courtier. But as a young man and against his father's wishes, Penn had converted to Quakerism, then an especially mystical, radical, and persecuted form of Protestantism. As a wealthy gentleman, Penn was an unusual Quaker, for most were tradesmen, shopkeepers, and small farmers, who distrusted conspicuous wealth and state power. In turn, the rich and powerful of the realm generally despised the Quakers.

Numbering about fifty thousand in Great Britain in 1680, the Quakers called themselves simply the Friends of God, but their opponents called them Quakers, because one had said that they quaked before the power of God. Inspired especially by the preaching of George Fox, the Quakers became numerous and controversial in England during the 1650s. Quakers carried the Puritan critiques of church hierarchy and ritual to their ultimate conclusion: a rejection of all sacraments, liturgies, and paid intermediaries—ministers as well as bishops—between a soul and God. Renouncing formal prayers, sermons, and ceremony of any sort, Quakers met together as spiritual equals and sat silently until the divine spirit inspired someone, anyone, to speak. Although they rejected a specially educated and salaried ministry, certain especially devout and articulate laymen (and women) served as "Public Friends," itinerant preachers supported by voluntary contributions.

In contrast to the Puritan emphasis on sacred scripture, Quakers primarily relied on mystical experience to find and know God. The Quakers sought an "Inner Light" to understand the Bible, which they read allegorically rather than literally. More than a distant divinity or an ancient person, their Jesus Christ was fundamentally here and now and eternal: the Holy

Spirit potentially dwelling within every person. Anyone truly awakened by that Spirit could thereafter live in sanctity.

By seventeenth-century standards, Quaker religious beliefs led to radical social conclusions. Insisting upon the equality of all persons before God, Quakers tried to dispense with the markers of social hierarchy. They wore plain clothes; refused to take oaths of allegiance or for testimony; rejected the payment of church tithes; used plain, familiar language with all people, even to address aristocrats or the king; and declined to doff their hats before their rulers as a conventional sign of respect. Considering women spiritually equal to men, Quakers established parallel men's and women's leadership for their meetings. Matrons exercised important powers within the Quaker meetings by guiding and disciplining the younger women and by regulating marriages. Pacifists, the Quakers refused to bear arms. Uneasy with slavery, most sought at least its amelioration, and some became the first people to urge its abolition.

Quakers were most radical during their early years, the 1650s, when the Puritans tried and failed to govern England as a republic. Especially zealous Friends disrupted Anglican and Puritan religious services, inviting prosecution and martyrdom to prove their convictions. By challenging political hierarchy and formal churches, the early Quakers meant to hasten the advent of Christ's millennial rule on earth. But, instead of the Millennium, the 1660s brought the Restoration of the king and a more systematic persecution of the Quakers. Local magistrates jailed, whipped, and fined thousands of Quakers for refusing oaths of allegiance, evading church tithes, or publishing their unorthodox ideas. Convicted four times for preaching or writing his beliefs, William Penn spent about half of the years 1667–71 behind bars.

Penn was both a devout Quaker and an ingrained elitist, both highly principled and habitually condescending. A tireless crusader for religious toleration, Penn traveled widely as a preacher, in Germany and Holland as well as Great Britain. He hosted Quaker meetings at his estate, published more than fifty devotional or polemical tracts, defended Quakers in the courts, and tirelessly lobbied the crown to liberate jailed Friends. For his expensive exertions, Penn expected honor and obedience from his social inferiors—which meant all other Quakers. Easily disappointed, Penn often wallowed in self-pity, styling himself misunderstood and unappreciated by many common Friends.

A relatively late Quaker, Penn converted in 1667, when the Quaker zeal was moderating, a trend that he furthered. Quakerism became more respectable after 1670, as many Friends prospered and as some wealthy merchants and gentry converted to that faith. Like the Puritans, the Quakers practiced the temperance, thrift, and exertion that enabled common men to accumulate prosperity and even wealth. Prosperity then gradually took the edge off their radicalism. Known as "weighty Friends," the wealthy Quakers helped by subsidizing meetings, preaching, publications, and legal defense funds, but their worldly ways compromised the Quaker commitment to a plain style, egalitarian manners, and spiritual spontaneity. To achieve greater discipline and uniformity, during the 1670s the Friends developed a network of local Monthly Meetings, which reported to regional Quarterly Meetings, and ultimately to the annual London Meeting.

As the Quakers became more respectable and moderate, they lowered their expectations and shifted their strategy away from provoking the Millennium in favor of securing a legally protected position as a permanent minority. Led by William Penn, the Quakers urged a national tolerance for all Protestant denominations as legal equals. This Quaker vision of Protestant pluralism and tolerance horrified the Anglican authorities as the road to atheism via anarchy. An Anglican clergyman reasoned that "to tollerate all [faiths] without controul is the way to have none at all."

But the Quaker cause found a powerful ally in the Duke of York, who became King James II in 1685. Although the legal head of the Church of England, James was a Catholic and so, like William Penn, a religious outsider in an officially Anglican nation. To emancipate Catholics from legal and political discrimination, James sought common cause with the dissenting Protestants, including Quakers, by announcing a new policy of toleration. The Anglican establishment was bitterly opposed, and most Puritans balked from fear of Catholicism and suspicion of the king's authoritarian motives. But Penn enthusiastically supported the king and his program. In return, James sought Penn's advice and encouraged his political activism.

Penn's plans for Pennsylvania expressed his double position as a Quaker and a gentleman, bent on sustaining his own fortune while benefiting his persecuted faith. Putting a Quaker twist on the Puritan concept of a colony as a "City upon a Hill," Penn spoke of Pennsylvania as a "holy experiment" and an "example to the Nations." But in stark contrast to Puritan Massachusetts, Pennsylvania would have no privileged church, no tax-supported religious establishment, not even for the Friends. Penn certainly meant to provide a haven for his persecuted people, but he spoke in universalistic terms of "a Free Colony for all Mankind that should go hither." In addition to recruiting Quakers from throughout the British Isles, Penn welcomed both non-Quakers and non-Britons, promising them all equal rights and opportunities.

Penn's financial interest also argued for hastening development by welcoming every productive emigrant. In founding a colony, Penn meant to enhance rather than to sacrifice his fortune. In promising a "Free Colony," he did not offer free land, for he meant to profit by selling real estate and by collecting annual quitrents. He explained, "Though I desire to extend religious freedom, yet I want some recompense for my trouble." To share the costs and risks of his colony, Penn needed other investors, primarily fellow Quakers who also wished to do well by doing good. During the early 1680s at least six hundred men subscribed for over 750,000 acres, raising about £9,000, which Penn needed to finance his new colony. About half of the investors eventually emigrated to Pennsylvania; the rest remained absentee speculators.

Masterfully employing that seed capital, Penn organized the fastest and most efficient colonization in the seventeenth-century English empire. During 1682, twenty-three ships from England reached the Delaware River, bearing about two thousand colonists and their tools, clothes, provisions, and livestock. A year later, twenty more ships brought another two thousand immigrants. By 1686, Pennsylvania's population exceeded eight thousand.

Most of the colonists settled along the western shore of the Delaware River just above the small, older settlements of New Sweden. At the juncture of the Schuylkill River with the Delaware, Penn established a city and capital named Philadelphia—"City of Brotherly Love." He designed a systematic grid of broad streets with spacious parks, an arrangement that distinguished Philadelphia from older colonial towns, like Boston or Bridgetown, with their rambling and narrow streets, crowded buildings, and frequent fires. Within two years, the instant city of Philadelphia had about 350 houses and 2,500 inhabitants.

Like the New England Puritans—but unlike the Chesapeake colonists—most early Pennsylvanians came in freedom as families of middling means. Only about a third of the early settlers were indentured. Most emigrants were Quakers, primarily from England, but many came from Ireland and Wales. The colony also attracted English Anglicans, German Pietists, and Dutch Calvinists. Most settled as farmers in the many rural townships, but some lingered in Philadelphia as artisans and merchants. The merchants tended to be "weighty Friends" with sound credit, sober reputations, and extensive trade contacts throughout the empire. Their shared faith endowed the far-flung Quaker merchants with a mutual trust that afforded a critical advantage in the competitive conduct of long-distance commerce. During the eighteenth century, Philadelphia's merchant community became the wealthiest in the colonies, providing Pennsylvania with an elite more like commercial New England than the planter Chesapeake.

Pennsylvania proved an ideal setting for colonial settlement by family farmers producing grains and livestock for the transatlantic market (and for merchants exporting that produce). The Delaware River offered cheap and easy transportation from the new farms to the port of Philadelphia. In contrast to rocky New England, southeastern Pennsylvania possessed a fertile soil and an easily tilled landscape of low, rolling hills. The new colony also enjoyed a relatively long growing season of 180 days, which offered a greater certainty that grains would ripen before the first killing frost of autumn. But that growing season was not long enough to tempt most colonists to compete with the Chesapeake in raising tobacco—a temptation that would have led to greater extremes of wealth and poverty, freedom and slavery. As in New England, family farms worked primarily by free labor prevailed in Pennsylvania, which meant a relatively egalitarian distribution of wealth.

Although warmer than New England, Pennsylvania possessed a healthier and more temperate climate than the hot, humid, and malarial Chesapeake. The healthy conditions, abundant economic opportunities, and relatively even gender division combined to encourage early marriages and numerous children. In 1698 a visitor reported that he seldom met "any young Married Woman but hath a Child in her belly, or one upon her lap." Although immigration slowed during the 1690s, natural increase sustained a population that nearly doubled from about 11,000 in 1690 to 18,000 by 1700.

Timing also favored Penn's colony, for it was far easier to develop a later rather than an early colony. Learning from the mistakes of the early seventeenth century, the Pennsylvanians avoided the golden delusions and "starving times" that had afflicted their predecessors in the Chesapeake. The Pennsylvanians also benefited from proximity to older colonies sufficiently developed to supply the new colonists until their farms became productive. And when those new farms did produce surpluses, the colonists could sell livestock and grain to the large West Indian market, which the older colonies had stimulated at mid-century.

Pennsylvania also enjoyed prolonged peace with the local Indians, avoiding the sort of native rebellion that had devastated Virginia, New England, and New Netherland (as well as Spanish New Mexico). The Pennsylvanians benefited because native peoples were relatively weak and few in the Delaware and Susquehanna valleys at the end of the seventeenth century. Pennsylvania commenced after the local natives had plunged in numbers and power from multiple epidemics, prolonged exposure to the alcohol of Dutch and Swede traders, and destructive raids by both the Iroquois Five Nations and the Chesapeake colonists. During the late 1670s the once formidable, but recently defeated, Susquehannock moved northward to live in subordination among their old enemies, the Five Nations.

After 1680, the Lenni Lenape were the principal Indians remaining in eastern Pennsylvania. Called Delawares by the English, the Algonquian-speaking Lenni Lenape numbered about five thousand. They dwelled in many small, autonomous bands along both banks of the Delaware River, shifting their encampments with the seasons and pursuing a mixed economy of fishing, hunting, gathering, and horticulture. Harassed by the Five Nations and recently deserted by their Susquehannock allies, the Lenni Lenape needed a colonial patron to provide trade goods.

Pennsylvania also derived security from the sincere and shrewd policy that William Penn adopted to cultivate Indian goodwill. In contrast to the blunt intimidation so characteristic of previous colonial leaders, Penn acknowledged the Lenni Lenape as the legitimate owners of the land, and he publicly treated their culture with respect. Penn assured the Indians, "I am very sensible of the unkindness and injustice that hath been too much exercised toward you." Penn promised to be different: "I desire to enjoy [this land] with your Love and Consent, that we may always live together as Neighbors and Friends." Penn permitted settlement only where he had first purchased the lands from the Indians, and he paid higher and fairer prices than had his predecessors in other colonies. Possessed of more land than their reduced numbers could use, the Lenni Lenape welcomed the opportunity to sell some for coveted trade goods.

During the late seventeenth and early eighteenth centuries, many native peoples fled from mistreatment in other colonies to settle in Pennsylvania. Penn's government welcomed Shawnees from South Carolina, the Nanticoke and Conoy of Maryland, the Tutelo from Virginia, and some Mahicans from New York. One refugee explained to the Quakers, "The People of Maryland do not treat the Indians as you & others do, for they make slaves of them & sell their Children for Money."

Welcoming the refugees was shrewd as well as benevolent. By locating the refugees along the Susquehanna River to replace the Susquehannock, the Pennsylvanians obtained a security screen to the west of their settlements in the Delaware Valley. The refugee villages provided a buffer against the French and their Indian allies. Such a screen was especially convenient to Quaker pacifists, who preferred that native clients bear the brunt of any frontier warfare. Behind a western buffer of Indian allies, Pennsylvania could grow and prosper, until the 1720s, when that growth began to encroach upon their native friends.

Blessed with hardworking colonists, a prime setting, perfect timing, and peace with the Indians, Pennsylvania prospered. Its multiple advantages enabled Pennsylvania to capture—at New England's expense—a growing share of the West Indian provisioning trade. Better soil, bigger farms, and a longer growing season enabled Pennsylvania's farmers to produce larger crops and herds at a lower cost. The most valuable grain for export, wheat, thrived in Pennsylvania at the same time that it withered in New England from a destructive blight. Since Pennsylvania was three hundred miles southwest of New England, its shipping also had a shorter and cheaper voyage to the West Indies. And the Pennsylvania farmers avoided their equivalent of King Philip's War, which had so devastated the farms of New England. During the early eighteenth century, economic growth endowed Pennsylvanians with a standard of living superior to New England's. Because family farms prevailed, the rural prosperity was broad-based, with few landless and fewer rich.

Despite its many economic advantages, early Pennsylvania suffered its full share of the political wrangling that characterized every new colony. In 1685, Penn pleaded with his colonists, "For the love of God, me, and the poor country, be not so Governmentish, so noisy and open in your dissatisfactions." A year later Penn sighed in frustration that there was "nothing but good said of the place, and little that's good said of the people."

One factional divide set the older, non-Quaker settlements of the lower Delaware (the three "Lower Counties") against the more numerous and mostly Quaker newcomers dwelling upriver in the three "Upper Counties." The Swedes, Finns, Dutch, and Anglicans of the Lower Counties resented political domination by the Quaker newcomers, and they feared the economic decline of their downriver ports as Philadelphia became the regional entrepôt. More vulnerable to French and pirate attacks by sea, the Lower Counties also demanded defense appropriations to arm their militia and strengthen their coastal fortifications. But the Quaker assemblymen balked, for their constituents were more securely located upriver, committed to pacifism, and determined to minimize their taxes. Unable to reconcile the two regions, Penn consented to their division in 1704 into the distinct colonies of Pennsylvania and Delaware, with separate legislatures but a common governor appointed by their proprietor.

A second factional divide erupted within the Quaker ranks during the early 1690s. Although contrary to the Quaker love of peace, the rancorous squabbling derived from the righteous assertion that characterized a people who had so long defied authority to defend their principles. Compelled to unite in England against their persecutors, the Quakers felt liberated in Pennsylvania to discover and exercise their theological differences, just as the Puritans had done in New England during the 1630s. In early 1693 rival factions seized opposite ends of the main Quaker meetinghouse in Philadelphia, erecting polarized galleries for their competing speakers. Instead of offering peace and meditation, the next Quaker meeting became a shouting contest that culminated in violence as each side took up axes to smash the other's gallery. Fortunately for Quaker harmony, the division healed in 1694 when the leader of one faction, George Keith, abruptly departed for England.

William Penn's sweeping claims to power provoked a third and more persistent division. Most colonists, Quaker and non-Quaker and in both the Lower and Upper Counties, chafed under Penn's patronizing authority, his apparent greed, and his capricious inconsistency. As the opposition saw it, Penn fleeced and restricted most of the colonists to further enrich himself and his official circle of cronies. The dissidents complained that although Penn denounced land speculation and favored close settlement, he reserved large tracts for himself or bestowed them upon his favorites.

In 1684, Penn departed Pennsylvania and returned to England, where he remained until 1699. During his long absence, his critics dominated the colonial assembly and council. They generally defied Penn's deputy governor, refused to pay their quitrents, and ignored Penn's letters of instruction. "After they are Read, there is no more notice taken of them," a loyal councillor reported in 1686. Feeling betrayed, Penn denounced his opponents as selfish ingrates indifferent to his extraordinary expenses and exertions in securing and colonizing Pennsylvania. He certainly needed the revenue from land sales and quitrents. Living beyond his means and donating generously to support Quaker meetings and Public Friends, Penn accumulated the debts that would consign him to an English debtors' prison in 1707.

DIVERSITY

Colonial empires sowed unintended and paradoxical consequences maddening to their rulers. In 1664 the English conquered the mid-Atlantic seaboard to consolidate a more homogeneous and docile empire stretching from Carolina to Canada. But that conquest absorbed a medley of non-English peoples: Dutch, Swedes, Finns, Walloons, Flemings, Huguenots, Germans, and Norwegians. This diversity contrasted markedly with both the Chesapeake and New England, where almost all of the white colonists came from England. That diversity also violated the traditional English conviction that social cohesion and political order depended on ethnic and religious uniformity. In 1692 an English New Yorker lamented, "Our chiefest unhappyness here is too great a mixture of nations, and English the least part." Xenophobic English officials did not adjust easily to the diversity of their new subjects.

The English conquest only compounded the region's ethnic, linguistic, and religious diversity as the victors created the new colonies of New Jersey and Pennsylvania, which attracted more non-English emigrants. That very diversity became the defining characteristic of the middle colonies, the collective name for New York, New Jersey, and Pennsylvania because they lay between the Chesapeake and New England. In the early eighteenth century, the middle colonists included Anglicans (mostly English), Presbyterians (Scots and Scotch-Irish), Congregationalists (relocated New English Puritans), Quakers (English and Welsh), Reformed (Dutch and German), Lutherans (the Scandinavians and some Germans), an array of pietistic sects (German and Swiss), and a few Catholics (primarily Irish) and Jews (from the Netherlands). In addition, most of the enslaved Africans preserved their traditional beliefs, which remained mysterious to their indifferent masters. Neither any single ethnic group nor any particular religious denomination enjoyed a majority in any middle colony.

Conventional political wisdom insisted that a polity should be organic and tradition-bound: a unified body of unequal parts ruled by a natural elite guided by long precedent. Defying those expectations, the middle colonies were new societies composed of diverse peoples who could not agree to give deference to a shared elite. Instead, ethnocultural groups were openly contentious and disrespectful of authorities, even within their own communities. In 1704, William Penn complained that the Pennsylvania colonists needed "to be humbled and made more pliable; for what with the distance and the scarcity of mankind there, they opine too much." In the mid-eighteenth century, a German immigrant reported, "They have a saying here: Pennsylvania is heaven for farmers, paradise for artisans, and hell for officials and preachers."

Although engaged in especially fractious political competition, the middle colonies avoided the violence that accompanied ethnic and religious difference in Europe. The rhetorical rancor of ethnocultural politics apparently vented resentments peacefully, which precluded a resort to house burnings and murder. The combination of contention and restraint appeared in the 1764 Pennsylvania election, when Benjamin Franklin criticized the bloc voting by German voters as "the Palatine Boors herding together." His opponents freely translated Franklin's words into the German complaint "that I call'd them a Herd of Hogs." Turning out in unprecedented numbers, the Germans ensured Franklin's defeat—but no one died or lost their home to a riot.

The middle colonies defined a distinctive culture and social order that precociously anticipated the American future. But the fractious diversity of the middle colonies also frustrated English visions of an empire responsive to command, especially during war. The middle colonies contributed little to an empire increasingly embroiled in massive conflicts with France.

Part III

EMPIRES

13

Revolutions

★

1685–1730

Detail of a mid-eighteenth-century engraving of the waterfront at Charleston, South Carolina, illustrating the prominence of shipping, fortifications (H), and church steeples (D and E) in the commercial entrepôts of a maritime empire. From London Magazine.

IN EARLY 1685, KING CHARLES II died without a legitimate son, leaving the English throne to his younger brother, the Duke of York, who reigned as James II. A vigorous man of powerful convictions and little tact, James openly practiced Catholicism and firmly avowed his royal absolutism. As the proprietor of New York, James had curtailed the liberties of the conquered Dutch and had denied the colony an assembly—precedents he meant to extend throughout the empire as king. To govern the royal colonies, James appointed military men accustomed to taking orders from above and dictating to subordinates below. He instructed his governors to treat colonial protests as insubordination and to bully or dispense with assemblies.

James II regarded the American colonies as cash cows meant to fund a more authoritarian crown. Endowed with a larger colonial revenue, the crown could dispense with Parliament, which was constitutionally necessary to levy taxes within England. Previously the crown had claimed a tenth of any treasures recovered from Spanish shipwrecks in the Caribbean; James demanded a full half. On Barbados, James sold the seats on the colonial council to anyone willing to pay, which appalled the great planters, who expected to monopolize the seats without paying for them and who disliked serving with men of lowly origins. For years, the West Indian planters had complained that the customs duty levied on their sugar was too high. Instead of heeding them, James doubled that duty. A sugar planter despaired, "They would use us like Sponges: or like Sheep. They think us fit to be squeezed and fleeced." James even increased the already extortionate duties levied on Chesapeake tobacco.

DOMINION

The new king took a particular interest in reducing New England to obedience, a process begun by his predecessor during the late 1670s, when the crown had demanded that Massachusetts accept a new charter with major concessions to royal authority. But in 1678 the defiant Massachusetts legislature announced, "The lawes of England are bounded within the fower seas, and does not reach America." Growing impatient, in 1684 the crown won an English court decision that revoked the Massachusetts charter. Then James consolidated the eight northern colonies—all five in New England plus New York and East and West Jersey—into a supercolony known as the Dominion of New England. Modeled on a Spanish viceroyalty, the Dominion extended from the Delaware River to Canada. The Dominion dispensed with assemblies, entrusting administration to a governor-general assisted by a lieutenant governor and an appointed council. The new arrangement radically reversed the previous trend toward greater colonial autonomy defended by powerful elected assemblies dominated by the wealthiest colonists. For governor-general, the king appointed Sir Edmund Andros, a military officer who had previously served

James as the competent but dictatorial governor of New York. A deputy governor, Francis Nicholson, took post in New York, while Andros and his Dominion council operated from Boston.

Arbitrary and centralized, the Dominion regime shocked the New English. Reorganizing the courts and the militia, Andros replaced Puritan judges and officers with Anglican newcomers. He also appointed the county sheriffs, who named the jurors—which did not bode well for the rights of defendants. "Foxes were made the Administrators of Justice to the Poultry," Cotton Mather grumbled. Andros also mandated that the superior court meet only in Boston, rather than in the rural counties, obliging plaintiffs, witnesses, and defendants to travel far from home, a major expense and hardship. In addition, he crimped the authority of local government by restricting town meetings to one per year. Determined to defund Puritanism, Andros forbade the Puritan clergy from drawing their salaries from town taxes. He also appropriated one of the Boston meetinghouses to conduct Anglican services.

Far more expensive than the old charter governments, the Dominion demanded unprecedented levels of taxation. Andros's lavish salary of £1,200 alone exceeded the entire annual cost of the former government of Massachusetts. Andros also brought along two companies of regular soldiers, who had to be paid and supplied. To raise revenue, Andros levied new taxes without an assembly and without even the support of a majority on his own council, which was composed largely of merchants.

Worse still, Andros challenged the legality of the land titles issued by the town governments under the old Puritan charter. He expected to reap windfall revenue in fees by demanding new land grants issued by his government. To secure a perpetual revenue for the crown, the new grants also required every property annually to pay quitrents of two shillings sixpence per hundred acres. Although routine in southern colonies (but poorly collected), quitrents were novel and provocative in New England. Because English folk regarded secure real estate as fundamental to their liberty, status, and prosperity, the colonists felt horrified by the sweeping and expensive challenge to their land titles.

In 1687 the Reverend John Wise rallied Ipswich, a town in Essex County, to protest and resist the new taxes. Wise claimed that the colonists carried their Magna Carta rights with them across the Atlantic. They therefore retained the fundamental right of Englishmen to pay no tax not levied by their own representatives. In response, Andros argued that the colonists had left English rights behind to enter an empire dependent upon the king's grace and command. A Dominion official provocatively declared, "Mr. Wise, you have no more priviledges Left you than not to be Sould for Slaves." Andros arrested, tried, convicted, and fined Wise and the other protest leaders.

The Dominion regime also vigorously enforced the Navigation Acts by establishing in Boston a new vice-admiralty court, which operated without juries. During the summer of 1686 the new court condemned at least six merchant ships, which depressed the port's business. With their currency and economy in contraction, the New English were hard pressed to pay the increased taxes and fees demanded by Andros. The spring of 1689, however, brought intriguing news of an upheaval in England that presented an opportunity to discontented colonists.

GLORIOUS REVOLUTIONS

In England, King James alarmed the Protestant majority by ruling arbitrarily and by favoring his fellow Catholics. Protestant gloom deepened in April 1688 when the queen gave birth to a son, a male heir to the throne, which threatened to perpetuate a Catholic dynasty. Several Anglican bishops and aristocrats secretly wrote to William, the Dutch Prince of Orange, urging that he come to England with an army to intervene on behalf of the Protestant cause. The plotters hoped to compel James to recognize Parliament's power and to accept a Protestant successor. William, however, saw an opportunity to seize the crown for himself.

As both the nephew and son-in-law of James, William was, along with his wife, Mary Stuart, a Protestant alternative for the English throne. As the military leader of the Netherlands, William also desperately needed to wean England from its pro-French policy. In 1688 the Dutch faced a renewed war with powerful France, under the aggressive rule of Louis XIV. In a bold and desperate gamble, William invaded England as a preemptive strike to capture that realm for a Dutch alliance. Aided by collusion in the disaffected English army and navy, William crossed the Channel and landed without resistance in November. Rallying to the stronger side, most English officers and aristocrats defected to join William, while James panicked and foolishly fled to France, finding sanctuary at the court of Louis XIV.

James's departure left a power vacuum that William was delighted to exploit. His Dutch regiments occupied London, and Parliament transferred the throne to William and Mary, as joint sovereigns (although Mary left governance to her husband). The new monarchs promised to cooperate with Parliament and to uphold the Anglican establishment. In the spring, they hedged that promise by ensuring religious toleration for dissenting Protestants, who had enthusiastically supported their coup, and for Catholics, who had not. William's English supporters, known as the Whigs, called the transfer of power a "Glorious Revolution," which they creatively depicted as a spontaneous uprising by a united English people. In fact, the revolution was fundamentally a coup spearheaded by a foreign army and navy.

Rumors of the Glorious Revolution reached the colonies in the spring of 1689, alarming the colonial appointees of King James. Unsure whether William and Mary had secured control over the realm and uncertain what to do,

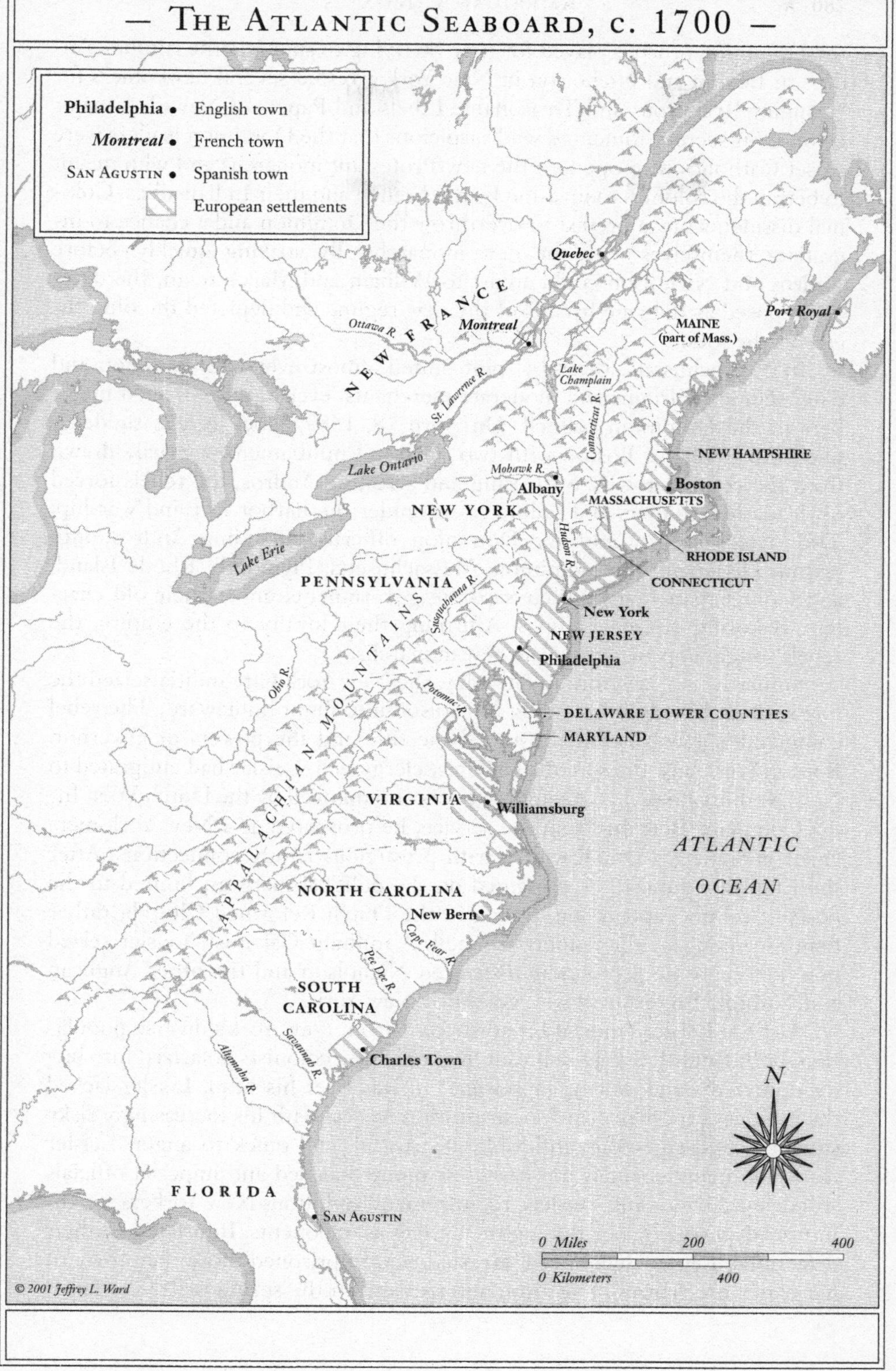
— The Atlantic Seaboard, c. 1700 —
Philadelphia • English town
Montreal • French town
San Agustin • Spanish town
European settlements
NEW FRANCE
Quebec
Montreal
Ottawa R.
St. Lawrence R.
Port Royal
MAINE (part of Mass.)
Lake Champlain
Connecticut R.
Lake Ontario
Mohawk R.
Albany
NEW HAMPSHIRE
Boston
MASSACHUSETTS
NEW YORK
Lake Erie
Hudson R.
RHODE ISLAND
CONNECTICUT
PENNSYLVANIA
Susquehanna R.
New York
NEW JERSEY
Philadelphia
Ohio R.
APPALACHIAN MOUNTAINS
Potomac R.
DELAWARE LOWER COUNTIES
MARYLAND
VIRGINIA
Williamsburg
ATLANTIC OCEAN
NORTH CAROLINA
New Bern
Cape Fear R.
Pee Dee R.
SOUTH CAROLINA
Charles Town
Savannah R.
Altamaha R.
N
FLORIDA
San Agustin
0 Miles 200 400
0 Kilometers 400
© 2001 Jeffrey L. Ward

the Dominion officials played for time by trying to suppress the rumors. Andros in Boston and Nicholson in New York arrested several newcomers for "bringing Traiterous and Treasonable Libels and Papers of News." A major error, their secrecy fomented wild suspicions that the Dominion leaders were closet Catholics who opposed the new Protestant monarchs and who meant to betray the colonies to invasion by the French and their Indian allies. Colonial dissidents saw a pretext to overthrow the Dominion and a chance to ingratiate themselves with the new monarchs. By striking quickly, before Andros and Nicholson could adjust to William and Mary's reign, the dissidents posed as the true friends of the new regime and depicted the old officials as the foes.

In Massachusetts, the rebel plot united almost everyone, common and elite, staunch Puritans and moderate merchants, even five disaffected members of the Dominion council. On April 18, 1689, rebel leaders suddenly filled the streets of Boston with two thousand militiamen, primarily drawn from the country towns. Surprising and arresting Andros, the rebels forced his leaderless soldiers and sailors to surrender the harbor fort and warship. The victors cast twenty-five Dominion officials, including Andros, into prison. Dissolving the Dominion, Massachusetts, Plymouth, Rhode Island, and Connecticut revived their separate governments under their old charters, restoring elected regimes. Affirming their loyalty to the empire, the rebels sought approval from the new monarchs.

Similarly, in New York in late May, the New York City militia seized the fort without bloodshed, sending Nicholson into flight homeward. The rebel commander, Jacob Leisler, assumed the title and the powers of governor. Born in Germany, the son of a Calvinist clergyman, Leisler had emigrated to New Netherland as a young military officer employed by the Dutch West India Company. Retiring from the service, he prospered as a New York merchant, marrying a Dutch widow with prestigious family connections. After the English conquest, he remained on the political margins, limited to the posts of militia captain and deacon in the Dutch Reformed Church, rather than ascending to the colonial council. A militant Calvinist, Leisler seized power because he profoundly distrusted Nicholson and the other Anglican and Catholic Englishmen who governed New York.

At first, Leisler enjoyed broad support from New York's diverse population, both English and Dutch. But over time, the colonists polarized into bitter opponents and defiant supporters. In way over his head, Leisler lacked the political experience and sophistication to deal with his increasingly risky situation. Self-righteous, inflexible, distrustful, and quick to anger, Leisler made too many enemies too easily. As months passed and imperial officials still delayed endorsing Leisler's regime, many ambitious New Yorkers sought future advantage by positioning themselves as opponents. Infuriated by their defections, Leisler denounced, arrested, and imprisoned more than forty of his critics on charges of sedition and treason. In the spring of 1690 a failed attempt to assassinate Leisler landed more men in prison and exposed their homes to plundering by militiamen. During the summer of 1690, Leisler lost still more support by botching an invasion of French Canada, in a desperate bid to demonstrate his usefulness to the English empire. Primarily motivated by his religious convictions, Leisler was no political visionary, no early proponent of colonial independence, and no republican reformer. With great reluctance he summoned an assembly, which he summarily dismissed as soon as the legislators raised embarrassing questions about his many political prisoners.

Contrary to Leisler's intentions, his controversial administration polarized the colony along ethnocultural and class lines. By the end of 1690, his enemies included almost all of the English-speaking colonists and some prominent Dutch merchants, who had made a profitable peace with the new order, mastering its language and customs and reaping political offices for their pains. The defections by the English and the Anglicizing Dutch reduced Leisler's supporters to the parochial Dutch majority of modest means and common manners. As both sides recognized the ethnic and class dimensions of their divide, they gave angry expression to long submerged suspicions, resentments, and fears against the other. By vociferously championing the Dutch-born King William III, the Leislerians expressed ethnic pride and vented their resentments over the English occupation of their colony. By default rather than intent, Leisler became the leader of a crusade by the most aggrieved Dutch to vindicate their culture and to reclaim the local power and respect taken away from them by the arrogant occupiers and elite collaborators.

The exception that proved the rule was Albany, the most securely Dutch community in the colony. The Albany burghers opposed Leisler precisely because they felt sufficiently confident in their cultural hegemony and local autonomy under English rule—and because they feared becoming subordinate to New York City under Leisler's arbitrary regime. In sum, they did not share the ethnocultural resentment that generated support for Leisler among the downriver Dutch, who lived in the offending presence of many English newcomers, soldiers, and officials. In 1690 the people of Albany belatedly and reluctantly submitted to Leisler only after a French and Indian raid devastated nearby Schenectady, exposing their insecurity to attack from the north.

Maryland hosted the third and smallest, but most successful, colonial uprising of 1689. The large Protestant majority resented the power of their proprietor, Lord Baltimore, who reserved the top offices in the colony for his fellow Catholics. Ambitious Protestant planters promoted popular suspicions that the Catholic regime was plotting to betray Maryland to the French and Indians. In 1689, the Catholic governor, William Joseph, fueled those rumors by refusing to acknowledge the revolution at home.

Seizing the opportunity, the planter John Coode armed and organized a rebel militia known as the Protestant Associators. In a public manifesto, the rebels promised to "vindicate and assert the Sovereign Dominion and right of King William and Queen Mary to this Province; to defend the Protestant Religion among us and to protect and shelter the Inhabitants from all manner of violence, oppression and destruction that is plotted and designed against them." Mustering 700 armed men, the Associators intimidated the 160 militia loyal to Governor Joseph, who surrendered without firing a shot on August 1. Professing their allegiance to the new monarchs, the rebels urged Maryland's conversion from a proprietary to a royal colony.

Virginia and the English West Indies did not rebel, despite their grievances with high taxes and arbitrary governors. Virginia escaped trouble because its royal governor had returned home, and, in his absence, his council promptly and astutely proclaimed their support for William and Mary on April 26. The proclamation and the arrest of a few agitators nipped in the bud an attempt to organize discontent in one Virginia county. In the West Indies, potential rebellion was deflated by the convenient death in October 1688 of Jamaica's domineering governor and by the rapid conversion of the Barbadian governor to enthusiastic support for William and Mary. Only the governor of the Leeward Islands, Sir Nathaniel Johnson, remained an unrepentant supporter of the old king. He essentially went on strike, doing nothing to stop the sack of English plantations on St. Kitts, first by rebellious Irish servants and then by French raiders. Although the Leeward Islands planters had far greater grounds to rebel than any other colonists, they patiently waited for Johnson to resign and sail away in late July. In general, the West Indian planters did nothing from a dread that upheaval would invite rebellion by the slave majority.

RESOLUTION

In Maryland, Massachusetts, and New York, the rebels all professed loyalty to England and vowed to abide by the determination of the new monarchs. But it was far from certain that William III would embrace the colonial rebellions. Above all, William wanted to consolidate his control in England and to mobilize colonial resources for a war against France. Both goals argued for bolstering, rather than retrenching, crown authority in the colonies. To solidify his support among the English magnates, William retained most high officials in London, including those in the colonial office who had helped design the Dominion. The colonial secretary, William Blathwayt, invoked class prejudice to blast the New English rebels as "a mean and mechanical sort of people" who presumed to "abuse the highest acts of royal government under the color of an imaginary charter they have justly forfeited." To bolster morale in the imperial service and discourage future colonial rebellions, the crown liberated and vindicated Sir Edmund Andros, appointing him to govern Virginia in 1692. The crown also cleared Francis Nicholson and rewarded him with a succession of important colonial posts. William III, however, was a pragmatic ruler who recognized that he had to compromise with the colonial leaders, lest their discontents obstruct his first priority: uniting the colonies for war.

It was easiest to find common ground in Maryland, for William distrusted the Catholic Lord Proprietor, and the rebels wanted a royal government. The crown permitted Lord Baltimore to retain his proprietorship over the colony's unsold lands but suspended his right to govern. William appointed an Anglican military officer, Lionel Copley, as governor and named the leading rebels to his governing council. They cooperated with a colonial assembly dominated by Anglicans to endow the Church of England with tax support and to bar Catholics (and Quakers) from holding public office. Not until 1715 did the fourth Lord Baltimore recover his right to appoint the governor (and only after the lord had converted to Anglicanism).

Although Pennsylvania had experienced no rebellion, William III treated Penn's colony similarly. A favorite of King James II, Penn fell from grace and into suspicion when William seized power. In 1691 the crown suspended Penn's charter, rendering Pennsylvania a royal colony. A year later, to the horror of the pacifist Quakers, the crown entrusted Pennsylvania to a military governor, Captain Benjamin Fletcher. Insisting that war taxes violated their consciences, the Quaker assemblymen obstructed every initiative by their new governor. In 1694 the crown gave up, restoring Penn's charter and authority in the vain hope that he could persuade the Pennsylvanians to provide men and money for the war against France. Governing as they liked, the Quaker elite virtually ignored Penn's governors and instructions—avoiding all but token contributions to the war effort. After a crippling stroke, Penn died in 1718, passing his colony to his sons.

Compromise between crown and colonists also proved difficult in Massachusetts, where the rebels wanted a restoration of the 1629 charter that permitted home rule, Puritan preeminence, and republican government. But King William was determined to retain Massachusetts as a crown colony. In 1691 his regime issued a new, compromise charter that mandated both a royal governor and an elected assembly. The governor held a complete veto over legislation, but the assembly controlled taxation and expenditures including the governor's salary. The charter even allowed the assembly to choose the members of the council, subject, however, to the governor's approval. In this, the Massachusetts assembly enjoyed greater power than its counterparts in other royal colonies, where the crown appointed the councillors. To further sweeten the deal, the king named a New English colonist, Sir William Phips, to become the first governor of Massachusetts under the new charter. Staunch Puritans grumbled because the new charter mandated toleration for all Protestants and opened the vote to all property-holders, rather than restricting it to the full members of Puritan churches. On the other hand, the colonists rejoiced that the 1691 charter required no quitrents and lifted the dark cloud of legal doubt cast by Andros on the old land titles. Finally, the new charter enlarged and strengthened the colony by dissolving the small Plymouth colony for incorporation into Massachusetts.

Although less than a restoration of the cherished 1629 charter, the new arrangement satisfied most colonists as a distinct improvement over the hated Dominion. Moreover, defying the crown was not feasible in 1691, when New England faced devastating frontier raids by the French and their Indian allies. Needing English assistance, the Massachusetts colonists recognized their military, commercial, and political dependence upon the empire.

Rather than bother with the smaller New England colonies, the crown simply let Rhode Island and Connecticut revive their old charters and autonomy. Alone among the English colonies, Rhode Island and Connecticut elected their governors and appointed their own executive officers. Save for paying customs duties and contributing small numbers of men to the imperial wars, the two surviving "charter colonies" preserved the virtual autonomy of their seventeenth-century origins.

Compromise proved most elusive in New York, where the rebellion exacerbated bitter internal divisions rooted in the English conquest of 1664. In the struggle to sway the new monarch, political sophistication and contacts in London mattered more than popular support in the colony. As a result, Leisler and his parochial Dutch supporters were at a profound disadvantage to their wealthier and more cosmopolitan rivals. Leisler's bungling and arbitrary government provided plenty of ammunition for his many enemies to use in lobbying the home government. Nor did King William feel any ethnic solidarity with his Dutch supporters in New York, for he could ill afford to confirm widespread suspicions that he was prejudiced against his English subjects. As a price of the throne, William cast Leisler to his enemies.

In September 1689 the home government designated a new governor, Colonel Henry Sloughter, an elitist army officer who endorsed the partisan view that New York had fallen into the hands of a "rabble." If Sloughter had immediately proceeded to New York, he might have restored order quickly, averting the worst turmoil, but he took a remarkably long time, well over a year, to reach his colony, with tragic consequences. During the prolonged interim, Leisler had enough rope to hang himself.

Sloughter's deputy, Major Richard Ingoldsby, reached New York in late January 1691 to demand that Leisler surrender the fort and release his many political prisoners. When Leisler refused, fighting erupted, with casualties on both sides. Finally, on March 19, Sloughter sailed into New York's harbor with additional ships and soldiers. Leisler's men deserted in droves, obliging Leisler to surrender. Sloughter's councillors—many of them newly released from jail—demanded Leisler's immediate trial for treason and murder. Living down to his name, Sloughter quickly tried, convinced, and executed Leisler and his chief lieutenant, Jacob Milborne, before they could appeal to

England. Sloughter imprisoned six other leading Leislerians and confiscated their property.

For the next two decades, the Leislerian and Anti-Leislerian factions persisted in a bitter struggle for power in New York. After Sloughter suddenly died in June, his successor, Governor Benjamin Fletcher, observed, "Neither Party will be satisfied with Less than the necks of their Adversaries." To ease the political strife in New York, in 1692 the crown pardoned the Leislerians, suspending additional prosecutions, freeing those in prison, and restoring confiscated property. Political memories, however, remained long and vindictive in colonial New York. Each successive royal governor had to choose one faction as allies and the other as enemies. Not until the 1710s did the deaths of old politicians and an unusually judicious governor dissipate the bitter legacy of Leisler's execution.

COMPROMISE

In sorting out the rebellions, the crown generally worked out a rough compromise between imperial power and colonial autonomy—a compromise that held until the imperial crisis of the 1760s. Except in Rhode Island and Connecticut, the colonists accepted royal (or proprietary) governors and their councils, as well as military coordination under English auspices. Except in Rhode Island and Connecticut, the colonies had to submit all legislation to approval first by their governors (either proprietary or royal) and then by the king and his privy council. The crown, however, accepted colonial assemblies elected by property-holders.

After 1689, the crown also exercised its powers more lightly, abandoning King James's ambitious and provocative program of consolidating multiple colonies into a viceroyalty. By appointing more conciliatory governors and moderating their demands for power, the crown hoped to reap more cooperation from the colonists. Even Andros and Nicholson behaved with greater restraint in their new posts as governors of Virginia and Maryland. The new regime especially favored the West Indies, considered the great colonial font of commercial wealth. In 1693 the crown dropped the sugar tax to its former level, before the doubling by James II, and terminated the slave trade monopoly previously held by the Royal African Company (in which the king had been a leading shareholder). Open competition doubled the flow of slaves, to the delight of sugar, tobacco, and rice planters. In all of its reforms, the crown favored the local oligarchies of great planters and merchants, rather than any colonial longing for democracy (which was not evident).

As a result of the compromises, the colonies and the mother country became more closely intertwined in a shared empire. The colonists recognized that they belonged to a transatlantic empire in which political, economic, cultural, and military initiatives derived primarily from the central metropolis of

London. Colonial leaders maintained that they were transplanted English endowed with all of the liberties enjoyed by propertied men at home. Indeed, they boasted that their English liberties rendered them superior to the colonists of the other, more arbitrary empires.

After 1691, colonial politics remained riven by factional disputes and heated rhetoric, but no longer interrupted by the violent rebellions that had characterized the 1670s and 1680s. Seats in the colonial assemblies became more stable, as fewer elections were contested and leading men clung to their seats for many years. As elite families intermarried, the leading councillors and assemblymen increasingly became related. More than ever before, ambitious colonists looked to London for approval and patronage. In particular, leading colonists influenced the appointment and recall of royal governors by lobbying the crown through correspondents and agents in London.

As New York's governor from 1702 to 1710, Lord Cornbury learned the hard way that leading colonists could effectively play the dirty politics of London. An indebted and grasping governor, Cornbury naturally sought every possible paying perquisite of his office, alienating subordinate officers and officials with their own needs and greed. The governor was an able administrator and had his share of colonial supporters, but his enemies were all too adept at the new game of transatlantic correspondence and intrigue. To discredit Cornbury at home, his foes collected and disseminated every shred of compromising evidence and every piece of malicious gossip, including the charge:

> My Lord Cornbury has and dos still make use of an unfortunate Custom of dressing himself in Women's Cloaths and of exposing himself in that Garb upon the Ramparts to the view of the public; in that dress he draws a World of Spectators upon him and consequently as many Censures, especially for exposing himself in such a manner [on] all the great Holy days and even in an hour or two after going to the Communion.

Although certainly overstated, and perhaps fabricated, the cross-dressing accusations proved useful to Cornbury's political enemies in London, who displaced the governor in 1709. His successor rewarded Cornbury's enemies by governing with their assistance.

Like Lord Cornbury, most royal governors were born and bred in England, ordinarily among the gentry or aristocracy, where they learned to live lavishly, accumulating mounting debts. They sought a colonial governorship as an opportunity to recoup their fortunes by reaping every possible salary and fee. Sojourners, they expected to return to London within a few years enriched to enjoy a more fashionable society and to reenter the higher-stakes politics of the mother country. While recouping their fortunes as governors, they struggled to perform a difficult balancing act, for the governors needed both to cultivate colonial cooperation and to satisfy their superiors in

London. Official instructions demanded their jealous protection of the crown's share of colonial power, known as "the prerogative," from aggressive assemblies. Governors were also supposed to secure increased colonial expenditures for the imperial wars against France. Unfortunately for the governors, colonial assemblies demanded more power in return for military appropriations.

The governors could not use military force to dictate to the colonists. After the collapse of the Dominion, the English reverence for the common law and for the distinction between the civil and military spheres precluded garrison government. And except for small garrisons in New York and the West Indies, the colonies lacked royal troops. British warships frequently visited the colonial seaports, but their commanders took orders only from their superiors in the royal navy, often to the great disappointment of the governors. Only one governor, Daniel Parke of the Leeward Islands, was foolish enough to employ troops to intimidate his assembly. For this, Parke suffered a brutal assassination by the leading sugar planters in 1710. No culprits were ever prosecuted. No other royal governor was assassinated, because none repeated Parke's folly.

Instead of force, governors had to rely upon persuasion and patronage to build "an interest" among the leading colonists in the assembly and on the council. At the provincial level, the governor made a few friends by appointing the attorney general, colonial secretary, surveyor general, and treasurer. At the county level, he named the sheriffs and clerks, justices of the peace, and militia officers. Colonists coveted these posts as sources of honor, influence, and income.

Governors also rewarded or punished colonial gentlemen by either awarding or withholding grants to large tracts of frontier lands taken from the Indians. Ultimately, most colonial fortunes depended upon the increased real estate value produced by expansion and farm-building on the frontier. Once granted thousands of acres of forest, a colonial land speculator stood to enhance his fortune by retailing farm-sized lots of one hundred to two hundred acres to settlers for clearing and cultivation. In 1767 a Pennsylvanian noted, "It is almost a proverb, that Every great fortune made here with in these 50 years has been by land [speculation]."

Despite this patronage, the governors failed to dominate the assemblies, where the representatives were loath to antagonize their constituents, who primarily wanted their taxes kept low and their governors kept weak. Moreover, no governor possessed enough offices, lands, and acquiescence to satisfy all of the ambitious and competitive colonial politicians. The dissatisfied became a vocal opposition. They could make abundant trouble by posing in the assembly and at elections as the champions of liberty and low taxes against a grasping governor and his corrupt minions. Colonial politics became an incessant scramble between a governor's faction ("court") and his opponents ("country"), with the arrival of each new governor usually rearranging the ins and the outs—while perpetuating the polarity and the libertarian rhetoric.

Exploiting their leverage from control over taxation and expenditure, the assemblies played a game of chicken with the governor by delaying the defense appropriations demanded by his instructions. They knew from experience that sooner rather than later, the crown would withdraw an ineffective governor. Assemblymen also could reward or punish a governor through their control over his annual salary. The crown expected the colonists to pay that salary but usually failed to persuade assemblies to render it permanent, for the representatives shrewdly recognized that an annually appropriated salary gave them the power to withhold payment from an uncooperative governor. After much wrangling, most governors eventually concluded that it was best to get along and go along with the leaders in their assemblies. The governors usually had little choice, given the demands of the expanding warfare with France. In this the governors followed the precedent set by the monarchs at home.

MEN AND MONEY

By overthrowing James II as king, William of Orange plunged England into a war with France of unprecedented scale and cost. In the first full flush of the Glorious Revolution, the English little realized how much that coup would cost them or where it would lead. To compete with France—the most powerful kingdom in Europe—the English had to build a much larger and more professional army and navy, managed by a state bureaucracy and funded by higher levels of taxation—measures long considered unthinkable in England. In the words of historian John Brewer, during the 1690s England developed a "fiscal-military state . . . dominated by the task of waging war." During subsequent periods of peace, Parliament could temporarily shrink, but never abolish, the expanded infrastructure of a militarized government.

The English fought the Nine Years War (1689–97) to uphold the Protestant regime, to maintain England's hold over Ireland, to preserve their American colonies, and to defend their new allies, the Dutch, from a massive French invasion. For means to achieve these ends, William persuaded Parliament to expand the English military to unprecedented dimensions. By 1694 the English sustained an army of 48,000 subjects plus 21,000 German mercenaries. Between 1689 and 1698, the English also built sixty-one new warships, rendering the royal navy the largest and best in Europe.

The massive military buildup demanded heavy new taxes. Prior to the Glorious Revolution, Parliament had held taxes down to weaken the crown by limiting its public purse. After 1688, however, Parliament became committed to a new monarch who required extraordinary new revenues to counter French power and prevent the return of a Catholic king. Formerly the bulwark against unpopular taxes and crown power, Parliament became the great collection agency for the new monarch, a Protestant succession, and a transatlantic empire. Formerly the lightest-taxed people in Europe, the English joined the French and the Dutch as the most heavily taxed.

Managing the expanded military and taxation required a revolution in the financial structures of the English empire. Despite their growth, the taxes failed to keep pace with the soaring military expenditures. Consequently, Parliament created a permanent, funded national debt that paid annual interest to private financiers. By 1698 the national debt reached £17 million and the annual interest payments absorbed nearly a third of the national revenues. To manage that debt, Parliament established the Bank of England, a mixed institution of private and public investment that dramatically increased the fiscal resources of the empire. The funded debt and the Bank of England also intertwined the interests of the government, the great capitalists of London, and a broader pool of smaller investors of middling means.

In stark contrast to France, England built a fiscal-military state without submitting to the despotism of an absolutist monarchy. Because the war was so expensive and increasingly unpopular, Parliament demanded greater control over expenditures, which King William had to concede in his desperation for military funding. The new fiscal powers enabled Parliament to control foreign and military policy, previously the most jealously guarded of royal prerogatives. In effect, during and because of the war, national sovereignty became vested in Parliament as well as in the crown. The two overlapped as never before, a formula the English called "King-in-Parliament." Before 1688, kings could dispense with Parliament for many years, ruling without its interference but also without the adequate funding that depended upon parliamentary statute. After 1688, the crown could no longer govern without an annual Parliament to approve the taxes that sustained an expanded state. In sum, the exigencies of war created both a formidable government and a new form of sovereignty that prevented the crown from exercising that expanded power without Parliament.

COLONIAL AND INDIAN WAR

During the Nine Years War, the enhanced English military proved of little benefit to the colonists. A sense of profound insecurity at home drove the English buildup, rather than an ambition to conduct offensives to expand the colonial empire. As a relatively small realm perilously close to powerful France, the English first had to protect themselves and their Dutch allies from invasion. Having posted most of their troops in Ireland or Flanders and most of their warships in the English Channel, the English could send few soldiers and vessels to the distant colonies. And almost all of the resources sent to the colonies defended the English West Indies, the crown jewels of the empire. Considered less valuable and less vulnerable, the mainland colonies were largely left to defend themselves. After 1682, the English crown maintained only one small, underfunded garrison on the mainland: about 150 badly trained and poorly equipped men at New York City. Surely, English officials reasoned, their 250,000 mainland colonists (black and white) could overwhelm the mere 12,000 French in Canada and Acadia.

Despite their numerical superiority, the English colonists suffered repeated defeats as New France mustered small but effective combinations of royal troops, Canadian militia, and Indians to raid and destroy frontier settlements in New York and New England. In response, the English tried to invade Canada both by land from Albany via Lake Champlain and by sea via the St. Lawrence River, but both invasions were expensive and humiliating failures.

By the end of the war, the New English were so starved for good news that they made a great deal of their only war hero, and an unlikely war hero she was. In March 1697, Abenaki Indian raiders captured Hannah Dustin, a Massachusetts woman of about forty years. After six weeks of captivity, Dustin persuaded two other captives—another woman and a boy—to surprise and slaughter their sleeping captors. Seizing hatchets, the three captives killed and scalped ten Abenaki, including two women and six children. Before making good their escape, Hannah Dustin carefully scalped the victims, for she knew that Massachusetts paid bounties for scalps: £10 for a child and £50 for an adult. Safely returned home, Hannah Dustin collected her bounty and reaped exuberant celebration from the Massachusetts assembly and Puritan ministers. In making a hero of a woman, colonial men contradicted their usual insistence on feminine submission, underlining how completely they had failed in the war.

The colonists bungled their war effort primarily because of bitter political infighting both within and between colonies. Bearing the brunt of the war, Massachusetts resented the indifferent effort made by New York, Connecticut, and Rhode Island. Crown officials concluded, "The King has subjects enough in those parts . . . to defend themselves against any attack of French and Indians, but they are so crumbled into little governments and so disunited in their interests that they have hitherto afforded but little assistance to each other." The imperial authorities regretted the demise of the Dominion, while the colonists discovered that the new crown regime embroiled them in an imperial war of unprecedented expense, destruction, and confusion against formidable northern foes. By 1697 the Nine Years War had exhausted the resources of the European belligerents, producing a peace treaty that reflected the military stalemate.

The Iroquois Five Nations especially suffered from the ineptitude of their English allies. In 1693 and 1696 the French and their Indian allies burned Iroquois towns and destroyed the ripening corn, sentencing the nations to hunger, while the New Yorkers did nothing to help their allies. An exasperated Iroquois demanded, "Pray let us know the reason why you do not come to Our assistance according to your former promise that We may live and die together."

After the English and French made a peace with one another in 1697, the Iroquois remained at war. Abandoned by their English allies, the Five Nations faced devastating raids by their Indian enemies. In defeat, the Iroquois suffered casualties instead of gathering the prisoners that they needed to appease mourning and recoup their losses. In 1700 a New Yorker reported, "The Indians I find much dejected and in a staggering condition, tho' they are so proud and will not own it."

By shrewd diplomacy in 1701, the Iroquois chiefs snatched partial victory from the jaws of defeat, making a peace with New France without alienating the English. As an alternative to dependence on either empire, the Iroquois chiefs developed a wary neutrality. By sustaining a balance of power between the French and English, the Five Nations meant, in the future, to reap respect, restraint, and generous presents from both. Rather than restrict their commerce to one empire, the Iroquois traded both north with Montreal and east with Albany, as shifting markets suited their interest. A New York official ruefully concluded, "To preserve the Ballance between us and the French is the great ruling Principle of the Modern Indian Politics." Fearful of alienating the Five Nations, both the French and the English lavished attention and presents to purchase a continued neutrality that was in the Iroquois' interest in any event. In 1711 the French governor-general explained that "the five Iroquois [nations] are more to be feared than the English colonies." A New Englander remarked that Iroquois delegations "are Courted and Caressed like the potentates of the Earth."

Neutrality did not bring a universal peace to Iroquoia. On the contrary, peace to the north and west obliged the Iroquois to find enemies elsewhere, for they remained committed to mourning wars to sustain their numbers, their spiritual power, and their warrior ethos. A colonist noted that "if you go to persuade them to live peaceably" the Iroquois "will answer you, that they cannot live without war." After 1701 the Iroquois focused their war parties southward to assail Indian foes on the distant Carolina frontier, primarily the Catawba. From the Iroquois perspective, the Catawba were ideal targets: few enough to be vulnerable, distant enough to discourage retaliation, proud enough to refuse submission, and brave enough to test the best warriors. By killing their share of Iroquois raiders, the Catawba added revenge to the motives driving their northern enemies.

English imperial officials disliked the southern raiding because the Catawba were allies and trading partners of the Carolinians and Virginians. Moreover, on their way to and fro, hungry Iroquois war parties passed through colonial settlements, occasionally killing and eating pigs and cattle, which sometimes led to firefights with settlers. In vain the governors of Virginia, North Carolina, and New York urged the Five Nations to desist.

Precisely because the southern raids kept the Iroquois preoccupied and made trouble for the English colonies, French officials encouraged the raiders with praise and presents. Thanks to the Iroquois' neutrality and southern raiding, New France enjoyed an unprecedented security—despite the new wars with the English.

WAR OF THE SPANISH SUCCESSION

The peace of 1697 lasted a mere five years for the Europeans and their colonists. By 1702, Louis XIV had rebuilt his military and renewed his ambitions for foreign expansion. By claiming the vacant throne of Spain for his grandson, Philip de Bourbon, Louis XIV threatened to unite the French and Spanish empires, armies, and fleets—which would destroy the balance of power in both Europe and the Americas. In England, the deaths of Queen Mary in 1694 and King William in 1702 without children left the throne to Mary's younger sister, Queen Anne. To defend both the Protestant Succession and the European balance of power, England revived the alliance against Louis XIV for an even longer and more expensive conflict, known as the War of the Spanish Succession. In contrast to the bloody stalemate of the previous war, the English army and navy won a surprising series of victories in Europe, marking England's emergence as a first-rank power.

But the English war effort again faltered in the colonies. In 1702 the Carolina colonists attacked San Agústin, the capital of Florida, but the Spanish garrison and fortifications proved too strong. Defeated, the Carolinians retreated in disarray, abandoning their artillery and burning their trapped ships. To the north, the French again rallied the Indians, including the Abenaki, to harass and burn the frontier towns of New England. Ineffectual at frontier war, the New English again favored action by sea, this time with some assistance from the mother country. In 1710 a combined force of royal navy ships and New English volunteers captured the weak French settlement of Port Royal in Acadia. In 1711, England sent an even larger expedition to assist New England in capturing Quebec from the sea, but the stormy, foggy, and treacherous mouth of the St. Lawrence defended New France, wrecking eight transports, with a loss of nine hundred lives. Timid and incompetent, the English admiral sailed for home, sparing Quebec for a second time, to the deep frustration of the New English.

Worn down by mounting casualties and extraordinary costs, the queen and Parliament decided to cash in their early European victories before further warfare reversed them. In 1713 the English abruptly abandoned their allies to negotiate their own advantageous treaties with France and Spain at Utrecht. The English accepted Philip de Bourbon as the Spanish king, with the proviso that the French and Spanish crowns and empires remain distinct. In return, Spain surrendered Gibraltar and the Mediterranean island of Minorca to England. Otherwise, the English preferred to take their gains in the Americas, although their forces had won victories in Europe but reaped defeat in the colonies. The French surrendered their claims to Acadia, Newfoundland, Hudson Bay, and the West Indian island of St. Kitts. In addition, English merchants won the coveted *asiento de negros:* a lucrative thirty-year monopoly contract to provide African slaves to the Spanish colonies. By giving a new priority to overseas expansion, the English committed their empire to maritime commerce rather than to European territory—a dramatic shift that elevated their American colonies to a new importance.

UNION

In the peace treaty the French and Spanish also recognized the new English union with Scotland. Since 1603, when the Scottish king ascended the English throne as James I, the crowns of Scotland and England had been united. But each kingdom remained legally distinct, retaining its own established church (Presbyterian in Scotland), legal system, and Parliament. After the Glorious Revolution, the Scots Parliament acted with greater independence and suggested that it would choose its own monarch if and when the Stuart dynasty ceased to reign in England. When all of Queen Anne's children died, the English faced the prospect of a new dynasty and Scottish secession. English leaders especially worried that the Scots might exploit the War of the Spanish Succession to choose James Edward Stuart, the son of the late James II, as their own king. An independent Scotland under a Catholic Stuart would place an enemy on England's northern border.

Scots pride urged political independence, but the country's economic dependence on England argued instead for a tighter union. Many Scots wanted improved access to the English market for their commodities, principally linen and cattle. Scots merchants also longed to share in the growing commerce of the North American colonies, which the Navigation Acts reserved for English exploitation.

During the 1690s, Scots merchants and politicians had sought their own commercial empire by forcing an entrepôt colony into the midst of Spanish America, at Darien on the strategic Isthmus of Panama, a transit point for trade between the Pacific and the Atlantic. The bold scheme attracted £400,000—nearly a quarter of all the liquid capital in Scotland—and almost all of the imperial ambitions of a small and fragile country. In 1698 a Scots investor observed, "The Ships of the Company are sailed" and "Scotland has now a greater venture at Sea than at any time since we have bin a Nation. . . . I may well say [that] all our hopes of ever being any other than a poor and inconsiderable People are imbarked with them." Undertaken in defiance of the English government, the Darien scheme represented a new assertion of sovereignty by the Scottish Parliament. In 1700, however, the Spanish destroyed

Darien, with English acquiescence. The Scots colonial company collapsed, ruining the investors and compounding a trade depression in Scotland. The Darien debacle also soured the investment of national hope and pride, reaffirming the Scots sense of economic inferiority to the English.

To resolve their Scottish problem, in 1705 the English threatened to close their border to trade unless the Scots negotiated a more complete union. A poorer and smaller country of only one million people, the Scots could also ill afford a rupture with the richer and more numerous (five million) English. Adding a carrot to the stick, the English promised large payments to Scots politicians who had invested in the Darien scheme. To avert a disastrous trade war and rescue their finances, in 1707 the Scottish Parliament narrowly embraced a union that created a new composite realm "by the name of Great Britain." Abandoning their own Parliament, the Scots received instead a few seats in both the House of Commons and the House of Lords in the hitherto English Parliament. Great Britain would have a common flag, coinage, measures, treasury, navy, army, and foreign policy, but England and Scotland would retain distinct legal, educational, and church establishments.

At the price of political subordination, the Scots won access to the thriving English colonies and overseas commerce. Frustrated in their own dream of colonial empire, the Scots instead made the best of the English empire, rendering it progressively more British over the course of the eighteenth century. Scots gentlemen became conspicuous as colonial officials, including the royal governors Robert Hunter of New York, Alexander Spotswood of Virginia, and Gabriel Johnston of North Carolina. Scots merchants also captured a growing share in the colonial commerce, especially the tobacco trade from the Chesapeake. And after 1707, the Scots outnumbered the English as emigrants to the colonies.

PIRATES

Enhanced in power and ambition, the British empire turned against the piracy that had been an English resource in earlier, weaker times. During the late sixteenth and early seventeenth centuries, as a relatively poor country with a limited navy, England had found piracy useful for attacking the more powerful Spanish empire. England's leaders, including Queen Elizabeth I and a long succession of colonial governors, protected and invested in pirate enterprises. New York, South Carolina, and Jamaica were especially notorious for hosting pirates. Needing more naval protection than the official navy could provide, colonial governors gave the pirates official cover as "privateers" licensed to plunder the enemy in wartime. By fencing pirate loot, governors procured the coveted gold and silver so desperately needed by the colonial economies.

At the end of the seventeenth century, as British commerce and naval might eclipsed the Spanish, British imperial officials reassessed their support for piracy. With Spanish shipping declining and British shipping growing, pirates became more indiscriminate, plundering vessels from their own country. In addition, by attacking Britain's foreign trading partners, the pirates disrupted the global reach of British merchants. For example, the emperor of India closed down British trade and held British officials hostage when British pirates ravaged Indian shipping. In 1696 a crown prosecutor explained the high stakes to an English jury: "For suffer Pirates, and the Commerce of the World must cease, which this nation has so deservedly a share in, and reaps such advantage by." By 1700, pirates had become liabilities to a successful empire.

As they became more disreputable, the pirates developed a distinctive counterculture that expressed their alienation from social conventions and structures of authority. For sailors who had previously lived by hard fare, low pay, and harsh discipline in the merchant marine or the royal navy, piracy offered an appealing release into excess. Bartholomew Roberts contrasted piracy with the merchant service, where "there is thin Commons, low Wages, and hard Labour; in this, Plenty and Satiety, Pleasure and Ease, Liberty and Power. . . . No, *a merry Life and a short one*, shall be my motto." Pirates took a special pride in their ability to eat, drink, dance, gamble, and whore with abandon, in a style that they called "living well." Although unstable and dangerous, piracy proved intoxicating and addictive. The governor of Jamaica noted, "These Indyes are so Vast and Rich, And this kind of rapine so sweet, that it is one of the hardest things in the World to draw those from it which have used it for long."

Piracy also invited offended sailors to strike back against the owners and operators of merchant ships, who exercised a severe discipline and cut wages to the bone in peacetime. One pirate explained that the "reasons for going a pirating were to revenge themselves on base Merchants and cruel commanders of ships." On captured vessels, pirates tried the merchant sea captains, to investigate their treatment of sailors. Those found guilty of abuse suffered whipping and sometimes execution. One pirate confessed to killing thirty-seven merchant ship captains. But if a captured crew vouched for good treatment, their master reaped the same from the pirates.

In an era when wealth and power accumulated at the top of the social pyramid, pirates maintained a distinctive egalitarianism. Each crew codified its rules in a written compact that every member signed. Instead of working for wages or an indenture, the pirates were equal risk-sharing and loot-dividing partners. In general, every man received one equal share of the loot, with the captain obtaining no more than a double share. In a form of social welfare, the pirates gave wounded and crippled men extra compensation before dividing their plunder. The pirate crews operated as democracies, in which majority vote determined who commanded, where to sail, and what to attack. But it was a rough form of democracy; after especially contentious debates and decisions, discredited captains and defeated minorities suffered harsh treatment, often set adrift in canoes or ashore on islands. In contrast to the navy or the merchant service, the pirate captain could punish no sailor without the consent of the majority. And the pirate captain enjoyed no privileged diet or berth, but had to sleep and mess with the rest of the crew. One observer noted: "They permit him to be Captain, on Condition, that they may be Captain over him."

Pirates were throwbacks to an eroding age of violent, open competition. They defied the consolidation of power and wealth in empires and large mercantile firms: the partnership that took control of maritime commerce during the early eighteenth century. The pirates were violent men defending their chance to participate in an age of exploitation. In a colonial world divided between masters and servants, the pirates defined freedom as their own opportunity to prey upon others. At a time when brutality with the whip maintained discipline on colonial plantations and merchant ships, the pirates relished the opportunity to wield rather than to suffer violence.

During the 1697–1701 interlude between the wars with France, the English empire first acted to suppress piracy in distant waters. The imperial government meant to demonstrate its new powers to control and defend colonial commerce. A war on the pirates also served as a vehicle to compel colonial merchants, legislators, and governors to acknowledge and cooperate with imperial authority. In 1700, Parliament passed tough new legislation exposing colonial merchants and governors to prosecution if they harbored or supplied the pirates. Thereafter, colonial governors demonstrated a new zeal to arrest pirates for shipment to London, where dozens were tried and executed during 1700 and 1701.

The most infamous convicted pirate was Captain William Kidd, who had raided in the Indian Ocean, with the connivance of his patron, the Earl of Bellomont, who governed New York. Recognizing that times were changing, Governor Bellomont sacrificed Kidd, luring him into an arrest and sending him in chains to London for trial, conviction, and execution before a huge crowd on May 23, 1701. As was common practice with executed pirates, the authorities had Kidd's body wrapped in chains and hoisted into an iron gibbet beside the Thames River, there slowly to rot, feed the crows, and warn passing mariners of the perils of piracy and the new power of the empire. Although Kidd had been a lesser pirate and a bit of a bungler, he became in public imagination the archpirate, which testified to the success of the authorities in staging his show trial and execution. An imperial official cynically explained, "Parliaments are grown into the habit of finding fault, and some Jonah or other must be thrown overboard. . . . Little men are certainly the properest for these purposes." Kidd died that Bellomont might live.

Between 1702 and 1713 the War of the Spanish Succession suspended the suppression of pirates, as imperial officials needed every available sailor for naval or privateer duty against the French and Spanish. But the struggle resumed with unprecedented vigor after the war ended. The peace brought a partial demobilization of the navy and privateers, which unleashed thousands of mariners into a glutted labor market. Widespread unemployment enabled merchants to slash their wages for common sailors to half the wartime level. Merchant sea captains also demanded harder work for the lower pay and inflicted more brutal whippings on sailors who balked. Some turned pirate by mutiny, seizing control of their merchant ship and killing or marooning their officers. From this genesis, pirate crews grew by recruiting volunteers from the sailors aboard captured merchant ships. By 1716 colonial authorities estimated that at least two thousand Anglo-American pirates were operating in the West Indies and along the Atlantic seaboard. They found havens on the unsettled islands of the Bahamas and in the secluded inlets of the Carolinas. A colonial customs officer in Philadelphia warned, "All the news of America is, the swarming of pirates not only on these coasts, but all the West Indies over, which doth ruin trade ten times worse than a war."

But the pirates had lost their former allies in colonial society as merchants, juries, and governors cooperated with the imperial authorities as never before. Leading colonists hired, armed, and manned their own vessels to supplement the royal navy in coastal patrols to seek and destroy pirates. Between 1716 and 1726 the British convicted and executed between four hundred and six hundred pirates; at least twice as many more died resisting capture. By 1730 the campaign virtually exterminated the pirates in the Bahamas, the Carolinas, and the West Indies, bringing a new security to colonial shipping. The suppression enabled merchants to cut shipping costs by eliminating the cannon and extra sailors formerly needed to defend their ships. The price of maritime insurance also fell dramatically during the 1730s. The seas belonged to the empire and to respectable merchants.

COMMERCE AND EMPIRE

The British triumphs in war, in the peace treaty, in crafting the British Union, and in crushing the pirates marked a revolutionary transformation in the realm's power. The British largely built their prowess at French expense, but the British also eclipsed their ostensible allies the Dutch, who reaped far less than they had sowed in staging William's coup in 1688–89. Initially, the Glorious Revolution had seemed a Dutch triumph that withdrew England from the French embrace and secured English military assistance to help defend the Netherlands in two massive wars. But those wars took an even heavier toll on Dutch taxpayers, ships, and commerce than on the English, a toll that the far smaller Netherlands could ill afford. Exhausted, the Dutch had little choice but to accept British primacy in their alliance and in the world's oceans. By 1713 the Dutch navy was only half the size of the British. And the

Treaty of Utrecht awarded the lucrative *asiento de negros* contract to the British, excluding the Dutch, who lost their former lead in the slave trade, so critical to overseas empire. During the early eighteenth century, London supplanted Amsterdam as Europe's premier center for commerce and high finance. In sum, although it seemed in 1688 that the Dutch had captured England, by 1713 it was clear that the English had captured and co-opted William, and through him had subordinated the Netherlands. The Dutch found themselves reduced to a second-rate power yoked in an unequal alliance with a more dynamic empire.

Of course, the British triumphs had not come cheap, as the long War of the Spanish Succession more than doubled the national debt to £36 million. In 1688 the crown captured about 3 percent of the national income as taxes; by 1715 that had tripled to 9 percent of an enlarged economy. Even during the subsequent years of peace, Great Britain annually spent an average of £6 million on its military, three times more than in 1688. For the rest of the century, the government devoted at least 75 percent of its annual expenditures to maintaining the military or servicing its war debts.

The lion's share of the military expenditure went into the navy, which became the material embodiment of British patriotism. As an island with an economy increasingly predicated on overseas commerce, Britain sought naval supremacy by maintaining a fleet at least as large as the combined navies of France and Spain. France reversed those priorities. Cursed with continental ambitions and with long and vulnerable borders with Germany and the Netherlands, France naturally favored its army, conceding naval supremacy to the British for most of the eighteenth century. Poorly protected, France's transatlantic commerce was more vulnerable to disruption by war, while British naval supremacy provided England's colonists with more secure shipping, avoiding the interruptions and shortages that racked French America during wars.

British naval supremacy primarily rested on superior financial resources and the political consensus for spending them on a fleet. The bigger budget enabled the British to build and maintain many more ships and to keep more of them at sea for longer periods, while the cash-starved French fleet often remained cooped up in port. Consequently, French sailors and officers could not match the sailing and combat experience of the British. Superior experience built a greater confidence and daring that enabled the British to seize the initiative in most naval combat. Hobbled by a sense of inferiority, the French usually avoided naval battle, for they were loath to risk ships that they could ill afford to replace.

The British military depended upon the flow of overseas commerce at least as much as trade depended upon protection from a powerful and versatile navy. Two-thirds of the British revenue came from taxes on commerce—customs and the excise—and the liquid capital of merchants primarily supplied the national loans. The merchant marine and fishing fleets also trained the thousands of sailors drawn upon for an expanded navy in war. Consequently, England risked financial crisis and military catastrophe if an enemy disrupted the maritime commerce that had become the lifeblood of the nation. In 1701, Lord Haversham assured the House of Lords:

> Your fleet and your trade have so near a relation, and such a mutual influence upon each other [that] they cannot be well separated; your trade is the mother and nurse of your seamen; your seamen are the life of your fleet, and your fleet is the security and protection of your trade, and both together are the wealth, strength, security and glory of Britain.

This did not mean that merchants governed the empire. Excluded by definition from the House of Lords, the merchants were also never more than a small minority in the House of Commons. Instead, Parliament belonged overwhelmingly to the landed aristocracy and gentry, who also dominated the upper ranks of the army and navy, the diplomatic and colonial services, the judicial bench, and the hierarchy of the Church of England. Confident in their own rule, the landed elite felt no threat from the men of commerce. Although the aristocrats and gentry regarded trade as vaguely dishonorable and beneath themselves, they applauded the commercial accomplishments of the middling sort. Britain's traditional elite recognized that the prowess of their realm had come to depend upon the wealth generated by commerce. Determined to govern a powerful empire, the landed elite needed the merchants to prosper to sustain the navy.

As commerce became fundamental to British power, the American colonies became more important to the empire, attracting increasing attention from the press, Parliament, and the imperial bureaucracy. Shared commercial and military interests also tied the colonies to the mother country as never before. During the mid-seventeenth century, the Navigation Acts had initially inflicted economic pain upon the colonists, who then depended upon Dutch credit, shipping, export markets, and manufactured imports. At that time, English merchants, shippers, markets, and manufacturers were not yet ready to fill the gap. But by the start of the eighteenth century, as British manufacturing, shipping, and finance outstripped the Dutch, the colonists could obtain better-quality goods from British suppliers at lower costs and on a more generous credit.

By 1720 the Navigation Acts became largely self-enforcing as the colonial and imperial economic interests converged. The enumerated colonial staples flowed almost entirely in the appropriate ships to a British port, and almost all the manufactures imported by the colonies came in British ships from British seaports. At one time or another, every colonial interest group protested some feature of the Navigation Acts, but no one wanted an abolition of the whole. By protesting particulars, they simply jockeyed for the best position within the mercantile framework.

Because maximizing shipping and sailors was the primary goal, the Navigation Acts did not entirely seal colonial trade within the empire. Except for the high-value "enumerated" commodities (principally sugar and tobacco), the colonists were free, indeed encouraged, to carry their produce to other lands, provided that they did so in ships owned and operated by British subjects (which, of course, included colonial shipping). Indeed, during the early eighteenth century, Portugal, Spain, and their Atlantic islands became prime markets for New England's fish, Carolina's rice, and Pennsylvania's wheat. The imperial authorities also encouraged the colonists to trade with New Spain to procure the gold and silver coins so essential to commerce but so precious and scarce in the English empire—although this trade violated Spanish law and risked Spanish punishment.

Overseas commerce and naval war also became central to the eighteenth-century patriotism of the British Union and empire. Between 1689 and 1713, prolonged warfare rendered the French a fearsome presence in British minds. Despite their many internal disputes over religion, the Scots, the English, and their colonists could see themselves as united Protestants when they focused outward upon Catholic France. Viewing the French as an "other," the British characterized them as economically backward, religiously superstitious, culturally decadent, aggressively militarist, and broken to despotic rule. By inverse definition, the British saw themselves as especially enlightened by commerce, individual liberties, the rule of law, and a Protestant faith.

In their intertwined commercial and military successes, the British and their colonists found the measure of their virtues. By prospering in both trade and war, the empire seemed to prove the equation that the Protestant Succession, the British Union, the common law, and individual liberties combined to create national wealth, imperial power, and individual happiness. Enthusiastic participants in this patriotism of empire, the American colonists felt more strongly tied to the mother country. The union, prosperity, and confidence of the eighteenth-century empire marked a major change, over the previous generation, from the severe tensions that had threatened to dissolve the empire into civil war as a consequence of James II's provocative effort to establish authoritarian rule at home and in the colonies.

14

The Atlantic

★

1700–80

African slaves ferried in canoes to a European ship at Manfroe, on the west coast of Africa. An engraving by Johannes Kip from John Churchill, ed., A Collection of Voyages and Travels *(London, 1732).*

DURING THE EIGHTEENTH CENTURY, a swelling volume of British shipping carried information, goods, and people more regularly across the Atlantic. The annual transatlantic crossings tripled from about five hundred during the 1670s to fifteen hundred by the late 1730s. The increasing shipping (and diminished piracy) reduced insurance costs and freight charges, which encouraged the shipment of greater cargos. More and larger ships, some dedicated to the emigrant trade, also cut in half the price of a passage from Europe to the colonies between 1720 and 1770.

The ocean became less of a barrier and more of a bridge between the two shores of the empire. Clustered close to the Atlantic, most colonists felt oriented eastward toward the ocean and across to Europe, rather than westward into the interior. The continental interior of dense forests, Indian peoples, and immense but uncertain dimensions was far more mysterious and daunting than an ocean passage. Colonists knew, often by direct and multiple experience, that the Atlantic was regularly traversed, but none had crossed the North American continent.

Far from dividing the colonists from the mother country, the ocean and the passage of time both worked to draw them closer together during the first two-thirds of the eighteenth century. The colonists became significantly better informed about events and ideas in Britain and especially London. The swelling volume of shipping also led to more complex trading patterns, which fed an impressive growth in the colonial economy. Consequently, most free colonists enjoyed rising incomes, which permitted their increased consumption of British manufactures. That consumption reinforced the ties between the mother country and the colonies, especially for the colonial elite. Paradoxically, as the Atlantic became more British in its shipping, information, and goods, it also became a conduit for a greater diversity of emigrants.

Despite the proliferation of British shipping, the overall number of emigrants declined in the early eighteenth century from its seventeenth-century peak. During the early decades of colonization, when the English economy and state were weak, ruling opinion regarded the realm as dangerously overpopulated. To reduce unemployment and discontent at home, England's rulers encouraged emigration to the colonies, where laborers could raise staple commodities for the mother country and where dissidents could be exiled from political influence. Late in the seventeenth century, however, ruling opinion shifted, as the home government became more tolerant of religious diversity; English manufacturing expanded, increasing the demand for cheap labor; and the realm frequently needed additional thousands for an enlarged military. Thereafter, English emigration seemed an economic and strategic loss to the mother country.

While discouraging English emigration, imperial officials wished to continue colonial development and bolster colonial defenses by procuring an alternative supply of colonists. By recruiting for colonists in Europe, imperial officials hoped to strengthen the colonies without weakening the mother country. William Penn explained that it had become "the interest of England to improve and thicken her colonys with people not her own." In 1740, Parliament passed the Plantation Act, which enabled foreign-born colonists to win British citizenship: a necessary prerequisite for legal ownership of land as well as for political rights. An immigrant qualified by residing for seven years in any colony, swearing allegiance to the king, taking communion in any Protestant church, and paying a two-shilling fee. Individual colonies also employed agents and subsidies aggressively to recruit and transport foreign Protestants, often for settlement on the frontiers.

The new recruitment invented America as an asylum from religious persecution and political oppression in Europe—with the important proviso that the immigrants had to be Protestants. Colonial laws and prejudices continued to discourage the emigration of Catholics and Jews to British America, from a fear that they would subvert Protestantism and betray the empire to French or Spanish attack. As a land of freedom and opportunity, British America had powerful limits.

More than any other eighteenth-century empire, the British relied on foreign emigrants for human capital. The new emigration included far fewer English but many more Scots and Germans. Even larger numbers of enslaved Africans poured across the Atlantic as the slave trade escalated, eclipsing the movement of all free emigrants to British America. Free and slave emigration were intertwined. The growing numbers of African slaves alarmed leading colonists as a grave internal security threat. Addicted to slave labor, most colonies dared not block further African imports. Instead, led by South Carolina, several colonies actively recruited and subsidized free white emigrants from Europe to help counterbalance the slave numbers and guard against a slave uprising.

As the colonial population became less English, it assumed a new ethnic and racial complexity, which increased the gap between freedom and slavery, privilege and prejudice, wealth and poverty, white and black. At the same time that high culture and consumer culture became more tied to English models, the colonial population and vernacular cultures became less homogeneous. Scots, Germans, and Africans struggled to maintain their cultural distinctiveness within an empire that generated an English model for how all elites were supposed to behave and appear.

NEWS

The increased volume and predictability of shipping improved the flow of transatlantic information, eroding the colonial sense of isolation. In 1690, William Byrd of Virginia had lamented, "We are here at the end of the World, and Europe may bee turned topsy turvy ere wee can hear a word of it." By the 1730s, however, ships arrived more frequently, bearing a greater volume of letters, pamphlets, and newspapers from England. Colonists felt better informed about European events at the same time that those events bore a greater importance to them as they became embroiled in the imperial wars.

Increased information from home—and greater colonial dependence upon it—stimulated the development of colonial newspapers. With one very brief exception in Boston in 1690, no seventeenth-century colony permitted a newspaper, because the authorities feared the press as a font of sedition and rebellion. After 1700, colonial officials and their British superiors felt more secure and less threatened by newspapers, permitting their development at home and in the colonies. The first enduring colonial newspaper, the *Boston News-Letter*, appeared in 1704. By 1739, British America had thirteen newspapers in seven seaports of seven colonies: Bridgetown (Barbados), Kingston (Jamaica), Charles Town (South Carolina), Williamsburg (Virginia), Philadelphia (Pennsylvania), New York (New York), and Boston (Massachusetts).

Newspapers both depended upon and contributed to the integration of the British Atlantic. Addressed primarily to the merchant community, the newspapers included very little local material, which consisted primarily of advertisements for newly imported goods or for the apprehension of runaway slaves and servants, as well as notices of ship arrivals, departures, and destinations. Avoiding local news stories, the colonial press primarily copied official items from the London press: diplomatic exchanges, parliamentary proceedings, and royal addresses. For filler, the colonial press drew upon English accounts of natural wonders, curious inventions, and brutal crimes, all usually from London. The cumulative effect was to draw colonial readers into an English perspective on the world. In 1717 the Boston newspaper publisher declared that the London news was what "most nearly concerns us." Sincere rather than ironic, he attested to the growing dependence of colonial merchants and officials upon a sense of the conditions in Europe. The London news afforded a barometer of political stability and foreign relations—both of great importance as the colonists became more involved in transatlantic commerce and more vulnerable to imperial warfare.

TRADE

During the eighteenth century, trade within the empire became increasingly complex. Rather than a simple, bilateral trade between the colonies and Britain, the empire developed a multilateral trading system that used bills of exchange drawn on London merchant firms to balance regional credits and debits. In the aggregate, the various regional surpluses and deficits eventually reached a near balance on the books of the London merchants, but there was a long-term trend toward increased debt owed by the mainland colonists, as

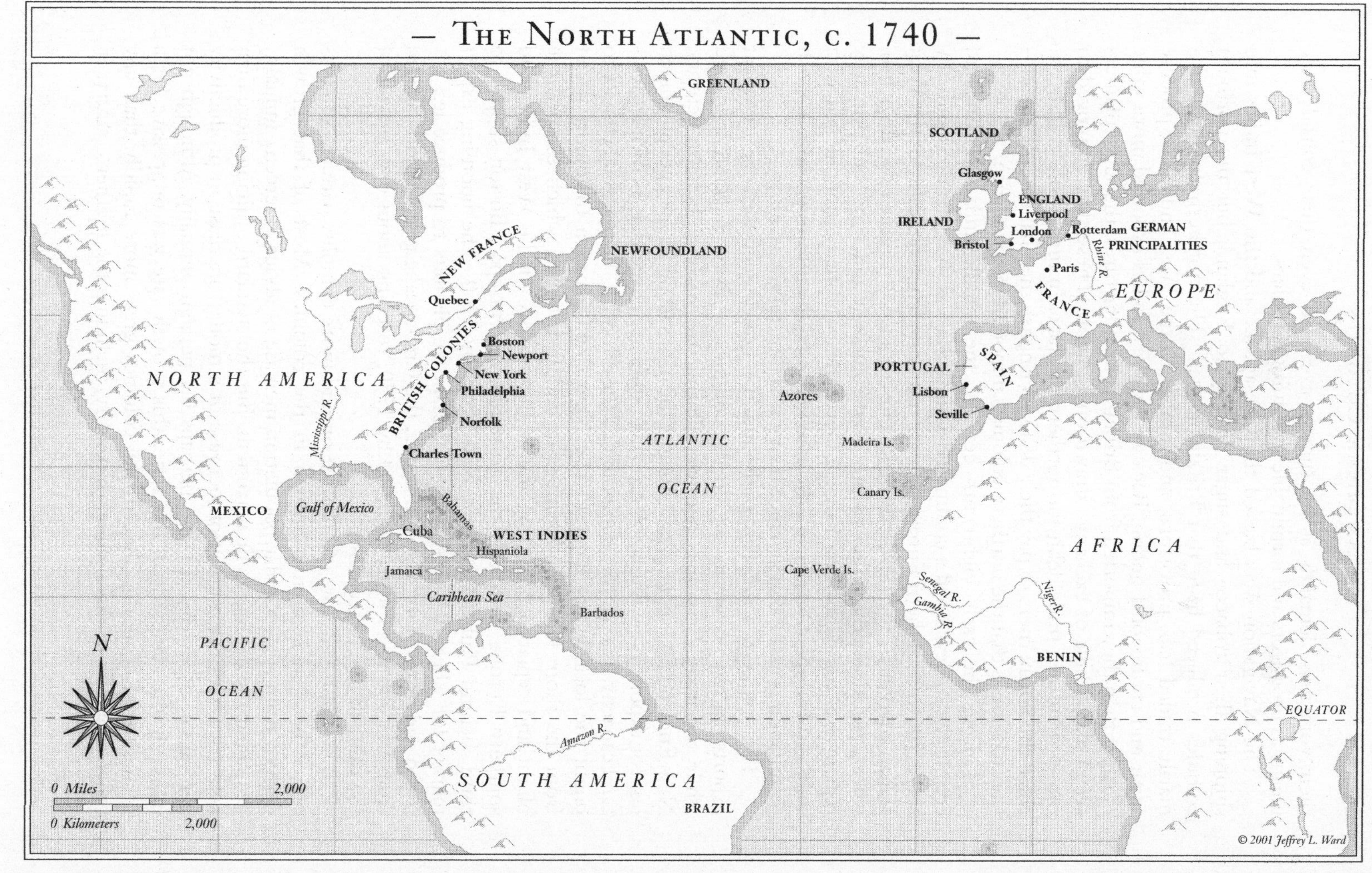
— THE NORTH ATLANTIC, C. 1740 —
GREENLAND
SCOTLAND
Glasgow
ENGLAND
Liverpool
IRELAND
London
Rotterdam
GERMAN PRINCIPALITIES
Bristol
Rhine R.
Paris
EUROPE
FRANCE
NEWFOUNDLAND
NEW FRANCE
Quebec
BRITISH COLONIES
Boston
Newport
New York
Philadelphia
Norfolk
Charles Town
NORTH AMERICA
Mississippi R.
PORTUGAL
SPAIN
Lisbon
Seville
Azores
ATLANTIC
OCEAN
Madeira Is.
Canary Is.
MEXICO
Gulf of Mexico
Bahamas
Cuba
WEST INDIES
Hispaniola
Jamaica
Caribbean Sea
Barbados
AFRICA
Cape Verde Is.
Senegal R.
Gambia R.
Niger R.
BENIN
N
PACIFIC
OCEAN
EQUATOR
Amazon R.
SOUTH AMERICA
BRAZIL
0 Miles 2,000
0 Kilometers 2,000
© 2001 Jeffrey L. Ward

their voracious demands as consumers exceeded even their considerable means as producers and formidable ingenuity as traders.

The Navigation Acts locked the Chesapeake and the West Indies into shipping their tobacco and sugar directly to England, but the northern colonies produced little that Britain needed. The northern colonists primarily traded fish, provisions, and lumber to the West Indies, to procure sugar and credits on London. Because the West Indies exported more value in sugar than they imported from Britain in manufactures, the sugar planters accumulated bills of exchange drawn on London. These they employed to cancel their own trade debit for northern produce. In turn, those credits enabled the northerners to pay their debts to English merchants for the manufactured goods that the northern colonists imported in abundance.

During the early eighteenth century, the middle and New England colonists also developed a commerce with Iberia and the Atlantic islands. By the 1770s this southern European trade nearly matched the value of the West Indian market to the northern mainland colonists. In return for their fish, wheat, and flour, the colonists procured some salt and wine, but primarily bills of exchange drawn on English merchants, who had a trade deficit with southern Europe. Once again, the colonists used the bills to procure English manufactures and Asian produce brought via the mother country.

The southern European trade and the growing importance of wheat exports shifted prosperity within the colonies, as New England stagnated while the middle colonies boomed. During the early eighteenth century, New England no longer grew enough wheat to sustain its own people, much less for export. New England's growing population exceeded its own agricultural capacity, as a parasite compounded the effects of the marginal climate to blight the local wheat harvest. The New English began to import wheat from the more fertile and temperate middle colonies, which escaped the blight and replaced New England as the granary of the West Indies and southern Europe. Formerly the great colonial entrepôt, Boston slipped to third, behind Philadelphia and New York, by 1760. The booming export market for wheat also encouraged Chesapeake planters to produce less tobacco and grow more wheat. In value, the Chesapeake grain exports surged from £11,500 in 1740 to £130,000 by 1770, reaching about one-quarter of the value of the tobacco crop.

The improved flow of information and more complex patterns of commerce boosted economic growth in the colonies. Most of that growth derived from a spectacular population increase of about 3 percent annually, just about the demographic maximum. But the standard of living more than kept pace with the population because of a modest increase in productivity per capita, of at least 0.3 and perhaps 0.5 percent annually. Although not much by the standards of our time, this growth rate was impressive for a preindustrial economy. Indeed, the colonies grew more rapidly than any other economy in the eighteenth century, including the mother country. In

1700 the colonial gross domestic product was only 4 percent of England's; by 1770 it had blossomed to 40 percent, as the colonies assumed a much larger place within the imperial economy.

The growing economy endowed free colonists with a higher standard of living than their counterparts in Europe. In 1774 on the North American mainland, the free colonists probably averaged £13 annually per capita, compared with £11 in Great Britain and £6 in France. In part, that prosperity reflected the colonial exploitation of African slaves, who amounted to a fifth of the population. Denied most of the profits of their labor, the enslaved Africans had to live in severe deprivation. In 1718 an Englishman remarked, "The labour of negroes is the principal foundation of riches from the plantations."

Indeed, the wealth of colonial regions varied directly and positively with the number of slaves. The West Indian planters lived in the greatest luxury because they conducted the harshest labor system with the greatest number of slaves. Next, in both wealth and slavery, came South Carolina, followed by the Chesapeake and the middle colonies. At the other extreme of the imperial spectrum, New England had the lowest standard of living and the fewest slaves. But even without many slaves, a common farmer or artisan lived better in New England than in the mother country. Slavery explained some, but not all, of the colonial prosperity. Access to abundant farmland accounted for the difference.

The free colonists also enjoyed a larger disposable income. Virtually exempt from imperial taxes, they paid less than a quarter of the burden borne by English taxpayers. Land-rich, the mainland colonies provided the necessities of life in cheap abundance. Surrounded by forests, the colonists paid little for lumber to build their homes and less for firewood to heat them. The relatively large farms and fertile soil enabled colonists to raise or to purchase cheaply the grains, vegetables, milk, and meat of a plentiful diet. The muster rolls for colonial military regiments recorded heights, revealing that the average colonial man stood two or three inches taller than his English counterpart. Stature depends upon nutrition, and especially protein, so the superior height of free colonists attested to their better diet, especially rich in meat and milk. On average, the tallest colonists were southern planters—those who profited most from African slavery and Indian land.

POVERTY

There were important exceptions to the rule of prosperity. Indeed, during the 1750s and 1760s the colonists reported growing numbers of the poor in the urban seaports. Especially in winter, when ice shut down shipping and employment shrank, the unemployed faced starvation unless they entered a grim almshouse maintained by the city as a last resort for the poor. In Boston, per capita expenditures on poor relief doubled between 1740 and 1760, only to double again by 1775—all despite a stagnation of the overall population at about sixteen thousand. In New York City, the number of poor receiving public relief increased fourfold between 1750 and 1775. In 1772 some 425 people crowded the almshouse built to house a hundred. That year the Philadelphia almshouse took in about nine hundred persons.

Although they were still a minority, the growing numbers of the urban poor alarmed contemporaries. The poverty seemed especially glaring because it was such a contrast with the increasingly conspicuous wealth of the lawyers, merchants, and government officials in the seaports. According to tax records, in 1771 the wealthiest tenth of Bostonians owned more than 60 percent of the urban wealth, while the bottom three-tenths owned virtually nothing. Urban radicals denounced the development of greater extremes of wealth and poverty as linked. In 1765 a New Yorker complained, "Men Frequently owe their Wealth to the impoverishment of their Neighbors."

The growth in urban poverty reflected the greater transatlantic integration of the British empire in three ways. First, the imperial wars swelled the numbers killed, incapacitated, or rendered alcoholic by military service. War's widows, orphans, and cripples strained poor relief, especially in the cities, which attracted and collected the most desperate people. Second, after 1763, emigration surged from Europe to the colonies, flooding the seaports with poor newcomers, depressing wages, and swelling unemployment for all. Third, the freer flow of credit, goods, and information across the Atlantic linked the colonies with the mother country in a shared market. Increasingly tied to the metropolitan economy of Britain, the colonial seaports became more vulnerable to the boom-and-bust business cycle. Market-driven unemployment compounded the more traditional seasonal cycle of cold-weather job loss. More entwined in a far-flung capitalist economy, the urban colonists could lose work at any time—whenever British creditors felt obliged to curtail credit and call for their debts, imperiling colonial merchants and artisans, and their laborers.

Although most conspicuous in the seaports, greater inequality also appeared in the older farm communities along the Atlantic seaboard. Only about 5 percent of the mainland colonists lived in the cities, which remained relatively small places, none exceeding thirty thousand inhabitants. Richer in land than in people and capital, British America was overwhelmingly rural and agricultural. Although still offering more opportunity than the mother country, the older counties of rural America afforded laboring people fewer prospects to get ahead in the mid-eighteenth century than in the past. In the long-settled places, the growing population pressed against the limited supply of land already secured from the Indians. Unable to buy or inherit farms, many young people faced three unpalatable alternatives. They could move to a city to work for wages, emigrate westward to fight the Indians for frontier land (and still have to pay a land speculator for his title), or rent eastern land from a wealthy landlord.

When eastern land had been more abundant, tenancy was rare and temporary—a way up for poor people to accumulate the means to buy their own farms. But during the mid-eighteenth century in the older eastern counties, tenancy became more widespread as a lifelong status—a trap rather than a ladder upward. Tenants were especially numerous in New York's Hudson Valley, in tidewater Maryland, and in eastern New Jersey. By 1770 in Maryland's Chesapeake counties, over half of the free inhabitants lived on tenant farms. Some tenants dwelled in substantial homes and accumulated thriving livestock, but just as many lived in deprivation. Maryland tenants often crowded their large families (an average of seven children per household) into small and flimsy wooden shacks of less than three hundred square feet, with dirt floors and stick-and-clay chimneys and without windows.

Whether we call them "poor" depends on what we compare them with. Relative to the beggars of London, the tenants lived in abundance—possessing roofs overhead and food on their tables. But compared with the colonial expectations of the recent past, the glowing rhetoric of colonial promoters, the urgent demands of the consumer revolution, and the increasingly conspicuous wealth of the colonial elite—by all of those standards, the rural tenants were poor and getting poorer.

Contrary to colonial promoters (and some historians), frontier settlement was neither an easy escape from tenancy nor an automatic path to prosperity. The thick forests, bad roads, distance from market, voracious wildlife, and resentful natives combined to consign new settlers to prolonged hardships and danger. Moreover, land speculators demanded payments that drained the resources that new settlers desperately needed to build barns, fences, and homes, and to acquire livestock and tools. After the first five years on the land, most settlers secured an ample diet, but paying off their debts remained difficult. Although usually cited to celebrate colonial prosperity, St. John de Crèvecoeur understood the hard labor and grave risks of frontier farm-building. He explained:

> Flourishing as we may appear to a superficial observer, yet there are many dark spots which, on due consideration greatly lessen that show of happiness which the Europeans think we possess. The number of debts which one part of the country owes to the other would greatly astonish you. The younger a country is, the more it is oppressed, for new settlements are always made by people who do not possess much. They are obliged to borrow, and, if any accidents intervene, they are not enabled to repay that money in many years. The interest is a canker-worm which consumes their yearly industry. Many never can surmount these difficulties. The land is sold, their labors are lost, and they are obliged

> to begin the world anew. Oh, could I have the map of the county wherein I live; could I point out the different farms on which several families have struggled for many years; [could I] open the great book of mortgages and show you the immense encumberances, the ramification of which are spread and felt everywhere—you would be surprised.

Crèvecoeur estimated that only about half of the frontier families paid for their farms and escaped from debt before death passed the burden to the next generation. Although frontier settlement gave laboring families a cherished opportunity, unmatched in Europe, to employ themselves on their own property, there was no guarantee of ultimate prosperity after years of hardship.

As increasingly numerous and visible minorities, the urban, rural, and frontier poor collectively attested to the greater social complexity of the eighteenth-century colonies. And their visibility heightened the anxiety with which the prosperous majority accumulated the goods and manners needed to claim and defend a higher status.

GOODS

During the eighteenth century, the expanding transatlantic commerce produced a "consumer revolution" that meant cheaper and more diverse goods in greater abundance, involving many more common people as consumers. At the same time, demand swelled to meet the improved supply, as consumers sought a wider array of new things. In the mother country, American and Asian produce became widespread at lower prices, which rendered the fruits of empire more attractive and important to a broader array of Britons. Their imports of tea from India increased a hundredfold, from a value of about £8,000 in 1700 to more than £800,000 by 1770. The British taste for tea contributed to a further surge in the consumption of West Indian sugar, from about four pounds per capita in 1700 to eleven by 1770. Similarly, the colonists experienced the empire as consumers of larger quantities of Asian tea and spices and of British manufactured goods.

During the mid-eighteenth century, colonial consumers usually had better credit than common Britons. Over time, the terms of trade shifted in favor of most colonists, especially in the middle colonies and the south, as their produce fetched higher prices while they paid essentially stable prices for English manufactures. During the 1740s, 100 bushels of colonial wheat could be exchanged for 150 yards of woolen cloth, but by the early 1760s, 100 bushels could procure 250 yards. Colonists also benefited from the increasing competition of British merchants, especially Scots, to capture consumer markets by extending credit more freely to colonial customers.

Taking advantage of their improved buying power, colonists procured growing quantities of British manufactures, usually on credit. Between 1720 and 1770, per capita colonial imports increased by 50 percent, and the aggregate value more than tripled from about £450,000 in 1700 to more than £1.5 million in 1750. In 1700 the American colonies consumed about 10 percent of British exports; that figure rose to 37 percent by 1772. In sum, the growing American market became critical to the profits and growth of British manufacturing.

Consumer goods became more conspicuous thanks to the proliferation of colonial stores, often with display windows, and of newspaper advertisements plugging the latest imports. Hundreds of itinerant peddlers also carried commodities far beyond the seaports into the rural hamlets and frontier settlements. In the early 1750s a German newcomer marveled that "it is really possible to obtain all the things one can get in Europe in Pennsylvania, since so many merchant ships arrive there every year."

Romantic mythology often miscasts the common colonists as self-sufficient yeomen who produced all that they needed or wanted. There is a germ of truth to this. Most colonists lived on farm households that produced most of their own food, fuel, and homespun cloth. In the mainland colonies (but not the trade-driven West Indies), about 90 percent of economic production remained within a colony for home consumption or local trade; only about 10 percent was exported. Even in the plantation colonies of the Chesapeake and Carolinas, the production of food—principally pork and corn—for domestic consumption employed more acres and labor than did the tobacco, rice, and indigo for export.

Although only about 10 percent of total production, the export sector made a critical difference in the standard of living and the pace of development. No farm could produce everything that a household needed, and by no means did mere subsistence satisfy colonists' desires or limit their production. On the contrary, every colonial farm produced crops both for household needs and for the market. The colonists needed to sell produce so that they might purchase imported consumer goods beyond their own means to make. Some derived from another climate, such as the West Indian sugar and Asian tea, but the colonists also imported products from the workshops of Britain. In the production of manufactures, which required abundant capital and cheap labor, the crowded mother country had an advantage over the land-rich but thinly populated colonies. Every colonial farm needed metal tools, including plows, hoes, axes, knives, and hammers. Beyond such necessities, the colonists also aspired to the pleasures and comforts of new niceties: pewter knives and forks, bed and table linens, ceramic cups and saucers, glasses and imported wines, metal buttons and silver buckles, and manufactured cloth and clothing.

In the new and fluid colonial societies, the display of finer consumer goods mediated claims to status. Because appearances mattered so much in regulating status and credit, colonists wished to see themselves, and to be seen by others, as something more than rude rustics. With so many people in motion over long distances, local elites especially sought a more cosmopolitan standard for demonstrating and testing claims to status in new settings.

Emulating the English gentry, the wealthier colonists cultivated "gentility": a conspicuous and self-conscious style that emphasized personal displays of harmony, grace, delicacy, and refinement. Gentility required considerable self-discipline, the financial means to procure fine goods, and the leisure to polish manners and conversation. Seeking stages on which to enact their gentility, the colonial elite abandoned the low, dark, unpainted, cramped, and undecorated wooden houses of the seventeenth century. Instead, they built lighter, finer, larger, and more ornamented houses, increasingly in brick and filled with fine furniture. The elite's houses provided spacious new rooms and expansive new grounds for greeting, impressing, and entertaining guests at afternoon tea, formal dinners, garden strolls, and evening balls. Although most common people continued to live in smaller, traditional houses, they began to fill them with some of the consumer goods associated with the new mansions.

While uniting elites throughout the colonies and on both sides of the Atlantic, gentility tried to define sharper boundaries within colonial communities, distinguishing the polite and refined from those excluded as rude and common. Throughout the British empire, traveling ladies and gentlemen felt a greater solidarity with one another at a distance than with their cruder neighbors. Claiming superior morals, taste, and talents, gentlemen and ladies looked down upon the common farmers and artisans as obtuse and mean.

The genteel performed constantly for one another, ever watching and ever watched for the proper manners, conversation, dress, furnishings, and home. Every action, every statement, every object was on display and subject to applause or censure. The well-trained eye and ear scrutinized details for the proper nuances of fashion. A faulty performance damned the unfortunate as impostors, as ridiculous as clowns. Pity the poor common man invited to eat and drink at the table of Robert "King" Carter, a great planter in Virginia. The family tutor dismissed the guest as dull and vulgar because "he held the Glass of Porter fast with both his Hands, and then gave an insignificant nod to each one at the Table, in hast[e], & with fear, & then drank like an Ox." His awkwardness and fear expressed the insecurity that the common people often felt in the presence of gentility.

At the same time, the common people strove, as consumers, to efface the insulting line between gentility and commonality. Indeed, maintaining gentility required constant expense and attention to fashion, for the middling sort blurred the distinction by stretching their budgets to buy some of the props of gentility. Rather than accept inferiority, artisan and farm families wanted to sip tea from ceramic teacups—because the elite did so.

The pursuit of fashion served as a coveted badge of membership in the elite, but that distinction inspired emulation by social climbers from the middling sort. In turn, that emulation fed the unease of colonial elites, already sensitive to how they looked to their counterparts in Britain. Longing for acceptance as equals with the English gentry, the colonial elite felt beleaguered by the avid consumerism of their common neighbors, who seemed determined to erase the class and taste distinctions essential to genteel superiority. Fashionable goods and their proper uses became both the exclusionary symbols of social superiority and the inclusive currency of social emulation. In that social tension lay the energy that drove accelerating consumption.

For example, the genteel Dr. Alexander Hamilton of Maryland delighted in his own consumption but denounced that of common colonists, remarking "that if Luxury was to be confined to the Rich alone, it might prove a great national good." During his 1744 tour of the colonies, Hamilton disliked seeing fine goods displayed in otherwise common dwellings. At one farm, he found "superfluous things which showed an inclination to finery . . . such as a looking glass with a painted frame, half a dozen pewter spoons and as many plates . . . a set of stone tea dishes, and a teapot." Far better, he thought, for farmers to make do with "wooden plates and spoons" and "a little water in a wooden pail might serve for a looking glass." Hamilton despised what the farmers cherished most about the consumer goods: the opportunity for ordinary people to express their aspirations.

Genteel moralists especially disliked the leading role of women in the consumer revolution. Women of middling means had the most to gain from increased consumption, for imported goods often reduced their long and arduous labor, especially in making candles and soap or in spinning and weaving cloth. By accumulating and displaying fashionable goods, middling women also obtained a new vehicle for self-expression and self-assertion. Astute storekeepers appealed to the growing influence of women over household consumption. In 1748 a Maryland factor wrote to a correspondent: "You know the influence of the Wives upon their Husbands, & it is but a trifle that wins 'em over, [and] they must be taken notice of or there will be nothing with them." Genteel moralizers, however, detected and denounced an erosion of patriarchal power that allegedly left men emasculated and financially ruined by their newly aggressive wives. This exaggerated concern found little echo among middling families, for most men felt proud that their wives could appear in better fashion.

Of course, the common folk could never fully match the consumption and taste of the colonial elite of great planters, merchants, and lawyers. Indeed, the common emulation constantly drove the gentility to reiterate their superior status by cultivating more expensive tastes in the most current fashions. In 1771 an Englishman in Maryland reported:

> The quick importation of fashions from the mother country is really astonishing. I am almost inclined to believe that a new fashion is adopted earlier by the polished and affluent American than by many opulent

> persons in the great metropolis. . . . In short, very little difference is, in reality, observable in the manners of the wealthy colonist and the wealthy Briton.

No other praise would have better pleased American gentlemen and ladies, so eager to prove their equality to wealthy Britons and their superiority to common colonists.

The status competition and consumer dynamic drove both commoners and the elite to buy more than they could well afford. Importing even more than they produced, the colonies had a chronic trade imbalance, and most colonists bore mounting debts. In 1762, William Smith of New York conceded, "Our importation of dry goods from England is so vastly great, that we are obliged to betake ourselves to all possible arts to make remittances to the British merchants . . . and yet it drains us of all the silver and gold we can collect." The shortage of cash and the increasing debts fed a nagging unease at odds with the overt colonial prosperity and general contentment with the empire.

ENGLISH EMIGRANTS

In addition to goods, the swelling volume of British shipping carried emigrants across the Atlantic. Relatively few, however, were English: only 80,000 between 1700 and 1775, compared with 350,000 during the seventeenth century. The decline is especially striking because after 1700 the colonies became cheaper and easier to reach by sea and safer to live in. But push prevailed over pull factors in colonial emigration. Beginning in the late seventeenth century, the English push weakened as a growing economy provided rising real wages for laboring families, enabling more to remain in the mother country. At the same time, the militarization of the empire absorbed more laboring men into the enlarged army and navy for longer periods. In wartime, many would-be emigrants also balked at the greater dangers of a transatlantic passage.

Especially depressed during war, colonial emigration partially revived during the intervals of peace, when the crown demobilized thousands of soldiers and sailors, temporarily saturating the English labor market. Unable to find work, some people entered indentures for service in the colonies. Other demobilized men went unwillingly as convicted and transported criminals. In England, crime surged with every peace as thousands of unemployed and desperate people stole to live. The inefficient but grim justice of eighteenth-century England imposed the death penalty for 160 crimes, including grand larceny, which was loosely defined as stealing anything worth more than a mere shilling.

In 1717, shortly after the military demobilization of 1713–14, Parliament began to subsidize the shipment of convicted felons to the colonies as an alternative to their execution. The crown generally paid £3 per convict to shippers, who carried the felons to America for sale as indentured servants with especially long terms, usually fourteen years. The shippers' profit came from combining the sales price (about £12) with the crown subsidy, less the cost of transportation (£5 to £6). The program recalled the logic of the West Country promotion of the 1580s: America could serve the mother country as a drain for the detritus of English society and a workhouse of rehabilitation.

Between 1718 and 1775, the empire transported about fifty thousand felons, more than half of all English emigrants to America during that period. The transported were overwhelmingly young, unmarried men with little or no economic skill: the cannon fodder of war and the jail fodder of peace. About 80 percent of the convicts went to Virginia and Maryland, riding in the English ships of the tobacco trade. Convicts provided a profitable sideline for the tobacco shippers, who had plenty of empty cargo space on the outbound voyage from England. At about a third of the £35 price of an African male slave, the convict appealed to some planters as a better investment. Most purchasers were small planters with limited budgets. In a pinch, however, great planters, including George Washington, bought a few convicts to supplement their slaves.

The planters employed the convicts as tobacco field hands, subject to the same treatment as slaves. Convicts who protested their harsh treatment to the courts usually received sentences of additional whipping and longer service for bringing false complaints. Those who lived long enough to become free found no land of opportunity. Studies of liberated convicts in Maryland and Virginia reveal that virtually none ever obtained real estate or social standing.

Despite their purchases, colonial leaders regarded the convict trade as an insult that treated the colonies as inferior to the mother country. The colonists wondered why they should have to accept convicts deemed too dangerous to live in England. The planters especially dreaded the possibility that white convicts would make common cause in rebellion with the black slaves. In 1736 the Virginia planter William Byrd wrote to an English friend, "I wish you would be so kind as to hang all your felons at home." Maryland, Virginia, New Jersey, and Jamaica tried to discourage the convict trade by levying heavy taxes per head, but the crown vetoed all such obstructions. In a political satire, Benjamin Franklin advocated sending, in exchange, American rattlesnakes to England. But ultimately, the colonists colluded in the convict trade. In 1725, Maryland's governor conceded, "While we purchase, they will send them, and we bring the Evil upon our selves."

SCOTS

While English emigration to the colonies flagged, Scots emigration soared to 145,000 between 1707 and 1775. Generally poorer than the English, the Scots had greater incentives to emigrate, and the British Union of 1707 gave them legal access to all of the colonies. The growth in Scots overseas shipping also provided more opportunities and lower costs for passage. After a few early emigrants prospered, their reports homeward attracted growing numbers in a chain migration. During a tour of northwestern Scotland, James Boswell and Samuel Johnson saw the locals perform a popular and symbolic new dance called "America," in which a few original dancers gradually drew the entire audience into the performance.

The Scottish diaspora flowed in three streams: Lowland Scots, Highland Scots, and Ulster Scots. Assimilated to English ways, the Lowland Scots were primarily skilled tradesmen, farmers, and professionals pulled by greater economic opportunity in America. They usually emigrated as individuals or single families, then dispersed in the colonies and completed their assimilation to Anglo-American ways. The Lowland Scots were especially conspicuous as colonial doctors, for more than 150 emigrated between 1707 and 1775. By the American Revolution, Scots doctors and their American apprentices dominated formal medical practice in the colonies.

More desperate than the Lowland Scots, the Highlanders responded primarily to the push of their deteriorating circumstances. In 1746 the British army brutally suppressed a rebellion in the Highlands, and Parliament outlawed many of the Highlanders' traditions and institutions, creating much discontent. At mid-century, the common Highlanders also suffered from a pervasive rural poverty worsened by the rising rents demanded by their landlords. The emigrants primarily came from the relatively prosperous peasants, those who possessed the means to emigrate and feared a fall into the growing ranks of the impoverished.

After 1750, emigration brokers and ambitious colonial land speculators frequented the northwest coast of Scotland to procure Highland emigrants. The brokers and speculators recognized that the tough Highlanders were especially well prepared for the rigors of a transatlantic passage and colonial settlement. One Scot observed:

> They launched out into a new World breathing a Spirit of Liberty and a Desire of every individual becoming a Proprietor, where they imagine they can still obtain land for themselves, and their flocks of Cattle at a triffling Rent, or of conquering it from the Indian with the Sword, the most desireable holding of any for a Highlander.

Preferring cheap if dangerous lands, the Highland Scots clustered in frontier valleys especially along the Cape Fear River in North Carolina, the Mohawk River of New York, and the Altamaha River in Georgia. By clustering, they preserved their distinctive Gaelic language and Highland customs, in contrast with the assimilating Lowland emigrants.

Nearly half of the Scots emigrants came from Ulster, in Northern Ireland, where their parents and grandparents had colonized during the 1690s. Like the Highlanders, the Ulster Scots fled from deteriorating conditions. During the 1710s and 1720s they suffered from interethnic violence with the Catholic Irish as well as from a depressed market for their linen, the hunger of several poor harvests, and the increased rents charged by grasping landlords. The Ulster emigration to the colonies began in 1718 and accelerated during the 1720s. In 1728 an opponent complained, "The humour has spread like a contagious distemper, and the people will hardly hear anybody that tries to cure them of their madness." The destitute sold themselves into indentured servitude, while the families of middling means liquidated their livestock to procure the cost of passage. Of course, most of the Ulster Scots remained at home, preferring the known hardships of Ireland to the uncertain prospects of distant America.

The Ulster Scots emigrated in groups, generally organized by their Presbyterian ministers, who negotiated with shippers to arrange passage. At first, the Ulster Scots emigrated to Boston, but some violent episodes of New English intolerance persuaded most, after 1720, to head for Philadelphia, the more welcoming seaport of the more tolerant colony of Pennsylvania. More thinly settled than New England, Pennsylvania needed more settlers to develop and defend the hinterland.

Once in the colonies, the Ulster Scots gravitated to the frontier, where land was cheaper, enabling large groups to settle together. Their clannishness helped the emigrants cope with their new setting, but it also generated frictions with the English colonists. Feeling superior to the Catholic Irish, the Ulster Scots bitterly resented that so many colonists lumped all the Irish together. In 1720 some Ulster Scots in New Hampshire bristled that they were "termed *Irish* people, when we so frequently ventured our all, for the British crown and liberties against the Irish Papists." As a compromise, they became known in America as the Scotch-Irish.

GERMANS

Outnumbering the English emigrants, the 100,000 Germans were second only to the Scots as eighteenth-century immigrants to British America. Most were Protestants, but they were divided into multiple denominations: Lutherans, Reformed, Moravians, Baptists, and Pietists of many stripes.

Drawn from both the poor and the middling sort, they emigrated primarily in families. Almost all came from the Rhine Valley and its major tributaries in southwestern Germany and northern Switzerland. Flowing north and east, the navigable Rhine channeled emigrants downstream to the Dutch port of Rotterdam, their gateway across the Atlantic to British America.

About three-quarters of the Germans landed in Philadelphia, the great magnet for colonial migration. During the late 1720s about three ships, bearing a total of 600 Germans, annually arrived in Philadelphia. By the early 1750s some twenty ships and 5,600 Germans landed every year. Seeking farms, most emigrants filtered into rural Pennsylvania. From there, some families headed south to settle on the frontiers of Maryland and Virginia. A second much smaller and less sustained migration flowed from Rotterdam to Charles Town, South Carolina, which served as a gateway to the Georgia and Carolina frontier.

The colonial emigration was a modest subset of a much larger movement of Germans out of the Rhineland. Between 1680 and 1780 about 500,000 southwestern Germans emigrated, but only a fifth went to British America. Many more headed east, seeking opportunities in Prussia, Hungary, and Russia. Receiving subsidies from the eastern rulers but nothing from the British, the Rhineland princes promoted the eastward movement while discouraging colonial emigration.

Why, then, did so many Rhinelanders undertake such a daunting journey across an ocean to a strange land? There were push factors. No united realm, Germany was subdivided into many small principalities, frequently embroiled in the great wars of the continent. To build palaces and conduct war, the authoritarian princes heavily taxed their subjects and conscripted their young men. Most princes also demanded religious conformity from their subjects, inflicting fines and imprisonment on dissidents. In addition, a swelling population pressed against the limits of the rural economy, blighting the prospects of thousands of young peasants and artisans.

Necessary but not sufficient for emigration, the push factors became pressing only once an uneasy people learned of an attractive alternative. In other words, they needed a pull as well as a push. They had to begin to perceive a great shortfall between their probable prospects at home and their apparent opportunities in a particular elsewhere.

Good news from Pennsylvania pulled many discontented Rhinelanders across the Atlantic. In 1682, William Penn recruited a few Germans to settle in Pennsylvania, where they prospered. Word of their material success in a tolerant colony intrigued growing numbers in their old homeland. Nothing was as persuasive as a letter from a prospering relative or friend who could make glowing comparisons from experience. The letters reported that wages were high and land and food cheap. The average Pennsylvania farm of 125 acres was six times larger than a typical peasant holding in southwestern Germany, and the colonial soil was more fertile, yielding three times as much wheat per acre. Lacking princes and aristocrats or an established church, Pennsylvania demanded almost no taxes, and none to support someone else's religion. And Pennsylvania did not conscript its inhabitants for war.

But even a pull and a push did not suffice to sustain a migration. Potential emigrants also needed an infrastructure to facilitate and finance their passage: a network of information, guides, ships, and merchants willing to provide passage on credit. Such an infrastructure began with the couriers carrying the letters from Pennsylvania to Germany. Known as Newlanders, the couriers were former emigrants returning home for a visit, often to collect debts or an inheritance. For a fee, they carried letters and conducted business in Germany for their neighbors who remained in Pennsylvania. By recruiting Germans to emigrate, the Newlanders could earn a free return passage to Philadelphia, and sometimes a modest commission too, from a British shipper. By speaking from experience and guiding the new emigrants down the Rhine to Rotterdam and onto waiting ships, the Newlanders eased the decision and passage of thousands who had balked at a journey on their own into the unknown. The opponents of German emigration denounced the Newlanders as dangerous charlatans, and a few unscrupulous men did live down to that reputation, but most provided accurate information and valuable services.

In addition to information and guides, the emigration depended upon British merchants at Rotterdam who saw a profitable opportunity to ship Germans to the colonies. Because of the Navigation Acts, only British (including colonial) ships could transport emigrants to the colonies. The merchants could profit by filling a ship with one hundred to two hundred emigrants at a charge of £5 to £6 per head. About two-thirds of the emigrants had sufficient means to pay their own way; the poorer third came as indentured servants. Sometimes parents could afford their own passage and that of younger children but had to indenture their adolescents, who had the highest value as laborers.

The German emigrant trade developed a relatively attractive form of indentured servitude adapted to the needs of families. Known as "redemptioners," the Germans contracted to serve for about four to five years. Unlike other indentured servants, the redemptioner families had to be kept together by their employers and not divided for sale. Most contracts also gave the emigrant family a grace period of two weeks, upon arrival in Pennsylvania, to find a relative or acquaintance who would purchase their labor contract. Often arranged by prior correspondence, these deals afforded the emigrants some confidence in their destination and employer. If the two-week period passed, the redemption became open to general bidding from any colonist who needed laborers. After serving out their indentures, the redemptioners became free to seek out their own farms, usually on the frontier where land was cheaper.

The system worked well, because successful German farmers in Pennsylvania needed labor, preferred fellow Germans, and favored intact families. The redemptioner system accelerated the chain migration as the early migrants succeeded, reported their gains, encouraged friends and relatives to follow, and helped finance their journey by purchasing their contracts upon arrival. No seventeenth-century indentured servants had been so fortunate.

The voyage was no picnic. The stormy North Atlantic terrified people who had never before been to sea; the vessels were crowded, dirty, and infested with lice, and the cheap food was often spoiled and repellent. After all, the shippers made their profit by packing their vessels tightly and by holding down the cost of feeding the passengers. But it was also in their interest to keep them alive, for a dead redemptioner yielded no payment in Philadelphia. In 1750, eyewitness Gottlieb Mittelberger described a voyage at its worst:

> During the journey the ship is full of pitiful signs of distress—smells, fumes, horrors, vomiting, various kinds of sea sickness, fever, dysentery, headaches, heat, constipation, boils, scurvy, cancer, mouth-rot, and similar afflictions, all of them caused by the age and the highly-salted state of the food, especially the meat, as well as by the very bad and filthy water, which brings about the miserable destruction and death of many.

But he exaggerated a tad, for the overall death rate for the voyage was only about 3 percent, a bit better than the 4 percent rate for convicts and far better than the 10 to 20 percent suffered by enslaved Africans. Germans probably risked more by staying at home in the path of the next European war. And most emigrants eventually found the journey worthwhile, for their favorable reports kept others coming.

Like the Highland and the Ulster Scots, the Germans preferred to settle in clusters and to cling to their language and customs. Most learned only a smattering of English, relying on a few bilingual leaders, usually ministers and schoolteachers, for more complicated transactions with outsiders. Their numbers and clannishness promoted a network of churches and schools conducted by fellow emigrants and coreligionists and financed by voluntary contributions. Highly literate, the Pennsylvania Germans also sustained a vibrant press that produced German-language almanacs, books, and a newspaper.

PLURALISM

Thanks primarily to the new waves of Scotch-Irish and German emigrants, Pennsylvania's population exploded from 18,000 in 1700 to 120,000 by 1750.

The Quakers became a minority in their own colony, slipping to just a quarter of the population by 1750. The Scotch-Irish accounted for an equal share of Pennsylvania's inhabitants, and the Germans were even more numerous, about 40 percent of the total.

The non-English and non-Quaker newcomers tested the commitment of the colonial elite to William Penn's ideal of tolerance. During the 1720s, when the emigration began, the numerous newcomers troubled the leading Pennsylvanians. In 1728 the lieutenant governor urged limiting the immigration "to prevent an English Plantation from being turned into a Colony of Aliens." But most leading Quakers soon concluded that the newcomers were hardworking assets to the prosperous development of their colony. After considering and ultimately rejecting proposals to tax, or otherwise limit, immigration, the Pennsylvania legislature instead passed a law to ease naturalization.

A plural society was also a challenging adjustment for most of the emigrants, who initially wished to avoid people different from themselves. The newcomers were often especially strong-willed and devout people who professed a demanding, perfectionist, and exclusive form of Protestantism. Their uncompromising convictions had irritated majorities and rulers in their homelands, and had emboldened them to venture across the Atlantic to a strange land. In Pennsylvania, they sought sufficient land to cluster in communities apart from everyone else, the better to perfect their version of the true faith.

The emigrants found, however, only half of what they sought. The seekers had escaped official persecution and often could form distinct local communities. But despite their best efforts, they could not avoid contact with an unprecedented and often shocking diversity of ethnic groups and Protestant beliefs, all pursuing their own version of purity. In 1736 the Swiss emigrant Esther Werndtlin denounced her new home, Pennsylvania: "Here are religions and nationalities without number; this land is an asylum for banished sects, a sanctuary for all evil-doers from Europe, a confused Babel, a receptacle for all unclean spirits, an abode of the devil, a first world, a Sodom, which is deplorable."

Although the diverse groups often disliked one another and longed for a more homogeneous society, none had the numbers and power to impose its own beliefs or to drive out others. By necessity, almost all gradually accepted the mutual forbearance of a pluralistic society as an economic boon and the best guarantee for their own faith. In 1739 a German emigrant concluded that "Liberty of conscience" was the "chief virtue of this land, and on this store I do not repent my immigration." He added, "But for this freedom, I think this country would not improve so rapidly."

While constraining direct and violent conflict, pluralism promoted a highly contentious politics as the ethnocultural groups jostled for patronage and priority. By mid-century, the Quaker leaders astutely made a political alliance with most of the Germans. Chastened by their harsh experiences with European militarism and heavy taxes, the Germans endorsed the Quaker policies of pacifism, no militia, and low taxes. An opponent complained that the Quakers persuaded the Germans "that a militia will bring them under as severe a bondage to governors as they were formerly under the princes in Germany."

With German votes, the Quaker party retained control over the Pennsylvania assembly, to the dismay of the Scotch-Irish, who felt ignored and maligned by the new coalition. Clustered on the frontier, the Scotch-Irish especially resented the refusal of the Quakers and Germans, who dwelled safely and prosperously around Philadelphia, to fund a frontier militia to attack the Indians. Feeling abandoned by the Pennsylvania government, the Scotch-Irish resolved to fight the natives on their own harsh terms. In killing Indians, the Scotch-Irish could vent their political resentments without overtly confronting the Germans and the Quakers.

By attracting thousands of immigrants seeking farms, Pennsylvania strained William Penn's policy of peace with the Indians. After Penn's death in 1718 his colony became the property of his sons, John, Richard, and Thomas, who usually remained in England, entrusting Indian diplomacy and land granting to the provincial secretary James Logan. Caring less for Indians than for the profits of land speculation, Logan and the Penn heirs steadily encroached upon the Lenni Lenape.

The settlers, especially the Scotch-Irish, invaded Indian lands even faster than the proprietors could buy them from the Lenni Lenape. Impatient over the frustrating delays of Pennsylvania's inefficient land office, many settlers abruptly occupied Indian lands and refused to pay either the natives or the Penn family for them. In 1729, James Logan warned the Penn heirs of the "vast numbers of poor but presumptuous People, who w[i]thout any License have entered on your Lands, & neither have, nor are like to have anything to purchase w[i]th."

To justify their conduct, the squatters adapted the rhetoric employed to dispossess the Indians. Colonizers had long insisted that the natives did not deserve to keep their lands because they did not "improve" them in the European mode. The squatters noted that the Penns and other land speculators made even less use of the lands that they held for future sale to actual settlers. Why then, the squatters asked, did the speculators deserve to demand payment from the people who actually did the improving? The squatters bluntly told colonial officials that it was "against the Laws of God & Nature that so much land should lie idle, while so many Christians wanted it to labour on and [to] raise their Bread."

In addition to seizing Indian lands, the squatters treated their Indian neighbors with violent contempt, often beating, robbing, cheating, or killing indiscriminately. In vain, the aggrieved Indians looked to the leaders of Pennsylvania to honor William Penn's legacy by removing the squatters. The proprietors preferred the cynical alternative of exploiting the squatter invasion as pressure to compel the Indians to sell the invaded tracts cheap. Then the proprietors meant to threaten lawsuits to force the squatters either to buy their homesteads or to move on.

In 1737, Thomas Penn and James Logan conducted the "Walking Purchase," perhaps the most notorious land swindle in colonial history—which is saying a great deal. Unable to stop invading squatters, the local Lenni Lenape band agreed to relinquish a tract that would be bounded by what a man could walk around in thirty-six hours. Of course, the Lenni Lenape expected to lose only a modest parcel, but Logan and Penn had made elaborate preparations to maximize their purchase. They employed scouts to blaze a trail, and they trained three runners. On the appointed September day, the runners astonished and infuriated the Lenni Lenape by racing around a tract of nearly twelve hundred square miles, including most of their homeland. Retail sale of farms within the tract ultimately earned the proprietors nearly £90,000.

Feeling cheated, the Lenni Lenape refused to move, thinking they were safe in the Quaker commitment to peace. But Logan and Penn sought out a third party to do their dirty work. They exploited Pennsylvania's link to the Covenant Chain alliance that served the mutual interests of the Six Nation Iroquois and the British colonial governments, at the expense of weaker Indian peoples. In return for generous presents from Pennsylvania's leaders, the Iroquois bluntly ordered the Lenni Lenape to move. Rather than fight the more numerous and better-armed Iroquois, the Lenni Lenape reluctantly withdrew westward. Nurturing a deep bitterness against both the Iroquois and the Pennsylvanians, Lenni Lenape raiders would return during the 1750s to take their revenge. The era of brotherly love was over in Pennsylvania—bringing that colony into line with the violent standard of the other colonies.

AFRICANS

Contrary to popular myth, most eighteenth-century emigrants did not come to America of their own free will in search of liberty. Nor were they Europeans. On the contrary, most were enslaved Africans forced across the Atlantic to work on plantations raising American crops for the European market. During the eighteenth century, the British colonies imported 1.5 million slaves—more than three times the number of free immigrants. And almost all of the imported Africans remained slaves for life, passing the status on to their children. Only about 1 percent of the blacks living in the British colonies became free prior to the American Revolution.

The slave trade diminished the inhabitants of West Africa, who declined from 25 million in 1700 to 20 million in 1820. At least two million people died in slave-raiding wars and another six million captives went to the New World as slaves. That demographic loss hampered economic development, rendering West Africa vulnerable to European domination during the nineteenth century.

While crippling Africa, the expanding slave trade and plantation agriculture jointly enriched the European empires, especially the British. The slave traders provided the labor essential to the plantations producing the commodities—sugar, tobacco, and rice—that drove the expansion of British overseas trade in North America. In 1737 a West Indian governor declared, "Slavery is among us not of choice but of necessity and unless (as it is not to be imagined) our mother country should quit the trade of the sugar colonies, Englishmen must continue to be masters of their slaves." Prior to 1775 very few Britons, at home or in the colonies, had any qualms about slavery, so long as Africans or Indians were the victims.

During the eighteenth century, the British seized a commanding lead in the transatlantic slave trade, carrying about 2.5 million slaves, compared with the 1.8 million borne by the second-place Portuguese (primarily to Brazil) and the 1.2 million transported by the third-place French. The British slavers sold about half of their imports to their own colonies and the other half to the French and Spanish colonies, often illegally. At first the West Indies consumed almost all of the slaves imported into British America: 96 percent of the 275,000 brought in the seventeenth century. During the next century, the West Indian proportion slipped to 81 percent, as the growing volume and competition of the slave trade carried more slaves (19 percent of the British imports) on to the Chesapeake and Carolinas.

The West Indies provided the greatest demand, because sugar plantations were especially profitable and especially deadly. The profits enabled the planters to pay premium prices for slaves to replace the thousands consumed by a brutal work regimen and tropical diseases. During the eighteenth century at least one-third of the slaves died within three years of their arrival on the island of Barbados. In addition to the high death rate, slaves suffered from a low birthrate, as a diet deficient in protein and the harsh field work under the tropical sun depressed female fertility and increased infant mortality. In the West Indies, half the slave women never bore a child that survived infancy. At least a quarter of their newborn died within ten days—many by the infanticide of mothers determined to spare their children a life in slavery.

On the colonial mainland, slave births exceeded their deaths, enabling that population to grow through natural increase. Especially in the Chesapeake, the slaves were better fed and less exposed to disease. During the colonial era, the mainland colonists imported 250,000 slaves but sustained a black population of 576,000 in 1780. In stark contrast, the British West Indies had only 350,000 slaves in 1780 despite importing 1.2 million during the preceding two centuries. It is revealing that *after* emancipation in the nineteenth century, the West Indian black population began to grow rapidly from natural increase.

Most British slave traders made triangular voyages, initially from Britain to the west coast of Africa, where they swapped British manufactures (and re-exported cloth and tea from India) for slaves. About three-quarters of the British colonial slave imports originated from the coast between the Senegal River on the north and the Congo River to the south. In the Americas, the shippers sold slaves for colonial produce and bills of exchange, before returning to the mother country. Such circuitous voyages took sailing ships at least a year, and sometimes eighteen months, to complete—with debilitating consequences for the health of the sailors.

On the coast of West Africa, the sojourning Britons suffered from the dank humidity, fierce heat, and frequent torrential rains. They also died by the hundreds from tropical diseases, for Africa reversed the immunological advantage that Europeans enjoyed as colonizers in more temperate climes. Referring to a center of the slave trade, sailors warned one another.

> Beware and take care
> Of the Bight of Benin;
> For one that comes out
> There are forty go in.

Because most mariners dreaded a voyage to West Africa, only especially generous pay, and the alternative of unemployment, could recruit captains and crews.

Popular myth has it that the Europeans obtained their slaves by attacking and seizing Africans. In fact, the shippers almost always bought their slaves from African middlemen, generally the leading merchants and chiefs of the coastal kingdoms. Determined to profit from the trade, the African traders and chiefs did not tolerate Europeans who foolishly bypassed them to seize slaves on their own initiative. And during the eighteenth century the Africans had the power to defeat Europeans who failed to cooperate. Contrary to the stereotype of shrewd Europeans cheating weak and gullible natives, the European traders had to pay premium, and rising, prices to African chiefs and traders, who drove a hard bargain. During the 1760s, traders paid about £20 per slave, compared with £17 during the 1710s.

The Europeans exploited and expanded the slavery long practiced by Africans. Some slaves were starving children sold by their impoverished parents. Others were debtors or criminals sentenced to slavery. But most were captives taken in wars between kingdoms or simply kidnapped by armed gangs.

Although they did not directly seize slaves, the European traders indirectly promoted the wars and kidnapping gangs by offering premium prices for captives. One victim, Olaudah Equiano, explained, “When a trader wants slaves, he applies to a chief for them, and tempts him with his wares." As in the North American slave trade with Indians, the traders provided guns that their clients could employ in raids for captives to pay for the weapons. Some kingdoms, principally Ashanti and Dahomey, became wealthy and powerful by slave-raiding their poorly armed neighbors. As guns became essential for defense, a people had to procure them by raiding on behalf of their suppliers, lest they instead participate in the slave trade as victims. By the end of the century, the British alone were annually exporting nearly 300,000 guns to West Africa.

The African raiders marched their captives to the coast in long lines known as coffles: dozens of people yoked together by the neck with leather thongs to prevent escape. Some marches to the coast exceeded five hundred miles and six months. About a quarter of the captives died along the way from some combination of disease, hunger, exhaustion, beatings, and suicide.

Upon reaching the coast, the captors herded their captives into walled pens called barracoons. Stripped naked, the slaves were closely examined by European traders, who wanted only reasonably healthy and young people, preferably male. Once purchased, slaves received the trader's brand with a hot iron, searing their new status as property into the flesh. The traders then ferried their slaves in large canoes to a ship at anchor in the harbor. An English captain remarked, "The Negroes are so wilful and loth to leave their own country, that they have often leap'd out of the canoes, boat, and ship into the sea [to drown themselves]; they having a more dreadful apprehension of Barbadoes than we can have of hell." A surgeon concluded, "I think it may be clearly deduced, that the unhappy Africans . . . have a strong attachment to their native country, together with a just sense of the value of liberty."

Dreading a violent uprising to seize the ship, the slavers took extreme precautions. They put the slaves belowdecks and shackled them in pairs, the right wrist and ankle of one to the left wrist and ankle of another. And the traders tried to assemble cargos of diverse ethnic groups and languages to discourage the communication and cooperation for a shipboard plot. For security, the slave ships also employed an especially large and well-armed crew, more than double the number needed simply to sail the vessel. In addition to providing more guards, the larger crew helped absorb the losses to tropical diseases on the West African coast.

The precautions sometimes failed, usually along the coast, before departure for the open ocean. One ship's doctor recalled that the slaves were "ever upon the watch to take advantage of the least negligence of their oppressors." Captain John Newton noted:

> One unguarded hour, or minute, is sufficient to give the slaves the opportunity they are always waiting for. An attempt to rise upon the ship's company brings on instantaneous and horrid war; for, when they are once in motion, they are desperate.

In most uprisings, the slavers regained bloody control, but sometimes the slaves overwhelmed and massacred their captors. To justify the brutal suppression of trouble, a slaver said, "The many acts of violence they have committed by murdering whole crews and destroying ships when they had it in their power to do so have made these rigors wholly chargeable on their own bloody and malicious disposition, which calls for the same confinement as if they were wolves or wild boars."

Once the ship set sail, the slaves entered the notorious "middle passage" across the Atlantic to colonial America. The shortest voyage was from Gambia to Barbados, a distance of about four thousand miles, which, with a fair wind, could be made in three weeks. But the equatorial winds were uncertain, sometimes stranding a ship for weeks in the dead air of the doldrums, inflicting severe suffering from thirst and hunger on crew and cargo. In especially desperate cases, the crew forced the captain to throw some slaves overboard to make the provisions and fresh water last longer for the sailors.

The shippers had two not entirely compatible goals: to cram as many slaves aboard as possible and to get as many as possible across the Atlantic alive and healthy. One school of thought, the "loose packers," argued that a little more room, better food, and some exercise landed a healthier and more profitable cargo in the colonies. But most slavers were "tight packers" who calculated that the greatest profits came from landing the largest number, accepting the loss of some en route as an essential cost.

On most ships, the slaves were jammed into dark holds and onto wooden shelves that barely allowed room to turn over. At six feet long by sixteen inches wide and about thirty inches high, the standard space for a slave was half that allowed to transported convicts. Lacking clothes and bedding, the slaves slept on their rough wooden shelves and in the wastes that their bodies produced overnight. A captain later recalled, "The poor creatures, thus cramped, are likewise in irons for the most part which makes it difficult for them to turn or move or attempt to rise or to lie down without hurting themselves or each other. Every morning . . . more instances than one are found of the living and dead fastened together." With good cause, the crew hated to go belowdecks. A ship's doctor recalled, "I was so overcome by the heat, stench, and foul air that I nearly fainted, and it was not without assistance, that I could get upon deck." But, of course, he was free to return above for fresh air.

The often violent motion of the ship compounded the distress in the dark, dank, and crowded hold. In a letter to his wife, Captain John Newton explained:

> Imagine to yourself an immense body of water behind you, higher than a house, and a chasm of equal depth just before you. . . . In the twinkling of an eye, the ship descends into the pit which is gasping to receive her, and with equal swiftness ascends to the top on the other side

> before the mountain can overtake her. And this is repeated as often as you can deliberately count to four.

Listening to the slaves in the hold, Newton added, "Dire is the tossing, deep the groans."

Twice a day, morning and late afternoon, the crew forced the chained slaves up on deck to eat. For security considerations, they usually brought up no more than ten at a time. The meals consisted of some combination of boiled rice, cornmeal, yams, beans, and salt meat, with water to drink. A few especially savvy captains fought scurvy by providing limes, lemons, or vinegar. Wielding whips, crew members also forced the slaves on deck to exercise by dancing and singing to the tune of a drum, fiddle, or bagpipe. A crewman recalled, "The captain ordered them to sing, and they sang songs of sorrow. Their sickness, fear of being beaten, their hunger, and the memory of their country, etc., are the usual subjects."

Of course such crowded, ill-fed, abused, and despondent people were prone to sicken and die, especially because the slave ships were junctures for the world's diseases. Olaudah Equiano described his fellow slaves as "a multitude of black people of every description chained together, every one of their countenance[s] expressing dejection and sorrow." The European crews exposed the slaves to smallpox, measles, gonorrhea, and syphilis. And the Africans brought along their own diseases to exchange with the crew: yellow fever, dengue fever, malaria, yaws, and especially a bacillary dysentery (a gastrointestinal disorder) known as the "bloody flux." One surgeon described the effects: "The floor of their rooms, was so covered with blood and mucus . . . that it resembled a slaughter house. It is not in the power of human imagination to picture to itself a situation more dreadful or disgusting." The sailors pitched the dead overboard, while the captain recorded the deaths. Deprived of their names, the dead bore the numbers assigned at shipment. For example, Captain Newton recorded, "Buried a slave No. 84. . . . This morning buried a woman slave, No. 47."

To discourage epidemics, some slavers threw overboard the first slaves who fell sick. But this practice encouraged despairing slaves to welcome or feign disease. Many slavers concluded that the fundamental killer was a profound depression called the "fixed melancholy." A doctor reported, "No one who had it was ever cured. The symptoms are a lowness of spirits and despondency. Hence they refuse food. Hence the belly ached, fluxes ensued, and they were carried off." A captain reported, "We had about 12 negroes [who] did wilfully drown themselves, and others starv'd themselves to death; for 'tis their belief that when they die they return home to their own country and friends again." With starving slaves, the captors employed a special instrument, the "mouth opener," to wrench open the jaws and force down food.

Seventeenth-century slave voyages probably killed about 20 percent of the slaves. During the eighteenth century, modest improvements in food, water, and cleanliness gradually cut the mortality rate in half to about 10 percent by the 1780s. Nonetheless, a 10 percent mortality was still a high rate for a population of young men, ordinarily the healthiest group. By comparison, only about 4 percent of the English convicts died during their passages across the Atlantic.

"NEW NEGROES"

After weeks, and even months, at sea, the ships reached their colonial destination. The captains conducted the sales, either by inviting buyers on board ship or by landing the slaves for auction by land. To enhance the slaves' appearance and price, they were cleaned, shaved, and greased with palm oil. To hide the signs of bleeding dysentery, some cunning captains had their surgeons stop the anus of each slave with oakum. The younger and healthier slaves, especially men, sold first and at the best prices. Older, weaker, and sicker slaves, especially females, were harder and slower to sell. As a rule, neither sellers nor purchasers made any effort to keep slave families together. Indeed, buyers preferred to break up families and ethnic groups to discourage the trust and communication that would facilitate plots to run away or rebel.

Most slaves were taken to a plantation and put to work in a strange new setting, obliged to respond to the orders and whims of a new master and overseer. Many did not survive the shock of the change. In the Chesapeake colonies during the early eighteenth century, one quarter of the new slaves died within their first year of arrival. Separated from friends and kin, ordered about in a language they did not understand, given tools they had not used before, and put to work beside strangers who shared only their complexion, the new slaves were strangers in a strange land. Arriving with distinct languages and identities as Ashanti, Fulani, Ibo, Malagasiy, Mandingo, and Yoruba (and many others), the slaves had to find a new commonality as Africans in America.

The masters tried to break their new slaves to a new identity and work regimen. The master often assigned and enforced a new name. Robert "King" Carter, Virginia's wealthiest planter, instructed his overseer, "I hope you will take care that the Negroes both men and women I sent you . . . always go by the names we gave them. I am sure we repeated them so often . . . that everyone knew their names & would readily answer to them." Although obliged to use their new names in front of whites, the slaves must have nurtured their African names with one another.

The masters also put the newcomers—children and women as well as the men—to the hardest, dirtiest, and least skilled jobs on the plantation. Many resisted by refusing to work or by blundering at their tasks, which led to a struggle of wills in which the master had the advantage of violent force. A Virginian complained, "A new Negro must be broke. . . . You would really be surpriz'd at their Perseverance. Let a hundred men show him how to hoe, or drive a wheelbarrow, he'll still take the one by the bottom and the other by the wheel; and they often die before they can be conquer'd."

The slave system required violence, for only fear and pain could motivate people without the incentives of working for their own benefit. In 1776 one planter explained, "The fear of punishment is the principle to which we must and do appeal, to keep them in awe and order." The most common punishment was a whipping to the bare back, often of fifty to seventy-five lashes, sometimes compounded by having salt literally rubbed into the wounds. Some masters escalated the punishment beyond whipping to include branding on the face, lopping off an ear, slitting the nose, and cutting the hamstrings or severing the foot of a chronic runaway. Masters usually meted out punishment without resorting to any court, and even when blacks died from their punishments, their masters or overseers almost always escaped legal punishment. One slave explained that his people suffered "unmerited and unprovoked punishment, without remedy, or the right to assist, or to remonstrate."

The power to inflict pain and to command people as if they were animals corrupted Thomas Thistlewood, a Jamaican estate manager during the 1750s. Although greatly outnumbered, he ruled his slaves through pain and terror. During one year he whipped thirty-five of his forty-two slaves (inflicting a total of fifty-two whippings), with fifty lashes the smallest punishment. He also forced himself upon ten of the sixteen female slaves on his plantation. He continued to rape slaves even after he picked up a painful venereal disease from one. Thistlewood was also proud to record the news that his intimidated slaves nicknamed him "No Play With."

Most masters recognized the advantages of making a few small concessions as rewards meant to inspire harder work. Over time, some rewards became entrenched in custom, and masters who omitted them confronted resentful and malingering slaves. The rewards included receiving every week at least a half day and usually a full day off from working for the master: time that the slaves generally devoted to their own gardens. After the harvest, slaves usually received a brief Christmas holiday accompanied by an extra allowance of food, some tobacco, and a little rum.

Masters also favored some slaves with greater privileges and responsibility. Especially strong and able male slaves became "drivers," who acted as foremen in the fields and who inflicted the punishments ordered by masters. For their services, drivers received better food, better clothing, and better access to slave women. Drivers often served as the master's eyes and ears in the quarters, reporting or discouraging runaways and rebels. But, as the most able and often the most powerful black man on a plantation, an alienated driver was the greatest danger to his master. When slaves did rebel or flee, they often relied on their drivers for leadership.

Other favored slaves, usually mulattoes with white fathers, received the less physically taxing jobs as house servants or the more fulfilling occupations as artisans. They too got a better diet, attire, and shelter, but they also lost a measure of the privacy from white supervision that field hands enjoyed in their quarters when not working. And because of their closer association with the masters, the domestics and artisans paid for their privileges by losing the trust of their fellow blacks.

To maximize their profits, masters demanded as much work as possible while minimizing their expenditures to maintain their slaves. But in the mainland colonies, if not in the West Indies, most masters were shrewd enough to see that it was in their long-term interest to sustain rather than break the health of their property. Most provided a bare minimum of food, shelter, and ragged clothing. Slaves usually lived in windowless log huts with earth floors and stick-and-clay chimneys. The furniture consisted of a few wooden benches and beds covered with mattresses stuffed with cornhusks. And their workday was long: at least twelve hours a day, six days a week under the close supervision of a white overseer. During harvest season, labor began before sunup and generally lasted fifteen hours.

The colonists liked to praise themselves as benevolent masters. A Virginia governor insisted that most slaves lived "much better than our poor laboring men in England." Although poor laboring men certainly led hard lives in England, none of them longed to change places with slaves, who could be bought and sold, whipped and mutilated at their owner's arbitrary dictate.

Despite all of their ingenuity and effort, masters and overseers could never break the slaves' longing to be free. Occasionally slaves risked a direct rebellion, a secret plot to rise up and kill their tormentors as the only means to freedom. Such rebellions were most plausible and common in the West Indies, where the African-born predominated and where blacks, as a whole, greatly outnumbered whites. The greatest uprising racked Jamaica in 1760, killing ninety whites. Ruthless repression then killed four hundred blacks; most were burned at the stake, belying the eighteenth century's reputation as an "Age of Enlightenment."

Despite the rarity of actual uprisings, planters suspected chronic plots to rebel. Acting on their fears, they periodically arrested, tried, and executed dozens of suspects. In the process, masters imagined themselves to be the victims of ungrateful and cruel slaves. Benjamin Franklin explained to an English friend, "Perhaps you may imagine the Negroes to be a mild-tempered, tractable Kind of People. Some of them indeed are so. But the Majority are of a plotting Disposition, dark, sullen, malicious, revengeful and cruel in the highest Degree." The slaves' bitter longing to be free was the germ of truth in Franklin's characterization.

Despite the great dangers, some slaves, usually newcomers from Africa, ran away to seek refuge in the forest or swamps as maroons. Anxious to avoid the Jamaican precedent, mainland authorities took special pains quickly to hunt down and destroy maroon camps, while they were still small and vulnerable. For a reward, local Indians often helped the white militiamen find and eliminate the runaways. In addition, finding food and shelter while on the run and in the woods was hard, especially for newcomers from another continent. The successful exception to the rule was Florida, where the Spanish welcomed several hundred runaways with land, provisions, and honors. The Spanish acted to weaken the British plantation colonies of Georgia and South Carolina and to strengthen their own frontier militia with black men.

By the mid-eighteenth century in the mainland colonies (but not in the West Indies), American-born slaves came to outnumber the African-born. At that point, resistance became more subtle. The second-generation "creole" slaves usually recognized that overt rebellion and maroon settlements were suicidal, given the superior numbers, arms, and organization of their oppressors. Shifting tactics, creole slaves ran away as individuals or pairs to try to disappear into the free black population of a seaport in another colony. Many more slaves stayed on their plantation but resisted covertly, by dragging out their tasks, feigning illness, pretending ignorance, and breaking tools—or by stealing their master's hogs and alcohol. With these tactics, the blacks cleverly exploited the prejudices of their masters, who considered blacks innately lazy, stupid, and dishonest. Landon Carter of Virginia complained, "I find it almost impossible to make a negro do his work well. No orders can engage it, no encouragement persuade it, nor no Punishment oblige it." His tone of resignation registered the small victory of his resisting slaves.

In sum, slave and master engaged in a contest of wills that determined the pace and volume of work on each plantation. One side, however, had far more power than the other. Slaves had to be careful not to overplay their resistance, especially when the master had a quick temper and a strong overseer or driver with a stinging whip. On the other hand, the wise planter had to watch for the limits of his own considerable power. If punished too brutally, slaves might lash out in deadly desperation. Some masters paid for their cruelty when arson consumed a house or barn, or when slaves slipped poison into their owners' food. Such acts rarely escaped detection and ruthless punishment, but they always left a restraining anxiety in planters' minds. Masters compelled enough labor and obedience to preserve a profitable slave system, but they did so with far greater difficulty and more anxiety than they had expected.

AFRICAN-AMERICANS

Within British America, slavery varied considerably by region. During the mid-eighteenth century, African slaves were small minorities in New England (about 2 percent) and the middle colonies (about 8 percent). Most northern slaves lived and worked in the countryside as farmhands or as laborers in the rural ironworks of Pennsylvania and New Jersey. But, given the overwhelmingly rural nature of the colonial population in general, northern slaves were disproportionately urban. Boston was home to one-sixth of the blacks in Massachusetts, and New York City held at least a fifth of the slaves in the colony of New York. Urban slaves generally belonged to wealthy families and served them either as domestic servants or as dockworkers and laundresses. They dwelled in back rooms, lofts, and alley shacks.

The northern blacks often found it difficult to form families and raise children. Many northern masters actively discouraged slave marriages and childbearing, considering children an unwarranted expense. The shortage of women among northern slave imports also frustrated black men. Many found relief by marrying women of the Indian enclave communities, where service in colonial wars had disproportionately killed native men, skewing the Indian population in favor of women.

As small minorities dispersed among many households, the northern slaves lived and worked beside and among whites, often sleeping and eating in the master's house. By necessity, the northern slaves absorbed Euro-American culture, including the English language and the Christian faith. In the process, they gradually lost most of their African culture, including their native languages. But, in an effort to sustain their own cultural space, northern blacks developed an annual ritual festival known as "Negro election day," when they gathered to drink, feast, play, and dance. The festivities culminated with the raucous election of local kings, governors, and judges, who acted throughout the next year as arbitrators of disputes within the black community. In this manner, blacks honored their own notables and enjoyed a day as free people. Masters cooperated by lending clothes and horses to their slaves for the day. By tolerating such a brief outlet, a temporary inversion of authority, northern whites expressed their self-assurance and helped to maintain slavery as the norm on the other 364 days of the year.

Cultural assimilation and smaller numbers rendered the northern blacks less alarming to their masters, who usually governed their slaves with less pain and terror than practiced where owners were greatly outnumbered. In 1717 a New York master complained to a West Indian friend, "The Custome of this Country will not allow us to use our Negroes as you doe in Barbadoes." In New England the law made few special provisions for slavery, even permitting slaves to press claims in court, to testify against whites, and (except in Massachusetts) to marry whites. Although mild when compared with the rigors of southern plantation slavery, northern slavery remained a hard lot that wore down black men and women, increasing their vulnerability to disease. During the mid-eighteenth century in northern seaports, blacks died at nearly twice the rate of whites.

And despite their relatively better circumstances and the numerical odds against them, some urban blacks conspired to rebel. In 1712 in New York City, two dozen especially desperate slaves set fire to buildings and killed fleeing whites with knives, axes, and guns. Soldiers subdued the rebels, and trials exacted deadly and medieval retribution. A lucky thirteen died on the gallows; another was hung up in chains to starve to death; one more was slowly broken on the wheel; three were burned at the stake. Six escaped further torture and execution by killing themselves. Nonetheless, the whites found little reassurance, for a generation later (1740–41) they detected, they thought, another plot to burn the city. Torture reaped confessions that confirmed their suspicions. In the name of the law, the New Yorkers burned thirteen slaves at the stake and hanged another seventeen (in addition to four white accessories). By sacrificing so much valuable property, the New Yorkers conceded that blacks had not fully submitted to slavery and never would—refuting a benign view of slavery, even at its "best" in the urban north.

Many more slaves endured the far harsher slavery of the West Indies, the grave of the great majority of the Africans imported into the British empire. Sugar plantations enforced work conditions more regimented and demanding than for any other crop grown in the empire. Only children under the age of six and a very few aged and invalids escaped from daily labor. Organized into a gang led by a driver, cane workers worked in a long line at a regulated pace, at the tasks of digging holes, planting, weeding, and harvesting. The whip stung anyone who lagged. The visitor Jane Schaw described the operation of a gang:

> The Negroes, who are all in troops, are sorted so as to match each other in size and strength. Every ten Negroes have a driver, who walks behind them, holding in his hand a short whip and a long one. . . . they are naked, male and female, down to the girdle, and you constantly observe where application [of the whip] has been made.

Initially shocked, Schaw soon accepted the dehumanizing equivocations of her gracious hosts:

> They would be as averse to [whipping] as we are, could it be avoided, which has often been tried to no purpose. When one comes to be better acquainted with the Negroes, the horrour of it must wear off. . . . As to the brutes, it inflicts no wound on their mind, whose Nature seems

> made to bear it, and whose sufferings are not attended with shame or pain beyond the present moment.

Of course, no whipped slave could or would explain his or her true feelings to Janet Schaw.

On the sugar islands, slaves outnumbered whites by more than three to one. That preponderance alarmed masters, as did the steady arrival of African newcomers, with alien ways and defiant attitudes. Seeking security, the West Indian planters devised the most draconian slave codes in the empire and periodically indulged in orgies of suspicion, torture, trial, and slow executions—despite the high value of the slaves destroyed.

A realm of extremes, the West Indies also featured more sexual liaisons between whites and blacks. Of course, those relations expressed the enormous imbalance of power between owner and property—and flourished in the absence of white women, who generally avoided the Caribbean. Law and custom strictly proscribed, and severely punished, sexual relations between black men and white women, but law was silent about, and custom encouraging of, white planters who raped black women or kept them as mistresses. In some cases, slave women negotiated better conditions for themselves and freedom for their offspring in return for submitting to the sexual demands of their owners.

Slave life in the marshy South Carolina and Georgia low country more closely resembled that in the West Indies than that in the northern colonies. As in the West Indies, only continued imports from Africa kept the slave population growing. Directly imported from Africa by the hundreds to work on rice and indigo plantations, the low-country slaves outnumbered whites by more than two to one. Dwelling in large concentrations on rural plantations, the Carolina and Georgia slaves could preserve (by adaptation) much of their African culture, including traditional African names. They developed a new, composite language, Gullah, based on several African languages and distinct in grammar and structure from English.

The Carolina and Georgia masters tried to impose the West Indian gang system, but the slaves resisted, obliging their masters to accept a compromise: the less rigorous "task system." Under the task system, the slave's day became his or her own once the daily task had been accomplished: so many rows of rice sowed, so many bushels of corn pounded into meal, or so many feet of canal cleared. The compromise gave masters a certain daily minimum, but no more. If they worked early and hard, slaves could leave the field in the afternoon, escaping from the most intense heat of the day. On their own time, they tended gardens and a few livestock, which they could sell to purchase goods, principally better clothing.

The urban slaves in Charles Town and Savannah were partial exceptions to the low-country rule. They lived in closer proximity to whites, working as house servants, boatmen, and skilled artisans. Unlike northern blacks, the low-country urban slaves even entered the higher trades as silversmiths and cabinetmakers. In the towns, black women dominated the marketing of produce. Mobile, skilled, and sometimes literate, the urban slaves understood white ways. Those with more lenient masters could earn wages for extra work, sometimes procuring the means to buy freedom for themselves and their children. Often the urban, skilled, and favored slaves were lighter-skinned mulattoes, the offspring of white masters and their female slaves. Adopting colonial words, ways, and clothes, the urban slaves usually felt little solidarity with the more numerous and African-born field hands of the rice and indigo plantations. But when frustrated in their aspirations for still greater freedom and privilege, the urban slaves could become especially formidable plotters against their masters.

In proportion and conditions, eighteenth-century Chesapeake slavery fell between the extremes manifest in the northern colonies, on the one hand, and in the West Indies or the Carolina-Georgia low country, on the other. In 1750 the Chesapeake hosted the great majority of slaves in mainland British America: 150,000 compared with 60,000 in the low country and 33,000 in the northern colonies. Slaves constituted about 40 percent of the population in Maryland and Virginia—a proportion large enough to concern, but rarely to terrify, their masters, and large enough to preserve some but not most African ways and words.

Chesapeake blacks enjoyed the best demographic conditions allowed slaves within the British empire. Although it was very hard work, cultivating tobacco was less brutal than slogging in a rice field or broiling in a cane field, and it exposed the worker to fewer mosquitoes bearing malaria and yellow fever. Chesapeake slaves also lived in sufficient concentrations to find marriage partners and bear children, in contrast to many northern slaves. Consequently, natural increase swelled the Chesapeake slave population, which enabled the planters to reduce their African imports after 1750. Thereafter, creole slaves predominated in the Chesapeake.

As the African infusion shrank, the Chesapeake slave culture became more American. Compared with northern blacks, the Chesapeake slaves were less surrounded and watched by whites. But compared with West Indian or low-country slaves, the Chesapeake blacks were more exposed to the culture of their masters. Chesapeake blacks developed no distinct language and rarely preserved African names for their children, but they put their own content into the cultural forms that they borrowed, selectively, from their masters. In the slave dialect, English words worked to an African grammar and syntax. The blacks gradually adapted evangelical Christianity to their own healing magic, emotional singing, and raucous funerals that celebrated death as a spiritual liberation and a restoration to Africa. They also added European instruments to their banjos, rattles, and drums to craft a music that expressed the African emphasis on rhythm and percussion. In turn, the new

African-American culture exercised an intimate influence over the white children raised by black servants on Chesapeake plantations. A British visitor complained that the planters "suffer [their children] too much to prowl amongst the young Negroes, which insensibly causes them to imbibe their Manners and broken Speech."

By crafting an African-American culture, Chesapeake slaves defended their creativity and identity within the confines of a brutal system of coerced labor. They successfully limited the dehumanization demanded by plantation slavery. But, at the same time, by creating consoling comforts within slavery, they made it harder to risk a violent uprising.

CONCLUSION

Eighteenth-century America was simultaneously and inseparably a land of black slavery and white opportunity. Primarily on the distinction of race, the colonies offered some emigrants greater liberty and prosperity, while others suffered the exploitation and deprivation of plantation slavery. Enslaved Africans dominated the eighteenth-century human flow across the Atlantic to British America, but the colonial white population remained more than twice as large. This paradox reflected the demographic stress of American slavery for Africans and the demographic rewards to the descendants of Europeans. In 1780 the black population in British America was less than half the total number of African emigrants received during the preceding century, while the white population exceeded its emigrant source by three to one, thanks especially to the healthy conditions in New England and the middle colonies. The black deaths primarily occurred in the West Indies, the principal destination of enslaved Africans, but even in the Chesapeake, where slave births did exceed deaths, their birthrate was lower and their death rate higher than those of their white masters.

15

Awakenings

★

1700–75

The Reverend Samson Occom (1723–92), a Mohegan Indian educated by the Reverend Eleazar Wheelock, who later founded Dartmouth College. This mezzotint was made in England in 1768 during Occom's preaching tour to raise funds meant for Wheelock's Indian school. Occom wears clerical garb and points to a passage in the Bible. The artist inserts an arrow hanging on the wall at top left as a reminder of Occom's native origins. The popularity of Occom and his print attests to the fascination of pious Anglo-Americans with the prospects of converting natives to their culture.

DURING THE MID-EIGHTEENTH CENTURY, British colonial America experienced a dramatic and sweeping set of religious revivals collectively known as the Great Awakening (or the First Great Awakening). After noting significant lags and regional exceptions, we find a dramatic, widespread, and increasingly synchronized outburst of revival religion that astonished and polarized the colonists. The evangelical revivalists undermined the traditional convictions that society must be stratified and corporate. They promoted a more pluralistic, egalitarian, and voluntaristic social order by defending the free flow of itinerant preachers and their converts across community and denominational lines. The revivalists also imagined an enlarged society: an intercolonial and transatlantic network of congregations united by a shared spirituality communicated over long distances by itinerants and print. That imagination rested upon a persistent hope that the revivals would spread around the globe to initiate Christ's triumphant millennial return to earth.

By no means did all colonists become evangelicals, but the latter were sufficiently numerous and interconnected to influence the entire culture and society. Evangelical revivals also brought Protestant conversion, for the first time, to thousands of Indians and enslaved Africans. In the evangelical emphasis on the individual encounter with the Holy Spirit, the poor and the marginal found a divine license for their own preachers, who adapted Christianity to assert the dignity and the rights of all people.

ESTABLISHMENTS

Myth insists that the seventeenth-century English colonists fled from religious persecution into a land of religious freedom. In addition to omitting economic considerations, the myth grossly simplifies the diverse religious motives for emigration. Not all colonists had felt persecuted at home, and few wanted to live in a society that tolerated a plurality of religions. Perfectly content with the official Anglican faith of the homeland, many colonists sought to replicate it in the colonies. And although some English dissenters, principally the Quakers, did seek in America a general religious freedom, many more emigrants wanted their own denomination to dominate, to the prejudice of all others. Indeed, at the end of the seventeenth century, most colonies offered *less* religious toleration than did the mother country.

Most colonies' founders believed that public morality, political harmony, and social order required religious uniformity. On pain of fines, jail, and whipping, they required the colonists to attend, and pay taxes for, one "established" church. The establishment varied by colony, depending upon the faith of the founders. The Puritan colonies of Plymouth, Massachusetts, and Connecticut established their Congregational Church. The Dutch Reformed Church enjoyed legal primacy in New Netherland. The Church of England also enjoyed official favor in Virginia, Barbados, Jamaica, and the Leeward Islands. Because the establishment varied from colony to colony, so did religious dissent. Where Anglicans held the establishment, Congregationalists ranked among the dissenters. New England reversed that relationship, putting the Anglicans there in the unusual and uncomfortable position of championing minority rights.

Between 1660 and 1690, establishments seemed to be waning, reduced by the founding of New Jersey, Pennsylvania, and Carolina and by the English conquest of New York. That trend, however, reversed between 1690 and 1720, with the creation of new Anglican establishments in Maryland (1692), the southern New York counties (1693), South Carolina (1706), and North Carolina (1715). The prime movers were ambitious royal governors and leading colonists who sought favor in England and political advantage in their colony over non-Anglican rivals. The proponents both exploited and contributed to the increased colonial integration into a transatlantic empire. In 1693, Governor Benjamin Fletcher pointedly reminded the New York assembly, "There are none of you but what are big with the privilege of Englishmen and Magna Charta, which is your right; and the same law doth provide for the religion of the church of England."

Congregationalists sustained an especially impressive establishment in New England, except for Rhode Island. Thanks to compact settlement by towns and laws mandating churches, few inhabitants lived more than six miles from a meetinghouse. And unlike other colonial regions, New England had plenty of official clergyman to fill the many pulpits. Most were graduates of Harvard (founded in 1636) or Yale (1701). Indeed, New England struck visitors as the most conspicuously devout and religiously homogeneous region in British North America. The New English towns enforced a Sabbath that restricted activity to the home and church, imposing arrests and fines on people who worked, played, or traveled on Sunday. An English visitor found the New England Sabbath "the strictest kept that ever I saw."

A mixed blessing, entanglement in an establishment meant clerical dependence upon selectmen and town meetings that proved both meddlesome and stingy. During the early eighteenth century, most towns refused to increase church taxes, although inflation cut the real value of ministers' fixed salaries, leading to protracted and divisive debates. In the poorer rustic towns, the Congregational ministers had to supplement their eroding salaries by running a farm or by doubling as country doctors. Clerical resentments bred counterresentments by laypeople, who grumbled that their minister cared more about money than souls.

The establishment also imposed a growing tension between the inclusion and exclusion of parishioners. As an established church dependent upon taxation, the church needed to be inclusive to justify town support and to provide universal moral instruction and supervision. As an established church in the world, Congregationalism also accepted and reflected social inequalities, arranging the pews in the meetinghouse to reflect the local hierarchy of family wealth and status. On the other hand, that inclusion and hierarchy contradicted the traditional Puritan goal of a "gathered church" limited to the "visible saints" by excluding the unworthy, regardless of their worldly status. During the later seventeenth century, the Puritans had compromised by adopting a two-tier system of membership: "halfway" for the baptized and full for those who proceeded on to spiritual "conversion" and communion. Because that tenuous compromise dissatisfied both the purists and the pragmatists, New England Congregationalism sat on a fault line that would shake the establishment during the Great Awakening of the 1740s.

Beyond New England, establishments were far weaker because official ministers were so few. The Anglican and Dutch Reformed churches demanded expensive ministries by relatively prestigious and learned men, who rarely left the comforts of England or the Netherlands for the instability, hardships, and uncertainties of the early colonies. In addition, beyond Congregational New England, the colonists were slow to found the colleges needed to train ministers. Not until 1693 did Anglicans found the College of William and Mary in Virginia, and it remained small, weak, and underfunded. Because an Anglican minister required ordination by a bishop and the colonies had no bishops, aspiring pastors faced the considerable expense and trouble of a transatlantic voyage for ordination in London. Consequently, the limited supply of Anglican pastors lagged behind the growing population and frontier expansion. In 1724, Virginia had 120,000 inhabitants but only twenty-eight Anglican pastors. Farther south the Anglican situation was even worse. In 1729, North Carolina had twelve Anglican parishes but no resident ministers.

Access to religious services was also difficult because the sprawling pattern of settlement stretched southern parishes, often beyond one hundred square miles (compared with an average of twenty-five in England). The horrendous state of southern roads and bridges compounded the difficulties of distance, often discouraging travel by ministers and attendance by parishioners. Studded with roots, stumps, and rocks, the roads were dust traps in summer and mud pits the rest of the year. Ice and sleet hindered passage in winter; a torrid sun and voracious mosquitoes afflicted travelers in summer. Periodic Indian wars added deadly dangers to the discomforts.

In Maryland and Virginia, the establishment proved a mixed blessing for Anglican clergymen, who depended financially upon vestries dominated by great planters. Anglican pastors complained of chronic meddling, disrespectful treatment, and insufficient pay from contemptuous vestrymen. In 1747 in Virginia, the Reverend William Kay preached a sermon against pride, which Colonel Landon Carter, a great planter, took personally. When Carter complained, Kay worsened matters by replying "that I was glad he applied it, for it was against everyone that was proud." Carter dominated the parish vestry, which promptly ousted the pastor and locked up his church. As Kay so unpleasantly learned, an establishment tended to increase the power of colonial elites over the church rather than the power of the church over the colonists.

In the middle colonies, ethnic and religious diversity precluded any church establishment and obliged every denomination to rely on voluntary attendance and contributions. Unparalleled in Europe or any other colonial region, the competition shocked orthodox ministers, who wished that their own denomination commanded a majority and enjoyed an establishment. With characteristic hyperbole, an Anglican minister denounced the middle colonies as a "soul destroying whirlpool of apostasy." In fact, despite the greater difficulties of supporting churches in the region, the middle colonists established more than their share. By 1750 the middle colonies sustained one congregation for every 470 colonists, compared with one per 600 in New England and one per 1,050 in the south. The denser network of middle colony churches reflected the ethnic and cultural diversity and their rivalries. Almost every denominational cluster of settlers sought its own local church to preserve its distinct identity.

In the middle colonies, prosperous farmers and artisans took the lead as governing elders who organized, funded, and supervised the local congregations. Lacking a sufficient supply of ministers, the elders annually hired devout schoolteachers to preach. During the 1730s and 1740s, however, educated ministers began to arrive in significant numbers from Scotland and Germany. They found that the leading colonial laymen had grown accustomed to governing their congregations and resented the air of command brought by the new clergymen used to the more hierarchical conditions of Europe.

GROWTH AND LIMITS

Despite the difficult conditions, every colonial region developed an extensive and conspicuous array of churches. In 1750 the mainland colonies sustained approximately 1,500 local congregations, each averaging about ninety families attending, which suggests that at least two-thirds of colonial adults were "churched" in the broad sense of affiliation. The Congregationalists composed the largest single denomination, with 450 churches, almost all in New England. The Anglicans ranked second, sustaining 300 parishes, primarily in the South, followed by the Quakers with 250 meetings and the Presbyterians with about 160 churches, most in the middle colonies. They competed with Baptists (100), Lutherans (95), Dutch Reformed (78), and German Reformed (51), all principally based in the middle colonies. Although overwhelmingly a Protestant society, the colonies also hosted a few Catholic churches (especially in Maryland) as well as Jewish synagogues in Newport, New York City, and Charles Town.

In a land of dispersed farms and plantations, church services filled a hunger for social gatherings and for information from the wider world. Church buildings also provided a forum for reading government proclamations, posting new laws, and holding elections to the assembly. Prior to 1750, most books published in the colonies (or imported from Britain) were religious tracts and sermons. Accepting and reflecting the inequalities of colonial society, every denomination included all social ranks but reserved lay leadership as vestrymen, deacons, and elders for the wealthiest and most prestigious men within each congregation.

Despite the impressive extensive growth in religion, many ministers complained that only a declining minority of adults qualified for full church membership and communion. The decline was especially conspicuous among Congregational men, who increasingly remained only halfway members. In most churches, full membership required an applicant to describe his spiritual experiences—a process that dismayed growing numbers of men, who preferred to keep their emotions private. Female full membership did not decline, because women remained more at ease discussing their spiritual feelings. By 1740, in most Congregational churches, the female full members exceeded men by more than two to one.

Despite the decline in full church membership, church attendance remained high, even in the rural south, the least "churched" region in the colonies. In 1724, Anglican ministers in Maryland, Virginia, and South Carolina reported that about 60 percent of the adults in their counties regularly attended Anglican services, although only 15 percent took communion. Many in the remaining 40 percent must have attended rival Presbyterian, Baptist, and Quaker churches, suggesting that at least two-thirds of the southern colonists participated in religious services.

Common people cherished preaching and access to the sacrament of baptism. Contrary to the teachings of their ministers, the common people regarded baptism as possessed of a magical power to fend off sickness and to invite God's saving grace. On the other hand, full membership stagnated because laypeople regarded communion more fearfully, from a conviction that God cursed hasty people who took it before they had been truly converted by grace. Devereux Jarratt, an Anglican, reported that most Virginians considered communion "a dangerous thing to meddle with." Even some vestrymen and deacons balked at full membership because of scrupulous doubts about their own spiritual readiness.

In addition to the many denominational divisions, colonial churches were developing an internal rift between evangelicals and rationalists. Evangelical clergy discounted formal, ceremonial, and sacramental worship in favor of cultivating a spontaneous, direct, and individual religious experience, which they called "experimental religion." Noting the dwindling full membership, evangelicals complained that worship had lost its former intensity, declining into empty formalism or utter indifference. They blamed the growing influence of Christian rationalism, especially among the colonial elite, including most Anglican and some Congregational, Presbyterian, and Dutch Reformed clergymen.

Favoring critical and empirical inquiry, the rationalists slighted the traditional foundations of Christian faith: scriptural revelation and spiritual experience. The rationalists instead found guidance in the science that depicted nature as the orderly and predictable operation of fundamental and discernible "laws," such as Isaac Newton's explication of gravity. Christian rationalism held that God created the natural universe and thereafter never interfered with its laws. God seemed less terrifying as learned people reinterpreted epidemics, earthquakes, and thunderbolts as "natural" rather than as direct interventions of divine anger. The Reverend Andrew Eliot, a New England Congregationalist, explained, "There is nothing in Christianity that is contrary to reason. God never did, He never can, authorize a religion opposite to it, because this would be to contradict himself."

The rationalists rejected the supernatural mysteries and overt emotionalism of evangelical worship. John Tillotson, the archbishop of Canterbury, argued that God asked "nothing but what is easy to be understood, and as easy to be practiced by an honest and willing mind." But the rationalists contradicted themselves by urging parishioners passively to accept instruction by a learned clergy who alone knew best. The Reverend Jonathan Mayhew, a Congregationalist, explained, "Those of the lower class can go but a little way with their inquiries into the moral constitution of the world."

Discarding the Calvinist notion of an arbitrary and punishing God, the rationalists worshiped a benign, predictable, forgiving, and consistent deity who rewarded good behavior with salvation, but who expected common people to defer to the learned and authoritative men at the top of the social hierarchy. The rationalist concept of God appalled the evangelicals as cold, distant, and irrelevant, for they sought direct, individual, and transforming contact with the Holy Spirit. They suspected that rationalists trumpeted their learning and prestige to mask their lack of conversion and to claim undue power over true believers. The latent conflict between the rational and evangelical emphases became manifest in the revivals of the 1730s and early 1740s.

REVIVALS

During the early eighteenth century, most Congregational and Presbyterian congregations had evangelical traditions that nurtured periodic "revivals": surges in fervor and new members. For example, the Congregational parish of Northampton in Massachusetts experienced six distinct revivals during the sixty-year pastorate of the Reverend Solomon Stoddard: in 1679, 1683, 1696, 1712, 1718, and 1727, with intervening lulls. Unpredictable, irregularly spaced, and of varying intensity, the Northampton revivals did not coincide in timing and velocity with their counterparts in other towns. Indeed, because Stoddard was an especially vigorous, evangelical, and effective preacher, Northampton experienced larger and more frequent revivals than did communities with less zealous ministers.

Revivals emphasized the emotional process of conversion that transformed sinners into saints who warranted eternal salvation. Committed to a Calvinist theology, the colonial evangelicals rejected the rationalists' suggestion that anyone could earn salvation by behaving well. On the contrary, the evangelicals insisted that God's grace alone could save and that he bestowed that grace as his free and arbitrary gift only upon some of those who accepted their own utter helplessness to save themselves. Yet the revivalists subtly contradicted their Calvinism by exhorting listeners to seek out evangelical preaching and to reform their conduct, as if such actions would help draw down God's saving grace.

To stimulate revivals, energetic ministers preached "soul-searching" sermons meant to shock their listeners into recognizing their impending and eternal sentence in hell. But the evangelicals balanced their images of terror with equally vivid depictions of eternal joy in heaven. These "awakening" sermons primarily appealed to the emotions, especially fear and hope, rather than to reason. A master of this style, Stoddard taught his grandson and successor the Reverend Jonathan Edwards, who explained, "Our people do not so much need to have their heads stored, as to have their hearts touched." A witness described hearing Edwards preach "a most awakening sermon, and before sermon was done there was a great moaning and crying through the whole house—What shall I do to be saved—oh, I am going to Hell—oh, what shall I do for Christ, etc., etc., so that the minister was obliged to desist—the shrieks and cries were piercing and amazing."

Evangelical preaching provoked conversion experiences that pulled a seeker through despair to an ecstatic experience of divine grace. In the first step, people had to forsake their false sense of security in their own good behavior and instead recognize their utter worthlessness and helplessness without God. Seekers then fell into a profound sense of despair, doubting that God would ever save them. Those who completed the process ultimately surrendered to God and felt an exhilarating and liberating infusion of saving grace called the New Birth. In 1741, Hannah Heaton, a Connecticut farm woman, recalled:

> The power of God came down. My knees smote together. . . . It seem[e]d to me I was a sinking down to hell. I tho[ugh]t the floor I stood on gave way and I was just a going, but then I began to resign and, as I resigned, my distress began to go off till I was perfectly easy, quiet, and calm. . . . It seem[e]d as if I had a new soul & body both.

Like Heaton, some evangelicals described their New Birth as so sudden and complete that they could identify the day and hour. Others experienced a more gradual and traditional ripening, over several weeks or months.

The cultivation of despair, however, was a dangerous business that imperiled the lives of the melancholy. Some seekers broke through to the New Birth, while others fell back into their worldly ways, but a few became trapped in despair and sought to escape through suicide. Unable to win any assurance in life, they sought immediately to face God and know their sentence. Such suicides dissipated the enthusiasm that sustained a revival, bringing the zeal and the conversions to a halt.

Congregational and Presbyterian revivals remained localized and episodic until the 1730s and early 1740s, when they began to interact and escalate as evangelical ministers cooperated over long distances as never before. The escalation of local into intercolonial revivalism began in the Raritan Valley of eastern New Jersey. Led by Theodore Frelinghuysen, a Dutch Reformed minister, and the Presbyterian brothers Gilbert and John Tennent and William Tennent, Jr., the Raritan evangelicals crossed denominational lines to cooperate in the face of opposition from more conservative ministers in their own churches.

In animated letters, Gilbert Tennent reported their success to his Congregational correspondents in New England, which inspired emulation especially by Jonathan Edwards. In turn, his success encouraged other ministers and devout laypeople throughout the Connecticut Valley, affecting at least thirty-two other towns by 1735. As the most extensive and synchronized set of revivals in colonial experience, the Connecticut Valley revivals seemed a miraculous outpouring of divine grace rather than anything wrought by humans. In mid-1735, however, the revivals ground to a halt after the shocking suicide of Joseph Hawley, Northampton's richest merchant and an uncle to Jonathan Edwards. Longing for, but despairing of, salvation, Hawley cut his throat.

WHITEFIELD

After fading in the Connecticut Valley, the revival assumed a new power and range by breaking into print. In London in 1737 and Boston in 1738, Edwards published a vivid account entitled *A Faithful Narrative of the Surprizing Work of God*. Linking the Connecticut Valley and Raritan Valley revivals, Edwards depicted God acting throughout the colonies, and perhaps the entire Protestant world. Widely and avidly read in Britain and the colonies, *A Faithful Narrative* provided models of preaching and conversion that guided subsequent revivals, imparting a greater similarity that evangelicals interpreted as a sure sign of God's uniform power, rather than as evidence of Edwards's influential account.

The English readers of *A Faithful Narrative* included George Whitefield, a young Anglican minister who developed an evangelical style at odds with the dominant rationalism of the Church of England. Inspired by God and Edwards, in 1739 Whitefield developed an innovative career as a tireless itinerant, touring England and Wales, seeking out the poor and laboring people usually ignored by Anglicans. Drawing immense crowds too large for churches and consisting of people uncomfortable in them, Whitefield preached conversion to thousands in the streets, fields, and parks, provoking outbursts of emotion. A charismatic and moving speaker, Whitefield directly engaged his audience by preaching without notes. Although short, slight, and cross-eyed, Whitefield compelled attention by his fluid and dramatic movements and by a magnificent voice that he modulated like a fine instrument. The contrast between Whitefield's insignificant appearance and commanding performance encouraged the impression that God inspired his preaching. A masterful promoter, Whitefield also exploited the marketing techniques of a commercial society, employing advance men, handbills, and newspaper notices to build his celebrity and audience expectation.

Edwards's words had crossed the Atlantic into London print to inspire Whitefield. In turn, London newsprint passed in ships to the colonies to convey vivid accounts of Whitefield's sensational impact in England. News of his immense crowds in London assured Whitefield of an eager audience in the colonies, for the colonists paid cultural deference to the great metropolis as the arbiter of all fashions. The more they read, the more the colonists longed to hear and see Whitefield preach.

In 1739, Whitefield crossed the Atlantic to tour the colonies, ostensibly to raise funds for an orphanage in Georgia but fundamentally to export his form of evangelical theater to new audiences. His American tour reflected the transatlantic integration of the British empire into an increasingly common market of goods and ideas. Whitefield exploited the proliferation of shipping and newspapers, the improved network of roads, and the greater density of settlement, which promised larger crowds, especially in the northern colonies. During his 1739–41 tour from Maine to Georgia, Whitefield furthered transatlantic and intercolonial integration by becoming the first celebrity seen and heard by a majority of the colonists.

In late 1739, Whitefield arrived in Philadelphia, which became his base for the next fourteen months spent in the colonies. In Philadelphia, Whitefield found an important friend and collaborator in Benjamin Franklin, the leading writer, publisher, and social reformer in the colonies. They made an odd couple, for Franklin was a confirmed rationalist who resisted Whitefield's evangelical message. But Franklin admired Whitefield as a shrewd entrepreneur and dazzling performer. Armed with skepticism, Franklin attended one of Whitefield's Philadelphia services determined to give nothing to the collection.

> I had in my Pocket a Handful of Copper Money, three or four silver Dollars, and five Pistoles in Gold. As he proceeded, I began to soften, and concluded to give the Coppers. Another Stroke of his Oratory made me ashamed of that, and determined me to give the Silver; and he finished so admirably, that I emptied my Pocket wholly into the Collector's Dish, Gold and all.

Above all, Franklin applauded Whitefield for improving the morals of the common people in Philadelphia. Whitefield also benefited Franklin's printing business by creating a sensation that sold newspapers and by commissioning Franklin to publish his sermons and journals. Profitable to Franklin, the joint venture served Whitefield by spreading his words far beyond the reach of his voice.

With Franklin's help, Whitefield escalated the print revolution in the colonies. Items featuring the great evangelist appeared in three-quarters of the issues of Benjamin Franklin's *Pennsylvania Gazette* published during the evangelist's fourteen-month stay in America. From 1738 to 1741, the number of colonial imprints increased 85 percent, primarily owing to works by or about Whitefield. He wrote brief, plain, and often autobiographical tracts accessible to common people who lacked the leisure and training to decipher long and learned treatises. Between 1739 and 1745, American printers produced at least eighty thousand copies of Whitefield's publications, or about one for every eleven colonists. A Bostonian marveled: "The Press here never had so full employ before, nor were people ever so busy in reading."

During 1740, Whitefield preached throughout the colonies, from Georgia to Maine. Although nominally an Anglican, Whitefield was primarily sponsored by Presbyterians and some Dutch Reformed in the middle colonies and by Congregationalists in New England. Sharing his evangelical Calvinism, they hoped that Whitefield's sensational preaching would provoke a renewed wave of conversions—and they were not disappointed.

Whitefield, however, evoked a relatively tepid response beyond the evangelical Calvinists. Because most Anglicans distrusted his emotional preaching and ecumenical support, Whitefield made little impact in the southern colonies, which also lacked the dense settlement and many printing presses so critical to his celebrity in the north. In Anglican Virginia, Colonel Landon Carter boasted that "Whit[e]field did but hum and buzz, and die away like the Insect of the Day." Even excepting the south, however, Whitefield did conduct the most dramatic, extensive, and controversial religious phenomenon ever to affect the British colonies.

Whitefield especially affected audiences in New England, where almost all adults were literate, newspapers and religious tracts were most abundant, and a dense network of ministers prepared for his sensational arrival. The combination drew unprecedented crowds primed with an electric anticipation. A Connecticut farmer, Nathan Cole, recalled:

> When I saw Mr. Whitefield come upon the Scaffold he Lookt almost angelical; a young, Slim, slender, youth before some thousands of people with a bold, undaunted Countenance, and my hearing how God was with him every where as he came along, it Solemnized my mind; and put me into a trembling fear before he began to preach; for he looked as if he was Clothed with authority from the Great God; *and a sweet sollome solemnity sat upon his brow*. And my hearing him preach, gave me a heart wound; by God's blessing: my old Foundation was broken up.

In Boston, a leading minister marveled, "The Grand Subject of Conversation was Mr. Whitefield, and the whole Business of the Town [was] to run, from Place to Place, to hear him preach." On October 12, Whitefield's farewell sermon in Boston drew about twenty thousand, more than the seaport's population, as hundreds of country people flocked in to see the great evangelist.

In addition to drawing unprecedented crowds and making a sensational impression, Whitefield stirred controversy by blaming rationalist ministers for neglecting their duty to seek, experience, and preach conversion. He charged, "The generality of preachers talk of an unknown and unfelt Christ. *The reason why congregations have been dead is, because they had dead men preaching to them.*" Such rebukes divided the ministry, inspiring some to adopt Whitefield's spontaneous, impassioned, evangelical style while hardening others in opposition.

In early 1741, Whitefield returned to England, leaving his American admirers and critics to cope with the upheaval he had expanded. Evangelical ministers worked to sustain Whitefield's sensational impact by effecting many local revivals, collectively called a Great Awakening. In Connecticut in 1741–42 the local churches added an average of sixty-six new members, compared with just sixteen biennially during the preceding decade. The evangelicals hoped that the revivals would expand exponentially and, in Edwards's words, "make New England a kind of heaven upon earth."

The conversions seemed especially impressive and divine because they included so many men and young people, the colonists ordinarily underrepresented in full church membership. In Massachusetts, the Reverend Peter Thacher reported:

> In the *ordinary* Excitations of Grace before this Time, there were more *Females* added than *Males*, . . . but in this *extraordinary* Season, the Grace of GOD has surprisingly seized and subdued the hardiest *Men*, and more *Males* have been added here than of the tenderer sex.

He added that the young people were "crying and wringing their hands, and bewailing their Frolicking and Dancing." During the early 1740s, the revivals temporarily corrected the skew in Congregational Church membership toward women and the elderly by drawing men and young people into the fold.

To highlight the universal and indiscriminate power of God, the revivalists emphasized the dramatic conversions of obscure, common people, the more marginal and previously sinful the better. In his *Faithful Narrative*, Jonathan Edwards set the pattern by featuring the emotional conversions of a four-year-old girl and a dying young woman—people ordinarily little noticed or heeded. The revivals offered a stage for otherwise obscure people to claim attention and even authority as channels for God's will and recipients of his saving grace.

Itinerating evangelicals generated increasing controversy. At Whitefield's special request, the Reverend Gilbert Tennent left New Jersey to tour New England during the winter of 1740–41. Partisan and confrontational, Tennent became celebrated among evangelicals and detested by their critics for his 1740 sermon *The Danger of an Unconverted Ministry*. In this evangelical manifesto, Tennent charged that rationalists lacked the evangelical experience with Christ that was a prerequisite for truly Christian preaching. Doomed to hell, the rationalist ministers covertly menaced souls by offering a dull and easy religion that distracted congregants from the hard, emotional work of seeking the New Birth: "They have not the Courage, or Honesty, to thrust the Nail of Terror into sleeping Souls." Tennent urged parishioners to desert such ministers who preached only a "dead" formalism and who opposed the revivals.

Tennent, however, was tame compared with the Reverend James Davenport. Caught up in the fervor, Davenport neglected his own parish to itinerate through Connecticut and Massachusetts. Denied access to most pulpits, Davenport gathered crowds in fields and streets to denounce their resident ministers as "unconverted hypocrites" and "the devil incarnate." During 1742, in Hartford and again in Boston, Davenport twice suffered arrest, trial, and verdicts of insanity from colonial courts. He culminated his itinerant career in March 1743 in New London, Connecticut, by gathering a throng around a bonfire to burn fashionable clothes and impious books, which, for Davenport, included religious tracts written by his many critics. Apparently burned out, a few weeks later Davenport publicly recanted his itinerant career "as enthusiastical and delusive."

Davenport's retreat did not stop the spread of evangelical preachers across the landscape and down the social ladder. Itineracy by well-educated and ordained ministers—such as Whitefield, Tennent, and Davenport—seemed bad enough to orthodox critics. Far worse were the poorly educated laypeople who itinerated as "exhorters." Finding a divine call to preach in their New Birth, they gathered audiences by testifying vociferously to their "experimental religion." Many exhorters claimed continuing communication with God in the form of trances, visions, and premonitions. Such certainty inspired common people to defy any minister or magistrate who opposed their preaching.

To the special horror of religious conservatives, some women became exhorters. Inspired by God's direct command, they felt obliged to defy the Biblical injunctions by the apostle Paul against female speaking in church. By claiming utter submission to God's command, and by speaking his words rather than their own, inspired women claimed a freedom from the social restraints placed on their gender. These women followed the precedent set by the Quakers, who had long recognized God's voice in their female preachers, known as Public Friends.

During the 1740s in western Massachusetts an inspired woman, Bathsheba Kingsley, defied her husband, stole a horse, and rode from town to town, preaching her "immediate revelations from heaven." Turning the tables, Kingsley rebuked men, including ministers, who commanded her to stop. When her husband resorted to "hard words and blows," she loudly and publicly prayed that he "might go quick to hell." Detecting a perversion of the revival, Jonathan Edwards denounced Kingsley as a "brawling Woman" who should "keep chiefly at home."

Sarah Haggar Osborne, a schoolteacher in Newport, Rhode Island, also felt too inspired to remain publicly silent. During the 1740s, she organized evening prayer meetings for younger women, a practice that did enjoy Biblical sanction. Later, during the mid-1760s, when another revival gripped Newport, Osborne's expanded her de facto ministry to hundreds of seekers: boys and girls, men and women, slave and free. Defying her own minister, Osborne refused "to shut up my mouth and doors and creep into obscurity." In evangelical preaching, she found an exhilarating new avenue for public expression and influence.

OLD LIGHTS AND NEW LIGHTS

Whitefield's controversial tour and its divisive aftermath manifested the latent rupture between rationalists and evangelicals. At the same time, the revivals promoted greater cooperation, across denominational lines, between evangelicals in different churches. Whitefield (Anglican), Edwards (Congregationalist), the Tennents (Presbyterian), Frelinghuysen (Dutch Reformed), and Henry M. Muhlenberg (Lutheran) shared encouragement, information, and pulpits. In reaction, rationalists in the various churches recognized their own affinities and made temporary alliances against revivalism. The evangelicals became known as New Lights, because they believed in new dispensations of divine grace, while their foes were Old Lights, who defended venerable institutions and scriptural traditions. Launched in acrimonious publications, their battle spread into ministerial conventions and colonial politics. A Congregational minister sadly concluded, "The glorious work appears to me now as changed into a ruinous war."

The bitter controversy between New Lights and Old Lights split both the colonial elite and the common people. Both camps included some learned ministers, powerful magistrates, and wealthy merchants as well as numerous common farmers, artisans, and laborers. But initially more men of education, prestige, wealth, and influence lined up with the Old Lights than with the New, which gave a more populist tone to the revivalists. Among the clergy, the split was partly generational. Most Old Light ministers were older men, well established in their careers and set in their ways. They felt rattled by the ambitious zeal of New Light ministers, who were usually younger and quicker to embrace "new measures." Among the Presbyterian clergy, the generational split divided older men trained in British universities from the younger ministers educated in America, usually at an evangelical academy run by Gilbert Tennent's father, the Reverend William Tennent, at Neshaminy, Pennsylvania.

The Old Lights defended the traditional form of learned sermons: carefully written in advance and designed to persuade with precedents and reason. By contrast, the New Lights preached emotionally and spontaneously to channel their immediate sense of the Holy Spirit and to shock and inspire their listeners. Such unstructured preaching appalled the Old Lights as "full of Words, but very confused and inconsistent." Counterattacking, John Henry Goetschius (Dutch Reformed) charged the Old Lights with "impos[ing] on many people, against their will, their old, rotten, and stinking routine religion."

Used to a dispassionate style of worship, the Old Lights despised the emotional and physical outbursts evoked by the revivals: weeping, crying out, twitching, and falling down during worship. Jonathan Edwards conceded that the conversions of the early 1740s were louder and more emotional than anything he had seen before: "It was a very frequent thing to see an house full of outcries, faintings, convulsions and such like, both with distress, and also with admiration and joy." The Old Lights called the outbursts "enthusiasm," then a pejorative term that meant human madness, at best, or Satan's manipulation, at worst. The Reverend Ezra Stiles commented that "multitudes were seriously, soberly and solemnly out of their wits."

The Old Lights especially distrusted the religious enthusiasm of children and women that so impressed revivalists. And where evangelicals celebrated the sudden conversions of conspicuous sinners, as proof of divine power, the critics countered that most unprepared converts promptly backslid into sin. For Old Lights, true grace ripened gradually and depended on patient study of the Bible, improved morality, and guidance by a learned and cautious minister.

Dismayed by evangelical itinerants, the Old Lights defended the traditional territorial parish that united all residents under the authority of an ordained and established minister who controlled public religious speech within his bounds. Because the New England establishment interwove church and state, the Congregational Old Lights charged that the invading itinerants were "endeavouring to overset the Government; to turn things *topsy, turvy;* and bring all into Convulsion." Another Old Light aptly noted that the itinerant evangelist "above all hates rules and good order, or *bounds and limits.*" Where the New Lights championed the uninhibited and disruptive flow of divine grace by inspired itinerants, the Old Lights regarded Christianity as a stable faith that needed barricades against intrusive innovations.

RADICALS

In addition to the fundamental divide between New and Old Lights, the evangelicals became subdivided into moderates and radicals. Both had a commitment to "experimental religion," but they differed over the implications for church and state institutions. Cherishing some measure of stability and security, the Congregational moderates clung to their establishment and its system of territorial parishes, which the radicals assailed as obstacles to the free flow of divine grace. The moderates asserted that church institutions necessarily belonged, in part, to this world and had to accommodate to its inequalities in wealth, status, and learning. The radicals, however, imagined otherworldly churches that brought heaven to earth during worship, temporarily dissolving the significance of all social distinctions.

The moderates embraced almost all of the professional clergy who supported the revivals, including Frelinghuysen, Muhlenberg, Whitefield, Edwards, and the Tennents. They favored evangelical preaching and conversions, but they also meant to preserve their own authority and privileges as educated and ordained ministers. In encouraging revivals, the moderates certainly had not bargained on unleashing poorly educated exhorters who urged parishioners to secede and found their own radical churches. The moderates felt caught between the Old Lights, who utterly rejected the revivals, and the radicals, who went too far. The moderates defended the revivals as the authentic work of God, but regretted the most emotional outbursts and censorious self-righteousness as unfortunate but incidental side effects. To vindicate the revivals from Old Light denunciation, the moderates felt compelled to denounce the radicals.

The radicals, however, rejected any church establishment as corrupting to both religion and government. They also gloried in the emotional and physical outbursts of the revivals as pure manifestations of God's overwhelming power. Regarding "experimental religion" as the only divine and true source of authority, they argued that no human institution of learning or government should interfere with God's commands felt in the souls of the converted. That conviction invited inspired common people of little education and low status to exhort and to denounce any officials who interfered. By emphasizing the overwhelming, miraculous, and fundamental power of God acting directly and indiscriminately upon souls, radical evangelicals weakened the social conventions of their hierarchical society.

In defying the established authority of minister and magistrate, the radical evangelicals championed individualism, a concept then considered divisive and anarchic. In matters of faith, a New Light minister asserted the "absolute Necessity for every Person to act singly . . . as if there was not another human Creature upon Earth." No matter how lowly in status or depressed by poverty, or how legally dependent upon another, everyone should choose how to find and worship Christ. A radical preacher insisted, "The common people claim as good [a] right to judge and act for themselves in matters of religion as civil rulers or the learned clergy."

Free choice had radical implications for a colonial society that demanded a social hierarchy in which husbands commanded wives, fathers dictated to sons, masters owned servants and slaves, and gentlemen claimed deference from common people. Although evangelicals avowed respect for all claims to service and deference in the secular world, they argued that no worldly authority could legitimately obstruct religious choice. Citing her husband's opposition, Relief Hooper, a Massachusetts woman, tried to excuse her long absence from her Baptist church, but her evangelical brothers and sisters replied, "When husbands' commands interfer[e]s with Christ's authority, we ought to obey God rather than man."

By distinguishing between worldly and spiritual duties, the evangelicals claimed to present no threat to the social order. But in an unequal society that interwove religious and social authority, the radical effort to separate the two alarmed men of prestige and property. Any elevation of individualism threatened elites, who felt that their authority depended upon the power to constrain the religious choices of their dependents.

Although the radicals invoked free choice to justify separations and itinerants, they were far from consistent in celebrating individualism. In summoning converts to desert their parish churches, the radicals urged them to defy all restraining bonds of family, neighborhood, and society. Then, however, the evangelicals formed their own, more demanding communities. The radical evangelicals considered themselves a spiritual family, calling one another "brother" and "sister." Old Light polemics charged that the radicals destroyed all moral restraints and wallowed in drink, contention, slander, and adultery. In fact, the radicals took great pains to supervise one another for strict morality and plain attire, for they knew that their enemies closely watched for any misdeed. The radicals rebuked or ousted anyone found wanting—a painful exclusion to those who had tasted the emotional intimacies of evangelical worship. Within the bounds of their own churches, the radicals meant to preserve the harmony of their worship from the individual assertion that had led them out of their former congregations.

The radical evangelicals sought to *include* every person in conversion, regardless of gender, race, and status, but they worked to *exclude* from church membership anyone they deemed unconverted by the New Birth. Impatient, the radicals demanded the immediate dismissal of ministers, and the ouster of all church members, whom they deemed unconverted hypocrites. A radical preacher exhorted, "O that the precious Seed might be preserved and *separated* from all gross Mixtures!" Of course, the radical attempts to distinguish and separate insulted and outraged those ministers and parishioners found wanting by the self-righteous. With good reason, the Old Lights and the moderate evangelicals worried that the divisive drive for purity would shatter the religious unity and establishment of Congregational New England.

When most Congregational churches balked at immediately adopting the higher standards of internal purity, the local radicals bolted to form their own "Separate" congregations or to join their fellow travelers the Baptists. A leading Separate announced his refusal "to Sit under the Stupid and Deceiving performances of unconverted ministers." Sometimes the radicals seceded from staunch Old Light ministers and congregations utterly opposed to the revivals. More often, the radicals deserted congregations led by moderate New Lights who preached conversion but clung to the inclusive principles of the establishment.

The Separates and Baptists took seriously the spiritual equality of all awakened people (and their spiritual superiority to all unconverted hypocrites). The radicals ordained their own preachers: poorly educated but charismatic laypeople. They worshiped in open fields, private homes, and barns: settings that reinforced their break from the traditional practice of arranging church pews in a hierarchy of family status that reflected the earthly inequalities of the local community. The radicals suspended social distinctions during worship, mixing together as poor and prosperous; Indian, white, and black; men and women. The radicals even tended to include converted women in the government of their churches. Women helped to choose ministers, to accept or reject potential members, to administer church discipline, and to debate and decide controversial practices and ideas. The radicals even encouraged women to exhort in their local churches but stopped short of ordaining them as ministers.

SOUTHERN REVIVALS

Revivalism came relatively late to Virginia. In 1743, three years after Whitefield's brief and ineffective passage through Virginia, moderate evangelicals organized in a single county—Hanover—under the leadership of a local bricklayer assisted by occasional Presbyterian itinerants from the middle colonies. In 1748 the Hanover dissenters obtained a resident Presbyterian minister, Samuel Davies, who had studied at the evangelical seminary in Pennsylvania conducted by William Tennent, Gilbert's father.

To discourage itinerants, the Anglican-dominated government of Virginia required, and then denied, special licenses. Governor William Gooch denounced the itinerants for seeking "not liberty of conscience but freedom of speech." His distinction was important and revealing. Gooch and other elitists accepted "liberty of conscience" as the passive persistence of longstanding denominational loyalties, but they dreaded "freedom of speech" for inviting people to rethink their allegiances, which seemed likely to disrupt social harmony. By this reasoning, Presbyterian preachers should limit their preaching to their traditional constituencies in Scots and Scotch-Irish settlements, rather than roam into other parishes to recruit Anglican defectors.

An educated man with good manners, Samuel Davies evoked far less hostility than did the poorly educated Baptist preachers from New England, who began to itinerate in North Carolina and Virginia during the mid-1750s. Accepting a low standard of living and working as farmers and tradesmen when not preaching, the Baptist elders needed only small contributions from their audiences, who rarely could afford to give much. Consequently, the Baptists could more rapidly and cheaply expand their ministry, especially on the frontier, than could the more orthodox denominations that depended upon a limited supply of expensive and college-educated ministers.

In the settlements, the preachers recruited followers by tapping into independent local prayer groups of devout seekers. Hungry for preaching, the unaffiliated seekers welcomed and hosted a variety of itinerant preachers touring the settlements. Although numerous, such pious "independents" have been underestimated in standard religious histories, naturally drawn by better documentation to the institutionalized denominations. Although certain that they were not Anglicans, the pious independents rarely knew what they were until impressed by the Baptist itinerants. Despite their late start in Virginia, the Baptists grew rapidly from only seven congregations in 1769 to fifty-four by 1774, embracing at least a tenth of white Virginians.

Used to reading character from external appearances, the Virginia Anglicans regarded the Baptists as somber and melancholy people, for they wore dark and plain clothing, cut their hair short, and wove their faith into every conversation. But their external sobriety and austerity covered a more emotional, intimate, and supportive community for worship. Gathered together, they shared their despair and ecstasy in a manner discouraged by ridicule in the highly competitive and gentry-dominated society of Anglican Virginia. Addressing one another as "brother" and "sister," the Baptists conducted an egalitarian worship that contrasted with the hierarchical seating and service of the Anglican churches. The Baptists even welcomed slaves into their worship as "brothers" and "sisters," and encouraged some to become preachers. To break down worldly pride and build solidarity, Baptist services included extensive physical contact: laying on of hands, the exchange of the "kiss of charity," and ritual foot-washing. A visceral distaste for such intimate contact with ordinary people discouraged gentlemen and ladies from becoming Baptists. Appealing primarily to common planters and some slaves, the Baptists drew them together while drawing them away from the gentry.

By calling upon converts to desert their Anglican churches, the Baptists threatened a foundation of Virginia society: the expectation that everyone in a parish would worship together in the established church supervised by the county gentry. Baptists also discouraged the public amusements that had long demonstrated the gentry's leadership as the finest dancers and the owners of the best racehorses and gamecocks. Landon Carter bitterly complained that the Baptists were "quite destroying pleasure in the Country; for they encourage ardent Prayer; strong & constant faith, & an intire Banishment of *Gaming*, *Dancing*, & Sabbath-Day Diversions." The withdrawal of common evangelicals from public diversions and Anglican services implicitly rebuked the gentry and parsons for leading worldly lives.

Anglican pastors and gentlemen defended the traditional conviction that secular authority depended upon a religious establishment. Rigorously enforcing the laws against itineracy, Anglican magistrates whipped and jailed dozens of unlicensed preachers. Far from avoiding or resisting confrontation, the Baptists welcomed opportunities to endure persecution conspicuously for their faith. In 1771 a county sheriff and a posse of gentry tried to break up a Baptist meeting by pulling the preacher, John Waller, from the stage to inflict twenty lashes with a horsewhip. In Waller's words, the congregation gathered around the whipping to sing psalms "so that he Could Scarcely feel the Stripes." Released, Waller "Went Back singing praise to God, mounted the Stage & preached with a Great Deal of Liberty." For evangelicals, to preach with "Liberty" meant to channel the Holy Spirit spontaneously. Astonished and ashamed, the posse rode away discredited. By enduring, Waller turned his whipping into a Baptist victory that impressed onlookers and made the case for toleration.

RACE

Prior to 1740, no ministers challenged the slave system and few even bothered to convert the enslaved Africans, deferring to the opposition of slave owners. Worried that their slaves considered Christianity a step toward freedom, masters feared that baptism would encourage resentment and resistance. Revivalists, however, longed to convert everyone, regardless of his or her race or lowly status in this world. Precisely because Indians and enslaved Africans had remained unchurched and seemed the most hardened of sinners, their conversion especially appealed to evangelicals as a sure sign of God's miraculous grace. The evangelicals also rendered Christianity more accessible and resonant to the illiterate and exploited by emphasizing feeling rather than learning.

Many slaves attended the revivals, to the considerable dismay of the Anglican clergy and magistrates. Indeed, the opposition of masters probably recommended evangelical preachers to slaves who distrusted Anglican pastors as allied to the planters. Ordinarily reminded of their inferiority in public encounters, the enslaved found in evangelical worship moments of equality with every other seeker. Fearful of where such slave spirituality might lead, in 1772 the Virginia assembly imposed stiff penalties on any preacher who baptized a slave without his master's written permission.

In fact, few white evangelicals overtly challenged the slave system. Jonathan Edwards owned slaves, and George Whitefield procured a Georgia plantation worked by slaves to support his orphanage. Even radical evangelicals said little against slavery as a system. Otherworldly in their priorities, the radicals demanded the right to convert slaves but declined to challenge slavery as a temporal condition. The evangelicals prepared slaves for an afterlife where they would be, at last, free and equal—an eternity that seemed far more important than a lifetime endured in slavery. Only later, after the American Revolution, did some southern evangelicals briefly challenge slavery as antithetical to Christianity's golden rule to do unto others as you would have them do unto you.

Only the Quakers tried to fulfill the radical racial implications of the revivals by challenging the twin injustices most fundamental to colonial society: Indian war and African slavery. Where other evangelicals temporized, the Quaker reformers obliged their meetings to take sweeping new stands against both. Under such pressure, most colonial Quaker leaders reaffirmed their pacifism by withdrawing from politics in wartime. In 1758 the Philadelphia Yearly Meeting also barred Quaker slaveholders from church leadership, and in 1776 it disowned them from membership. In colonies premised on slavery, the Quakers became the lone denomination to seek abolition systematically. However, their greater unity, discipline, and moral principle came at a cost, for the Quaker meetings shrank, as worldly members left or were forced out for colluding with war or clinging to slavery.

The Great Awakening also revived the long-dormant efforts by colonial Protestants to convert the Indians. After the collapse in 1675 of most of the Puritan "praying towns," almost all of the colonial clergy dismissed Indian missions as time, effort, and money squandered on immutable savages. During the 1740s, however, the millennial enthusiasm of the Great Awakening inspired evangelicals to target Indians for conversion, as a critical step toward realizing Christ's return to govern humanity on earth. Evangelical worship also provided a new basis for spiritual conversations across the cultural divide between native and colonial peoples.

The evangelicals enjoyed their greatest success among the small Indian groups dwelling in enclaves surrounded by the colonial settlements, especially in southern New England. Long resistant to orthodox Christian preaching, the Narragansett (Rhode Island), Mohegan and Pequot (Connecticut), and Montauk (Long Island) suddenly warmed to the new, more evangelical mode of preaching. From service on colonial farms and sailing ships and in colonial wars, most enclave Indians had become familiar with English words and ways, rendering Christian preaching more comprehensible. Then the Great Awakening disseminated itinerants bearing a more accessible and relevant form of Christianity. The evangelical practices of musical intonation, bodily responses to worship, and reverence for spiritual visions brought Christianity closer to the traditional shamanism of the northeastern tribes. Learning to think and see in a more Christian vein, native adepts began to experience visions of angels rather than the animal spirits of tradition. The radical evangelicals also inspired native converts to organize congregations led by their own exhorters.

Far more than Old Light Congregationalism, evangelicalism permitted Indians to make Christianity their own. Rather than experiencing conversion as a cultural surrender, the enclave Indians exploited it to revitalize their culture. Conversion on their own terms brought them a new source of discipline to resist the worst vices of the dominant society. In particular, converted Indians reduced the alcohol consumption that rendered enclave Indians so poor, indebted, and exploited by their colonial neighbors. By creating their own local congregations, enclave Indians also limited the cultural control of outsiders. In effect, evangelical conversion and church organization helped enclave Indians build their own bridge between tradition and assimilation into the dominant society.

That bridge, however, did little to weaken the racism practiced by the larger society, even by white evangelicals, who were far quicker to detect pride or backsliding in Indians than in themselves. During the mid-eighteenth century, Samson Occom, a Mohegan convert, became the most celebrated Indian in the empire, but he repeatedly and painfully confronted white prejudice in, and exploitation by, his evangelical mentors. Born in 1723, Occom experienced conversion at age sixteen after hearing James Davenport preach near the Mohegan reservation. During the mid-1740s, Occom became the first student in an academy for Indian youths founded by Davenport's brother-in-law and fellow New Light, Eleazar Wheelock. From 1749 to 1760, Occom worked for a missionary society as a preacher and schoolteacher among the Montauk of Long Island. For this double duty, Occom received the poverty-level salary of £15, compared with the £100 paid to the society's white missionaries, who performed half of his duties. Occom bitterly observed, "I believe it is because I am a poor Indian; I Can't help that God has made me so; I did not make myself so."

In 1766, Wheelock sent Occom to England on a preaching tour to raise contributions for educating Indians. Occom's sincerity and eloquence impressed English crowds drawn by curiosity to see an American native preach Christianity. A sensation, Occom raised £11,000—an unprecedented fund-raising success for an American charity. But when Occom returned to Connecticut in 1767, he found poverty and neglect, rather than the triumph he deserved. Feeling used and abandoned, in 1771 Occom assured Wheelock:

> This makes me think of what that great man of God said to me, Mr. Whitefield, just before I left England. . . . "ah," Says he, "you have been a fine Tool to get Money for them, but when you get home, they won't Regard you; they'll Set you a Drift." I am ready to believe it Now.

Occom's outrage deepened when Wheelock used the £11,000 to found a new college (Dartmouth) that educated whites and only a few Indians.

The evangelical culture encouraged by the Great Awakening also spilled across the frontier to influence the still independent Indians seeking new spiritual resources to fend off the settler invasion. During the late 1730s, a German emigrant and mystic, Gottlieb Priber, became profoundly disillusioned with the materialism and inequalities of colonial society. Defecting to the Cherokee, Priber promoted a visionary scheme, called the Kingdom of Paradise, to unite the Indians into a confederacy that would draw strength from the colonies by welcoming runaway servants, slaves, and debtors. Alarmed, South Carolina officials demanded that the Cherokee arrest and surrender Priber. The Cherokee refused, but their Creek rivals captured Priber in 1743 and surrendered him to the colonists, who held the dangerous mystic in prison until his death, probably in 1744.

Evangelical discourse also influenced the Indians on the Pennsylvania frontier. During the 1750s and 1760s several Lenni Lenape (Delaware) prophets preached moral reform and Pan-Indian unity. The visionaries urged forsaking trade goods, especially alcohol. They also promoted a new code of morality evidently indebted to Christianity, especially its emphasis on marital monogamy. And their visions showed considerable Christian content in their concepts of heaven and hell, moral sin and eternal judgment, and a supreme God and an interceding "Son, or Little God."

The Indian prophets developed their syncretic ideas from animated discussions with devout settlers and missionaries, especially Quakers and Moravians, who found common ground in their shared interest in the spiritual meaning of trances and dreams. Of course, the Indian visionaries preferred to adapt rather than to adopt Christianity, the better to preserve the cultural autonomy of their people while obtaining the moral discipline needed to repel colonial vices. By co-opting selected Christian elements, the native prophets fortified their people against the missionaries who demanded acceptance of their full program, including political submission to colonial rule. In surprising forms, the energy of evangelical religion spread far and wide, often beyond the expectations and against the wishes of the original revivalists.

LEGACIES

Revivals were too emotionally demanding to last. As northern revivalism receded after 1743, the moderate evangelicals and most Old Light clergy regretted their animosities, which had weakened public respect for a learned clergy. Even Gilbert Tennent denounced "everything which tends to enthusiasm and division." Although still differing in their modes of preaching, the Old Lights and the moderate New Lights agreed to disagree without impugning each other's salvation and godliness. The New England Congregational clergy quietly reconciled during the late 1740s; the Presbyterians followed suit in 1758, and the Dutch Reformed in 1772. The clergies of all three denominations were brought together, first, by the clear victories of the moderates in attracting more listeners and in training the next generation of ministers. Second, both groups recognized their shared antipathy toward the radical evangelicals who championed lay exhorters, anti-intellectualism, latter-day visions, and church separations.

The educated clergy also worked to regain popular support by reaffirming the fundamental power of the laity to govern each local church. Most clergymen wisely paid a new tribute to the piety and wisdom of their congregants, especially their role in judging the authentic conversions of applicants for membership. By 1775 these concessions to popular authority and conversion religion eased the return of about half of the Separates to the Congregational fold. The remaining radicals took refuge in Baptist congregations, while the most hard-line rationalists found havens in Anglican churches. Indeed, Anglicanism experienced a modest boom in the northern colonies by welcoming Old Lights opposed to any compromise with evangelical ways.

The renewed consensus within the leading denominations failed to reverse the greatest change wrought by the Great Awakening: the popular enthusiasm for sampling an array of traveling preachers of remarkable social and theological diversity. In her diary for 1769, Mary Cooper of Long Island recorded attending a Quaker "woman preach[er] that lately came from England," a "New Light meeten to here a Black man preach," and two Indian preachers holding "verry happy meetens" as "grate numbers flocked to here them." Ecumenical seekers like Mary Cooper cherished their expanding religious choices. Such a free flow of itinerants and audiences—and the spiritual authority of some Africans and Indians over whites—would have been inconceivable thirty years earlier.

Multiple itinerants offered a perpetual source of religious fluidity and innovation, which, however, was counteracted by the tendency of evangelical groups eventually to institutionalize in search of greater stability and respectability. At their genesis in a revival, evangelical groups defied the social order in hopes of bringing heaven to earth, but as their own revivalism cooled and millennial hopes faded, evangelical groups either institutionalized or dissolved. The persistent affiliated with a denomination and compromised with the inequalities and conventions of their larger society. To finance their churches and to attain respectability, they recruited converts farther up the social ladder, abandoning radical practices that might offend. For example, at the end of the eighteenth century most Baptists forbade female exhorting and voting, restricted lay exhorting, reduced rituals of physical contact, founded colleges to educate their ministers, accepted slavery, and enhanced the authority and prestige of their clergy.

The changes made it easier for gentlemen and ladies to become Baptists. But the changes also alienated purists, who usually bolted into some emerging evangelical group that privileged spiritual spontaneity over institutional regularity. During the 1790s, for example, alienated Baptists found haven among the newer and more radical Freewill Baptists or the Methodists. In sum, the Great Awakening accelerated a religious dialectic that pulled seekers and their congregations between the spiritual hunger to transcend the world and the social longing for respect in it.

16

French America

1650–1750

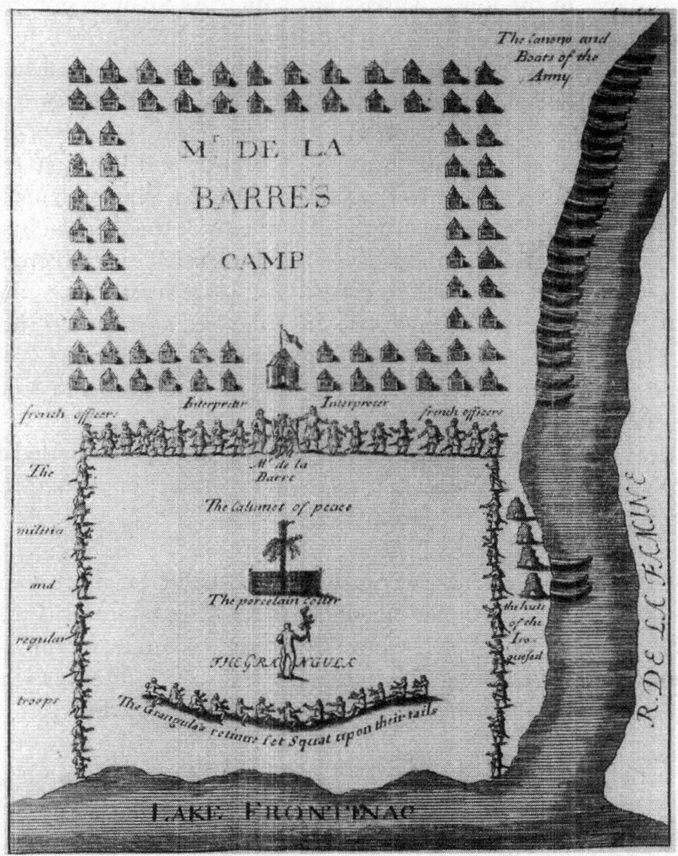

In 1684 the Iroquois spokesman Grangula (Otreouti) addresses the French governor-general de la Barre on the shores of Lake Frontenac (now Lake Ontario). The image conveys the prominence of native protocols of diplomacy in the attempted French exercise of empire in the vast reaches of the North American interior. From Baron Lahontan, New Voyages to North America *(London, 1703).*

AS BRITAIN'S PRINCIPAL colonial rivals, the Canadian French found paradoxical strengths in their weaknesses: their northern setting and small population. The colder climate and difficult access complicated British invasions, while New France's limited numbers reduced frictions with the Indians. As the British colonies grew in numbers, power, and ambition, the French increasingly looked to the Indians to protect Canada. Usually (but not always) less threatening to natives, the French could more readily recruit them against the expansive British. Although deficient for economic development, New France worked well as a militarized colony for harassing and hindering British expansion.

At the end of the seventeenth century, the French founded a new colony, named Louisiana, in the lower Mississippi Valley. As Spanish power faded in Florida after the destruction of their missions, the French in Louisiana became the chief rival for British Carolina in the American southeast. Like New France, Louisiana remained thinly populated and dependent upon Indian allies to counter the superior and growing numbers of British Americans. Together the French colonies of New France and Louisiana stretched from the Gulf of St. Lawrence to the Gulf of Mexico, sweeping around British America, confined to the Atlantic seaboard east of the Appalachian mountains. Despite their small numbers, the French claimed and affected more of the continent than did any other empire. In the vast Great Lakes country and Mississippi Valley, the thin French presence depended more on Indian consent than French power. By adapting to that reality, the French developed a distinctive mode of empire that long held the vast interior against their more numerous rivals, the British.

In Europe, French diplomats pretended that they commanded the Indians as subjects. In North America, French commanders knew better. In 1731 a governor-general informed his superior in Paris:

> I grant you [that] these nations would have become far more useful to the colony had we been able to subdue them little by little. If this has not been done, it is because we have found the task to be an impossible one; nor are there signs that it will become less so. Kindly apprise me of any means you should conceive of for securing such obedience.

Through generosity and restraint, the French could exercise some influence, but they could never command their Indian allies. The trader Nicolas Perrot grumbled at the natives' "arrogant notion that the French cannot get along without them and that we could not maintain ourselves in the colony without the assistance that they give us." But Perrot knew both to be true. Although more subtle and patient than their British rivals, French officials and priests only grudgingly accepted the limits on their power. In private correspondence, they vented their frustrations at, and even contempt for, the native peoples whom they had to treat publicly with great respect. Indeed, the proud individualism of the Indians contradicted the fundamental assumption of the French *ancien régime:* that a proper society had a status and power hierarchy that ranked everyone into relations of superiority and inferiority.

EMIGRANTS

Until 1663, Canada belonged to the fur-trading Company of New France, rather than to the French crown. The company saw little purpose and no profit in the costly business of transporting people to a colony dedicated to the fur trade. Because Indians did the work of the beaver hunt, the company needed only a few French employees, primarily soldiers to defend the post and clerks to handle the furs and the manufactured goods that purchased them. Moreover, additional colonists would probably set up in the fur trade for themselves, driving up the price of furs and driving down the company's profits.

Too late, the French learned that they needed more colonists to defend Quebec, not from the Indians, but from their English rivals, eager for easy pickings. In 1627, after nearly two decades of colonization, Quebec still had only eighty-five French colonists. Two years later, they were easily overwhelmed by three English privateers that sailed up the St. Lawrence River. In 1632 a peace treaty restored to the French a thoroughly plundered set of ruins.

Fearful of losing the colony again, the French crown ordered the Company of New France to recruit more inhabitants. The company farmed out the task to ambitious men of means, who could obtain immense colonial estates and titles of nobility as "seigneurs" by organizing and financing shipments of new colonists. During the 1660s many army officers posted in Canada also received "grants of seigneurie," provided that they stayed in the colony. By 1675, seventy seigneuries divided most of the land between Quebec and Montreal in the St. Lawrence Valley.

The seigneurs brought the first farm families to Canada, initiating a period of modest growth. Known as "habitants," the farmers introduced the northern European mode of agriculture, featuring crops of wheat and small herds of livestock. Although blessed with a fertile soil, the St. Lawrence Valley had the short growing season of a northern climate, which, in some years, brought killing frosts before the grains could ripen. In part because of the marginal growing season, New France grew slowly, from seven hundred colonists in 1650 to three thousand by 1663 (when another five hundred French inhabited Acadia).

Crown officials worried that the French were losing the demographic race to colonize North America. By 1660 the English had 58,000 colonists in New England and the Chesapeake. Growing impatient with New France's slow development and lingering insecurity, the crown took control of the colony in 1663. During the next decade, the crown stimulated emigration by paying for transatlantic passages.

The new emigrants came primarily from the northern and western seaports of France: Rouen, Nantes, Saint-Malo, La Rochelle, and Bordeaux, where merchant and crown recruiters could link poor and footloose young men with waiting ships. During the seventeenth century, fewer than 250 families emigrated to Canada, and only 12 percent of the immigrants were female. Instead, most emigrants were poor single young men like those who settled the English Chesapeake and West Indies. In search of work and food, these French men had moved to a port before some became sufficiently desperate to engage for service across the Atlantic in Canada. Most were urban laborers and artisans rather than rural peasants, which complicated their adjustment to a colony where most had to raise crops. Most of the female emigrants came from an orphanage in Paris and were known as *filles du roi* ("daughters of the king"). In addition to paying their passage, the crown provided a cash marriage dowry: an alluring incentive for orphan girls lacking family money.

Most male emigrants arrived in servitude, as either soldiers or indentured servants, known as *engagés*. Generally serving only a three-year term, the *engagés* were purchased and employed by seigneurs, habitants, merchants, or religious orders. The *engagés* loaded and unloaded ships, rowed boats, constructed buildings, and cleared the forest to make farms. Soldiers served long and indeterminate terms until the crown decided to demobilize some, when a rare peace permitted and exhausted royal finances demanded. During their service, the soldiers drilled, hauled supplies, constructed and repaired forts, and fought the Iroquois. The *filles du roi* were technically free but expected to marry within a few weeks of their arrival. They then became subject to the legal authority of their new husbands and served as housekeepers.

The expensive program of subsidized emigration produced relatively little long-term benefit. At the end of their terms, two-thirds of the *engagés* and three-quarters of the soldiers returned to France, despite official efforts to discourage their departure from Canada. Many men refused to indenture themselves without a prior commitment from their employer to pay for their return to France at the end of three years. Married men and women tended to stay, but the more numerous single men usually left.

The transient nature of most Canadian immigration contrasted with the English, who sent thousands of indentured servants overseas to stay. Unlike the English colonies, New France failed to develop a self-sustaining and self-financing chain migration as relatives and friends followed the first emigrants in growing numbers. Instead, the French colonial migration depended upon crown initiative and subsidy. After 1673, when the government retrenched to save money, the emigration ground to a halt.

Thereafter, the colonists' numbers grew through natural increase by the seed population introduced between 1663 and 1673. Fortunately, New

— French America, c. 1740 —

MIAMI	Native people
New York •	British town
New Orleans •	French town
PENSACOLA •	Spanish town

Hudson Bay
NEW FRANCE
Saguenay R.
Tadoussac
Quebec
MICMAC
Trois-Rivières
ABENAKI
OJIBWA
Lake Superior
Ottawa R.
Montreal
Kennebec R.
OTTAWA
St. Lawrence R.
Michilimackinac
Lake Huron
Fort Fontenac
BRITISH COLONIES
Albany
Mohawk R.
Green Bay
Lake Michigan
Mississippi R.
Lake Ontario
Connecticut R.
Boston
SAUK
Fort Niagara
SIX NATIONS
POTAWATOMI
Hudson R.
FOX
Detroit
Lake Erie
Susquehanna R.
Delaware R.
LENNI LENAPE
New York
Philadelphia
Fort St.-Louis
Illinois R.
Fort Crèvecœur
Potomac R.
SHAWNEE
ILLINOIS
Ohio R.
Missouri R.
MIAMI
James R.
ATLANTIC OCEAN
OSAGE
Cumberland R.
CHEROKEE
QUAPAW
Arkansas R.
Mississippi R.
Fort Prudhomme
Pee Dee R.
CHICKASAW
CATAWBA
Arkansas Post
UPPER CREEK
Coosa R.
Tallapoosa R.
LOUISIANA
Tombigbee R.
Savannah R.
Altamaha R.
Charles Town
NATCHEZ
Pearl R.
CHOCTAW
Alabama R.
Fort Toulouse
Chattahoochee R.
N
Red R.
Fort Rosalie
LOWER CREEK
PETITES NATIONS
Mobile
Biloxi
FLORIDA
PENSACOLA
St. Johns R.
SAN AGUSTIN
New Orleans
Gulf of Mexico
0 Miles 200 400
0 Kilometers 400

France enjoyed an especially high rate of natural increase that made the most of the emigrant minority that had persisted. Because the women married early and bore many healthy children, the birthrate of 55 per 1,000 inhabitants was a third higher than in France. From about 3,000 in 1663, the population grew to 15,000 in 1700: an impressive rate but from a very low base. This growth was too little too late to compete with the swelling number of English colonists, who numbered 234,000 whites plus 31,000 enslaved Africans by 1700.

Why did France, with a population of twenty million, the largest in western Europe and four times larger than England's five million, send far fewer emigrants to America? There was no higher standard of living in France to keep people at home (as there was in the Netherlands). On the contrary, if the push of hunger and poverty sufficed to generate emigration, France should have outdone England, for the French peasantry lived even closer to the bone than did the English poor. Indeed, recurrent famines killed thousands in rural France during the seventeenth century.

Cultural values and institutional obstacles blocked the overseas emigration by the more numerous and desperate masses of France. In contrast to England, in France the peasantry remained rooted to their land. The peasants' resistance, often violent, prevented their lords from adopting the English program of rural rationalization and enclosure that dispossessed and dislocated the English rural poor. Most French peasants clung to their little farms, which continued to shrink over the generations as parents divided them among several sons, for they knew no other way of life or form of security. In the mid-seventeenth century, 85 percent of French peasant families possessed fewer than thirteen acres—about the bare minimum for subsistence.

Despite the abundant miseries of French rural life, the peasants preferred to endure the known rather than risk the strange and distant. In 1636 a Jesuit priest promoted Canadian colonization: "There are so many strong and robust peasants in France who have no bread to put in their mouths; is it possible that they are so afraid of losing sight of the village steeple, as they say, that they would rather languish in their misery and poverty, than to place themselves some day at their ease among the inhabitants of New France?" Despite the hunger, the peasants did prefer to remain near their village steeple. Short-range moves to nearby villages were common; longer-distance migration beyond a region was not. Even men who left for a few years to obtain paying work usually returned home with their savings to buy a little land.

In tapping France's surprisingly small pool of long-distance roamers, Canada's recruiters faced some stiff competition from Spain, the West Indies, and the French army. Potential emigrants found a cheaper, closer, and far warmer alternative by walking to Spain (especially Catalonia and Valencia), where there was considerable demand for French artisans and laborers. In

1669 about 200,000 French lived in Spain, compared with only about 5,000 in New France. Most of the French who would emigrate to the Americas preferred the warmer climes of the West Indies, moving there in about ten times the numbers that went to Canada. Of course, like the English West Indians, most of the Caribbean French died within a few years as their penalty for bypassing healthier Canada. Finally, the swelling army of Louis XIV absorbed many of the poor and single men who might otherwise have emigrated as *engagés* to New France. Building the largest military in Europe, Louis XIV expanded his army from 20,000 men in 1661 to 300,000 in 1710. The crown did send a few regiments to Canada, but the great majority remained to fight in Europe.

And although France had plenty of religious dissidents, who might have been eager to emigrate, French policy forbade their settlement in New France after 1632. That restrictive policy deprived Canada of an especially promising set of colonists, the Protestant minority known as Huguenots, who resembled the English Puritans in their Calvinist faith and middling status as artisans, shopkeepers, and merchants. Instead of strengthening the French empire, at least 130,000 alienated Huguenots fled to the Protestant states of Switzerland, Germany, Holland, and England, especially after 1685, when King Louis XIV outlawed their faith. France's loss was Britain's gain, for about 10,000 Huguenots moved on across the Atlantic to strengthen British America.

Seventeenth-century New France also did not offer much of a pull for potential emigrants. Canada suffered from an especially daunting (although much overstated) reputation as an immoral, cold, and unprofitable land. Although very few criminals or prostitutes went to seventeenth-century New France, popular opinion insisted that they abounded, a gross exaggeration that deterred moralistic emigrants. From a lack of experience with frontier conditions, many French also balked at the hard work of clearing dense forests to make new farms. Worse still, the long and cold Canadian winter shocked newcomers from temperate France. A visitor commented that a Canadian needed glass eyes, a brass body, and brandy for blood to endure the bitter cold. When winter at last receded, warm weather unleashed tormenting clouds of mosquitoes and blackflies—denser and fiercer than any in Europe.

Because of the short growing season, Canadians could not produce the warm-climate staples in greatest European demand. Only a fool would attempt a sugar or tobacco plantation in Canada. Instead, the habitant raised European livestock and grains, especially wheat. Bulky hides and grains, however, could not profitably bear the high transportation costs dictated by Canada's northern isolation far up a long river, the St. Lawrence, which froze shut for half the year. A voyage from France to Quebec took twice as long and cost twice as much as one from the mother country to the West Indies. It rarely paid to ship Canadian livestock and grains to either France or the

French West Indies, and few ships visited Quebec in the early eighteenth century: only about twenty a year, arriving exclusively in the summer and early fall, primarily to haul furs away to France. In 1748 the governor-general conceded:

> We should never delude ourselves that our colonies on the continent . . . could ever rival the neighbouring English colonies in wealth, nor even be commercially very lucrative, for with the exception of the fur trade, the extent of which is limited and the profits continually declining, these colonies can furnish only goods similar to those of Europe at higher prices and of poorer quality.

Deprived of an export market for grain, the habitants relied on the limited local market, feeding fur traders and soldiers. Ultimately, the Canadian economy depended on the gold and silver spent by the crown to pay soldiers, purchase their supplies, and build forts. In most years the military expenditures exceeded the value of the fur trade. In effect, French taxpayers sustained the Canadian economy.

Potential emigrants also balked because of New France's reputation as a perilous land with especially savage enemies, the Iroquois. A frustrated Canadian governor described them:

> They are everywhere. They will stay hidden behind a stump for ten days, existing on nothing but a handful of corn, waiting to kill a man, or a woman. It is the cruelest war in the world. They are not content to burn the houses, they also burn the prisoners they take, and give them death only after torturing them continually in the most cruel manner they can devise.

The same Jesuit publications that exhorted emigration to New France also grimly detailed, without any sense of irony, Iroquois atrocities against settlers. Prior to 1663, New France suffered from a dilemma: the colony could not attract enough people for effective defense because the French balked at emigrating to such a dangerous land.

OPPORTUNITY

Most of the French who did emigrate to Canada (and stayed) significantly improved their status and standard of living, escaping their former poverty as landless laborers. At least 80 percent of the colonists lived as habitants, leasing farms of about one hundred acres—far larger than the peasant plots of the homeland. Indeed, a French officer noted:

> The ordinary habitants would be scandalized to be called peasants. In fact, they are of a better stuff, have more wit, more education, than those of France. This comes from their paying no taxes, that they have the right to hunt and fish, and that they live in a sort of independence.

Habitants took pride in their regular consumption of meat and white bread, which few French peasants could afford. Thanks to small, tight houses and plentiful firewood, the New French also kept warmer in the winter, despite its rigors and duration. And in contrast to their French relatives, the New French could afford horses, another cherished mark of higher status among peasants. Finally, the Canadian habitant enjoyed privileges of hunting and fishing—both of which were environmentally and legally denied to the peasants in crowded, depleted, and hierarchical France, where the aristocrats monopolized the limited supply of game.

Although greater than in the British colonies, the exactions of church and state in New France were much lighter than those endured by the captive peasantry of France. Chronically at war, the colony routinely conscripted habitants to serve in the military, to build roads and fortifications, to house and feed troops, and to provide grains or livestock at fixed rates to the army. But, in sharp contrast to France, there was no direct tax on either people or lands—merely export duties on furs and import duties on alcohol and tobacco. In Canada, the Catholic church also collected a so-called tithe, but it was set at only a twenty-sixth of the grain harvest—half the level taken in France. To make up the difference, the crown subsidized the Canadian church, paying a third of its expenses.

Lacking freehold land titles, the habitants leased their farms, paying annual rents to a seigneur, but so long as they paid, their tenure was secure and could be passed on to heirs or sold to others. Moreover, the rents were modest, usually less than 10 percent of the annual crop, for the seigneur had to offer attractive terms to draw people into an uncertain life so far from home. In the eighteenth century, after the population had grown and land assumed a higher value, the seigneur collected a more significant income from a second financial right: to one-twelfth of the purchase price when a habitant sold his farm to another. The habitant also had to mill his grain at the seigneur's gristmill, paying a toll of one sack of flour out of every fourteen. All three of these habitant payments to their seigneurs were significantly smaller than those that the French aristocrats extorted from their peasants.

Although most habitants lived comfortably, few became distinctly wealthier than their neighbors. A rough equality prevailed in rural New France, because of the limited opportunities to hire laborers or to sell a surplus on the market. The farms produced a diverse set of crops, usually in abundance, primarily for family subsistence and the local market rather than for export. The colony's limited economy and authoritarian government also discouraged entrepreneurial initiative and thrift in favor of leisure, consumption, spontaneity, and vivacity. Adapting to the cold, the habitants transformed winter into a cherished season of festive visiting, facilitated by horse-drawn sleighs, known as *carioles.* In 1749, after passing through the British colonies and New France, the Swedish traveler Peter Kalm declared:

> The inhabitants of Canada, even the ordinary man, surpasses in politeness by far those people who live in these English provinces. . . . On entering one of the peasants' houses, no matter where, and on beginning to talk with the men or women, one is quite amazed at the good breeding and courteous answers which are received, no matter what the question is.

Similarly, Pierre de Charlevoix, a Jesuit priest, concluded, "The English colonist amasses means and makes no superfluous expense; the French enjoys what he has and often parades what he has not."

Canadian emigration and settlement improved the status and conditions of the peasantry but had little effect on the legal and cultural subordination of women. As in France, people took for granted the patriarchal authority of the husband and father as divinely ordained and immutable. In a society where women were relatively few (until 1710), almost all quickly married. When widowed, they just as rapidly remarried. Many women vigorously defended their interests within marriage, but the law sided with any husband who resorted to force, provided it was "reasonable correction."

Most couples had to modify the power of patriarchy in their own daily practices. To operate a farm, men and women had to cooperate, dividing and sharing the immense and diverse labors of a household that produced almost all that they ate and wore. Women tended the poultry, cows, and garden as well as the kitchen and house. Given the chronic scarcity of labor, women also had to help in the field work, especially during harvest. Women married to artisans routinely made and sold goods for the market, and when a patriarch died, his widow ran the family enterprise until she remarried, or until a son came of age to assume the role.

Like Dutch law, French law treated wives as equal economic partners with their husbands—in contrast to English common law, which dissolved the wife's identity into that of her spouse. Civil contracts in New France (as in New Netherland) required the signatures of both husband and wife. At death, the widow inherited half the assets (and debts), while the children obtained the other half—a better split than the one-third that English widows ordinarily received.

In contrast to the Protestant British colonists, women in Catholic New France had an alternative to marriage and childbearing. They could embrace a life of celibacy and religious devotion in a convent in Montreal or Quebec, where nuns ran schools, asylums, and hospitals, providing a thicker network of social welfare than in the British colonies. Women governed these female organizations and kept them largely independent of control by the men who governed church and state. Because each novice had to pay a substantial dowry to enter a convent, most came from seigneurial or mercantile families. By paying convent dowries to place some daughters, parents could vest most of the family estate in fewer heirs, especially an elder son. In addition, the daily prayers of nuns for their families were a good investment for eternal salvation. Because of the entry cost and the demanding life of a nun, fewer than 4 percent of Canadian women entered a convent.

AUTHORITY

Compared with their British rivals, the French colonies reflected a more militaristic, paternalistic, and centralized form of authority. The demographic weakness and military peril of New France demanded a more frequent and total mobilization for defense. But the colony also reflected the greater concentration of power in the French monarchy, especially under the hyperambitious, resourceful, and egocentric Louis XIV, who reigned from 1661 to 1715. Ruling at home without any parliament, Louis relied upon the largest and best army in Europe to reward the nobility with officer commissions and to intimidate his common subjects. At the point of the bayonet, Louis raised extraordinary tax revenues from an impoverished population to sustain his vast army and growing navy. In the colonies, as at home, Louis expected his officials to govern by command.

The power of the crown, however, consistently fell short of total control. Although a despot, Louis also thought of himself as a benevolent father to his common subjects. To sustain that conceit, he and his officials occasionally exercised their power to protect the common people from some exactions and injustice inflicted by the aristocracy and merchants. In both France and New France, crown power was also diluted by its reliance on aristocratic officers and officials, who sometimes pursued their own interests at the expense of their royal master. Ambitious men looked to the crown for patronage, while common people expected the government to regulate prices to protect them from inflation and shortages. In New France as in France, the governing ethos was paternalistic and monarchical rather than commercial and libertarian.

To govern New France, the crown appointed three rival officials: a military governor-general, a civil administrator known as the intendant, and a Catholic bishop. The three were supposed to cooperate to enforce crown orders while competing for crown favor by jealously watching one another for corruption, heresy, and disloyalty. In theory, the governor-general was supreme, but the intendant controlled the finances and civil patronage that often endowed the seigneurs and habitants with greater wealth and influence.

The bishop supervised the parish clergy, the convents, and the seminaries. Competing for power, the three top officials attracted rival coteries of lesser officials and merchants, each striving for contracts and promotions. As in New Spain, this rivalry served the crown's interest in checking the governor-general from grasping sole power, but it also impeded efficient administration.

The bishop, governor-general, and intendant conducted an overlapping partnership between church and state. Hardened by long civil wars over religion, the crown regarded Catholic uniformity as essential to the political subserviency of its subjects. The New French authorities tolerated no other faith and punished as crimes the violation of Catholic social customs (by, for example, eating meat during Lent). On the other hand, Catholic New France conducted no witch-hunts, executing no one for occult practices, in sharp contrast to New England. Nor did the New French live up to their stereotype, in British minds, of docile and credulous dupes to manipulative priests. Although active religious dissidents were virtually unknown, the authorities frequently complained of popular indifference and even disrespect during services. In general, most colonists wore their Catholic faith lightly but comfortably, taking it for granted as essential to their way of life.

As in New Spain, but in contrast to the British colonies, the French established no elective assembly to represent the colonists. Instead the crown appointed a sovereign council, consisting of five to seven seigneurs, as well as the governor-general, bishop, intendant, and attorney general. Combining executive, legislative, and judicial functions, the sovereign council advised the governor-general, enacted local legislation, and served as the supreme court of appeal. Occasionally the governor-general and intendant convened public meetings in the three major towns—Montreal, Trois-Rivières, and Quebec—to air pressing issues. But these meetings were rare, purely advisory, and readily ignored. Because neither church nor state saw any point in educating the common people, there were no schools beyond the three major towns. Less than a quarter of the habitants could read and write. The colony published neither books nor newspapers, discouraging the development of a provincial intellectual life.

New France also lacked the town or county governments that permitted so much local autonomy in the British colonies. Instead, the French divided the St. Lawrence Valley into parishes, which combined civil, military, and ecclesiastical functions. Each had a church, a priest, and a militia company under a captain appointed by the intendant. Chronic warfare demanded, and the law required, every male between the ages of sixteen and sixty to serve in the militia, for mobilization on the frequent occasion of emergencies. The captains also served as agents of civil administration, informing the intendant of local problems, arresting criminals, and disseminating official ordinances. By design, the militia captain was a habitant rather than a seigneur—from a well-founded official fear that a seigneur invested with command would develop too much local power. Bypassing the seigneurs in the chain of military authority prevented the development of a true feudalism in the colony. Given the extensive autonomy of the habitants and the lack of seigneurial control over military fiefs, historians exaggerate when they characterize New France as a feudal society.

But that characterization has a germ of truth, for the seigneurial system enabled the French to transplant a version of Europe's hierarchical social order more successfully than did their British rivals. In New France, most officials and regular army officers were colonial aristocrats; in contrast, the other empires rarely considered any colonists good enough for ennoblement. About 5 percent of the Canadians belonged to seigneurial families. Pierre de Charlevoix noted that "in New France there are more nobles than in all the other colonies put together." Eschewing the rustic and sometimes dangerous life on their country estates, the seigneurs usually dwelled in Montreal and Quebec, where they could sustain a genteel society of dinner parties and balls. There the seigneurial families displayed their superior rank, serenely confident that God mandated subordination upon, and deference from, the common folk.

Noble birth and aristocratic honor, rather than acquired wealth, were the primary criteria of status and authority in New France. Indeed, both social custom and French law worked to perpetuate wealth and power in inherited hands, rather than to encourage the creation of new fortunes by ambitious commoners. Seigneurs were not supposed to compromise their honor by engaging in manual labor or entrepreneurial trade, and very rarely could habitants or merchants become seigneurs. Meant primarily to sustain rank and only secondarily to generate economic development, a seigneury could not legally be subdivided and sold, only leased to habitants. Consequently, the seigneurial system discouraged the land speculation so rampant in the British colonies with their more commercial ethos. In theory, social rank was immutable and law discouraged social mobility. The exception that proved the rule was Charles Le Moyne, who arrived in New France a penniless *engagé*, but eventually prospered in the fur trade and bought the rights to a seigneury, including the title and privileges of colonial nobility.

In New France, the crown also worked to reinforce social rank with assured prosperity. The colonial authorities favored the seigneurs with almost all of the commissions as regular army officers, salaries as civil officials, and coveted licenses to conduct the fur trade (although bourgeois managers did the work). The authorities reasoned that only men of aristocratic honor could command respect from the common people. In turn, the salaries of office or the profits of the fur trade were supposed to bolster the wealth that sustained honor in the proper people. When officers or officials died, their widows received annual government pensions to uphold their noble standard of living.

But the number of army commissions, civil offices, and fur trade licenses lagged behind the proliferating children of seigneurial families. Inhibited from entering trade by their code of nobility, growing numbers dwelled in genteel indolence and poverty. In 1737 a priest reported that many seigneurial families were "as poor as artists and as vain as peacocks." Charlevoix noted, "There is a great fondness for keeping up one's position, and nearly no one amuses himself by thrift. Good cheer is supplied, if its provision leaves means enough to be well clothed; if not, one cuts down on the table in order to be well dressed." Appearances mattered in New France.

THE UPPER COUNTRY

During the early eighteenth century, New France consisted of two very different sectors: the narrow, cultivated St. Lawrence Valley and the vast interior of forest and lakes known as the upper country. In the valley the French practiced colonization by settlement; in the interior they exercised a dispersed empire of trade.

The great majority of the New French dwelled on a long but narrow thread of farms strung along both banks of the St. Lawrence River between Quebec and Montreal. A visitor traveling by boat along the river could see most of the farms in the colony: an impressive succession of whitewashed stone houses and wooden barns roofed with thatch. Periodically, the traveler also saw larger stone structures: windmills, steepled churches, and the manor houses of seigneurs. The roads were few and bad, but people and their goods primarily moved by sleighs in winter and by canoe or boat along the river in summer.

After 1700, hard labor, rapid reproduction, and peace with the Iroquois brought greater security, prosperity, and development to the valley. From 15,000 in 1700, the population grew to 52,000 by 1750. The amount of cleared and cultivated land, the size of the wheat harvest, and the number of mills all tripled.

In the valley, natives persisted in several mission reserves beside the larger settler population. A mix of Montagnais, Huron, Abenaki, Algonkin, and Mohawk, the mission Indians had reached a compromise with their priests, who tacitly accepted much traditional custom and ritual that did not directly contradict Catholic worship. The mission Indians also remained highly mobile, freely coming and going from their mission villages. At home, they practiced a mix of Indian and European horticulture, but they continued to disperse annually for months to hunt for meat and furs in the hinterland.

Because the mission Indians provided warriors essential to the defense of Canada, the French felt obliged to respect their autonomy. A French official warned, "If we do not agree, or do not pretend to agree, to their rights over the country which they occupy, never will we be able to engage them in any war for the defense of this same country, which is the first line of defense of Canada." The measure of French restraint came when a mission Indian killed an unlucky Frenchman, usually a trader in a drunken dispute. The colonial authorities dared not attempt an arrest and trial, for the mission Indians refused to submit to French law. Instead, the officials had to accept the native ceremony of "covering the grave": the ceremonial delivery of presents from the Indians to the relatives of the deceased to settle the murder. These ceremonies indicate that even where outnumbered and converted to Catholicism, the Canadian Indians remained sovereign peoples rather than French subjects. This certainly contrasted with the legal treatment of those Indians who remained on enclaves within the British settlements.

Beyond Montreal across the Great Lakes to the Mississippi, the immense hinterland of New France hosted only a few scattered colonists dependent upon the fur trade with their Indian hosts. In the upper country, the French were a mix of missionaries, traders, soldiers, and habitants. The upper-country French lived in a few far-flung settlements near forts, principally at Cahokia, Kaskaskia, and Vincennes in the Illinois country or at Detroit between Lakes Huron and Erie. In 1750 a mere 261 French soldiers garrisoned all of the posts around the Great Lakes. Perhaps another 2,000 French were traders or habitants in the upper country. The largest town, Detroit, had only 600 residents.

Powerful at Quebec, the fortified colonial capital, the authority of the crown progressively dissipated over the immense distances of the Great Lakes country. In the vast reaches of forest, prairie, and lakes, the French lived as a small minority on reserves among about eighty thousand native inhabitants. The distant post commandants operated as petty barons, often ignoring the uninformed orders of their distant superiors in Quebec and Paris. The commandants felt far more constrained by the superior power of Indian numbers—given their critical importance to prosecuting the fur trade and defending the posts.

In the upper country, the Indians and the French gradually developed an effective alliance based upon mutual accommodations on what the historian Richard White has called "the middle ground." A middle ground could develop and endure only where neither natives nor colonizers could dominate the other, but instead they had to join together to craft new customs and rhetoric to deal with each other as near equals. Already at odds with the formidable Iroquois, the French needed the western Indians as allies and could not afford them as enemies. In the weakness of colonial power, the upper country contrasted sharply with the Chesapeake and New England, where the English rapidly and callously settled in numbers that overwhelmed the natives.

During the 1640s and 1650s, the Iroquois' attacks had destroyed or dispersed their many native enemies dwelling around the eastern Great Lakes. The outgunned and desperate survivors fled westward to refuges on the upper Illinois River, the southern shore of Lake Superior, and the western shore of Lake Michigan. Each cluster of refugee villages hosted diverse peoples: a mix of Fox, Sauk, Mascouten, Potawatomi, Kickapoo, Miami, Ojibwa, Ottawa, Wyandot, Winnebago, Menominee, and Illinois. The Wyandot were Iroquian-speakers and the Winnebago had a Siouan language, but most of the refugee peoples were Algonquian-speakers.

Life was hard in the refugee villages. Despite the broad depopulated buffer zone created by their flight, the inhabitants faced continuing attacks from the relentless Iroquois. The refugees also suffered from famines, because, crowding together for safety in numbers, they exhausted local supplies of fish, deer, and maize. Often hungry, they were especially vulnerable to the diseases introduced by French traders and priests.

The refugees also fought among themselves, for the diverse peoples had long traditions of distrust as well as new frustrations. Disputes over fishing places and hunting grounds, as well as accusations of witchcraft, led to murders, which provoked revenge killings in an apparently unbreakable cycle. Some especially embittered bands even conspired with Iroquois raiders to destroy other refugees. The peoples needed both a means to settle their many disputes and access to trade goods, especially firearms. During the 1680s they obtained both from the French, who needed the refugees as trading partners and allies to consolidate their control over the fur trade of the interior.

The Iroquois destruction of the Huron during the 1640s had disrupted the French fur trade. In 1653 the Jesuits reported, "For a year the warehouse at Montreal has not bought a single beaver from the Indians." Unable to rely on Huron purveyors to bring Great Lakes furs to Montreal, the French traders instead had to travel hundreds of miles westward to seek out the "far Indians" of the Great Lakes and Illinois countries. During the 1660s and 1670s, French priests and traders crossed the Great Lakes in canoes to find and follow the river routes to the Mississippi.

During the 1670s and 1680s French traders established a far-flung network of small fortified posts around the Great Lakes and in the Illinois country. The most important post was at Michilimackinac, an island near the strategic intersection of Lakes Michigan, Huron, and Superior. At Michilimackinac the French freely traded guns for furs, enabling the refugees to close their arms gap with the Iroquois. In 1683 the crown took responsibility for the posts, providing small garrisons. Despite their isolation and dangers, these distant posts attracted ambitious officers eager to make their fortune by engaging in the fur trade on the side (although this was contrary to their explicit orders from France).

The better to supervise and tax, French officials tried to limit the fur trade to the forts, but a growing number of young, independent, and defiant traders, known as *coureurs de bois*, paddled their canoes far beyond the posts to trade with the natives at their own villages. In 1680 the intendant investigated but complained, "I have been unable to ascertain the exact number because everyone associated with them covers up for them."

From the natives, the *coureurs de bois* learned the patterns of the rivers and seasons, the rudiments of Indian languages, and the native ways of trade, war, and love. Alone or in small groups, these traders ventured into a dangerous world, where even native allies sometimes killed to steal their goods, to keep weapons from reaching their enemies, to avenge a previous killing by another Frenchman, or to satisfy a drunken rage. In 1684 alone, thirty-nine French traders died at the hands of their allies. A trader lived longer and did more business if he entered a partnership with an Indian woman and obtained her kin network, which provided the best security in the native world. She was also the best teacher of native ways and languages, a helpmate in the labors of the fur trade, and a source of friendship and pleasure.

Far more readily than their English or Dutch competitors, the French traders married native women, which proved critical to their persistent predominance in the fur trade of the Great Lakes country. Indian women overcame their initial dislike of the pale and bearded French as ugly. Owing to war losses, Indian men had become relatively scarce, and the *coureurs de bois* offered their wives and Indian kin privileged access to the coveted trade goods of Europe. Over the generations, these relationships produced a distinctive mixed-blood people known as the *métis*, who spoke multiple languages, lived in their own villages, and acted as intermediaries between their French and Indian relatives.

The officials of church and state regarded the *coureurs de bois* with profound ambivalence. On the one hand, they were disreputable and insubordinate people who traded brandy, slept with native women, and evaded oversight by priest and seigneur. In 1680, *coureurs de bois* employed in Illinois by Sieur de La Salle ran away, demolished his fort, stole his goods, and left a graffito: *Nous sommes touts Sauvages* ("We are all savages"). This declaration played upon the greatest fear among the official French: that their common people would prefer anarchic barbarism to hierarchical civilization. On the other hand, their contact with the natives rendered the *coureurs de bois* essential sources of information and conduits for influence. In sum, the *coureurs de bois* simultaneously represented and blurred the power of empire projected far from Quebec. After failing to recall the *coureurs de bois*, the colonial authorities had to make the best of them.

To build a native alliance, the French needed more than a supply of trade guns and a network of *coureurs de bois*. Above all, the French had to unify the fractious refugees of the Great Lakes and Illinois countries, which required the arbitration of their many disputes. A Jesuit noted, "It is absolutely necessary to keep all these tribes . . . in peace and union against the common enemy—that is, the Iroquois." In the Indians' dissensions, the French saw an opportunity to make themselves indispensable. In 1681 the intendant advised the French to "take cognizance of all their differences, . . . to watch carefully that not one of them terminate without our mediation and to constitute ourselves in all things their arbiters and protectors."

In the native world there was no mediation, no meaningful public action, without the delivery of gifts. Words were pointless and no agreement was binding unless accompanied by presents. The greater the ceremony and the offerings involved, the more serious and binding the agreement. Unlike the refugee peoples, who suffered from deprivation as well as violence, the French alone possessed the means—trade goods—essential to the ceremonies and agreements needed to reconcile so many clashing peoples. French brandy, cloth, blankets, kettles, knives, hatchets, guns, shot, and gunpowder became critical to restoring peace.

To put an end to their divisive cycle of revenge killings, the French assumed the ritual role of bestowing presents to "cover the graves" of the dead. The ritual and the gifts persuaded the kin of the murdered to forsake revenge, and it obligated the relatives of the murderer to reciprocate by seeking Iroquois scalps. Reluctantly, the French officers even had to accept ritual compensation from natives who killed French traders, rather than attempt to punish the suspects as criminals.

The middle ground rested on creative misunderstandings. The French said that their king and his officials, especially the governor-general, were the "fathers" to Indian "children." Of course, the French understood the relationship as hierarchical, enabling them as superiors to command their native inferiors as the dutiful children of a European patriarch. The Indians accepted the terminology only because they understood it very differently, for they did not have patriarchal families. In their matrilineal kinship systems, mothers and uncles had far more authority than did fathers. The natives happily called the French their "fathers" in the expectation that they would behave like Indian fathers: indulgent, generous, and weak. Among Indians, a father gave much more than he received.

In return for their presents, the French expected to buy Indian obedience. In fact, the chief who received French presents usually could influence only his particular lineage within a given village. He could not, as the French wished, command an entire village, much less a whole tribe. Chiefs repeatedly tried to explain to the governor-general:

> Father: It is not the same with us as with you. When you command, all the French obey and go to war. But I shall not be heeded and obeyed by my nation in a like manner. Therefore, I cannot answer except for myself and for those immediately allied or related to me.

To sway an entire village, the French had to reward multiple chiefs with sufficient presents to satisfy their several lineages. The presents did carry French influence into native villages, for the chiefs with presents had more clout than those without. But the French could not demand too much of their clients, for a heavy-handed chief quickly lost influence and risked assassination. The French always felt that they expended too much in presents to purchase too little in control.

Armed by and allied with the French, the upper-country Indians inflicted bloody defeats on their former tormentors, the Iroquois, during the 1680s and 1690s. In 1701 the beleaguered Iroquois made a peace that conceded the upper country to the French and their allies. Although an apparent French triumph, the peace of 1701 actually weakened their native alliance. Deprived of a common Iroquois enemy, the allies felt secure enough both to disperse and to find new grievances against one another. Abandoning their refuges in Illinois and Wisconsin, several native peoples headed east, reoccupying the former buffer zone north of the Ohio River and south of the Great Lakes. In 1701 the French foolishly assisted that drift by founding a new, stockaded settlement at Detroit, which replaced the more distant Michilimackinac as the principal French post in the Great Lakes country. Unfortunately for the French, the shift eastward brought their allies closer to Iroquois diplomats and British traders, who worked to seduce the allies by proffering British manufactured goods, which were cheaper than their French counterparts.

The French also miscalculated by reducing their expenditures for western forts and Indian presents. With the Iroquois apparently defeated, the French indulged in the fantasy that the Indians of the upper country would have to accept French dictation. In fact, diminished mediation and presents dissipated French influence among their dispersing and wrangling allies. Without mediation by the French, revenge killings accelerated among the Indians, who also killed French traders for any perceived partiality to their enemies.

In 1712 the crisis came at Detroit, where the French had attracted too many Indians from diverse tribes, too many for their limited presents to mediate or for the local deer and beaver to sustain. The Indian frictions polarized as an alliance of Fox and Mascouten antagonized a larger array of Illinois, Miami, Ojibwa, Wyandot, Potawatomi, and Ottawa peoples. The latter array demanded French assistance, threatening to destroy Detroit if denied. Unable to prevent war, the French chose the stronger side, supplying arms, ammunition, and some soldiers. Driven from their villages, the Fox suffered about one thousand killed or captured. The survivors fled west to their kin who had remained in the Wisconsin country. Seeking revenge, the western Fox killed French traders and their Indian friends.

When it served their interest, the French could match the brutality of the British and Spanish toward their Indian enemies. Determined to prove French power, Governor-General Beauharnois vowed to obliterate the Fox, ordering his subordinates to "kill them without thinking of making a single prisoner, so as not to leave one of the race alive in the upper country." Satisfied with crippling the Fox, the other Indians of the upper country saw no point in destroying them. Indeed, they took fright at the French intransigence. In 1712 the Indian allies had launched the Fox wars and obliged the reluctant French to assist, but the allies wisely deserted during the 1730s, when the French took command and turned the war into an exercise in imperial fantasies. In 1737 a frustrated Beauharnois explained to his superior in France, "You may imagine, Monseigneur, that the Savages have their policy as we have Ours, and that they are not greatly pleased at seeing a nation destroyed for Fear that their turn may come."

Abandoned by their allies, the French again had to recognize the real limits on their power by making a grudging peace with the Fox. Yet another governor discovered that the French could exercise a limited empire only by patiently and expensively providing trade, mediation, and presents. Never stable, the middle ground alliance required constant attention from, and generosity by, the French.

LOUISIANA

During the 1670s and 1680s, at the same time that the English founded Carolina, French traders and priests probed southwestward from their trading posts along the Great Lakes into the Mississippi Valley. In 1682 the Sieur de La Salle led a party of French and allied Indians down the river to the Gulf of Mexico. Returning to France, La Salle impressed King Louis XIV with the Mississippi's enormous strategic and economic potential. To flatter his king, La Salle named the valley and adjoining Gulf Coast "Louisiana." But he warned that the French needed to act quickly before the English could occupy the river's mouth.

In 1684, La Salle returned to the Gulf of Mexico by sea from France. Unable to locate the river's mouth, La Salle planted his fortified settlement at Matagorda Bay on the Texas coast, miscalculating that the Mississippi lay nearby. Poorly located and led, the colony collapsed as the starving French mutinied, assassinating La Salle in 1687. The remaining colonists then succumbed to attack by the local Karankawa Indians, who more than a century before had hosted Cabeza de Vaca.

Despite La Salle's debacle, the French sent additional expeditions, both south from Canada and by sea from France, to occupy Louisiana. In 1686, Canadian traders established Arkansas Post, a fur-trading post among the Quapaw people near the juncture of the Arkansas River with the Mississippi. Pierre Le Moyne d'Iberville led two naval expeditions to explore the Gulf Coast. He rediscovered the mouth of the Mississippi and founded small fortified settlements at Biloxi Bay (1699) and Mobile Bay (1702). Upon returning home in 1702, Iberville entrusted the colony to his brother, Jean Baptiste le Moyne, Sieur de Bienville, who usually governed Louisiana thereafter, until 1740.

Lacking settlers, the French hoped to dominate the interior of North

America by linking Canada with Louisiana via a system of fortified trading posts attached to a network of Indian allies. Small and dispersed, the posts could not survive without native support. Instead of intimidating the Indians, the posts served as nodes of trade and negotiation for maintaining alliances.

In Louisiana, the French made expanding trade, rather than religious conversions, their priority in Indian relations. Unlike Canada's French in the mid-seventeenth century, the Louisiana French sustained no significant missionary effort. The shift registered the apparent lesson learned in the destruction of the Jesuit missions in Huronia during the 1640s and of the Franciscan missions in Florida between 1704 and 1706. In both cases, Indian traditionalists armed with trade muskets devastated native peoples weakened and divided by the provocative presence of Christian missionaries. From Carolina's success and Florida's failure, the French concluded that a commerce in guns better secured native support than did missionaries. Determined to compete with the Carolina traders, the French in Louisiana wooed the Indians with trade goods, especially firearms.

But rather than copy the Carolina traders, the French initially promised that an alternative system of commerce would reduce slave-raiding. With good cause, the French regarded the Carolina slave trade as dangerously unstable. And the French saw an opportunity to unite and arm the many southeastern natives who had long suffered from English-led slavers. Instead of consuming native peoples, the French wished to stabilize most of them, to serve as enduring allies defending the margins of their colony and keeping the English at a safe distance.

In designing their alternative to the Spanish mission system and the Carolina slave trade, the French drew upon their experience in rallying the upper-country Indians against the Iroquois. As in the middle ground of the Great Lakes, the Louisiana French built an alliance by providing arbitration and presents to make peace between enemies. In particular, the French initially tried to reconcile the Choctaw and Chickasaw, who shared the hinterland east of the Mississippi and north of the Gulf. The Choctaw and Chickasaw possessed kindred cultures and spoke dialects of a common language. They had shared a confederacy until a bitter rupture during the mid-seventeenth century. Although smaller in number, the Chickasaw were winning their bloody civil war because they had obtained English muskets in return for slaves taken from the poorly armed Choctaw. Iberville estimated that during the 1690s the Chickasaw had suffered eight hundred casualties in killing eighteen hundred Choctaw and enslaving another five hundred.

In 1702, Iberville convened Chickasaw and Choctaw delegations at Mobile Bay for a peace council. He proposed that the Choctaw and Chickasaw engage only in deer hunting and deliver the skins exclusively to a new French trading post. To demonstrate the wages of peace, Iberville bestowed generous presents of guns, powder, shot, axes, knives, kettles, and beads in equal quantities on both delegations. The Chickasaw and Choctaw agreed to make peace—and Louisiana seemed secured to France. But both that peace and the infant colony remained weak and vulnerable to the growing strength of Carolina, which worked to reclaim the Chickasaw as clients and raiders.

During the long and hard-fought War of the Spanish Succession (1702–13), the French could spare few men and resources to defend and develop their newest colony. Far from its mother country, Louisiana languished as the most peripheral colony in an overstretched empire. In 1708, Louisiana consisted of merely 122 soldiers and sailors, 80 slaves, and 77 habitants, scattered along the Gulf Coast. Instead of developing plantations, the early colonists lived by a mix of fishing, subsistence gardening, livestock herding, wildlife hunting, and petty trading with the natives.

After the war, to stimulate development, the crown entrusted Louisiana to a private corporation, the Company of the Indies, which promoted plantations to cultivate tobacco and indigo. In 1718, the company shifted the focus of the colony from the sandy Gulf Coast to the fertile Mississippi Valley by establishing New Orleans about 125 miles above the mouth of the river. Set amid rich alluvial lands reclaimed from the swamps, New Orleans became the colony's largest town, principal seaport, and government headquarters. To attract settlers, the Company of the Indies freely granted long but narrow riverfront farms of about 170 acres each.

Between 1717 and 1730, at considerable expense, the Company of the Indies transported 5,400 European colonists and 6,000 African slaves to Louisiana. The slaves primarily came from the coasts of Senegal and Benin in West Africa. Most of the Europeans were French, but a substantial minority (about 1,300) were German Catholics, who proved the most industrious and prosperous of the early colonists. Because few French volunteered to colonize distant and alien Louisiana, the company relied on military conscripts and convicted criminals (a mix of vagrants, blasphemers, thieves, smugglers, tax evaders, political prisoners, and prostitutes). To a far greater degree than in Canada, the French used Louisiana as a penal colony, which further undermined its reputation. In 1720 a colonial official complained, "What can one expect from a bunch of vagabonds and wrong-doers in a country where it is harder to repress licentiousness than in Europe?" Regarded with contempt by most officials and officers, the common colonists reciprocated with insubordination.

The early colonists were overwhelmed by the daunting challenge of making farms in a subtropical environment with extreme variations of temperature and rainfall. The swampy landscape and the hot and humid summers promoted dysentry and malaria, while the dense vegetation exhausted axmen. Regular spring flooding of the Mississippi and periodic hurricanes ruined crops and hard-built farms, necessitating laborious reconstruction. After the floods, it seemed a cruel joke that summer sometimes brought droughts that withered the crops. In 1734, Louisiana officials moaned, "This country is subject to such great vicissitude that one can almost not count on the crops at all. Now there is too much drought, now too much rain."

The hardships of the ocean crossing, chronic food shortages, and the shock of a challenging new environment took a grim toll. Hundreds died, while others fled to Spanish Florida—never previously considered an attractive destination. In 1721, Bienville reported, "Death and disease are disrupting and suspending all operations and, if the famine does not end, all is lost. The best workers are dead." Pierre de Charlevoix noted, "Numbers died of misery or disease, and the country was emptied as rapidly as it had filled." Only a third of the European emigrants remained alive in Louisiana in 1731, when the colonial population numbered two thousand whites and four thousand Africans. In 1733 a gloomy official warned, "Little by little, the colony is destroying itself."

Conditions, however, improved during the 1740s as the surviving colonists acquired partial immunities to the fevers and developed sufficient farms to feed themselves. A priest described the course of a successful farmer:

> A man with his wife or his partner clears a little ground, builds himself a house on four piles, covers it with sheets of bark, and plants corn and rice for his provisions; the next year he raises a little more for food, and has also a field of tobacco; if at last he succeeds in having three or four Negroes, then he is out of his difficulties.

Despite the virtual cessation of both European emigration and slave imports after 1731, the Louisiana population grew by natural increase to 4,100 slaves, 3,300 settlers, and 600 soldiers by 1746. Nearly three-quarters of the colonists lived on the lower Mississippi near New Orleans. At its core, Louisiana was a plantation colony with an enslaved African majority, a much poorer and smaller version of South Carolina, which had 41,000 slave and 20,000 free colonists in 1745.

Louisiana failed to develop a profitable export staple. The planters raised inferior grades of tobacco and indigo that sold in France for less than the high costs of production and shipment. Shipping was usually scarce and always expensive, because the voyage around Florida and across the Atlantic was very long and dangerously exposed to pirates, sandbars, and hurricanes. Because many mariners refused to sail to Louisiana, planters often could not ship their crop before it spoiled and usually had to pay prohibitive freight charges. Only crown subsidies sustained the plantation sector, and the colony continued to depend upon the deerskin trade with the Indians. During the 1720s the Louisiana French collected about fifty thousand deerskins annually, compared with the sixty thousand obtained by the Carolina traders.

In addition to its underdeveloped economy, Louisiana suffered from an arbitrary government. A governor commanded the troops and conducted

Indian diplomacy, while the commissary (the equivalent of Canada's intendant) served as the chief fiscal officer, overseeing funds and supplies. After 1712 they also convened a council of leading colonists, which served as an advisory body and supreme court, but Louisiana had no elected assembly.

Unchecked by an electorate and far from imperial supervision, the Louisiana officials were notoriously corrupt. Appalled at their low salaries and the high cost of living, the officials seized every opportunity to line their own pockets, embezzling crown funds and misappropriating government supplies, ships, and labor. Violating their instructions, the governors also invested in pirate ships and smuggled contraband to and from the Spanish colonies. In 1723 a colonist complained, "In short, this is a country which, to the shame of France be it said, is without religion, without justice, without discipline, without order, and without police."

Lacking a profitable economy and suffering from corrupt government, the colony cost much more to administer than it yielded in revenue. After losing 20 million livres on Louisiana, the bankrupt Company of the Indies surrendered the colony to the French crown in 1731. Thereafter Louisiana remained a financial liability, costing the government a net loss of 800,000 livres annually at mid-century. In the French imperial scheme, Louisiana was the least valuable colony, lagging behind even Canada, to say nothing of the valuable French West Indies. Indeed, the jealous and powerful planters of St. Domingue, Martinique, and Guadeloupe exerted their considerable influence to hamper the development of Louisiana as a competitor. As with New France, the crown retained Louisiana primarily for its strategic value in confining the British colonies to the east.

Like the Carolinians, the Louisiana officials worked to keep Indians and Africans apart, lest they combine to destroy the colony. The French fostered animosity to employ each against the other. In 1731, Bienville observed:

> The greatest misfortune which could befall the colony and which would inevitably lead to its total loss would be a union between the Indian nations and the black slaves, but happily there has always been a great aversion between them which has been much increased by the war, and we take great care to maintain it.

To sow antipathies, the French conspicuously employed especially trusted blacks in their militias sent to fight the Indians. A few particularly courageous black soldiers won their freedom as a reward. On the other hand, colonial leaders periodically punished rebel slaves by turning them over to Indians for burning to death. A French priest said that the executions "inspired all the Negroes with a new horror of the Savages, . . . which will have a beneficial effect in securing the safety of the Colony."

But in Louisiana, in contrast to Carolina, the elite also distrusted their own lower-class whites as little better (and perhaps worse) than Indians or enslaved Africans. The French elite regarded their soldiers with particular contempt. Bienville lamented, "It is exceedingly painful for an officer, who is entrusted with the destinies of a colony, to have nothing better to defend her [with] than a band of deserters, of smugglers, and of rogues, who are ever ready, not only to abandon their flag, but to turn their arms against their country." When a slave assaulted a planter or officer, he could expect to be broken on the wheel, but a slave who crippled a common soldier merely suffered the loss of an ear and a flogging. The elite reasoned that a slave was too valuable to be executed for injuring a cheaper and more expendable soldier.

The rigid class system of eighteenth-century France led officers and officials to exploit and punish common soldiers as brutes. Their woefully inadequate pay was a quarter of what Spanish colonial soldiers received. Worse still, corrupt officers often embezzled their pay and resold provisions and clothing meant for them. A sympathetic observer wrote, "It is pitiful to see them as they are all naked and most living on crushed and boiled Indian corn. . . . Besides these said soldiers are not paid at all, so they can only be very dissatisfied." Despite incredible dangers and hardships, many deserted to seek refuge among the Indians, the Spanish in Florida, or the English in Carolina. In 1739, some soldiers and slaves cooperated to escape by boat to Spanish Cuba. In the longest flight, in 1748, three deserters crossed the Great Plains to find refuge in Spanish New Mexico.

Instead of alleviating the harsh conditions that spawned desertion, the commanders relied on brutal punishments to intimidate their soldiers. If convicted of mutiny, the lucky died on the gallows; others suffered slow deaths as their backs were broken on the wheel or severed by saws. To maintain the racial divisions essential to Louisiana's security, the officers relied on Indians and blacks to track down and punish deserters. Military tribunals often specified that insubordinate soldiers be flogged by a black man. In 1721 the garrison at Fort Toulouse, in the Creek country, mutinied and fled eastward, seeking escape to Carolina. Offered French rewards, Creek warriors pursued and overwhelmed the deserters, killing eighteen and returning the rest to their post. A court-martial sentenced the leading deserter, a sergeant, to be tomahawked by the Creek.

Regarded as felons and vagrants, the settlers and soldiers of Louisiana found that a white skin brought them far less privilege than it did the common people of Carolina. Louisiana officials routinely used torture to execute white soldiers and indentured servants. By contrast, the British colonists reserved such treatment exclusively for their African property. To execute convicted whites, Louisiana employed a black man, Louis Congo, who drove a hard bargain for his services as executionor: freedom for himself and his wife, a plot of land, a steady supply of alcohol, and generous fees levied in pounds of tobacco—ten for a flogging or branding, thirty for a hanging, and forty for breaking on the wheel or burning alive.

In sum, the Louisiana elite pitted *all* of the races against one another, relying on blacks and natives to control lower-class whites, just as they employed Africans and Indians against one another. This contrasted with the British colonial tendency toward a greater, formal equality and liberty for all white men, as they increasingly equated freedom with the white race and their property rights over Africans. Relative to the French, the British colonists enjoyed greater liberties from, and voice within, their government—and more shared power over slaves.

In part, the differing equations of race and class represented the contrasting cultural heritages of their different mother countries: Britain's libertarian tradition compared with the more authoritarian ethos of France. And in part, the differences reflected the persistent demographic and economic weakness of the Louisiana colony. Lacking numbers, Louisiana officials felt deeply vulnerable to attack, especially as the English colonial population soared. To compensate, the French maintained a regular military garrison in Louisiana, which had no English counterpart in the southern colonies. Vulnerability and a garrison government reinforced the French authoritarian tradition. As the English colonists grew even more numerous, prosperous, and confident, they developed their white racial solidarity and popular government, which compounded the insecurity of the French officials, who clung more tightly to their harsh and divisive methods of social control.

REBELS AND ALLIES

Selective settlement divided the vast colony of Louisiana into two very different landscapes: a small plantation core remade by settlers; and an immense hinterland dominated by Indians. In the interior, the French presence was confined to a few small and scattered forts, each garrisoned by fewer than fifty men and all held hostage to the goodwill of the surrounding natives. French officials claimed that they had a particular gift for understanding and conciliating Indians, but their claim was only half true. In fact, the bifurcated colonial landscape of Louisiana drove two very different French policies toward the Indians (as had the similarly bifurcated landscape of New Netherland). In the hinterland, where the French lacked numbers, they made a virtue of their weakness by cultivating some natives as their cherished allies (while manipulating others as necessary enemies). But in the plantation core, where the colonists and their slaves were numerous, the French treated natives as callously as did any other Europeans.

Along the Gulf Coast and the Mississippi Delta, the French dealt with many small tribes, including the Acolapissa, Atakapa, Bayogoula, Biloxi, Capina, Chaouacha, Chitimacha, Colapissa, Houma, Mobile, Moctobi, Mongoulacha, Ouacha, Opelousa, Pascagoula, and Tohome. For convenience, the French lumped them together as the "Petites Nations." Once numerous, these peoples had been depleted during the seventeenth century by exposure to the diseases and slave raids introduced by Spanish explorers and English traders. The Petites Nations welcomed the French as potential liberators, offering the arms and other trade goods that the coastal natives desperately needed. By providing food, the Petites Nations preserved the vulnerable French settlements during their difficult early years.

But, as soon as the French grew secure in greater numbers, they abandoned gratitude. On their periphery, the French posed as emancipators of Indians enslaved by the English, but at the core they imposed slavery on any of the Petites Nations that defied their power. In 1706, when some Chitimacha killed a French priest, the French destroyed their village and enslaved the women and children. In 1729, the governor armed black slaves to massacre the sleeping Chaouacha in their village, as a grim example to keep "the other little nations up the river in a respectful attitude." Ignoring an imperial prohibition, Bienville developed a slave trade with the French West Indies, exchanging two Indians for one African.

Exposed to alcohol, disease, and violence, the Petites Nations dwindled from 24,000 in 1685 to just 4,000 in 1730. Bienville noted:

> It is known that this country . . . was formerly the most densely populated with Indians, but at present of these prodigious quantities of different nations one sees only pitiful remnants . . . which are diminishing every day because of the different diseases that the Europeans have brought into the country and which were formerly unknown to the Indians.

Rendered a weak minority in their former homelands, the survivors accepted French domination, surrendering most of their land to provide plantations and farms for the colonists. Dwelling in small enclaves on the margins of a plantation society, the Petites Nations survived by trading fish, venison, garden produce, and baskets to their colonial neighbors and by laboring as boatmen, porters, and slave-catchers.

Farther up the Mississippi, at Natchez, a dangerous uncertainty developed over the relative power of the French and the local Indians. The Natchez people preserved substantial elements of the Mississippian culture, including ceremonial mounds, painted and carved temples, and powerful chiefs who, in death, were honored with the human sacrifice of their servants. During the 1720s the French expanded their tobacco plantations up the Mississippi and built Fort Rosalie near the Natchez villages. Although the local French numbered only about 550 colonists and 200 slaves, they bullied the 1,800 Natchez as if they were a subjugated Petite Nation. Encroaching French planters provoked growing friction, especially when their roaming livestock invaded Natchez cornfields. When the Natchez began to kill and eat the offending animals, the French commandant demanded a tribute payment to compensate the colonists.

Outraged by the demands and indignities, the Natchez blamed themselves for welcoming the newcomers and depending upon their trade. In 1725 a Natchez war chief complained to a European visitor:

> Why did the French come into our country? Before they came, did we not live better than we do [now], seeing we deprive ourselves of a part of our corn, our game, and fish, to give a part to them? . . . In fine, before the arrival of the French, we lived like men who can be satisfied with what they have; whereas at this day we are like slaves, who are not suffered to do as they please.

The Natchez longed for an opportunity to redeem their pride by restoring the world they had known before the French colonized their land.

In 1729 the callous commander at Fort Rosalie provoked a crisis by ordering one of the Natchez villages to relocate, for he meant to replace it with a tobacco plantation worked by his slaves. In a secret council, a Natchez chief exhorted rebellion: "We walk like slaves, which we shall soon be, since the French already treat us as if we were such." He asked, "Is not death preferable to slavery?" On the morning of November 28, 1729, the Natchez staged a well-planned uprising, quickly killing the commander and most of the soldiers and colonists in the vicinity. The 145 men, 36 women, and 56 children killed amounted to one-tenth of Louisiana's white population. The Natchez also took captive 50 white women and children and absorbed more than 200 African slaves as allies. This deadly surprise attack was the Louisiana equivalent of Opechancanough's 1622 uprising in Virginia and of Popé's 1680 rebellion in New Mexico.

The Natchez uprising especially terrified the French because African slaves joined the Indian rebels, combining the two greatest nightmares of a colonial people: an Indian massacre and a slave rebellion. To save Louisiana, the officials felt driven to crush the rebels quickly, lest their victory embolden the Indian and slave majorities throughout the colony. Lacking sufficient troops to suppress the rebels, the French had to rely on native allies. In return for generous presents, the Choctaw attacked their old enemies the Natchez, destroying their villages in early 1730. For the next two years, the French and Choctaw pursued the Natchez fugitives, killing hundreds and enslaving at least five hundred for sale to the French West Indies. When it served their purposes, the French massacred and enslaved natives as vigorously as did the British. Some Natchez escaped to find refuge among the Creek, Catawba, and Chickasaw. Celebrating the Natchez defeat and dispersal, a French priest exulted, "God wishes that they yield their place to new peoples"—the standard conclusion of victorious colonizers.

The rebellion demonstrated the French dependence upon the Choctaw to defend Louisiana. In 1746 the French commandant at New Orleans noted "the impossibility of keeping a country as vast as the one we occupy with the few troops and settlers who are there . . . if the Choctaws refused us their assistance and decided to act against us." In contrast to their abrupt handling of the Petites Nations and the Natchez, the French had to treat the interior Indians seriously, as either essential allies or formidable enemies.

In the hinterland east of the Mississippi (and west of the Carolinas), the natives remained numerous and powerful. During the seventeenth century, they formed five loose confederations for protection: from east to west, the Catawba, Cherokee, Creek, Chickasaw, and Choctaw. In 1730 about two thousand Catawba lived in the South and North Carolina Piedmont. To their northwest, the twelve thousand Cherokee dwelled in the southern Appalachian Mountains. A like number of Creek inhabited the fertile river valleys of what is now western Georgia and eastern Alabama. The twelve thousand Choctaw occupied the hilly pinewoods country of east-central Mississippi, while their close kin but bitter enemies the three thousand Chickasaw dwelled to their north.

Unable to strike directly at each other, the English and the French competed for influence over the native confederacies. The Indians were capable of devastating either colony and critical to the survival of both. To woo the natives, the empires needed to supply their demand for European manufactures, either by trade or by present.

The confederations had emerged in response to the more violent world wrought by the European invasion. Relatively isolated from early contacts with the colonizers, the interior villages had suffered less severely than had the coastal peoples, who more quickly and directly faced the new epidemics and the slave raids. The interior peoples also mitigated their own losses by absorbing many refugees, who fled from the coastal and riverine villages. As a result, each hinterland confederacy included ethnically and linguistically diverse people, drawn together primarily by their shared need for security. For example, the Catawba gradually united more than a dozen previously distinct peoples who spoke various Siouan languages

Each major southeastern Indian town included about two hundred houses made of cane withes, plastered and whitewashed with clay and roofed with a grass thatch. During the hot months, the occupants shifted into adjoining rectangular summer houses raised above the ground on posts for better ventilation. The towns featured a central plaza of beaten earth, where men regularly played *chunky* (a spear-tossing game) and a ball sport akin to lacrosse, both accompanied by heavy betting. To help keep the peace within their confederacies, southeastern Indians channeled their internal aggression into ball play between their villages. Upon the return of a successful war party, the plaza also hosted the prolonged torture-executions of captured warriors. Beside the plaza stood a public granary, filled in good times by donations from every successful family and drawn upon in hungry times by the unfortunate.

The margin of the plaza also featured a conical council house, where the leading men gathered around a central fire to discuss diplomacy and war and to arrange religious rituals.

The landscape of each confederation consisted of a relatively tight core of horticultural villages surrounded by a much broader forested periphery dedicated to hunting and gathering. In the nearby fields, the women cultivated maize, beans, squash, and pumpkins, while the Indian men ventured dozens, and sometimes hundreds, of miles away in pursuit of the deer and buffalo that abounded in the broad borderlands. The borderlands served as an environmental insurance policy. When droughts or pests curtailed the village crops, the inhabitants dispersed into the hinterland to subsist by hunting and by gathering nuts, berries, and roots.

But the confederations claimed overlapping borderlands, which produced violent conflicts. Because hunters avoided the most dangerous locales, war allowed wildlife there a respite that enabled their numbers to recover. However, such renewed abundance rendered the war zones especially valuable and contested by the Indian rivals, keen to harvest deerskins. The advent of European trade escalated the stakes of war, for the winners of large hunting territories reaped guns, while the losers suffered raids by the better-armed.

In their trade competition with the French, the British consistently had the advantages of price, quantity, and quality in the supply of cloth, guns, and alcohol. In 1744 the governor of Louisiana complained that the inferior quality of his guns had convinced the Indians "that the French are entirely poor and do not know how to make goods as the English do." Because of the especially long and dangerous shipping route from France, shipments of trade goods were also expensive and irregular, pushing up prices and producing shortages in Louisiana. By comparison, the Carolina traders enjoyed more predictable shipments at a lower cost via the shorter and safer route from London to Charles Town—or in the case of rum, from Jamaica and Barbados. Because the French empire protected the mother country's brandy distilleries, mercantile legislation forbade the production of rum in the French West Indies. This prohibition weakened the French trade with the Indians, for English rum was cheaper than French brandy.

On the other hand, the Carolinians often squandered their trade advantages by treating their Indian clients with contempt. Indians repeatedly complained that English settlers refused them hospitality, that Carolina officials skimped on their presents, and that Carolina traders cheated them and abused their women. A Louisiana governor noted that the English traders were "restless and quarrelsome spirits who cause division everywhere and who[m] the Indians tolerate only because they bring them goods and supply them abundantly with them. If the French could do the same thing, they would without contradiction be preferred."

Put on the defensive commercially, the French had to compensate by treating their hinterland Indian customers with greater respect and generosity. A Louisiana official explained that Indian loyalty depended upon "the presents that are given them, the justice that is done them, and even more the food that one must not let them lack when they come on visits, together with caresses and evidences of friendship." Presents, however, always cost more and purchased less than the French wished, primarily because authority was so weak and decentralized among the Indians. To increase their control and reduce their costs, the French tried to name one Choctaw head chief to distribute patronage and command all the villages. Of course, the Choctaw deeply distrusted centralized authority, especially when pushed upon them by outsiders. They clung to the virtual autonomy of their villages, the multiplicity of their chiefs, and the limits on their authority. In 1732 a French Jesuit complained, "All the villages are so many little republics in which each one does as he likes."

Frustrated in the great chief scheme, the French governor had to hold a long and expensive annual council to consult and reward more than a hundred Choctaw chiefs drawn from forty villages. During the 1730s, the presents distributed at the Choctaw council annually cost the crown nearly 50,000 livres, about twice the value of the deerskins received in trade from the Choctaw. The French ran their relationship with the Choctaw at a financial loss because strategic considerations took primacy in Louisiana. The French paid dearly to retain the Choctaw as their border guards, to keep runaway Africans and deserting soldiers within Louisiana and to keep the Carolina traders out.

At such a rate, the French could not afford to befriend all of the southeastern Indians. Forsaking their early ambition to unite the Indians, the French had to pick and choose their allies more selectively. The French generally wrote off the Catawba and Cherokee as too distant from Louisiana and too close to Carolina to draw into the French orbit. Through Fort Toulouse, in central Alabama, the French did trade with and influence the Creeks, which helped preserve their neutrality. That left the nearby Choctaw and Chickasaw. Obliged by scarce resources to choose one over the other, the French naturally opted for the Choctaw, who lived closer to Louisiana's core settlements and were more numerous (twelve thousand in 1730, versus three thousand Chickasaw).

Persuaded that peace between the Chicakasaw and Choctaw would only facilitate the extension of British trade, Governor Bienville concluded that a permanent state of wasting war between the two confederacies best served the French interest. Because putting "these barbarians into play against each other is the sole and only way to establish any security in the colony," he coldly concluded that "the more of them who are killed on both sides the greater will be our safety." In 1721, Bienville began to pay the Choctaw 80 livres for every Chickasaw slave and to swap a gun, a pound of gunpowder, and two pounds of shot for every Chickasaw scalp. During the next two years, the Choctaw brought in four hundred scalps and one hundred captives for payment.

But the Chickasaw proved more formidable enemies than the French had expected. Chickasaw warriors afflicted Choctaw villages and waylaid French riverboats and outposts. In 1734 a frustrated Bienville urged a genocidal escalation, warning his superiors in Paris:

> As long as the Chickasaws exist we shall always have to fear that they shall entice away the others from us in favor of the English. The entire destruction of this hostile nation therefore becomes every day more necessary to our interests, and I am going to exert all diligence to accomplish it.

In 1736 and again in 1739, Bienville invaded the Chickasaw country with mixed forces of French soldiers, Choctaw warriors, and armed slaves, but twice the well-armed Chickasaw inflicted humiliating defeats.

The defeats emboldened a Choctaw peace faction led by a chief known as Red Shoes, who announced that "for too long a time the French have been causing the blood of the Indians to be shed." In 1746, under his leadership, several Choctaw villages rebelled, killing three French men while welcoming Carolina traders. With especially generous presents, the French rallied most of the Choctaw to assassinate Red Shoes and attack his supporters. The allied Choctaw collected French bounties for 233 scalps taken from the western rebels (and for three heads formerly worn by English traders). In November 1750 the surviving rebels submitted, restoring a semblance of the French-Choctaw alliance.

DEPENDENCE

From the imperial perspective of Paris, French America was an economic disappointment. New France and Louisiana annually cost the crown more to administer than they generated in revenue from the fur and deerskin trades. Imperial officials especially resented the heavy costs to maintain forts and to bestow presents on the Indians. Weary of the financial drain, the crown abruptly ordered a withdrawal from the upper-country posts in 1696. The order provoked a storm of protest from Canadian merchants and officials, who personally profited from the fur trade and feared that British traders would fill the vacuum. They insisted that imperial honor required the retention of the west and its native alliance. The home authorities backed down.

That retreat demonstrated that as the Indians became dependent upon French trade, the French empire became captive to Indian demand. No longer able to live comfortably without metalware, firearms, and gunpowder, the Indians faced hunger and destitution if denied access to European goods.

In 1753 Skiagunsta, a Cherokee chief, observed, "The Cloaths we wear, we cannot make ourselves, they are made [for] us. We use their Amunition with which we kill deer. We cannot make our Guns. Every necessary Thing in Life we must have from the White People." Harsh experience had taught them that any people cut off from the gun trade faced destruction by their native enemies. Consequently, they considered any cessation of trade or escalation of prices to be acts of hostility, demanding war.

Colonial officials nervously warned their French superiors to accept a trade and alliance on Indian terms. In 1717 a Canadian official explained:

> The Trade with the Indians is a necessary commerce; and even if the colonists were able to manage without it, the State is virtually forced to maintain it, if it wishes to maintain Peace. . . . There is no middle course; one must have the natives either as friend or foe; and whoever wants him as friend, must furnish him with his necessities at conditions which allow him to procure them.

Beginning in the late 1720s, the French posts on the Great Lakes sold goods at below market value to dissuade the Indians from trading with the British colonists. The program reveals that the French strategic dependence on the Indians exceeded the Indians' dependence on French trade.

The crown subsidized the Indian trade primarily because it served political ends. The French needed native allies to hold the interior and so contain the British colonies on the Atlantic seaboard. Otherwise, the French feared that proliferating British settlers would break into the fertile Mississippi watershed to enrich and empower that empire to the detriment of France. At considerable expense, and with great frustrations, the French became entangled in complex relationships with Indian peoples, who had adapted resourcefully to the new world wrought by the colonial intrusions.

17

The Great Plains

★

1680–1800

The interior of a Mandan earth lodge, sketched in 1833 and later engraved by the Swiss artist Karl Bodmer, who visited the Missouri River valley. The engraving shows the interplay of human and animal life, with dogs and horses taking refuge from the winter inside a lodge that features the hides and skulls of buffalo. People gather around the central hearth, illuminated by the skyhole above. From Prince Alexander Philip Maximilian, Travels in the Interior *(Paris, 1840-43).*

POOR, ISOLATED, AND THINLY SETTLED, Hispanic New Mexico depended for survival upon both alliance with the Pueblo peoples of the Rio Grande and war with the nomads of the western Great Plains and southern Rocky Mountains. The shared threat from the nomads obliged the colonists and the Pueblo to cling together for mutual defense. Without external enemies, the Hispanics risked another internal rebellion by the Pueblo like that which had devastated New Mexico in 1680. New Mexico needed some Indian enemies that it might have other Indians as friends—however reluctant.

But the warfare that kept the colony alive also kept it weak by discouraging new colonists. In 1765 only 9,600 Hispanics dwelled in New Mexico, half of them in the two major towns: El Paso (2,600) to the south and Santa Fe (2,300) to the north. The rest lived on farms and ranches scattered through the long Rio Grande Valley between the two. Meanwhile, disease continued to diminish the Pueblo; their numbers fell from 14,000 in 1700 to 10,000 in 1765. That decline secured the Hispanics from another internal rebellion, but it rendered them more vulnerable to attacks by the many nomadic Indians around the little colony.

The Spanish possessed a vast American empire of extremes: alluring wealth and daunting power at its core in Mexico and Peru but great poverty and vulnerability on the northern margins. The extremes were related, for Spanish imperial policy favored the mother land over the colonies and the colonial core over the frontier periphery.

The crown retained New Mexico primarily as a military buffer zone meant to maximize the distance between valuable Mexico to the south and the rival European empires, which were growing more powerful, to the northeast. The Spanish felt uneasy as French Louisiana drove a wedge between Florida and northern New Spain, imperiling Spanish control of the Gulf of Mexico. Meanwhile, far to the northeast, at subarctic Hudson Bay, the British established trading posts, whose influence on native peoples extended southwestward onto the northern Great Plains. To counteract an exaggerated fear of the British approach, the French extended their own traders deeper onto the Great Plains, which further impinged upon Spanish New Mexico. Through their trade competition, the rival empires were increasingly affecting native peoples deep within the continent as colonization generated far-reaching and overlapping spheres of influence and violence.

Although usually allies in Europe, the French and Spanish bitterly competed to influence the native peoples in the vast grassy borderland between Louisiana and New Mexico. Noting the growing French gun trade with the Indians, in 1716 a Spanish priest complained, "They are slipping in behind our backs in silence, but God sees their intentions." He understood that trade bought influence and redirected Indian warfare against natives in a rival trade orbit. Long finding security in their monopoly over firearms and horses, the Spanish reacted with horror as the Indians on the southern Great Plains obtained both.

In the eighteenth century, an Indian trade was the key to expanding a North American empire. Although commercially weaker than the British of Carolina, the French of Louisiana had the edge as Indian traders over the Spanish of New Mexico. Compared with the French, Spanish workshops were less productive and Spanish shipping was more expensive. Spanish regulations also forbade most colonial manufacturing and limited imports into New Spain to a single Mexican port, Veracruz, on the Gulf Coast. This policy favored Spanish manufacturers and merchants by crippling their colonial competitors. The restrictions also facilitated the royal collection of import duties at a single port. But the regulations stifled economic development and depressed the standard of living in northern New Spain. From Veracruz, trade goods had to make a long, circuitous, and arduous journey over bad roads and mountains to Santa Fe, inflating the costs of Spanish cloth and metal tools, to the detriment of the New Mexicans and the benefit of their competitors in Louisiana.

The Great Plains Indians also preferred the French trade for cultural reasons. While the Spanish badgered their trading partners to accept missionaries, the French came to the Great Plains solely to trade, leaving their priests behind. Determined to retain their own culture, while adding European trade goods, the Indians favored French traders over Spanish missionaries.

By arming the Comanche, Wichita, and Pawnee of the Great Plains, the French indirectly threatened the New Mexicans and their Pueblo allies. In raiding the Hispanics and the Pueblo, the Plains Indians aggressively pursued their own interests—with French weapons. They sought revenge for Hispanic slave-raiding as well as horses and captives to pay for French goods. As nomadic raids took a heavy toll, New Mexico seemed doomed to wither.

But what looked like impending disaster to the Hispanic colonists was a brave new world for native peoples on the Great Plains. By combining Hispanic horses with French guns, many native bands reinvented themselves as buffalo-hunting nomads, which brought them unprecedented prosperity and power. In sum, the Great Plains exacerbated the paradoxical impact of colonialism so manifest throughout North America. In general, the effects of colonial intrusion—germs, weeds, livestock, soldiers, missionaries, and trade—spread far and wide, extending beyond imperial control and affecting native peoples in wildly unanticipated ways. Reacting creatively to the colonial invasions, natives selectively adopted new animals, weapons, and techniques to strengthen their position. This, in turn, obliged the colonists to respond to the native adaptations. For example, at the end of the eighteenth century, Indian success on the Great Plains obliged the Hispanics to deemphasize their system of missions in favor of adopting the French program of building native alliances through trade and diplomacy.

VILLAGERS AND NOMADS

Two thousand miles long (north and south) by several hundred miles wide (east and west), the Great Plains is an immense, windy, and arid grassland in the heart of the continent. Many long, low, swells of earth alternate with vast stretches of virtually flat land. The boundaries are the Rio Grande on the south, the subarctic forest of the Canadian Shield to the north, the Rocky Mountains on the west, and the forested hills of the Mississippi Valley to the east. Subtly tilted, the plains rise gradually in altitude from about one thousand feet above sea level on the east to six thousand feet at their western margin. In the rain shadow of the Rockies, the Great Plains receive, on average, an annual rainfall of only twelve to twenty inches—less than half of what falls on the humid eastern third of North America. Because the rain comes to the Great Plains in fits and starts, most of the many small streams are intermittent, drying up in the warmer months, but raging with floods after intense storms. Only the major rivers, principally the Red, Arkansas, Kansas, Platte, and Missouri, run permanently to reach the Mississippi.

For want of sufficient water and because of the prevailing high winds, only a few species of trees, primarily cottonwood and willow, grew on the Great Plains, and only along the narrow, sheltered margins beside the permanent rivers. Instead of trees, hardy and drought-resistant grasses covered most of the Great Plains. On the drier western half of the plains, known as the "high plains," buffalo and grama grasses, four to five inches tall, prevailed in a tough fibrous mat with deep roots. The slightly wetter eastern half, the "low plains," sustained tall-grass prairies, with some grasses exceeding six feet in height.

This landscape favored grazers: the pronghorn antelope and, especially, the bison (or buffalo), the largest mammal in North America. Possessing thick hides and strong stomachs, the buffalo adapted to the abundant but tough grass and to the extremes of temperature and wind that characterized the Great Plains. Bison weighed over a ton, resembling oversized cattle with humps on their backs and shaggy hair around their heads and neck. Shortsighted and hard of hearing, the buffalo relied on a keen sense of smell to warn of danger, and they herded in numbers for safety.

Scholars calculate that the Great Plains sustained more than twenty million buffalo in 1600. They usually lived in scattered herds of fifty to two hundred animals, but in late summer they congregated by the thousands for their mating season, creating masses astonishing to newcomers. During the 1830s the artist George Catlin reported that the buffalo formed "such masses in some places, as literally to blacken the prairies for miles together." An immense herd was "in constant motion; and all bellowing . . . in deep and hollow sounds; which, mingled together, appear, at the distance of a mile or two, like the sound of distant thunder." Possessing a spiritual rather than a scientific imagination, the natives believed that the buffalo swarmed like bees from subterranean hives every spring, and that their annual numbers depended primarily upon human rituals that managed their relationship with the supernatural.

Until about A.D. 800 the Great Plains belonged to many small and dispersed bands of hunter-gatherers, who traveled on foot. Thereafter, the climate became a bit wetter, pushing westward the possibilities of horticulture in the major river valleys. Horticultural peoples from the Mississippi Valley shifted up the Red, Arkansas, Republican, Platte, and Missouri rivers to build villages, plant crops, and hunt the buffalo. The river valleys were elongated oases where the permanent water and the alluvium of spring flooding produced a fertile floodplain, up to four hundred feet wide in some pockets. The stands of cottonwood and willow provided the Indians with firewood, stockades, and lodge frames. Where cleared of trees and brush, the fertile soil sustained crops of corn, squash, beans, and sunflowers.

The villagers were ethnically and linguistically diverse. Along the rivers of the southern plains, the Caddo, Pawnee, and Wichita spoke a Caddoan language. In the northern valleys, the horticulturalists were generally Siouan-speakers, including the Mandan, Hidatsa, Omaha, and Ponca. There were exceptions to the general pattern: the Arikara dwelling on the upper Missouri were Caddoan-speakers who had broken away from the Pawnee to the south. On the central plains, the Kansa and Osage were Siouans who intruded south of the Pawnee. In general, the Caddoans seem to have arrived first, with the Siouans relative latecomers to the Great Plains.

In the horticultural villages, dozens of lodges clustered together for convenience and safety. In the hotter southern climes, the Caddo and Wichita lived in well-ventilated beehive-shaped wooden frames covered with grass thatch. In the colder northern valleys, the villagers built well-insulated earth lodges: mounds of earth banked around and over a wooden frame, with a smoke hole at the top and a door flap facing east, toward their former homelands. The earth lodges were dark, smoky, and crowded, but warm and usually dry. Whether grass or earth, each lodge belonged to a senior woman and included her husband, unmarried children, married daughters and their husbands, and her grandchildren. As owners of the lodges and the crops, the women sustained the community. More mobile, men were also more peripheral to the village.

Twice annually the villagers walked far out onto the plains to hunt buffalo. The first hunt came in July and August, after the spring planting and before the September harvest of their crops. Following that harvest and its festivals, they briefly returned to the plains in November for another hunt. While hunting, the people lived in mobile encampments of tipis: conical tents of tanned buffalo hides stretched over frames of cottonwood poles. By combining hunting with horticulture, the village peoples diversified their

— The Great Plains, c. 1750 —

OMAHA	Native people
York Factory •	British post
New Orleans •	French town
San Antonio •	Spanish town

diet, which provided security when either the herds proved elusive or a pest or drought withered the crops.

Life in permanent, substantial, and prosperous villages encouraged the development of an elaborate annual cycle of religious ceremonies meant to ensure the continued success of crops and hunting. Doubling as priests, the chiefs were ritual leaders drawn from a few high-status families who dominated the public life of each village. They inherited, maintained, and augmented sacred congeries of found objects known as "medicine bundles." A white observer saw nothing but random and dead matter within one, describing

> a buffalo robe, fancifully dressed, [containing] skins of several fur-bearing animals . . . the skull of a wild cat, stuffed skins of a sparrow-hawk . . . and the swallow-tailed fly catcher, several bundles of scalps and broken arrows taken from enemies, a small bundle of Pawnee arrows, some ears of corn, and a few wads of buffalo-hair.

But to the natives each object recalled some especially significant manifestation of supernatural power in a vision, battle, hunt, or good harvest from ages past. Collected together, they served a people who knew the proper time and ritual to unleash their magical power. Every significant aspect of life required resort to the medicine bundle, lest offended spirits inflict defeat, withhold buffalo, or wither the corn. Consequently, every collective enterprise was simultaneously and inseparably spiritual and material. Indeed, the loss of a bundle was a catastrophe that would break up a people and unhinge the cosmos that they ritually sustained.

As with all Native American religions, the villagers subscribed to a profound dualism that reflected upon the alternation of death and life, construction and destruction, reproduction and disintegration in their nature (which included themselves). Because no positive could exist without its negative, they performed an always tense balancing act as the essential managers of a world constantly ebbing and flowing with spiritual power, ever poised between chaos and order—and requiring people to survive.

As the owners of the bundles, the priest-chiefs enjoyed superior status and influence. During the major ceremonial feasts through the year, the people gave them hides, meat, and corn to honor their successful management of the medicine bundles. But most of this wealth paused only briefly at the top of the hierarchy, for a chief preserved and enhanced his status by redistributing. Because what he received was his due, everything that he gave was a gift, and his status lay in that unreciprocated difference, in the obligations he imposed on those who received his largesse. Consequently, among the village dwellers there were large gradations of status but only modest differences in material prosperity. And the former depended upon the latter. "It is hard to be a chief" was a common saying among the villagers, a comment on the burdens of maintaining the village and its world.

Although every village was virtually autonomous, people who spoke a common language and who intermarried and practiced similar ceremonies shared an identity. Such a people ordinarily refrained from attacking one another and cooperated in war against others who differed in language and customs.

Especially different were the nomadic buffalo hunters who came onto the Great Plains from the opposite direction, from the Rocky Mountains to the west. At first, most were Athapaskan speakers, who over many generations had slowly migrated southward down the Rockies from northwestern Canada. During the fifteenth century, many Athapaskan migrants turned eastward onto the southwestern Great Plains. Among their native enemies and the Hispanics, the diverse Athapaskans became known collectively as the Apache. Armed with bows and arrows, assisted by dogs, and guided by the visions of shamans, the nomads adapted to their new life as buffalo hunters. Hunting on foot, the Apache used magic, stealth, cooperation, and skilled archery to find, approach, surround, and attack the bison.

Supplemented by the gathering of wild berries and roots, buffalo hunting provided almost all that the nomads ate, wore, and used. Indeed, both the villagers and the nomads carefully exploited the entire buffalo, regarding waste with horror as a dangerous affront to the guardian spirits of the bison. The natives wore some hides in winter as robes, and they dried and tanned others to make tipis. The rough side of a dried tongue served as a comb, while a stiffened tail worked as a flyswatter. The Indians reworked the horns into spoons and the bones into tools. The bison flesh abounded in protein with relatively little fat, and the internal organs supplied many vitamins and minerals. Cut into thin strips and dried in the hot summer sun, the meat could be preserved for months and even years. Indian women pounded cherries and other wild fruit into the dried meat to make pemmican, which provided sufficient vitamin C to preserve the people from scurvy. The dried dung, known as "buffalo chips," served as fuel on the treeless plains. In a pinch, the blood of a newly killed bison substituted for water to revive parched hunters.

Unlike the villagers, the nomads lived year-round in many small and mobile camps with few possessions, little time for ceremonies, and scant surplus food. Obliged to move frequently and lacking beasts of burden other than small dogs, the nomads could accumulate little. Strong but light, a tipi could be quickly taken down, placed on a travois, and dragged away by dogs or women. Rather than class, the most important distinction in nomad society was gender. Women gathered seeds and fruits, fetched wood and water, and cured and tanned animal hides to make clothing and tipis. Although men led the hunts, these often involved everyone in a band, young and old, women and men, to surround, drive, and kill the buffalo.

The fundamental unit was an extended family: parents, their unmarried sons, their daughters, and the husbands and children of their daughters. Several extended families formed a band that camped and hunted together within a broad territory that they defended as their own. Several nomad bands came together periodically for trade, ceremonies, and marriages. Those ties rendered band membership highly fluid, as the dissatisfied could readily shift into another band where they had relatives. Occasionally several bands cooperated to raid a common enemy. In particular, as the nomadic bands shifted eastward they came into conflict with the horticulturalists when the latter came out onto the plains to hunt.

When the hunting failed and starvation loomed, the nomads had to eat their dogs. Thereafter, if the buffalo remained elusive, the people of a nomadic band began to die. When seen at their low ebb, the buffalo nomads struck Spanish explorers as the poorest of Indians. In his 1541 journey across the Great Plains in search of Quivira, Coronado described them as possessing "nothing but little villages, and . . . they do not plant anything and do not have any houses except of skins and sticks, and they wander around with the cows." The Spanish explorer hastened on, dismissing the nomads, for they lacked gold and maize and seemed too elusive for the mission life.

In search of a more secure subsistence, some Apachean nomads diversified their way of life. When unusually abundant rains permitted, these bands spent the spring and early summer in sheltered valleys around streams, where they raised small crops of corn, beans, and squash. The nomads also visited the pueblos in the Rio Grande and Pecos valleys to trade buffalo hides, dried meat, and human captives for maize, beans, squash, turquoise, pottery, and cotton blankets. Other nomads turned eastward to trade with the Wichita, horticulturalists dwelling on the Arkansas River in central Kansas. When rainfall was scarce and the Pueblo or the Wichita lacked the surplus to trade, the nomads raided the horticultural villages, taking what they needed. Consequently, nomad relations with the Pueblo and Wichita varied from village to village and from year to year, with peaceful trade alternating with violent raiding. But whether as trading partners or as raiding victims, the settled Pueblo and Wichita became essential to the nomads on their periphery.

GENIZAROS

During the seventeenth century, the Spanish empire commandeered the Pueblo people by founding the colony of New Mexico in their midst. By exacting tribute from the Pueblo, the Hispanics captured their surplus, which reduced their trade with the nomads, provoking increased frictions. By conscripting the Pueblo to raid the nomads, the Hispanics further alienated them from one another. The raids procured the one paying commodity in New Mexico: slaves. But the predation went both ways, for nomads sought revenge by killing and capturing Hispanics and Pueblo. In the ebb and flow of captives and livestock, some colonists came out ahead while others suffered severely. In general, the governors and other officials thrived, while the Pueblo and common colonists bore the brunt of nomad revenge.

To add to the complexity, some nomads sold to the Hispanics the captives taken from their Indian enemies farther east on the Great Plains. In 1761 a Franciscan priest described a trade fair conducted at Taos by the Hispanic governor with visiting Comanche:

> Here in short, is gathered everything possible for trade and barter with these barbarians in exchange for deer and buffalo hides, and what is saddest, in exchange for Indian slaves, men and women, small and large, a great multitude of both sexes, for they are gold and silver and the richest treasure for the governors, who gorge themselves first with the largest mouthfuls from this table, while the rest eat the crumbs.

Two horses and a few knives could usually purchase an adolescent Indian girl—the preferred commodity of the slave trade. Male captives were worth half as much. The purchased captives labored for the New Mexicans or were sent south to work in the silver mines of northern Mexico. The Hispanics rationalized the trade by claiming that their purchases rescued slaves from death and paganism—for Catholic conversion and Hispanic education. Masters were supposed to indoctrinate the captives in Hispanic ways and Catholic beliefs, providing baptism and new names. Known as *genizaros*, the detribalized captives formed the lowest caste of New Mexican society, constituting at least 10 percent of the population in the mid-eighteenth century.

Usually captured as children, most *genizaros* lacked the means to return home. They generally labored as ranch and domestic laborers, and often suffered sexual exploitation. A fortunate and persistent few acquired property and respect, often by brokering trade and negotiations between the diverse peoples of the southwest. After 1740, freed *genizaros* formed communities and obtained lands on the frontier margin, where they served New Mexico as border guards against the Great Plains nomads.

HORSES AND GUNS

Today the predominant image of the American Indian is a warrior and buffalo hunter, wearing an eagle-feather bonnet and riding across the Great Plains. We imagine that the mounted warrior defended a timeless, deeply rooted way of life, independent of the European invasion of America. In fact, the association of Great Plains Indians with the horse is relatively recent and depended upon the colonial intrusion. Although horses first evolved in North America, before spreading eastward into Asia and Europe about twelve thousand years ago, they had become extinct in this continent by about ten thousand years ago. During the sixteenth century, the horse returned to North America as a domesticated animal kept by the Hispanic colonists.

Not until the late seventeenth century did the Pueblo and Apache acquire horses from the New Mexicans, by a mixture of illicit trade and nocturnal raiding. The most dramatic infusion followed the Pueblo revolt of 1680, which drove the Hispanics from New Mexico; they left behind hundreds of horses for native appropriation. From Pueblo and Apache middlemen, the horses filtered northward, reaching other natives through trade and theft. Common among the Indians of the southern plains by 1720, horses spread to the northern plains by 1750. Hardy grazers, the horses thrived on the immense grassy plains, especially the southern reaches, where the winters were milder. By converting the abundant grass into flesh and energy, horses provided people with an immense and versatile new source of power.

The proliferation of horses seemed a godsend to people who lived, either partly or primarily, by buffalo hunting on the Great Plains. On horseback, men could cover far more ground in much less time, and they could see farther, finding herds more easily. Faster and nimbler than the buffalo, the horses enabled mounted men armed with bows to maneuver and attack with deadly rapidity.

By killing more buffalo, the Great Plains peoples became better fed, clothed, and housed. A horse could haul loads four times larger than could a dog, enabling the Indians to acquire and transport more possessions over longer distances. They accumulated buffalo hides, made larger tipis, and ate more meat. And in a starving emergency, people could eat their horses, which provided far more flesh than did dogs. The great material benefits fed into a new psychology, a sense of liberation from old limits into an intoxicating sense of speed, power, and range—an offering of both security and immense, open possibility.

In the short run, the horse improved life substantially for the village dwellers and immensely for the nomads. Most horticultural peoples clung to their traditional seasonal and ceremonial cycle, with over half their year spent in permanent villages near their productive fields. The horse simply enabled them to extend their seasonal hunts deeper into the plains and to bring more meat and robes back to their villages. There was a conspicuous exception to the general pattern: on the upper Missouri River some Hidatsa bands broke away westward, abandoning horticulture to become nomads, assuming a new identity as the Crow.

During the eighteenth century the rich new possibilities of the mounted life on the Great Plains attracted newcomers and competitors. From the Rockies to the northwest emigrated the Kiowa, a Uto-Aztecan people, and the Comanche, a Shoshonean-speaking people. From the east in the upper Mississippi Valley came a succession of Siouan-speaking peoples: the Assiniboine and the seven Lakota (or Dakota) tribes. Especially numerous, the Lakota totaled some 25,000 people in 1790. Their own word *lakota* means "allies," but their foes, including the French, called them the Sioux, which meant "enemies." Obtaining horses, seeking buffalo, and retreating from eastern enemies, the Assiniboine and Lakota gradually migrated westward onto the northern Great Plains. In addition, several Algonquian-speaking peoples, including the Blackfoot, Plains Cree, Gros Ventre, Arapaho, and Cheyenne, moved westward from homelands at the headwaters of the Mississippi or in the southern reaches of the Hudson Bay watershed. In sum, most of the Indian peoples we now associate with the Great Plains were relative newcomers who arrived during the eighteenth century.

The migrations greatly increased the number of buffalo hunters on the Great Plains. Because the village dwellers occupied and defended the river bottoms that could sustain native horticulture, the newcomers generally remained on the vast grasslands, living primarily in pursuit of the buffalo herds (except in winter, when they sought refuge in sheltered stream beds). Unwelcome intruders in the eyes of the longer-term residents, the newcomers provoked frictions that led to widespread warfare between men on horseback. For, in addition to promoting the hunting of buffalo, the horses facilitated the killing of people. In 1800 a trader on the northern plains marveled at the abundant buffalo and remarked, "This is a delightful country, and were it not for perpetual wars, the natives might be the happiest people on earth."

During the eighteenth century, as they obtained horses, the Great Plains peoples also acquired firearms. They sought guns to defend their villages and raid their enemies, but they continued to rely on the bow for hunting buffalo. Loud and smoky, gunfire spooked the herds, and the single-shot muzzle-loaded flintlock was slow to reload and difficult to aim from horseback when compared with the bow. But guns had a longer range and inflicted gaping wounds, rendering firearms advantageous in battle against people armed only with bows. Moreover, guns conveyed a spiritual terror beyond even their material impact, for their novel and frightening flash, smoke, and roar seemed akin to the supernatural power in thunder and lightning.

In the shifting conflicts and alliances of the Great Plains, the most common pattern was for the various newcomers to cooperate against alliances of the older residents. For example, on the northern plains the westward-migrating Cheyenne, Arapaho, and Lakota tended to cooperate against the Crow, Hidatsa, and Mandan. But there were exceptions to every rule, for although Siouan and newly arrived, the Assiniboine preferred trade and alliance with the earth-lodge peoples against their fellow nomads. And the newcomers often alternated their raiding upon horticultural villages with peaceful trading, depending upon shifting needs, resentments, and opportunities.

In warfare, the villagers initially prevailed over the nomads. More attractive and accessible to French and native traders, the village dwellers were better armed and mounted. The horticulturalists also enjoyed the protection of their concentrated numbers in palisaded villages.

But over time, the nomads caught up in horses and guns, while the traders introduced European diseases to the villages. Once an advantage, the concentration in villages became a deadly liability as the villagers suffered disproportionately from the contagious epidemics. As their numbers dwindled, the horticulturalists could no longer effectively defend many of their villages, much less their claim to the surrounding buffalo herds. Because the more mobile and dispersed nomads suffered smaller losses to the epidemics, they grew in relative power as the villagers waned. For example, in 1780–81 a smallpox epidemic killed two-thirds of the Mandan, inviting the Lakota to escalate their raids with devastating effect. The surviving Mandan consolidated into fewer villages, relocated into a tighter cluster beside their equally beleaguered allies, the Hidatsa.

Young males avidly sought the name and reputation of a warrior by success in taking scalps, captives, and horses from an enemy. Boys early learned to covet the prestige enjoyed by the most successful warriors, who were the celebrities of their band or village. In the nineteenth century, Francis Parkman described a returning and victorious Lakota war party:

> The warriors rode three times round the village; and as each noted champion passed, the old women would scream out his name, to honor his bravery, and excite the emulation of the younger warriors. Little urchins, not two years old, followed the warlike pageant with glittering eyes, and gazed with eager admiration at the heroes of their tribe.

The prevalence of epidemics also promoted a fatalism about early death and a zeal to prove courage and prowess before it was too late. In 1796 a French trader watched Pawnee mothers ceremonially celebrate the return of their sons as corpses killed in battle with the Comanche:

> [H]olding a bow in one hand and an arrow in the other, [the mothers] sang near the bodies of their sons an air both gay and martial, thanking them for having given them the satisfaction of seeing them die at the hands of the enemy while fighting valiantly for the defense of their country, a death a thousand times preferable to the fate of him who on a wretched mat expires consumed by some deadly disease.

Through such testimonials, women played key roles in sustaining the warrior cult.

The nomads became less egalitarian as the most successful men accumulated larger herds of horses and a greater number of wives. They needed more women to tan the extra hides and to dry the meat of their increased kill. A young man also sought horses to provide the dowry to procure a wife from her father. Horses and women became interdependent markers of high status. A prosperous warrior displayed twenty or more horses, while a poor man possessed one or two (or none)—a discrepancy in private property unprecedented in their societies. Individual property in horses also fluctuated wildly over time, as a severe winter or an enemy raid could suddenly deplete one man's horse herd.

The greater rewards of successful manhood came at a high price, for Great Plains warriors led shorter lives of increased violence. Because so many males died in their youth or prime, women outnumbered men, which encouraged polygamy by the most successful warriors.

The horse-centered way of life proved a mixed blessing for women. Horses liberated them from bearing the heaviest burdens, and better hunting meant more food for everyone. But women also reaped relatively lower status as their tribes elevated male hunters and warriors. In addition, women had to work harder, feeding and tending horses, scraping and tanning more hides, drying more buffalo meat, and making larger stocks of pemmican. Among the horticultural peoples there was additional resentment over the damage that hungry roaming horses wreaked on the village crops that the women cultivated. A nineteenth-century missionary among the Pawnee observed, "There are more broils, jealousy, and family quarrels caused by horses than all other troubles combined. The horse frequently causes separation between man and wife, sometimes for life." Finally, women became the targets of raids meant to enhance the wealth and status of the enemy men who captured them.

Environmentally, the horse-centered way of life was highly unstable. Near their encampments the Indians concentrated horses in numbers greater than the local grass could bear. The strain was greatest in the winter, when the people were least mobile and the grass was less nutritious, but the horses needed more calories to stay warm. Consequently, the horse herds depleted the most fragile, scarce, and important niches on the Great Plains: the river and stream valleys that provided the winter refuges. The growing numbers of hunters also exceeded the reproductive capacity of the buffalo herds. That pressure was compounded by newly arrived French traders, who offered guns and other manufactures in return for buffalo hides. As natives increased their hunt to serve commerce as well as subsistence, the buffalo died in unprecedented numbers.

The diminished herds intensified the violent competition between native peoples. Where the violence peaked, hunting temporarily eased, permitting the buffalo herds to recover (like the deer herds in the war zones of the American southeast). More human death meant longer buffalo life. For example, bison abounded between the Arkansas and North Canadian rivers of western Kansas, a region hotly contested between the Pawnee to the east and the Cheyenne and Arapaho newcomers to the north and west. But such zones of enlarged herds became even more coveted and contested by the rival peoples, who needed more hides to buy guns for an edge in their increasingly violent world.

TEXAS

During the early eighteenth century, French traders ascended the Great Plains rivers to trade with the village peoples, offering guns and ammunition for buffalo hides and slaves. Soon the Wichita and Pawnee villagers became better armed than the mission Indians within the Hispanic orbit. In 1719, Spanish missionaries complained, "We do not have a single gun, while we see the French giving hundreds of arms to the Indians." With French weapons, the Pawnee and Wichita began raiding the Apache and Pueblo for captives to sell to the French for more guns. When facing east, the French opposed the British slave trade based in Carolina, but in facing west, the French encouraged their Great Plains clients to prey on poorly armed natives at a distance.

The attacks dismayed the Hispanics, who needed the Pueblo as allies. Overreacting, Governor Valverde of New Mexico imagined that the French meant to lead the Pawnees across the Great Plains to attack Santa Fe. During the summer of 1720, as a preemptive strike, Valverde sent Pedro de Villasur with forty-five Hispanics and sixty Pueblo on an expedition northeastward across the Great Plains to attack the Pawnee. In early August, Villasur approached their villages on the Platte River in present-day Nebraska. At dawn, however, the Pawnee surprised the Hispanic-Pueblo encampment, killing half the invaders, including Villasur. The survivors fled back to New Mexico. Sobered and weakened by the sudden loss of one-third of his garrison, Governor Valverde did not dare a second strike across the Great Plains.

Overmatched in a trade war for Indian favor, the Spanish tried instead to expand their traditional combination of Franciscan missions and military presidios eastward into the contested border zone. The Hispanics wishfully believed that God would reward them for extending the faith—rather than favor those impious French traders indifferent to the souls of Indians. The Spanish failed to recognize how outmoded their mission system had become once horses and guns spread among the natives.

In 1716 the Spanish built new missions in the hill country of east Texas, where the Caddo were settled horticulturalists—the people deemed most appropriate for conversion. The Caddo, however, disappointed Hispanic illusions. After the missionaries unwittingly introduced a deadly smallpox epidemic, the Caddo refused Catholic baptism because, in the words of a friar, "they have formed the belief that the [holy] water kills them."

Caddo threats obliged the missionaries and their soldiers to retreat to San Antonio, in south-central Texas, where in 1718 the Spanish founded a town, mission, and presidio. By 1722, Hispanic Texas consisted of the town of San Antonio, ten nearby missions, and 250 soldiers in four scattered presidios. After the growth spurt of 1718–22, Hispanic Texas stagnated as few Hispanics moved to a colony even more distant, dangerous, and impoverished than New Mexico. In 1760 only about 1,200 colonists lived in Texas, nearly half of them (580) at San Antonio. The Hispanic colonists sustained a hardscrabble existence by supplying their presidios with provisions, by driving longhorn cattle south for sale to the silver miners of northern New Spain—and by smuggling with French Louisiana, which defeated the colony's official purpose. Already stretched perilously thin in New Mexico, the Spanish had compounded their exposed frontier by adding a second cluster of weak and unprofitable settlements in Texas.

Only at San Antonio did the missions prosper, and only for one generation. By 1750 the Franciscans had gathered about a thousand Indian converts. Most were Coahuiltecan speakers, nomadic hunting and gathering bands under attack from their more numerous and better-mounted foes the Apache and Comanche, who were pressing southward deep into Texas. In desperation, the Coahuiltecans sought safety and food by learning agriculture at the missions. "They are more concerned about having goods in abundance than with any fear of life eternal," one priest grumbled. Crowded into San Antonio for safety, however, the Coahuiltecans were vulnerable to epidemic diseases, which shrank their numbers during the 1750s. At the same time, the Apache and Comanche raiders pressed closer to the Hispanic missions and ranches.

COMANCHE AND APACHE

On the Great Plains, the eighteenth century was a period of violent flux as native peoples competed to exploit the buffalo and to steal horses and women. The influx of horses and guns flowed unevenly, favoring some native peoples at the expense of others. If a people captured a territory rich with buffalo, their advantages became compounded, to the detriment of their rivals. The victors grew in population, horses, and firearms while the losers shrank in all three.

On the southern plains, the Comanche were the big winners. During the early eighteenth century, the Comanche steadily acquired horses as they moved southeastward onto the southern plains: the western third of Kansas and Oklahoma, as well as northeastern New Mexico and northwestern Texas. The acquisition of horses and Comanche migration reinforced each other. By trading for or stealing Hispanic horses, the Comanche obtained the means to force their way farther south and east. By procuring enlarged hunting territories, they improved their bargaining position as traders and their might as warriors.

The aggressive newcomers provoked a deadly competition with their Apache predecessors. They especially clashed over the limited number of river valleys, which provided critical concentrations of water, grass, wood, and shelter. Although the Comanche bands were fluid and independent, they usually cooperated in raiding the Apaches to take horses, women, children, and buffalo territory. Primarily women and children, the captives strengthened the Comanche as their loss weakened the Apache. The adopted captives and an improved diet of abundant buffalo meat fueled a population growth that starkly contrasted with the demographic decline afflicting most other native peoples. By 1800 the Comanches numbered about twenty thousand—twice as many as all other native peoples on the southern plains.

Expansion endowed the Comanche with surplus horses, buffalo hides, and human captives to trade for French guns and ammunition. By allying with the Wichita, who lived along the lower Arkansas and Red rivers, the Comanche obtained access to the French traders. Determined to keep their enemies vulnerable, the Comanche and Wichita blocked efforts by French gun traders to push through them to deal with the desperate Apache. Success enabled the Comanche to dominate the southern plains and to broker the growing trade both north to the earth-lodge dwellers on the upper Missouri River and east to the French in Louisiana. Comanche expansion set off a domino effect as defeated rivals fled and came into conflict with new neighbors. Reeling from Comanche raids, Apache bands headed westward across the Rio Grande into western New Mexico or pushed southward deeper into Texas.

Many westering Apache refugees found a more secure haven in the canyons of northwest New Mexico. Along their way west, they raided the Pueblo, taking horses, sheep, cattle, and captives. Pueblo influence led the western bands to adopt weaving, pottery-making, and the herding of domestic animals, especially sheep. Having become a composite people, they syncretized new ceremonies and religious concepts by adapting Pueblo traditions to their own. As they became distinctive from the other Apaches, these composite and increasingly prosperous western bands became known to the Hispanics as the Apache de Navihu, which soon became shortened to Navajo.

During the 1720s and early 1730s other Apache bands moved southward, pressing closer to the Hispanic settlements of New Mexico and Texas. To recoup their losses to the Comanche, the Apache raided Hispanic ranches and missions. No longer able to hunt buffalo to the north, they stole and ate Spanish cattle and horses to the south. In 1732 the commander at San Antonio begged his superior, the governor of Texas, to negotiate peace with the Apache. "Otherwise, this Presidio, with its towns and Missions will be exposed to total destruction," he warned.

But the Hispanic losses to the Apache paled by comparison to Apache sufferings at the hands of the Comanche and their Wichita allies. Some Apache became so desperate that they sought Hispanic protection by entering the mission system. In 1749 the Lipan Apache formalized their submission in a ceremony at San Antonio at which they symbolically buried a hatchet, a lance, six arrows, and a living horse beneath the town plaza. In 1757 the Hispanics built a new mission and presidio for the Lipan Apache on the San Saba River, north of San Antonio.

Instead of bringing peace, the alliance and mission increased the danger to Texas as the Hispanics became a party to the Apache conflict with the Comanche and Wichita. In 1758, hundreds of Comanche and Wichita, mounted on horses and bearing French muskets, attacked and destroyed the San Saba mission, killing the Hispanics, including two priests. In 1759 the Spanish counterattacked, sending Apache warriors and Hispanic soldiers north to the Red River, where they found a stockaded Wichita village bearing a provocative French flag given by Louisiana officials. The Spanish expedition suffered defeat and fifty-two casualties from the Comanche and Wichita gunfire. Formerly dominant over Indians without guns and horses, the Hispanics saw that the tables had turned as the Great Plains tribes became armed and mounted. A presidio commander in Texas gloomily noted, "The enemy [is] so superior . . . in firearms as well as in numbers that our destruction seems probable."

New Mexico also suffered as displaced Apache bands pressed closer to the Pueblo missions and Hispanic ranches of the Rio Grande Valley. Stealthy in approach, ruthless in attack, secretive in retreat, and formidable in defense, the Apache acquired a fearsome reputation among the Hispanics and Pueblo. In 1777 the governor sadly reported that the Indian raids had reduced New Mexico "to the most deplorable state and greatest poverty." Increasingly beleaguered, Texas and New Mexico became shrinking Hispanic pockets amid increasingly powerful Indian enemies. During the mid-eighteenth century on the northern frontier of New Spain, the colonial conquest seemed to shift into reverse, as Hispanic defenses weakened.

THE BOURBON REFORMS

During the 1770s and 1780s, Spanish officials rescued New Mexico by adopting reforms that bolstered the frontier defenses. Drawn from the Bourbon family, the eighteenth-century monarchs of Spain were influenced by the Enlightenment, a European intellectual movement meant to rationalize and secularize government, society, and the economy. In that spirit, King Carlos III (1759–88) appointed reform-minded officials determined to strengthen the defenses and increase the revenues of New Spain at the expense of the church.

The Bourbon reformers recognized that the Spanish mission system had failed to counter native peoples armed by imperial rivals—the British in the southeast and the French on the Great Plains. As an alternative, the reformers relied on improved presidios and a more flexible diplomacy that treated autonomous native peoples with a new combination of respect, generosity, and cunning. Recognizing that Spanish private enterprise could not provide sufficient trade goods at competitive prices, the reformers adopted the French policy of wooing Indians with crown-funded presents. By providing weapons, the Spanish hoped to purchase some Indians as allies to fight against the others as enemies.

Reform did not come easily or quickly. The apparently intractable problem of defending a long frontier without sufficient manpower wore down the inspector general, José de Galvez. In 1769, Galvez cracked under the strain of a formidable rebellion by the Seri and Pima Indians in Sonora (which included southern Arizona). One morning he bolted from his tent to announce a plan to "destroy the Indians in three days simply by bringing 600 monkeys from Guatemala, dressing them like soldiers, and sending them against Cerro Prieto," a Seri stronghold. Galvez proceeded to assume the identity of Moctezuma, the king of Sweden, Saint Joseph, and finally God. The concerned viceroy of New Spain recalled Galvez to Mexico City, where he slowly recovered his mental health; sent home, he later rose to higher office in Spain.

During the 1770s and 1780s, frontier reform began to progress under the able leadership of Teodoro de Croix (the military commander of the northern frontier), Bernardo de Galvez (the viceroy of New Spain and the nephew and protégé of José de Galvez), and Juan Bautista de Anza (the governor of New Mexico). De Croix increased the frontier army by 900 men to a total of 2,800 and dramatically improved their training, equipment, pay, and morale. But the Hispanic troops remained far too few to defend the eighteen-hundred-mile frontier against all of the nomads. Because the Apache were more immediately threatening, the Spanish cultivated the Comanche and Navajo with presents of arms, ammunition, clothing, hats, mirrors, knives, sugar, body paint, and cigars. In return, the Comanche and Navajo attacked the Apache. Bernardo de Galvez frankly characterized the new policy of division as "peace by deceit." For their part, the Comanche and Navajo felt that they had manipulated the Hispanics to obtain an edge over the Apache and primacy over the Pueblo, as well as procuring presents in the bargain.

During the early 1790s, some (but by no means all) Apache bands sued for peace. The governor of New Mexico resettled about two thousand Apache near presidios in eight new reservations known as *establecimientos de paz* ("peace establishments"), where they received weekly rations of corn, meat, tobacco, and sugar, as well as instruction in agriculture, the Spanish language, and other Hispanic ways. Hispanic authorities hoped that the reservation Apache would prosper and lure down from the mountains the defiant bands that remained, in the words of New Mexico's governor, "dispersed in the empty Sierras with nothing but wild foods to eat, stealing to live." As a secular alternative to the old mission system, the *establecimientos de paz* dismayed the Franciscan priests, who longed for their former primacy in Indian policy.

Although it fell far short of this official hope, the reservation program combined with the Comanche alliance to reduce the Apache raiding. During the 1790s, travel to and settlement in New Mexico became safer and more attractive. At last, New Mexico began, modestly, to prosper and grow. Only 9,600 in 1765, the Hispanic population doubled to 20,000 by 1800. But this new growth and security should not be overstated. By no means had New Mexico become strong enough to dominate the surrounding native peoples. And the Comanche did not regard their peace with New Mexico as binding them in Texas. Indeed, they continued to raid Texan ranches to procure horses for sale to their New Mexican allies. With Comanche help, the Hispanics of New Mexico had secured a modest advantage rather than a complete victory.

THE NORTHERN PLAINS

On the Great Plains, the trade competition of rival European empires provided new opportunities and new dangers for native peoples. Where the southern plains featured competition between the Spanish and the French, the northern Indians maneuvered between the clashing interests of British and French traders. That new contest first emerged during the 1670s far to the north and east of the Great Plains.

During the late seventeenth century, the French had pursued the beaver trade westward across the Great Lakes to present-day Minnesota, where the French traded with the Algonquian-speaking Ojibwa. English merchants, however, saw an opportunity to outflank the French to the north by sending traders by sea around Labrador to Hudson Bay, an immense subarctic body of water that intruded into northern Canada. Usually locked by ice, Hudson Bay was accessible by ships only during two months in the summer. But the bay compensated for its short season by collecting the vast and intricate river systems of the Canadian Shield: a watershed of 1.4 million square miles where beaver abounded in an immense black-spruce forest broken by thousands of swamps, lakes, and streams. Obliged by the northern climate to specialize in hunting and gathering, the local Cree were especially adept at finding and killing beaver. Finally, Hudson Bay's more direct access by sea to Britain meant lower transportation costs than the French bore in carrying furs from the Great Lakes via the St. Lawrence to the Atlantic and France.

In 1670, London merchants organized the Hudson's Bay Company and procured a crown monopoly to trade with the Indians dwelling along its waterways. During the 1670s and 1680s, the company established fortified trading posts (known as "factories") on the bay's western shore—principally Fort

Albany, at the mouth of the Albany River, and York Factory, at the mouth of the Nelson River. This enterprise was the great exception to the apparent rule that the British came in greater numbers (than other colonial powers) to dispossess the natives and rework their land. The company employed no more than two hundred British, all male and determined to return home. Many were orphan teenagers who contracted for seven years of service in a distant land, enduring the brutal cold of the long, dark winter and the intense mosquito clouds of the short (but surprisingly hot) summer.

Few in number and bearing coveted goods, the Hudson's Bay Company traders were an asset, rather than a threat, to the Cree, who felt enriched by their new source of metals, cloth, alcohol, and guns. In 1749 a company official explained, "The Indians near the Factories Consider their Factories as their Home [because] the Company relieves their distresses." Far from displacing the Indians, the company encouraged Cree bands to settle around the posts. In addition to delivering prime beaver pelts, the Cree supplied moose meat and guarded the posts against French attack.

The Hudson's Bay Company forbade marriages to natives as a drain on corporate resources, but the employees recognized that life was unpleasant and trade difficult without the comforts, expertise, and kin connections offered by Indian women. Eager to tie themselves to the British, the Cree offered their women to the company men. Known as marriages "after the custom of the country," these relationships cemented alliances with particular Cree families and provided essential instruction in native ways of trading, speaking, and traveling. The women also made moccasins and snowshoes and treated beaver pelts, all essential tasks to the northern trade. Many Cree women welcomed trade marriages for offering a more secure life, relative to the hardships of nomadic life in a hunting band.

The Hudson's Bay Company built its trade by offering an abundant stock of guns, selling more than four hundred a year during the early 1690s. As the Cree became well armed, they overawed their neighbors in the southwestern interior, the Assiniboine, who dwelled along the environmental transition between the northern forest and the Great Plains. Accepting peace on Cree terms, the Assiniboine broke with their fellow Siouans the Lakota. In return for helping the Cree raid the Lakota, the Assiniboine won partial access to the company's trading posts, where they procured the coveted guns.

But the gun trade created a dangerous dependence. Formidable aggressors when the gun trade was open, the Assiniboine and Cree became especially vulnerable when it lapsed. In 1697 the French seized the Hudson's Bay Company posts, breaking up the British gun trade until 1714, when a peace treaty returned the posts to the company. Upon recovering their posts, the British found the Assiniboine much reduced by warfare. A factor reported:

> They told me this Reason for it, that they had lost the Use of their Bows and Arrows by having Guns so long amongst them, and when they were

> disappointed of Powder [&] Shott, . . . their Enemies found They had no Guns to Defend themselves with [and] made Warr Upon them & Destr[o]y[e]d above 100 Tents [of] Men, Women, and Children.

The return of the British gun trade rescued the Assiniboine, who resumed raiding their Lakota enemies.

Like most fur-trading enterprises, the Hudson's Bay Company preferred to provide guns rather than missionaries, from a conviction that Christianity ruined hunters. The company also meant to keep the Cree from learning much about the English culture, lest that knowledge render them too savvy as traders. In 1724 the directors rebuked a factor for teaching a few Cree to read and write, lest they "prye into ye Secrets of their affairs." In fact, the Cree quickly learned the tricks of the trade and used French competition to demand fair prices and quality goods. In 1728 a factor warned the directors, "Never was any man so upbraided with our powder, kettles, and hatchets, than we have been this summer by all the natives, especially by those that border near the French . . . for the natives are grown so politic in their way of trade, so as they are not to be dealt by as formerly." As they became dependent upon guns and other metal goods, Indians also became more canny and critical consumers, lest faulty items threaten their survival.

In contrast to the aggressive French traders, who ventured deep into Indian country, the British factors cautiously stuck to their posts beside the bay, wary of the forbidding (to the British) interior maze of rivers, forests, swamps, and lakes. They expected the Indians to come to them, bearing the hardships to travel hundreds of miles in canoes along dangerous waters. Nonetheless, the French believed that the Hudson's Bay Company was expanding southwestward to seduce Indians throughout the interior. Because trade and alliance were inseparable in native America, the French worried that the Hudson's Bay Company could then turn the Indians against New France. To keep the Indians away from the British, the French had to intercept them as customers and allies.

The imaginative French also feared that the Indians would help the British discover an easy route across the continent to the Pacific and the trade riches of China. Underestimating the width of the continent and blissfully ignorant of the Rocky Mountains, the French imagined an interior sea, somewhere just west of Lake Superior, that communicated directly with the Pacific. Driven by alarm and fantasy, the French worked to contain the Hudson's Bay Company by extending their own trade westward, beyond Lake Superior. The governor-general of New France reasoned, "If the savages find the French on their passage, they will not go in search of the English." And Indians who traded with the French would become allies rather than enemies.

In 1727 the governor-general entrusted western expansion to Pierre Gaultier de Varennes, Sieur de la Vérendrye, a veteran fur trader and military officer. Vérendrye was supposed to finance exploration and new trading posts by collecting furs along the way. Obliged to trade first and explore later, Vérendrye proceeded incrementally. During the early 1730s his men steadily unraveled the best routes by canoe through the lakes and rivers west of Lake Superior as far as Lake Winnipeg (in present Manitoba), a key spot at the transition between the southern watershed of Hudson Bay and the northeastern margin of the Great Plains. Along that route, Vérendrye built small, stockaded posts, well supplied with French goods, which captured much of the western Cree, Monsoni, and Assiniboine trade, reducing the number of beaver pelts that reached Hudson Bay.

But trade meant alliance, which brought dangerous complications. The western Cree and Monsoni demanded that Vérendrye supply and assist their war parties, just as the Huron, Algonkin, and Montagnais had compelled Samuel de Champlain to join them against the Iroquois in 1609. Like Champlain, Vérendrye submitted to immediate necessity and thereby created an enduring enemy. He supplied munitions and his eldest son, Jean-Baptiste, as a military adviser to a war party that inflicted heavy casualties on the Lakota. Vérendrye also accepted Lakota captives in payment from his allies for French goods. He conveyed the captives eastward for sale at Montreal, where labor was preciously scarce and a Lakota slave sold for 351 livres, the equivalent of an entire pack of prime beaver pelts. Although it yielded the immediate profits needed to fund his enterprise, the slave trade alienated the Lakota, who threatened Vérendrye's venture in the long term.

In 1736 the Lakota took revenge by ambushing and exterminating a party of twenty-one French who worked for Vérendrye. As a message of contempt for the French and their fur trade, the Lakota decapitated the dead, wrapped each head in a beaver skin, and left the parcels conspicuously beside the waterway for Vérendrye to find. One of those heads had belonged to his son Jean-Baptiste. For the French, the Lakota became the western equivalent of the Iroquois (and the northern counterpart to the Chickasaw): formidable enemies.

Vérendrye hoped to circumvent the Lakota to the west with help from the Assiniboine, who enthralled him with embroidered tales about the Mandan, who dwelled in earth-lodge villages on the upper Missouri River (in present-day North Dakota), about three hundred miles southwest of Lake Winnipeg. As Vérendrye wishfully interpreted these stories, the Mandan were a wealthy and civilized people who understood all of the mysteries of the interior, including the route to the Pacific. In late 1738, Vérendrye and a small French party attached themselves to the annual Assiniboine trading expedition that traveled beyond the northern forest onto the Great Plains to visit the Mandan.

Despite their great distance from European trading posts, the Mandan were not an isolated people unaffected by the new commerce. On the contrary, the French found that the Mandan already possessed some metal tools, including a few guns. Most they obtained secondhand from the Assiniboine, who had procured them at Hudson Bay, more than a thousand miles away to the northeast. But the French also found metal items that originated in New Mexico—another thousand miles to the southwest. Shortly after Vérendrye's visit, the Mandan also acquired horses from the southwest. Their villages became the great trading centers for natives both north and south to swap guns for horses. In sum, the Mandan dwelled at the midpoint of a two-thousand-mile-long trade corridor that extended from Hispanic New Mexico to British Hudson Bay, passing across the new French presence at Lake Winnipeg. During the eighteenth century, long-distance native and European trade routes and networks were intersecting, bringing colonial influence and rivalries to every corner of the continent. But the bearers of that influence were often natives pursuing their own interests—sometimes at odds with the schemes of the colonizers.

After a brief visit, Vérendrye returned northeastward to Lake Winnipeg. He never revisited the Mandan villages, but in 1742 Vérendrye dispatched four other Frenchmen, including two of his sons, to retrace and extend his steps. With the help of various plains nomads, the younger Vérendryes crossed the plains, probably reaching the Black Hills of western South Dakota before turning back. Their long, difficult, and unprofitable journey frustrated wishful thinking that a narrow continent or an interior sea offered an easy path to the Pacific. The Vérendryes instead learned the hard way that wide plains and formidable mountains dominated the vast interior of the continent. Thereafter, the French desisted from further attempts to cross the northern plains. Indeed, after 1744 they had to conserve their resources to the east, in Canada and the Great Lakes, where they struggled to repel British invaders determined to conquer New France.

18

Imperial Wars and Crisis

1739–75

The Shawnee and Lenni Lenape Indians of the Ohio Valley surrender their adopted captives, former colonial children, to Colonel Henry Bouquet in 1764. Demanded by the British commanders as a prerequisite of peace, the surrender was traumatic for the Indian families and for the youngest captives. A secretary records the names of the children while British troops loom in the right background. The engraving is based on a drawing by famed artist Benjamin West. From William Smith, An Historical Account of the Expedition Against the Ohio Indians in the Year 1764 *(Philadelphia, 1766).*

BETWEEN 1689 AND 1763 THE BRITISH EMPIRE waged four wide-ranging wars with the French. The empires fought for predominance in Europe and for mastery of the colonies and control over the shipping lanes across the Atlantic and Indian oceans. The wars came in two cycles, on either end of a long interlude of peace. The first cycle, 1689–1713, featured the Nine Years War (1689–97) and the War of the Spanish Succession (1702–13). That cycle so exhausted the belligerents that they avoided another major conflict for twenty-six years. In 1739 the British renewed war with Spain, which broadened to include France five years later, spawning the second cycle of war, which endured until 1763. During the first cycle, North America was a sideshow in wars fought primarily in Europe. In the second, the colonies assumed a new military importance, especially to the British. During the ultimate imperial conflict, the Seven Years War, the British decided to expand their empire deep into North America by investing men and money as never before to conquer New France.

British success threatened the Indian peoples of the interior, for they depended upon playing off rival empires to maintain their own autonomy. Deprived of a French counterweight, the British empire could sweep settlements deep into the continent, pushing the Indians aside and transforming their land into farms and towns. The victory of the British introduced a dangerous new stage in the colonization of North America, when their large colonial population on the Atlantic seaboard would break through the Appalachian Mountains into the great heartland of the continent, the vast Mississippi watershed.

But that new stage challenged colonial allegiance to the British empire. After making such a major investment of money and lives in North America during the Seven Years War, the British were not about to resume their former policy of benign neglect. During the 1760s, Parliament and the crown worked to strengthen imperial management of an enlarged domain that threatened to spin beyond control. Concluding that the empire was too weak and the colonists too insubordinate, the British tightened enforcement of the trade laws, maintained a permanent garrison in North America, and imposed new taxes to pay for it. That shift in imperial policy shocked the colonial leaders of the Atlantic seaboard into recognizing and defending their distinctive way of life. Push came to shove as both colonists and imperialists belatedly recognized the contradiction, long overlooked, between the growth in imperial ambition and the persistence of colonial autonomy. By 1775 a majority of the colonial elite felt a new confidence in their ability to defy the British empire—if necessary—and to conquer and develop the continent for their own purposes.

RENEWED WAR

During the 1720s and 1730s the dominant British politician, Sir Robert Walpole, preferred stability and peace over the costly uncertainties of a renewed war with France. After the long, expensive, and destructive War of the Spanish Succession (1702–13), the British public and Parliament initially welcomed Walpole's peace program. By the mid-1730s, however, Britons began to forget the costs of war as they instead noted, with growing alarm, the renewed wealth and power of France. The French empire grew especially rich in the West Indies, where French sugar plantations surged past the British in productivity and production. Not yet willing to challenge the French directly, British warmongers hoped instead to catch up by plundering France's ally Spain. By seizing Spanish shipping, ports, and islands around the Caribbean, the war party hoped to restore Britain's predominance in the West Indies. British imperialists perceived Spain as a rich but decadent power, a bloated and tempting victim for fleecing, rather than as a dangerous adversary.

In the press and Parliament, the war party fanned public outrage over the severe treatment of British sailors and smugglers by Spanish colonial authorities. In particular, the war partisans lamented that Captain Robert Jenkins, a smuggler, had lost an ear to Spanish colonial justice. Overriding Walpole, in 1739 a belligerent Parliament ordered British warships to seize Spanish shipping as a reprisal. One of Walpole's principal critics, Admiral Edward Vernon, commanded a British fleet that captured the valuable Caribbean seaport of Portobello in November. The victory inflamed British and colonial fantasies of easy pickings in a full-scale war with Spain. Popularly called the War of Jenkins's Ear, this was the first imperial conflict that began over a colonial issue and was primarily waged on the American side of the Atlantic.

Unfortunately for the British, the Spanish failed to live down to their lowly stereotype as easy victims. Resourceful commanders and valiant soldiers effectively defended well-designed fortifications to frustrate the two major British assaults: in 1740 on San Agustín in Florida and in 1741 on the Caribbean seaport of Cartagena. The British forces also suffered from bungling commanders and heavy losses to disease, especially yellow fever. Lured by fantasies of golden plunder, 3,500 colonists joined the Cartagena expedition, but fewer than half survived to return home in defeat. The debacle persuaded the surviving colonists that the British officers were incompetent martinets; the Britons concluded that the Americans were undisciplined cowards. The only significant British victory came on defense, in repelling a Spanish assault on the new colony of Georgia in 1742.

Fearing that the British would recoup their losses and expand their attacks, the French government belatedly rallied to support Spain in 1744, which widened the conflict under a new name: the War of the Austrian Succession. Thereafter the conflict shifted back to the traditional setting in Europe, where massive armies clashed in Flanders and Germany. Except for supplying a few warships, after 1744 the British left colonial warfare to the colonists, expecting nothing better than a stalemate in America. As in the past wars, the French Canadians and their Indian allies devastated the exposed frontier settlements of New England from Maine to western Massachusetts. To the immense surprise of the British, however, the New English also won the one great victory in the war: the capture of the French fortress at Louisbourg.

By the 1713 Treaty of Utrecht, the French had surrendered Acadia to the British, who renamed the colony Nova Scotia. Because the Acadians lingered and retained the best farmland, few Britons came to colonize in Nova Scotia, leaving the population small (six thousand) and overwhelmingly French. The Nova Scotia officials exercised little authority beyond their small garrison at Annapolis, and they confronted a far more formidable French position at Louisbourg, a fortified seaport built on Cape Breton Island, in the Gulf of St. Lawrence.

The French designed Louisbourg to defend their long supply line up the St. Lawrence River to Quebec, to protect the lucrative French fisheries in the gulf, and to harass New English shipping in wartime. Begun in 1718, the construction cost the French 3.5 million livres, about four times the ordinary annual budget for all of New France. Surrounded by massive stone walls, bristling with cannon, and garrisoned by about 1,500 regulars, Louisbourg was the most formidable American fortress north of Cuba. Home to about 4,200 colonists, Louisbourg eclipsed Quebec as the largest town in New France. Louisbourg shifted the front line of Canada's maritime defense beyond Quebec into the Atlantic; any renewed British assault on New France would first have to capture the new fortress.

In 1744, upon learning of the new war between France and Britain, the Louisbourg commander attacked the fishing stations and boats of Nova Scotia, and he unleashed his privateers to seize New English ships. The able and ambitious royal governor of Massachusetts, William Shirley, seized the opportunity to win both colonial popularity and British respect by organizing an expedition to seize Louisbourg. Assisted by a British naval squadron, four thousand New English volunteers besieged and captured the formidable fortress in 1745. After so many failures in war against New France, the capture of Louisbourg thrilled the New English, who felt a new sense of pride in, and importance to, the British empire.

Consequently, they were dismayed when the British government used the fortress as a bargaining chip in the 1748 peace negotiations. To secure a French withdrawal from conquests in India and Flanders, the British restored Louisbourg to France. Begun in 1739 in hopes of winning a golden empire in America from the Spanish, the war ended nine years later as a bloody stalemate without any colonial gains to the British. The peace treaty also proved surprisingly unpopular in Britain. Denouncing the return of Louisbourg, opposition politicians hammered the administration for neglecting the colonies. Noting the growing importance of the colonists as consumers of British manufactures, the critics charged that a sleeping administration risked losing America to French aggression. Wounded by the criticism, the imperial authorities resolved to pay closer attention to North America in the next war, and to keep any gains made there.

BALANCE OF POWER

Savvy imperialists recognized that Indians determined the military balance of power within North America. In 1755 an English trader observed:

> The importance of the Indians is now generally known and understood. A Doubt remains not, that the prosperity of our Colonies on the Continent will stand or fall with our Interest and favour among them. While they are our Friends, they are the Cheapest and Strongest Barrier for the Protection of our Settlements; when Enemies, they are capable of ravaging in their method of War, in spite of all we can do, to render those Possessions almost useless.

Skilled at guerrilla warfare, Indians dominated the forest passages between the rival empires. They could obstruct the advance of their colonial enemy and terrify and destroy outlying settlements.

Divided into many tribes and subdivided into hundreds of autonomous villages, the Indian peoples were further riven by factional divisions led by rival chiefs. Nonetheless, the natives shared a broad interest in exploiting and perpetuating their strategic position between the French and the British colonies. Benefiting from the competition between the traders and officials of rival empires, the Indians sought favorable prices and abundant presents from both sides.

The Six Nation Iroquois enjoyed the most strategic location along the major waterways between French Canada and the British colony of New York. In a rough and forested continent, colonial armies with cannon could barely move overland. Far better to proceed in boats via the larger rivers and lakes, which channeled most military operations along a few strategic corridors, where the colonists built forts and cultivated Indian allies. The two principal corridors ran through Iroquoia: first, the north-south passage along Lake Champlain between Albany on the Hudson and Montreal on the St. Lawrence; and second, the east-west route along the Mohawk and Oswego rivers that linked Albany with the Great Lakes.

Although numbering only about two thousand warriors in 1720, the Iro-

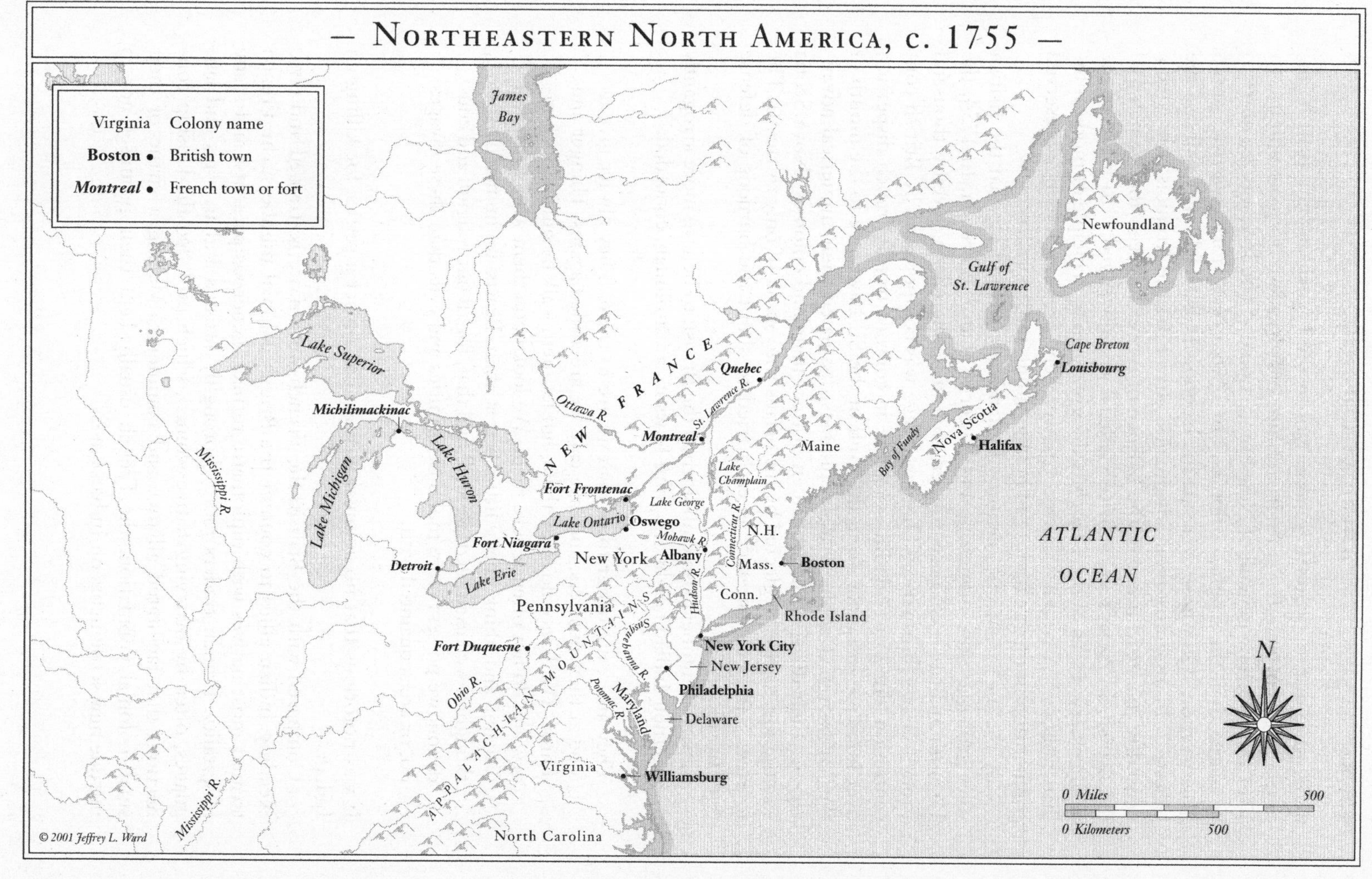
— Northeastern North America, c. 1755 —
Virginia Colony name
Boston • British town
Montreal • French town or fort
James Bay
Newfoundland
Gulf of St. Lawrence
Cape Breton
Louisbourg
Lake Superior
NEW FRANCE
Quebec
St. Lawrence R.
Ottawa R.
Michilimackinac
Montreal
Nova Scotia
Halifax
Bay of Fundy
Maine
Mississippi R.
Lake Michigan
Lake Huron
Lake Champlain
Fort Frontenac
Lake George
Lake Ontario
Oswego
Mohawk R.
Connecticut R.
N.H.
Fort Niagara
New York
Albany
Mass.
Boston
ATLANTIC OCEAN
Detroit
Lake Erie
Hudson R.
Conn.
Rhode Island
Pennsylvania
APPALACHIAN MOUNTAINS
Susquehanna R.
New York City
Fort Duquesne
New Jersey
N
Ohio R.
Potomac R.
Maryland
Philadelphia
Delaware
Virginia
Williamsburg
0 Miles 500
0 Kilometers 500
© 2001 Jeffrey L. Ward
Mississippi R.
North Carolina

quois were disproportionately important to the French and the British empires. Both coveted Iroquois friendship and dreaded Iroquois enmity. In 1711 the governor-general of New France noted, "The Iroquois are more to be feared than the English colonies." In 1746 a New York colonist assured his governor, "On whose ever side the Iroquois Indians fall, they will cast the balance." To maximize their advantages, after 1701 the Iroquois cultivated a neutrality meant to preserve the balance of power between the French and the British. In New York, a British official acknowledged, "To preserve the balance between us & the French is the great ruling principle of modern Indian politics." A rough balance of power kept presents flowing, preserved competition in the fur trade, and held invading settlers at bay.

By the mid-eighteenth century, Indian leaders could see that the British were growing more numerous and powerful than the French. In 1754, the 1.5 million British colonists immensely outnumbered the seventy thousand French in North America. That advantage was compounded by British concentration along the Atlantic seaboard, in contrast to the French dispersion over immense distances, from the Gulf of the St. Lawrence to the mouth of the Mississippi. But the British colonists dissipated their numerical advantage by their division into fourteen distinct mainland colonies (Nova Scotia was the fourteenth, neglected by historians who speak of only thirteen). The fourteen rarely cooperated, as each tried to shunt the burdens of defense onto the others.

Superior numbers also emboldened the British to behave more arrogantly toward their Indian neighbors. John Lawson, a Carolinian, conceded:

> They are really better to us than we are to them. They always give us food at their quarters, and take care we are armed against Hunger and Thirst. We do not do so by them, but let them walk by our Doors hungry, and do not often relieve them. We look upon them with scorn and disdain, and think them little better than Beasts in human shape, though, if well examined, we shall find that, for all our religion and education, we possess more moral deformities and evils than these savages do, or are acquainted with.

It was notorious that no colonial jury would convict a settler for killing an Indian.

Compared with the British, the French were more restrained and civil. Needing Indian allies to counter the British colonial numbers, the French treated most natives with diplomatic respect, generous presents, and ready hospitality. French traders more thoroughly learned Indian ways and languages, often by marrying native women, which provided the kinship connections that facilitated alliance and commerce. Making a virtue of their small colonial population, the French usually kept their promises not to intrude new settlements on Indian lands.

French officials regarded the Indians as both indispensable and insufferable, for they were the colony's best defense, but their demands demonstrated that they knew it. To mobilize war parties required French arms, ammunition, presents, and feasts. During expeditions with French forces, the Indians acted independently, taking no orders, fighting in their own fashion, and returning home whenever they felt insulted or weary. The officials also had to buy scalps and prisoners, at no small expense. All of these expenditures maddened colonial officials, who were under constant pressure from the crown to economize. In 1747 one long-suffering intendant lamented:

> Persuaded of their usefulness to the colony (which is true), more often than not they are so boastful as to greet our hospitable treatment with complaints. . . . Indeed, I could carry on forever were I to convey the ceaseless importunities with which they try us. . . . Still, one has to admit that their continued forays against the enemy have bred such horror as to prevent—for the time being—plots against the colony from bearing fruit.

Although native warriors cost considerably less than French soldiers, the officials of a hierarchical society resented the need to treat Indians with tact and generosity.

Grudgingly accepting these frustrations, the French shaped their military strategy in North America to construct a network of Indian alliances. Lacking settlers, the French had to rely on the natives to hold the interior against British settlers, traders, and soldiers. To cultivate Indian support, the French established a long string of small forts and trading posts that stretched around the Great Lakes and down the Ohio and Mississippi valleys. Lightly built and garrisoned, the posts depended upon the local Indians for protection and paid for it with presents and mediation. In general, the natives welcomed the French posts as assets, instead of resenting them as threats. An Indian reassured his compatriots:

> Brethren, are you ignorant of the difference between our Father [the French] and the English? Go and see the forts our Father has created, and you will see that the land beneath their walls is still hunting ground, . . . whilst the English, on the contrary, no sooner get possession of a country than the game is forced to leave; the trees fall down before them, the earth becomes bare.

Similarly (but more cynically) another chief preferred French neighbors because, he explained, "we can drive away the French when we please."

In sum, by 1750 the Indians faced a greater threat of settler invasion and environmental transformation from the numerous and aggressive English than from the few and more generous French. Noting the French advantage,

Governor Shirley of Massachusetts warned, "A few Indians do more execution, as we see, than four or five times their number of our men, and they have almost all the Indians of the continent to join them."

That Indian support, however, was soft, because the British colonists had one great countervailing advantage; although rude and intrusive, they offered superior trade goods in abundant quantities and at relatively attractive prices. Dependent upon European cloth, metals, and alcohol, native peoples often embraced the better deals that British traders offered for their deerskins and beaver pelts. In wartime, the British navy compounded the trade advantage by controlling the sea lanes and destroying French merchant shipping. A prolonged war depleted the supplies in New France and Louisiana, obliging more Indians to make peace with British officials so that they could obtain trade goods.

THE SEVEN YEARS WAR

The peace of 1748 proved short-lived, as both the French and the British overreacted to local aggressions as if they were part of some grand power play by the other empire. In Nova Scotia, the British established a fortified town and navy base at Halifax in 1749 to counter nearby Louisbourg. Alarmed, the French promptly built two new forts at the head of the Bay of Fundy to hem in Nova Scotia to the west, which the British resented as an intrusion on their colony. Farther west, Virginia land speculators coveted the immense and fertile valley of the Ohio river which began beyond the Appalachian Mountains in western Pennsylvania and flowed southwestward into the Mississippi. And Pennsylvania traders crossed the Ohio to capture a growing share of the fur trade with the Indians. To protect their native alliance and communications between Canada and Louisiana, in 1753–54 the French sent troops to plunder and oust the Pennsylvania traders and to build a new set of forts, principally Fort Duquesne at the forks of the Ohio (present Pittsburgh). In turn, British colonial officials interpreted the French moves as aggression: as a conspiracy to confine and strangle the coastal colonies. For both empires, the colonies had assumed a greater importance that elevated their frictions into the grounds for global war.

The climactic imperial war for North America erupted in 1754, when the British governor of Virginia, Robert Dinwiddie, tried to oust the French from the forks of the Ohio. In addition to asserting Virginia's jurisdiction, Dinwiddie promoted his own interest in a company of land speculators determined to sell Ohio Valley lands to settlers. Dinwiddie sent a small regiment of colonial troops commanded by his fellow land speculator, the young and ambitious George Washington, to evict the French.

Embarked on his first command, Washington promptly displayed his inexperience. Although superior French numbers were building Fort Duquesne, Washington foolishly attacked and destroyed a small French patrol. Understandably upset, the main French force and their Indian allies surrounded Washington's camp, a crude stockade that he had built in a swamp surrounded by high ground. When it began to rain heavily, his soldiers wallowed in water as the French and Indians fired on them from the hills. Compelled to surrender on July 4, Washington was fortunate to receive generous terms from the victors. Hoping to avoid a full-scale war, the French commander allowed Washington and his men to limp back to Virginia.

Imperial officials in Paris and London were already preparing for a new war, subsequently known as the Seven Years War. Informed of Washington's defeat, the British government resolved to escalate the conflict and make war in North America its highest priority. In 1755 the British sent unprecedented numbers of troops to the mainland colonies to seize control of their frontier from the French. One combined force of British regulars and New English volunteers won an easy but modest victory by overwhelming the two French posts at the head of the Bay of Fundy in Nova Scotia. The victors then deported most of the Acadian French and confiscated their farms and livestock for appropriation by New English land speculators and settlers. By treating the Acadians so harshly, the British stiffened the resolve of the Canadians to resist invasion.

Meanwhile, the primary British expedition reaped disaster. To recoup Washington's setback, a veteran British general, Edward Braddock, marched 2,200 regular and colonial troops against Fort Duquesne. Although brave and energetic, Braddock was also arrogant, stubborn, and inexperienced at warfare in the American forests. Unwilling to adapt, Braddock expressed contempt for both Indians and colonists. He assured Benjamin Franklin, "These savages may, indeed, be a formidable enemy to your raw American militia, but upon the king's regular and disciplined troops, sir, it is impossible to believe they should make any impression." They made quite an impression when Braddock marched his men directly into an ambush within ten miles of Fort Duquesne. Although the French and Indians had only half as many men, they exploited the forest, firing from behind trees and rocks into the massed and exposed British and colonial ranks. The French and the Indians suffered only about forty casualties while killing or wounding nearly a thousand men in the British force. The dead included General Braddock. The British debacle had one silver lining: George Washington inherited the command and redeemed his military reputation by resourcefully conducting a retreat that saved half the army.

Braddock had blundered into the ambush because he lacked the Indian allies needed to supply scouts and partisans for forest warfare. Only eight natives accompanied his army, and Braddock ignored their advice. One Indian recalled, "He looked upon us as dogs and would never hear anything [we] said to him." No expedition through the forest could prosper without significant Indian support and without heeding Indian expertise.

Braddock's defeat emboldened the Lenni Lenape and Shawnee of the Ohio Valley to attack the hated colonial settlements in Virginia, Maryland, and Pennsylvania. By the spring of 1756, the raiders had killed or captured at least seven hundred settlers. In a panic, the survivors abandoned their farms and fled eastward, pushing the frontier back to within a hundred miles of Philadelphia. The Indian raids also pinned down colonial troops, which enabled the French to take the offensive in 1756 and 1757, under the able leadership of Governor-General Pierre de Rigaud de Vaudreuil and General Louis-Joseph de Montcalm. They mustered small but effective forces that combined French regulars, Canadian militia, and Indian warriors to capture British forts on Lake Ontario in 1756 and on Lake George in 1757. In both cases, the nearby but alienated Iroquois provided little or no help to the British defenders. Short of men and provisions, Montcalm could not garrison the captured forts; instead he destroyed both and withdrew to Canada.

Montcalm also weakened his victories by alienating many of his Indian allies. A regular officer trained in Europe, Montcalm despised the disorder and atrocities of frontier raiding—a mode of war that the Canadian-born Vaudreuil championed as essential to the defense of undermanned New France. At Lake George, Montcalm enraged the Indians with his well-intentioned but ineffectual attempts to liberate their prisoners. The Indians promptly killed many prisoners and returned home in anger. Most refused to assist the French in future campaigns, which weakened the front lines of Canadian defense. Vaudreuil denounced Montcalm, producing a bitter feud that ruined their cooperation—with fatal consequences for New France.

In Great Britain the embarrassing military setbacks of 1755–57 brought to power a new and more competent administration headed by William Pitt, a blunt man whose ability matched his towering ego. In 1757, Pitt boasted, "I believe that I can save this nation and that no one else can." Despite the expansion of the war in 1756 to include Europe, Pitt clung to the America-first policy, investing even more troops and money in North America. Pitt also defused tensions between colonial governments and British commanders over their requisitions of men and supplies. Instead of ordering colonial cooperation, Pitt bought it by reimbursing in cash their expenditures, which dramatically increased the colonial contributions. Although politically expedient, Pitt's policy was financially reckless: by augmenting the monstrous public debt, Pitt saddled the colonists and Britons with a burden that would violently disrupt the empire after the war.

For the North American campaign of 1758 the British employed some 45,000 troops, about half British regulars and half colonial volunteers. Against such large numbers, New France could muster only 6,800 regulars and 2,700 provincials, supplemented by volatile Indian warriors and drafted Canadian militiamen. Their morale flagged as hunger prevailed in Canada after the disappointing harvests of 1757 and 1758. The French troops received less than half their usual rations, while many habitants faced starvation. The skyrocketing price of food devastated the Canadian economy and virtually bankrupted the colonial government. Putting a higher priority on operations in Europe, the French government virtually wrote off Canada, leaving Vaudreuil and Montcalm to muddle and squabble through with their small and shrinking forces.

Pitt also appointed more competent and adaptable generals to command the growing forces deployed against New France. Regular troops, heavy artillery, and siege warfare remained at the core of every British expedition, but the new commanders diversified their forces to counter the Canadian irregulars and Indian warriors. The British recruited colonists into new ranger units that used Indian tactics and trained some British light infantry units to use rifles and tomahawks instead of the customary muskets and bayonets.

The British war effort in North America also thrived as the royal navy won control of the Atlantic, reducing the reinforcements and supplies that reached New France. As trade goods became scarce at French posts, many Indians sought an alternative supply, especially of the guns, gunpowder, and shot needed for hunting and war. In the Ohio Valley in 1758, as a new British army advanced on Fort Duquesne, the Shawnee and Lenni Lenape deserted the French and reopened trade with the Pennsylvanians. Abandoned by the Indians, the French blew up Fort Duquesne and fled northward. To the Indians' dismay, the British replaced Fort Duquesne by building Fort Pitt, which was ten times larger than its French predecessor—an ominous sign of British intentions.

In 1758 a massive British fleet and thirteen thousand regulars, commanded by General Jeffrey Amherst, besieged and captured fortress Louisbourg. This cleared the way for General James Wolfe to ascend the St. Lawrence to attack Quebec, the key to Canada, in 1759. Frustrated by the massive fortifications and Montcalm's resourceful defense, Wolfe made one last desperate gamble, scaling a cliff at night to assemble his troops on a field, called the Plains of Abraham, just outside the city walls. Lacking an easy retreat, the British forces faced destruction if defeated. Fortunately for the British, Montcalm also gambled, marching out of the relative security of the city to give battle in the open field. As European veterans, neither Wolfe nor Montcalm could resist the fatal temptation of a conventional battle: the first in the colonies. After a half-hour battle, the French broke and ran back to Quebec.

Both Montcalm and Wolfe suffered mortal wounds, leaving other commanders to offer and receive Quebec's surrender on September 18. In death, Wolfe became larger than life—a martyr for the British empire. The London writer Horace Walpole saw an infusion of nationalism as the "whole people . . . triumphed—and they wept—for Wolfe had fallen in the hour of victory!"

The British mopped up the remaining French in Canada during 1760. British regulars and colonial volunteers advanced on Montreal in overwhelming numbers from three directions: Quebec, Lake Champlain, and

Lake Ontario. Convening at Montreal in early September, the British forces, led by Amherst, obliged Governor-General Vaudreuil to surrender all of New France, including the remaining forts around the Great Lakes to the west.

The British overwhelmed New France with sheer numbers of soldiers and sailors, warships and cannon. That ability to project military power across the Atlantic reflected British superiority in shipping, finance, and organization. And that superiority reflected the more advanced nature of Britain as a capitalist society endowed with far more liquid capital and financial acumen. The British had more money, spent it with wild abandon, and concentrated their expenditures in North America (while the French had to invest most of their resources in their army in Germany). The conquest of Canada cost the British empire about £4 million, more than ten times what the French spent to defend it. Never before had any empire spent so much money to wage war on a transoceanic scale.

And the conquest of Canada was only part of a global set of British victories in the largest war ever waged by Europeans. In 1759 the British reaffirmed their naval supremacy by crippling the Spanish and French fleets in battles at Lagos, off Portugal, and Quiberon Bay, on the west coast of France. In the Caribbean, a British amphibious operation captured the lucrative sugar island of Guadeloupe. In West Africa, the British seized the French slaving entrepôt at Senegal. The British also secured a dominant position in India by routing the French and their local allies.

Until 1762 the Spanish remained on the sidelines, but they became alarmed as continued British victories shattered the old balance of power. Instead of reversing the British victories, the Spanish entry escalated them. British forces captured Manila in the Philippines and the great port of Havana on Cuba, where the Spanish had stored much of their Mexican bullion. Another British fleet and army seized the sugar-rich French West Indian islands of Martinique, Dominica, St. Lucia, Grenada, and St. Vincent. So many victories embarrassed British diplomats striving to draw the proud French and Spanish to negotiate peace.

At last, in early 1763, the belligerents concluded the Treaty of Paris. The French conceded Canada and all of their claims east of the Mississippi, including the Ohio Valley. The British also retained the lesser of their French West Indian conquests: Dominica, Grenada, St. Vincent, and Tobago. To mollify the French, the British returned the major islands of Guadeloupe, Martinique, and St. Lucia. The victors also restored French access to the valuable fishing waters off Newfoundland by conceding two small, unfortified islands in the Gulf of St. Lawrence. As a sop to their Spanish allies, the French gave them New Orleans and most of Louisiana (west of the Mississippi River). Although Louisiana was a troublesome money-loser, the Spanish hoped that it would enhance the security of New Spain by providing a frontier buffer zone. To regain Havana, the Spanish ceded Florida to the

British. The various swaps made the Mississippi the boundary between the British and the Spanish claims in North America. Of course, most of the interior remained in the possession of Indian peoples, who denied the European power to dispose of their lands.

In preparing for negotiations, the British considered keeping most of the French West Indies and returning Canada. Although much smaller, the sugar islands were far more lucrative. But the influential British West Indian lobby did not want to weaken its advantageous position within the empire by accepting new competition from the more productive plantations on Guadeloupe and Martinique. The British West Indians lobbied to keep Canada instead, which reassured the mainland colonists, who feared a grander version of the 1748 giveaway of Louisbourg. By taking vast new territories in the Treaty of Paris, the British broke with a previous imperial policy that had sought to maximize maritime commerce while minimizing continental entanglements. Somehow they would have to raise the money to administer and garrison their expensive new domains in Canada, the Great Lakes, the Ohio Valley, and Florida.

In surprising ways, the peace benefited the war's losers more than the British victors. Generating scant revenue, Louisiana, New France, and Florida had drained the French and Spanish of funds and soldiers, all better spent and employed on more valuable colonies in the Caribbean. While losing little of real (immediate) value, the French and the Spanish recovered their most valuable losses: Guadeloupe, Martinique, Cuba, and access to the Newfoundland fisheries.

Humiliated by their defeats, the French and Spanish resolved to strike back and restore the balance of power at their next opportunity. Learning from defeat, they rebuilt and reformed their armies and navies. In the next conflict with Britain, the French and the Spanish would be far leaner and meaner adversaries. And in the next war, the British could not count on assistance from any European allies, for all concluded that Great Britain had grown too rich and too powerful. The British had replaced the French as the expansionist power considered most dangerous to the rest of Europe. Nor would the British be able to count on their own colonists, who would find in the victory the grounds for their own rebellion. Instead, in the War of the American Revolution, the British would have to recruit allies from among the Indians who had formerly defended Canada and harried British America.

INDIAN REBELLIONS

The collapse of New France was dreadful news to the Indians of the interior. No longer could they play the French and the British off against one another to maintain their own independence, maximize their presents, and ensure trade competition. When British troops occupied the French forts, colonial traders flocked into the Ohio and Great Lakes countries. Most cheated and abused Indians in pursuit of immediate profit, rather than cultivating long-term relationships as the French had done. Colonial governors also did little to restrain the flood of settlers into the Carolina backcountry and the Ohio Valley. And the British military commander, Jeffrey Amherst, cut off the delivery of presents, deeming them a waste of money, given the removal of the French competition. Amherst suffered from the imperial delusion that his scattered forces could impose a new order on the vast Indian country and its messy tangle of relationships involving diverse villages, contentious traders, rival missionaries, and intruding settlers. Feeling insulted and aggrieved by the intrusions and the cutbacks, the Indian chiefs began to cultivate a new cooperation between their peoples in search of a common redress.

The Indian discontent first erupted into war in an unexpected place: the South Carolina frontier, where the Cherokee had long allied with the colonists. Late in the Seven Years War, with the French facing defeat, reckless Carolina settlers invaded Cherokee lands and poached their deer. Some especially ruthless frontiersmen killed Cherokee to procure scalps to collect the large bounties offered by the colony of Virginia. It was impossible to tell a Cherokee scalp from that of a hostile Shawnee—and far easier to kill an unsuspecting people than one prepared for war. The £50 bounty for an adult scalp allured settlers who rarely could make that much in a year. They rationalized that all Indians were their enemies, if not immediately, then inevitably.

In 1759, the Cherokee warriors took revenge by killing about thirty settlers. Escalating the conflict, the South Carolina authorities demanded that the Cherokee surrender the warriors as murder suspects for colonial trial and execution. The chiefs proposed the traditional alternative: they would compensate for every settler death with a French scalp or prisoner. The South Carolina governor abruptly rejected that offer, for he wanted a Cherokee submission to colonial law more than additional dead Frenchmen. His intransigence appalled the Cherokee, who recognized that submission would sacrifice their independence. The impatient Carolinians completed the rupture by seizing and executing twenty-two chiefs who had come to the colony for further negotiations.

A numerous people (twelve thousand) inhabiting about forty villages in the defensible valleys of the southern Appalachian mountains, the Cherokee were a formidable enemy. In 1760 they ravaged the South Carolina frontier settlements, captured a British fort (Fort Loudon), and frustrated an invasion by a mixed force of British regulars and Carolina volunteers.

In 1761, however, the tide turned against the Cherokee. British and colonial forces invaded the Cherokee country to destroy fifteen towns and their crops, sentencing the survivors to severe hunger. Cherokee resistance had faltered for want of sufficient gunpowder and shot for their guns. The

Cherokee had hoped to procure a supply from the French, but the British fleet blocked French shipments to Louisiana. The Cherokee had also expected assistance from the Creek Confederacy, the most numerous and powerful set of native peoples in the southeast. The Creek, however, depended upon their Carolina suppliers for trade goods. Showered with British presents, the Creek remained neutral. Deprived of corn, gunpowder, and allies, the Cherokee had to make peace. Although they ceded additional lands to South Carolina, the Cherokee avoided surrendering the murder suspects to colonial trial.

In Cherokee defeat, the northern Indians saw their own fate if they did not unite against the British occupation of the former French forts. But the northern Indians could also find inspiration in the Cherokee ability to take a major British fort. During the spring of 1763 the Indians in the Ohio Valley and the Great Lakes covertly prepared for war. The defiant peoples included Mississauga, Ottawa, Potawatomi, Huron, Ojibwa, Wyandot, Miami, Kickapoo, Mascouten, Lenni Lenape, Illinois, Shawnee, and even one of the Iroquois Six Nations, the westernmost Seneca. Despite their linguistic and traditional differences, the natives found a new common ground in their shared grievances against the British traders, soldiers, and settlers.

The natives also felt a new commonality as Indians, above and beyond their traditional tribal and village identities. This Pan-Indian sensibility emerged from the teaching of a new set of religious prophets, led by a Lenni Lenape named Neolin. Adapting Christian ideas selectively to update native traditions, the prophets proclaimed a double creation: one for all Indians, the others for whites. In defense of their own divinely ordained way of life, Indians were supposed to resist colonial innovations, especially the consumption of alcohol and the cession of lands.

During the spring of 1763, far-flung native peoples surprised and captured most of the British forts around the Great Lakes and in the Ohio Valley. Through the summer and fall, they also raided the settlements of western Pennsylvania, Maryland, and Virginia, killing or capturing about two thousand colonists. By routing the British and the colonists, the Indian rebels hoped to lure the French back into North America. But the Indians failed to capture the three largest and strongest British posts: at Detroit, Niagara, and Fort Pitt.

The British preferred to blame Indian rebellions on a single mastermind, just as they had done with Metacom (King Philip) in New England in 1675 to concoct King Philip's War. Similarly, in 1763 they called the new uprising Pontiac's Rebellion, after an Ottawa chief prominent in the siege of Detroit. Although more influential than most chiefs, Pontiac could not command the diverse peoples dwelling in dozens of scattered villages. For their own, shared reasons and under their own chiefs, the various native peoples rose up in a rebellion that had no central command.

The brutal war hardened animosities along racial lines. Outraged by the atrocities of frontier war, the settlers treated all Indians, regardless of allegiance, as violent brutes best exterminated. In Pennsylvania, the peaceful Indians of the eastern enclaves suffered for the violence of the western frontier. Shortly before dawn on a snowy December 14, 1763, fifty armed Pennsylvania settlers surprised the Indian village at Conestoga. Dwelling on a small reservation amid the settlements, the natives slumbered in false security. Avoiding the war, they hoped to live in peace by raising hogs, hunting deer, tending their gardens, and making and peddling brooms and baskets to their settler neighbors. But the vigilantes, known as the Paxton Boys, insisted that all Indians were their enemies. Unable to come to grips with the frontier Indians, whose raids massacred farm families, the Paxton Boys surprised and butchered the nearby sleeping Conestoga and set ablaze the bloodied cabins.

Later that day, colonists rummaged through the smoldering ashes and scorched bones to find a bag containing the Conestoga's most precious possessions: two wampum belts and six old documents, all produced at past treaty councils to certify their status as allies of Pennsylvania. The longest and oldest document was a cherished copy of a treaty made in 1701 with William Penn, the colony's Quaker founder. The treaty pledged that the Indians and colonists "shall forever hereafter be as one Head & One Heart, & live in true Friendship & Amity as one People."

Determined to be thorough, the Paxton Boys next attacked the county jail in Lancaster, where the governor had gathered fourteen surviving Conestoga for their own protection. The vigilantes broke into the jail and killed and mutilated all fourteen. Seeking more blood, in early 1764 about five hundred armed settlers marched on Philadelphia determined to kill 140 Indian refugees gathered there. Blocked by royal troops, the Paxton Boys backed down and returned home when promised immunity from prosecution. Although spared from massacre, a third of the Indian refugees died of smallpox contracted while crowded in their Philadelphia barracks.

During the summer of 1764, the western rebels ran short on gunpowder, shot, and guns. Indians could not maintain their resistance for long without a European supplier. Unable to take the major forts, most of the Indians longed to resume a peaceful trade. At the same time, the British government eagerly sought to end the expensive and frustrating war. The crown blamed Amherst for the crisis, recalling him in disgrace. The new commander, Thomas Gage, followed the more pragmatic advice of the Indian superintendent, Sir William Johnson. Recognizing that presents and respect for Indians were far cheaper than military expeditions against them, Johnson adopted the French practices of the "middle ground" alliance. From 1764 to 1766, the various villages gradually made peace with Johnson, who distributed presents with a lavish hand.

Although they allowed the British to reoccupy the captured forts, the Indians continued to insist that they were independent peoples. In 1766, Pontiac assured Johnson:

> We tell you now [that] the French never conquered us, neither did they purchase a foot of our Country, nor have they a right to give it to you. We gave them liberty to settle for which they always rewarded us & treated us with great Civility. . . . [I]f you expect to keep these Posts, we will expect to have proper returns from you.

To avoid another expensive and bloody war, British military officers practiced a new policy of presents and conciliation at their western garrisons.

To further mollify the Indians, the crown tried to enforce a new boundary line, running north-south along the ridge of the Appalachians, a line meant to keep settlers east of the mountains. But the ten thousand British soldiers scattered through North America could never restrain the dozens of cunning land speculators (including most royal governors) and the thousands of determined settlers, who continued to flock westward into the Ohio Valley. British troops sometimes burned the log cabins of squatters, but the latter soon returned in greater numbers to rebuild. As a result, the ineffectual new boundary line merely irritated the colonists. But by trying to replicate the French role as generous and mediating "Fathers," the British won numerous Indian allies in 1776, when the colonies revolted against their "Mother Country."

IMPERIAL CRISIS

The conquest of Canada, which made the Indians so anxious, initially delighted the British colonists. After so many past wars of futile bloodshed, victory lifted the danger of French and Indian raids and seemed to open a vast and fertile continent to colonial settlement. In 1763 a farmer's almanac in New England celebrated, "But now behold! The farmer may have land for nothing. . . . Land enough for himself and all his sons, be they ever so many." Of course that land would be taken from the Indians of the interior (and it would not be had "for nothing," because settlers always found a frontier land speculator demanding payment).

The colonists felt pride in their contributions to the war effort and in belonging to such a powerful, prosperous, and relatively free empire. Celebrating the conquest of Canada, Benjamin Franklin rejoiced "not merely as I am a colonist, but as I am a Briton." By public subscription, the city of New York erected triumphant statues of both King George III and William Pitt. In Salem, Massachusetts, the Reverend Thomas Barnard depicted the victories as vindicating Protestant liberty against French absolutism, Catholic superstition, and savage violence. He predicted a glorious colonial future within a perpetual empire:

> Safe from the Enemy of the Wilderness, safe from the griping Hand of arbitrary Sway and cruel Superstition; Here shall be the late founded Seat of Peace and Freedom. Here shall our indulgent Mother [Country], who has most generously rescued and protected us, be served and honoured by growing Numbers, with all Duty, Love, and Gratitude, till Time shall be no more.

In nearby Boston a minister foretold that British America would "become in another century or two, a mighty empire," but he promptly added, "I do not mean an independent one."

And yet, within thirteen years of the treaty of peace, thirteen Atlantic seaboard colonies would revolt to wage a long war for their independence. That shocking conflict between the colonies and the mother country developed from strains initiated by winning the Seven Years War. The conquest of Canada deprived the mainland colonists and the British of a common enemy that had united them in the past. Victory invited the British to redefine the empire and to increase the colonists' burdens. But victory also emboldened the colonists to defy British demands because they no longer needed protection against the French. In 1773 the royal governor of Massachusetts noted that had Canada "remained to the French none of the spirit of opposition to the Mother Country would have yet appeared."

During the Seven Years War, British authorities began to pay closer attention to the North American colonies and to rethink how best to administer them. Impressed by the apparent prosperity of the free colonists, British concluded that they could pay higher taxes to support the empire that benefited them so greatly. This seemed only fair to the British, who had spent so much blood and treasure making the continent safe for the prospering colonists. After all, British taxpayers were already paying far heavier taxes than were the colonists: in 1763 imperial taxation averaged twenty-six shillings per person in Britain, where most subjects were struggling, compared with only one shilling per person in the colonies, where most free people were prospering.

During the war, British officers and officials were also appalled to discover that the colonists routinely ignored imperial regulations that hurt their economic interest, particularly the 1733 Molasses Act. Imposed by Parliament at the request of the powerful West Indian sugar lobby, the act imposed discriminatory duties meant to prevent the New English from importing molasses from the French West Indies to make rum. Ignoring the law, New English shippers continued to trade with the French islands, even during the Seven Years War. By feeding the French colonists and their slaves, the trade prolonged their resistance to British attacks. Shocked imperial officers and officials vowed to tighten enforcement of the trade laws, to teach discipline to the colonists, and to reap a greater revenue for the empire.

Victory had not come cheap, doubling the British debt from a prewar £73 million to a postwar £137 million. Interest payments on that debt consumed more than 60 percent of Great Britain's annual budgets during the mid-1760s. Moreover, the expanded empire in North America was far more expensive to garrison and administer. Before the Seven Years War, the British posted only a few hundred troops in North America. In 1763, however, the crown decided to maintain ten thousand men in the colonies, primarily in Canada and the Great Lakes country. With the British people already taxed to the limit, Parliament hoped to pay for the new army by levying new taxes on the colonists.

But the colonists balked at the new taxes, detecting a dangerous precedent ominous to their prosperity and liberties. Paradoxically, by protesting British taxation, the colonists affirmed their cherished identity as liberty-loving Britons, as they rallied behind the most cherished proposition of their shared political culture: that a free man paid no tax unless levied by his own representatives. The colonists devoutly believed that without such protection from arbitrary taxation, people gradually but inevitably became enslaved by domineering rulers. The colonists would pay taxes levied by their own assemblies but not by the distant Parliament, where no colonist sat. In 1764, Boston's town meeting protested Parliamentary taxation:

> This we apprehend annihilates our charter right to govern and tax ourselves. It strikes at our British privileges which, as we have never forfeited them, we hold in common with our fellow subjects who are natives of Britain. If taxes are laid upon us in any shape without ever having a legal representation where they are laid, are we not reduced from the character of free subjects to the miserable state of tributary slaves?

Colonists were quick to speak of "slavery" because they knew from their own practice on Africans where unchecked domination ultimately led. The conspicuous presence of slavery rendered liberty the more dear to the colonial owners of human property.

The colonists also began to recognize and defend the considerable autonomy that they had gained—despite the simultaneous growth, during the eighteenth century, of the empire's power and ambition. The financial and military demands of the imperial wars had strengthened the government at home but weakened its power over the colonies. Desperate to raise funds and troops for war, royal governors had to appease colonial assemblies by conceding greater control over expenditures. Of course, the assemblies were loath to surrender their gains after 1763, when Parliament and the crown abruptly demanded a new subservience.

The increased British demands also coincided with a postwar depression in the colonial economy. That crash followed the boom produced by the wartime investment of British men and money in the colonies. Long troubled by a lack of currency, the colonial economy thrived during the war from the infusion of British coin and the official indulgence of paper money issued by colonial assemblies. That boom, however, created a dependence that proved painful when Parliament stopped the transfer payments at the end of the war and forbade further issues of paper money. In the subsequent hard times of the mid-1760s, incomes fell and creditors sued for collection, just when debtors found it most difficult to pay. In 1764 a New Yorker lamented, "Everything is tumbling down, even the merchants themselves." In sum, the new parliamentary taxes on sugar (1764) and stamps (1765) and the tighter enforcement of customs regulations all came at an especially bad time for the colonists. Struggling with public and private debts, a commercial depression, and surging litigation, the colonists resented the new policies and taxes.

Instead of seeing the new permanent army in North America as a source of protection, colonial leaders felt threatened as those troops became both the pretext for raising new taxes and the means for enforcing them. In addition, after the British made peace with the Indians, the colonists concluded that the army served to protect natives from settlers rather than to help them dispossess the Indians. Rather than preserving the North American empire, the new postwar garrisons (and their associated taxes) provoked the crisis that lost most of that empire.

From 1763 to 1776 the colonial leaders conducted a prolonged and increasingly rancorous constitutional debate with Parliament over the new taxes and the army of occupation. As never before, that debate revealed to both Britons and Americans the divergent development of their societies. In Britain, most common men were "dependents" upon a patron: either tenants reliant upon an aristocratic landlord, or landless laborers dependent upon an employer. Forgetting their own slaves, colonial visitors were shocked at the extremes of wealth and poverty in the white population of Great Britain. Addressing the few colonists who aspired to Britain's industrial development, Benjamin Franklin observed:

> Let them with three-fourths of the People of Ireland, live the Year round on Potatoes and Butter Milk, without Shirts, then may their Merchants export Beef, Butter, and Linnen. Let them with the Generality of the Common People of Scotland go Barefoot, then may they make large Exports in Shoes and Stockings. And if they will be content to wear Rags like the Spinners and Weavers of England, they may make Cloths and Stuffs for all Parts of the World.

Compared with Britain, the American colonies offered greater opportunity for free people to become landowning farmers. In 1767, Governor Sir Henry

Moore of New York explained that former indentured servants accepted frontier hardships to become landowners:

> As soon as the time stipulated in their indentures is expired, they immediately quit their masters and get a small tract of land, in settling which for the first three or four years they lead miserable lives, and in the most abject poverty. But all this is patiently borne and submitted to with the greatest cheerfulness, the satisfaction of being land holders smooths every difficulty and makes them prefer this manner of living to that comfortable subsistence which they could procure for themselves and their families by working at the trades in which they were brought up.

In sum, colonial conditions permitted most adult, free men to own sufficient land to employ themselves and their families, a cherished condition called "independence," which starkly contrasted with the dependence of laborers and tenant farmers in Great Britain. Knowing the difference, the colonists clung to independence as a precious state in a world where dependence was the norm. Of course, this did not mean any withdrawal from market transactions into pure subsistence farming. Nor did it stop the most prosperous farmers from buying their own dependent people: indentured servants, convicts, or slaves. The best free man's country was a hard land for the unfree.

The imperial crisis called British official attention to the unconventional nature of the colonial social structure. To British eyes, a land of so many independent common men and so many chattel slaves seemed doubly strange and threatening to proper order. No wonder the colonists were so insubordinate: their leaders were vulgar men grown too wealthy and arrogant from dominating slaves, and yet the colonial gentlemen were also far too solicitous of their independent constituents who did not fully understand deference to their betters.

Some imperial officials became alarmed during the late 1760s and early 1770s as emigration increased from Great Britain to the colonies. From a trough at mid-century, emigration soared to new heights after the war, especially from Scotland and northern England as tenants sought the independence of American farms. Elite observers, however, saw no profit to the mother country in the loss of British laborers and tenants into the woods of America. After all, the British economy needed many common people to keep wages low, which would keep factories and farms productive and competitive. Members of Parliament suspected that the discrepancy between Britain's high taxes and America's low ones encouraged emigration. Narrowing that gap would, they hoped, keep more laborers and tenants at home while rendering the colonists more dutiful.

In the ill-concealed British jealousy, leading colonists detected both their own advantages and their vulnerability to losing them. Ambitious colonists took personally the imperial efforts to tighten control. In late 1765 the young lawyer John Adams saw the Stamp Act as a plot against his own aspirations: "I have groped in dark Obscurity, till of late, and had but just become known, and gained a small degree of Reputation, when this execrable Project was set on foot for my Ruin as well as that of America in General, and of Great Britain."

Adams expressed a widespread fear that the small new taxes set precedents that would inevitably lead to ever increasing levies that would enrich an official elite around the royal governors while impoverishing common taxpayers and obstructing their social mobility. The free colonists intently defended their property rights because property alone made men truly independent and free. In turn, the free colonists clung to their liberties as the means to protect the property that endowed their self-employed independence. Without property they would become "slaves," a state they knew all too well from local observation. Broadly defined, "slavery" meant to labor for a master without reaping the rewards. In sum, the colonists translated the constitutional abstractions of the imperial debate into the implications for their property and social structure.

Adams and other free colonists began to see that their good fortune as middling property-holders was unusual within the empire. Inequality and dependence were the norm in the British empire (and the rest of the world). The colonial nightmare scenario of common white people dominated by landlords and factory owners was all too real in Great Britain. And although prosperity remained the colonial norm for free people, there were nagging signs, especially in the seaports and the older farm communities, of increasing unemployment and poverty. In the context of the imperial crisis, those signs profoundly alarmed colonists of middling means who dreaded the erosion of their own good fortune. Material anxieties gave constitutional issues an intense emotional resonance.

EMPIRE OF LIBERTY

Until the American Revolutionary War began in 1775, few colonists aspired to national independence, for they felt great pride in the empire, derived great economic benefits from trading within its network, and dreaded the death and destruction of a civil war. Instead of national independence, the colonists had wanted to preserve their privileged position within the empire as virtually untaxed beneficiaries of imperial trade and protection. Until the British began to tighten the empire in the 1760s, the colonists had a very good deal—and they knew it. They resisted the new taxes in the hope that the British would back down, preserving their loose relationship with the mother country. But, of course, the British would not back down, which brought on a long and bloody war that no one really wanted. That war obliged the mainland colonial leaders to declare independence, converting thirteen colonies into states with elected governments bound into a confederation.

When the civil war within the empire erupted in 1775, the less populous and more marginal colonies to the north—Nova Scotia, Newfoundland, and Quebec—remained loyal, for they depended upon British protection and markets. Similarly, to the south, the West Indian sugar planters felt too inhibited by their slave majority and too reliant upon the British market for sugar to consider rebellion. By 1775, however, the Atlantic seaboard colonists felt a new confidence in their own power as they noted their growing population. Postwar immigration and continued natural increase pushed their numbers from 1.5 million in 1754 to 2.5 million by 1775. In their swelling population, colonial leaders detected an importance and maturity that deserved greater respect from Parliament. When denied that respect, many (but not all) mainland colonists felt a new capacity to reject British rule. John Adams warned that the British risked provoking a colonial rebellion: "They will find it a more obstinate War, than the Conquest of Canada and Louisiana."

That greater colonial assurance directly clashed with its British counterpart: an imperial arrogance enhanced by so many victories over the powerful French and Spanish. British officials boasted that the conquest of Canada had depended exclusively on the royal navy and army, and that the colonial troops had been no more than expensive cowards. Therefore the British had a dangerous certitude that their forces could easily suppress any colonial rebellion. Impressed with their own might and contemptuous of their colonists, British imperialists were blind to the compromises needed to avoid a civil war within the empire.

By 1763 the British had, at last, at great cost in money and lives, prevailed in the imperial wars to dominate North America. During the subsequent two decades, however, they promptly alienated and lost their most important colonies to rebellion. Triumphant in the War of the American Revolution (1775–83), the new United States embraced the continental expansion that the British had unleashed only to regret. Learning from the abject failure of the British to slow frontier settlement, the American leaders shrewdly dedicated their nation to creating new farms by the thousands to accommodate the proliferating population. In western lands, the Americans meant to reproduce a society of family farmers endowed with household independence, which would postpone the dreaded emergence of a propertyless proletariat of white people. That vision of white liberty depended upon the systematic dispossession of native peoples and, until the Civil War of the 1860s, upon the perpetuation of black slavery. Thomas Jefferson aptly described the United States as an "empire of liberty," by and for the white citizenry. The new American empire liberated their enterprise as it provided military assistance to subdue Indians and Hispanics across the continent to the Pacific.

19

The Pacific

★

1760–1820

The Mission of San Carlos, near Monterey, sketched in 1792 by John Sykes, an English sailor participating in George Vancouver's voyage of Pacific exploration. The engraving captures the rambling and makeshift nature of early missions made of adobe brick with thatched roofs. From George Vancouver, Voyage of Discovery *(London, 1798).*

Indian vaqueros lasso cattle, with Mission San José in the background, in an engraving based on a watercolor made in the 1820s by William Smyth, a sailor on a British voyage of exploration. The image shows the more regimented scale of missions in their last years and highlights the new predominance of raising livestock to export their hides. From Frederick W. Beechey, Narrative of a Voyage to the Pacific *(London, 1831).*

DURING THE 1760S THE OFFICIALS of New Spain heard alarming rumors of Russian and British advances toward the west coast of North America. Vague in their knowledge of that vast region, the Spanish prematurely concluded that the Russians and British were closing in on California and would soon outflank New Mexico to attack precious Mexico. In fact, the British and Russians were fewer and farther away than the Spanish imagined. Far to the northwest in subarctic Alaska, a few dozen Russian traders pursued the commercial harvest of sea otter pelts. As for the British, their Hudson's Bay Company had not yet tried to breach the Rocky Mountains to find the Pacific, and the royal navy had only just begun scientific voyages into the South Pacific.

The rumors reverberated through the distorting echo chamber of diplomacy in distant London, Madrid, and St. Petersburg. All parties acted in expectation of the worst, because none recognized the real weakness of the others on the peripheries of their overstretched domains. In imperial ventures, fearful misunderstanding was more motivating than reassuring truth.

During the mid-eighteenth century, the rival empires began to dispatch naval vessels accompanied by scientists to develop maps, categorize the natives, classify the wildlife, and describe the geology of the Pacific. By subsidizing exploration and publishing their findings, European empires claimed to serve a universal good—scientific knowledge—as they bolstered their particular geopolitical claims to distant territory and peoples. Of course, the Spanish ambassador was not persuaded when a British official insisted that "the English Nation is actuated merely by desiring to know as much as possible with regard to the planet which we inhabit."

During the eighteenth-century "Enlightenment," educated Europeans assumed that the universe of both mind and matter obeyed predictable natural laws, rather than the arbitrary dictates of an inscrutable God. Rejecting ancient texts as a sufficient proof, enlightened Europeans sought more systematically to collect and organize new information about everything on earth (and beyond). European leaders increasingly concluded that wealth and power accrued to nations that discovered and analyzed new information. In publications circulating through the learned circles of the European elite, new discoveries became a medium for the competitive pursuit of national prestige.

Scientific adepts formed a new interest group that urged governments to spend money on science. In Britain the Royal Society united leading scientists, prominent merchants, and powerful aristocrats into a body with a growing political influence in Parliament. In 1768, when the Royal Society wanted astronomers sent to the South Pacific to view the transit of Venus, the British Admiralty was happy to provide a naval vessel and crew, at public expense. Of course, it helped that such an expedition also served an important political goal: to beat the French in exploring and exploiting the unknown reaches of the Pacific.

During the late eighteenth century, the rival probes of France, Britain, Spain, and Russia increasingly intersected in the North Pacific. That competition brought the diverse peoples around the Pacific rim into new relationships over very long distances through the medium of European ships. And that growing integration of the Pacific into a European-managed market economy obliged native peoples to adapt to unprecedented and traumatic changes in their world.

RUSSIANS

During the sixteenth and seventeenth centuries, as western Europeans headed westward across the Atlantic to colonize North America, Russians expanded eastward across Siberia. A vast northern region of long and frigid winters, Siberia varied from grassy tundra on the north to evergreen forests on the south. By subduing the native peoples and erecting fortified towns, Russian fur traders worked their way east to the Pacific Ocean by 1639. During the 1680s, they began to occupy the Kamchatka Peninsula, which became their base for forays into the North Pacific. The traders primarily sought sable, the premier fur-bearing mammal of Siberia. At first, the Russians marketed their furs in western Europe, but in 1689 they opened an even more lucrative trade with China, via the Siberian border town of Kaikhta, where the Russians obtained, in return, Chinese porcelains, teas, and silks.

As the French depended upon Indian hunters to harvest beaver, the Russians relied on Siberian tribal peoples to kill sable. Living in many bands of highly mobile hunter-gatherers with animist beliefs, the native Siberians resembled their distant kin the Inuit and the Indians of subarctic Canada. The Siberian natives also lacked steel and firearms, and they employed dogs as their only domesticated mammal. But, in contrast to Canada, where the French used trade to induce Indians to hunt voluntarily for the market, the Russian fur traders, known as *promyshlenniki*, came in well-armed numbers to intimidate the Siberians. By exacting an annual tribute, generally five to seven sable per man per year, the *promyshlenniki* compelled the natives to become market hunters. In their reliance on tribute rather than trade to capture native labor, the Russians resembled the Spanish conquistadores of Mexico rather than the French traders in Canada.

The *promyshlenniki* became notorious for their brutality to native peoples and for the rapidity with which their operations harvested wild animals to local extinction. When natives resisted or rebelled, they were massacred. When they submitted, the Siberians became exposed to deadly new diseases and a debilitating new dependency on alcohol, a combination that devastated their population. The Siberians also confronted the contempt of their conquerors. A Russian said of the Kamchadal people of Kamchatka, "Only in their power of speech do they differ from animals." Just as Spain's treatment of the Guanche in the Canaries foreshadowed its conduct in the Americas and the English behavior in Ireland became a precedent in Virginia, so too the Russian handling of the Kamchadal set patterns repeated in the Aleutians and Alaska.

During the early eighteenth century, the Russian imperial court at St. Petersburg organized and financed official expeditions of oceanic exploration beyond Kamchatka in search of North America. Russian imperialists envied the western European success in geographic discovery and in developing profitable colonies in North America. By joining the competition for knowledge and commerce in North America, the Russians hoped to prove that they belonged, culturally and politically, to Europe. In search of respect to the west, the Russians pursued science and colonial power to their east.

Russian geographers reasoned that the northwest coast of North America could be found by ships sailing eastward from the coast of Siberia. Such naval exploration might, at last, reveal the coveted maritime passage through North America, so long suspected and so vainly sought from the Atlantic side by the western Europeans. In 1729 and 1741 the Russian crown sponsored exploration by the Danish mariner Vitus Bering and his Russian lieutenant, Alexeii Chirikov. The Russian crown sent along two renowned international scientists: Georg Wilhelm Steller, a German naturalist, and Louis Delisle de la Croyere, a French astronomer. By gathering and publishing their data, the scientists would strengthen the Russian claim to newfound lands.

Like the French and the English, leading Russians longed to believe that they could easily establish an American empire by appearing before the Indians as kinder and gentler colonizers. Subscribing to the "Black Legend" of peculiar Spanish brutality, the Russians predicted that the American Indians would welcome them as liberators. In 1734 a high Russian official, Ivan Kirilov, argued that Russia could "extend its possessions as far as California and Mexico. . . . [W]ithout preparing for war, we can in time acquire them through kindness." This conviction was especially delusional among Russians, who had exploited the Siberian natives at least as ruthlessly as the conquistadores had the Aztecs. Indeed, to bolster Russian claims, imperial officials instructed Bering and Chirikov to compel the natives to give hostages and pay an annual tribute in furs—following the Siberian precedents.

In 1729, Bering and Chirikov determined that an extension of the Pacific Ocean, now known as the Bering Sea, bounded Asia on the east. They failed to detect the nearby Alaskan shore, shrouded by dense fogs. Bering and Chirikov tried again in 1741, departing in June from the port of Petropavlosk on Kamchatka in two ships, the *St. Peter* and the *St. Paul*. Chirikov and the *St. Paul* proceeded farther east to the heavily wooded shore of the Alaska panhandle, arriving in mid-July. Instead of welcoming the Russians as liberators, the local Tlingit Indians ambushed and destroyed two small boats filled with fifteen men sent to probe the shallow waters. In alarm, Chirikov promptly sailed back to Kamchatka, bearing neither hostages nor tribute.

In the *St. Peter*, Bering was even less fortunate. In mid-July he reached the south-central shore of Alaska and began a slow return to Kamchatka, discovering and following westward the Aleutians, a thirteen-hundred-mile-long chain of about fifty foggy, rainy, grassy, but treeless islands, all originally volcanic. Bering and his crew ran low on food and began to suffer from both scurvy and malnutrition. In November, dangerously late in the subarctic year, they ran aground on an uninhabited island in the Bering Sea. Compelled to spend the long, dark winter in huts dug into the earth, Bering and half his men died from frostbite, hunger, disease, and exhaustion.

The naturalist Georg Steller kept alive and busy observing, killing, dissecting, and naming wildlife previously unknown to Europeans, including Steller's eagle, Steller's jay, Steller's white raven, and Steller's sea cow, the last an immense northern manatee unique to the western Aleutians. Steller's sea cows were, when mature, thirty-five feet long and exceeded four tons. Steller and the other survivors endured by hunting sea cows and sea otters and by grubbing for roots with sufficient vitamin C to ease their scurvy. In the

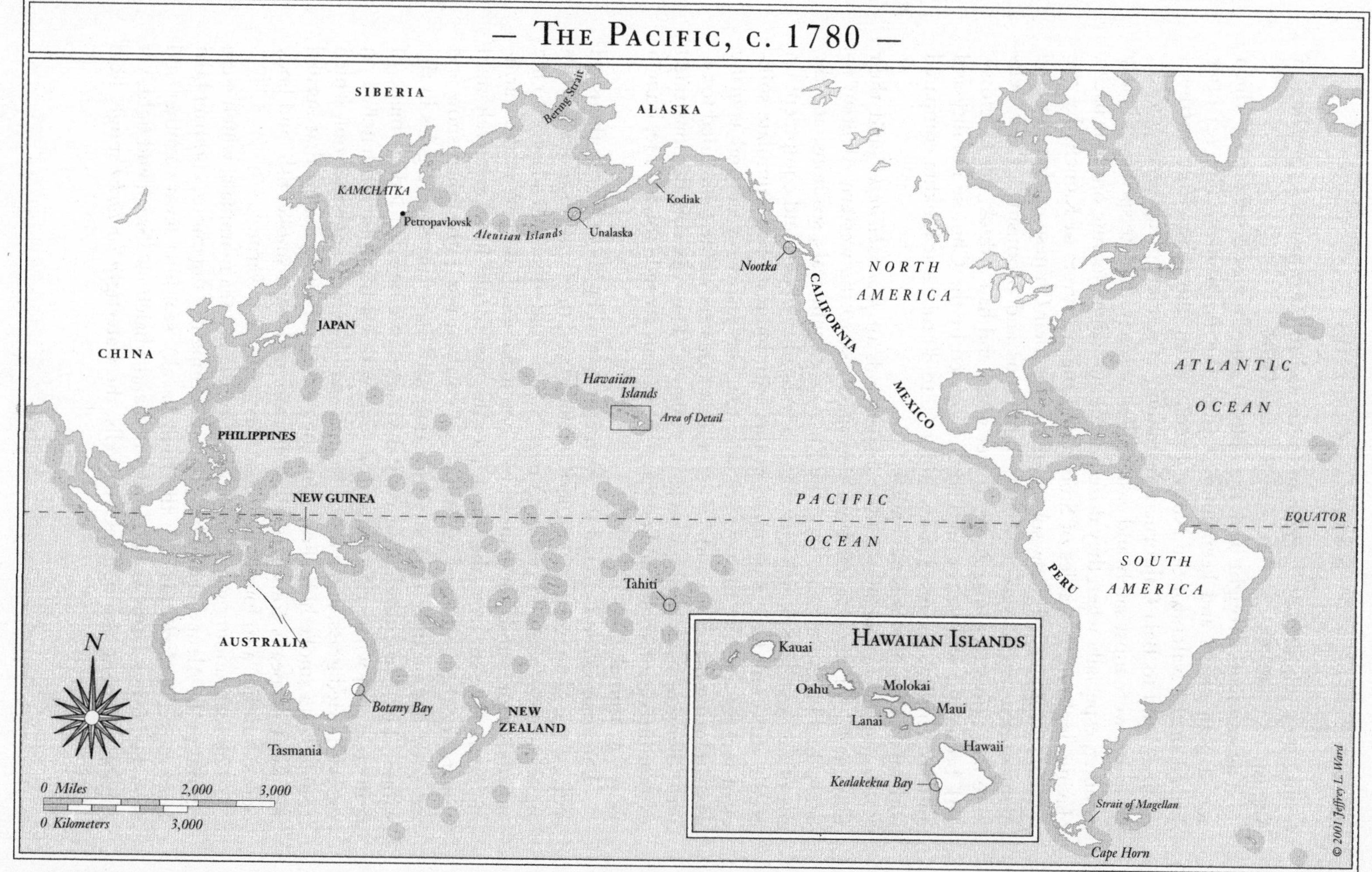
— The Pacific, c. 1780 —
SIBERIA
Bering Strait
ALASKA
KAMCHATKA
Petropavlovsk
Aleutian Islands
Unalaska
Kodiak
Nootka
CALIFORNIA
NORTH AMERICA
MEXICO
JAPAN
CHINA
Hawaiian Islands
Area of Detail
PHILIPPINES
NEW GUINEA
PACIFIC OCEAN
EQUATOR
ATLANTIC OCEAN
SOUTH AMERICA
PERU
Tahiti
AUSTRALIA
Botany Bay
Tasmania
NEW ZEALAND
N
0 Miles 2,000 3,000
0 Kilometers 3,000
HAWAIIAN ISLANDS
Kauai
Oahu
Molokai
Maui
Lanai
Hawaii
Kealakekua Bay
Strait of Magellan
Cape Horn
© 2001 Jeffrey L. Ward

spring, they rebuilt the *St. Peter* and returned to Petropavlovsk, arriving in August.

The survivors brought back the pelts of nine hundred sea otters, which netted high prices and keen interest from the fur traders. The sea otter thrived in the waters of the North Pacific, along the coasts from northern Japan around to Baja California. Swimming in schools of up to a hundred, sea otters were most safely and easily killed at sea in the late spring and early summer, especially when they dozed in the sun while floating on their backs. Having depleted the sables of Siberia and the sea otters of Kamchatka, the *promyshlenniki* needed a new source of furs for their Chinese market. And the Aleutian sea otters were especially numerous and promising. Their pelts were large (five feet long and two feet wide) and had a thick, dense, glossy, dark brown fur with silver highlights. Coveted by the Chinese nobility and imperial family, a sea otter pelt sold for 60 to 80 rubles at Kaikhta compared with 10 to 15 rubles in Kamchatka.

Beginning in the mid-1740s, small bands of *promyshlenniki* (and their Kamchadal servants) sailed from Petropavlovsk to the western Aleutian islands. In addition to sea otters, the Russians sought seals, sea lions, and the fox of the islands. Siberian merchants advanced the boats and equipment on credit, expecting later repayment in furs with interest. To accumulate sufficient furs for a profit, the voyages were long: at least two years and as many as six. During the 1740s and 1750s, at least a quarter of the men failed to return, dying of disease, shipwreck, or violence. The survivors demonstrated extraordinary endurance and developed a callous attitude toward life, human as well as animal.

The *promyshlenniki* found the Aleutians settled by about fifteen thousand natives, the Aleut, relatives of the Kamchadal and the Inuit (Eskimos). Arriving about five thousand years ago from Siberia, the Aleut had adapted to life on windswept islands surrounded by a bountiful ocean. Because of the warming Japan Current from the south, the Aleutian Islands had a relatively mild climate for their subarctic setting. Cool rain and fog, rather than snow and ice, prevailed on most days at all seasons, with especially severe gales in the winter. The Aleut dwelled in coastal villages in elongated lodges made of driftwood and whale ribs, banked around with warming earth, thatched on top with dried grass, and entered from a small hatch through the roof, which doubled as a smoke hole. For light, they relied on smoky lamps that burned seal oil. Europeans considered the interiors rank with smoke, fish, and body odors, but they also found the houses dry, tight, and warm.

The surrounding waters abounded in fish and sea mammals, which were central to the Aleut diet and life. They developed an ingenious, compact boat known as a *baidarka* (akin to the Inuit kayak): sealskins sewn together and stretched over a framework of driftwood and whalebone. Small and light, yet capable of riding through severe swells, the watertight *baidarka* snugly held one man or two. In 1788 an English visitor, Martin Sauer, admired the Aleut *baidarka:* "If perfect symmetry, smoothness, and proportion, constitute beauty, they are beautiful: to me they appeared so beyond any thing I ever beheld." Wearing watertight parkas made of seal gut or bird skins, the Aleut quickly, silently, and smoothly paddled into the swimming masses of seals or sea otters to kill with stone-tipped harpoons attached to an inflated bladder to hinder the wounded animal's flight.

The Aleut divided into castes of chiefs, commoners, and slaves (principally war captives). The chiefs enjoyed larger dwellings and more prominent burials, with executed slaves as their companions in the afterworld. Gender strictly divided the roles and work of the Aleut, with men hunting and fishing, and women tending to the lodges and villages. By strict partition, men exclusively worked with wood, bone, and (later) metal to make tools, weapons (spears, bows, and daggers), houses, and boats. Women alone could rework animal skins and plant fibers into baskets, clothing, bedding, and partitions.

Divided into many small and independent villages, the Aleut had considerable experience fighting one another in blood feuds, but they had never dealt with firearms or an external market—an inexperience that rendered them doubly vulnerable to the newcomers. Following Siberian precedent, the standard *promyshlenniki* practice was to surprise and storm an Aleut village. Martin Sauer reported, "If the least opposition was made, they were silenced by the muskets of the hunters." At gunpoint, the victors held the native women and children for ransom, while releasing the Aleut men to fill a large quota of furs (which took months). Once the furs were delivered, the *promyshlenniki* released the children and the women. In the interim, the Russians exploited the Aleut women as sex slaves. Upon departing, the traders left behind venereal diseases and some trade goods—wool, beads, knives, and hatchets—in token payment for the sea otter pelts.

The new, forced commerce took a heavy environmental toll. For food, the *promyshlenniki* relentlessly hunted the slow and vulnerable Steller's sea cows to extinction by 1768. Deaths of thousands of sea otters also rapidly exceeded their reproduction, for a female bore only one or two pups, sometimes annually but usually biennially. As the market hunting exterminated the sea otter in the western Aleutians, the *promyshlenniki* extended their operations eastward during the 1760s to the large islands of Umnak, Unalaska, and Kodiak, which lay at the eastern end of the Aleutian chain or off the southern coast of Alaska.

During the winter of 1763–64 the Aleut on Umnak and Unalaska rebelled, seizing and burning four Russian ships and killing most of their crews (perhaps 150 men in all). The outnumbered but better-armed Russians responded with a massive retribution meant to kill enough Aleut to intimidate the survivors. In 1766, the Russians, led by Ivan Soloviev, returned to Umnak and Unalaska to bombard and burn eighteen villages and to massacre prisoners by the hundred. Acknowledging the grim power of the Russians, the Aleut never mounted another rebellion.

Hunger, new diseases, labor exploitation, and violent retribution combined to depopulate the Aleutians. Conscripted for months to hunt sea otter for the Russians, the Aleut men were distracted from pursuing and killing the fish, seals, sea lions, and whales that their people needed to eat. Hunger compounded the debilitating and deadly inroads of venereal and contagious diseases in their villages. From a contact population of about 20,000, the Aleut dwindled to only 2,000 by 1800. In the western Aleutians, entire islands became depopulated, as the Russians ordered the few survivors to shift eastward in pursuit of the receding sea otter.

During the 1780s a cartel of Siberian merchants, led by Grigorii Ivanovich Shelikhov, tried to control, regulate, and reorganize the chaotic and destructive exploitation of the sea otter and the Aleut. Shelikhov believed that a permanent settlement would facilitate more intensive, continuous, predictable, and profitable hunting. And, as on other fur-trade frontiers, a fortified base might scare away competitors, *promyshlenniki* as well as foreign. In 1784, Shelikhov led 130 Russians to Kodiak Island to found the first permanent Russian settlement east of Siberia. Kodiak offered a large harbor, abundant sea otters, and proximity to the Alaska mainland. By 1794 Kodiak had 331 colonists, all of them men and almost all company employees who usually departed after serving a five-year term. The small settlement was strictly a company operation meant to serve the sea otter hunt, by staffing warehouses, smithies, and other shops; by tending livestock; and by raising turnips and potatoes, the only crops that could mature in the short subarctic growing season.

When resisted, Shelikhov treated the natives with overwhelming force, bombarding one Kodiak village with cannon. He also adopted the *promyshlenniki* practice of holding women and children hostage to command the services of Kodiak and Aleut men as sea otter hunters. But Shelikhov reduced the sexual exploitation of women, and he paid the natives a better rate in trade goods for the pelts.

By reducing violence and subsidizing missionaries at Kodiak, Shelikhov hoped to impress the Russian empress and the influential leaders of the Russian Orthodox Church. By embracing the new priests, the Kodiak and the Aleut procured new champions against the most extreme forms of labor exploitation. For his (relatively) good deeds, Shelikhov sought an imperial charter and a fur-trading monopoly of the sort enjoyed by the Hudson's Bay Company in northeastern Canada. At last in 1799, four years after Shelikhov's death, the Russian government belatedly rewarded his firm with a charter as the Russian-American Company. It procured a twenty-year monopoly over Aleutian and Alaskan fur-trading, and the powers to govern the colony.

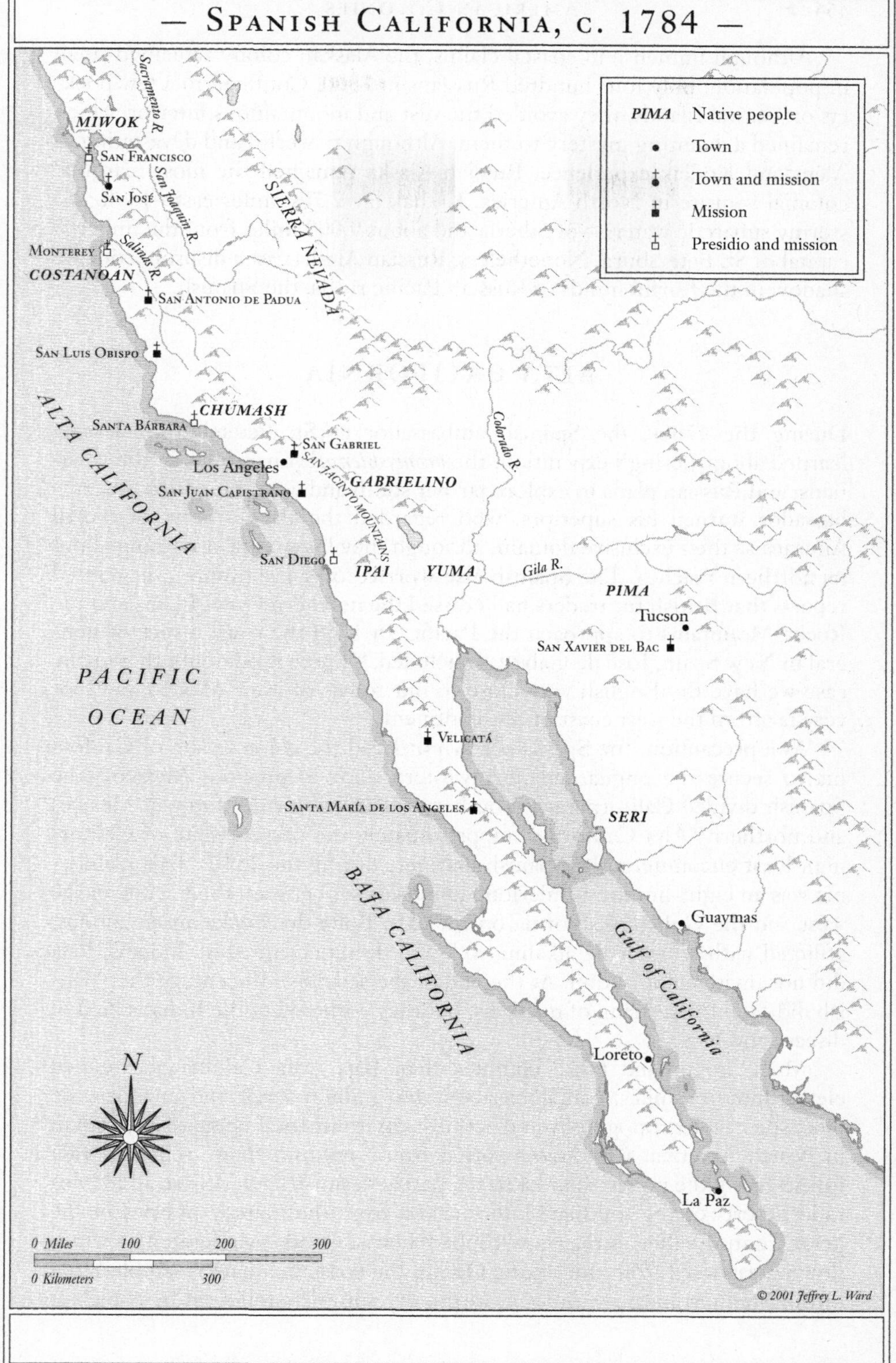
— Spanish California, c. 1784 —
PIMA Native people
Town
Town and mission
Mission
Presidio and mission
MIWOK
Sacramento R.
San Francisco
San José
San Joaquin R.
SIERRA NEVADA
Monterey
Salinas R.
COSTANOAN
San Antonio de Padua
San Luis Obispo
ALTA CALIFORNIA
CHUMASH
Santa Bárbara
San Gabriel
Los Angeles
San Jacinto Mountains
GABRIELINO
San Juan Capistrano
Colorado R.
San Diego
IPAI
YUMA
Gila R.
PIMA
Tucson
San Xavier del Bac
PACIFIC OCEAN
Velicatá
Santa María de los Angeles
SERI
BAJA CALIFORNIA
Guaymas
Gulf of California
Loreto
N
La Paz
0 Miles 100 200 300
0 Kilometers 300
© 2001 Jeffrey L. Ward

Although immense in coastal claims, the Alaskan colony remained small in population: only four hundred Russians in 1800. Confined to a few pockets on coastal islands, they avoided the vast and mountainous interior, which remained a daunting mystery to them. Although powerful and devastating in Aleut and Kodiak experience, Russian Alaska remained the most marginal colonial venture in North America. Kodiak lay 2,700 miles east—by foggy, stormy subarctic waters—of Siberia and about 9,000 miles from the imperial capital of St. Petersburg. Nonetheless, Russian Alaska cast a disproportionate shadow in the fearful minds of Russia's Pacific rivals, the Spanish.

ALTA CALIFORNIA

During the 1760s, the Spanish ambassador at St. Petersburg belatedly learned about Bering's expedition, the *promyshlenniki* operations in the Aleutians, and Russian plans to explore farther south and west. Horrified, the ambassador warned his superiors, who regarded the Pacific coast of North America as their exclusive domain, although they knew almost nothing about its northern reaches. The Spanish also worried over even more exaggerated reports that British fur traders had crossed the northern Great Plains and the Rocky Mountains to approach the Pacific. In 1768 the royal inspector general in New Spain, José de Galvez, concluded, "There is no doubt that in any case we have the English very close to our towns of New Mexico, and not very far from the west coast of this continent."

As a precaution, the Spanish crown ordered the colonization of California to secure the unguarded northwestern door to precious Mexico. The Spanish divided California into southern "Baja California" (now in Mexico) and northern "Alta California" (approximately the present state of California). First encountered by Spanish mariners during the 1530s, Baja California was an eight-hundred-mile-long peninsula set between the Pacific on the west and the Gulf of California on the east. Bone-dry, rocky, mountainous, afflicted with an infertile alkaline soil, and thinly occupied by Indians, Baja did not invite colonization. At the end of the seventeenth century the Spanish did establish a string of missions, but they withered as the Indians died of disease and hunger.

Much larger and more complex than Baja, Alta California extended eleven hundred miles, contained about 100 million acres, and included the most spectacular topography and greatest environmental range of any region in North America. Conditions varied from cool and foggy redwood rain forests along the northern coast to the parched, sun-baked Mojave and Colorado deserts of the southern interior, and from the marshy prairies in the great Central Valley to the snow-topped Sierra Nevada. Moderated by winds flowing eastward from the Pacific Ocean, the coastal climate resembled that of the Mediterranean, with long, warm, dry summers followed by cool, wet winters. Only the mountains received frost and snow, while the summer heat rarely exceeded one hundred degrees Fahrenheit except in the deserts and the Central Valley. An extraordinary diversity of plants and animals had adapted to this broad range of environments, generating a succession of localized and distinctive mosaics of life.

In 1768 about 300,000 natives dwelled in Alta California: an especially impressive number given that only a few practiced horticulture. The great majority lived by a complex and seasonally shifting mix of hunting and gathering that made the most of their abundant environment. Armed with bows and snares, the men pursued elk, deer, antelope, and rabbit. With weirs, nets, and spears, they trapped and killed salmon by the thousand during spring runs. In the coastal bands, the men also hunted for marine mammals along the beaches or built plank canoes to take them in the ocean. Native women accumulated most of the diet by gathering and processing an array of edible seeds, roots, nuts, mushrooms, berries, and acorns, which they rendered into cakes or porridge.

The Spanish regarded Alta California as a wilderness, but, in fact, the natives had subtly reshaped and enhanced their environment. Many bands approached horticulture by weeding and irrigating patches of especially valued wild plants. And like most other Indians, the California natives regularly set low-level fires to drive rabbits for hunting or to trap and roast grasshoppers and caterpillars—considered great delicacies. The fires also reduced brush and insects. Above all, fire facilitated the seeding of many useful plants, especially the oaks, whose acorns fed the people.

In sum, much of the California landscape was subtly anthropogenic (human influenced) long before colonizers arrived with their own even more demanding system of manipulating nature, which they called civilization. In general, the natives encouraged a mix of grasslands, meadows, and open forests characterized by especially large trees, widely spaced. These human-tended landscapes sustained larger numbers of plants and animals and were healthier than today's forests in California. Indeed, for lack of regular fires, contemporary forests are crowded with small trees, cluttered with deadwood, infested with pests, and vulnerable to destruction by huge and catastrophic fires.

Alta California also sustained the greatest cultural diversity of any region in North America. Adapting to the environmental variation, the Indians subdivided into dozens of bands and tribes, which developed great linguistic differences. In 1768, Alta California hosted at least ninety languages, drawn from seven different language families. The northwestern coast belonged primarily to the Hupa, Yurok, Tolowa, Karok, and Wiyot peoples. In the northern interior dwelled the Shasta, Modoc, Achumawi, and Atsugewi. The central coast natives included the Pomo, Costanoan, Esselin, and Salinan. Behind them, in the Central Valley and its surrounding foothills, the leading language groups were the Miwok, Wintun, Nomiaki, Konkowa, Nisenan,

Maidu, Yana, Yuki, Mono, and Yokut. Farther east, beyond the Sierra Nevada, the Paiute, Washo, Mono, and Chemehuevi dwelled in the arid Great Basin. The south coast sustained the Chumash, Gabrielino, Luiseno, Ipai, and Tipai. Behind them, in the interior valleys, lived the Serrano, Cupeno, and Cahuilla. Farther east still, the lower Colorado River belonged to the Quechan, Mohave, and Halchidhoma. As the only California natives to cultivate maize, beans, and squash, the Colorado River peoples showed their proximity to, and the influence of, the southwestern horticulturalists.

The names convey only linguistic affiliations, for none of the "tribes" were politically unified. Instead, the natives lived in hundreds of autonomous bands. For example, the Pomo consisted of at least seventy-two bands, ranging from 125 to 1,500 persons. Because the land belonged collectively to the villagers rather than to individuals, there was no market in land, no buying and selling of real estate.

Most bands rotated with the seasons around a precisely understood territory, returning annually for a prolonged stay in their home village. Their housing varied with the local environment. On the heavily timbered northwest coast, the natives built substantial homes from redwood planks. In the northern Central Valley, they banked earth around circular wooden frames. In the southern portions of that valley, they wove conical huts from bulrushes (known as tule), and in the foothills they used redwood bark and pine slabs to construct the same shape.

Like most native cultures, the California Indians had powerful shamans but weak chiefs. Empowered by dreams, visions, and an apprenticeship to an elder, the shaman was responsible for maintaining the proper relationship of his people with the network of supernatural power manifest in plants, animals, and other peoples. Held in both awe and dread, the shaman was at once healer, priest, magician, and witch. The village chief was almost always male, usually inheriting his status from his father. The chief properly acted only upon securing a consensus in a village and derived influence from his generosity rather than from any coercive power. The chief worked to arbitrate local disputes, to supervise religious ceremonies, to provide charity for the unfortunate, and to regulate trade, diplomacy, and war with neighboring peoples. Relations between the many bands were usually, but not invariably, peaceful. Fighting usually began when a hungry band intruded into the territory of another to hunt, fish, or harvest acorns.

CROSSINGS

During the 1540s and again during the early seventeenth century, the Spanish explored the Alta California coast. On both occasions, however, they concluded that the coast was too poor, distant, and inaccessible to justify colonization. Although the coastal Indians were numerous and well-fed, they lacked the horticulture, precious metals, and adobe towns that the Spanish considered prerequisites for conquest and missions. The long and mountainous coast also provided few secure harbors to shelter shipping from storms and to provide access to the interior. Moreover, the prevailing northwest-to-southeast flow of winds and ocean currents rendered a voyage from Mexico to Alta California a long, hard struggle for sailing ships. Sixteenth-century attempts to reach Alta California by land from New Mexico also failed because the distance was too great, the terrain too rugged, the desert too harsh, and the Indian resistance too fierce.

In 1768 the Spanish revived their interest in Alta California in response to premature reports that the Russians and British were planning their own colonies there. The royal inspector general in New Spain, José de Galvez, ordered Captain Gaspar de Portola to find and occupy the best harbors on the Alta California coast. Galvez, however, could spare few soldiers and could recruit few colonists. Lacking Hispanics to colonize California, Galvez meant to turn the native Indians into Hispanics by reeducating them in missions. Although the Franciscan mission system was in decay and discredit in New Mexico and Texas, the Spanish hoped to revive it in California—a measure of their desperation.

In Fray Junipero Serra, Galvez found the perfect leader to breathe new life into an anachronistic institution. Serra admired and emulated an earlier generation of missionaries who had courted pain and martyrdom for their faith. He wore rough hair shirts augmented with metal wire points, periodically flagellated his bare back until it was bloody, and burned the hair on his chest with a lighted candle. Upon developing an ulcerous sore in one leg, he refused treatment, preferring further mortification of the temporal body that he so hated. Serra welcomed the inevitable hardships of a new colony meant to convert Indians to the Catholic faith.

In the spring of 1769, Portola and Serra reached San Diego Bay with about one hundred Hispanics, all of them men. At San Diego they founded the first mission and the first presidio in Alta California. During the summer and early fall, Portola led an overland party up the coast in search of Monterey Bay, which Spanish mariners erroneously considered the best harbor on the northern coast. Along the way, Portola belatedly discovered the far larger and better harbor that he named San Francisco. Because fog often obscured its relatively narrow entrance, San Francisco Bay had escaped previous notice by Spanish mariners. Despite San Francisco's superiority, Portola scrupulously obeyed his official instructions and established the colonial capital of Alta California at Monterey.

Portola described the new Monterey presidio as meant "to occupy the port and defend us from attacks by the Russians, who were about to invade us." In fact, there were no Russians within fifteen hundred miles. Ironically, news of Monterey alarmed the Russians into a dread that the Spanish were coming to attack *them* in Alaska and Kamchatka. Just as the Spanish had overreacted to overstated reports of the Russian advance, the Russians hastened to bolster their defenses in Kamchatka against the supposed Spanish threat. Pacific colonization had the elements of a farce—although natives experienced it as tragedy.

Far from plotting to attack Alaska, the few Spanish in Alta California were preoccupied with trying to control the immense native population. Undisciplined soldiers complicated matters by plundering, beating, and raping Indians. Native resentments erupted into occasional local uprisings, which then evoked a disproportionate retribution, meant to terrify, lest (in the words of an officer) the Indians "come to know their power." In 1771 at Mission San Gabriel, a soldier lassoed and raped the wife of a local chief. In revenge, the chief attacked another soldier, but suffered a fatal gunshot. Rather than punish his own troops, the commander decapitated the chief and impaled the head on a stake for display outside the mission as a warning to other Indians.

Although greatly outnumbered, the Hispanics possessed an intimidating monopoly of horses and guns, as well as a formal command structure. The California Indians were subdivided into many bands and lacked traditions of alliance and institutions of military coordination. Because they were unable to concert an extensive resistance, their rebellions were few, sporadic, localized, and—with one exception—quickly suppressed. The Hispanics hoped to keep the sort of military superiority that the New Mexicans had enjoyed in the sixteenth century but lost in the eighteenth as the nomadic Indians of the Great Plains acquired guns and horses.

From their two bases at San Diego and Monterey, the Spanish gradually expanded their missions along the intervening coast. By 1774 Alta California had two presidios, at San Diego and Monterey, and five missions, from south to north: San Diego, San Gabriel, San Luis Obispo, San Antonio de Padua, and San Carlos Borromeo (near Monterey). All remained small and weak, with a total colonial population of only 180.

The colony seemed doomed to stagnate unless the Hispanics could find an overland route from Sonora, in northern Mexico. In 1774 the astute presidio commander at Sonora, Juan Bautista de Anza, learned that a California Indian named Sebastian Tarabal had fled from the San Gabriel mission and arrived in Sonora. Anza realized that Tarabal could reveal the long-sought land route from Sonora back to Alta California. Conscripting Tarabal as a guide, Anza crossed, mapped, and reported the six-hundred-mile route across the Colorado River and the Colorado Desert and through the San Jacinto Mountains to Mission San Gabriel.

The new route permitted a modest burst of development. In 1775, Anza returned to Alta California with 240 colonists, mostly women and children, an unprecedented surge of emigrants. A year later he ventured north from San Gabriel to establish a presidio and mission beside strategic San Francisco

Bay. By Fray Serra's death in August 1784, Alta California had two agricultural towns (San Jose and Los Angeles), four presidios, and nine missions. The Spanish simply took the land they wanted without the bother of a formal purchase from the natives. The colonizers reasoned that the towns, presidios, and missions all benefited the Indians by introducing Hispanic civilization and the Catholic faith.

Beginning in 1784, the governors began to allocate lands to a fourth institution, the *rancho*, a private, landed estate dedicated to raising horses and cattle. The governors granted *ranchos* to reward their favorites, mostly army officers. Located in the hinterland around Los Angeles or Monterey, the *ranchos* embraced vast tracts of grazing land. The first three granted consisted of 36,000, 75,000, and 150,000 acres. In the mid-nineteenth century the *ranchos* became romantically celebrated for their graceful, rich way of life, but in their early years they were poorly capitalized adobe farms without pretensions. Nonetheless, they spawned a new interest group that, after 1820, would grow in number, wealth, and political power to challenge the primacy of the missionaries.

Critical to Alta California's development, Anza's promising new route from Sonora remained vulnerable to the Indians' hostility, especially at the critical Yuma crossing of the Colorado River. To secure the goodwill of the three thousand Quechan Indians around that crossing, Anza brought their leading chief, Olleyquotequiebe, to Mexico City in the fall of 1776. Determined to impress, Spanish authorities gave the chief lavish hospitality, splendid clothing, a Catholic baptism, and the new Christian name Salvador Palma. No mere pawn, Palma sought material benefits for his people: presents of manufactured goods and assistance in war against their native enemies. In early 1780, with Palma's consent, the Spanish established two small villages of soldiers, settlers, and four Franciscan missionaries at the Yuma crossing.

The Indians thought that they had procured protection, but the Spanish meant the villages to control the Quechan. The colonists soon alienated their hosts by aggressively appropriating scarce fields to pasture their livestock. Worse still, some soldiers raped Quechan women and brutally whipped native men who protested. Led by Palma, the Quechan suddenly rebelled on the morning of July 17, 1781. Destroying both villages, the Indians killed fifty-five Hispanics, including all four priests. Chronically short of soldiers, the Spanish authorities dared not reestablish their destroyed villages at the Yuma crossing.

Briefly opened by Tarabal and Anza in 1774, the overland route to California closed down after the Quechan uprising of 1781. Whereas the opening had encouraged a temporary boom in Alta California, the closing stunted the colony's further growth. Officials and potential colonists balked at the costs, dangers, and delays of the difficult maritime passage from Mexico. The subsequent growth in the Hispanic population derived primarily from natural increase by those who had arrived during the brief window of overland opportunity between 1774 and 1781.

During the late eighteenth century, isolation from Mexico sentenced Alta California to little more than a subsistence economy. Spanish manufactured goods were prohibitively expensive because they were imported via distant Mexico. That distance also discouraged exports of California's bulky produce, primarily livestock and grains. Unattractive to private merchant enterprise, the maritime commerce from Mexico to California depended upon a few vessels owned and operated by the crown. The ships were usually delayed, were always unpredictable, and often arrived with damaged cargos. Unable to ship their produce to Mexico profitably, the colonists were limited to the local market provided by the small presidio garrisons (a total of 218 men in 1794). Without the infusion of royal money to pay and supply the presidio soldiers, the Hispanic economy of Alta California would have collapsed.

In 1790, Alta California had only a thousand Hispanic colonists, stretched thin along a five-hundred-mile coast from San Francisco to San Diego and scattered among thousands of Indians. For want of colonists, the survival and development of the colony continued to depend upon remaking the native inhabitants into approximations of Hispanics.

MISSIONS

The subtle ingenuity of the California Indian cultures did not impress the Hispanics. Instead, they labeled the natives as *gente sin razón* ("people without reason") in contrast to themselves, the *gente de razón.* A Franciscan said of the Indians:

> Their characteristics are stupidity and insensibility; want of knowledge and reflection; . . . in fine, a most wretched want of everything which constitutes the real man, and renders him rational, inventive, tractable, and useful to himself and society.

The Hispanics insisted that the hallmarks of reason were the Catholic faith, the Castilian language, obedience to the Spanish king, and a Hispanic mode of agricultural labor.

This polarity was primarily cultural and only secondarily racial. Indeed, most of the California colonists were themselves people of mixed ancestry, mestizos or mulattoes, from northwestern Mexico. By asserting their *razón* and defining themselves against the California Indians, the Hispanic Californios claimed a relatively higher status than they could have enjoyed had they remained in Mexico, where colonial law defined a complex hierarchy of fifty-six racial *castas* with varying degrees of honor and privilege. When the authorities in Spain inquired about the *castas* in California, the missionary at San Gabriel frankly replied, "How many these *castas* are, and precisely which *castas* they are, we do not know because, as we have said, they are all known as *gente de razón*." All but the Indians.

By emphasizing *razón* as the basis of privilege, the Hispanics conceded, in theory, that the natives could become *gente de razón* with the proper education. For *gente sin razón* were the equivalent of children, inferior today but potentially equal tomorrow. Through the medium of the mission, the Spanish officials and priests meant to rescue the Indians from their cultural childhood by remaking them into especially pious Hispanics.

The friars planned first to draw the Indians into baptism and the mission and then to render them a captive audience. To allure the Indians, the Franciscans displayed religious paintings and carvings and performed the pageantry of the mass and the holy day processions. The Franciscans also made a show of their metal goods, domesticated livestock, and new crops to argue that conversion offered a richer and more secure way of life. Because merchants were so few and trade goods so scarce and expensive in California, the missions offered Indians the best, and often the only, access to the new metals, cloths, and animals.

Like the priests, the Indians regarded the rituals and objects as pregnant with a powerful magic. Associating that magic with the Hispanic mastery of steel, firearms, and sailing ships, Indians sought to learn the secrets to employ against their enemies and to manage the newcomers. And because their shamans failed to cure the introduced diseases, natives tried the Franciscans as an alternative source of healing magic.

Like the Pueblo peoples of New Mexico, the California converts covertly maintained many of their traditional beliefs and rituals, treating their Christianity as a supplement rather than a substitute. Today archaeologists find shamans' whistles and crystals in the ruins of the Indian quarters at missions, and art historians detect Indian spiritual symbols smuggled by native artisans into the Christian frescoes decorating the missions. An especially observant Franciscan sadly conceded, "As all their operations are accompanied by stratagems and dissimulation, they easily gain our confidence, and at every pass we are deluded."

In principle, the missionaries considered all conversions voluntary. But they were made by people with dwindling choices. An exasperated Fray Fermín Lasuen rebuked his converts, "Why, you make me think that if one were to give you a young bull, a sheep, a *fanega* of grain every day, you would still be yearning for your mountains and your beaches." A convert replied, "What you say is true, Father. It's the truth."

By introducing free-ranging livestock, the Hispanics narrowed the Indians' ability to live outside the missions. Foraging horses, cattle, mules, sheep, and pigs consumed the wild plants and seeds, including acorns, critical to the native diet. In response, Indians shot arrows into the voracious livestock at night, infuriating the Hispanics, who often avenged their lost property with brutal force. To further protect their livestock, the Hispanics also banned in their vicinity the native practice of setting fires. Because these fires were critical to traditional hunting and gathering, their restriction further eroded Indian autonomy.

By alienating native peoples from their traditional role in structuring nature, the newcomers distressed the California environment. Because many grasses and trees had, over the centuries, adapted to the Indian fire management, they suffered from its decline. In addition, trampling and grazing by cattle traumatized native grass species (such as chia and red maids), which created much bare and eroded earth for aggressive opportunists, the European weeds, especially filaree, mustard, ripgut, and wild oats. Beginning near the coastal missions during the 1770s, this plant transition broke into the Central Valley by 1800.

A few native plants and animals, however, adapted all too well to the new conditions. In the presence of livestock and the absence of regular fire, a tough but flammable bush, chaparral, covered many hillsides denuded of grass. To the dismay of the colonists, the chaparral provided little fodder for cattle but much fuel for a catastrophic fire if ignited. Grizzly bears also multiplied, as Indian hunting declined and as spreading livestock provided more meals. Becoming bold, voracious, and numerous, the grizzly bears menaced their benefactors—the colonizers, who had reduced the Indians and spread the cattle. In sum, the environmental trauma was all the greater because it disrupted a nature long shaped by native peoples, rather than the pristine "wilderness" imagined by the Hispanics (and by romantics ever since).

As the environment was transformed and autonomous subsistence strategies decayed, the mission seemed to offer relative security, attracting more converts. At San Gabriel a Franciscan observed, "These Indians are usually caught by the mouth." Such conversions especially surged during the periods of drought. Cyclical droughts had long affected the natives by periodically depleting wild plants and animals, leading to widespread hunger. But after 1770, those droughts were especially devastating where the wild plants and animals were already in decline from the inroads of livestock, the lapse in fire management, and the proliferation of new weeds.

Conversions were cumulative, for as growing numbers entered the mission, their kin felt increasing pressure to follow to maintain the cohesion of their lineage. The number of mission Indians (called "neophytes") more than doubled, from about 2,000 in 1776 to 4,650 in 1784. The Franciscans especially cultivated the chiefs, anticipating that their influence would help convert the rest of their people. The priests appointed cooperative chiefs to the mission post of *alcalde*, charged with keeping order among the converts, but such appointments cut two ways, by perpetuating native authority within the mission framework.

For close supervision, the Franciscans required the new converts to live in or near the mission and apart from their old village and the unconverted. At the missions, the priests meant to reshape the Indians into replicas of Hispanics. Fray Fermín Lasuen explained:

> Here then we have the greatest problem of the missionary: how to transform a savage race such as these into a society that is human, Christian, civil, and industrious. This can be accomplished only by "denaturalizing" them. It is easy to see what an arduous task this is, for it requires them to act against nature.

They had to adopt Spanish clothing, attempt the Castilian language, memorize a catechism, practice celibacy before marriage and monogamy within it, forsake animist rituals and magic, and honor and obey their new fathers, the friars. Fray Serra assured the viceroy, "They are our children. . . . We shower all our love and care upon them."

And the neophytes could never leave their new fathers, except for brief sojourns when authorized by a pass signed by a priest, for the Franciscans regarded the decision to join a mission as final and irreversible. They sent soldiers to retrieve runaways for public punishment and restoration to the mission. In 1797, Fray Fermín Lasuen (Serra's successor as president of the California missions) protested a proposal to withdraw soldiers from Alta California:

> The majority of our neophytes have not yet acquired much love for our way of life; and they see and meet their pagan relatives in the forest, . . . enjoying complete liberty. They will go with them, then, when they no longer have any fear and respect for the force, such as it is, which restrains them.

Lasuen understood that, fundamentally, the mission system depended on a reserve of military force.

It also depended upon a regulation of female sexuality. To control Indian women and protect them from rape by colonists, the priests segregated all unmarried females over the age of seven in a locked barracks at night, disrupting the traditional organization of households around extended kin and encouraging the spread of infectious disease. At one mission, a California governor found the women's quarters so "small, poorly ventilated, and infested" that it "was not possible for me to endure them, even for a minute."

The mission revolved around an enclosed quadrangle, which included the church, the priests' apartments, kitchens, and the single women's quarters. Indian families dwelled in an adjacent village, initially composed of traditional lodges that were ultimately replaced with adobe row houses, divided into apartments. To protect the mission and discipline the Indians, a squad of five or six soldiers lived in a nearby barracks. The perimeter also featured mills, tanneries, tile and brick kilns, corrals and pastures for livestock, and fields of grain. Most missions built and maintained complex systems of dams, ditches, flumes, and reservoirs to bring water to the quarters and the fields. As the missions developed large herds of livestock, they also acquired their own *ranchos* in the hinterland.

By cultural as well as commercial imperative, the missions were economic as well as religious institutions. The Franciscans regarded work as a moral discipline at the heart of a proper civilization and therefore essential for true conversion to Christianity. The priests regarded sustained, structured, and supervised work as the only antidote to the indolence deemed innate to Indians. And pure otherworldliness was a luxury neither the priest nor the neophytes could afford. They needed to eat, and to generate a marketable surplus to procure imported manufactures, especially cloth and steel.

The Franciscans put the neophytes to work constructing buildings, digging irrigation ditches, erecting fences, herding cattle, and cultivating grain. The priests also imposed a more rigid structure and pace on the workday, employing a succession of bells to communicate the hourly dictates of the mission clock. Such agricultural work in a fixed setting to the rigid progression of the clock was all very new and disorienting to people who had previously lived as hunters and gatherers, moving in a seasonal cycle about their homelands and alternating ease with exertion as immediate need dictated.

The Franciscans punished overt resistance to the work regimen with the whip and shackles. Indians could subtly resist by feigning illness or misunderstanding of their orders. These deceptions were especially effective because real sickness and misunderstanding were all too common at the missions. In sum, the missions faced considerable difficulties in adapting the land and a native people to an essentially European mode of agricultural production. Like all Hispanic enterprise in Alta California, the missions also struggled to make ends meet on the periphery of a market economy, at an expensive distance from essential capital and consumer goods.

Given these grave difficulties, the missions proved surprisingly successful as economic enterprises, becoming self-sustaining in food by 1778. In 1775 the missions had only 427 head of cattle, but these grew phenomenally to at least 95,000 by 1805. In addition, the missions of 1805 possessed 130,000 sheep, 21,000 horses, 1,000 mules, and 800 pigs. During the 1790s the missions also developed workshops capable of producing many trade goods previously imported at considerable expense. In addition to servicing the mission, the new crafts supplied the presidios with saddles, shoes, boots, soap, candles, beds, blankets, and even coffins. The presidios paid by issuing a credit to the missions, which the missionaries redeemed in Mexico City to purchase imported goods.

As legal wards, the mission Indians did not individually receive the fruits of their labors, collecting neither wage nor dividend. Instead, the priests provided their food, housing, and clothing. Any profits yielded by market sales accrued to the mission fund managed by the priests. They used the income primarily to expand the mission buildings and fields and to ornament the church. In theory, the mission was a trust, holding the Indians and their property for return once they had become Hispanic in thought and behavior (as determined by the Franciscans).

The neophytes, however, died with a shocking rapidity from exposure to new diseases and from the shocks of a more intensive labor regimen. Living in closer quarters in the missions than they had as members of free bands, the mission Indians were easy prey to infectious diseases. Although known among Indians elsewhere, syphilis was introduced to California by the Hispanics. Rape by colonists infected women with the disease, which they passed on to their husbands, debilitating entire families. Syphilis inflicted infertility and stillbirths on Indian women and afflicted newborns with fatal birth defects. In 1814 a Franciscan reported, "Of every four children born, three die in their first or second year, while those who survive do not reach the age of twenty-five." Misunderstanding many of the stillbirths as abortions, some insensitive priests punished the women with whippings. Statistical analysis of mission registries confirms that women and children died in disproportionate numbers, creating a skewed mission population heavy in adult men unable to form families.

In 1769 the California coast between San Diego and San Francisco had a native population of 72,000, which declined to just 18,000 by 1821. One Franciscan conceded, "They live well free but as soon as we reduce them to a Christian and community life . . . they fatten, sicken, and die." The mission diet did offer more calories more steadily through the year, but the fare was heavy on beef and maize, which was more monotonous and vitamin-deficient than the diverse foods of hunting and gathering. Consequently, the new diet did weaken resistance to disease, particularly for women and infants.

Maintaining the mission population required a constant effort by priests and soldiers to recover runaways and to recruit new Indians by force. Running short on coastal Indians, in 1797 presidio commanders began to send troops into the Central Valley to capture potential neophytes. From 1797 to 1817 the Franciscans also established seven new missions closer to autonomous villages, to draw more Indians into the system. For a generation, the sweeps and the new missions kept the aggregate mission numbers growing a bit faster than disease killed. In 1821, when Spanish rule ended, the system had grown to twenty missions with more than 21,000 neophytes.

The growth and prosperity of the missions provoked growing tensions between the colonists and the priests. In general, the Franciscans regarded the colonists and the soldiers as moral dregs, best kept away from the missions, lest they corrupt the Indians. The friars especially detested the sexual predation of Hispanic men, primarily soldiers, on Indian women. But the civil and military leaders distrusted the Franciscan demands for distance and autonomy. Officials suspected that the missionaries simply wanted to monopolize the exploitation of Indian labor. Hispanic farmers complained that they could not compete in supplying the garrisons because the missions enjoyed a large pool of cheap Indian labor and had taken the best lands for agriculture and grazing.

Siding with the colonists, the governors repeatedly urged the Franciscans to prepare Indians for the colonial world promptly and then to divide the communal property of the mission among them. When rebuffed, the governors complained that the priests infantilized the neophytes to perpetuate Franciscan control. In 1796 the governor grumbled, "The mission Indians should be free from guardianship in ten years, but those of New California, at the rate they are progressing, will not become so in ten centuries."

In response, the Franciscans persistently argued that their converts were not yet ready to compete in the Hispanic world. Indeed, the priests regarded the Indians as perpetual children who would probably never thrive outside of mission paternalism. "No matter how old they are, California Indians are always children," a priest observed in 1818. When the governors meddled, Franciscans bristled and mobilized their considerable political influence with the viceroy in New Spain. A host unto himself, Fray Serra got one governor sacked and another excommunicated.

Despite their bitter arguments, the friars and the soldiers needed one another to dominate the more numerous Indians. The Franciscans helped the military by consolidating Indians into mission communities, rendering the colony more secure from an uprising, while the missionaries needed soldiers to recapture and punish wayward converts. In addition, despite repeatedly insisting that soldiers and Indians be kept apart, the friars readily sent Indian laborers to work at the presidios—because their wages went into the mission coffers.

In 1800, Alta California remained the most marginal colony on the long northern frontier of New Spain. During the nineteenth century, this Hispanic weakness would attract growing attention from covetous Anglo-Americans, who detected an economic potential in California that had eluded Hispanic exploitation. Impatient and ruthless, the nineteenth-century newcomers would decimate the remaining Indians and further degrade the environment of California. And the newcomers would expand and exploit the commercial links around and across the Pacific that Captain James Cook had initiated on behalf of the British Empire during the 1760s and 1770s.

ISLANDS

To Europeans, the Pacific Ocean long remained the most mysterious part of the temperate earth. On the other side of the planet, the Pacific was especially distant and hard to reach from Europe. During the colonial era, the only western access by sea came via the narrow, rocky, and stormy Strait of Magellan at the southern tip of South America. The Pacific was also so huge—covering a third of the earth—that mariners readily got lost for want of accurate techniques for determining longitude. Once they found a secure track across the Pacific, they clung to it, which discouraged new discoveries. Distance and difficulty also rendered the Pacific impractical for plantations or fisheries producing in bulk for a European market. Preoccupied with closer colonial ventures, Europeans largely neglected the Pacific until the mid-eighteenth century.

During the early sixteenth century, the Spanish mariner Magellan discovered the western route into the Pacific via the strait that bears his name. Following up on Magellan's discoveries, the Spanish established a colony at Manila in the Philippines, and during the 1560s they initiated a trade across the Pacific to Mexico. Along the way, their mariners discovered a few inhabited islands, principally Guam in the Marianas, where they established a small settlement to resupply their passing ships with water and provisions. But by the end of the century the Spanish feared that further Pacific discoveries would only overstretch their limited means. By following the same narrow trade passage in a single vessel once a year from the Philippines to Mexico, the Spanish preserved their ignorance of most of the Pacific.

The Spanish also wanted to keep the ocean's secrets from other Europeans, lest Pacific information benefit their piracy. By burying in secret files the charts and reports of their explorers, the Spanish unwittingly hurt their own later mariners, who frequently repeated the mistakes as well as the "discoveries" of forgotten predecessors. For nearly two centuries the Spanish hostility and secrecy did minimize other European ventures into the Pacific unknown. Beginning with Sir Francis Drake in 1578–79, sea marauders occasionally broke into the Pacific via the Strait of Magellan to plunder Spanish shipping and seaports on the west coast of South America, but hit-and-run raids generated no lasting benefit to the rival empires.

During the 1760s, the British and French governments became serious about probing the Pacific Ocean. In the name of science, they asserted their right to explore anywhere in the world. Determined to collect information more empirically and systematically, their mariners brought along cartographers, astronomers, naturalists, and skilled draftsmen to study and depict the waters, skies, plants, animals, weather, and peoples of distant coasts and islands. Claiming allegiance to pure science, the British and French officials denounced the Spanish secrecy and protectiveness as intellectual crimes against humanity.

The collection and publication of geographic and scientific information became essential to claim new lands. Captain James Cook of Britain asked that his Pacific findings be quickly "published by Authority to fix the prior right of discovery beyond dispute." By promptly and officially publishing Cook's maps and journals, the British government reaped European credit for "discovering" much of the Pacific northwest in 1778, when, in fact, secretive Spanish expeditions had already visited that coast in 1774 and 1775. The frustrated Spanish had to send more conspicuous expeditions in 1788–89 to gather evidence from the northwestern Indians that the 1774–75 voyages had taken place.

While claiming pure objectivity, the scientific inquiries asserted the superiority of the new European modes of measurement, description, and categorization over the traditional native ways of knowing as practiced in the Pacific. The systematic collection of data about new plants and animals also provided marketable commodities for commercial exploitation. And new knowledge of distant peoples promised to facilitate their pacification as imperial subjects.

Although serving an imperial agenda, the sojourning scientists were also observant and often sympathetic men affected by their encounters with new cultures. The shock of the new sometimes revealed the psychic losses accepted in their own increasingly artificial, anxious, materialistic, and competitive societies. The Pacific islanders seemed to possess a worthy simplicity that Europeans had lost. While accepting that the islanders would, inevitably, have to change, the explorers often romantically mourned what they saw as a doomed paradise of natural people.

During the 1760s, Britain's rulers feared that the French would find and exploit some great new opportunity for trade and colonies in that immense and mysterious quarter of the globe, the Pacific Ocean. No British politician wished to be accused later of losing something valuable in the Pacific to the national enemy. British exploration seemed a cost-effective insurance policy against a comeback by France as a colonial and naval power. National pride and fear, as much as national interest, drove both the British and the French in a race to explore the Pacific, just as similar anxieties pushed the Spanish into Alta California during the same decade.

By the 1760s, political and technological developments rendered the Pacific significantly more accessible to British (and French) ships. New and more precise instruments—quadrant, sextant, and chronometer—enabled mariners to ascertain their longitude in distant oceans, solving the most important and persistent difficulty in navigation. Precise location and measurement allowed the development of far more accurate maps and charts, which were critical to navigating the vast reaches of the open Pacific and returning to small and far-flung islands. The decline of Spanish naval might also enabled rival vessels to venture more securely into the Pacific.

In 1768 the British Admiralty and the Royal Society entrusted Pacific exploration to Captain James Cook. The ambitious son of a Yorkshire farm laborer, Cook enjoyed a social mobility unusual for eighteenth-century Britain, rising in the royal navy from a common seaman to the officer corps. Through diligent study and hard work, he became adept in mathematics, navigation, and mapmaking, the primary talents needed for exploration. In 1768–71 and again in 1772–75, Cook crisscrossed the South Pacific. He rediscovered and more thoroughly probed the coasts of Australia and New Zealand, the largest islands in the South Pacific, previously known only vaguely from hasty Dutch encounters a century before. Cook's reconnaissance facilitated subsequent British colonization of Australia, which began with the arrival of 723 convicts at Botany Bay in early 1788.

The two voyages established Cook's reputation as the preeminent explorer of the eighteenth century. In the process, he transformed the role from swashbuckling adventurer into professional man of science. More methodical and thorough than any other mariner, Cook developed maps and charts of unprecedented precision, defining the Pacific in print for distant Europeans. In addition to his technical skills, the levelheaded and resourceful Cook was masterful at organizing and leading the complex little society of a ship's crew. Attentive to the well-being of his men, Cook twice returned home without the loss of a single sailor to scurvy (the scourge of long-distance voyages)—a remarkable accomplishment.

An eighteenth-century man of the Enlightenment, Cook was no conquistador come to plunder, conquer, enslave, and convert. He usually treated the Polynesian peoples of the Pacific islands with public respect and tried (in vain) to prevent his sailors from spreading venereal disease. Cook also recognized that "the too frequent use" of guns would teach "them that Fire Arms were not such terrible things as they had imagined. They are very sensible of the superiority they have over us in numbers and no one knows what an enraged multitude might do." Cook was more prophetic than he then knew.

Although relatively restrained and reflective, Cook could never entirely transcend the fundamental arrogance of imperial exploration. Whenever push came to shove, he insisted that the natives would have to respect his power and serve his mission. Ultimately that conviction would kill him—to the deep regret of most Polynesians, who recognized his many sterling qualities. And no matter how well-meaning, the eighteenth-century mariners inevitably introduced dangerous new diseases, animals, weeds, weapons, and missionaries that cascaded into sweeping and rapid environmental and cultural changes that troubled the Polynesians.

In 1776–79, for his third and final voyage, Cook probed the North Pacific in search of the fabled Northwest Passage around North America. Sailing north by northwest from Tahiti in January 1778, Cook was pleasantly surprised to stumble upon the Hawaiian Islands, a midoceanic and subtropical range of volcanic peaks. Located 2,700 miles beyond Tahiti and 2,400 miles southwest of California, the Hawaiian Islands were the most geographically isolated cluster in the Pacific. The eight major islands formed an arc, 350 miles long, anchored at the southeast by the largest, Hawaii. Aggregating to 6,435 square miles of land, the Hawaiian Islands collectively matched the area of

Connecticut plus Rhode Island. Many fertile and lush valleys intersected the rugged terrain of steep hills and lofty volcanoes, some over ten thousand feet above sea level and topped by snow in winter.

The Hawaiian people were the farthest extension of the great northeastward migration of the Polynesians, which began in Indonesia about two thousand years ago. Skilled builders and navigators of double canoes propelled by both paddles and sails, the Polynesians steadily discovered and colonized a succession of island chains. About one thousand years ago, some especially daring mariners and their families ventured far beyond Tahiti into the open ocean—and were skilled and lucky enough to find the Hawaiian islands. Other Tahitians followed to help colonize the newfound islands, until contact between the two chains lapsed, about the year 1200, creating the isolation broken by Captain Cook in January 1778.

Adept fishers and farmers, the Hawaiians enjoyed an abundant diet. In irrigated terraces, they cultivated a tuber known as taro. On drier fields, the Hawaiians raised sweet potatoes, yams, breadfruit, bananas, and coconuts. They also kept chickens, dogs, and pigs, all brought by the original Polynesian emigrants, but they had neither horses nor cattle. Women cared for the children and made mats and clothing, primarily by treating and softening the fibrous inner bark of the mulberry tree. The Hawaiians lived in many small villages and in houses composed of light wooden frames with grass-thatch walls and roofs to keep off the frequent rains. Lacking metallurgy, the natives exercised their ingenuity in crafting tools and weapons from wood and stone. They did occasionally recover bits of iron, mostly nails, from driftwood that apparently originated with Japanese and, perhaps, Spanish wrecks. Cherishing this metal, they longed to obtain more.

Dependent upon a bountiful but volatile nature, the Hawaiians maintained their harmony with the supernatural by worshiping an array of divine spirits, each manifesting some aspect of their environment. In particular, Lono dispensed the nourishing rain, while Ku had to be propitiated with human sacrifice to secure victory in war. A strict and complicated system of taboos (known as *kapu*) regulated behavior and maintained a strict gender distinction and a complex hierarchy of social castes. For example, men and women ate different foods and ate apart from one another. Only men could eat pig and only chiefs could eat dog. Essential to maintain good relations with the sacred, obeying *kapu* ensured the health and prosperity of the people. Violators faced death sentences imposed by the priests and enforced by the chiefs. As quasi-divine figures, the most powerful chiefs could announce and impose new *kapu* meant to change the behavior of their subjects.

Although the chiefs governed with the power of life and death, they had to remain within the broad bounds of customary law, lest they offend their people and alienate them into rebellion. The chiefs consulted priests, who tended the open-air temples and predicted the future. Like the chiefs, the priests lived in relative leisure and abundance upon the surplus produce of the common people, who fished the sea and worked the land. The bottom of the social ladder belonged to a small and despised caste of slaves, who could be sacrificed to appease Ku.

In 1778 there were four major chiefdoms, each dominating a major island: Hawaii, Maui, Oahu, and Kauai. The head chiefs maintained a form of feudalism, assigning lands and their commoners to subordinate chiefs, in return for tribute and assistance in war. The pride and rivalries of chiefs provoked frequent wars between the chiefdoms and rebellions within them. Lacking firearms, the Hawaiians fought with stone-headed spears, daggers, and clubs.

Cook's arrival created a sensation among the Hawaiians, who had probably never seen such large and complex sailing ships. Entranced by the metals of the newcomers, the Hawaiians avidly offered abundant fresh produce and pork in trade. A subordinate officer noted, "This is the cheapest market I ever yet saw, a moderate sized Nail will supply my Ship's Company very plentifully with excellent Pork for the Day, . . . such is these People's avidity for Iron." But when some Hawaiians tried to pilfer pieces of the alluring metal, the British mariners responded with rough and in one case fatal force. After two weeks of mostly harmonious exchanges, Cook sailed northward in renewed search of the elusive Northwest Passage.

In November, the British mariners returned from Alaskan waters to Hawaii, seeking a warm-weather base to rest and resupply through the winter. Good relations soured in mid-February, when a few natives grabbed some iron tools and a small boat, and the British officers resolved, in classic imperial fashion, to demonstrate their superior power. Cook led a small party of only ten marines to seize the preeminent chief of Kealakekua Bay on the big island (Hawaii) as a hostage for the return of the stolen items. The British bungled the operation, killing a subordinate chief, which infuriated a large crowd armed with daggers, clubs, spears, and stones. The frightened British fled to their boats at the beach, where Cook shot another Hawaiian dead, further enraging the crowd. Engulfed, Cook suffered fatal blows from clubs and daggers. Four marines also died, but the remaining six made a narrow escape to the ships. After another week of sporadic fighting, with heavy Hawaiian casualties, the two sides made a formal peace, for both regretted the violent rupture and sought renewed trade. In mid-March, the British mariners sailed for Alaska to complete their northern coastal survey. In Britain, Cook became a legendary martyr to imperial duty and scientific progress.

NOOTKA

During the spring and summer of 1778, between his visits to Hawaii, Captain Cook sojourned along the northwest coast of North America. From

Vancouver Island (now part of British Columbia), Cook sailed steadily northeastward to Alaska and the Bering Strait before returning to the Hawaiian Islands to die. Mapping with his usual obsessive detail, Cook closed the cartographic gap between the Spanish coastal probes of California and the Russian investigation of Alaska. For the first time, Europeans basically understood the entire coastal arc from Siberia to California. In the process, Cook demolished the myth of an accessible Northwest Passage.

In the Pacific northwest, Cook found an elaborate native culture adapted to a mild and rainy climate abounding in timber, fish, sea otters, seals, and whales. Amply supported by fishing and marine hunting, the 200,000 raincoast inhabitants had never needed to develop horticulture. Although divided into at least six language groups and hundreds of villages, the raincoast peoples shared important cultural elements, including complex social hierarchies, elaborate ceremonies, and a highly stylized art expressed in wood carving.

Claiming and defending particular rivers and bays, the raincoast peoples had developed localized languages and distinct tribal identities. Proceeding from north to south, the principal linguistic groups were the Tlingit on the mainland and islands of the Alaska panhandle, the Haida on the Queen Charlotte Islands of British Columbia, the Tsimshian on the adjacent mainland coast, the Kwakiutl on northern Vancouver Island, the Moachat (or Nootka) on southern Vancouver Island and the northern Olympic Peninsula, the Salish and Chinook on the coast of Washington, the Tillamook and Tolowa of Oregon, and the Hupa, Karok, and Yorok of northwestern California. For want of tribal unions, almost every village was independent and organized along kinship lines. Each village had multiple chiefs, but one enjoyed local preeminence for his superior achievements in war, trade, and gift-giving.

The raincoast natives worked most intensely in the late spring, when the salmon returned from the ocean to ascend the rivers and streams in search of spawning beds. The thousands of concentrated fish invited a concerted community effort to harvest, eat, dry, and store an immense supply of salmon for the winter. Men caught the fish, and women dried or smoked them for preservation.

Far from taking for granted the nourishing salmon, the natives developed elaborate taboos and rituals deemed essential to ensure their return. If the people neglected or showed disrespect to the salmon, they would vanish and the people would starve. Casting fish bones, scales, or guts back into the water was an insult to the spirits guarding the salmon. Indeed, any dead animal part thrown into the stream could doom the fishery. When a visiting fur trader threw the bone of a dead horse into the Columbia River, the salmon vanished until the alarmed Indians sent a diver to retrieve the offending bone. The salmon returned a few hours later. The natives also could neither cut the salmon crosswise nor leave any cooked salmon uneaten before sundown. Other taboos prohibited women from fishing and forbade menstruating woman even to enter a river.

The damp raincoast environment sustained immense trees, especially Douglas fir. With stone axes and chisels the natives felled, split, and worked tree trunks to build large and solid plank houses and cedar-plank canoes, as well as food trays and storage boxes. Abundant food and wood endowed the natives with the time and materials to develop an elaborate religious art featuring carved masks, house ridgepoles, and totem poles. They also combined fibers from the inner bark of spruce and cypress trees with the wool from mountain goats to make clothing.

The well-fed natives also had the leisure time to compete violently for prestige. The victors in their endemic warfare collected numerous slaves and the skulls of the dead for prominent display in their villages. In the late eighteenth century, European visitors calculated that at least a fifth of the raincoast inhabitants were slaves. A victorious chief had the power of life and death over his slaves, periodically sacrificing some to demonstrate that power. But relations with neighbors were not always violent, for the natives developed elaborate chains of trade, along the coast with one another and up the major rivers with the Indians of the mountainous interior.

Abundance encouraged a complex social hierarchy regulated and maintained by the lavish and ritualistic gift-giving known as the potlatch. Chiefs built or maintained their status by periodically hosting a potlatch to bestow abundant gifts of food, clothing, and wood carvings on their honored guests. The most lavish givers reaped superior prestige and influence. Sometimes rivals for power held a competitive potlatch, in which each destroyed property, including slaves, until only one chief had any left. The competitive passion to accumulate, give, and destroy goods also led to a certain gamesmanship in trying to take items from visitors, as Captain Cook discovered.

In the spring of 1778, Cook brought his two ships and crews into the complex world of the Pacific raincoast. He spent a month at Nootka, an inlet on the west coast of Vancouver Island, to repair and refit his ships and to obtain fresh water and provisions. The local natives called the place Yuquot and themselves the Moachat, but Cook's misnomer, "Nootka," has stuck ever since to both place and people. Having learned the usefulness of European metals from Spanish mariners, the Moachat paddled out in many canoes to meet Cook's ships and initiate trading. They took possession of the trade and forcibly kept other native bands from dealing directly with Cook and his men. Exploiting their profitable position as middlemen, the Moachat sold some of their metal acquisitions to neighboring peoples for sea otter pelts, which they then traded to the British for more metal.

Experienced traders and devoted to property, the raincoast peoples belied the classic stereotype of naive natives easily cheated by European traders bearing a few beads. Although eager to get metal knives, chisels, and arrowheads, the Moachat drove a hard bargain for their pelts and salmon. An expedition scientist noted that the raincoast natives were "very keen traders, getting as much as they could for everything they had; always asking for more, give them what you would." The expedition artist John Webber had to pay for the right to draw the interior of a Nootka house. In contrast to the ready availability of Polynesian women, the Moachat provided the crewmen with only a few, always slaves, and for a high price. When Cook's men cut grass to feed the livestock held aboard ship, the Indians demanded payment. Cook ruefully discovered that "there was not a blade of grass that had not a separate owner." He concluded that "no people had higher ideas of exclusive property."

Inverting the usual colonial equation, the Moachat regarded their rights to property as superior to those of the European newcomers. Whenever they were allowed on board the ships, the Moachat tested British vigilance by taking anything they could lay their hands on. In stark contrast to the shipboard game, the visitors suffered no thefts when visiting the village, because the Moachat, as hosts, felt honor-bound by a strict code of hospitality. Focusing on the shipboard behavior, Cook considered the Moachat "as light-fingered as any people we had before met with"—no small compliment, given his experiences in the Hawaiian islands.

In contrast to his later hard line in Hawaii, Cook reacted with restraint to the lost items at Nootka. His subordinate Lieutenant Charles Clerke explained that it was better to "put up with the loss of some trifles, than bring matters to a serious decision." But other officers grumbled at the restraint. Lieutenant James King complained, "In all our intercourse with Indians, we never gave so great [a] latitude to insolent behaviour as we did to these." Feeling diminished as white men by any concession to natives, these officers longed to punish and intimidate the Moachat. A hotheaded marine officer, John Williamson, arranged a public demonstration that fired a musket ball through a dummy wearing the wooden war armor of the Moachat. More savvy than Williamson, the natives watched with a calculated indifference that persuaded another officer that the Moachat had not "the least fear of us or our fire Arms."

Ultimately, Cook and his crew had no reason to complain of their transactions with the Moachat. The British purchased fifteen hundred sea otter pelts for about sixpence apiece in English goods. A year later, en route homeward, they stopped in China, where each pelt sold for goods worth about $100 to $120. Launched as science, Cook's voyage evolved into commerce. The easy transition demonstrated the cozy relationship of capitalism and science in British thought and practice.

Published in 1783 and 1784, crewmen's accounts and Cook's official journals aroused intense interest in western Europe and New England. British and New English merchants, intrigued by the profits made by selling sea otter pelts in China, dispatched ships to trade at Nootka and other raincoast harbors. Proceeding on to China with the pelts, the traders purchased Chinese porcelain, tea, spices, and silks for conveyance to, and sale in, western Europe and northeastern America. Once the rare experience of government-sponsored explorers, circumnavigation became a commercial commonplace.

KAMEHAMEHA

After 1786, maritime contact with the Hawaiian Islands became annual and increasing, for they proved ideally located to facilitate the new transpacific trade. Both inbound to the Pacific northwest and outbound to China, the fur-trade ships stopped at the Hawaiian Islands for rest, repairs, and a resupply of water, wood, and provisions. The Hawaiian Islands became the nexus in an emerging market integration of the Pacific by European shipping and shippers.

Formerly isolated by the ocean, the Hawaiians quickly found themselves living at a busy crossroads of North Pacific trade and in a hothouse of cultural encounters and transformations. Growing numbers of Hawaiians volunteered to serve in the crews of short-handed European vessels, which enabled Hawaiians to discover China, Europe, and northeastern North America. Meanwhile, some European mariners deserted their ships to enter the service of Hawaiian chiefs eager to procure their skills as artisans and military advisers. Forsaking the rigorous discipline, hard fare, poor pay, and limited sex of the British navy or merchant marine, the deserters obtained, instead, land, wealth, prestige, and a Hawaiian wife. In addition to recruiting military advisers, the chiefs sought guns and gunpowder to secure an edge in their conflicts with one another. Endowed with new weapons, the Hawaiian chiefs escalated their wars to an unprecedented scale of death and destruction.

During the 1780s and 1790s, Chief Kamehameha of Hawaii won the local arms race to become the dominant chief in the islands. A man of powerful build, restless intelligence, voracious ambition, and ruthless opportunism, Kamehameha exploited the newcomers and their technology for his own ends. George Vancouver, a British naval officer, even provided Kamehameha with a European-style warship. Vancouver reasoned that Kamehameha was the probable and, from a British perspective, the best victor in the Hawaiian wars. Regarding the islands as their protectorate, the British government bet on Kamehameha's ability to unify them.

During the late 1780s, Kamehameha forcibly united his home island, Hawaii. In 1795 he invaded and conquered, in quick succession, the islands of Maui, Molokai, and Oahu and their satellite islands, Lanai and Kahoolawe. Kamehameha used his artillery to deadly and decisive advantage, ultimately driving his foes over a cliff in Oahu. Attentive to ancient tradition as well as new technology, Kamehameha ritually sacrificed defeated chiefs to Ku. In 1810 the last independent chiefdom (on Kauai) submitted, completing the unification of the islands under the new monarchy established by Kamehameha. Thereafter, until his death in 1819, King Kamehameha presided over a period of peace and prosperity that helped the islands recover from his wars of conquest.

Like the other Polynesians, the Hawaiians experienced the shocks of European encounter: germs, livestock, weeds, weapons, and missionaries. But Hawaiians in general, and Kamehameha in particular, managed to mitigate the shocks, retaining control of their land until later in the nineteenth century. Dealt a difficult new hand by the strangers, for half a century the Hawaiians adapted well enough to compel concessions and respect from the intruders.

CONCLUSION

Despite their long head start in the Pacific, the Spanish lost much ground (and more water) to their many rivals at the end of the eighteenth century. They lacked the commitment to entrepreneurial commerce that drove the European penetration of the Pacific after Cook and his scientists showed the way. Wedded to Catholic absolutism, economic monopolies, and a highly bureaucratic and hierarchical government, the Spanish authorities simply did not trust independent merchants and their aggressive pursuit of self-interest. By contrast, the British and especially their spawn the Americans dedicated their governments to promoting commerce. And trade drew native peoples into imperial webs more smoothly than did missions.

Hispanic California could have profited by harvesting the abundant sea otter along the coast for shipment and sale in China. Such a trade would have filled a major economic need by procuring in China the mercury essential to Mexican silver production. And exploiting the California sea otter would have served the Spanish imperial interest by discouraging the Russians, British, and Americans from expanding their hunting and trading into California. During the 1780s a Hispanic entrepreneur did try to develop a sea otter trade with China by hiring California Indians as hunters, but the enterprise offended a powerful corporation, the Philippine Company, which had a crown monopoly to trade with China. The company protested to the crown, which terminated the California sea otter venture in 1790. That decision left the California sea otters open to subsequent exploitation by Anglo-American and Russian interlopers.

During their brief military occupation of two posts in the Pacific northwest, in 1792–95, the Spanish again adhered to an older imperial logic at odds with the entrepreneurial enterprises of the British, Americans, and Russians. A government operation without merchants, the Spanish posts failed commercially to exploit the local sea otter to develop a transpacific trade. Instead the Spanish primarily spent their limited funds to buy 150 to 200 Indian slaves, mostly children, from their native owners. At a further cost, the Spanish carried the children south to Mexico for religious education and conversion as Catholics. For Spanish officials, saving souls from paganism remained a more appealing investment than enlisting natives into the emerging global market economy. By investing in children's souls instead of the sea otter trade, the Spanish ensured their own long-term irrelevance in the north Pacific.

Instead, the dominant colonial power on the Pacific rim became the United States, the hypercommercial nation founded by the Americans who won their independence from the British by revolution and war in the years 1775–83. Far from ending with the American Revolution, colonialism persisted in North America, but from a new base on the Atlantic seaboard. During the early nineteenth century, the Americans crossed their continent to invade the Pacific. They absorbed half of the Pacific raincoast in 1846 (leaving the other half to British Canada), conquered California in 1846–48, purchased Russian Alaska in 1867, and subverted the Hawaiian monarchy in 1898. In their ambitions and their grasp, the Americans proved worthy heirs to the British as the predominant colonizers of North America.

ACKNOWLEDGMENTS

I am grateful to Eric Foner for the opportunity to write his book—and for his savvy advice, which improved it. At Viking Penguin, Wendy Wolf, Bruce Giffords, and Clifford J. Corcoran oversaw the final stages with consummate professionalism.

At the University of California at Davis I have benefited immensely from the intellectual support and challenge provided by my colleagues: especially Ted Margadant and Karen Halttunen. I have explored the many ideas and books shared by Clarence Walker—my most regal friend (as well as a generous host and gourmet cook). My colleagues in the history of borders and borderlands—Arnie Bauer, Lorena Oropeza, Andres Resendez, Chuck Walker, and Louis Warren—have broadened my understanding of the history of the Americas. I am especially grateful to Andres for improving several of my chapters with his close, careful reading and suggestions. The department's staff—Charlotte Honeywell, Debbie Lyon, and Eteica Spencer—performed wonders under duress and with remarkable grace and good humor. My graduate students have contributed by their individual interests. In particular, I have been stretched by the promising work on Indians by Kathleen Duval and Jill Hough and on early California by Albert Amador-Lacson and Rosamaria Tanghetti. Ably led by Peter Lindert, the Agricultural History Center has been a stimulating forum for many ideas that have filtered into this book. I similarly benefited from a fellowship at the Davis Humanities Institute, under the adept guidance of Georges Van den Abbeele and Ron Saufley. It has been a great relief and pleasure to work with the administration at UC Davis—including Larry Vanderhoef, Bob Grey, Barry Klein, Barbara Metcalf, and Steve Sheffrin.

I put the finishing touches on this book at the American Antiquarian Society, a scholar's paradise. In addition to the extraordinarily rich collections, I benefited from the generous assistance of Nancy Burkett, Joanne Chaison, Ollie Chapdelaine, Ellen Dunlap, Christine Estabrook, Alice Gardner, John Hench, Phil Lampi, Dennis Laurie, Jim Moran, Ann-Catherine Rapp, Caroline Sloat, Laura Wasowicz, and Bill Young. With insight, grace, and efficiency, Gigi Barnhill helped secure most of the illustrations. I am especially grateful to Marie Lamoureux for her extraordinary expertise and generosity.

Elsewhere, several scholars gave generously of their scarce time and abundant insights to read, correct, and improve several chapters. For that, I thank James Brooks, Richard D. Brown, Richard Dunn, David D. Hall, Sheila McIntyre, Jean M. O'Brien, Dan Richter, Neal Salisbury, Rosamaria Tanghetti, and Len Travers. On top of years of sage advice and encouraging example, David provided a place to stay and write during part of one summer. On that score, I am also grateful to Lucia and Michael Gates (and, of course, to the late and lamented Sandy, who helped morale by his inexhaustible delight in playing ball). Martha D. Shattuck provided invaluable advice on New Netherlands and its scholars.

In securing illustrations, I received generous assistance from Catherine H. Grosfils (Colonial Williamsburg Foundation), Nasrine Rohany (Peabody Museum of Harvard University), David R. Brigham (Worcester Art Museum), Vicky Wells and David Perry (University of North Carolina Press), and Sarah Hartwell (Dartmouth College Special Collections). Leon Wieseltier of *The New Republic* provided a venue for developing many of the themes in this book.

Thoughtful and encouraging friends have—by their own interests and generosity—influenced my thinking and improved my life. I am especially grateful to Alessa and Chris, Ana and Pablo, Ted and Jo B., Louis and Spring, Cecelia and Bob, Chuck and Zoyla, Rosamaria and Emil, Beverly and James, Sheila and Michael (and the Magpie!), Lucy (and Curtis), Krystyna and Luis, Pedro and Kristen, Jim(bo) and Sandy, Nina and Jim, David and Judy, Kevin and Kathy, Laurie and Jonathan, Katherine and Michael (and Francine), Shelley and Peter, Nina and Louis, Allan and Linda, Dennis and Laurie, Wendy and Bruce, Barry and Jan, Chris and Margaret, and Frank and Mimi. Once again, Kevin Convey shared his considerable insights into pirate life. My mother has been an enduring source of love and support—as have been Carole and Marty. Emily Elizabeth, Doris, Jim, Rhonda, Tom, and Pat have warmly welcomed me into their fold. And Emily Albu is my greatest inspiration.

BIBLIOGRAPHY

A European fantasy of the American landscape as first encountered by Spanish explorers. An engraving from Caspar Plautius, Nova Typis Transacta Navigatio *(n.p., 1621).*

Introduction

For the classic statement of American exceptionalism applied to the colonial past, see Oscar Handlin, "The Significance of the Seventeenth Century," in James Morton Smith, ed., *Seventeenth-Century America: Essays in Colonial History* (Chapel Hill: University of North Carolina Press, 1959), 3–12.

American exceptionalism owes much to the lyrical account by the colonist J. Hector St. John de Crèvecoeur, *Letters from an American Farmer and Sketches of Eighteenth-Century America* (New York: Penguin Books, 1963), and to the historian Frederick Jackson Turner's essay "The Significance of the Frontier in American History," in Turner's *The Frontier in American History* (New York: Henry Holt, 1920).

For the tragic dimensions of colonial America, see John M. Murrin, "Beneficiaries of Catastrophe: The English Colonies in America," in Eric Foner, ed., *The New American History* (Philadelphia: Temple University Press, 1997), 3–30.

For a critique of traditional colonial history, see James A. Hijiya, "Why the West Is Lost," *William and Mary Quarterly*, 3d Ser., LI (Apr. 1994), 276–92; "Forum: Comments on James A. Hijiya's 'Why the West Is Lost,' " *William and Mary Quarterly*, 3d Ser., LI (Oct. 1994), 717–54.

For samples of the leading recent scholarship, see Jack P. Greene and J. R. Pole, eds., *Colonial British America: Essays in the New History of the Early Modern Era* (Baltimore: Johns Hopkins University Press, 1984), 317–44; and Stanley N. Katz, John M. Murrin, and Douglas Greenberg, eds., *Colonial America: Essays in Politics and Social Development*, 4th ed. (New York: McGraw-Hill, 1993).

For the multicultural foundations of colonial America, see T. H. Breen, "Creative Adaptations: Peoples and Cultures," and Gary B. Nash, "Social Development," in Greene and Pole, *Colonial British America*, 195–232 and 233–61; James H. Merrell, *The Indians' New World: Catawbas and Their Neighbors from European Contact Through the Era of Removal* (Chapel Hill: University of North Carolina Press, 1989); Gary B. Nash, *Red, White, and Black: The Peoples of Early America* (Englewood Cliffs, N.J.: Prentice-Hall, 1982).

For the neglected importance of Indians to colonial history, see the correctives by James H. Merrell, "Some Thoughts on Colonial Historians and American Indians," *William and Mary Quarterly*, 3d Ser., XLVI (Jan. 1989), 108–12; James Axtell, *Before 1492: Encounters in Colonial North America* (New York: Cambridge University Press, 1992).

For the nature of empires, see Eric Hinderaker, *Elusive Empires: Constructing Colonialism in the Ohio Valley, 1673–1800* (New York: Cambridge University Press, 1997); John Robert McNeill, *Atlantic Empires of France and Spain: Louisbourg and Havana, 1700–1763* (Chapel Hill: University of North Carolina Press, 1985).

Chapter 1: Natives, 13,000 B.C.–A.D. 1492

In general, see Neal Salisbury, "The Indians' Old World: Native Americans and the Coming of Europeans," *William and Mary Quarterly*, 3d Ser., LIII (July 1996), 435–58.

For the Beringian migration, the Paleo-Indians, and the Archaic Indians, see Alfred W. Crosby, *Ecological Imperialism: The Biological Expansion of Europe, 900–1900* (New York: Cambridge University Press, 1986); Brian M. Fagan, *The Great Journey: The Peopling of Ancient America* (London: Thames & Hudson, 1987); Stuart J. Fiedel, *Prehistory of the Americas* (New York: Cambridge University Press, 1992); Dean R. Snow, "The First Americans and the Differentiation of Hunter-Gatherer Cultures," in Bruce G. Trigger and Wilcomb E. Washburn, eds., *The Cambridge History of the Native Peoples of the Americas*, vol. 1, *North America*, part 1 (New York: Cambridge University Press, 1996), 125–200.

For the Hohokam and Anasazi, see Linda S. Cordell, *Prehistory of the Southwest* (New York: Academic Press, 1984); Linda S. Cordell, *Archaeology of the Southwest*

(New York: Academic Press, 1997); Stuart J. Fiedel, *Prehistory of the Americas* (New York: Cambridge University Press, 1992).

For the Mississipians, see Linda S. Cordell and Bruce D. Smith, "Indigenous Farmers," and Bruce D. Smith, "Agricultural Chiefdoms of the Eastern Woodlands," in Trigger and Washburn, eds., *North America*, part 1, 201–66, 267–323; David H. Dye and Cheryl Anne Cox, eds., *Towns and Temples Along the Mississippi* (Tuscaloosa: University of Alabama Press, 1990); Charles Hudson and Carmen Chaves Tesser, eds., *The Forgotten Centuries: Indians and Europeans in the American South, 1521–1704* (Athens: University of Georgia Press, 1994); Peter Nabokov and Dean Snow, "Farmers of the Woodlands," and Francis Jennings, "American Frontiers," in Alvin M. Josephy, Jr., ed., *America in 1492* (New York: Alfred A. Knopf, 1992), 119–46, 339–67; Timothy R. Pauketat and Thomas E. Emerson, *Cahokia: Domination and Ideology in the Mississippian World* (Lincoln: University of Nebraska Press, 1997); Lynda Norene Shaffer, *Native Americans Before 1492: The Moundbuilding Centers of the Eastern Woodlands* (Armonk, N.Y.: M. E. Sharpe, 1992).

For the supernatural and environmental beliefs of native people, see Eric Hinderaker, *Elusive Empires: Constructing Colonialism in the Ohio Valley, 1673–1800* (New York: Cambridge University Press, 1997); Alvin M. Josephy, Jr., ed., *America in 1492: The World of the Indian Peoples Before the Arrival of Columbus* (New York: Alfred A. Knopf, 1992); Shepard Krech III, ed., *Indians, Animals, and the Fur Trade: A Critique of Keepers of the Game* (Athens: University of Georgia Press, 1981); Shepard Krech III, *The Ecological Indian: Myth and History* (New York: W. W. Norton, 1999); Neal Salisbury, *Manitou and Providence: Indians, Europeans, and the Making of New England, 1500–1643* (New York: Oxford University Press, 1982); Richard White, *The Organic Machine: The Remaking of the Columbia River* (New York: Hill & Wang, 1995).

For the spiritual ideas of Europeans and their economic and environmental implications, see William Cronon, *Changes in the Land: Indians, Colonists, and the Ecology of New England* (New York: Hill & Wang, 1983); Stephen Innes, *Creating the Commonwealth: The Economic Culture of Puritan New England* (New York: W. W. Norton, 1995); Carolyn Merchant, *Ecological Revolutions: Nature, Gender, and Science in New England* (Chapel Hill: University of North Carolina Press, 1989); Timothy Silver, *A New Face on the Countryside: Indians, Colonists, and Slaves in South Atlantic Forests, 1500–1800* (New York: Cambridge University Press, 1990).

Chapter 2: Colonizers, 1400–1800

For fifteenth-century Europe and Iberia, see Fernand Braudel, *Civilization and Capitalism, Fifteenth to Eighteenth Centuries*, 3 vols., trans. Sian Reynolds (New York: Harper & Row, 1982–84), esp. 3: 92–173; J. H. Elliott, *Imperial Spain, 1469–1716* (London: Edward Arnold, 1963); J. H. Elliott, *The Old World and the New, 1492–1650* (New York: Cambridge University Press, 1970); Bernard Lewis, *Cultures in Conflict: Christians, Muslims, and Jews in the Age of Discovery* (New York: Oxford University Press, 1995); J. H. Parry, *The Age of Reconnaissance* (Berkeley: University of California Press, 1981); Miguel Angel Ladero Quesada, "Spain, circa

1492: Social Values and Structures," in Stuart B. Schwartz, ed., *Implicit Understandings: Observing, Reporting, and Reflecting on the Encounters Between Europeans and Other Peoples in the Early Modern Era* (New York: Cambridge University Press, 1994), 96–133.

For the expansion of Europe, see Alfred W. Crosby, Jr., *Ecological Imperialism: The Biological Expansion of Europe, 900–1900* (New York: Cambridge University Press, 1986); Philip D. Curtin, *The Rise and Fall of the Plantation Complex* (New York: Cambridge University Press, 1990); John Thornton, *Africa and Africans in the Making of the Atlantic World, 1400–1680* (New York: Cambridge University Press, 1992).

For the Atlantic islands, see Seymour Phillips, "The Outer World of the European Middle Ages," and Eduardo Aznar Vallejo, "The Conquests of the Canary Islands," in Stuart B. Schwartz, ed., *Implicit Understandings: Observing, Reporting, and Reflecting on the Encounters Between Europeans and Other Peoples in the Early Modern Era* (New York: Cambridge University Press, 1994), 23–63, 134–56.

For Columbus, see Stephen Greenblatt, *Marvelous Possessions: The Wonder of the New World* (Chicago: University of Chicago Press, 1991); William D. Phillips, Jr., and Carla Rahn Phillips, *The Worlds of Christopher Columbus* (New York: Cambridge University Press, 1992); Delno West, "Christopher Columbus and His Enterprise to the Indies: Scholarship of the Last Quarter Century," *William and Mary Quarterly*, 3d Ser., XLIX (April 1992), 254–77.

For the Norse explorations and colonization, see G. J. Marcus, *The Conquest of the North Atlantic* (Bury St. Edmunds: Boydell Press, 1980); J. R. S. Phillips, *The Medieval Expansion of Europe* (New York: Oxford University Press, 1988); David B. Quinn, *North America from Earliest Discovery to First Settlements: The Norse Voyages to 1612* (New York: Harper & Row, 1977).

For the voyages of John Cabot, see Patrick McGrath, "Bristol and America, 1480–1631," in K. R. Andrews, N. P. Canny, and P. E. H. Hair, eds., *The Westward Enterprise: English Activities in Ireland, the Atlantic, and America, 1480–1650* (Detroit: Wayne State University Press, 1979), 81–102.

For the conquest of Hispaniola and Cuba, see Charles Gibson, *Spain in America* (New York: Harper & Row, 1966); John E. Kicza, "Patterns in Early Spanish Overseas Expansion," *William and Mary Quarterly*, 3d Ser., XLIX (April 1992), 229–53.

For global overviews of the post-Columbian transformation, see Crosby, *Ecological Imperialism;* Alfred W. Crosby, Jr., *The Columbian Exchange: Biological and Cultural Consequences of 1492* (Westport, Conn: Greenwood, 1972); Jared Diamond, *Guns, Germs, and Steel: The Fates of Human Societies* (New York: W. W. Norton, 1998).

For the debate over the pre-Columbian population, see John D. Daniels, "The Indian Population of North America in 1492," *William and Mary Quarterly*, 3d Ser., XLIX (April 1992), 298–320.

For the post-encounter population collapse, see Noble David Cook and W. George Lovell, eds., *"Secret Judgments of God": Old World Disease in Colonial Spanish America* (Norman: University of Oklahoma Press, 1991); Kenneth F. Kiple and Stephen V. Beck, eds., *Biological Consequences of the European Expansion,*

1450–1800 (Brookfield, Vt.: Ashgate Publishing, 1997); Kenneth F. Kiple, ed., *The Cambridge World History of Human Disease* (New York: Cambridge University Press, 1993), especially the essays by Jane E. Buikstra, Ann G. Carmichael, Alfred W. Crosby, Jr., and Ann Ramenofsky; William H. McNeill, *Plagues and Peoples* (New York: Doubleday, 1977); John M. Murrin, "Beneficiaries of Catastrophe: The English Colonies in America," in Eric Foner, ed., *The New American History* (Philadelphia: Temple University Press, 1997), 3–30; Marvin T. Smith, "Aboriginal Depopulation in the Postcontact Southeast," in Charles Hudson and Carmen Chaves Tesser, eds., *The Forgotten Centuries: Indians and Europeans in the American South, 1521–1704* (Athens: University of Georgia Press, 1994), 257–75; John W. Verano and Douglas H. Ubelaker, eds., *Disease and Demography in the Americas* (Washington, D.C.: Smithsonian Institution Press, 1992).

For the impact of the Columbian exchange on the populations of Europe and Africa, see Kenneth F. Kiple, *The Caribbean Slave: A Biological History* (New York: Cambridge University Press, 1984); Alfred W. Crosby, Jr., *Germs, Seeds, and Animals: Studies in Ecological History* (Armonk, N.Y.: M. E. Sharpe, 1994).

For the environmental transformation of America, see Colin G. Calloway, *New Worlds for All: Indians, Europeans, and the Remaking of Early America* (Baltimore: Johns Hopkins University Press, 1997); William Cronon, *Changes in the Land: Indians, Colonists, and the Ecology of New England* (New York: Hill & Wang, 1983); Elinor G. K. Melville, *A Plague of Sheep: Environmental Consequences of the Conquest of Mexico* (New York: Cambridge University Press, 1994); Carl Ortwin Sauer, *The Early Spanish Main* (Berkeley: University of California Press, 1966).

For the enduring importance of native peoples in colonial America, see James Axtell, *After Columbus: Essays in the Ethnohistory of Colonial North America* (New York: Oxford University Press, 1988); Richard White, *The Middle Ground: Indians, Empires, and Republics in the Great Lakes Region, 1650–1815* (New York: Cambridge University Press, 1991).

Chapter 3: New Spain, 1500–1600

For the conquest of Mexico, see Inga Clendinnen, *Aztecs: An Interpretation* (New York: Cambridge University Press, 1991); Inga Clendinnen, " 'Fierce and Unnatural Cruelty': Cortés and the Conquest of Mexico," *Representations*, No. 33 (Winter 1991), 65–100; J. H. Elliot, "The Spanish Conquest," in Leslie Bethell, ed., *Colonial Spanish America* (New York: Cambridge University Press, 1987), 1–58; John E. Kicza, "Patterns in Early Spanish Overseas Expansion," *William and Mary Quarterly*, 3d Ser., XLIX (April 1992), 229–53; J. H. Parry, *The Age of Reconnaissance* (Berkeley: University of California Press, 1981); Carl Ortwin Sauer, *The Early Spanish Main* (Berkeley: University of California Press, 1966).

For the consolidation of New Spain, see Peter Bakewell, "Conquest After the Conquest: The Rise of Spanish Domination in America," in Richard L. Kagan and Geoffrey Parker, eds., *Spain, Europe and the Atlantic World: Essays in Honour of John H. Elliott* (New York: Cambridge University Press, 1995), 296–315; J. H. Elliot, "Spain and America Before 1700," in Leslie Bethel, ed., *Colonial Spanish America*

(New York: Cambridge University Press, 1987), 59–111; J. H. Elliott, *Spain and Its World, 1500–1700, Selected Essays* (New Haven: Yale University Press, 1989); James Lockhart and Stuart B. Schwartz, *Early Latin America: A History of Colonial Spanish America and Brazil* (New York: Cambridge University Press, 1983); Elinor G. K. Melville, *A Plague of Sheep: Environmental Consequences of the Conquest of Mexico* (New York: Cambridge University Press, 1994); John Lynch, *Spain, 1516–1598: From Nation State to World Empire* (Cambridge, Mass.: Blackwell, 1992); David J. Weber, *The Spanish Frontier in North America* (New Haven: Yale University Press, 1992).

For emigration to New Spain, see Ida Altman, "A New World in the Old: Local Society and Spanish Emigration to the Indies," and Auke Pieter Jacobs, "Legal and Illegal Emigration from Seville, 1550–1650," in Ida Altman and James Horn, eds., *"To Make America": European Emigration in the Early Modern Period* (Berkeley: University of California Press, 1991), 30–58, 59–84; Nicolás Sánchez-Albornoz, "The First Transatlantic Transfer: Spanish Migration to the New World, 1493–1810," in Nicholas Canny, ed., *Europeans on the Move: Studies on European Migration, 1500–1800* (New York: Oxford University Press, 1994), 26–36.

For the empire's gold and silver (and the predation of other European powers upon it), see Kenneth R. Andrews, *Trade, Plunder, and Settlement: Maritime Enterprise and the Genesis of the British Empire, 1480–1630* (New York: Cambridge University Press, 1984); Anthony Pagden, "The Struggle for Legitimacy and the Image of Empire in the Atlantic to c. 1700," in Nicholas Canny, ed., *The Oxford History of the British Empire*, vol. 1, *The Origins of Empire, British Overseas Enterprise to the Close of the Seventeenth Century* (New York: Oxford University Press, 1998), 34–54; Geoffrey Parker, "David or Goliath?: Philip II and His World in the 1580s," in Kagan and Parker, eds., *Spain, Europe, and the Atlantic World*, 245–66; Parry, *The Age of Reconnaissance*.

Chapter 4: The Spanish Frontier, 1530–1700

For the natives and the Spanish in the American southeast in general, see David Hurst Thomas, ed., *Columbian Consequences*, vol. 1, *Archaeological and Historical Perspectives on the Spanish Borderlands East* (Washington, D.C.: Smithsonian Institution Press, 1990); David J. Weber, *The Spanish Frontier in North America* (New Haven: Yale University Press, 1992); J. Leitch Wright, Jr., *The Only Land They Knew: The Tragic Story of the American Indians in the Old South* (New York: Free Press, 1981).

For Cabeza de Vaca and Soto, see also Alvar Núñez Cabeza de Vaca, *Castaways: The Narrative of Alvar Núñez Cabeza de Vaca*, ed. Enrique Pupo-Walker, trans. Frances M. López-Morillas (Berkeley: University of California Press, 1993); Paul E. Hoffman, "Lucas Vazques de Ayllon's Discovery and Colony" and "Narváez and Cabeza de Vaca in Florida," in Charles Hudson and Carmen Chaves Tesser, eds., *The Forgotten Centuries: Indians and Europeans in the American South, 1521–1704* (Athens: University of Georgia Press, 1994), 36–49, 50–73; David A. Howard, *Conquistador in Chains: Cabeza de Vaca and the Indians of the Americas* (Tuscaloosa: University of Alabama Press, 1997).

For the collapse of the Mississippian chiefdoms and the rise of loose confederations, see Marvin T. Smith, "Aboriginal Depopulation in the Postcontact Southeast," Vernon James Knight, Jr., "The Formation of the Creeks," and Patricia Galloway, "Confederacy as a Solution to Chiefdom Dissolution: Historical Evidence in the Choctaw Case," in Hudson and Tesser, eds., *The Forgotten Centuries*, 257–75, 373–92, 393–420; Marvin T. Smith, "Aboriginal Population Movements in the Early Historic Period Interior Southeast," in Peter H. Wood, Gregory A. Waselkov, and M. Thomas Hatley, eds., *Powhatan's Mantle: Indians in the Colonial Southeast* (Lincoln: University of Nebraska Press, 1989), 21–34.

For the Indians and the colonization of Florida, see James Axtell, *The Indians' New South: Cultural Change in the Colonial Southeast* (Baton Rouge: Louisiana State University Press, 1997); Amy Turner Bushnell, "Ruling 'the Republic of Indians' in Seventeenth-Century Florida," in Wood, Waselkov, and Hatley, eds., *Powhatan's Mantle*, 134–50; Paul E. Hoffman, *A New Andalucia and a Way to the Orient: The American Southeast During the Sixteenth Century* (Baton Rouge: Louisiana State University Press, 1990); Jerald T. Milanich, "Franciscan Missions and Native Peoples in Spanish Florida," and John H. Hann, "The Apalachee of the Historic Era," in Hudson and Tesser, eds., *Forgotten Centuries*, 276–303, 327–54.

For Coronado, the Pueblo and Apachean peoples, and the colonization of New Mexico, see Jack D. Forbes, *Apache, Navaho, and Spaniard* (Norman: University of Oklahoma Press, 1994); Ramón A. Gutiérrez, *When Jesus Came, the Corn Mothers Went Away: Marriage, Sexuality, and Power in New Mexico, 1500–1846* (Stanford: Stanford University Press, 1991); Elizabeth A. H. John, *Storms Brewed in Other Men's Worlds: The Confrontation of Indians, Spanish, and French in the Southwest, 1540–1795* (Norman: University of Oklahoma Press, 1996); Andrew L. Knaut, *The Pueblo Revolt of 1680: Conquest and Resistance in Seventeenth-Century New Mexico* (Norman: University of Oklahoma Press, 1997); Edward H. Spicer, *Cycles of Conquest: The Impact of Spain, Mexico, and the United States on the Indians of the Southwest, 1533–1960* (Tucson: University of Arizona Press, 1962); David J. Weber, *The Spanish Frontier in North America* (New Haven: Yale University Press, 1992).

For the Pueblo revolts, see also J. Manuel Espinosa, ed., *The Pueblo Indian Revolt of 1696 and the Franciscan Missions in New Mexico: Letters of the Missionaries and Related Documents* (Norman: University of Oklahoma Press, 1988); Alvin M. Josephy, Jr., *The Patriot Chiefs: A Chronicle of American Indian Resistance* (New York: Penguin, 1976), 63–94.

Note: In estimating the 1680 Hispanic population of New Mexico at 1,000 and their losses to revolt at 200, I have followed the calculations by Andrew Knaut rather than the usual, higher figures of 2,400 and 400 found in most accounts. Knaut makes a persuasive case that the higher counts are inflations wrought by Otermín's alarmist reports.

Chapter 5: Canada and Iroquoia, 1500–1660

In general, this chapter relies upon Denys Delage, *Bitter Feast: Amerindians and Europeans in Northeastern North America, 1600–1664*, trans. Jane Brierly (Vancouver:

University of British Columbia, 1993); Olive Patricia Dickason, *Canada's First Nations: A History of Founding Peoples from Earliest Times* (Norman: University of Oklahoma Press, 1992); W. J. Eccles, *France in America* (East Lansing: Michigan State University Press, 1990); W. J. Eccles, *The Canadian Frontier, 1534–1760* (Albuquerque: University of New Mexico Press, 1983); Cornelius J. Jaenen, *Friend and Foe: Aspects of French-Amerindian Cultural Contact in the Sixteenth and Seventeenth Centuries* (Toronto: University of Toronto Press, 1976); Bruce G. Trigger, *Natives and Newcomers: Canada's "Heroic Age" Reconsidered* (Montreal: McGill–Queen's University Press, 1986).

For the explorers, see J. H. Parry, *The Age of Reconnaissance: Discovery, Exploration and Settlement, 1450–1650* (Berkeley: University of California Press, 1963); David B. Quinn, *North America from Earliest Discovery to First Settlements: The Norse Voyages to 1612* (New York: Harper & Row, 1977).

For the early fur trade, see James Axtell, "At the Water's Edge: Trading in the Sixteenth Century," in his *After Columbus: Essays in the Ethnohistory of Colonial North America* (New York: Oxford University Press, 1988), 144–81; Colin G. Calloway, ed., *Dawnland Encounters: Indians and Europeans in Northern New England* (Hanover, N.H.: University Press of New England, 1991); William Cronon, *Changes in the Land: Indians, Colonists, and the Ecology of New England* (New York: Hill & Wang, 1983); Shepard Krech III, *The Ecological Indian: Myth and History* (New York: W. W. Norton, 1999); Neal Salisbury, *Manitou and Providence: Indians, Europeans, and the Making of New England, 1500–1643* (New York: Oxford University Press, 1982).

For the Iroquois and the French, see José Antonio Brandao, *"Your Fyre Shall Burn No More": Iroquois Policy Toward New France and Its Native Allies to 1701* (Lincoln: University of Nebraska Press, 1997); Matthew Dennis, *Cultivating a Landscape of Peace: Iroquois-European Encounters in Seventeenth-Century America* (Ithaca, N.Y.: Cornell University Press, 1993); Daniel K. Richter, *The Ordeal of the Longhouse: The Peoples of the Iroquois League in the Era of European Colonization* (Chapel Hill: University of North Carolina Press, 1992); Dean R. Snow, *The Iroquois* (Cambridge, Mass.: Blackwell, 1994); Ian K. Steele, *Warpaths: Invasions of North America* (New York: Oxford University Press, 1994); Anthony F. C. Wallace, *The Death and Rebirth of the Seneca* (New York: Alfred A. Knopf, 1969).

For the Jesuit missions, see James Axtell, *The Invasion Within: The Contest of Cultures in Colonial North America* (New York: Oxford University Press, 1985); and Delage, *Bitter Feast.*

Chapter 6: Virginia, 1570–1650

In general, this chapter relies on Warren M. Billings, John E. Selby, and Thad W. Tate, *Colonial Virginia: A History* (White Plains, N.Y.: KTO Press, 1986); Wesley Frank Craven, *The Southern Colonies in the Seventeenth Century, 1607–1689* (Baton Rouge: Louisiana State University Press, 1970); James Horn, *Adapting to a New World: English Society in the Seventeenth-Century Chesapeake* (Chapel Hill: University of North Carolina Press, 1994); and Edmund S. Morgan, *American Slavery, American Freedom: The Ordeal of Colonial Virginia* (New York: W. W. Norton, 1975).

For the West Country colonial promoters, see Peter C. Mancall, ed., *Envisioning America: English Plans for the Colonization of North America, 1580–1640* (New York: Bedford Books/St. Martin's Press, 1995); Anthony Pagden, "The Struggle for Legitimacy and the Image of Empire in the Atlantic to c. 1700," in Nicholas Canny, ed., *The Oxford History of the British Empire*, vol. 1, *The Origins of Empire: British Overseas Enterprise to the Close of the Seventeenth Century* (New York: Oxford University Press, 1998), 34–54; J. H. Parry, *The Age of Reconnaissance* (Berkeley: University of California Press, 1981); David B. Quinn, *North America from Earliest Discovery to First Settlements: The Norse Voyages to 1612* (New York: Harper & Row, 1977).

For English conditions, see E. L. Jones, "The European Background," in Stanley L. Engerman and Robert E. Gallman, eds., *The Cambridge Economic History of the United States*, vol. 1, *The Colonial Era* (New York: Cambridge University Press, 1996), 95–133; Mark Kishlansky, *A Monarchy Transformed: Britain, 1603–1714* (New York: Penguin, 1996); Carole Shammas, "English Commercial Development and American Colonization, 1560–1620," in K. R. Andrews, N. P. Canny, and P. E. H. Hair, eds., *The Westward Enterprise: English Activities in Ireland, the Atlantic, and America, 1480–1650* (Detroit: Wayne State University Press, 1979), 151–74.

For the Irish precedent, see Nicholas P. Canny, "The Ideology of English Colonization: From Ireland to America," *William and Mary Quarterly*, 3d ser., XXX (1973), 575–98; Nicholas P. Canny, "The Permissive Frontier: Social Control in English Settlements in Ireland and Virginia, 1550–1650," in Andrews, Canny, and Hair, eds., *Westward Enterprise*, 17–44; Nicholas A. Canny, "The Origins of Empire: An Introduction," and Jane H. Ohlmeyer, "Civilizinge of Those Rude Partes': Colonization Within Britain and Ireland, 1580s–1640s," in Canny, ed., *Origins of Empire*, 1–33, 124–47.

For the first English attempts to colonize Virginia, see Kenneth R. Andrews, *Trade, Plunder, and Settlement: Maritime Enterprise and the Genesis of the British Empire, 1480–1630* (New York: Cambridge University Press, 1984); Karen Ordahl Kupperman, *Roanoke: The Abandoned Colony* (Totowa, N.J.: Rowman & Allanheld, 1984).

For the Powhatan Indians, see James Axtell, "The Rise and Fall of the Powhatan Empire," in *After Columbus: Essays in the Ethnohistory of Colonial North America* (New York: Oxford University Press, 1988), 182–221; Frederic W. Gleach, *Powhatan's World and Colonial Virginia: A Conflict of Cultures* (Lincoln: University of Nebraska Press, 1997); Helen C. Rountree, *Pocahontas's People: The Powhatan Indians of Virginia Through Four Centuries* (Norman: University of Oklahoma Press, 1990); Helen C. Rountree, *The Powhatan Indians of Virginia: Their Traditional Culture* (Norman: University of Oklahoma Press, 1989); Helen C. Rountree and E. Randolph Turner III, "On the Fringe of the Southeast: The Powhatan Paramount Chiefdom in Virginia," in Charles Hudson and Carmen Chaves Tesser, eds., *The Forgotten Centuries: Indians and Europeans in the American South, 1521–1704* (Athens: University of Georgia Press, 1994), 355–72.

For Jamestown, see Carville V. Earle, "Environment, Disease, and Mortality in Early Virginia," in Thad W. Tate and David L. Ammerman, eds., *The Chesapeake in the Seventeenth Century: Essays on Anglo-American Society* (Chapel Hill: University of

North Carolina Press, 1979), 96–125; Alden T. Vaughan, *American Genesis: Captain John Smith and the Founding of Virginia* (Boston: Little, Brown, 1975).

For the demography, economy, and society of Virginia and Maryland, see Nicholas Canny, "English Migration into and Across the Atlantic During the Seventeenth and Eighteenth Centuries," in Nicholas Canny, ed., *Europeans on the Move: Studies on European Migration, 1500–1800* (Oxford: Clarendon Press, 1994), 39–75; Lois Green Carr, Russell R. Menard, and Lorena S. Walsh, *Robert Cole's World: Agriculture and Society in Early Maryland* (Chapel Hill: University of North Carolina Press, 1991); David W. Galenson, "The Settlement and Growth of the Colonies: Population, Labor, and Economic Development," in Engerman and Gallman, eds., *Colonial Era*, 135–208; Gloria L. Main, *Tobacco Colony: Life in Early Maryland, 1650–1720* (Princeton: Princeton University Press, 1982); Russell R. Menard, "Economic and Social Development of the South," in Engerman and Gallman, eds., *Colonial Era*, 249–96; Menard, "British Migration to the Chesapeake Colonies in the Seventeenth Century," in Lois Green Carr, Philip D. Morgan, and Jean B. Russo, eds., *Colonial Chesapeake Society* (Chapel Hill: University of North Carolina Press, 1988), 99–132.

For gender relations, see Kathleen M. Brown, *Good Wives, Nasty Wenches, and Anxious Patriarchs: Gender, Race, and Power in Colonial Virginia* (Chapel Hill: University of North Carolina Press, 1996); Mary Beth Norton, *Founding Mothers and Fathers: Gendered Power and the Forming of American Society* (New York: Alfred A. Knopf, 1996).

Chapter 7: Chesapeake Colonies, 1650–1750

For the political history of the Chesapeake colonies, see Bernard Bailyn, "Politics and Social Structure in Virginia," in James Morton Smith, ed., *Seventeenth-Century America: Essays in Colonial History* (Chapel Hill: University of North Carolina Press, 1959); Warren M. Billings, John E. Selby, and Thad W. Tate, *Colonial Virginia: A History* (White Plains, N.Y.: KTO Press, 1986); Wesley Frank Craven, *The Southern Colonies in the Seventeenth Century, 1607–1689* (Baton Rouge: Louisiana State University Press, 1970); and, especially, Edmund S. Morgan, *American Slavery, American Freedom: The Ordeal of Colonial Virginia* (New York; W. W. Norton, 1975).

For the demography, economy, and society of Virginia, see Kathleen M. Brown, *Good Wives, Nasty Wenches, and Anxious Patriarchs: Gender, Race, and Power in Colonial Virginia* (Chapel Hill: University of North Carolina Press, 1996); James Horn, *Adapting to a New World: English Society in the Seventeenth-Century Chesapeake* (Chapel Hill: University of North Carolina Press, 1994); John J. McCusker and Russell R. Menard, *The Economy of British America, 1607–1789* (Chapel Hill: University of North Carolina Press, 1985); Darrett B. Rutman and Anita H. Rutman, *A Place in Time: Middlesex County, Virginia, 1650–1750* (New York: W. W. Norton, 1984).

For Maryland, see Lois Green Carr, Russell R. Menard, and Lorena S. Walsh, *Robert Cole's World: Agriculture and Society in Early Maryland* (Chapel Hill: University of North Carolina Press, 1991); Aubrey C. Land, *Colonial Maryland: A History*

(Millwood, N.Y.: KTO Press, 1981); Gloria L. Main, *Tobacco Colony: Life in Early Maryland, 1650–1720* (Princeton: Princeton University Press, 1982); David B. Quinn, ed., *Early Maryland in a Wider World* (Detroit: Wayne State University Press, 1982).

For emigration, see Nicholas Canny, "English Migration into and Across the Atlantic During the Seventeenth and Eighteenth Centuries," in Nicholas Canny, ed., *Europeans on the Move: Studies on European Migration, 1500–1800* (Oxford: Clarendon Press, 1994), 39–75; James Horn, " 'To Parts Beyond the Seas': Free Emigration to the Chesapeake in the Seventeenth Century," in Ida Altman and James Horn, eds., *"To Make America": European Emigration in the Early Modern Period* (Berkeley: University of California Press, 1991), 85–130; Russell R. Menard, "British Migration to the Chesapeake Colonies in the Seventeenth Century," in Lois Green Carr, Philip D. Morgan, and Jean B. Russo, eds., *Colonial Chesapeake Society* (Chapel Hill: University of North Carolina Press, 1988), 99–132.

For Bacon's Rebellion and its legacies, see also Ian K. Steele, *Warpaths: Invasions of North America* (New York: Oxford University Press, 1994).

For Virginia's transition to slavery, see Richard N. Bean and Robert P. Thomas, "The Adoption of Slave Labor in British America," in Henry A. Gemery and Jan S. Hogendorn, eds., *The Uncommon Market: Essays in the Economic History of the Atlantic Slave Trade* (New York: Academic Press, 1979), 377–98; Ira Berlin, *Many Thousands Gone: The First Two Centuries of Slavery in North America* (Cambridge, Mass.: Harvard University Press, 1998); Richard S. Dunn, "Servants and Slaves: The Recruitment and Employment of Labor," in Jack P. Greene and J. R. Pole, eds., *Colonial British America: Essays in the New History of the Early Modern Era* (Baltimore: Johns Hopkins University Press, 1984), 157–94; Winthrop D. Jordan, *White over Black: American Attitudes Toward the Negro, 1550–1812* (New York: W. W. Norton, 1977).

For Virginia in the eighteenth century, see T. H. Breen, *Tobacco Culture: The Mentality of the Great Tidewater Planters on the Eve of Revolution* (Princeton: Princeton University Press, 1985); Rhys Isaac, *The Transformation of Virginia, 1740–1790* (Chapel Hill: University of North Carolina Press, 1982); Allan Kulikoff, *Tobacco and Slaves: The Development of Southern Cultures in the Chesapeake, 1680–1800* (Chapel Hill: University of North Carolina Press, 1986); Charles S. Sydnor, *American Revolutionaries in the Making: Political Practices in Washington's Virginia* (New York: Free Press, 1965).

Chapter 8: New England, 1600–1700

For England and Puritanism, see Patrick Collinson, *The Birthpangs of Protestant England: Religious and Cultural Change in the Sixteenth and Seventeenth Centuries* (London: Macmillan, 1988); Collinson, *The Religion of Protestants: The Church in English Society, 1559–1625* (Oxford: Clarendon Press, 1982); Christopher Hill, *The Century of Revolution, 1603–1714* (New York: W. W. Norton, 1961); William Hunt, *The Puritan Moment: The Coming of Revolution in an English County* (Cambridge, Mass.: Harvard University Press, 1983); Mark Kishlansky, *A Monarchy Transformed: Britain, 1603–1714* (New York: Penguin, 1996).

For the influence of English Puritanism on New England, see Charles Lloyd Cohen, *God's Caress: The Psychology of Puritan Religious Experience* (New York: Oxford University Press, 1986); Stephen Foster, *The Long Argument: English Puritanism and the Shaping of New England Culture, 1570–1700* (Chapel Hill: University of North Carolina Press, 1991).

For the exploration and first settlement of New England, see Kenneth R. Andrews, *Trade, Plunder, and Settlement: Maritime Enterprise and the Genesis of the British Empire, 1480–1630* (New York: Cambridge University Press, 1984); J. H. Parry, *The Age of Reconnaissance* (Berkeley: University of California Press, 1981); David B. Quinn, *North America from Earliest Discovery to First Settlements: The Norse Voyages to 1612* (New York: Harper & Row, 1977).

For the Puritan migration, see Virginia DeJohn Anderson, *New England's Generation: The Great Migration and the Formation of Society and Culture in the Seventeenth Century* (New York: Cambridge University Press, 1991); Richard Archer, "New England Mosaic: A Demographic Analysis for the Seventeenth Century," *William and Mary Quarterly*, 3d Ser., XLVII (Oct. 1990), 477–502; David Cressy, *Coming Over: Migration and Communication Between England and New England in the Seventeeth Century* (New York: Cambridge University Press, 1987).

For Puritanism in New England, see Theodore Dwight Bozeman, *To Live Ancient Lives: The Primitivist Dimension in Puritanism* (Chapel Hill: University of North Carolina Press, 1988); Richard S. Dunn, *Puritans and Yankees: The Winthrop Dynasty of New England, 1630–1717* (Princeton: Princeton University Press, 1962); David D. Hall, *Worlds of Wonder, Days of Judgment: Popular Religious Belief in Early New England* (New York: Alfred A. Knopf, 1989); David D. Hall, "Narrating Puritanism," in Harry S. Stout and D. G. Hart, eds., *New Directions in American Religious History* (New York: Oxford University Press, 1997), 51–83; David D. Hall and Ann S. Brown, "Family Strategies and Religious Practice: Baptism and the Lord's Supper in Early New England," in David D. Hall, ed., *Lived Religion in America: Toward a History of Practice* (Princeton: Princeton University Press, 1997), 41–68; Edmund S. Morgan, *The Puritan Dilemma: The Story of John Winthrop* (Boston: Little, Brown, 1958).

For the Plymouth colony, see William Bradford, *Of Plymouth Plantation, 1620–1647*, ed. Francis Murphy (New York: Random House, 1981); John Demos, *A Little Commonwealth: Family Life in Plymouth Colony* (New York: Oxford University Press, 1970); George D. Langdon, *Pilgrim Colony: A History of New Plymouth, 1620–1691* (New Haven: Yale University Press, 1966).

For Rhode Island, see Bruce C. Daniels, *Dissent and Conformity on Narragansett Bay: The Colonial Rhode Island Town* (Middletown, Conn.: Wesleyan University Press, 1983); Sydney V. James, *Colonial Rhode Island: A History* (New York: Charles Scribner's Sons, 1975); William G. McLoughlin, *Rhode Island: A Bicentennial History* (New York: W. W. Norton, 1978).

For Maine and New Hampshire, see Charles E. Clark, *The Eastern Frontier: The Settlement of Northern New England, 1610–1763* (New York: Alfred A. Knopf, 1970); Jere R. Daniel, *Colonial New Hampshire: A History* (Millwood, N.Y.: KTO Press, 1981).

For Connecticut, see Bruce C. Daniels, *The Connecticut Town: Growth and Development, 1635–1790* (Middletown, Conn.: Wesleyan University Press, 1979); Robert J. Taylor, *Colonial Connecticut: A History* (Millwood, N.Y.: KTO Press, 1979).

For women's experience, see Cornelia Hughes Dayton, *Women Before the Bar: Gender, Law, and Society in Connecticut, 1639–1789* (Chapel Hill: University of North Carolina Press, 1995); Mary Beth Norton, *Founding Mothers and Fathers: Gendered Power and the Forming of American Society* (New York: Alfred A. Knopf, 1996); Laurel Thatcher Ulrich, *Good Wives: Image and Reality in the Lives of Women in Northern New England, 1650–1750* (New York: Alfred A. Knopf, 1982).

For witchcraft, see Paul Boyer and Stephen Nissenbaum, *Salem Possessed: The Social Origins of Witchcraft* (Cambridge, Mass.: Harvard University Press, 1974); John P. Demos, *Entertaining Satan: Witchcraft and the Culture of Early New England* (New York: Oxford University Press, 1982); Richard Godbeer, *The Devil's Dominion: Magic and Religion in Early New England* (New York: Cambridge University Press, 1982); Carol F. Karlsen, *The Devil in the Shape of a Woman: Witchcraft in Colonial New England* (New York: W. W. Norton, 1987).

For the economic development of New England, see Christine Leigh Heyrman, *Commerce and Culture: The Maritime Communities of Colonial Massachusetts, 1690–1750* (New York: W. W. Norton, 1984); Stephen Innes, *Creating the Commonwealth: The Economic Culture of Puritan New England* (New York: W. W. Norton, 1995); John J. McCusker and Russell R. Menard, *The Economy of British America, 1607–1789* (Chapel Hill: University of North Carolina Press, 1985); Daniel Vickers, *Farmers and Fishermen: Two Centuries of Work in Essex County, Massachusetts, 1630–1850* (Chapel Hill: University of North Carolina Press, 1994).

Chapter 9: Puritans and Indians, 1600–1700

For the Indians of New England, see Kathleen J. Bragdon, *Native People of Southern New England, 1500–1650* (Norman: University of Oklahoma Press, 1996); Laurence M. Hauptman and James D. Wherry, eds., *The Pequots in Southern New England: The Fall and Rise of an American Indian Nation* (Norman: University of Oklahoma Press, 1990); William S. Simmons, *Spirit of the New England Tribes: Indian History and Folklore, 1620–1984* (Hanover, N.H.: University Press of New England, 1986).

For the economic culture of the colonists and the environmental transformation of New England, see Virginia DeJohn Anderson, "King Philip's Herds: Indians, Colonists, and the Problem of Livestock in Early New England," *William and Mary Quarterly* 3d Ser., LI (Oct. 1994), 601–24; William Cronon, *Changes in the Land: Indians, Colonists, and the Ecology of New England* (New York: Hill & Wang, 1983); Stephen Innes, *Creating the Commonwealth: The Economic Culture of Puritan New England* (New York: W. W. Norton, 1995); Carolyn Merchant, *Ecological Revolutions: Nature, Gender, and Science in New England* (Chapel Hill: University of North Carolina Press, 1989).

For Indian-Puritan relations, see James Axtell, *The European and the Indian:*

Essays in the Ethnohistory of Colonial North America (New York: Oxford University Press 1981); Alfred A. Cave, *The Pequot War* (Amherst: University of Massachusetts Press, 1996); Francis Jennings, *The Invasion of America: Indians, Colonialism, and the Cant of Conquest* (Chapel Hill: University of North Carolina Press, 1975); Ronald Dale Karr, " 'Why Should You Be So Furious?': The Violence of the Pequot War," *Journal of American History* LXXXV (Dec. 1998), 876–909; Kenneth M. Morrison, *The Embattled Northeast: The Elusive Ideal of Alliance in Abenaki-Euroamerican Relations* (Berkeley: University of California Press, 1984): Neal Salisbury, *Manitou and Providence: Indians, Europeans, and the Making of New England, 1500–1643* (New York: Oxford University Press, 1982); Alden T. Vaughan, *New England Frontier: Puritans and Indians* (Norman: University of Oklahoma Press, 1995).

For the praying towns, see James Axtell, *The Invasion Within: The Contest of Cultures in Colonial North America* (New York: Oxford University Press, 1985); Dane Morrison, *A Praying People: Massachusett Acculturation and the Failure of the Puritan Mission, 1600–1690* (New York: Peter Lang, 1995); Jean M. O'Brien, *Dispossession by Degrees: Indian Land and Identity in Natick, Massachusetts, 1650–1790* (New York: Cambridge University Press, 1997); Neal Salisbury, "Red Puritans: The 'Praying Indians' of Massachusetts Bay and John Eliot," *William and Mary Quarterly*, 3d ser., XXXI (Jan. 1974), 27–54. I also drew upon an unpublished conference paper by Len Travers, "John Cotton, Jr., Among the Indians: Martha's Vineyard, 1664–1667," from the October 15, 1999, conference "Microhistory: Advantages and Limitations for the Study of Early American History," sponsored by the Omohundro Institute of Early American History and Culture and the University of Connecticut.

For King Philip's War, see Douglas Edward Leach, *Flintlock and Tomahawk: New England in King Philip's War* (New York: Macmillan, 1958); Jill Lepore, *The Name of War: King Philip's War and the Origins of American Identity* (New York: Alfred A. Knopf, 1998); Patrick M. Malone, *The Skulking Way of War: Technology and Tactics Among the New England Indians* (New York: Madison Books, 1991); Richard I. Melvoin, *New England Outpost: War and Society in Colonial Deerfield* (New York: W. W. Norton, 1989); Mary Rowlandson, *The Sovereignty and Goodness of God, Together with the Faithfulness of His Promises Displayed, Being a Narrative of the Captivity and Restoration of Mrs. Mary Rowlandson and Related Documents*, ed. Neal Salisbury (Boston: Bedford Books, 1997); Ian K. Steele, *Warpaths: Invasions of North America* (New York: Oxford University Press, 1994).

For the lot of New England Indians after Metacom's rebellion, see, Richard R. Johnson, "The Search for a Usable Indian: An Aspect of the Defense of New England," *Journal of American History* LXIV (Dec. 1977), 623–51; Daniel Mandell, "To Live More Like My Christian English Neighbors': Natick Indians in the Eighteenth Century," *William and Mary Quarterly*, 3d Ser., XLVIII (Oct. 1991), 552–79; Jean M. O'Brien, " 'Divorced' from the Land: Resistance and Survival of Indian Women in Eighteenth-Century New England," in Colin G. Calloway, ed., *After King Philip's War: Presence and Persistence in Indian New England* (Hanover, N.H.: University Press of New England, 1997), 144–61; O'Brien, *Dispossession by Degrees.*

Chapter 10: The West Indies, 1600–1700

For the English West Indies in general, see Hilary McD. Beckles, "A 'Riotous and Unruly Lot': Irish Indentured Servants and Freemen in the English West Indies, 1644–1713," *William and Mary Quarterly*, 3d Ser., XLVII (Oct. 1990), 503–22; Carl and Roberta Bridenbaugh, *No Peace Beyond the Line: The English in the Caribbean, 1624–1690* (New York: Oxford University Press, 1972); Barbara Bush, *Slave Women in Caribbean Society, 1650–1838* (Bloomington: Indiana University Press, 1990); Michael Craton, "Reluctant Creoles: The Planters' World in the British West Indies," in Bernard Bailyn and Philip D. Morgan, eds., *Strangers Within the Realm: Cultural Margins of the First British Empire* (Chapel Hill: University of North Carolina Press, 1991), 314–62; Richard S. Dunn, *Sugar and Slaves: The Rise of the Planter Class in the English West Indies, 1624–1713* (Chapel Hill: University of North Carolina Press, 1972); Kenneth E. Kiple, *The Caribbean Slave: A Biological History* (Cambridge: Cambridge University Press, 1984).

For Barbados, see also Hilary [McD.] Beckles, *Black Rebellion in Barbados: The Struggle Against Slavery, 1627–1838* (Barbados: Antilles Publications, 1984); Hilary McD. Beckles, *Natural Rebels: A Social History of Enslaved Black Women in Barbados* (New Brunswick, N.J.: Rutgers University Press, 1989); Hilary McD. Beckles, *White Servitude and Black Slavery in Barbados, 1627–1715* (Knoxville: University of Tennessee Press, 1989); Jack P. Greene, "Changing Identity in the British Caribbean: Barbados as a Case Study," in Nicholas Canny and Anthony Pagden, eds., *Colonial Identity in the Atlantic World, 1500–1800* (Princeton: Princeton University Press, 1987), 213–66.

For piracy in the West Indies, see Kenneth R. Andrews, *Trade, Plunder, and Settlement: Maritime Enterprise and the Genesis of the British Empire, 1480–1630* (New York: Cambridge University Press, 1984).

For the economic development of the West Indies, see Philip D. Curtin, *The Rise and Fall of the Plantation Complex: Essays in Atlantic History* (New York: Cambridge University Press, 1998); K. G. Davies, *The North Atlantic World in the Seventeenth Century* (Minneapolis: University of Minnesota Press, 1974); John J. McCusker and Russell R. Menard, *The Economy of British America, 1607–1789* (Chapel Hill: University of North Carolina Press, 1985); Richard B. Sheridan, *Sugar and Slavery: An Economic History of the British West Indies, 1623–1775* (Baltimore: Johns Hopkins University Press, 1973).

For Jamaican maroons, see Barbara Klamon Kopytoff, "The Early Political Development of Jamaican Maroon Societies," *William and Mary Quarterly*, 3d Ser. XXXV (April 1978), 287–307.

Chapter 11: Carolina, 1670–1760

For overviews of early Carolina, see Daniel C. Littlefield, *Rice and Slaves: Ethnicity and the Slave Trade in Colonial South Carolina* (Baton Rouge: Louisiana State University Press, 1981); Robert M. Weir, *Colonial South Carolina: A History* (Millwood, N.Y.: KTO Press, 1983); Peter H. Wood, *Black Majority: Negroes in Colonial South Carolina from 1670 Through the Stono Rebellion* (New York: Alfred A. Knopf, 1974).

For the origins of Carolina, see also Wesley Frank Craven, *The Colonies in Transition, 1660–1713* (New York: Harper & Row, 1968); Wesley Frank Craven, *The Southern Colonies in the Seventeenth Century, 1607–1689* (Baton Rouge: Louisiana State University Press, 1970).

For the development of the Carolina deerskin and slave trades, see James Axtell, *The Indians' New South: Cultural Change in the Colonial Southeast* (Baton Rouge: Louisiana State University Press, 1997); David H. Corkran, *The Carolina Indian Frontier* (Columbia, S.C.: University of South Carolina Press, 1970); Verner W. Crane, *The Southern Frontier, 1670–1732* (New York: W. W. Norton, 1981); John Lawson, *A New Voyage to Carolina*, ed. Hugh Talmadge Lefler (Chapel Hill: University of North Carolina Press, 1967); James H. Merrell, *The Indians' New World: Catawbas and Their Neighbors from European Contact Through the Era of Removal* (Chapel Hill: University of North Carolina Press, 1989); J. Leitch Wright, Jr., *The Only Land They Knew: The Tragic Story of the American Indians in the Old South* (New York: Free Press, 1981).

For the destruction of the Florida missions, see Ian K. Steele, *Warpaths: Invasions of North America* (New York: Oxford University Press, 1994); David J. Weber, *The Spanish Frontier in North America* (New Haven: Yale University Press, 1992).

For the demographic and economic consequences of colonization, see Timothy Silver, *A New Face on the Countryside: Indians, Colonists, and Slaves in South Atlantic Forests, 1500–1800* (New York: Cambridge University Press, 1990); Peter H. Wood, "The Changing Population of the Colonial South: An Overview by Race and Region, 1685–1790," in Wood, Gregory A. Waselkov, and M. Thomas Hatley, eds., *Powhatan's Mantle: Indians in the Colonial Southeast* (Lincoln: University of Nebraska Press, 1989), 35–103.

For Georgia, see Harvey H. Jackson and Phinizy Spalding, eds., *Forty Years of Diversity: Essays on Colonial Georgia* (Athens: University of Georgia Press, 1984); Trevor Richard Rees, *Colonial Georgia: A Study in British Imperial Policy in the Eighteenth Century* (Athens: University of Georgia Press, 1963); Phinizy Spalding and Harvey H. Jackson, eds., *Oglethorpe in Perspective: Georgia's Founder After Two Hundred Years* (Tuscaloosa: University of Alabama Press, 1989); Betty Wood, *Slavery in Colonial Georgia, 1730–1775* (Athens: University of Georgia Press, 1984).

Chapter 12: Middle Colonies, 1600–1700

For the Dutch empire, see Jonathan I. Israel, *The Dutch Republic: Its Rise, Greatness, and Fall, 1477–1806* (New York: Oxford University Press, 1998); J. L. Price, *The Dutch Republic in the Seventeenth Century* (New York: St. Martin's Press, 1998).

For New Netherland, see Stefan Bielinski, "The People of Colonial Albany, 1650–1800: The Profile of a Community," in William Pencak and Conrad Edick Wright, eds., *Authority and Resistance in Early New York* (New York: New-York Historical Society, 1988), 1–26; Patricia U. Bonomi, *A Factious People: Politics and Society in Colonial New York* (New York: Columbia University Press, 1971); Patricia U. Bonomi and Eric Nooter, eds., *Colonial Dutch Studies: An Interdisciplinary Approach* (New York: New York University Press, 1988); David Cohen, "How Dutch Were the Dutch of New Netherland?" *New York History* LXII (1981), 51; Michael Kammen, *Colonial New York: A History* (New York: Oxford University Press, 1975); Jan Lucassen, "The Netherlands, the Dutch, and Long-Distance Migration in the Late Sixteenth to Early Nineteenth Centuries," in Nicholas Canny, ed., *Europeans on the Move: Studies on European Migration, 1500–1800* (Oxford: Clarendon Press, 1994), 153–91; David E. Narrett, *Inheritance and Family Life in Colonial New York City* (Ithaca, N.Y.: Cornell University Press, 1992); Oliver A. Rink, *Holland on the Hudson: An Economic and Social History of Dutch New York* (Ithaca, N.Y.: Cornell University Press, 1986); Allen W. Trelease, *Indian Affairs in Colonial New York: The Seventeenth Century* (Ithaca, N.Y.: Cornell University Press, 1960).

For New Sweden, see John A. Munroe, *Colonial Delaware: A History* (Millwood, N.Y.: KTO Press, 1978); C. A. Weslager, *Dutch Explorers, Traders, and Settlers in the Delaware Valley, 1609–1664* (Philadelphia: University of Pennsylvania Press, 1961).

For the English empire in the seventeenth century and the Navigation Acts, see Robert M. Bliss, *Revolution and Empire: English Politics and the American Colonies in the Seventeenth Century* (New York: Manchester University Press, 1990); John J. McCusker, "British Mercantilist Policies and the American Colonies," in Stanley L. Engerman and Robert E. Gallman, eds., *The Cambridge Economic History of the United States*, vol. 1, *The Colonial Era* (New York: Cambridge University Press, 1996), 337–62; Nuala Zahediah, "Overseas Expansion and Trade in the Seventeenth Century," in Nicholas Canny and Alaine Low, eds., *The Origins of Empire: British Overseas Enterprise to the Close of the Seventeenth Century* (New York: Oxford University Press, 1998), 398–422.

For the conquest of New Netherland and its effects, see Randall H. Balmer, *A Perfect Babel of Confusion: Dutch Religion and English Culture in the Middle Colonies* (New York: Oxford University Press, 1989); Linda Biemer, *Women and Property in Colonial New York: The Transition from Dutch to English Law, 1643–1727* (Ann Arbor: University of Michigan Press, 1983); Joyce D. Goodfriend, *Before the Melting Pot: Society and Culture in Colonial New York City, 1664–1730* (Princeton: Princeton University Press, 1992); Lawrence H. Leder, *Robert Livingston, 1654–1728, and the Politics of Colonial New York* (Chapel Hill: University of North Carolina Press, 1961); Donna Merwick, *Possessing Albany, 1630–1710: The Dutch and English Experiences* (New York: Cambridge University Press, 1990); John M. Murrin, "English Rights as Ethnic Aggression: The English Conquest, the Charter of Liberties of 1683, and Leisler's Rebellion in New York," in William Pencak and Conrad Edick Wright, eds., *Authority and Resistance in Early New York* (New York: New-York Historical Society, 1988), 56–94; Robert C. Ritchie, *The Duke's Province: A Study of New York Politics and Society, 1664–1691* (Chapel Hill: University of North Carolina Press, 1977).

For the Covenant Chain, see Matthew Dennis, *Cultivating a Landscape of Peace: Iroquois-European Encounters in Seventeenth-Century America* (Ithaca, N.Y.: Cornell University Press, 1993); Francis Jennings, *The Ambiguous Iroquois Empire* (New York: W. W. Norton, 1984); Richard R. Johnson, "The Search for a Usable Indian: An Aspect of the Defense of New England," *Journal of American History* LXIV (Dec. 1977), 623–51; Daniel K. Richter, *The Ordeal of the Longhouse: The Peoples of the Iroquois League in the Era of European Colonization* (Chapel Hill: University of North Carolina Press, 1992); Daniel K. Richter and James H. Merrell, eds., *Beyond the Covenant Chain: The Iroquois and Their Neighbors in Indian North America, 1600–1800* (Syracuse, N.Y.: Syracuse University Press, 1987).

For the colonization of New Jersey, see Ned C. Landsman, *Scotland and Its First American Colony, 1683–1765* (Princeton: Princeton University Press, 1985); John E. Pomfret, *The Province of East New Jersey, 1609–1702: The Rebellious Proprietary* (Princeton: Princeton University Press, 1962); John E. Pomfret, *The Province of West New Jersey, 1609–1702* (Princeton: Princeton University Press, 1956); John E. Pomfret, *Colonial New Jersey: A History* (New York: Charles Scribner's Sons, 1973).

For Penn and Pennsylvania, see Mary Maples Dunn, *William Penn, Politics and Conscience* (Princeton: Princeton University Press, 1967); Richard S. Dunn and Mary Maples Dunn, eds., *The World of William Penn* (Philadelphia: University of Pennsylvania Press, 1986); Joseph Illick, *Colonial Pennsylvania: A History* (New York: Charles Scribner's Sons, 1976); Barry Levy, *Quakers and the American Family: British Settlement in the Delaware Valley* (New York: Oxford University Press, 1988); Gary B. Nash, *Quakers and Politics: Pennsylvania, 1681–1726* (Boston: Northeastern University Press, 1993); Sally Schwartz, *"A Mixed Multitude": The Struggle for Toleration in Colonial Pennsylvania* (New York: New York University Press, 1988); Frederick B. Tolles, *Meeting House and Counting House: The Quaker Merchants of Colonial Philadelphia, 1682–1763* (Chapel Hill: University of North Carolina Press, 1948).

For Pennsylvania and the Indians, see Eric Hinderaker, *Elusive Empires: Constructing Colonialism in the Ohio Valley, 1673–1800* (New York: Cambridge University Press, 1997); Francis Jennings, *The Ambiguous Iroquois Empire: The Covenant Chain Confederation of Indian Tribes with English Colonies from Its Beginnings to the Lancaster Treaty of 1744* (New York: W. W. Norton, 1984); C. A. Weslager, *The Delaware Indians: A History* (New Brunswick, N.J.: Rutgers University Press, 1972).

For the distinctive nature of the middle colonies, see Wayne Bodle, "Themes and Directions in Middle Colonies Historiography, 1980–1994," *William and Mary Quarterly*, 3d Ser., LI (July 1994), 355–88; Patricia U. Bonomi, "The Middle Colonies: Embryo of the New Political Order," in Alden T. Vaughan and George Athan Billias, eds., *Perspectives on Early American History: Essays in Honor of Richard B. Morris* (New York: Harper & Row, 1973), 63–92; Douglas Greenberg, "The Middle Colonies in Recent American Historiography," *William and Mary Quarterly*, 3d Ser., XXXVI (July 1979), 396–427; A. G. Roeber, " 'The Origin of Whatever Is Not English Among Us': The Dutch-Speaking and the German-Speaking Peoples of Colonial British America," in Bernard Bailyn and Philip D. Morgan, eds., *Strangers Within the Realm: Cultural Margins of the First British Empire* (Chapel Hill: University of North Carolina Press, 1991), 220–83.

Chapter 13: Revolutions, 1685–1730

For the Dominion of New England, see T. H. Breen, *The Character of the Good Ruler: A Study of Puritan Political Ideas in New England, 1630–1730* (New Haven: Yale University Press, 1970); Michael G. Hall, *Edward Randolph and the American*

Colonies, 1676–1703 (Chapel Hill: University of North Carolina Press, 1960); Michael G. Hall, *The Last American Puritan: The Life of Increase Mather, 1639–1723* (Middletown, Conn.: Wesleyan University Press, 1988); Richard R. Johnson, *Adjustment to Empire: The New England Colonies, 1675–1715* (New Brunswick, N.J.: Rutgers University Press, 1981); David S. Lovejoy, *The Glorious Revolution in America* (New York: Harper & Row, 1972); Jack M. Sosin, *English America and the Revolution of 1688* (Lincoln: University of Nebraska Press, 1982).

For the Glorious Revolution in England, see Robert Beddard, ed., *The Revolutions of 1688* (Oxford: Clarendon Press, 1991); Dale Hoak and Mordechai Feingold, eds., *The World of William and Mary: Anglo-Dutch Perspectives on the Revolution of 1688–89* (Stanford: Stanford University Press, 1996); Jonathan I. Israel, ed., *The Anglo-Dutch Moment: Essays on the Glorious Revolution and Its World Impact* (New York: Cambridge University Press, 1991).

For overviews of the Glorious Revolution in America, see K. G. Davies, "The Revolutions in America," in Beddard, ed., *Revolutions of 1688*, 246–70; Richard S. Dunn, "The Glorious Revolution in America," in Nicholas Canny and Alaine Low, eds., *The Origins of Empire: British Overseas Enterprise to the Close of the Seventeenth Century* (New York: Oxford University Press, 1998), 445–66; Richard R. Johnson, "The Revolution of 1688–9 in the American Colonies," in Israel, ed., *The Anglo-Dutch Moment*, 215–40; Lovejoy, *Glorious Revolution in America*; Sosin, *English America and the Revolution of 1688*; Ian Steele, "Governors or Generals: A Note on Martial Law and the Revolution of 1689 in English America," *William and Mary Quarterly*, 3d Ser., XLVI (April 1989), 304–14. I disagree with Sosin's characterization of the Leislerians as "frustrated and resentful opportunists" who cynically masqueraded behind an insincere Anti-Catholic rhetoric.

For the Glorious Revolution in New England, see also Breen, *Character of the Good Ruler;* Hall, *Edward Randolph and the American Colonies, 1676–1703*; Hall, *Last American Puritan*; Johnson, *Adjustment to Empire*.

For Leisler's Rebellion, see especially David William Voorhees, "The 'Fervent Zeale' of Jacob Leisler," *William and Mary Quarterly*, 3d Ser., LI (July 1994), 447–72.

For Coode's Rebellion, see Lois Green Carr and David William Jordan, *Maryland's Revolution of Government, 1689–1692* (Ithaca, N.Y.: Cornell University Press, 1974); Aubrey C. Land, *Colonial Maryland: A History* (Millwood, N.Y.: KTO Press, 1981); Gloria L. Main, *Tobacco Colony: Life in Early Maryland, 1650–1720* (Princeton: Princeton University Press, 1982).

For the impact of the Glorious Revolution on the West Indies, see also Richard S. Dunn, *Sugar and Slaves: The Rise of the Planter Class in the English West Indies, 1624–1713* (Chapel Hill: University of North Carolina Press, 1972).

For the political consequences of the Glorious Revolution in the colonies, see Patricia U. Bonomi, *The Lord Cornbury Scandal: The Politics of Reputation in British America* (Chapel Hill: University of North Carolina Press, 1998); Richard L. Bushman, *King and People in Provincial Massachusetts* (Chapel Hill: University of North Carolina Press, 1985); Edmund S. Morgan, *Inventing the People: The Rise of Popular Sovereignty in England and America* (New York: W. W. Norton, 1988); John Murrin,

"Political Development," in Jack Greene and J. R. Pole, eds., *Colonial British America: Essays in the New History of the Early Modern Era* (Baltimore: Johns Hopkins University Press, 1984), 408–56; Ian K. Steele, "The Anointed, the Appointed, and the Elected: Governance of the British Empire, 1689–1784," in P. J. Marshall, ed., *The Oxford History of the British Empire*, vol. 2, *The Eighteenth Century* (New York: Oxford University Press, 1998), 105–27; Allan Tully, "Quaker Party and Proprietary Policies: The Dynamics of Politics in Pre-Revolutionary Pennsylvania, 1730–1775," and Jessica Kross, " 'Patronage Most Ardently Sought': The New York Council, 1665–1775," in Bruce C. Daniels, ed., *Power and Status: Officeholding in Colonial America* (Middletown, Conn.: Wesleyan University Press, 1986), 75–105, 205–31.

For European war and the development of the fiscal-military state, see Jeremy Black, *Britain as a Military Power, 1688–1815* (London: University College London Press, 1999); Jeremy Black and Philip Woodfine, eds., *The British Navy and the Use of Naval Power in the Eighteenth Century* (Leicester: Leicester University Press, 1988); John Brewer, *The Sinews of Power: War, Money, and the English State, 1688–1783* (New York: Alfred A. Knopf, 1989); Mark Kishlansky, *A Monarchy Transformed: Britain, 1603–1714* (New York: Penguin, 1996); Patrick K. O'Brien, "Inseparable Connections: Trade, Economy, Fiscal State, and the Expansion of Empire, 1688–1815," and N. A. M. Rodger, "Sea-Power and Empire, 1688–1793," in Marshall, ed., *Eighteenth Century*, 53–77, 169–83; Lawrence Stone, ed., *An Imperial State at War: Britain from 1689 to 1815* (New York: Routledge, 1994).

For the Nine Years War and the War of the Spanish Succession in the colonies, see W. J. Eccles, *The Canadian Frontier, 1534–1760* (Albuquerque: University of New Mexico Press, 1983); Douglas Edward Leach, *Arms for Empire: A Military History of the British Colonies in North America, 1607–1763* (New York: Macmillan, 1973); Douglas Edward Leach, *Roots of Conflict: British Armed Forces and Colonial Americans, 1677–1763* (Chapel Hill: University of North Carolina Press, 1986); Bruce P. Lenman, "Colonial Wars and Imperial Instability, 1688–1793," in Marshall, ed., *Eighteenth Century*, 151–68; Ian K. Steele, *Warpaths: Invasions of North America* (New York: Oxford University Press, 1994).

For the Iroquois crisis and neutrality, see Richard Aquila, *The Iroquois Restoration: Iroquois Diplomacy on the Colonial Frontier, 1701–1754* (Detroit: Wayne State University Press, 1983); William N. Fenton, *The Great Law and the Longhouse: A Political History of the Iroquois Confederacy* (Norman: University of Oklahoma Press, 1998); Daniel K. Richter, *The Ordeal of the Longhouse: The Peoples of the Iroquois League in the Era of European Colonization* (Chapel Hill: University of North Carolina Press, 1992); Daniel K. Richter and James H. Merrell, eds., *Beyond the Covenant Chain: The Iroquois and Their Neighbors in Indian North America, 1600–1800* (Syracuse, N.Y.: Syracuse University Press, 1987).

For the British Union, see David Armitage, "Greater Britain: A Useful Category of Historical Analysis?" *American Historical Review* CV (April 1999), 427–45; David Armitage, "Making the Empire British: Scotland in the Atlantic World," *Past and Present*, No. 155 (May 1997), 34–63; Eric Richards, "Scotland and the Uses of the Atlantic Empire," in Bernard Bailyn and Philip D. Morgan, eds., *Strangers*

Within the Realm: Cultural Margins of the First British Empire (Chapel Hill: University of North Carolina Press, 1991), 67–114; John Robertson, ed., *A Union for Empire: Political Thought and the British Union of 1707* (New York: Cambridge University Press, 1995); John Robertson, "Union, State, and Empire: The Britain of 1707 in Its European Setting," in Stone, ed., *An Imperial State at War*, 224–57.

For the Scots tobacco trade and emigration, see Warren M. Billings, John E. Selby, and Thad W. Tate, *Colonial Virginia: A History* (White Plains, N.Y.: KTO Press, 1986); Ned C. Landsman, "The Provinces and the Empire: Scotland, the American Colonies and the Development of British Provincial Identity," in Stone, ed., *Imperial State at War*, 258–87; Ned C. Landsman, "Nation, Migration, and the Province in the First British Empire: Scotland and the Americas, 1600–1800," *American Historical Review* CV (April 1999), 463–75; T. C. Smout, N. C. Landsman, and T. M. Devine, "Scottish Emigration in the Seventeenth and Eighteenth Centuries," in Nicholas Canny, ed., *Europeans on the Move: Studies on European Migration, 1500–1800* (Oxford: Clarendon Press, 1994), 76–112.

For the war against the pirates, see Hugh T. Lefler and William S. Powell, *Colonial North Carolina: A History* (New York: Charles Scribner's Sons, 1973); Marcus Rediker, *Between the Devil and the Deep Blue Sea: Merchant Seamen, Pirates, and the Anglo-American Maritime World, 1700–1750* (New York: Cambridge University Press, 1987); Robert C. Ritchie, *Captain Kidd and the War Against the Pirates* (Cambridge: Harvard University Press, 1986); David J. Starkey et al., eds., *Pirates and Privateers: New Perspectives on the War on Trade in the Eighteenth and Nineteenth Centuries* (Exeter: University of Exeter Press, 1997); Ian K. Steele, *Politics of Colonial Policy: The Board of Trade in Colonial Administration, 1696–1720* (Oxford: Clarendon Press, 1968).

For the commercial empire, see Linda Colley, *Britons: Forging the Nation, 1707–1837* (New Haven: Yale University Press, 1992); Jack P. Greene, "Empire and Identity from the Glorious Revolution to the American Revolution," in Marshall, ed., *Eighteenth Century*, 208–30; John J. McCusker, "British Mercantilist Policies and the American Colonies," in Stanley L. Engerman and Robert E. Gallman, eds., *The Cambridge Economic History of the United States*, vol. 1, *The Colonial Era* (New York: Cambridge University Press, 1996), 337–62; John J. McCusker and Russell R. Menard, *The Economy of British America, 1607–1789* (Chapel Hill: University of North Carolina Press, 1985).

Chapter 14: The Atlantic, 1700–80

For the British Atlantic, see Marilyn C. Baseler, *"Asylum for Mankind": America, 1607–1800* (Ithaca, N.Y.: Cornell University Press, 1998); Richard S. Dunn, "Servants and Slaves: The Recruitment and Employment of Labor," in Jack P. Green and J. R. Pole, eds., *Colonial British America: Essays in the New History of the Early Modern Era* (Baltimore: Johns Hopkins University Press, 1984), 157–94; John J. McCusker, "British Mercantilist Policies and the American Colonies," in Stanley L. Engerman and Robert E. Gallman, eds., *The Cambridge Economic History of the United States*, vol. 1, *The Colonial Era* (New York: Cambridge University Press,

1996), 337–62; Ian K. Steele, *The English Atlantic, 1675–1740: An Exploration of Communication and Community* (New York: Oxford University Press, 1986).

For the colonial economy, see John J. McCusker and Russell R. Menard, *The Economy of British America, 1607–1789* (Chapel Hill: University of North Carolina Press, 1985); Edwin J. Perkins, *The Economy of Colonial America* (New York: Columbia University Press, 1980); Jacob M. Price, "The Imperial Economy, 1700–1776," in P. J. Marshall, ed., *The Oxford History of the British Empire*, vol. 2, *The Eighteenth Century* (New York: Oxford University Press, 1998), 78–104.

For urban poverty, see Gary B. Nash, *The Urban Crucible: Social Change, Political Consciousness, and the Origins of the American Revolution* (Cambridge, Mass.: Harvard University Press, 1979); Billy G. Smith, "The Material Lives of Laboring Philadelphians, 1750 to 1800," *William and Mary Quarterly*, 3d Ser., XXXVIII (April 1981), 163–202; Billy G. Smith, "The Vicissitudes of Fortune: The Careers of Laboring Men in Philadelphia, 1750–1800," in Stephen Innes, ed., *Work and Labor in Early America* (Chapel Hill: University of North Carolina Press, 1988), 221–51.

For the pockets of rural poverty, see Paul G. E. Clemens and Lucy Simler, "Rural Labor and the Farm Household in Chester County, Pennsylvania, 1750–1820," in Innes, ed., *Work and Labor in Early America*, 106–43; Dennis P. Ryan, "Landholding, Opportunity, and Mobility in Revolutionary New Jersey," *William and Mary Quarterly*, 3d Ser., XXXVI (Oct. 1979), 571–92; Gregory A. Stiverson, *Poverty in a Land of Plenty: Tenancy in Eighteenth-Century Maryland* (Baltimore: Johns Hopkins University Press, 1977).

For frontier poverty, see J. Hector St. John de Crèvecoeur, *Sketches of Eighteenth-Century America: More "Letters from an American Farmer,"* Henri L. Bourdin, Ralph H. Gabriel, and Stanley T. Williams, eds. (New Haven: Yale University Press, 1925); Alan Taylor, *Liberty Men and Great Proprietors: The Revolutionary Settlement on the Maine Frontier, 1760–1820* (Chapel Hill: University of North Carolina Press, 1990).

For gentility and the consumer revolution, see T. H. Breen, "An Empire of Goods: The Anglicization of Colonial America, 1690–1776," in Stanley N. Katz, John M. Murrin, and Douglas Greenberg, eds., *Colonial America: Essays in Politics and Social Development* (New York: McGraw-Hill, 1993), 367–98; Richard Bushman, *The Refinement of America: Persons, Houses, Cities* (New York: Alfred A. Knopf, 1992); Cary Carson, Ronald Hoffman, and Peter J. Albert, eds., *Of Consuming Interests: The Style of Life in the Eighteenth Century* (Charlottesville: University of Virginia Press, 1994); Linda Colley, *Britons: Forging the Nation, 1707–1837* (New Haven: Yale University Press, 1992).

For eighteenth-century English emigration, see Bernard Bailyn, *Voyagers to the West: A Passage in the Peopling of America on the Eve of the Revolution* (New York: Alfred A. Knopf, 1986); A. Roger Ekirch, *Bound for America: The Transportation of British Convicts to the Colonies, 1718–1775* (Oxford: Clarendon Press, 1987); James Horn, "British Diaspora: Emigration from Britain, 1680–1815," in Marshall, ed., *Eighteenth Century*, 28–52.

For Scottish emigration to the colonies, see William R. Brock, *Scotus Americanus: A Survey of the Sources for Links Between Scotland and America in the Eighteenth*

Century (Edinburgh: Edinburgh University Press, 1982); Ian C. C. Graham, *Colonists from Scotland: Emigration to North America, 1707–1783* (Ithaca, N.Y.: Cornell University Press, 1956); Alan L. Karras, *Sojourners in the Sun: Scottish Migrants to Jamaica and the Chesapeake, 1740–1800* (Ithaca, N.Y.: Cornell University Press, 1992); Ned C. Landsman, *Scotland and Its First American Colony, 1683–1765* (Princeton: Princeton University Press, 1985); Ned C. Landsman, "The Provinces and the Empire: Scotland, the American Colonies and the Development of British Provincial Identity," in Lawrence Stone, ed., *An Imperial State at War: Britain from 1689 to 1815* (New York: Routledge, 1994), 258–87; Ned C. Landsman, "Nation, Migration, and the Province in the First British Empire: Scotland and the Americas, 1600–1800," *American Historical Review* CV (April 1999), 463–75; T. C. Smout, N. C. Landsman, and T. M. Devine, "Scottish Emigration in the Seventeenth and Eighteenth Centuries," in Nicholas Canny, ed., *Europeans on the Move: Studies on European Migration, 1500–1800* (Oxford: Clarendon Press, 1994), 76–112.

For Ulster Scots emigration to the colonies, see R. J. Dickson, *Ulster Emigration to Colonial America, 1718–1775* (London: Routledge, 1966); Maldwyn A. Jones, "The Scotch-Irish in British America," in Bernard Bailyn and Philip D. Morgan, eds., *Strangers Within the Realm: Cultural Margins of the First British Empire* (Chapel Hill: University of North Carolina Press, 1991), 284–313; James G. Leyburn, *The Scotch-Irish: A Social History* (Chapel Hill: University of North Carolina Press, 1962).

For the German migration, see Georg Fertig, "Transatlantic Migration from the German-Speaking Parts of Central Europe, 1600–1800: Proportions, Structures, and Explanations," in Canny, ed., *Europeans on the Move*, 192–235; Aaron Spencer Fogleman, *Hopeful Journeys: German Immigration, Settlement, and Political Culture in Colonial America, 1717–1775* (Philadelphia: University of Pennsylvania Press, 1996); A. G. Roeber, "In German Ways?: Problems and Potentials of Eighteenth-Century German Social and Emigration History," *William and Mary Quarterly*, 3d Ser., XLIV (Oct. 1987), 750–74; A. G. Roeber, "The Origin of 'Whatever Is Not English Among Us': The Dutch-Speaking and the German-Speaking Peoples of Colonial British America," in Bailyn and Morgan, eds., *Strangers Within the Realm*, 220–83; Marianne Wokeck, "Harnessing the Lure of the 'Best Poor Man's Country': The Dynamics of German-Speaking Immigration to British North America, 1683–1783," in Ida Altman and James Horn, *"To Make America": European Emigration in the Early Modern Period* (Berkeley: University of California Press, 1991), 204–43.

For the Lenni Lenape and the Walking Purchase, see Eric Hinderaker, *Elusive Empires: Constructing Colonialism in the Ohio Valley, 1673–1800* (New York: Cambridge University Press, 1997); Francis Jennings, *The Ambiguous Iroquois Empire: The Covenant Chain Confederation of Indian Tribes with English Colonies from Its Beginnings to the Lancaster Treaty of 1744* (New York: W. W. Norton, 1984); C. A. Weslager, *The Delaware Indians: A History* (New Brunswick, N.J.: Rutgers University Press, 1972).

For overviews of slavery and the transatlantic slave trade, see Robin Blackburn, *The Making of New World Slavery: From the Baroque to the Modern, 1492–1800* (New

York: Verso, 1997); John Thornton, *Africa and Africans in the Making of the Atlantic World, 1400–1680* (New York: Cambridge University Press, 1992); James Walvin, *Black Ivory: A History of British Slavery* (London: HarperCollins, 1992).

For the slave trade, see Philip D. Curtin, *The Atlantic Slave Trade: A Census* (Madison: University of Wisconsin Press, 1969); Henry A. Gemery and Jan S. Hogendorn, eds., *The Uncommon Market: Essays in the Economic History of the Atlantic Slave Trade* (New York: Academic Press, 1979); Herbert S. Klein, *The Atlantic Slave Trade* (New York: Cambridge University Press, 1999).

For colonial slavery and African-American culture, see Ira Berlin, "Time, Space, and the Evolution of Afro-American Society on British Mainland North America," *American Historical Review* LXXXV (Jan. 1980), 44–78; Ira Berlin, *Many Thousands Gone: The First Two Centuries of Slavery in North America* (Cambridge, Mass.: Harvard University Press, 1998); Barbara Bush, *Slave Women in Caribbean Society, 1650–1838* (Bloomington: Indiana University Press, 1990); Sylvia R. Frey, *Water from the Rock: Black Resistance in a Revolutionary Age* (Princeton: Princeton University Press, 1991); Allan Kulikoff, *Tobacco and Slaves: The Development of Southern Cultures in the Chesapeake, 1660–1800* (Chapel Hill: University of North Carolina Press, 1986); Philip D. Morgan, "British Encounters with Africans and African-Americans, circa 1600–1780," in Bailyn and Morgan, eds., *Strangers Within the Realm*; Philip D. Morgan, *Slave Counterpoint: Black Culture in the Eighteenth-Century Chesapeake and Lowcountry* (Chapel Hill: University of North Carolina Press, 1998); Mechal Sobel, *The World They Made Together: Black and White Values in Eighteenth-Century Virginia* (Princeton: Princeton University Press, 1987).

Chapter 15: Awakenings, 1700–75

For colonial religion in general, see Patricia U. Bonomi, *Under the Cope of Heaven: Religion, Society, and Politics in Colonial America* (New York: Oxford University Press, 1986); Jon Butler, *Awash in a Sea of Faith: Christianizing the American People* (Cambridge, Mass.: Harvard University Press, 1990); Edwin Scott Gaustad, *Historical Atlas of Religion in America* (New York: Harper & Row, 1962); David D. Hall, "Religion and Society: Problems and Reconsiderations," in Jack P. Green and J. R. Pole, eds., *Colonial British America: Essays in the New History of the Early Modern Era* (Baltimore: Johns Hopkins University Press, 1984), 317–44; Richard Hofstadter, *America at 1750: A Social Portrait* (New York: Alfred A. Knopf, 1971); Henry F. May, *The Enlightenment in America* (New York: Oxford University Press, 1976); John M. Murrin, "Religion and Politics in America from the First Settlements to the Civil War," in Mark A. Noll, ed., *Religion and American Politics: From the Colonial Period to the 1980s* (New York: Oxford University Press, 1990), 19–43; Mark A. Noll, *A History of Christianity in the United States and Canada* (Grand Rapids, Mich.: Eerdmans, 1992).

For religion in the middle colonies, see Randall Balmer, *A Perfect Babel of Confusion: Dutch Religion and English Culture in the Middle Colonies* (New York: Oxford University Press, 1989); Aaron Spencer Fogleman, *Hopeful Journeys: German Immigration, Settlement, and Political Culture in Colonial America, 1717–1775* (Philadelphia: University of Pennsylvania Press, 1996); Rebecca Larson, *Daughters of Light: Quaker Women Preaching and Prophesying in the Colonies and Abroad, 1700–1775* (New York: Alfred A. Knopf, 1999); Marilyn J. Westerkamp, *Triumph of the Laity: Scots-Irish Piety and the Great Awakening, 1625–1760* (New York: Oxford University Press, 1988).

For religion in New England, see Richard L. Bushman, *From Puritan to Yankee: Character and the Social Order in Connecticut, 1690–1765* (Cambridge, Mass.: Harvard University Press, 1970); Michael J. Crawford, *Seasons of Grace: Colonial New England's Revival Tradition in Its British Context* (New York: Oxford University Press, 1991); Barbara E. Lacey, "Gender, Piety, and Secularization in Connecticut Religion, 1720–1775," *Journal of Social History* XXIV (Summer 1991), 799–821; Harry S. Stout, *The New England Soul: Preaching and Religious Culture in Colonial New England* (New York: Oxford University Press, 1986).

For overviews of the Great Awakening, see Richard L. Bushman, ed., *The Great Awakening: Documents on the Revival of Religion, 1740–1745* (Chapel Hill: University of North Carolina Press, 1970); Jon Butler, "Enthusiasm Described and Decried: The Great Awakening as Interpretive Fiction," *Journal of American History* LXIX (1982), 305–25; Frank Lambert, *Inventing the "Great Awakening"* (Princeton: Princeton University Press, 1999); Susan O'Brien, "Eighteenth-Century Publishing Networks in the First Years of Transatlantic Evangelicalism," in Mark A. Noll, David W. Bebbington, and George A. Rawlyk, eds., *Evangelicalism: Comparative Studies of Popular Protestantism in North America, the British Isles, and Beyond, 1700–1990* (New York: Oxford University Press, 1994), 38–57.

For Jonathan Edwards, see David D. Hall, ed., *Works of Jonathan Edwards*, vol. 12, *Ecclesiastical Writings* (New Haven: Yale University Press, 1994); C. C. Goen, ed., *Works of Jonathan Edwards*, vol. 4, *The Great Awakening* (New Haven: Yale University Press, 1972); Patricia J. Tracy, *Jonathan Edwards, Pastor: Religion and Society in Eighteenth-Century Northampton* (New York: Hill & Wang, 1979).

For George Whitefield, see Frank Lambert, *"Pedlar in Divinity": George Whitefield and the Transatlantic Revivals, 1737–1770* (Princeton: Princeton University Press, 1994); Louis Masur, ed., *The Autobiography of Benjamin Franklin* (Boston: Bedford Books/St. Martin's Press, 1993); Harry S. Stout, *The Divine Dramatist: George Whitefield and the Rise of Modern Evangelicalism* (Grand Rapids, Mich.: Eerdmans, 1991).

For radical evangelicals, especially in New England, see Catherine A. Brekus, *Strangers and Pilgrims: Female Preaching in America, 1740–1845* (Chapel Hill: University of North Carolina Press, 1998); Timothy D. Hall, *Contested Boundaries: Itinerancy and the Reshaping of the Colonial American Religious World* (Durham, N.C.: Duke University Press, 1994); Susan Juster, *Disorderly Women: Sexual Politics & Evangelicalism in Revolutionary New England* (Ithaca, N.Y.: Cornell University Press, 1994); William G. McLoughlin, *New England Dissent, 1630–1833: The Baptists and the Separation of Church and State*, 2 vols. (Cambridge, Mass.: Harvard University Press, 1971); Marilyn J. Westerkamp, *Women and Religion in Early America, 1600–1850: The Puritan and Evangelical Traditions* (New York: Routledge, 1999).

For the Great Awakening in the south, see Sylvia R. Frey, *Water from the Rock:*

Black Resistance in a Revolutionary Age (Princeton: Princeton University Press, 1991); Sylvia R. Frey and Betty Wood, *Come Shouting to Zion: African American Protestantism in the American South and British Caribbean to 1830* (Chapel Hill: University of North Carolina Press, 1998); Christine Leigh Heyrman, *Southern Cross: The Beginnings of the Bible Belt* (New York: Alfred A. Knopf, 1997); Rhys Isaac, *The Transformation of Virginia, 1740–1790* (Chapel Hill: University of North Carolina Press, 1982); Marjoleine Kars, *"Breaking Loose Together": How North Carolina Farmers Came to Fight the War of the Regulation* (Chapel Hill: University of North Carolina Press, 2001); Donald G. Mathews, *Religion in the Old South* (Chicago: University of Chicago Press, 1977).

For enclave Indians and the Great Awakening, see Bernd C. Peyer, *The Tutor'd Mind: Indian Missionary-Writers in Antebellum America* (Amherst: University of Massachusetts Press, 1997); William S. Simmons, "Red Yankees: Narragansett Conversion in the Great Awakening," *American Ethnologist* X (May 1983), 253–71.

For frontier Indians and the Great Awakening, see David H. Corkran, *The Cherokee Frontier: Conflict and Survival, 1740–1762* (Norman: University of Oklahoma Press, 1962); Gregory Evans Dowd, *A Spirited Resistance: The North American Indian Struggle for Unity, 1745–1815* (Baltimore: Johns Hopkins University Press, 1992); Richard White, *Indians, Empires, and Republics in the Great Lakes Region, 1650–1815* (New York: Cambridge University Press, 1991).

Chapter 16: French America, 1650–1750

For emigration to New France, see Leslie Choquette, "Recruitment of French Emigrants to Canada, 1600–1760," in Ida Altman and James Horn, *"To Make America": European Emigration in the Early Modern Period* (Berkeley: University of California Press, 1991), 131–71; R. Cole Harris, "The Colonists of Seventeenth-Century Canada," in J. M. Bumsted, ed., *Interpreting Canada's Past*, vol. 1, *Pre-Confederation* (Toronto: Oxford University Press, 1993), 108–20; Peter Moogk, "Manon's Fellow Exiles: Emigration from France to North America Before 1763," in Nicholas Canny, *Europeans on the Move: Studies on European Migration, 1500–1800* (Oxford: Clarendon Press, 1994), 236–60.

For the society and government of New France, see W. J. Eccles, *France in America* (East Lansing: Michigan State University Press, 1990); W. J. Eccles, *The Canadian Frontier, 1534–1760* (Albuquerque: University of New Mexico Press, 1983); Allan Greer, *The People of New France* (Toronto: University of Toronto Press, 1997); Jan Noel, *Women in New France* (Ottawa: Canadian Historical Association, 1998); Gilles Paquet and Jean-Pierre Wallot, "Nouvelle-France/Quebec/Canada: A World of Limited Identities," in Nicholas Canny and Anthony Pagden, eds., *Colonial Identity in the Atlantic World, 1500–1800* (Princeton: Princeton University Press, 1987), 95–114.

For the bifurcated geography of New France, see Winstanley Briggs, "Le Pays des Illinois," *William and Mary Quarterly*, 3d Ser., XLVII (Jan. 1990), 30–56; Catherine M. Desbarats, "The Cost of Early Canada's Native Alliances: Reality and Scarcity's Rhetoric," *William and Mary Quarterly*, 3rd ser., LII (Oct. 1995), 609–30; W. J. Eccles, *Essays on New France* (Toronto: Oxford University Press, 1987).

For the Middle Ground, see Eric Hinderaker, *Elusive Empires: Constructing Colonialism in the Ohio Valley, 1673–1800* (New York: Columbia University Press, 1997); Helen Hornbeck Tanner, ed., *Atlas of Great Lakes Indian History* (Norman: University of Oklahoma Press, 1987); Richard White, *The Middle Ground: Indians, Empires, and Republics in the Great Lakes Region, 1650–1815* (New York: Cambridge University Press, 1991).

For the Fox Wars, see Olive Patricia Dickason, *Canada's First Nations: A History of Founding Peoples from Earliest Times* (Norman: University of Oklahoma Press, 1992); R. David Edmunds and Joseph L. Peyser, *The Fox Wars: The Mesquakie Challenge to New France* (Norman: University of Oklahoma Press, 1993); White, *Middle Ground*.

For La Salle, see Patricia K. Galloway, ed., *La Salle and His Legacy: Frenchmen and Indians in the Lower Mississippi Valley* (Jackson: University Press of Mississippi, 1982); Peter H. Wood, "La Salle: Discovery of a Lost Explorer," *American Historical Review* LXXXIX (April 1984), 294–323.

For the colonization of Louisiana, see Eccles, *France in America*; Daniel H. Usner, Jr., *Indians, Settlers, and Slaves in a Frontier Exchange Economy: The Lower Mississippi Valley Before 1783* (Chapel Hill: University of North Carolina Press, 1992); Patricia Dillon Woods, *French-Indian Relations on the Southern Frontier, 1699–1762* (Ann Arbor, Mich.: UMI Research Press, 1980).

For the Catawba, see James H. Merrell, *The Indians' New World: Catawbas and Their Neighbors from European Contact Through the Era of Removal* (Chapel Hill: University of North Carolina Press, 1989).

For the Cherokee, see David H. Corkran, *The Cherokee Frontier: Conflict and Survival, 1740–1762* (Norman: University of Oklahoma Press, 1962); M. Thomas Hatley, "The Three Lives of Keowee: Loss and Recovery in Eighteenth-Century Cherokee Villages," in Peter H. Wood, Gregory A. Waselkov, and M. Thomas Hatley, eds., *Powhatan's Mantle: Indians in the Colonial Southeast* (Lincoln: University of Nebraska Press, 1989), 223–48.

For the Chickasaw, see Arrell M. Gibson, *The Chickasaw* (Norman: University of Oklahoma Press, 1971).

For the Choctaw, see Patricia Galloway, " 'The Chief Who Is Your Father': Choctaw and French Views of the Diplomatic Relation," in Wood, Waselkov, and Hatley, eds., *Powhatan's Mantle*, 254–78; Patricia Galloway, *Choctaw Genesis, 1500–1700* (Lincoln: University of Nebraska Press, 1995); Richard White, *The Roots of Dependency: Subsistence, Environment, and Social Change among the Choctaws, Pawnees, and Navajos* (Lincoln: University of Nebraska Press, 1983).

For the Creek, see Kathryn E. Holland Braund, *Deerskins and Duffels: The Creek Indian Trade with Anglo-America, 1685–1815* (Lincoln: University of Nebraska Press, 1993); David H. Corkran, *The Creek Frontier, 1540–1783* (Norman: University of Oklahoma Press, 1967); Claudio Saunt, " 'Domestick . . . Quiet Being Broke': Gender Conflict Among the Creek Indians in the Eighteenth Century," in

Andrew R. L. Cayton and Fredrika J. Teute, eds., *Contact Points: American Frontiers from the Mohawk Valley to the Mississippi, 1750–1830* (Chapel Hill: University of North Carolina Press, 1998), 151–74.

For the contrasting racial and class systems of Louisiana and the British colonies, see Ira Berlin, *Many Thousands Gone: The First Two Centuries of Slavery in North America* (Cambridge, Mass.: Harvard University Press, 1998); Gwendolyn Midlo Hall, *Africans in Colonial Louisiana: The Development of Afro-Creole Culture in the Eighteenth Century* (Baton Rouge: Louisiana State University Press, 1995); Usner, *Indians, Settlers, and Slaves.*

Chapter 17: The Great Plains, 1680–1800

In general, this chapter relies on Paul H. Carlson, *The Plains Indians* (College Station: Texas A&M University Press, 1998); Loretta Fowler, "The Great Plains from the Arrival of the Horse to 1885," in Bruce G. Trigger and Wilcomb E. Washburn, eds., *The Cambridge History of the Native Peoples of the Americas*, vol. 1, *North America*, part 2 (New York: Cambridge University Press, 1996), 1–55; David J. Weber, *The Spanish Frontier in North America* (New Haven: Yale University Press, 1992); Richard White, *"It's Your Misfortune and None of My Own": A New History of the American West* (Norman: University of Oklahoma Press, 1991).

For the captive trade and the *genizaros,* see James F. Brooks, " 'This Evil Extends Especially to the Feminine Sex': Captivity and Identity in New Mexico, 1700–1846," in Elizabeth Jameson and Susan Armitage, eds., *Writing the Range: Race, Class, and Culture in the Women's West* (Norman: University of Oklahoma Press, 1997), 97–121; Ramón A. Gutiérrez, *When Jesus Came, the Corn Mothers Went Away: Marriage, Sexuality, and Power in New Mexico, 1500–1846* (Stanford: Stanford University Press, 1991); Russell M. Magnaghi, "The *Genizaro* Experience in Spanish New Mexico," in Ralph H. Vigil, Frances W. Kaye, and John R. Wunder, eds., *Spain and the Plains: Myths and Realities of Spanish Exploration and Settlement on the Great Plains* (Niwot: University Press of Colorado, 1994), 114–30.

For villagers and nomads, see Linda S. Cordell, "Durango to Durango: An Overview of the Southwest Heartland," in David Hurst Thomas, ed., *Columbian Consequences*, vol. 1, *Archaeological and Historical Perspectives on the Spanish Borderland West* (Washington, D.C.: Smithsonian Institution Press, 1989), 17–40; Howard L. Harrod, *Becoming and Remaining a People: Native American Religions on the Northern Plains* (Tucson: University of Arizona Press, 1995); Preston Holder, *The Hoe and the Horse on the Plains: A Study of Cultural Development Among North American Indians* (Lincoln: University of Nebraska Press, 1970); Roy W. Meyer, *The Village Indians of the Upper Missouri: The Mandans, Hidatsas, and Arikaras* (Lincoln: University of Nebraska Press, 1977); Virginia Bergman Peters, *Women of the Earth Lodges: Tribal Life on the Plains* (North Haven, Conn.: Archon Books, 1995); Katherine A. Spielmann, ed., *Farmers, Hunters, and Colonists: Interaction Between the Southwest and the Southern Plains* (Tucson: University of Arizona Press, 1991); Walter Prescott Webb, *The Great Plains* (Lincoln: University of Nebraska Press, 1981); Richard White, *The*

Roots of Dependency: Subsistence, Environment, and Social Change Among the Choctaws, Pawnees, and Navajos (Lincoln: University of Nebraska Press, 1983).

For the impact of horses and the new migrations, see James F. Brooks, "Sing Away the Buffalo: Faction and Fission on the Northern Plains," in Philip Duke and Michael C. Wilson, eds., *Beyond Subsistence: Plains Archaeology and the Post-processual Critique* (Tuscaloosa: University of Alabama Press, 1995); Dan Flores, "Bison Ecology and Bison Diplomacy: The Southern Plains from 1800 to 1850," *Journal of American History* LXXVIII (Sept. 1991), 465–85; Dan Flores, "The Great Contraction: Bison and Indians in Northern Plains Environmental History," in Charles E. Rankin, ed., *Legacy: New Perspectives on the Battle of the Little Bighorn* (Helena: Montana Historical Society Press, 1996), 3–22; Elliott West, *The Way to the West: Essays on the Central Plains* (Albuquerque: University of New Mexico Press, 1995); Elliott West, *The Contested Plains: Indians, Goldseekers, and the Rush to Colorado* (Lawrence: University Press of Kansas, 1998); Richard White, "The Winning of the West: The Expansion of the Western Sioux in the Eighteenth and Nineteenth Centuries," *Journal of American History* LXV (Sept. 1978), 319–43.

For the Spanish response to the French trade, see Elizabeth A. H. John, *Storms Brewed in Other Men's Worlds: The Confrontation of Indians, Spanish, and French in the Southwest, 1540–1795*, 2d ed. (Norman: University of Oklahoma Press, 1996); Vigil, Kaye, and Wunder, eds., *Spain and the Plains.*

For Texas, the Comanche, and the Apache, see Morris Foster, *Being Comanche: A Social History of an American Indian Community* (Tucson: University of Arizona Press, 1991); Pekka Hamalainen, "The Western Comanche Trade Center: Rethinking the Plains Indian Trade System," *Western Historical Quarterly* XXIX (Winter 1998), 485–513; Thomas R. Hester, "Texas and Northeastern Mexico: An Overview," and James E. Corbin, "Spanish-Indian Interaction on the Eastern Frontier of Texas," in David Hurst Thomas, ed., *Columbian Consequences*, vol. 1, *Archaeological and Historical Perspectives on the Spanish Borderland West* (Washington, D.C.: Smithsonian Institution Press, 1989), 191–212, 269–76; Thomas W. Kavanagh, *Comanche Political History: An Ethnohistorical Perspective, 1706–1875* (Lincoln: University of Nebraska Press, 1996).

For the Hudson's Bay Company, see Olive Patricia Dickason, *Canada's First Nations: A History of Founding Peoples from Earliest Times* (Norman: University of Oklahoma Press, 1992); W. J. Eccles, *The Canadian Frontier, 1534–1760* (Albuquerque: University of New Mexico Press, 1983); Arthur J. Ray, *Indians in the Fur Trade: Their Role as Trappers, Hunters, and Middlemen in the Lands Southwest of Hudson Bay, 1660–1870* (Toronto: University of Toronto Press, 1974); Sylvia Van Kirk, *Many Tender Ties: Women in Fur-Trade Society, 1670–1870* (Norman: University of Oklahoma Press, 1980).

For French western exploration and commerce, see Bernard DeVoto, *The Course of Empire* (Boston: Houghton Mifflin, 1952); W. J. Eccles, "La Mer de l'Ouest: Outpost of Empire," in *Essays on New France* (Toronto: Oxford University Press, 1987), 96–109; G. Hubert Smith and W. Raymond Wood, eds., *The Explorations of the La Vérendryes in the Northern Plains, 1738–43* (Lincoln: University of

Nebraska Press, 1980); W. Raymond Wood and Thomas Thiessen, eds., *Early Fur Trade on the Northern Plains: Canadian Traders Among the Mandan and Hidatsa Indians, 1738–1818* (Norman: University of Oklahoma Press, 1985).

For the Indians of the northern plains in the eighteenth century, see John C. Ewers, *Indian Life on the Upper Missouri* (Norman: University of Oklahoma Press, 1968); John C. Ewers, *Plains Indian History and Culture: Essays on Continuity and Change* (Norman: University of Oklahoma Press, 1997); Meyer, *Village Indians of the Upper Missouri*.

Chapter 18: Imperial Wars and Crisis, 1739–75

For the British military in the mid-eighteenth century, see Jeremy Black, *Britain as a Military Power, 1688–1715* (London: University College London Press, 1999); Jeremy Black and Philip Woodfine, eds., *The British Navy and the Use of Naval Power in the Eighteenth Century* (Leicester: Leicester University Press, 1988); Richard Harding, *The Evolution of the Sailing Navy, 1509–1815* (London: St. Martin's Press, 1995); Lawrence Stone, ed., *An Imperial State at War: Britain from 1689 to 1815* (New York: Routledge, 1994).

For overviews of the imperial wars, see Bruce P. Lenman, "Colonial Wars and Imperial Instability, 1688–1793," N. A. M. Rodger, "Sea-Power and Empire, 1688–1793," and John Shy, "The American Colonies in War and Revolution, 1748–1783," in P. J. Marshall, ed., *The Oxford History of the British Empire*, vol. 2, *The Eighteenth Century* (New York: Oxford University Press, 1998), 151–68, 169–83, 300–24; Douglas Edward Leach, *Arms for Empire: A Military History of the British Colonies in North America, 1607–1763* (New York: Macmillan, 1973); ; Ian K. Steele, *Warpaths: Invasions of North America* (New York: Oxford University Press, 1994).

For Louisbourg, see John Robert McNeill, *Atlantic Empires of France and Spain: Louisbourg and Havana, 1700–1763* (Chapel Hill: University of North Carolina Press, 1985).

For more detailed treatment of the Seven Years War, see Fred Anderson, *A People's Army: Massachusetts Soldiers and Society in the Seven Years War* (Chapel Hill: University of North Carolina Press, 1984); Fred Anderson, *Crucible of War: The Seven Years' War and the Fate of Empire in British North America, 1754–1766* (New York: Alfred A. Knopf, 2000); Richard Pares, *War and Trade in the West Indies, 1739–1763* (London: Frank Cass & Co., 1963).

For Canadian perspectives on the war, see W. J. Eccles, *The Canadian Frontier, 1534–1760* (Albuquerque: University of New Mexico Press, 1969); W. J. Eccles, *Essays on New France* (New York: Oxford University Press, 1987); W. J. Eccles, *France in America* (East Lansing: Michigan State University Press, 1990); George F. G. Stanley, *New France: The Last Phase, 1744–1760* (Toronto: McClelland and Stewart, 1968).

For the impact of the war on Louisiana, see Daniel H. Usner, Jr., *Indians, Settlers, and Slaves in a Frontier Exchange Economy: The Lower Mississippi Valley Before 1783* (Chapel Hill: University of North Carolina Press, 1990).

For the war in the interior and the Indian rebellions, see John Richard Alden, *John Stuart and the Southern Colonial Frontier* (New York: Gordian Press, 1966); Gregory Evans Dowd, *A Spirited Resistance: The North American Indian Struggle for Unity, 1745–1815* (Baltimore: Johns Hopkins University Press, 1992); Eric Hinderaker, *Elusive Empires: Constructing Colonialism in the Ohio Valley, 1673–1800* (New York: Cambridge University Press, 1997); Warren R. Hofstra, " 'The Extention of His Majesties Dominions': The Virginia Backcountry and the Reconfiguration of Imperial Frontiers," *Journal of American History* LXXXIV (March 1998), 1281–1312; Michael N. McConnell, *A Country Between: The Upper Ohio Valley and Its Peoples, 1724–1774* (Lincoln: University of Nebraska Press, 1992); James H. Merrell, *Into the American Woods: Negotiators on the Pennsylvania Frontier* (New York: W. W. Norton, 1999); Richard White, *The Middle Ground: Indians, Empires, and Republics in the Great Lakes Region, 1650–1815* (New York: Cambridge University Press, 1991).

For the new strains on the empire and their ties to the war, see Theodore Draper, *A Struggle for Power: The American Revolution* (New York: Random House, 1996); Lawrence Henry Gipson, "The American Revolution as an Aftermath of the Great War for Empire, 1754–1763," *Political Science Quarterly* LXV (1950), 86–104; Douglas Edward Leach, *Roots of Conflict: British Armed Forces and Colonial Americans, 1677–1763* (Chapel Hill: University of North Carolina Press, 1986); John J. McCusker, "British Mercantilist Policies and the American Colonies," in Stanley L. Engerman and Robert E. Gallman, eds., *The Cambridge Economic History of the United States*, vol. 1, *The Colonial Era* (New York: Cambridge University Press, 1996), 337–62; Gary B. Nash, *The Urban Crucible: Social Change, Political Consciousness, and the Origins of the American Revolution* (Cambridge, Mass.: Harvard University Press, 1979).

For the divergence of British and colonial societies, see Bernard Bailyn, *Voyagers to the West: A Passage in the Peopling of America on the Eve of the Revolution* (New York: Alfred A. Knopf, 1986); Richard L. Bushman, *King and People in Provincial Massachusetts* (Chapel Hill: University of North Carolina Press, 1985); Gordon S. Wood, *The Radicalism of the American Revolution* (New York: Alfred A. Knopf, 1992).

For the empire of liberty, see Hinderaker, *Elusive Empires*; Drew McCoy, *The Elusive Republic: Political Economy in Jeffersonian America* (Chapel Hill: University of North Carolina Press, 1980); Alan Taylor, "Land and Liberty on the Post-Revolutionary Frontier," in David Konig, ed., *Devising Liberty: Preserving and Creating Freedom in the New American Republic* (Stanford: Stanford University Press, 1995), 81–108.

Chapter 19: The Pacific, 1760–1820

For Russian America in general, see Hector Chevigny, *Russian America: The Great Alaskan Venture, 1741–1867* (New York: Viking Press, 1965); Raisa V. Makarova, *Russians on the Pacific, 1743–1799*, trans. Richard A. Pierce and Alton S. Donnelly (Kingston, Ontario: Limestone Press, 1975).

For the Siberian precedent and connection, see Benson Bobrick, *East of the Sun:*

The Conquest and Settlement of Siberia (London: Heinemann, 1992); William W. Fitzhugh and Aron Crowell, eds., *Crossroads of Continents: Cultures of Siberia and Alaska* (Washington, D.C.: Smithsonian Institution Press, 1988), especially the essays by Lydia T. Black and by Fitzhugh.

For Russian exploration and exploitation of the Aleutians and Alaska, see Glynn Barratt, *Russia in Pacific Waters, 1715–1825* (Vancouver: University of British Columbia Press, 1981); Raymond H. Fisher, *Bering's Voyages: Whither and Why* (Seattle: University of Washington Press, 1977); William R. Hunt, *Arctic Passage: The Turbulent History of the Land and People of the Bering Sea, 1697–1975* (New York: Charles Scribner's Sons, 1975); Georg W. Steller, *Journal of a Voyage with Bering, 1741–1742*, ed. O. W. Frost (Stanford: Stanford University Press, 1988).

For the colonial development of Russian Alaska, see James R. Gibson, *Imperial Russia in Frontier America: The Changing Geography of Supply of Russian America, 1784–1867* (New York: Oxford University Press, 1976); Barbara Sweetland Smith and Redmond J. Barnett, eds., *Russian America: The Forgotten Frontier* (Tacoma: Washington State Historical Society, 1990).

For California in general, see Julia G. Costell and David Hornbeck, "Alta California: An Overview," in David Hurst Thomas, ed., *Columbian Consequences*, vol. 1, *Archaeological and Historical Perspectives on the Spanish Borderland West* (Washington, D.C.: Smithsonian Institution Press, 1989), 303–32; David J. Weber, *The Spanish Frontier in North America* (New Haven: Yale University Press, 1992).

For Spanish exploration of the Pacific coast see Warren L. Cook, *Flood Tide of Empire: Spain and the Pacific Northwest, 1543–1819* (New Haven: Yale University Press, 1973); Iris H. W. Engstrand, "Seekers of the 'Northern Mystery': European Exploration of California and the Pacific," in Ramón A. Gutiérrez and Richard J. Orsi, eds., *Contested Eden: California Before the Gold Rush* (Berkeley: University of California Press, 1998), 78–110.

For the California environment, see M. Kat Anderson, Michael G. Barbour, and Valerie Whitworth, "A World of Balance and Plenty: Land, Plants, Animals, and Humans in a Pre-European California," and William Preston, "Serpent in the Garden: Environmental Change in Colonial California," in Gutiérrez and Orsi, eds., *Contested Eden*, 12–47, 260–98; M. Kat Anderson and Thomas C. Blackburn, eds., *Before the Wilderness: Environmental Management by Native Californians* (Menlo Park, Calif.: Ballena Press, 1992); Robert F. Heizer and Albert Elsasser, *The Natural World of the California Indians* (Berkeley: University of California Press, 1980).

For the California natives, see Albert L. Hurtado, *Indian Survival on the California Frontier* (New Haven: Yale University Press, 1988); Howard R. Lamar and Sam Truett, "The Greater Southwest and California from the Beginning of European Settlement to the 1880s," in Bruce G. Trigger and Wilcomb E. Washburn, eds., *The Cambridge History of the Native Peoples of the Americas*, vol. 1, *North America*, part 2 (New York: Cambridge University Press, 1996), 57–116; George Harwood Phillips, *Chiefs and Challengers: Indian Resistance and Cooperation in Southern California* (Berkeley: University of California Press, 1975); George Harwood Phillips, *Indians and Intruders in Central California, 1769–1849* (Norman: University of Oklahoma Press, 1993); William S. Simmons, "Indian Peoples of California," in

Gutiérrez and Orsi, eds., *Contested Eden*, 48–77; Phillip L. Walker, Patricia Lambert, and Michael J. DeNiro, "The Effects of European Contact on the Health of Alta California Indians," and Edward D. Castillo, "The Native Response to the Colonization of Alta California," in Thomas, ed., *Archaeological and Historical Perspectives on the Spanish Borderland West*, 349–64, 377–94.

For the California mission experience, see Michael J. Gonzalez, "The Child of the Wilderness Weeps for the Father of Our Country': The Indian and the Politics of Church and State in Provincial California," James A. Sandos, "Between Crucifix and Lance: Indian-White Relations in California, 1769–1848," and Antonia I. Castaneda, "Engendering the History of Alta California, 1769–1848: Gender, Sexuality, and the Family," in Gutiérrez and Orsi, eds., *Contested Eden*, 147–72, 196–229, 230–59; Steven W. Hackel, "The Staff of Leadership: Indian Authority in the Missions of Alta California," *William and Mary Quarterly*, 3rd Ser., LIV (April 1997), 347–76; John R. Johnson, "The Chumash and the Missions," Robert L. Hoover, "Spanish-Native Interaction and Acculturation in the Alta California Missions," David Hornbeck, "Economic Growth and Change at the Missions of Alta California, 1769–1846," and Julia G. Costell, "Variability among the Alta California Missions: The Economics of Agricultural Production," in Thomas, ed., *Archaeological and Historical Perspectives on the Spanish Borderland West*, 365–76, 395–406, 423–33, 435–50.

For the economic and social development of Alta California, see Lisbeth Haas, *Conquests and Historical Identities in California, 1769–1936* (Berkeley: University of California Press, 1995); Steven W. Hackel, "Land, Labor, and Production: The Colonial Economy of Spanish and Mexican California," and Douglas Monroy, "The Creation and Re-creation of Californio Society," in Gutiérrez and Orsi, eds., *Contested Eden*, 111–46, 173–95; Douglas Monroy, *Thrown Among Strangers: The Making of Mexican Culture in Frontier California* (Berkeley: University of California Press, 1990).

For Pacific exploration, see Hugh Cobbe, *Cook's Voyages and the Peoples of the Pacific* (London: British Museum, 1979); Robin Fisher and Hugh Johnston, eds., *Captain James Cook and His Times* (Seattle: University of Washington Press, 1979); Alan Frost and Jane Samson, *Pacific Empires: Essays in Honour of Glyndwr Williams* (Vancouver: University of British Columbia Press, 1999); Derek Howse, ed., *Background to Discovery: Pacific Exploration from Dampier to Cook* (Berkeley: University of California Press, 1990); Glyndwr Williams, "The Pacific: Exploration and Exploitation," in P. J. Marshall, ed., *The Oxford History of the British Empire*, vol. 2, *The Eighteenth Century* (New York: Oxford University Press, 1998), 552–75; Lynne Withey, *Voyages of Discovery: Captain Cook and the Exploration of the Pacific* (New York: William Morrow, 1987).

For the Hawaiian Islands, see Gavan Daws, *Shoal of Time: A History of the Hawaiian Islands* (New York: Macmillan, 1968); Ralph S. Kuykendall, *The Hawaiian Kingdom, 1778–1854: Foundation and Transformation* (Honolulu: University of Hawaii Press, 1957); Marshall Sahlins, *Historical Metaphors and Mythical Realities: Structure in the Early History of the Sandwich Islands Kingdom* (Ann Arbor: University of Michigan Press, 1981).

For the Pacific Northwest, see Robin Fisher, "The Northwest from the Beginning of Trade with Europeans to the 1880s," in Trigger and Washburn, eds., *North America*, part 2, 117–82; Stephen Haycox, James K. Barnett, and Caedmon A. Liburd, eds., *Enlightenment and Exploration in the North Pacific, 1741–1805* (Seattle: University of Washington Press, 1997); Richard White, *The Organic Machine: The Remaking of the Columbia River* (New York: Hill & Wang, 1995).

INDEX